COMMUNICATION MATTERS

Fourth Edition

KORY FLOYD

University of Arizona

DEDICATION   Most books are dedicated to people, but I wish to dedicate this one to a
principle. To compassion, wherever it is needed and no matter how well it
may be hidden.

COMMUNICATION MATTERS, FOURTH EDITION

Published by McGraw Hill LLC, 1325 Avenue of the Americas, New York, NY 10121. Copyright ©2022 by McGraw Hill LLC. All rights reserved. Printed in the United States of America. Previous editions ©2018, 2014, and 2011. No part of this publication may be reproduced or distributed in any form or by any means, or stored in a database or retrieval system, without the prior written consent of McGraw Hill LLC, including, but not limited to, in any network or other electronic storage or transmission, or broadcast for distance learning.

Some ancillaries, including electronic and print components, may not be available to customers outside the United States.

This book is printed on acid-free paper.

1 2 3 4 5 6 7 8 9 LWI 24 23 22 21

ISBN 978-1-260-00708-4 (bound edition)
MHID 1-260-00708-1 (bound edition)
ISBN 978-1-264-03356-0 (loose-leaf edition)
MHID 1-264-03356-7 (loose-leaf edition)

Executive Portfolio Manager: *Sarah Remington*
Product Development Manager: *Dawn Groundwater*
Product Developer: *Elizabeth Murphy*
Content Project Managers: *Lisa Bruflodt*

Buyer: *Sandy Ludovissy*
Designer: *Matt Diamond*
Content Licensing Specialists: *Brianna Kirschbaum*
Compositor: *MPS Limited*

All credits appearing on page or at the end of the book are considered to be an extension of the copyright page.

Library of Congress Cataloging-in-Publication Data

Names: Floyd, Kory, author.
   Title: Communication matters / Kory Floyd, University of Arizona.
   Description: Fourth edition. | New York, NY : McGraw Hill Education, [2022]
   Identifiers: LCCN 2020034468 | ISBN 9781260007084 (hardcover; acid-free paper) |
   Subjects: LCSH: Communication. | Interpersonal communication.
   Classification: LCC P94.7 .F56 2022 | DDC 302.2—dc23 LC record available at https://lccn.loc.gov/2020034468

The Internet addresses listed in the text were accurate at the time of publication. The inclusion of a website does not indicate an endorsement by the authors or McGraw Hill LLC, and McGraw Hill LLC does not guarantee the accuracy of the information presented at these sites.

mheducation.com/highered

Dear Readers:

I can still recall how my family reacted when I said I wanted to study communication. *You already know how to communicate,* I remember one relative saying. Communication seemed like common sense to my family members, so they weren't entirely sure why I needed a Ph.D. just to understand it.

As it turns out, my relatives are like a lot of other people in this regard. Because each of us communicates in some form nearly every day of our lives, it's hard not to think of communication as completely intuitive. What can we possibly learn from research and formal study that we don't already know from our lived experience? Aren't we all experts in communication already?

For the sake of argument, let's say we were. Why, then, do we so often misunderstand each other? Why is our divorce rate so high? How come it seems like women and men speak different languages? What accounts for the popularity of self-help books, relationship counselors, and talk shows? If we're all experts at communicating, why do we often find it so challenging? Maybe communication isn't as intuitive as we might think.

When I wrote earlier editions of *Communication Matters*, my goal was to help readers see how communication not only affects their social relationships, but also influences their happiness, career objectives, and quality of life. I wanted to guide students through their personal experience of communication, illuminate the value of engaging in a critical investigation of processes and behaviors, and help readers actively apply the course material to their own life experiences.

Our world is changing quickly these days—and so, too, are the ways we communicate. In the last few years, we've seen people use computer-mediated communication in unprecedented ways. Deployed servicemen watch the birth of their children live via Skype or FaceTime. Political protestors organize rallies with less than a day's notice on Twitter. Adults given up for adoption as infants use Facebook to find their biological parents. And despite the growth of these newer platforms, e-mail is far from dead: Most adults in a recent survey said their e-mail load either stayed the same or increased over the past year. Each new technology shrinks our world just a little more, requiring effective communicators to adapt their behaviors accordingly. This new edition of *Communication Matters* focuses on teaching the adaptability skills students need in an ever-changing communication world.

An ideal textbook not only engages and excites students; it also provides relevant, contemporary, and high-quality support for instructors. *Communication Matters*, Fourth Edition, offers Connect, a flexible, groundbreaking, online learning platform that features SmartBook, a personalized learning system; hands-on learning activities; quizzes; and a fully integrated e-book. Connect enables instructors to better tailor class time to student needs and gives students more opportunities than ever for communication skills practice and assessment. I hope you will find this new edition of *Communication Matters* and its extensive instructional support to comprise a well-integrated package of engaging and contemporary materials for the introductory course.

Courtesy of Michael Chansley

Name: Kory Floyd

Education: I got my undergraduate degree from Western Washington University, my Master's degree from the University of Washington, and my PhD from the University of Arizona

Current jobs: Professor, book writer

Favorite job growing up: Singing busboy

Worst childhood memory: Getting sent to the principal's office in third grade. [It's possible I haven't told my parents about that.]

Best childhood memory: The birth of my sister and brother

Hobbies: Playing piano, singing, reading, traveling

Pets: Three wonderful dogs, Cruise, Buster and Champ, and a large family of goldfish

Favorite recent book: Talking to Strangers, by Malcolm Gladwell

Favorite TV show: The Big Bang Theory

Places I love: Iceland, Starbucks, my brother's house

BRIEF CONTENTS

These three chapters are available exclusively through McGraw Hill Create, where you can customize your version of *Communication Matters*. Talk to your McGraw Hill representative or visit www.mcgrawhillcreate.com for more information.

CONTENTS

Three chapters, written by Kory Floyd for Communication Matters, *are available exclusively through McGraw Hill's Create customization site:*

CHAPTER 16 Communicating in Organizations

CHAPTER 17 Communication and Media

CHAPTER 18 Communication and Health

BOXES

THE COMPETENT COMMUNICATOR

PUTTING COMMUNICATION TO WORK

McGraw Hill Connect: An Overview

McGraw Hill Connect offers full-semester access to comprehensive, reliable content and learning resources for the Introduction to Communication course. Connect's deep integration with most learning management systems (LMS), including Blackboard and Desire2Learn (D2L), offers single sign-on and gradebook synchronization. Data from Assignment Results reports synchronize directly with many LMS, allowing scores to flow automatically from Connect into school-specific grade books, if required.

Instructor's Guide to Connect for *Communication Matters*

When you assign **Connect**, you can be confident—and have data to demonstrate—that the learners in your courses, however diverse, are acquiring the skills, principles, and critical processes that constitute effective communication. This leaves you to focus on your highest course expectations.

TAILORED TO YOU. Connect offers on-demand, single sign-on access to learners—wherever they are and whenever they have time. With a single, one-time registration, learners receive access to McGraw Hill's trusted content. Learners also have a courtesy trial period during registration.

EASY TO USE. Connect seamlessly supports all major learning management systems with content, assignments, performance data, and SmartBook, the leading adaptive learning system. With these tools, you can quickly make assignments, produce reports, focus discussions, intervene on problem topics, and help at-risk learners—as you need to and when you need to.

Communication Matters SmartBook 2.0

A PERSONALIZED AND ADAPTIVE LEARNING EXPERIENCE WITH SMARTBOOK 2.0. Boost learner success with McGraw Hill's adaptive reading and study experience. The *Communication Matters* SmartBook 2.0 highlights the most impactful communication concepts the learner needs to study at that moment in time. The learning path continuously adapts and, based on what the individual learner knows and does not know, provides focused help through targeted assessments and Learning Resources.

ENHANCED FOR THE NEW EDITION! With a suite of new Learning Resources and adaptive assessments, as well as highlights of key chapter concepts, SmartBook 2.0's intuitive technology optimizes learner study time by creating a personalized learning path for improved course performance and overall learner success.

HUNDREDS OF INTERACTIVE LEARNING RESOURCES. Presented in a range of interactive styles, *Communication Matters* Learning Resources support learners who may be struggling to master, or simply wish to review, the most important communication concepts. Designed to reinforce the most important chapter concepts—from competent online self-disclosure and nonverbal communication channels to detecting deceptive communication and managing relationships—every Learning Resource is presented at the precise moment of need. Whether a video, audio clip, or interactive mini-lesson, each of the 200-plus Learning Resources was created for the new edition and was designed to give learners a lifelong foundation in strong communication skills.

The Connection Between Relationships and Communication

Do you expect your relationships with family members to fill the same needs as your relationships with friends? Why or why not?

In addition to physical needs, every person has **relational needs**, the essential elements we look for in our relationships with other people.

Communication scholar Rebecca Rubin and her colleagues have identified several relational needs:

- Companionship
- Affection
- The ability to relax and escape our problems

Ariel Skelley/Blend Images LLC

MORE THAN 1,000 TARGETED ASSESSMENTS. Class-tested at colleges and universities nationwide, a treasury of engaging adaptive assessments—new and revised, more than 1,000 in all—gives learners the information on communication they need to know, at every stage of the learning process, in order to thrive in the course. Designed to gauge learners' comprehension of the most important *Communication Matters* chapter concepts, and presented in a variety of interactive styles to facilitate learner engagement, targeted assessments give learners immediate feedback on their understanding of the material. Each question identifies a learner's familiarity with the instruction and points to areas where additional review is needed.

A SUITE OF APPLICATION-BASED ACTIVITIES. At the higher level of Bloom's, McGraw Hill's Application-Based Activities are highly interactive, automatically graded, online learn-by-doing exercises that provide students a safe space to apply their knowledge and problem-solving skills to real-world scenarios. Each scenario addresses key concepts that students must use to work through to solve communication problems, resulting in improved critical thinking and development of relevant skills.

RESEARCH-BASED. We all communicate, all the time. Consequently, many of us believe we're experts, and that good communication is based on personal instincts. *Communication Matters* became one of the most successful new offerings in introductory communication because it debunks that myth, using sound and relevant research to help students think critically about the communication they take part in every day.

- **Updated with more than 60 percent new scholarly references,** the fourth edition of *Communication Matters* continues to emphasize communication as a discipline of study and ensures that students are exposed to the most recent and pertinent research.
- ***Fact or Fiction*** boxes invite learners to challenge their own assumptions about human communication, and to rethink seemingly self-evident communication

questions in light of what the scholarship reveals. New and revised topics include how texting does (or doesn't) affect language (language chapter) and how group support can aid in quitting smoking (small groups chapter).

- *Dark Side* features in each chapter offer an in-depth, well-researched look at a specific dark side topic and promote discussion of mature, effective ways of dealing with its challenges. New and revised topics include hurtful communication, such as bullying and cyberbullying (introductory chapter), a new evidence-based strategy for reducing collective blame (communication and culture chapter), and the relationship between power and coercion (decision-making and leadership chapter).

REAL-WORLD BACKED. *Communication Matters* doesn't just offer research—it shows, clearly and consistently, why the research is important. Whether students are reading a chapter, working through a SmartBook 2.0 assignment, or reviewing key concepts in a Learning Resource, their every instructional moment is rooted in the real world. McGraw Hill research shows that high-quality examples reinforce academic theory throughout the course. Relevant examples and practical scenarios—reflecting interactions in school, the workplace, and beyond—demonstrate how effective communication informs and enhances students' lives and careers.

- **Relevant, timely chapter opening examples.** In addition to fresh examples integrated throughout, each chapter in *Communication Matters* opens with a familiar and provocative example that primes students for what's to come. New topics include an inspiring public art project spanning the border between Mexico and the U.S. (culture chapter), the use of nonverbal behaviors to protest social inequity (nonverbal chapter), the "chosen family" working relationship between comedians Tina Fey and Amy Poehler (intimate relationships chapter), the life-or-death consequences of small group communication among surgery team members (small groups chapter), the climate activism of Greta Thunberg (research chapter), and the effects of disinformation on public health (informative speaking chapter).
- **EXPANDED coverage of the power of language.** It is perhaps more urgent than ever for students to appreciate the power of language, including understanding what qualifies as hate speech and developing skills for practicing civil discourse. The fourth edition of *Communication Matters* incorporates this coverage and emphasizes the effects of language on individuals and on culture. Inclusive language is explained and used throughout, with new coverage reflecting current cultural conventions for applying gender-neutral pronouns.
- **UPDATED guidance on finding and evaluating sources for a speech.** *Communication Matters* meets students where they are, emphasizing the importance of evaluating critically the information they find online. This new edition includes expanded coverage of "fake news" and the spread of disinformation, as well as additional guidance on using sources responsibly.

SKILLS-FOCUSED. *Communication Matters* stakes research and relevance a step further, providing learners with clear takeaways that integrate into their everyday lives. In every chapter, learners are introduced to research-based strategies for improving communication skills and applying those skills to a variety of real-life situations, making *Communication Matters* a real tool for real life.

- *Difficult Conversations* boxes invite students to consider specific—and not uncommon—real-life situations that are uncomfortable or awkward and then provide useful strategies for managing the communication competently.

Topics include dealing with an angry customer (introductory chapter), offering condolences (language chapter), defusing political arguments on social media (perception chapter), writing a eulogy (developing and researching a topic), and making a public apology (persuasive speaking chapter).

- **The Competent Communicator** boxes in each chapter present students with a self-assessment of a particular communication skill or tendency. These boxes were designed with the underlying idea that for students to improve their communication skills and ability, they need to reflect on how they communicate now. Topics include determining whether you are a high self-monitor (introductory chapter), Googling yourself to manage your online image (perception chapter), and determining your level of extroversion (decision making and leadership chapter).
- **Sharpen Your Skills** boxes, which appear throughout each chapter, are stand-alone skill-builders comprising active-learning exercises that may be carried out in a group or individually. Activities include watching and reacting to a TED Talk (perception chapter) and examining co-cultural norms (culture chapter).

Video Capture Powered by GoReact

With just a smartphone, tablet, or webcam, students and instructors can capture video of presentations with ease. Video Capture Powered by GoReact, fully integrated in McGraw Hill's Connect platform, doesn't require any extra equipment or complicated training. Create your own custom Video Capture assignment, including in-class and online speeches and presentations, self-review, and peer review.

With our customizable rubrics, time-coded comments, and visual markers, students will see feedback at exactly the right moment, and in context, to help improve their speaking and presentation skills and confidence.

- The Video Capture tool allows instructors to easily and efficiently set up speech assignments for their course that can easily be shared and repurposed, as needed.
- Customizable rubrics and settings can be saved and shared, saving time and streamlining the speech assignment process.
- Allows both students and instructors to view videos during the assessment process. Feedback can be left within a customized rubric or as time-stamped comments within the video-playback itself.

Connect Reports

Instructor Reports allow instructors to quickly monitor learner activity, making it easy to identify which learners are struggling and to provide immediate help to ensure those learners stay enrolled in the course and improve their performance. The Instructor Reports also highlight the concepts and learning objectives that the class as a whole is having difficulty grasping. This essential information lets you know exactly which areas to target for review during your limited class time.

Some key reports include:

Progress Overview report—View learner progress for all modules, including how long learners have spent working in the module, which modules they have used outside of any that were assigned, and individual learner progress.

Missed Questions report—Identify specific assessments, organized by chapter, that are problematic for learners.

Most Challenging Learning Objectives report—Identify the specific topic areas that are challenging for your learners; these reports are organized by chapter and include specific page references. Use this information to tailor your lecture time and assignments to cover areas that require additional remediation and practice.

Metacognitive Skills report—View statistics showing how knowledgeable your learners are about their own comprehension and learning.

Classroom Preparation Tools

Whether before, during, or after class, there is a suite of products designed to help instructors plan their lessons and keep learners building upon the foundations of the course.

Instructor's Manual. Written and updated by the author, the Instructor's Manual provides a range of tools for each chapter to help structure the course and use the *Communication Matters* text effectively for particular course needs— discussion questions, assignment ideas, lecture ideas, and other resources.

Test Bank and Test Builder. The Test Bank offers multiple choice questions, true/false questions, fill-in-the-blank questions, and essay questions for each chapter. New to this edition and available within Connect, Test Builder is a cloud-based tool that enables instructors to format tests that can be printed and administered within a Learning Management System. Test Builder offers a modern, streamlined interface for easy content configuration that matches course needs, without requiring a download. Test Builder enables instructors to:

- Access all test bank content from a particular title
- Easily pinpoint the most relevant content through robust filtering options
- Manipulate the order of questions or scramble questions and/or answers
- Pin questions to a specific location within a test
- Determine the preferred treatment of algorithmic questions
- Choose the layout and spacing
- Add instructions and configure default settings

Accessible PowerPoints for each chapter created and updated by the author.

Remote Proctoring. New remote proctoring and browser-locking capabilities are seamlessly integrated within Connect to offer more control over the integrity of online assessments. Instructors can enable security options that restrict browser activity, monitor student behavior, and verify the identity of each student. Instant and detailed reporting gives instructors an at-a-glance view of potential concerns, thereby avoiding personal bias and supporting evidence-based claims.

Support to Ensure Success

Support at Every Step—McGraw Hill's Support at Every Step site offers a wealth of training and course creation guidance for instructors and learners alike. Instructor support is presented in easy-to-navigate, easy-to-complete sections. It includes the popular Connect how-to videos, step-by-step guides, and other materials that explain how to use both the Connect platform and its course-specific tools and features. https://www.mheducation.com/highered/support.html

Implementation Consultant—These specialists are dedicated to working online with instructors—one-on-one—to demonstrate how the Connect platform works and to help incorporate Connect into a customer's specific course design and syllabus. Contact your local McGraw Hill representative to learn more.

Digital Faculty Consultants—Digital Faculty Consultants are experienced instructors who use Connect in their classroom. These instructors are available to offer suggestions, advice, and training about how best to use Connect in your class. To request a Digital Faculty Consultant to speak with, please e-mail your McGraw Hill learning technology consultant.

CONTACT OUR CUSTOMER SUPPORT TEAM

McGraw Hill is dedicated to supporting instructors and learners. To contact our customer support team, please call us at 800-331-5094 or visit us online at http://mpss.mhhe.com/contact.php

Chapter-by-Chapter Changes to the Fourth Edition

Communication: A First Look New chapter-opening example looking at the challenges of communicating online; new example of digital communication reflecting the #MeToo movement; new discussion about the frequency of loneliness among younger Americans; new research on marital benefits to health; new Dark Side box on the effects of hurtful communication, such as bullying and cyberbullying; updated table of most-sought qualities for employees; greatly expanded section on online communication competence.

Communication and Culture New chapter-opening example illustrates cross-cultural exchange using a public art project; updated Dark Side box with new evidence-based strategy for reducing collective blame; updated discussion of immigration conflicts; new section on cultural universals.

Perceiving Ourselves and Others New chapter-opening example on the variety of public opinions surrounding the case of actor Jussie Smollett; new explanation on the science of stereotyping; new material on online image management and Instagram envy.

How We Use Language Updated examples of loaded language, defamation, and the effects of such language on individuals and on culture; expanded and updated coverage of separating opinions from factual claims; greatly expanded

coverage of hate speech and a new section on practicing civil dialogue.

Communicating Nonverbally New chapter-opening example on nonverbal behaviors used for social protest; new sections on situational and cultural awareness, with attention to groups of nonverbal behaviors; expanded guidance on improving nonverbal communication skills.

Listening Effectively New chapter-opening example on listening on a suicide support hotline; revised discussion of listening styles including updated Competent Communicator box; new example of misunderstood listening; updated data on information overload, as well as tips for managing it online; new section on effective listening online.

Communicating in Social and Professional Relationships Revised discussion of celebrity privacy invasions; updated research on online and offline relationships, and new discussion of niche dating apps; new discussion of parasocial relationships; new coverage of romantic relationships in the workplace and workplace bullying; added section on "Friendships are usually platonic," including coverage of friends-with-benefits relationships.

Communicating in Intimate Relationships New section on relational repair and forgiveness; new coverage of online behaviors such as ghosting, orbiting, and catfishing; updated discussion of arranged marriage and cultural expectations for love, as well as added discussion of polyamory; new table on social media and relationships.

Communicating in Small Groups New chapter-opening example on the life-and-death consequences of communication in a surgery team; updated discussion of social networking and social media; new Fact or Fiction? box on how group support can help people quit smoking.

Decision Making and Leadership in Groups Updated examples of groupthink and community decision-making; new discussion of the leadership strengths of introverts; new Dark Side box on the relationship between power and coercion.

Choosing, Developing, and Researching a Topic New chapter-opening example featuring climate activist Greta Thunberg; new examples of contemporary speech topics; updated discussion of generational differences including a new figure on research sources; new section on conference papers; new example of speech of introduction.

Organizing and Finding Support for Your Speech Expanded treatment helps students distinguish between their specific speech purpose and their thesis; updated coverage of copyright infringement and fair use; table on bibliography entries includes new citation models and updated APA and MLA style guidelines; new coverage of "fake news" and expanded coverage of objectivity.

Presenting a Speech Confidently and Competently New chapter-opening example looking at a commencement speech delivered by author Chimamanda Ngozi Adichie; new material on virtual reality apps for managing public speaking anxiety.

Speaking Informatively New chapter-opening story on the effects of inaccurate health news; updated examples of speech topics throughout.

Speaking Persuasively New persuasive speech example; new Dark Side box about how persuasion that misleads is damaging to a speaker's credibility; updated examples of speech topics throughout.

Appendix: Workplace Communication and Interviewing Updated example of lawmaker communication; updated statistics on workplace internet use and new suggestions for online job searches, including tips for drafting compelling cover letters.

CREATE YOUR OWN CUSTOMIZED COMMUNICATION MATTERS AT WWW.MCGRAWHILLCREATE.COM.

The following are available exclusively through McGraw Hill's Create customization site:

Communication in Organizations Added section on workplace romances, and new examples throughout.

Communication and Media Thoroughly updated, with updated statistics and examples throughout.

Communication and Health Updated claims about empathy during medical education and refreshed example of sensationalistic health news.

CONTRIBUTORS

I am very grateful to the thoughtful, astute instructors across the country who offered insights and suggestions that improved and enhanced Communication Matters, *Fourth Edition:*

Bakari Akil, *Florida State College at Jacksonville*

Sherrill Ashely, *Central Piedmont Community College*

Lisa Heller Boragine, *Cape Cod Community College*

Sandra Brisiel, *Delaware Technical Community College*

Pamela Brooks, *Arizona State University Polytechnic*

Christy Burns, *Jacksonville State University*

Anna Carmon, *Indiana University–Purdue University Columbus*

Natalia Cherjovsky, *Kirkwood Community College*

Margaret Chojnacki, *Barry University*

William Davis, *Westchester Community College*

Jenny Erikson, *Normandale Community College*

Jodi Gaete, *Suffolk County Community College*

Mattea Garcia, *Indiana State University*

Terri Gibson, *Anderson University*

Mary Gill, *Buena Vista University*

Charles Goehring, *San Diego State University*

Karly Goen, *Tarleton State University*

Brent Goken, *Illinois Central College*

Joni Gray, *Fairmont State University*

Lysia Hand, *Phoenix College*

Chris Harper, *Arkansas State University*

Heather Heritage, *Cedarville University*

Ronald Hochstatter, *McLennan Community College*

Milton Hunt, *Austin Community College*

Mohammad Islam-Zwart, *Eastern Washington University and Spokane Falls Community College*

Brent Kice, *Frostburg State University*

Kimberly Kline, *University of Texas at San Antonio*

Kurt Lindemann, *San Diego State University*

Kathryn Lookadoo, *University of Oklahoma, Norman*

Laura Marqua, *Joliet Junior College*

Anne McIntosh, *Central Piedmont Community College*

Laurie Metcalf, *Blinn College*

Shawn Miklaucic, *Johnson C. Smith University*

Steven Montemayor, *Northwest Vista College*

Teresa Morales, *Suffolk County Community College*

Thomas Morra, *Northern Virginia Community College*

Diane Nicodemus, *University of Pittsburgh at Johnstown*

Liz O'Brien, *Phoenix College*

Laura Oliver, *University of Texas at San Antonio*

Susan Olson, *Mesa Community College*

Karen Otto, *Florida State College at Jacksonville*

Marcie Pachter, *Palm Beach State College*

Carol Paulnock, *Saint Paul College*

Marisa Penkauskas, *University of Oklahoma*

Tami Phillips, *University of Central Arkansas*

Whitney Pisani, *Collin College*

Tonia Pope, *Houston Community College*

Elsha Ruminski, *Frostberg State University*

Kevin Ryals, *Mississippi State University*

Shari Santoriello, *Suffolk County Community College*

David C. Schrader, *Oklahoma State University*

David K. Scott, *Northeastern State University*

Pam Solberg, *Western Technical College*

Karen Stevens, *Austin Community College*

Kelly Stockstad, *Austin Community College*

Christy Takamure, *Leeward Community College*

Raymond Taylor, *Blue Ridge Community College*

Richard Underwood, *Kirkwood Community College*

Curt Van Geison, *St. Charles Community College*

Adam Vellone, *Miami Dade College*

Myra Walters, *Florida SouthWestern State College*

Jenny Warren, *Collin College*

Charlene Widener, *Hutchinson Community College*

Karin Wilking, *Northwest Vista College*

Karen Wolf, *Suffolk County Community College*

Arnold Wood, *Florida State College at Jacksonville*

Emily R. Workman, *Guilford Technical Community College*

David Worth, *Lone Star College*

ACKNOWLEDGMENTS

Few endeavors of any significance are achieved in isolation. There are always others who help us rise to—and exceed—our potential in nearly everything we do. I am delighted to acknowledge and thank those whose contributions and support are responsible for the book you are now reading.

This was the second book I wrote with McGraw Hill, and I could not ask for a better team of editors, managers, and publishers to work with. I am indebted to Sarah Remington, Kelly Ross, Dawn Groundwater, Lisa Bruflodt, David Patterson, and Mike Ryan for their consistent, professional support. I'm also grateful for the excellent contributions of Meghan Campbell and George Theofanopoulos to the digital components available for the book in Connect.

Elizabeth Murphy is a development editor *par excellence*. She made nearly every word of this book more interesting, more relevant, and more compelling than it was when I wrote it. I have been exceedingly grateful for her insights, her humor, and her patience throughout this revision process.

Special thanks go out to the team behind the scenes who built and continue to maintain speech assignment/video submission assignment functionality on Connect: Irina Blokh-Reznik, Vijay Kapu, Swathi Malathi, Rishi Mehta, Bob Myers, Bhumi Patel, Dan Roenstch, Ayeesha Shaik, Kapil Shrivastava, and Udaya Teegavarapu.

My students, colleagues, and administrators at the University of Arizona are a joy to work with and a tremendous source of encouragement. Undertaking a project of this size can be daunting, and it is so valuable to have a strong network of professional support on which to draw. I am also indebted to Jeannette Maré, Leslie Decker, Jennifer Linde, Teles Machibya, and Mark Dowley for their subject matter expertise and guidance.

Finally, I am eternally grateful for the love and support of my family and my lifelong friends. One needn't be an expert on communication to understand how important close personal relationships are—but the more I learn about communication, the more appreciative I become of the people who play those roles in my life. You know who you are, and I thank you from the bottom of my heart.

COMMUNICATION MATTERS

1

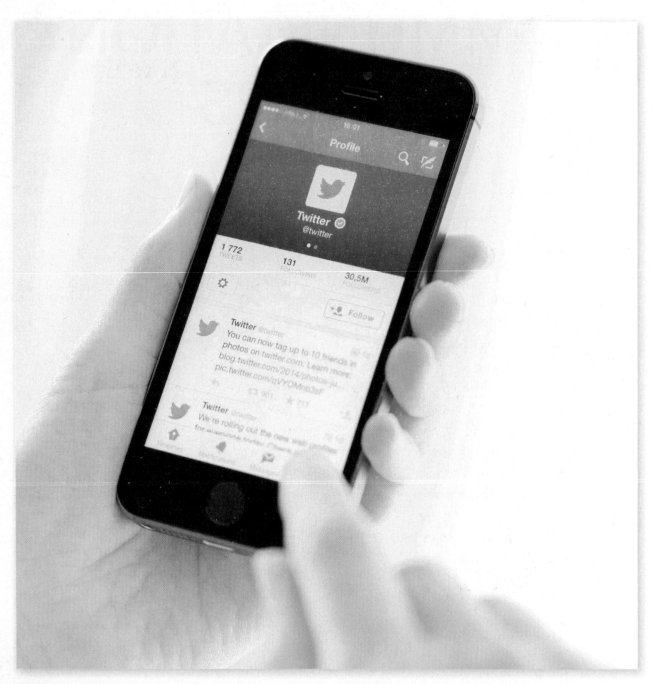

Bloomicon/Shutterstock

COMMUNICATION: A FIRST LOOK

#misinterpreted

We've probably all had the experience of being misunderstood. Others don't always take our words to mean what we intend for them to mean, and that risk is magnified when we communicate via social media. When we speak to people in person, we can usually tell by their facial expressions and tone of voice whether they are joking or being serious. Without these cues to guide us, however, we can more easily misinterpret what someone says in an e-mail, text message, or tweet. In 2017, Alex McDaniel tweeted about a funny conversation with her 3-year-old son, then jokingly offered to sell her son for $12. An anonymous caller reported her tweet to Mississippi's Child Protective Services, who then investigated McDaniel for suspected human trafficking. Although the case against her was eventually dropped, McDaniel's ordeal underscores the point that what we *mean* isn't always what people *interpret*.[1] Even as social media has greatly expanded our opportunities for interaction, McDaniel's experience demonstrates just how challenging human communication can be.

As You READ

- What needs does communication help us meet?
- How does communication work, and what misconceptions do we have about it?
- What particular skills characterize competent communicators?

Why We Communicate

Scarcely a day goes by when we don't communicate for one purpose or another. For example, we communicate to form personal relationships, to maintain them, and to end them. We communicate to order dinner at a restaurant, negotiate a car loan, and buy music online. Through communication behaviors, teachers instruct us, advertisers persuade us, and actors entertain us. In truth, very little about our everyday lives isn't influenced by the way we communicate.

Because communication affects so many aspects of our existence, learning how to communicate effectively helps improve our lives in multiple ways. As you will see, effective communication depends not only on having the right message but also on shaping that message to meet the needs of your audience. Alex McDaniel knew that her tweet was meant to be a joke, but she failed to consider how others—having only the text of her message to go on—might react. To **adapt** means to modify your behavior to accommodate what others are doing. This course will help you develop the tools you need to understand the communication process and the skills you need to adapt your communication behavior to others.

Communication is the process by which we use signs, symbols, and behaviors to exchange information and create meaning.[2] Digital technologies such as Twitter and Instagram give us unprecedented communication abilities. In the wake of widespread sexual misconduct allegations against film producer Harvey Weinstein in 2017, actress Alyssa Milano tweeted the phrase #MeToo to show solidarity with sexual assault victims. Civil rights activist Tarana Burke had initiated the phrase MeToo 11 years earlier to raise awareness of sexual abuse and assault. Within 24 hours of Milano's text, the hashtag had appeared more than 500,000 times on Twitter and more than 4.7 million times on Facebook. Tens of thousands of people—including many high-profile celebrities—shared their own stories of sexual assault, and a social movement was born. Several spin-off movements emerged, such as MeTooMilitary for service members and MeTooK12 for primary and secondary schoolchildren. Despite concerns that some men and women may be falsely accused, the MeToo hashtag has trended in at least 85 countries and the movement has attracted millions of dollars in corporate support. By encouraging victims to share their stories—and by reminding them that they are not alone—the MeToo movement has empowered women and men across the globe to stand up for their rights.

Never before has it been so easy to communicate with others—but what draws us to do so? *Why* do we communicate? As you will see in this section, communication is vital to many different aspects of life, from meeting physical and practical needs to experiencing relationships, spirituality, and identity.

- **adapt** To modify one's behavior to accommodate what others are doing.

- **communication** The process by which people use signs, symbols, and behaviors to exchange information and create meaning.

Andrew Burton/Getty Images

COMMUNICATION ADDRESSES PHYSICAL NEEDS

We humans are such social beings that when we are denied the opportunity for interaction, our mental and physical health can suffer. That is a major reason solitary confinement is considered such a harsh punishment. Several studies have shown that when people are prevented from having contact with others for an extended period, their health can quickly deteriorate.[3] One study even showed that feeling rejected reduces the rate at which a person's heart beats.[4] Similarly, individuals who feel socially isolated because of poverty, homelessness, mental illness, or other stigmatizing situations can suffer emotional distress and even physical pain owing to their lack of interaction with others.[5]

We literally cannot survive without human communication, as shown in a bizarre experiment in the thirteenth century. Frederick II, emperor of Germany, wanted to know what language humans would speak naturally if they weren't taught any particular language. To find out, he placed 50 newborns in the care of nurses who were instructed only to feed and bathe the babies, but not to speak to or hold them. The emperor never discovered the answer to his question, however, because all the infants died.[6] Frederick's experiment was clearly unethical by modern standards, meaning that it did not follow established guidelines for right and wrong. Such an experiment would not be repeated today. However, more recent studies in orphanages and adoption centers, conducted in an ethical manner, have convincingly shown that human interaction—especially touch—is critical for infants' survival and healthy development.[7]

Positive social interaction keeps adults healthy, too. Research shows that people without strong social ties, such as close friendships and family relationships, are more likely to suffer major ailments (such as heart disease and high blood pressure) and to die prematurely than are people who have close, satisfying relationships.[8] They are also more likely to suffer basic ailments, such as colds, and they often take longer to recover from illnesses and injuries.[9] Communication researchers Chris Segrin and Stacey Passalacqua have even found that loneliness is related to sleep disturbances and stress.[10] That connection matters to many college students, as young adults ages 18 to 22 report higher levels of loneliness than any other age group.[11] Although we can't say for sure why social interaction and health are related, it is clear that communication plays an important role in keeping us healthy, both physically and mentally.

COMMUNICATION MEETS RELATIONAL NEEDS

Besides our physical needs, each of us also has **relational needs**—the essential elements we look for in our relationships with other people. As communication scholar Narissra Punyanunt-Carter and her colleagues have found, relational needs include companionship, affection, and the ability to relax and get away from our problems.[12] We don't necessarily have the same needs in all our relationships—you probably value your friends for somewhat different reasons than you value your relatives, for instance. The bottom line, though, is that we need relationships in our lives, and communication is a large part of how we establish and maintain these relationships.[13]

Many features of our day-to-day lives are designed to promote the development of human relationships. Neighborhoods, schools, workplaces, malls, theaters, and restaurants are all social settings in which we regularly interact with others in some way. Technology is also an avenue for promoting our relationships. Smartphones let us call or exchange text messages with virtually anyone at the touch of a button. The Internet offers multiple ways of connecting with others, and many people have met new friends or romantic partners online.[14] Table 1 provides an idea of how much of our lives are spent communicating in electronically mediated ways. Just imagine how challenging it would be to form and maintain strong social relationships if you did not have the ability to communicate with others. The lack of communication opportunity is a common experience for many immigrants, who often struggle to adapt to their new culture and to learn its language—and who may feel lonely or ignored in the process.[15]

Some scholars believe our need for relationships is so fundamental that we can hardly get by without them.[16] For example, research has shown that having an active social life is one of the most powerful predictors of a person's

> • **relational needs** The essential elements people seek in their relationships with others.

Communication technology connects us in unprecedented ways. Social networking sites and chat apps make it easy for us to maintain close relationships, regardless of physical distance.

Oliver Rossi/Getty Images

TABLE 1	
COMMUNICATING ELECTRONICALLY	
1.9	Average number of e-mail accounts per U.S. e-mail user
74	Percentage of Facebook users who check their account at least once per day
83	Percentage of U.S. teenagers who sleep with, or next to, their cell phone
338	Number of friends the average Facebook user has
4,900,000	Number of Skype users per day
118,000,000	Number of users following Barack Obama (@barackobama), the most followed account on Twitter
360,000,000	Number of active blogs on Tumblr
246,500,000,000	Average number of e-mail messages sent worldwide per day

HOW DO YOU COMPARE? ⟶ Take note of how you compare to these averages. Do you have more e-mail accounts or Facebook friends than average, or fewer? Do you sleep next to your cell phone? Are you an average communicator in these ways, or do you differ from the averages?

SOURCES: Radicati Group; Pew Research Center; Common Sense; Brandwatch; Digital Marketing Research; Twitter Analytics; Mediakix. Statistics are from August 2019.

overall happiness.[17] In fact, the single most important predictor of happiness in life—by far—is the degree to which an individual has a happy marriage.[18] Marital happiness is more important than income, job status, education, leisure time, or anything else in accounting for how happy people are with their lives. On the negative side, people in distressed marriages are much more likely to suffer from major depression, and they even report being in worse physical health than their happily married counterparts.[19]

The cause-and-effect relationship between marriage and happiness isn't a simple one. It may be that strong marriages promote happiness and well-being, or it may be that happy, healthy people are more likely than others to be happily married. Whatever the reason, personal relationships clearly play an important role in our lives, and communication helps us form and maintain them.

People's relational needs were challenged in 2020 when the novel coronavirus (SARS-CoV-2) infected millions around the world. Every U.S. state imposed requirements for quarantine that forced many to work or go to school entirely online and prevented people from spending time with friends or loved ones in person. Even when people were around one another in public, obligations to practice *social distancing* kept many from shaking hands, hugging, or interacting in close proximity. As a result, feelings of loneliness and isolation were common during the coronavirus pandemic.

COMMUNICATION FILLS IDENTITY NEEDS

Are you curious? Laid-back? Caring? Impatient? Each of us can probably come up with a long list of adjectives to describe ourselves, but here's the critical question: How do you *know* you are those things? In other words, how do you form an identity?

The ways we communicate with others—and the ways others communicate with us—play a major role in

Research indicates that the strongest predictor of happiness in life is the degree to which an individual has a happy marriage.

Purestock/Alamy Stock Photo

shaping how we see ourselves.[20] As we'll consider in the chapter on perceiving ourselves and others, people form their identities partly by comparing themselves to others. If you consider yourself intelligent, for instance, what that really means is that you see yourself as more intelligent than most other people. If you think you're shy, you see most other people as more outgoing than you are.

One way we learn how we compare to others is by communicating with those around us. If people treat you as intelligent or shy, you may begin to believe that you have those characteristics. In other words, those qualities will become part of your self-image. As you will see in the perceiving chapter, identity develops over the course of life, and communication plays a critical role in driving that process. Good communicators also have the ability to emphasize different aspects of their identities in different situations. For example, at work it might be important for you to portray your organized, efficient side, whereas at a pool party you might choose to project your fun-loving nature and sense of humor.

COMMUNICATION MEETS SPIRITUAL NEEDS

An important aspect of identity for many people is their spirituality. Spirituality includes the principles someone values in life ("I value loyalty" or "I value equal treatment for all people"). It also encompasses a person's *morals*, or notions about right and wrong ("It's never okay to steal, no matter what the circumstances" or "I would lie to save a life, because life is more important than honesty"). Finally, spirituality includes beliefs about the meaning of life, such as personal philosophies, awe of nature, belief in a higher purpose, and religious faith and practices ("I trust in God" or "I believe I will reap what I sow in life").

Communication lets people express their faith and spirituality.
Melba Photo Agency/Alamy Stock Photo

One survey of college students around the United States found that many consider some form of spirituality to be an important part of their identity.[21] Almost half said they consider integrating spirituality into their lives to be essential or very important. For those in the study, spirituality didn't necessarily include formal religion; over 70 percent of students who considered themselves to be spiritual said people can have good values and morals without being religious. For people who include spirituality as a part of their identity, communication provides a means of expressing and sharing spiritual ideas and practices with one another.

COMMUNICATION SERVES INSTRUMENTAL NEEDS

Finally, people communicate to meet their practical, everyday needs, which researchers call **instrumental needs**. Some instrumental needs have short-term objectives, such as ordering a drink in a bar, scheduling a haircut on the telephone, filling out a rebate card, and raising your hand when you want to speak in class. Others encompass longer-term goals, such as getting a job and earning a promotion. The communicative behaviors entailed in serving instrumental needs may not always contribute directly to our health, relationships, identity, or spirituality. Each behavior is valuable, however, because it serves a need that helps us get through daily life.

• **instrumental needs**
Practical, everyday needs.

Meeting instrumental needs may not seem as interesting as forging new relationships or as meaningful as expressing spiritual beliefs, but it is important for two reasons. The first reason is simply that we have many instrumental needs. In fact, most of the communication we engage in on a day-to-day basis is probably mundane and routine—not heavy, emotionally charged conversations but instrumental interactions such as talking to professors about assignments and taking customers' orders at work. The second reason instrumental needs are important is that many of them—such as buying food at the store and ordering clothes online—have to be met before other needs—for example, maintaining high-quality relationships and finding career fulfillment—can be satisfied.[22]

The Nature and Types of Communication

When 14-year-old Santiago Ventura left his home in the Mexican state of Oaxaca for farm work in Oregon, he had no way of foreseeing the tragedy that would befall him. After the fatal stabbing of a fellow farm worker at a party, Ventura was questioned by a Spanish-speaking police officer. Ventura spoke neither Spanish nor English, however, but only the native language of the Mixtec Indians. During questioning, he never made eye contact with the officer, because Mixtec Indians believe that it is rude to look people directly in the eye. Due to his poor grasp of Spanish, Ventura simply answered "yes" to all the officer's questions, leading the officer to presume his guilt. After a trial in which his lawyer forbade him to testify because of his English-language limitations, Ventura was convicted of murder and sentenced to 10 years to life in prison. Only after 5 years of protests by immigration advocates and jurors who were unconvinced of Ventura's guilt did another judge set aside the verdict, freeing Ventura from his wrongful imprisonment.

Had we been involved in Ventura's case, many of us would have interpreted his words and behaviors the same way the arresting officer did. If they asked Ventura whether he had committed a crime and he replied "yes" while also avoiding eye contact, most reasonable people would conclude that he was guilty. As his story illustrates, however, it is easy to misunderstand others when we don't adapt to their communication styles. Even seemingly straightforward communication behaviors can easily be misinterpreted, sometimes with tragic consequences. Ventura's problems began when the officer interpreted his words and behaviors incorrectly. How do people express and interpret meaning accurately? What accounts for our ability to communicate in the first place?

We begin this section by examining different ways to understand the communication process. Next, we look at some important characteristics of communication and consider various approaches to thinking about communication in social interaction. Finally, we explore five types of communication in which humans engage. Even though you communicate all the time, you will find there is still much to learn about communication's central role in life.

VARIOUS MODELS EXPLAIN THE COMMUNICATION PROCESS

How would you describe the process of communicating? Even researchers have answered that question in different ways over the years. A formal description of a process such as communication is called a **model**. In this section we look at three different models that communication scholars have developed over the years: the action, interaction, and transaction models. The action model was developed first, then the interaction model, and finally the transaction model. In that sense, those models demonstrate how communication researchers have defined and described communication over time.

· **model** A formal description of a process.

Communication as Action In the **action model**, we think of communication as a one-way process.[23] To illustrate, let's say that you need to leave work early next Tuesday to pick up a friend from the airport, and you're getting ready to ask your

· **action model** A model describing communication as a one-way process.

supervisor for permission. The action model starts with the **source**—the individual who has a thought that he or she wishes to communicate. In our example, the source is *you*. To convey the idea that you'd like to leave early, you must **encode** it, which means to put your idea in the form of language or a gesture that your supervisor can understand. Through that process, you create a **message**, which consists of the verbal and/or nonverbal elements of communication to which people give meaning.[24] In this example, your message might be the question, "Would it be alright if I left work a couple of hours early next Tuesday?"

According to the action model, you would then send your message through a communication **channel**, which is a type of pathway for conveying messages. For example, you can pose your question to your supervisor face-to-face, or you can send it by e-mail or through a text message. Selecting the most appropriate channel is a matter of adapting to the communication context. You adapt to a context when you identify your goals, consider the options available to you at the time, and make a strategic decision about how to communicate. If your message is brief and unambiguous—such as an announcement about a meeting location—you might choose to send that message by e-mail or text message in order to be efficient and save time. When asking if you can leave work early, however, you realize that your supervisor may have questions about who will cover for you during that time. A face-to-face or telephone conversation might let you address your supervisor's questions better than a text message or e-mail would, and may also allow you to pay attention to your supervisor's facial expressions or tone of voice, to make sure he or she understands you.

In the action model, your supervisor acts as the **receiver** of the message, the person who will **decode** or interpret it. The communication process also includes **noise**, which is anything that interferes with a receiver's ability to attend to your message. The major types of noise are *physical noise* (such as background conversation in the office or static on the telephone line), *psychological noise* (such as other concerns your supervisor is dealing with that day), and *physiological noise* (such as fatigue or hunger). Any of these could prevent your supervisor from paying full attention to your question.

You can see that the action model is linear: a source sends a message through some channel to a receiver, and noise interferes with the message somehow (Figure 1). Many of us talk and think about the communication process in that linear manner. For example, when you ask someone "Did you get my message?," you are implying that communication is a one-way process. However, human communication is usually more of a back-and-forth exchange than a one-way process—more similar to tennis than to bowling. Over time, researchers responded to that observation by creating an updated model of communication known as the interaction model.

- **source** The originator of a thought or an idea.

- **encode** To put an idea into language or gesture.

- **message** Verbal and nonverbal elements of communication to which people give meaning.

- **channel** A pathway through which messages are conveyed.

- **receiver** The party who interprets a message.

- **decode** To interpret or give meaning to a message.

- **noise** Anything that distracts people from listening to what they wish to listen to.

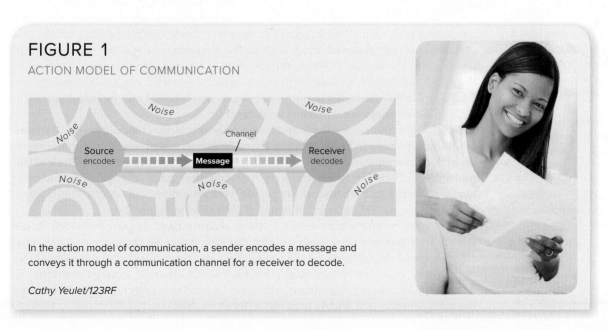

FIGURE 1
ACTION MODEL OF COMMUNICATION

In the action model of communication, a sender encodes a message and conveys it through a communication channel for a receiver to decode.

Cathy Yeulet/123RF

FIGURE 2

INTERACTION MODEL OF COMMUNICATION

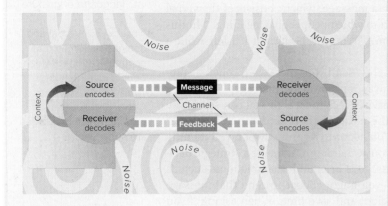

The interaction model of communication explains that our messages are shaped by the feedback we receive from others and by the context in which we interact.

Ingram Publishing

• **interaction model** A model describing communication as a process shaped by feedback and context.

• **feedback** Verbal and nonverbal responses to a message.

• **context** The physical or psychological environment in which communication occurs.

Communication as Interaction

The **interaction model** picks up where the action model leaves off. It includes all the same elements: source, message, channel, receiver, noise, encoding, and decoding, but it differs from the action model in two basic ways. First, the interaction model recognizes that communication is a two-way process. Second, it adds two elements to the mix: feedback and context.

If you've studied physics, you know that every action has a reaction. A similar rule applies to communication. Let's say you are talking to your friend Simone about a conflict you recently had with your romantic partner. As you relate your story, Simone nods along and says "Uh-huh" to show she's listening. She might also ask you questions about what prompted the argument and how you felt afterward. In other words, Simone *reacts* to your story by giving you **feedback**, or various verbal and nonverbal responses to your message. Thus, Simone is not just a passive receiver of your message—instead, she is an active shaper of your conversation.

Now let's imagine that you are sharing your story with Simone while you are having coffee in a crowded café. Would you tell your story any differently than if the two of you were alone? What if you were in a classroom on campus? What if your parents were in the same room? All those situations are part of the **context**, or the environment you are in. Your environment includes both the physical and the psychological context. The *physical context* reflects where you are physically interacting with each other. In contrast, the *psychological context* includes factors that influence people's states of mind, such as the formality of the situation, the level of privacy, and the degree to which the situation is emotionally charged. According to the interaction model, we take context into account when we engage in conversation. That is, we realize that what is appropriate in certain contexts may be inappropriate in others, and we adapt our behaviors accordingly.

By taking account of feedback and context, the interaction model presents the communication process more realistically than the action model does. In telling Simone about your relationship conflict, for instance, your story and Simone's feedback would probably be affected by where you were speaking, how many other people could overhear you (if any), and whether those people were coworkers, classmates, family members, or strangers. The interaction model is illustrated in Figure 2.

Although the interaction model is more realistic than the action model, it still doesn't truly represent how complex communication can be. During conversations, it often seems as though both people are sending and receiving information simultaneously rather than simply communicating back and forth, one message at a time. To understand that aspect of communication, we turn to the transaction model, currently the most complete and widely used of the three models.

Communication as Transaction

Unlike the action and interaction models, the **transaction model** of communication doesn't distinguish between the roles of source and receiver, nor does it represent communication as a series of messages going back and forth. Rather, it maintains that both people in a conversation are simultaneously sources *and* receivers. In addition, it illustrates that the conversation flows in both directions at the same time.[25] As a consequence, each person must continuously adapt his or her communication behaviors to those of the other person, in order to keep the conversation flowing smoothly.

To understand the transaction model, imagine that you have taken your car in for service and you are describing to the mechanic the noise your engine has been making. As you speak, a confused look falls across the mechanic's face. According to the interaction model, that facial expression would constitute feedback to your message. The transaction model recognizes that you will interpret that expression not only as feedback to your message, but also as a message in and of itself, making the mechanic a source and you a receiver. Note that this process occurs while you are describing your car problems to the mechanic. In other words, you are both sending messages to, and receiving messages from, the other at the same time. Figure 3 depicts the transaction model.

Not only does the transaction model reflect the complex nature of communication, but it also leads us to think about context more broadly. It suggests that our communication is affected not just by the physical or psychological environment but also by our experience, gender, social class, and even the history of our relationship with the person or persons to whom we are talking. As we'll see throughout this book, communication is also influenced by our culture—the collection of shared values, beliefs, and behaviors of a group of people.

If you have a history with the car mechanic, you might help him understand your problem by referring to car trouble you've had in the past. If he isn't a native speaker of your language, you might have to speak more slowly and clearly than you otherwise would. Sometimes it's a challenge to consider how cultural aspects of context might affect the way you communicate. According to the transaction model, however, they are always with you.

Adapting to the Communication Context Clearly, then, researchers have different ways of understanding the communication process. Instead of debating which model is right, it's more helpful to look at the useful ideas each model offers. When we do so, we find that each model fits certain situations better than others. You can use that information to adapt to the communication constraints of each model.

FIGURE 3
TRANSACTION MODEL OF COMMUNICATION

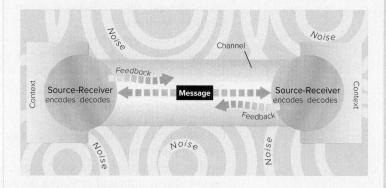

The transaction model recognizes that both people in a conversation are simultaneously senders and receivers.

Thinkstock/Getty Images

• **transaction model**
A model describing communication as a process in which everyone is simultaneously a sender and a receiver.

For instance, sending an e-mail message to your instructor is a good example of the action model. You are the source, and you convey your message through a written channel to a receiver (your instructor). Noise includes any difficulty your instructor experiences in opening the e-mail or understanding the intent of your message because of the language you have used. When the linear model is in use, you can remember that the likelihood of misunderstanding is high because there is no opportunity for feedback.

An apt example of the interaction model is the communication that occurs when you submit a report for your job, and a team of coworkers comments on it in writing. You (the source) have conveyed your message through your report, and your coworkers (the receivers) provide written feedback. Noise includes any difficulties that either you or your coworkers experience in understanding what everyone has said. In that situation, your coworkers and you send messages to one another, but not at the same time. You, therefore, have time to interpret, and perhaps misinterpret, one another's meanings.

Most conversations are good examples of the transaction model, because both parties are sending and receiving messages simultaneously. That process occurs, for instance, when you strike up a conversation with someone sitting next to you on a bus. You might make small talk about where each of you is traveling that day or how the weather has been. As you do so, each of you is sending verbal and nonverbal messages and feedback to the other, and is simultaneously receiving and interpreting such messages from the other. Your conversation is affected by the context, in that you may communicate only to pass the time until you arrive. It is also affected by noise, including traffic sounds and the bus driver's announcements. A face-to-face conversation requires you to adapt your communication behaviors to the other person's on an ongoing basis, as each of you helps to construct the conversation you are having.

Each model, then, is more useful in some situations than in others. The action and interaction models are too simplistic to describe most face-to-face conversations, but when you are just leaving a note for someone or submitting a report for feedback, those models can describe the situation quite well. The transaction model, which many experts consider the most comprehensive of the three models, better describes complex face-to-face communications. As you come across examples of different communication situations in this book, you might ask yourself how well each model fits them.

Now that we've looked at different models of communication, let's consider some of communication's most important characteristics.

COMMUNICATION HAS MANY CHARACTERISTICS

Describing the communication process requires more than just mapping out how it takes place. We also need to catalog its important features. In this section, we will discover that

- Communication relies on multiple channels.
- Communication passes through perceptual filters.
- People give communication its meaning.
- Communication has literal meanings and relational implications.
- Communication sends messages, whether intentional or unintentional.
- Communication is governed by rules.

Communication Relies on Multiple Channels How many different ways do people communicate with one another? Facial expressions convey how a person is feeling. Gestures and tone of voice help others to interpret his or her messages. Touch can signal feelings such as affection and aggression. Even a person's clothing and physical appearance communicate messages about that individual to others. Each of these is an example of a different communication channel, and we often use multiple channels when communicating with others.

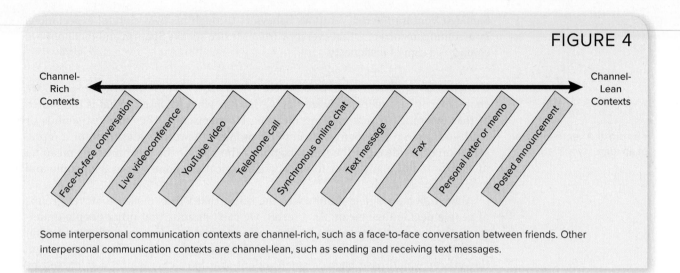

FIGURE 4

Channel-
Rich
Contexts

Channel-
Lean
Contexts

Face-to-face conversation

Live videoconference

YouTube video

Telephone call

Synchronous online chat

Text message

Fax

Personal letter or memo

Posted announcement

Some interpersonal communication contexts are channel-rich, such as a face-to-face conversation between friends. Other interpersonal communication contexts are channel-lean, such as sending and receiving text messages.

Some situations are **channel-rich contexts**—environments that incorporate many communication channels at once (see Figure 4). In face-to-face conversations, for instance, you can pay attention to people's words, see their expressions and gestures, hear their tone of voice, and feel their touch at the same time. Similarly, Zoom and FaceTime conversations depict words, facial cues, gestures, and vocal tones. Because you experience multiple communication channels at once, you can evaluate the information from all those channels simultaneously. Other situations are **channel-lean contexts**—environments that use relatively fewer channels.[26] Text messaging and instant messaging, for example, rely much more heavily on text, so we don't experience a person's voice or gestures. As a consequence, we may pay more attention to that person's words.

- **channel-rich contexts** Communication environments involving many channels at once.

- **channel-lean contexts** Communication environments involving few channels at once.

Communication Passes through Perceptual Filters
Anything you put through a filter—such as air, water, or light—comes out a little bit differently than how it went in. The same happens when we communicate: what one person says is not always exactly what the other person hears. The reason is that we all "filter" incoming communication through our perceptions, experiences, biases, and beliefs.

Let's say you're listening to a senator speak on television. The way you process and make sense of the speech probably depends on how much you agree with the senator's ideas or whether you belong to the same political party. Two people with different political viewpoints may listen to the same speech yet hear something very different. One may hear a set of logical, well thought-out ideas, while the other hears nothing but empty promises and lies.

Perceptual filters can also influence how different people understand the same words. For instance, some trains in New Jersey's transit system are designated "quiet cars." Since the quiet car program started, passengers have disagreed about the proper meaning of "quiet." Some believe it calls for complete silence, whereas others believe they have a right to talk quietly, or whisper. Everyone agrees on which cars are the quiet cars, but their perceptual filters give them different interpretations of what that designation means.

Many aspects of our lives can influence our perception of communication. Whether we are aware of it or not, our ethnic and cultural background, gender, religious beliefs, socioeconomic status, intelligence, education, level of physical attractiveness, and experiences with illness, disease, and death can all act as filters, coloring the way we see the world and the way we make sense of communication. The officer who questioned

Because of people's different perceptual filters, the definition of "quiet" in the quiet cars of public transportation systems has been a point of debate and contention.

TravelCouples/Moment/ Getty Images

Santiago Ventura filtered Ventura's behaviors through his own cultural expectations by assuming, incorrectly, that everyone from Mexico speaks Spanish and that poor eye contact is a sign of dishonesty.

People Give Communication Its Meaning When we write or speak, we choose our words deliberately so that we can say what we *mean.* What is the source of that meaning? Words have no meaning by themselves; they are just sounds or marks on a piece of paper or a computer monitor. A word is a **symbol**, or a representation of an idea, but the word itself isn't the idea or the meaning. The meaning of words—and of many other forms of communication—comes from the people and groups who use them.

- **symbol** A representation of an idea.

Almost all language is arbitrary in the sense that words mean whatever groups of people decide they mean. As a result, we can't assume that other people understand the meanings we intend to communicate just because we understand what we mean. For instance, what is a mouse? If you asked that question 40 years ago, the answer would have been "a small rodent that likes cheese and gets chased by cats." Today, however, many people know a mouse as a pointing device for navigating within a computer screen. As another example, what is a robot? In the United States, it's a humanlike machine that performs mechanical tasks, but in South Africa, it's a traffic light.

Communication Has Literal Meanings and Relational Implications
Nearly every verbal statement has a **content dimension**, which is the literal information the communicator is communicating.[27] When you say to your friend, "I'm kind of unhappy today," the content dimension of your message is that you're feeling sad, angry, or depressed. When your housemate says, "We're out of cereal again," the content dimension of the message is that you have no cereal left.

- **content dimension** Literal information that is communicated by a message.

There's often more to messages than their literal content, though. Many messages also carry signals about the nature of the relationship in which they are shared. Those signals make up the **relational dimension** of the message. For example, by telling your friend that you are feeling unhappy, you may also be sending the message, "I feel comfortable enough with you to share my feelings," or "I want you to help me feel better." Likewise, you might interpret your housemate's statement that you're out of cereal as also saying, "I'm sure you're aware of this, but I'm just reminding you," or you might take it as meaning, "I'm irritated that you never replace the food you use up." Even though messages like those are unspoken, we often infer meanings about our relationships from the tone and manner in which the statements are made.

- **relational dimension** Signals about the relationship in which a message is being communicated.

One way we distinguish between content and relational dimensions is through **metacommunication**, which is communication about communication. Let's say that Jude asks her husband, Han, to read over the speech she is preparing to give at a conference for small-business owners. Han reads the speech and marks it up with critical comments such as, "This argument isn't convincing," "Awkward wording," and "I can't tell what you're trying to say." After reading Han's comments, Jude is disheartened, and Han is confused by her reaction.

- **metacommunication** Communication about communication.

> **Han:** *I thought you wanted my feedback. I was just trying to help you make your speech better; that's what you asked for. Why are you taking my comments so personally?*
>
> **Jude:** *It's not what you said; it's how you said it.*

By focusing his attention on Jude's request for feedback, Han is attending to the content dimension of their conversation. He can't understand why Jude is upset, because Jude had asked him for his feedback. To Jude, however, Han's comments are overly harsh and insensitive, and they imply that he doesn't care about her feelings. Jude is focusing on the relational dimension of their conversation. To highlight that distinction, she metacommunicates with Han by explaining that her hurt feelings were caused not by what Han said but by *the way he said it*. That phrase conveys Jude's thoughts about her communication with Han; thus, it is metacommunicative.

Communication Sends Messages, Intentional and Unintentional Much of what we communicate to others is deliberate. When you order lunch at a restaurant, for instance, you do so intentionally, having thought about what what you want to eat and how much money you want to spend.

Dozing off during class sends messages to others, even if those messages are unintentional.
Cathy Yeulet/123RF

You may communicate a number of other messages, however, without intending to do so. For example, have you ever tried to stay awake in an important meeting? Despite your efforts to look engaged and interested, you might not have been aware that your slouching posture and droopy eyelids were signaling your fatigue, perhaps after a long day of working at a part-time job and attending classes. In that instance, your behavior was sending unintentional messages.

Whether unintentional messages should qualify as communication has been a focal point of debate among communication scholars for many years. Some researchers believe that only deliberate, intentional messages are a part of communication and that if you don't intend to communicate, you aren't communicating.[28] Others subscribe to the belief that "you cannot *not* communicate," meaning that absolutely everything you do has communicative value.[29] The validity of that idea is addressed in the "Fact or Fiction?" box.

Communication Is Governed by Rules Rules tell us which behaviors are required, preferred, or prohibited in various social contexts.[30] Some rules for communication are **explicit rules**, meaning someone has clearly articulated them. Perhaps your parents used to say, "Don't talk with your mouth full." Many universities have explicit rules banning hate speech, such as statements that degrade ethnic or sexual minorities, at campus events and in school publications. Facebook enforces specific guidelines regarding the content of text and photos. Those examples are all explicit communication rules because they directly express expectations for communicative behavior.

In contrast, many communication rules are **implicit rules**—rules that almost everyone in a certain social group knows and follows, even though no one has formally articulated them. People in North American cultures, for instance, follow implicit rules when riding in an elevator, such as "Don't get on if it's already full" and "Don't make eye contact with others while you're riding." Implicit rules also govern taking turns when you are waiting for some type of service, such as at a bank or grocery store; those rules include "Get into an orderly line" and "Don't cut ahead of someone else."

Most people seem to know and accept implicit rules, even though they usually aren't posted anywhere. They are just a part of everyone's cultural knowledge. Because those rules are implicit, however, their interpretations are likely to vary more from person to person than do understandings of explicit rules. For example, some people believe it is an implicit rule that you shouldn't talk on a cell phone in a crowded environment such as a subway train during rush hour, whereas other people don't see that behavior as inappropriate.

• **explicit rules** Rules that have been clearly articulated.

• **implicit rules** Rules that have not been clearly articulated but are nonetheless understood.

SHARPEN Your Skills: *Communication rules*

Choose a specific communication situation, such as listening to a distraught friend, talking to a professor about a grade, or watching a speech at an awards ceremony. Write down at least five implicit communication rules that apply to that situation. For each, note what would likely happen if someone violated the rule in that situation.

Fact or *fiction*?

You Cannot *Not* Communicate

Some of the research findings you'll encounter in this course will make intuitive sense to you, and others will be more challenging. Although our intuition is right much of the time, it can also fail us, and that is just one reason why the systematic study of communication is so useful. In the "Fact or Fiction?" boxes throughout this book, we'll examine some of the more intuitively appealing ideas we hold about communication to see how valid they are.

For instance, Paul Watzlawick, an Austrian-born communication theorist, proposed that "one cannot *not* communicate." He believed that every behavior sends some message, whether intentional or not, so all behavior has communicative value. Because people are engaged in some type of behavior—watching television, crying, sleeping, dancing—at every moment, they cannot help but continuously communicate, according to Watzlawick. Other researchers have pointed out, however, that Watzlawick's idea treats all behavior as communication, and they have argued

instead that unintentional behaviors are not necessarily communicative. If you don't *intend* for your behavior to convey a message, they believe, you aren't engaging in communication.

In this book, I've endeavored to take a position that reflects my own conclusions, which fall somewhere in between those of Watzlawick and his critics. Although I don't believe every possible behavior is a form of communication, neither do I think behaviors must be intentional to have communicative value. I would suggest that even unintended messages—such as the ones you might have expressed while trying to stay awake during a meeting—are forms of communication because they still convey meaning. Many aspects of appearance illustrate that idea. For instance, seeing someone in a wheelchair probably leads you to different conclusions than seeing someone in a white lab coat or an orange prison jumpsuit, yet those messages might be unintentional on the other person's part.

ASK YOURSELF

- What do you think about Watzlawick's idea? Did it seem reasonable or unreasonable to you at first? Why?

- When and how do you communicate messages unintentionally?

SOURCES: Clevinger, T. (1991). Can one not communicate? A conflict of models. *Communication Studies, 42*(4), 340–353. https://doi.org/10.1080/10510979109368348; Andersen, P. A. (1991). When one cannot not communicate: A challenge to Motley's traditional communication postulates. *Communication Studies, 42*(4), 309–325. https://doi.org/10.1080/10510979109368346

FIVE TYPES OF COMMUNICATION

Communication occurs as five basic types: intrapersonal, interpersonal, small group, public, and mass. They differ primarily with respect to the size of the audience, but they also call for different communication skills.

Intrapersonal Communication The form of communication that addresses the smallest audience is **intrapersonal communication**, the communication you have with yourself. When you mentally remind yourself to do something or you rehearse an upcoming conversation in your mind, you are engaging in intrapersonal communication.

Although it may be tempting to equate intrapersonal communication with *cognition*—the act of thinking—your thoughts and memories become communicative only when you put them into words in your mind. Perhaps you have the thought "Don't

• **intrapersonal communication** Communication with oneself.

forget to e-mail Mom about my holiday travel plans." In this instance, you have expressed your thought in words directed at yourself; that is, you have communicated intrapersonally. The same would not be true if you were simply to think of an image, such as a ski slope or a sandy beach, without translating that image into words in your mind.

Interpersonal Communication When you exchange instant messages with a friend, talk on the phone with a relative, or meet face-to-face with your supervisor, you are engaging in interpersonal communication. **Interpersonal communication** occurs between two people in the context of their ongoing relationship, and it is the most common form of communication we enact.[31] Even in larger social groups, such as families and organizations, much of our communication is typically interpersonal in nature. We delve more deeply into interpersonal communication in the chapters on social and professional relationships and intimate relationships.

Small Group Communication Almost all of us interact in small groups of people, such as sports teams, study groups, organizational departments, and teams of students working on a class project. When we communicate with groups of about 3 to 20 people who are working interdependently to accomplish a task, we are engaging in **small group communication**. As we will discover in the chapters on small groups and decision making and leadership, groups have specific ways of making decisions, negotiating power, and working together in the service of their common goals.

Public Communication **Public communication** occurs when we speak or write to an audience larger than a small group. If you give the welcome speech at a convention for your fraternity or sorority or write a column for the convention's newsletter, you are engaging in public communication. Because your communication targets a larger audience, you might spend more time preparing and practicing your remarks than if you were talking only to a friend or a small group. We will examine skills that are helpful for successful public communication when we discuss public speaking.

Mass Communication Communication delivered to a large audience is considered public communication unless it is being transmitted via electronic or print media, such as magazines, television, newspapers, blogs, radio, and websites. Communication transmitted by such media is considered **mass communication**. Newspaper journalists, television personalities, bloggers, and podcasters are among those whose words are disseminated to vast audiences of people with whom they have little or no personal connection. Because its audience is so large, mass communication works well for distributing news, commentary, and entertainment. It also is effective for marketing products and services through advertisements, but its breadth makes mass communication unsuited for developing relationships or making collective decisions.

Now that we've surveyed the nature and basic types of communication, we'll shift gears and look at some common beliefs about communication that are not as valid as they might seem.

Interpersonal communication occurs between people in the context of their relationships.
Thinkstock

• **interpersonal communication**
Communication that occurs between two people in the context of their relationship.

• **small group communication**
Communication occurring within small groups of approximately 3 to 20 people.

• **public communication**
Communication directed at an audience that is larger than a small group.

• **mass communication**
Communication to a large audience that is transmitted by media.

Dispelling Some Communication Myths

In one way or another, you've communicated practically every day of your life. You might therefore feel that you already know what there is to know about communication. As you will see, however, people have many different ideas about communication. Some of those ideas are not very accurate, which can lead people to make mistakes when communicating with others. In this section we will examine five common communication myths so that you will be better able to separate fact from fiction:

1. Everyone is a communication expert.
2. Communication will solve any problem.
3. Communication can break down.
4. Communication is inherently good.
5. More communication is always better.

MYTH: EVERYONE IS A COMMUNICATION EXPERT

Because people communicate constantly, it's easy to believe that just about everyone is an expert in communication. Indeed, in a nationwide survey of American adults conducted by the National Communication Association, fully 91 percent of participants rated their communication skills as above average.[32] Keep in mind, though, that having *experience* with something is not the same as having *expertise*. Many people drive, but that doesn't make them expert drivers. Many people have children, but that doesn't make them parenting experts. Experience can be invaluable, but expertise requires knowledge and ability that go beyond personal experience. Thus, experts in driving, parenting, or communication have training in their fields and a level of understanding that most people who drive, raise children, or communicate don't have.

SHARPEN Your Skills: *Communication experts*

Identify three communication experts outside your college or university. Read about each person's background, and list the training, education, and/or work experiences that make that person an expert in communication. In a brief report, share your findings with your instructor to ensure that you have identified appropriate markers of expertise for each person.

MYTH: COMMUNICATION WILL SOLVE ANY PROBLEM

The classic Paul Newman movie *Cool Hand Luke* (1967) featured a prison warden who had his own special way of dealing with inmates. Whenever things went wrong, he would say, "What we've got here is a failure to communicate,"[33] after which he would beat the inmate unconscious and send him to solitary confinement. Sometimes it seems as though we could solve almost any problem—especially in our relationships—if only we could communicate better. It's easy to blame a lack of communication when things go wrong. Yet the fact is that poor communication isn't the cause of every problem.[34]

On his television talk show *Dr. Phil*, psychologist Phil McGraw often counsels couples encountering difficulties in their relationships. Suppose Connie and Andy appear on *Dr. Phil* complaining that they have been drifting apart for some time. When they discuss their problems on the show, Connie says she feels they need to communicate better to save their relationship. In the course of their conversation, however, Andy states very clearly that he is no longer in love with Connie and he wishes to explore a new relationship with someone else.

Will communication ultimately solve this couple's marital problems? No—in fact, it will probably cause Connie to realize that their relationship is already over. Going their separate ways might be better for both of them in the long run, so we could say that communication will help them to come to that realization. Nevertheless, it won't solve the problem of their drifting apart in the first place. Therefore, we must be careful not to assume that better communication can resolve any problem we might face in our relationships.

AF archive/Alamy Stock Photo

MYTH: COMMUNICATION CAN BREAK DOWN

Just as we sometimes blame our problems on a lack of communication, many of us also point to a "breakdown" in communication as the root of problems. When marriages fail, the spouses may say it was a breakdown in communication that led to their relational difficulties. When government agencies are slow to respond to a natural disaster, people frequently blame their sluggish response on communication breakdowns within those agencies.

The metaphor of the communication breakdown makes intuitive sense to many of us. After all, our progress on a journey is halted if our car breaks down, so it's easy to think that our progress in other endeavors is halted because our communication has broken down. But communication isn't a mechanical object like a car, a refrigerator, or an iPad. Instead, it's a process that unfolds between and among people over time. It may be easy to blame a breakdown in communication for problems we face in personal relationships or during crisis situations. What is actually happening in those contexts is that we are no longer communicating *effectively*. In other words, the problem lies not with communication itself but with the way we are using it. That is one reason why learning about communication—as you are doing in this class—can be so beneficial.

MYTH: COMMUNICATION IS INHERENTLY GOOD

In many instances, people feel they are *talking* but not really *communicating*.
Steve Debenport/Getty Images

Listen to people who are having relationship problems, and you will hear them say they no longer communicate with their romantic partners, parents, or friends. "Sure, we talk all the time," someone might say, "but we don't really *communicate* anymore." Reflected in that statement is the idea that *talking* means just producing words, but *communicating* means sharing meaning with another person in an open, supportive, and inherently positive manner.[35]

Thinking that communication is inherently good is similar to thinking that money is inherently good. Sometimes money is put to positive uses, such as providing a home for your family and donating to a worthy charity. At other times it is put to negative uses, such as providing funding for a terrorist group and gambling away hard-earned income. In either case, it isn't the money itself that is good or bad—rather, it's the way it is used.

We can make the same observation about communication. We can use communication for positive purposes, such as expressing love for our parents and comforting a grieving friend. We can also use it for negative purposes, such as intimidating and deceiving people. In fact, bullying has become a prevalent problem for many

THE DARK SIDE OF COMMUNICATION

Hurtful Communication: Bullying and Cyberbullying

Recent years have brought increased attention to the problems associated with bullying. Bullying can occur in person and often involves teasing, name-calling, threats, spreading rumors, and physical behaviors such as hitting, kicking, or pushing. In the United States, approximately 20 percent of young people report experiencing bullying in school. Bullying also occurs online—a behavior known as *cyberbullying*—and can involve harassing or stalking people and sending humiliating photos of them to others. Approximately 15 percent of young people in the United States report being the target of cyberbullying, but that figure is likely low because many cyberbullying incidents go unreported.

One reason we are paying more attention to bullying is that we better understand its health risks. According to research, adolescent and adult bullying targets are at elevated risk of experiencing anxiety and depression,

inflammation, sleep problems, body pain, and frequent headaches. They are also more likely to smoke heavily and are even more likely to contemplate or attempt suicide.

There is evidence, in fact, that experiencing bullying actually changes the structure of our brains. One study examined brain scans of more than 600 young people in Europe, nearly a third of whom had endured chronic bullying. According to the research, parts of the brain that allow people to learn from their experiences were demonstrably smaller in bullying targets than in non-targets. The scientists who conducted the study speculated that these differences could help explain why bullying is associated with mental health problems such as anxiety.

If you or someone you know is a target of bullying or cyberbullying, the website StopBullying.gov offers information and resources that can help.

SOURCES: National Center for Education Statistics. (2019, April). Indicator 10: Bullying at school and electronic bullying. https://nces.ed.gov/programs/crimeindicators/ind_10.asp; Quinlan, E. B., Barker, E. D., Luo, Q., Banaschewski, T., Bokde, A. L. W., Bromberg, U., Büchel, C., Desrivières, S., Flor, H., Frouin, V., Garavan, H., Chaarani, B., Gowland, P., Heinz, A., Brühl, R., Martinot, J.-L., Paillère Martinot, M.-L., Nees, F., Orfanos, D. P., Paus, T., . . . IMAGEN Consortium. (2018). Peer victimization and its impact on adolescent brain development and psychopathology. *Molecular Psychiatry*, article 1. https://doi.org/10.1038/s41380-018-0297-9; Wolke, D., & Lereya, S. T. (2015). Long-term effects of bullying. *Archives of Disease in Childhood, 100*(9), 879–885. https://doi.org/10.1136/archdischild-2014-306667

adolescents and adults, and one with the potential to cause enormous harm, as "The Dark Side of Communication" explains.

Regarding the "dark side" terminology: in recent years, several scholars in the area of interpersonal communication have been studying what they call the "dark side" of communication, or the ways in which people sometimes use communication to hurt or manipulate others. As you encounter "The Dark Side of Communication" box in each chapter of this book, remember that communication itself is not positive or negative—it's what individuals do with it that makes it good or bad.

MYTH: MORE COMMUNICATION IS ALWAYS BETTER

Antonio thinks that if others don't agree with him, the reason is that they just don't understand him. In those situations, he talks on and on, figuring that others will eventually see things his way if he gives them enough information. Perhaps you know someone like Antonio. Does more communication always produce a better outcome?

When people have genuine disagreements, more talk doesn't always help. In some cases, it can just lead to frustration and anger. A study of consultations between doctors and patients found that the more doctors talked, the more likely they were to get off-track and forget about the patients' problems, a pattern that can translate into worse care for the patient.[36] Another study found that the more people communicated with one another on cell phones, the less happy they were, the less satisfied they were with their families, and the more likely they were to say that their work lives "spilled over" into their family lives.[37]

We've already considered that communication cannot solve every problem, so it shouldn't surprise you to learn that more of it isn't always preferable. Indeed, sometimes it seems as though the less said, the better. As you'll learn in this book, the *effectiveness* of our communication—rather than the *amount*—is often what matters. That fact explains why learning to be a competent communicator is so advantageous.

Building Your Communication Competence

Recently, the National Association of Colleges and Employers asked employers around the United States which skills and personal qualities they most look for in new college graduates whom they are considering hiring. As you can see in Table 2, communication skills topped the list.[38] That survey—along with several others like it over the past decade—indicates that being an effective communicator gives job applicants a sizable advantage.[39]

None of us is born a competent communicator. Rather, like driving a car, playing a sport, or designing a web page, communicating competently requires skills we must learn and practice. That doesn't mean that nature doesn't give some people a head start. Indeed, research shows that genes partly contribute to some of our communication traits, such as how sociable, aggressive, or shy we are.[40] No matter which traits we are born with, though, we can still learn how to communicate competently. In this section, we probe what it means to be a competent communicator, which skills are necessary for competent communication, and how we learn them.

Companies seek to hire employees with excellent communication skills.

Abel Mitja Varela/The Agency Collection/Getty Images

• **communication competence** Communication that is effective and appropriate for a given situation.

COMPETENT COMMUNICATION IS EFFECTIVE AND APPROPRIATE

Think about five people you consider to be really good communicators. Who's on your list? Any of your friends or relatives? Classmates or teachers? Politicians? Celebrities? Yourself? You probably recognize that identifying good communicators means first asking yourself what a good communicator is. Even communication scholars find that a tricky question. Nevertheless, most researchers seem to agree that **communication competence** means communicating in ways that are *effective* and *appropriate* in a given situation.[41] Communication scholars Brian Spitzberg and Bill Cupach have spent much of their careers studying effective, appropriate communication. Let's take a closer look at what it means to communicate effectively and appropriately, and also at how we can engage in effective and appropriate communication online.

Communicating Effectively Effectiveness describes how well your communication achieves its goals.[42] Suppose you want to persuade your neighbor to donate money to a shelter for abused animals. There are many ways to achieve that goal. You could explain how much the shelter needs the money and identify all the services it provides to animals in need. You could offer to do yard work in exchange for your neighbor's donation. You could even recite the times when you have donated to causes that were important to your neighbor.

TABLE 2
PERSONAL QUALITIES MOST SOUGHT BY EMPLOYERS AMONG NEW COLLEGE GRADUATES

1. Communication skills

2. Problem-solving skills

3. Ability to work in a team

4. Initiative

5. Analytical/quantitative skills

SOURCE: National Association of Colleges and Employers. (2019). *Job Outlook 2019*. Author.

Your choice of strategy may partly depend on what other goals you are trying to achieve at the same time. If maintaining a good relationship with your neighbor is also important to you, then asking politely may be the most effective course of action. If all you want is the money, however, and your neighbor's feelings are less important to you, then making your neighbor feel obligated to donate may help you achieve your goal, even though it might not be as acceptable morally.

The point is that no single communication strategy is effective in all situations. Because we often pursue more than one goal at a time, being an effective communicator means using behaviors that meet all the goals we have, in the specific context in which we have them.

Communicating Appropriately for the Social and Cultural Context

Besides being effective, competent communication should also be appropriate. That means it adheres to the rules and expectations that apply in a social situation, as we considered earlier in this chapter. For instance, when a coworker asks, "How are you?" you know that it's appropriate to say, "Fine, how are you?" in return. The coworker probably isn't expecting a long, detailed description of how your day is going, so if you launch into one, he or she may find that response inappropriate. Similarly, it's appropriate in most classrooms to raise your hand and wait to be called on before speaking, so it would be inappropriate in those cases to blurt out your comments.

Communicating appropriately can be especially challenging when you're interacting with people from other cultures. The reason is that many communication rules are culture-specific, so what might be perfectly appropriate in one culture may be inappropriate or even offensive in another.[43] If you are visiting a Canadian household and your hosts offer you food, it's appropriate to accept if you are hungry. In many Japanese households, however, it is inappropriate to accept until you have declined the food twice and your hosts offer it a third time.

Even within a specific culture, expectations can vary according to the social situation. Communication that's appropriate at home might be inappropriate at work and vice versa. Moreover, communication that's appropriate for a socially powerful individual is not necessarily appropriate for everyone. It might not be unexpected for your manager to make you wait before a meeting, although making your manager wait for you may be considered out of line.

High self-monitors pay close attention to the way they look, sound, and act.
Ghislain and Marie David de Lossy/Cultura/Getty ImagesC

People who know how to communicate effectively can use their abilities to succeed in a wide range of fields. Throughout this book, you'll find descriptions of careers that can make excellent use of communication training. In the "Putting Communication to Work" box, you'll also discover the diversity of options available to students who hone their communication skills.

Whether face-to-face or online, communication competence implies both effectiveness and appropriateness. Note that those are characteristics of *communication*, not of people. Thus, the logical follow-up question is whether competent *communicators* share any traits. They do, as we will see next.

COMPETENT COMMUNICATORS SHARE MANY CHARACTERISTICS AND SKILLS

Look again at your list of five people who are good communicators. What do they have in common? Of course, competence is situation-specific, so what works in one context may not work in another. Good communicators, however, tend to have certain characteristics that help them to behave competently in most situations: they are self-aware, adaptable, empathic, cognitively complex, and ethical.

putting**communication**to**work**

Search

Job Title >

Work Responsibilities >

Public Information Officer for Nonprofit Organization

A public information officer, or PIO, is the public face and voice of an organization. This person speaks to the media and to representatives from government and business about the organization's activities and priorities. On any given day, the PIO might be writing a press release, taking part in a live televised interview, making an announcement to an organization's employees, or giving a presentation about the organization to a group of schoolchildren. The job requires excellent public speaking skills, an ability to consider how messages should be framed, and a high level of skill at adapting to the communication needs of different audiences.

Competent Communicators Are Self-Aware Good communicators are aware of their own behavior and its effects on others.[44] Researchers call that awareness **self-monitoring**. People who are "high self-monitors" pay close attention to the way they look, sound, and act in social situations. In contrast, people who are "low self-monitors" often seem oblivious to both their own behaviors and other people's reactions to them. For instance, you may know someone who never seems to notice that he dominates the conversation or who seems unaware that she speaks louder than anyone around her.

> • **self-monitoring** Awareness of one's behavior and how it affects others.

Self-monitoring usually makes people more competent communicators because it enables them to see how their behavior fits or doesn't fit in a given social setting. In addition, high self-monitors often have the ability to understand people's emotions and social behaviors accurately.[45]

How high of a self-monitor are you? Take the quiz in "The Competent Communicator" box to find out.

Competent Communicators Are Adaptable It's one thing to be aware of your own behavior; it's quite another to be able to adapt it to different situations. We have seen that what works in one situation might not be effective in another. Competent communicators are able to assess what will be appropriate and effective in a given context and then modify their behaviors accordingly.[46] As we'll discover in the chapter on choosing, developing, and researching a topic, part of delivering a good speech is being aware of the audience and adapting our behavior accordingly. A competent communicator would speak differently to a group of senior executives than to a group of new hires, for example.

Competent Communicators Are Empathic Good communicators practice **empathy**, or the ability to be "other-oriented" and to understand other people's thoughts and feelings.[47] When people say "Put yourself in my shoes," they are asking

> • **empathy** The ability to think and feel as others do.

Are You a High Self-Monitor?

One of the ways to improve your communication ability is to think about how you communicate now. Each "The Competent Communicator" box will help you to do so by presenting a self-assessment quiz covering a specific communication skill or tendency. For instance, how high a self-monitor are you? Indicate how well each of the following statements describes you by assigning it a number between 1 ("not at all") and 7 ("very well").

Design Pics/Don Hammond

_____ I tend to show different sides of myself to different people.

_____ I would probably make a good actor.

_____ I can usually tell when I've said something inappropriate by reading it in the listener's eyes.

_____ I pay attention to how other people react to my behavior.

_____ I can adjust my behavior to meet the requirements of any situation I'm in.

_____ I am often able to read people's true emotions through their eyes.

_____ I can usually tell when others are lying to me.

_____ I am not always the person I appear to be.

When you're finished, add up your scores. Your total score should fall between 8 and 56. A score of 8–22 suggests that self-monitoring is a skill you can work on, as you are doing in this class. If you scored between 23 and 38, you are already a moderate self-monitor, with a good sense of self-awareness. Continued practice can strengthen that skill. If you scored above 38, you are a high self-monitor, which usually makes your communication more effective.

Remember that your score on this quiz—and on every "The Competent Communicator" quiz in this book—reflects only how you see yourself at this time. If your score surprised you, take the quiz again later in the course to see how studying communication may have changed the way you assess your communication abilities.

SOURCE: Lennox, R. D., & Wolfe, R. N. (1984). Revision of the self-monitoring scale. *Journal of Personality and Social Psychology, 46*(6), 1349–1364. https://doi.org/10.1037/0022-3514.46.6.1349

you to consider a situation empathically, from *their* perspective rather than your own. Because people often think and feel differently than you do about the same situation, empathy helps you understand and adapt to their communication behaviors.

Suppose you want to ask your instructor for a one-week extension on an assignment. You might think, "What's the big deal? It's only a week." To your instructor, however, the extension might mean that she will be unable to complete her grading in time for her planned vacation. If the situation were reversed, how would you feel? An empathic approach would help you consider the situation from the instructor's perspective and tailor your behavior accordingly. People who don't practice empathy tend to assume that everyone thinks and feels the same way they do, and they risk creating problems when that assumption isn't accurate.

Empathy is a particular challenge for individuals with conditions such as autism and Asperger's disorder, both of which impair the ability to interpret other people's nonverbal behaviors. You may have little difficulty judging when a friend is being sarcastic, for instance, because you infer that from his facial expressions and tone of voice. For people with autism or Asperger's disorder, however, the meaning of those nonverbal signals may not be as evident, making it more challenging to understand and adopt another person's perspective.

Children with autism often have difficulty interpreting other people's nonverbal behaviors.

Maskot/Getty Images

Competent Communicators Are Cognitively Complex

Let's say you see your friend Annika coming toward you in the hallway at school. You smile and get ready to say hi, but she walks right by as if you're not there. How would you interpret her behavior? Maybe she's mad at you. Maybe she was concentrating on something when she passed by and didn't notice anyone around her. Maybe she actually did smile at you and you just didn't see it.

The ability to consider a variety of explanations and to understand a given situation in multiple ways is called **cognitive complexity**. Cognitive complexity is a valuable skill because it keeps you from jumping to the wrong conclusion and responding inappropriately.[48] Someone with little cognitive complexity might feel slighted by Annika's behavior and might therefore ignore her the next time they meet. In contrast, someone with more cognitive complexity would remember that behaviors do not always mean what we think they mean. That person would be more open-minded, considering several possible interpretations of Annika's behavior.

Competent Communicators Are Ethical

Finally, competent communicators are ethical communicators. **Ethics** are principles that guide us in judging whether something is morally right or wrong. Ethical communication generally dictates that we treat people fairly, communicate honestly, and avoid immoral or unethical behavior. Communicating ethically can be easier said than done, however, because people often have very different ideas about right and wrong. What may be morally justified to one person or one culture may be considered completely unethical to another.

Ethical considerations are often particularly important when we are engaged in compliance-gaining strategies, trying to change the way another person thinks or behaves. Referring back to a previous example: is it ethical to make your neighbor feel obligated to contribute money to your cause? To some people, that strategy would seem unfair, because it may lead your neighbor to donate even if he or she doesn't want to. Depending on why you need the money, however, or what you have done for your neighbor in the past, you might not consider it unethical even if others do. Competent communicators are aware that people's ideas about ethics vary. They are also aware of their own ethical beliefs, and they communicate in ways that are consistent with those beliefs.

Take one last look at your list of five good communicators. Are they generally aware of their own behaviors and able to adapt them to different contexts? Can they adopt other people's perspectives and consider various ways of explaining situations? Do

SHARPEN Your Skills: *Evaluating competence*

Choose a reality TV show, and consider the cast members and their communication behaviors. Based on what you have learned in this section, how would you rate each participant in terms of communication competence? What makes some individuals more communicatively competent than others? Try to identify specific skills, such as empathy and cognitive complexity, that distinguish each individual. Consider how each person might improve his or her communication competencies. Share your thoughts in a brief report.

• **cognitive complexity** The ability to understand a given situation in multiple ways.

• **ethics** Principles that guide judgments about whether something is morally right or wrong.

Difficult Conversations

Dealing with an Angry Customer

Imagine this: You are working at a car rental counter at the airport when a customer approaches you to complain. She says your website listed the cost of her rental car at $39.95 per day, so she is frustrated about getting charged more than twice that amount. As you explain that taxes, insurance, and fuel fees account for the added costs, she blames you for trying to scam her. You get angry and consider calling security to have her escorted away.

In your situation, it is natural to feel attacked and to respond with anger. After all, the customer seems to be blaming you for the cost of the car, when you know she was clearly shown the costs at the time of the rental.

Now, consider this: You could respond to this customer's anger with anger of your own, and call security to have her escorted out. A more constructive approach to this difficult conversation may be to respond to the customer in an empathic way.

- Begin by putting aside your own feelings for a moment and considering how you would feel if you were this customer. Have you ever felt cheated or taken advantage of by a business? If so, then you understand how this woman feels right now.

- Remember that it's not important whether you think her feelings are justified. All that matters in this moment is identifying how she feels.

- Look for ways to communicate that you recognize the customer's feelings. Statements such as "I understand how frustrating this must be" convey your *empathy* for the other person's situation. Comments such as "I would feel the same way if I were in your situation" show the customer that you can take her perspective.

Tyler Olson/123RF

Recognizing the customer's feelings won't, by itself, solve her problem. Communicating with empathy, however, can help you identify acceptable solutions because it lets you consider the situation from her point of view. Empathic communication can also keep the customer's emotions from becoming more negative.

they behave ethically? These aren't the only characteristics that make someone a competent communicator, but they are among the most important. That's especially true when we deal with tricky situations, as the "Difficult Conversations" box illustrates. To the extent that we can develop and practice these skills, we can all become better at the process of communication.

When it comes to communication competence, the mode of communication matters. People who grew up before the invention of the Internet may feel comfortable talking to others face-to-face or by telephone, for instance, but they may be less competent at using Snapchat, sending tweets, or posting to Instagram. For some others, it's just the opposite. Because social media have greatly expanded our options for communication, it pays to consider specifically what makes people competent online communicators.

COMPETENT ONLINE COMMUNICATION

These days, much of our interpersonal communication takes place in electronically mediated contexts. These include e-mail, instant messaging, and text messaging; social networking (such as on Facebook and LinkedIn); tweeting; image sharing (such as on YouTube and Instagram); and videoconferencing (such as on Skype and FaceTime), among others. As you'll see in this section, communicating competently in these venues requires paying attention to their unique capabilities and pitfalls.

Beware of the Potential for Misunderstanding Face-to-face conversations allow you to pay attention to behaviors that help to clarify the meaning of a speaker's words. People's facial expressions, gestures, and tone of voice, for example, generally provide clues about what they are trying to say. Are they speaking seriously or sarcastically? Are they upset or calm, tentative or self-assured? We can usually tell a lot about people's meaning by considering not only *what they say* but *how they say it*.

We saw earlier that some channel-lean forms of communication—such as tweeting and instant messaging—rely heavily on text, restricting our access to facial expressions and other clues. As a result, these forms of communication increase the potential for misunderstanding. Many of us have had the experience of teasing or joking with someone in a text message, for instance, only to discover that the person took our words seriously and felt offended or hurt. Similarly, recall from the chapter-opening story that Alex McDaniel even faced potential legal action because someone misunderstood her tweet.

To communicate competently when using channel-lean media, follow these guidelines:

- *Review your message before you share it.* Although the meaning of your words is clear to you, think about the ways in which it may be unclear to your recipient. In particular, identify words or phrases in your message that could have more than one meaning.

- *Clarify your meaning wherever possible.* When you find parts of your message that could be misinterpreted, consider whether using a different word or phrase would be clearer.

- *Use emoji to convey emotion.* Adding symbols to express your emotional state—such as a smiling face, a winking face, or a crying face—can help receivers understand how to interpret your message.

Presume that Everything Is Permanent and Nothing Is Secret Perhaps you've had the embarrassing experience of sending a text message to the wrong person. Words you intended for one recipient are therefore read by someone else, who may choose either to delete them or to save them. That situation illustrates an important characteristic of electronically mediated communication: Everything you say and do leaves behind a record. That creates the possibility that your messages can be seen or heard by virtually anyone. Sometimes this occurs by accident, as when you send your text message to the wrong person. On other occasions, however, people can copy or forward your messages to others without your knowledge or permission.

It is best, therefore, to remember that anything you communicate via electronically mediated channels could reach people other than your intended receivers, and to modify your messages accordingly. Here are some specific tips:

- *Write as though others will read your words.* Psychologist Ken Siegel, who advises companies on workplace efficiency, offers this advice: "send e-mail with the assumption that the person you really don't want to read it *will* read it."[49]

- *Double-check your recipients before hitting "Send."* When drafting a text message, make sure you have chosen the proper receiver. Before you send an e-mail message, ensure that you haven't hit "Reply All" when you intended to reply only to one person.

- *Take sensitive messages offline.* When your message includes sensitive information, communicate it face to face whenever possible. Never send private financial information, personal evaluations of others, or similarly sensitive details in an e-mail or instant message that could easily be saved and shared with others.

Avoid Communicating in Anger When someone else's words or actions upset us, it can be easy to lash out by sending a nasty text message or posting words of anger online. Doing so may soothe our feelings in the short run, but our words can continue to wound and upset others long after our anger is gone. That's important to remember, because anger can cloud our ability to think clearly and make us less likely to care about the repercussions of our words. Because electronically mediated messages can be read—and misunderstood—by broad audiences, however, competent online communicators recognize this danger and avoid communicating in anger.

To do the same, consider these suggestions:

- *Consider whether your anger springs from misunderstanding.* We have seen that electronically mediated messages—especially channel-lean forms such as e-mails and texts—are easy to misinterpret. If your anger was sparked by a message you received from someone else, consider the possibility that you misunderstood what he or she was saying. Before lashing out at the person, think about whether you might have misinterpreted his or her meaning.

- *Write a draft, then set it aside.* There's nothing wrong with *composing* messages while you're in an emotional state. You just want to be cautious about sending them. A good option is to write a draft of your message and then set it aside, without sending it. Later, after you feel less angry, read your draft carefully and consider how you want to modify it, if at all.

Considering the potential for misunderstanding, remembering the scope of your audience, and avoiding communication while angry can be helpful in most any social context. They are particularly important while communicating in electronically mediated ways, however. Although they aren't the only components of online communication competence, these suggestions can help you communicate in effective and appropriate ways across a range of contexts.

For REVIEW

- **What needs does communication help us meet?**

We use communication to help us stay physically healthy, form and maintain important relationships, understand and express our identities, convey our spiritual beliefs, and accomplish mundane, instrumental tasks.

- **How does communication work, and what misconceptions do we have about it?**

Communication can be described as action, interaction, or transaction, depending on the situation. Many people mistakenly believe that everyone is a communication expert, communication will solve any problem, communication can break down, communication is inherently good, and more communication is always better.

- **What particular skills characterize competent communicators?**

Competent communicators express themselves effectively and appropriately in whatever situation they are in. They are self-aware, adaptable, empathic, cognitively complex, and ethical.

KEY TERMS

NOTES

1. McDaniel, A. (2017, October 9). I tweeted about my toddler and someone called Child Protective Services. *Time.* https://www.msn.com/en-us/lifestyle/whats-hot/i-tweeted-about-my-toddler-and-someone-called-child-protective -services/ar-AAtaGvl?ocid=se

2. See, e.g., Graham, S. A., Deriziotis, P., & Fisher, S. E. (2015). Insights into the genetic foundations of human communication. *Neuropsychology Review, 25*(1), 3–26. https://doi.org/10.1007/s11065-014-9277-2

3. Shankar, A., McMunn, A., Demakakos, P., Hamer, M., & Steptoe, A. (2017). Social isolation and loneliness: Prospective associations with functional status in older adults. *Health Psychology, 36*(2), 179–187. https://doi.org/10.1037/hea0000437; Walker, J., Illingworth, C., Canning, A., Garner, E., Woolley, J., Taylor, P., & Amos, T. (2014). Changes in mental state associated with prison environments: A systematic review. *Acta Psychiatrica Scandinavica, 129*(6), 427–436. https://doi.org/10.1111/acps.12221

4. Gunther Moor, G., Bos, M. G. N., Crone, E. A., & van der Molen, M. W. (2014). Peer rejection cues induce cardiac slowing after transition into adolescence. *Developmental Psychology, 50*(3), 947–955. https://doi.org/10.1037/a0033842

5. Cacioppo, J. T., & Cacioppo, S. (2018). The growing problem of loneliness. *The Lancet, 391*(10119), P426. https://doi .org/10.1016/S0140-6736(18)30142-9

6. Perry, B. D. (2002). Childhood experience and the expression of genetic potential: What childhood neglect tells us about nature and nurture. *Brain and Mind, 3*(1), 79–100. https://doi.org/10.1023/A:1016557824657

7. Bales, K. L., Witczak, L. R., Simmons, T. C., Savidge, L. E., Rothwell, E. S., Rogers, F. D., Manning, M. J., Heise, M., Englund, M., & del Razo, R. A. (2018). Social touch during development: Long-term effects on brain and behavior. *Neuroscience & Biobehavioral Reviews, 95,* 202–219. https://doi.org/10.1016/j.neubiorev.2018.09.019

8. Marcus, A. F., Illescas, A. H., Hohl, B. C., & Llanos, A. A. M. (2017). Relationships between social isolation, neighborhood poverty, and cancer mortality in a population-based study of U.S. adults. *PLoS One, 12*(3), e0173370. https://doi.org/10.1371 /journal.pone.0173370

9. LeRoy, A. S., Murdock, K. W., Jaremka, L. M., Loya, A., & Fagundes, C. P. (2017). Loneliness predicts self-reported cold symptoms after a viral challenge. *Health Psychology, 36*(5), 512–520. https://doi.org/10.1037/hea0000467

10. Segrin, C., & Passalacqua, S. A. (2010). Functions of loneliness, social support, health behaviors, and stress in association with poor health. *Health Communication, 25*(4), 312–322. https://doi.org/10.1080/10410231003773334

11. Polack, E. (2018, May 1). New Cigna study reveals loneliness at epidemic levels in America. *Cigna.* https://www.cigna.com /newsroom/news-releases/2018/new-cigna-study-reveals-loneliness-at-epidemic-levels-in-america

12. Punyanunt-Carter, N. M., & Wagner, T. R. (2018). Interpersonal communication motives for flirting face to face and through texting. *Cyberpsychology, Behavior, and Social Networking, 21*(4), 229–233. https://doi.org/10.1089/cyber.2017.0608

13. Hall, J. A., & Davis, D. C. (2017). Proposing the Communicate Bond Belong Theory: Evolutionary intersections with episodic interpersonal communication. *Communication Theory, 27*(1), 21–47. https://doi.org/10.1111/comt.12106

14. Punyanunt-Carter, N. M., & Wrench, J. S. (Eds.). (2017). *The impact of social media in modern romantic relationships.* Lexington Books.

15. Sirin, S. R., Sin, E., Clingain, C., & Rogers-Sirin, L. (2019). Acculturative stress and mental health: Implications for immigrant-origin youth. *Pediatric Clinics, 66*(3), 641–653. https://doi.org/10.1016/j.pcl.2019.02.010

16. Adamczyk, K. (2018). Direct and indirect effects of relationship status through unmet need to belong and fear of being single on young adults' romantic loneliness. *Personality and Individual Differences, 124,* 124–129. https://doi.org/10.1016 /j.paid.2017.12.011

17. Demir, M., Vento, I., Boyd, R., & Hanks, E. (2018). My relationships are my estate: Relationships with kin and voluntary bonds as predictors of happiness among emerging adults. In M. Demir, & N. Sümer (Eds.), *Close relationships and happiness across cultures* (pp. 105–129). Springer. https://doi.org/10.1007/978-3-319-89663-2_7

18. Popenoe, D. (2007). *The state of our unions: The social health of marriage in America.* The National Marriage Project.

19. Wong, C. W., Kwok, C. S., Narain, A., Gulati, M., Mihalidou, A. S., Wu, P., Alasnag, M., Myint, P. K., & Mamas, M. A. (2018). Marital status and risk of cardiovascular disease: A systematic review and meta-analysis. *Heart, 104*(23), 1937–1948. https://doi.org/10.1136/heartjnl-2018-313005

20. Sinigaglia, C., & Rizzolatti, G. (2011). Through the looking glass: Self and others. *Consciousness and Cognition, 20*(1), 64–74. https://doi.org/10.1016/j.concog.2010.11.012

21. Kosmin, B. A., & Keysar, A. (2013). *Religious, spiritual, and secular: The emergence of three distinct worldviews among American college students.* Trinity College.

22. Tripathi, N. (2018). A valuation of Abraham Maslow's theory of self-actualization for the enhancement of quality of life. *Indian Journal of Health and Wellbeing, 9*(3), 499–504.

23. Shannon, C. E. (1948). A mathematical theory of communication. *Bell System Technical Journal, 27*(3), 379–423. https://doi.org/10.1002/j.1538-7305.1948.tb01338.x

24. See, e.g., O'Sullivan, P. B., & Carr, C. T. (2018). Mass-personal communication: A model bridging the mass-interpersonal divide. *New Media & Society, 20*(3), 1161–1180. https://doi.org/10.1177/1461444816686104

25. Paige, S. R., Stellefson, M., Krieger, J. L., Anderson-Lewis, C., Cheong, J., & Stopka, C. (2018). Proposing a transactional model of eHealth literacy: Concept analysis. *Journal of Medical Internet Research, 20*(10), e10175. https://doi.org/10.2196/10175

26. Ziegele, M., & Reinecke, L. (2017). No place for negative emotions? The effects of message valence, communication channel, and social distance on users' willingness to respond to SNS status updates. *Computers in Human Behavior, 75*(C), 704–713. https://doi.org/10.1016/j.chb.2017.06.016

27. Eriksson, L. (2016). Components and drivers of long-term risk communication: Exploring the within-communicator, relational, and content dimensions in the Swedish forest context. *Organization & Environment, 30*(2), 162–179. https://doi.org/10.1177/1086026616649647

28. Nadin, M. (2001). One cannot not interact. *Knowledge-Based Systems, 14*(8), 437–440. https://doi.org/10.1016/S0950-7051(01)00138-1; Motley, M. T. (1991). How one may not communicate: A reply to Andersen. *Communication Studies, 42*(4), 326–339. https://doi.org/10.1080/10510979109368347

29. Clevinger, T. (1991). Can one not communicate? A conflict of models. *Communication Studies, 42*(4), 340–353. https://doi.org/10.1080/10510979109368348

30. Denzin, N. K. (2017). Rules of conduct and the study of deviant behavior: Some notes on the social relationship. In G. J. McCall, M. M. McCall, N. K. Denzin, G. D. Suttles, & S. B. Kurth (Eds.), *Friendship as a social institution* (pp. 62–95). Routledge. https://doi.org/10.4324/9780203791493

31. Floyd, K. (2021). *Interpersonal communication* (4th ed.). McGraw-Hill.

32. National Communication Association. (1999). *How Americans communicate* [online]. https://www.natcom.org/research/Roper/how_americans_communicate.htm

33. Quote from *Cool Hand Luke* by Warner Bros. Seven Arts, Inc.

34. Pillay, S. (2014, May 21). 3 problems talking can't solve. *Harvard Business Review.* https://hbr.org/2014/05/3-problems-talking-cant-solve

35. For a classic text, see Katriel, T., & Philipsen, G. (1981). "What we need is communication": "Communication" as a cultural category in some American speech. *Communication Monographs, 48*(4), 300–317. https://doi.org/10.1080/03637758109376064

36. McDaniel, S. H., Beckman, H. B., Morse, D. S., Silberman, J., Seaburn, D. B., & Epstein, R. M. (2007). Physician self-disclosure in primary care visits: Enough about you, what about me? *Archives of Internal Medicine, 167*(12), 1321–1326. https://doi.org/10.1001/archinte.167.12.1321

37. Chesley, N. (2005). Blurring boundaries? Linking technology use, spillover, individual distress, and family satisfaction. *Journal of Marriage and Family, 67*(5), 1237–1248. https://doi.org/10.1111/j.1741-3737.2005.00213.x

38. National Association of Colleges and Employers. (2019). *Job Outlook 2019.* Author.

39. Worthington, R. E. (2019). *2019 corporate recruiters survey report.* Graduate Management Admission Council.

40. York, C. (2020). Behavior genetics and twin studies: Principles, analytical techniques, and data resources for innovative communication research. In K. Floyd, & R. Weber (Eds.), *The handbook of communication science and biology* (pp. 78–92). Routledge.

41. Titsworth, S., & Okamoto, K. (2017). Communication competence. In C. R. Scott, & L. Lewis (Eds.), *The international encyclopedia of organizational communication* (pp. 321–330). John Wiley & Sons. https://doi.org/10.1002/9781118955567

42. Spitzberg, B. H. (2013). (Re)introducing communication competence to the health professions. *Journal of Public Health Research, 2*(3), 126–135. https://doi.org/10.4081/jphr.2013.e23

43. de Hei, M., Tabacaru, C., Sjoer, E., Rippe, R., & Walenkamp, J. (2020). Developing intercultural competence through collaborative learning in international higher education. *Journal of Studies in International Education, 24*(2), 190–211. https://doi.org/10.1177/1028315319826226

44. Lou, H. C., Changeux, J. P., & Rosenstand, A. (2017). Towards a cognitive neuroscience of self-awareness. *Neuroscience & Biobehavioral Reviews, 83*, 765–773. https://doi.org/10.1016/j.neubiorev.2016.04.004

45. Makkar, S., & Basu, S. (2019). The impact of emotional intelligence on workplace behaviour: A study of bank employees. *Global Business Review, 20*(2), 458–478. https://doi.org/10.1177/0972150917713903

46. See Pitts, M. J., & Harwood, J. (2015). Communication accommodation competence: The nature and nurture of accommodative resources across the lifespan. *Language & Communication, 41*, 89–99. https://doi.org/10.1016/j.langcom.2014.10.002

47. Weisz, E., & Zaki, J. (2018). Motivated empathy: A social neuroscience perspective. *Current Opinion in Psychology, 24*, 67–71. https://doi.org/10.1016/j.copsyc.2018.05.005

48. Wildemuth, B. M., Kelly, D., Boettcher, E., Moore, E., & Dimitrova, G. (2018). Examining the impact of domain and cognitive complexity on query formulation and reformulation. *Information Processing & Management, 54*(3), 433–450. https://doi.org/10.1016/j.ipm.2018.01.009

49. Novak, C. (2008). 7 ways your e-mail can get you fired. *U.S. News & World Report.* https://money.usnews.com/money/careers/articles/2008/08/04/7-ways-your-e-mail-can-get-you-fired

ART FOXALL/Newscom

COMMUNICATION AND CULTURE

A Brief Triumph of Cultural Unity

Conflicts about immigration into the United States have reached a fevered pitch in recent years. Many U.S. Americans argue that the United States has a moral obligation to welcome those fleeing poverty, violence, and oppression in their home countries and that the inclusion of immigrants enriches cultural and political life for all. Others claim that immigration contributes to overpopulation and crime, and that it strains already-limited welfare and law-enforcement resources. This contentious debate has unfortunately fueled hate crimes against people of Mexican descent, such as a mass shooting in El Paso, Texas, in August 2019.[1]

Believing that people can be united instead of divided, however, artists in Sunland Park, New Mexico, installed seesaws in July 2019 across the city's border with Ciudad Juárez, Mexico. Each allowed one rider in Mexico and another in the United States to play simultaneously. The seesaws were the brainchild of Ronald Rael, a professor of architecture at the University of California, Berkeley, and Virginia San Fratello, an associate professor of design at San Jose State University. The pair had conceived of the idea a decade earlier while writing a book about the futility of borders.[2]

··▶ As You READ

- What is culture?
- How does culture influence communication behavior?
- In what ways can we improve our cultural communication skills?

The seesaws were an instant hit, bringing together adults and children alike to share in a few moments of cooperation and play across what has become a tense national border. Although they were in place for only a short while, the seesaws allowed people on both sides of the wall an opportunity to come together in unity, excitement, and joy.

Nearly all of us will communicate with people from different cultures at some point. Today's global marketplace makes that increasingly likely. Culture is a powerful influence on communication behavior. It can affect not only how we express ourselves but also how we interpret and react to others. In this chapter, we examine many ways that culture influences us as communicators. We begin by defining culture and considering the sources of our cultural ideas. We then look at some key ways in which cultures differ, focusing in particular on how communication behavior varies from society to society. Finally, we explore strategies for improving our communication with people of other cultures.

Understanding Cultures and Co-Cultures

- **culture** The totality of learned, shared symbols, language, values, and norms that distinguish one group of people from another.

- **societies** Groups of people who share the same culture.

Even if we don't realize it, our cultural traditions and beliefs influence how we make sense of communication behavior. Each of us is affected by the culture in which we grew up, and we tend to notice other cultures only when they differ from ours. To many people, culture—like an accent—is something that only *other* people have. Let's begin by understanding in what sense we *all* have cultural traits and biases.

SHARPEN Your Skills: *Communication challenges*

Role-play an interaction you have had with someone whose language, values, or traditions differed markedly from your own. Consider what communication challenges each of you faced. How did you manage those challenges? Ask your instructor and classmates for feedback on how you might have managed them more effectively.

WHAT IS CULTURE?

We use the term *culture* to mean all sorts of things. Sometimes we connect it to a place, as in "South African culture" and "Syrian culture." Other times we use it to refer to an ethnic or a religious group, as in "Asian American culture" and "Jewish culture." We also speak of "hip-hop culture" and the "culture of the rich." What makes a culture?

Although the word *culture* can have different meanings, we define **culture** as the totality of learned, shared symbols, language, values, and norms that distinguish one group of people from another. That definition tells us that culture is not necessarily tied to countries or ethnicities or economic classes. Rather, it's a characteristic of *people.* Groups of people who share a culture with one another are called **societies**.

Naturalized citizens bring many different cultural beliefs and practices to the United States.

Drew Angerer/Getty Images

Each of us identifies with one or more societies, and we are usually keenly aware which ones. It is fundamental to our human nature, in fact, to notice people's similarities and differences with respect to ourselves, so that we know which groups of people we belong to and which ones we are separate from. That distinction comprises the difference between in-groups and out-groups. Who belongs in your in-groups? Take a look at Table 1 to see how you compare to the average citizen of the world.

TABLE 1

THE ULTIMATE IN-GROUP: THE AVERAGE WORLD CITIZEN

More than 7 billion people live on planet Earth. How well do you represent the average person? If we were to identify the single most representative citizen of the planet, that person would:

- **Live in China,** as 19 percent of the world's population does.

- **Be Christian,** as 33 percent of the world's population is.

- **Be male,** as 50.5 percent of the world's population is.

- **Live in a town or city,** as 55 percent of the world's population does.

- **Be 30.4 years old,** which is the median age of the world's population.

- **Make $18,120 per year,** which is the per capita gross world income.

- **Not use the Internet,** as 52 percent of the world's population does not.

Science Photo Library - NASA/ NOAA/Brand X Pictures/Getty Images

In what ways do you fit into this in-group? In what ways do you differ?

◀ ······························

HOW DO YOU COMPARE?

SOURCES: United Nations; Statistics Times; Population Reference Bureau. https://www.prb.org/2018-world-population-data-sheet-with-focus-on-changing-age-structures/; CIA *World Factbook*, www.cia.gov/library/publications/the-world-factbook/

DISTINGUISHING BETWEEN IN-GROUPS AND OUT-GROUPS

Researchers use the term **in-groups** to refer to groups we identify with and **out-groups** to describe groups we see as different from us.[3] If you grew up in the American South, for example, you probably see other Southerners as part of your in-group, whereas if you were raised in the Northwest, you do not. Similarly, when you are traveling in foreign countries, the residents may perceive you as an out-group member if you look or sound different from them or if you behave differently.

In-Groups and Out-Groups in Social Media If you're an active social networker, you already have an understanding of the difference between in-groups and out-groups. Your Facebook friends list and your groups on messaging apps like Snapchat or Kik are your in-groups. In contrast, your out-group includes people who are not in those circles—among them, those you have "unfriended" or blocked from messaging apps. Do these social networks qualify as their own cultures? Check out Table 2 and see what you think.

The Challenges of Out-Group Status For some people, being perceived as different can be an exciting or intriguing experience, particularly if they do not typically stand out in their regular environments. For others, however, their differences can be stressful. Research shows that many immigrants experience abnormally high levels of stress during their first year in their new homeland.[4]

Some researchers point out that our ability to distinguish between people who are similar to, and different from, ourselves probably helped our ancestors survive by encouraging them to associate with people whose goals and priorities were aligned with their own.[5] These feelings can make it uncomfortable for an individual to live or work where he or she is considered a minority, especially if the person experiences discrimination on the basis of cultural or ethnic background. For example, read about the experiences of some Muslim Americans in "The Dark Side of Communication."

- **in-groups** Groups of people with which a person identifies.

- **out-groups** Groups of people with which a person does not identify.

TABLE 2	Has Facebook become so large that it should qualify as its
THE UNITED STATES OF FACEBOOK	own culture? Consider the following:

Has Facebook become so large that it should qualify as its own culture? Consider the following:

- Facebook has more than 2.4 billion active users. If Facebook were its own country, it would be the most populous nation in the world.

- Although Facebook began in the United States, 85 percent of users today are from other countries.

- Facebook is available in over 100 different languages.

- Five new Facebook profiles are created every second.

- Each minute, 510,000 comments are posted, 405 statuses are updated, and 136,000 photos are uploaded.

Denis Rozhnovsky/Alamy Stock Photo

CONSIDER THIS: What symbols, language, values, and norms would you identify as being unique to the Facebook culture?

SOURCE: Data from Zephora Digital Marketing; Statista; statistics from August 2019.

The in-group/out-group distinction is a major reason so many countries struggle with the issue of immigration. How open should a country be to letting people from other societies—whom its own citizens consider to be out-groups—become part of its culture and in-group? Some countries, including Sweden and France, have relatively lenient policies that allow many applicants for immigration to enter their borders and eventually become citizens. Other countries have much stricter policies. Denmark, for instance, has drawn sharp criticism for significantly toughening its immigration policies and making it harder for foreign-born people to become citizens.[6]

As the chapter-opening story suggested, the question of how best to manage immigration—and the population of immigrants living in the country illegally—is currently a highly controversial issue in the United States. In 2018, for instance, the administration of president Donald Trump drew intense bipartisan criticism for its policy of separating children from their parents at the U.S.–Mexico border when the parents were suspected of crossing the border illegally. The policy resulted in at least 2,600 children being detained while their parents were held in federal jail awaiting trial.[7] Advocacy groups such as Human Rights Watch have warned that such separations cause long-term physical and psychological trauma for both children and parents.[8] The experiences of Sweden, France, the United States, Mexico, and Denmark all illustrate the complex and sometimes contentious relationship between national in-groups and out-groups.

ACQUIRING A CULTURE

- **ethnicity** People's perceptions of ancestry or heritage.

- **nationality** One's status as a citizen of a particular country.

- **enculturation** The process of acquiring a culture.

How does each of us acquire a culture? Because cultures and societies vary so broadly around the world, it might seem as though we simply inherit our culture genetically, the same way we inherit our eye color and other physical characteristics, but that isn't the case. Culture is not necessarily related to or based on our **ethnicity**, which is our perception of our ancestry or heritage. Neither is culture necessarily related to our **nationality**, which is our status as a citizen of a particular country. Rather, culture is learned. We acquire our culture by learning the traditions, values, and language of the people who raised us. Researchers use the term **enculturation** to describe the process of acquiring a culture.

THE DARK SIDE OF COMMUNICATION

Cultural Intolerance: Discrimination against Muslim Americans

Nineteen-year-old college senior Nohayia Javed was walking to her residence hall on a Saturday night when she was grabbed from behind, thrown to the ground, and kicked in the ribs by a young man yelling anti-Islamic slurs. An emergency room exam later revealed that Javed had sustained multiple bruises and a dislocated shoulder. It's fortunate that few Muslim students at U.S. colleges and universities have endured similar physical attacks—yet since the U.S. wars in Iraq and Afghanistan, many have felt like outsiders. Some receive hostile looks or threatening e-mail messages. Others feel excluded from social events where they once would have felt welcome.

Distinguishing between in-groups and out-groups may be a natural tendency among humans, but it can lead us to make erroneous judgments. During times of stress or uncertainty, it may be especially easy to make broad generalizations about groups of people. In the wake of terror attacks committed in the United States and abroad by a very small number of radical Islamic groups, this kind of stereotyping presents a particular burden for Muslim Americans. Many Muslim Americans—even those born in the United States, such as Javed—are treated with suspicion or outright contempt by those who fail to recognize that the vast majority of Muslims have nothing to do with terrorism.

In fact, many major Islamic organizations explicitly condemn terrorist acts. But many non-Muslim Americans remain distrustful of Islam, and continue to treat those who adhere to the faith with suspicion or contempt. As atrocities committed by the group calling itself "Islamic State" unfolded in the Middle East and around the world, many Muslim Americans found themselves on the receiving end of behaviors ranging from subtle exclusion, to verbal and online attacks, to outright abuse by others who blame all Muslims for the destructive actions of a few.

For competent communicators, however, it is vitally important not to condemn an entire group based on the actions of a few individuals. In fact, research shows that collective blame can be significantly reduced when people are asked to reflect on their own cultural groups. For instance, U.S. Americans are less likely to blame all Muslims for the terrorist actions of the Islamic State when they are asked if all white Americans should be blamed for the actions of domestic terrorists such as Dylann Roof, who murdered nine African American parishioners during a church service in June 2015. When people realize they are not at fault for the bad behaviors of others in their own cultural groups, they are less likely to blame all Muslims for individual terrorists acts.

MOHD KHAIRI IBRAHIM/123RF

SOURCES: Svokos, A. (2015, April 7). What it's like to be a Muslim college student today. *Huffington Post*. http://www.huffingtonpost.com/2015/04/07/muslim-college-students_n_6864910.html; Resnick, B. (2017, November 30). All Muslims are often blamed for single acts of terror. Psychology explains how to stop it. *Vox*. https://www.vox.com/science-and-health/2017/11/30/16645024/collective-blame-psychology-muslim; Woods, T. (2006, April 5). Muslim student believes attacker came from off campus. *Waco Tribune-Herald*. http://www.wacotrib.com/news/content/news/stories/2006/04/05/04052006wacmuslim.html

For instance, a Cambodian-born citizen raised in the United States will likely adopt the language and practices common to the place where she is brought up. Her ethnicity and citizenship are Cambodian, but her culture is the U.S. culture. Likewise, someone born in New Zealand but raised in Nigeria may adopt the Nigerian culture as his own, even if he is Caucasian.

Culture is learned. Regardless of our citizenship, most of us learn the language and cultural practices common to the place where we grow up.

Monkey Business Images/ Shutterstock

We learn some of our cultural messages through direct instruction. When a parent tells us to say "thank you" after receiving a gift, or a teacher helps us learn the pledge of allegiance, those experiences impart cultural knowledge in a direct and conscious manner. We learn other cultural lessons through imitation. Perhaps no one had to teach you to face forward and stay quiet while riding in a crowded elevator; instead you learned that cultural norm by observing others. We can even pick up cultural practices subconsciously, such as when we begin speaking with the accent of those around us without realizing we are doing so.

Although culture is learned, our biology gives us the capacity to learn it. Our genes give us the brains capable of learning and remembering cultural practices and the hands capable of writing cultural stories. They give us the eyes capable of seeing cultural symbols and the mouths capable of using language. Our genes don't *determine* our communication behavior, however. Rather, they interact with our cultural environment to shape who we are and how we communicate.

WHAT IS A CO-CULTURE?

When you think about culture as shared language, beliefs, and customs, it may seem as though you belong to many different cultures at once. If you grew up in the United States, you likely feel a part of the U.S. culture. At the same time, if you enjoy comic books, vintage cars, or skateboarding, you may notice that the people who share your interests appear to have their own customs and vocabularies. Or perhaps you observe that people in your generation have different values and customs than people who are older than you—or that different ethnic or religious groups at your school seem to have their own traditions and beliefs. Does each of those groups have a culture of its own? In a manner of speaking, the answer is yes.

Defining Co-Cultures Within many national cultures—such as the Kenyan, Thai, and U.S. cultures—is a host of other cultural groups that researchers call co-cultures. **Co-cultures** are groups of people who share values, customs, and norms related to mutual interests or characteristics other than their national citizenship. Your co-culture isn't based on the country in which you were born or raised. Instead, it is composed of smaller groups of people with whom you identify. In many cases, you may identify with your co-cultures as strongly as—or more strongly than—you identify with your national culture.

The Bases of Co-Cultures Some co-cultures form around shared activities or beliefs. If you're into fly fishing, organic gardening, or political activism, there are co-cultures for those interests. Similarly, Buddhists have beliefs and traditions that distinguish them from Baptists, regardless of where they grew up.

Some co-cultures develop around differences in mental or physical abilities. Many deaf populations have values and customs that differ from those of hearing populations, including social customs.[9] Deaf co-culture also places a strong emphasis on the distinctions between in-group and out-group members. Many individuals who are deaf point out that a person cannot genuinely understand the physical or social experience of deafness unless he or she is deaf. Consequently, people who are deaf often express a strong preference for interacting with other deaf individuals, because that enhances their ability to understand one another and to share their co-cultural values and traditions. They may treat sign language interpreters, the hearing parents of deaf children, and the hearing children of deaf parents as "honorary deaf people," but they may be hesitant to accept hearing people as part of the Deaf co-culture.[10]

Such reluctance was evident in 1988, when students at Gallaudet University in Washington, D.C., the world's only liberal arts university for the Deaf, staged an

James Woodson/Getty Images

• **co-cultures** Groups of people who share values, customs, and norms related to mutual interests or characteristics other than their national citizenship.

eight-day protest demanding the appointment of a deaf president for the university. The board of trustees responded by appointing the first deaf president in the school's 130-year history.

Identifying with Multiple Co-Cultures

Many people identify with several co-cultures at once. You might relate to a co-culture for your age group, ethnicity, religion, sexual orientation, musical tastes, athletic interests, and even your college major. Each may have its own values, beliefs, traditions, customs, and ways of using language that distinguish it from other groups. Some co-cultures even contain smaller co-cultures within them. For example, the Deaf co-culture includes people who advocate using only sign language and others who advocate the use of cochlear implants, devices surgically inserted in the ear to help a person hear.

The Deaf co-culture often places a strong emphasis on the distinctions between in-group and out-group members.
New Africa/Shutterstock

The Internet offers multiple opportunities for people to develop and participate in co-cultures that are specific to the online world. Those who are interested in online games or science fiction, or in the development of free software, can find extensive communities of people with similar interests on the web. Each such community may develop its own terminology, values, and communication practices, and interact as a co-culture even though its members may be geographically dispersed.

The Internet also provides opportunities for people to find others who share co-cultural interests that are not unique to the online world. For instance, thousands of Usenet groups exist online, where people can communicate with others who share their passion for Japanese anime, environmentalism, fan fiction, or African art. Although not all co-cultures are specific to the Internet environment—in the way that, say, online gaming is—they often thrive on the web, where people separated by thousands of miles can communicate whenever they wish.

Components of Cultures and Co-Cultures

Cultures and societies vary enormously. Imagine a group composed of people raised in Saudi Arabia, Vietnam, Iceland, Botswana, Paraguay, Israel, and the U.S. Southwest. The members of that group would differ not only in their native languages, but also, most likely, in their religious beliefs, political viewpoints, sports interests, food preferences, clothing, and beliefs about education, marriage, money, and sexuality. Indeed, we might have a harder time identifying the members' similarities than their differences. That's how powerful an influence culture can be.

Culture distinguishes people with different interests. Opera lovers and country music fans—even if they live in the same community—often seem more different than similar.
Comstock Images/Getty Images; David Becker/ Getty Images

Fact or *fiction?*

Change Is Inevitable: The United States Is Becoming More Culturally Diverse

Communication professors often encourage students to learn more about intercultural communication on the argument that the United States is becoming more diverse over time. Is that notion fact or fiction?

Projections from the U.S. Census suggest that it's a fact. Using data compiled from previous census counts, the U.S. Census Bureau predicts that, over the next half century, the United States will have greater diversity with respect to both ethnicity and age. The accompanying table presents the percentages of the U.S. population that fit each ethnic and age category in 2000 and are projected to fit each category in 2025 and 2050.

As the table illustrates, the U.S. Census Bureau forecasts greater ethnic and age diversity over the next 30 years. For instance, whereas Asian Americans made up 3.8 percent of the population in 2000, they are expected to rise to 7.8 percent of the population in 2050. Similarly, senior citizens 65 years of age and older were only 12.4 percent of the U.S. population in 2000 but are expected to make up 20.6 percent—slightly more than one-fifth—just five decades later. Given this growth, the ability to communicate effectively with people from other demographic groups will be increasingly advantageous in the years to come.

Year	Ethnic Category				Age Category		
	African American	White/Caucasian	Asian American	Other Ethnicities	0–19	20–64	65+
2000	12.7	81.0	3.8	2.5	28.5	59.0	12.4
2025	13.0	77.3	5.9	3.8	26.3	55.5	18.2
2050	13.0	74.0	7.8	5.3	26.0	53.4	20.6

2025 percentages for ethnicity represent aggregates of 2020 and 2030 projections. Owing to rounding, some percentages do not sum to 100.

ASK YOURSELF

- What communication challenges will people in the United States face as ethnic and age diversity increases?
- What particular communication skills do you think might help people meet those challenges?

SOURCE: Shrestha, L. B., & Heisler, E. J. (2011, March 31). *The changing demographic profile of the United States.* Congressional Research Service report for Congress, accessed from www.fas.org/sgp/crs/misc/RL32701.pdf

As we'll see later, values, beliefs, and preferences often vary even among different groups of people within the same country. For example, native Hawaiians, native Texans, and native New Yorkers might vary considerably in their customs and values, even though they were all raised in the United States. Similarly, opera buffs might seem to have more differences than similarities with country music lovers and jazz fans, even if they grew up in the same community. In short, culture can distinguish not only people with different nationalities but also those with different interests and social characteristics.

The United States has often been called a melting pot to acknowledge that it includes multiple cultural groups. In fact, students are frequently encouraged to learn more about intercultural communication precisely because of the notion that the country's cultural diversity continues to increase. Is that assumption true, though? Check out the "Fact or Fiction?" box to find out.

No matter what their differences, cultures have some common components, as our definition of culture made clear. Those components are symbols, language, values, and norms. Let's take a closer look at each one.

CULTURES VARY IN THEIR SYMBOLS

As we saw in the introductory chapter, a symbol is something that represents an idea. Words are symbols, for example. In addition, every culture has its own symbols that stand for ideas that are vital to that culture. When we hear that something is "as American as baseball and apple pie," the speaker is using baseball and apple pie as symbols of U.S. life. The U.S. flag, the bald eagle, and "The Star-Spangled Banner" are also common symbols of the United States.

Each society uses symbols that carry particular meanings for its members. For instance, the Chinese national anthem, "Yìy ngjūn Jìnxíngqǔ" ("March of the Volunteers"), serves as a symbol of Chinese culture. Similarly, "Die Stem van Suid-Afrika" ("The Call of South Africa"), the national anthem of South Africa, symbolizes that country's culture. The tartan—a criss-crossed pattern of dyed threads woven together in a textile—serves as an important symbol of Scottish culture, whereas the crescent moon and star is a symbol of Islamic culture.

ying wang/Alamy Stock Photo

In August 2018, protesters at the University of North Carolina at Chapel Hill toppled an eight-foot-tall statue, dubbed Silent Sam, depicting a Confederate soldier from the U.S. Civil War.[11] For some, the statue—which had stood at the university's main entrance for more than a century—represented a deep sense of pride in their Southern heritage; for others, it reflected a history of slavery and racial oppression. Unsurprisingly, the decision to remove the statue drew both strong support and vocal opposition, even though research shows that most Americans have neither a strongly positive nor a strongly negative reaction to such symbols.[12]

CULTURES VARY IN THEIR LANGUAGES

Researchers believe there are approximately 7,100 languages used in the world today.[13] The nation of Papua New Guinea uses the most, with 839 living languages.[14] Furthermore, according to the New York State Comptroller's Office, more languages are spoken in Queens, New York, than in any other city on Earth: 179 at last count, prompting Queens to call itself "The World's Borough."[15] Language allows for written and spoken communication, and it also ensures that cultures and cultural ideas are passed from one generation to the next.

Today, Chinese, Spanish, and English—in that order—are the three most commonly spoken languages in the world. Nearly 2 billion people speak one or more of those three languages. Unfortunately, many other languages are in danger of extinction. In fact, researchers believe that at least 10 percent of the world's languages are currently spoken by fewer than 100 people each.[16] We examine language use further in the language chapter.

CULTURES VARY IN THEIR VALUES

A culture's *values* are the standards it uses to judge how good, desirable, or beautiful something is. In other words, values are cultural ideas about *what ought to be*. Psychological research indicates that U.S. culture values ideas such as equal opportunity, material comfort, practicality, efficiency, achievement, democracy, free enterprise, and individual choice.[17]

Whereas values can vary considerably across cultures, 10 in particular are widely shared and similarly interpreted:[18]

1. *Power:* having prestige, social status, and control over resources
2. *Achievement:* acquiring personal success through your own competence
3. *Hedonism:* experiencing fun and pleasure
4. *Stimulation:* having novelty, excitement, and challenge in life
5. *Self-direction:* being able to engage in independent thought and action
6. *Universalism:* appreciating and caring about all people and about nature
7. *Benevolence:* enhancing the welfare of people with whom you have contact
8. *Tradition:* respecting the customs and ideas of your culture and religion
9. *Conformity:* observing social norms and inhibiting actions that are likely to harm others
10. *Security:* having safe and stable relationships

Although these 10 values exist across cultures, not every culture emphasizes them to the same degree. As you'll discover in this chapter, tradition, power, and conformity are strongly emphasized in some cultures, whereas achievement and self-direction are more privileged in others.

CULTURES VARY IN THEIR NORMS

Finally, *norms* are rules or expectations that guide people's behavior in a culture. As an example, consider the norms for greeting people when you first meet them. In North American countries, people typically shake hands and make a courteous statement such as "Nice to meet you." In another culture it may be normal to hug, bow, kiss on both cheeks or, in some cases, even to kiss on the lips.

Cultures also vary in their norms for politeness. A behavior that is considered very polite in one culture may be frowned on in another. When receiving a compliment, for instance, people in the United States consider it polite to say "Thank you." In comparison, a Chinese person may consider that reply boastful and would instead respond by suggesting that he or she was not worthy of the compliment.[19]

Even the Internet has its own norms. Netiquette—or network etiquette—consists of the expectations that guide people's online behaviors. Those norms include not forwarding junk mail (also known as *spam*), respecting others' privacy by not forwarding personal messages without permission, using appropriate language and acronyms (such as LOL for "laughing out loud"), and not "flaming," or making hostile and insulting remarks about other Internet users.

DISTINCTIVE FEATURES OF CO-CULTURES

Like cultures, co-cultures often adopt distinctive symbols, language, values, and norms that distinguish their members from outsiders. A co-cultural symbol might be a logo, such as the rainbow flag used by the LGBT (lesbian, gay, bisexual, and transgender) community, or an action, such as genuflecting (bending at least one knee to the ground), a common symbol in certain religious communities. Although co-cultures may not adopt entirely distinctive languages, they frequently use terminology—called *jargon*—that is understood only by others in the same co-culture. Surfers, for instance, might say "getting tubed" to describe being completely covered by the top of a wave, and firefighters call

SHARPEN Your Skills: *Co-cultural norms*

Select a co-culture with which you are largely unfamiliar. Using the Internet, research the values and norms common in that co-culture. Create a PowerPoint or video presentation describing them and identifying how others can use that knowledge to communicate effectively with people of that co-cultural background.

someone who always has trouble gearing up for a fire a "door dancer." We will delve further into the topic of jargon later in this chapter.

Co-cultural groups often arise precisely because their members share specific values. The co-culture of veganism—which promotes diets free of animal products—largely shares values related to the preservation of animal life, whereas the co-culture of Civil War re-enactors—who stage dramatizations of famous Civil War battles to preserve the accurate history of the period—shares values related to recognizing that major event in U.S. history. Finally, co-cultures adopt their own norms, such as silent worship among Quakers and dressing alike among the community of twins.

CULTURAL UNIVERSALS

Given the number of ways in which cultures differ from one another, it can be easy to believe that people from different cultures have virtually nothing in common. Cultural anthropologist Donald Brown and linguist Steven Pinker remind us, however, that some ideas and experiences are culturally universal.[20] According to their work, people in all known cultures

- Enforce a sense of fairness and punish cheaters
- Value loyalty and reciprocate favors
- Divide labor on the basis of sex
- Defer to legitimate authority
- Experience pride and shame
- Have beliefs about death and experience mourning
- Express emotions through facial expressions
- Play, dance, and sing
- Distinguish right and wrong
- Classify ages, colors, kinships, and behavioral tendencies
- Share gossip

This is just a short list of the ideas and experiences that people share across cultures. Brown and Pinker's work helps us understand that even though cultural groups differ in many ways, they also have much in common.

How Culture Affects Communication

If you've ever had difficulty communicating with someone from a different cultural background, then you know how challenging it can be. Dutch social psychologist Geert Hofstede and American anthropologist Edward T. Hall have pioneered the study of cultures and cultural differences in behavior. Their work and that of others points to six cultural differences that influence how people communicate with one another. Those differences—our focus in this section—are related to (1) the emphasis placed on individuals versus groups, (2) the communicative context, (3) power distance, (4) views about masculinity and femininity and about men's and women's roles, (5) orientation toward time, and (6) uncertainty avoidance. We discuss these variations as comparisons—individualistic versus collectivistic, for example—for simplicity's sake. It's better to think of them as sliding scales, however, in which each culture scores higher or lower on each dimension.

1. INDIVIDUALISTIC VERSUS COLLECTIVISTIC CULTURES

• **individualistic culture**
A culture in which people believe that their primary responsibility is to themselves.

• **collectivistic culture**
A culture in which people believe that their primary responsibility is to their families, their communities, and their employers.

The phenomenal popularity of *American Idol* and the quick rise to fame of many of its winners reflect the highly individualistic nature of U.S. culture. Season 17 winner Laine Hardy is shown here.

Amy Sussman/Staff/Getty Images

Cultures differ in how much they emphasize individuals rather than groups. In an **individualistic culture**, people believe their primary responsibility is to themselves. Children in individualistic cultures are raised hearing messages such as "Be yourself," "You're special," and "There's no one else in the world who's just like you." Those messages emphasize the importance of knowing yourself, being self-sufficient, and being true to what you want in life.[21] Indeed, the motto in an individualistic culture might be "I gotta be me!" People in individualistic societies also value self-reliance and the idea that people should help themselves instead of waiting for others to come to their aid. Research shows that the United States, Canada, Great Britain, and Australia are among the most individualistic societies in the world.[22] The United States is so individualistic that *American Idol*—the talent show in which undiscovered singers compete to land lucrative recording contracts and achieve superstar status—has been one of television's top-rated programs over its 17-season run.

In contrast, people in **collectivistic cultures** are taught that their primary responsibility is to their families, their communities, and their employers. These cultures focus on the importance of taking care of the needs of the group rather than the individual. People place a high value on duty and loyalty and see themselves not as unique or special but as a part of the group or groups to which they belong. Among the Kabre of Togo, for instance, individuals try to give away many of their material possessions in order to build relationships and benefit their social groups.[23] In the collectivistic societies of Saudi Arabia and North Korea, parents are prohibited from giving their children names that contradict the culture of those countries.[24] The motto in a collectivistic culture might be "I am my family and my family is me." Collectivistic cultures include North and South Korea, Japan, and many countries in Africa and Latin America.[25]

How individualistic or collectivistic a culture is can affect communication behavior in several ways. When people in an individualistic culture experience conflict with one another, for instance, they are expected to express it and work toward resolving it. In comparison, people in a collectivistic culture are taught to be much more indirect in the way they handle disagreements, to preserve social harmony. For instance, they may avoid the conflict and hope it will resolve itself or hint at their problems with other people instead of describing them explicitly.[26]

Another difference between the two types of culture centers on people's comfort level with public speaking. Many people feel anxious when they have to give a speech, but especially those in collectivistic societies, where people are taught to blend in rather than to stand out. Asserting yourself and standing up for yourself are valued in individualistic cultures, but pressure to adopt these norms can cause embarrassment and shame for people in a collectivistic culture.

Some researchers suggest that the individualistic–collectivistic distinction is the most fundamental way in which cultures differ from one another. Other researchers disagree, maintaining that this distinction by itself cannot adequately characterize the differences between cultures.[27] Read on and see what you think.

2. LOW-CONTEXT VERSUS HIGH-CONTEXT CULTURES

If you have traveled much, perhaps you have noticed that people in various parts of the world differ in how direct and explicit their language is. You may have spent time in both low- and high-context cultures in your travels, with *context* here referring to the broad range of factors surrounding every act of communication.

In a **low-context culture**, people are expected to be direct and to say what they mean. Individuals in low-context cultures prefer precise, concrete language for sending and receiving messages, and are unlikely to rely on the context of a message to determine its meaning.[28] The United States is an example of a low-context society, as are Canada, Israel, and most northern European countries.

In contrast, people in a **high-context culture**—such as North and South Korea and the cultures of Native Americans and the Maori of New Zealand—are taught to speak in a much less direct way. In such cultures, maintaining harmony and avoiding offense are more important than expressing true feelings.[29] Speech is more ambiguous and people convey much more of their meaning through subtle behaviors and contextual cues, such as their facial expressions and tone of voice.

The difference between low-context and high-context cultures is evident in the ways in which people handle criticism and disagreement. In a low-context culture, a supervisor might reprimand an irresponsible employee openly, to make an example of the individual. The supervisor would probably be direct and explicit about the employee's shortcomings, the company's expectations for improvement, and the consequences of the employee's failing to meet those expectations.

In a high-context culture, however, the supervisor probably wouldn't reprimand the employee publicly for fear that it would put the employee to shame and cause the worker to "lose face." Criticism in high-context cultures is more likely to take place in private. The supervisor would also likely use more ambiguous language to convey what the employee was doing wrong, "talking around" the issue instead of confronting it directly. To reprimand an employee for repeated absences, for example, a supervisor might point out that responsibility to coworkers is important and that letting down the team would be cause for shame. The supervisor may never actually say that the employee needs to improve his or her attendance record. Instead, the employee would be expected to understand that message by listening to what the supervisor says and paying attention to the supervisor's body language, tone of voice, and facial expressions.

When people from low- and high-context cultures communicate with one another, the potential for misunderstanding is great. To appreciate that point, imagine that you've asked two of your friends to meet you tomorrow evening for a coffee tasting at a popular bookstore café. Tina, an American, says, "No, I've got a lot of studying to do, but thanks anyway." Lee, who grew up in South Korea, nods his head and says, "That sounds like fun." Thus, you're surprised later when Lee doesn't show up.

How can you account for those different behaviors? The answer is that people raised in a high-context culture (such as that of South Korea) are often reluctant to say no—even when they mean no—for fear of causing offense. Another person raised in the South Korean culture might have understood from Lee's facial expression or tone of voice that he didn't intend to go to the coffee tasting. If you, like Tina, grew up in a low-context society, however, then you probably interpreted his answer and his nods to mean he was accepting your invitation.

3. LOW-POWER-DISTANCE VERSUS HIGH-POWER-DISTANCE CULTURES

Cultures also differ from one another in the degree to which power is distributed within society. Several types of assets can give someone power, including money or other valuable resources, education or expertise, age, popularity, talent, intelligence, and experience. In democratic societies such as the United States and western European nations, people generally believe in the value of equality across the sexes and groups.

• **low-context culture** A culture in which people are expected to be direct and to say what they mean.

• **high-context culture** A culture in which people are taught to speak in an indirect, inexplicit way.

The belief that all men and women are equal and that no one person or group should have excessive power is characteristic of a **low-power-distance culture**. The United States and Canada fall in that category, as do Israel, New Zealand, Denmark, and Austria.[30] People in low-power-distance societies are raised to believe that although some individuals are born with more advantages (such as wealth or fame), no one is inherently better than anyone else. That doesn't necessarily mean people in those societies *are* treated equally, only that they value the idea that they *should* be.

In a **high-power-distance culture**, power is distributed less evenly. Certain groups, such as members of the royal family or the ruling political party, have great power, and the average citizen has much less. People in high-power-distance societies are taught that certain people or groups deserve more power than others and that respecting power is more important than respecting equality. Mexico, Brazil, India, Singapore, and the Philippines are all examples of high-power-distance societies.[31]

Power distance affects many aspects of communication. For example, people in low-power-distance cultures usually expect friendships and romantic relationships to be based on love rather than social status. In contrast, people in high-power-distance cultures often feel pressure to choose friends and mates from within their social class.[32]

Another difference appears in the way people talk to authority figures. Individuals in a low-power-distance society are often taught that it is their right—even their responsibility—to question authority. In such a society it's not unexpected for people to ask "Why?" when a parent or teacher tells them to do something. In comparison, individuals in a high-power-distance society learn to obey and respect those in power, such as parents and teachers, without question.[33]

Cultural norms about power distance can change over time. A few generations ago, Britons would have been shocked by Prince Harry's marriage to Meghan Markle, an American commoner.

Jada Images/Alamy Stock Photo

That difference is also evident in individuals' relationships and communication patterns with their employers. Workers in a low-power-distance culture value *autonomy*, which is their ability to choose how they do their jobs and to influence decisions that affect them. They might provide their input, for example, through union representatives or employee satisfaction surveys. In contrast, employees in a high-power-distance culture are used to having little or no say about how to do their jobs. Instead, they expect their employers to make the decisions and are more likely to follow those decisions without question.

4. MASCULINE VERSUS FEMININE CULTURES

We usually use the terms *masculine* and *feminine* when we are referring to people. Hofstede has suggested that we can also apply those terms to cultures.[34] In a highly **masculine culture**, people tend to cherish stereotypically masculine values, such as ambition, achievement, and the acquisition of material goods. They

In masculine cultures, professional success is often equated with achievement, status, and wealth, regardless of whether one is male or female.

gstockstudio/123RF

also value sex-specific roles for women and men, preferring that men hold the wage-earning and decision-making positions (such as corporate executive) while women occupy the nurturing positions (such as homemaker). Examples of masculine cultures are Austria, Japan, and Mexico.

In a highly **feminine culture**, people tend to value nurturing behavior, quality of life, and service to others, all of which are stereotypically feminine qualities. They also tend *not* to believe that men's and women's roles should be strongly differentiated. Therefore, in a feminine culture, it is not unusual for a man to care for children or for a woman to be her family's primary wage earner. Most feminine cultures also provide new parents with more paid parental leave than do masculine cultures, so that those parents can focus their attention on their new infants. Examples of feminine cultures are Sweden, Chile, and the Netherlands.

According to Hofstede's research, the United States has a moderately masculine culture. U.S. adults tend to value sex-differentiated roles—although not as strongly as Austrians, Japanese, and Mexicans do—and they place a fairly high value on stereotypically masculine qualities such as achievement and the acquisition of resources.[35]

5. MONOCHRONIC VERSUS POLYCHRONIC CULTURES

Cultures also vary with respect to their norms and expectations concerning the use of time. Societies that have a **monochronic** concept of time—such as Swiss, Germans, and most Americans—view time as a commodity. People in these cultures save time, spend time, fill time, invest time, and waste time as though time were tangible. They treat time as valuable, believe that "time is money," and talk about making time and losing time.[36]

A monochronic orientation toward time influences several social behaviors. People who think of time as valuable hate to waste it. Therefore, they expect meetings and classes to start on time, and if that doesn't happen, they are willing to wait only so long before leaving. They also expect others to show up when they say they will.

In contrast, societies with a **polychronic** orientation—which include Latin America, the Arab part of the Middle East, and much of sub-Saharan Africa—conceive of time as more holistic and fluid and less structured. Instead of treating time as a finite commodity that must be managed properly to avoid wasting it, people in a polychronic culture perceive it more like a never-ending river, flowing infinitely into the future.[37]

In societies with a polychronic time orientation, schedules are more fluid and flexible than in monochronic societies. In Pakistan, for instance, if you are invited to a wedding that begins at 4:30 in the afternoon and you arrive at 4:25, you will most likely be the first one there. A bank or restaurant may not open at a specified time—as it would be expected to do in a monochronic society—but whenever the owner or manager decides to open. Students in a polychronic society would not expect a professor to begin class at an appointed hour; instead, students would arrive over a period of time, and the class would begin whenever the professor was ready. Further, people in a polychronic culture don't prioritize efficiency and punctuality but, instead, attach greater value to the quality of life and to their relationships with others.

Check out "Putting Communication to Work" for an example of a career in which communication training can help you interact effectively with people from a wide variety of cultures.

- **low-power-distance culture** A culture in which people believe that no one person or group should have excessive power.

- **high-power-distance culture** A culture in which certain groups, such as the royal family or the members of the ruling political party, have much greater power than the average citizen.

- **masculine culture** A culture in which people cherish traditionally masculine values and prefer sex-specific roles for women and men.

- **feminine culture** A culture in which people cherish traditionally feminine qualities and prefer little differentiation in the roles of women and men.

- **monochronic culture** A culture that sees time as a valuable commodity that should be used wisely and not wasted.

- **polychronic culture** A culture that views time as holistic, fluid, and infinite.

SHARPEN Your Skills:
Adapting to time management

Interview someone whose career depends heavily on maintaining a tightly managed schedule (such as a person in the travel or broadcast industries). Ask how he or she would work effectively with a customer or coworker who took a polychronic approach to time management.

Design Pics/Don Hammond

6. UNCERTAINTY AVOIDANCE

Humans have a natural tendency to avoid unfamiliar and uncomfortable situations. In other words, we dislike uncertainty—in fact, uncertainty causes many of us a good deal of stress.[38] Not all cultures find uncertainty to be equally problematic,

Job Title >

International Student Life Coordinator, College or University

Work Responsibilities >

Most U.S. colleges and universities have programs to help international students adapt to life in the United States. A student life coordinator may communicate with student applicants from a wide variety of cultures, assist them with immigration and customs documents, meet them on arrival, and help them acclimate to the routines and cultural customs they will experience as students in the United States. This job requires excellent written and oral communication skills, a friendly and patient personality, and a working knowledge of the communication patterns of people from other cultures.

• uncertainty avoidance
The extent to which people try to avoid situations that are unstructured, unclear, or unpredictable.

Although the United States is relatively accepting of uncertainty, particular groups—such as the Amish—are highly uncertainty-avoidant.
George Sheldon/ Shutterstock

however. Rather, cultures vary in what Hofstede called **uncertainty avoidance**, or the extent to which people try to avoid situations that are unstructured, unclear, or unpredictable.[39]

Individuals from cultures that are highly uncertainty-avoidant are drawn to people and situations that are familiar, and they are relatively unlikely to take risks, for fear of failure. They are also uncomfortable with differences of opinion, and they tend to favor rules and laws that maximize security and reduce ambiguity. Argentina, Portugal, and Uruguay are among the countries whose cultures are the most uncertainty-avoidant.

In comparison, people in uncertainty-accepting cultures are more open to new situations and more accepting of people and ideas that are different from their own. They take a "live and let live" approach, preferring as few rules as possible that would restrict their behaviors. Societies with cultures that are highly accepting of uncertainty include Hong Kong, Jamaica, and New Zealand. Hofstede determined that the U.S. culture is more accepting than avoidant of uncertainty, but it is closer to the midpoint of the scale than many countries are. Co-cultures within the United States, however, vary in how tolerant they are of uncertainty. For instance, Amish communities—which adhere to strict guidelines regarding dress, behavior, and the use of modern technology—are often highly uncertainty-avoidant. In comparison, actors, sculptors, and other artists may have a high tolerance for uncertainty if it facilitates their creativity.

Communicating with Cultural Awareness

The opportunity to know and communicate with people from other cultures is greater now than at any time in history. Many U.S. colleges and universities enroll large populations of international students, and social networking makes it as easy to connect with someone in New Guinea as with someone in New Jersey. Consequently, the ability to communicate effectively with people from different cultural backgrounds has never been a greater advantage. In this section, we explore some essential qualities for communicating with cultural awareness: being open-minded about cultural differences, knowledgeable about cultural communication codes, and flexible and respectful when interacting with others.

BE OPEN-MINDED ABOUT CULTURAL DIFFERENCES

People with different cultural backgrounds don't just communicate differently—in many cases, they truly *think* differently. Those differences in communicating and thinking can present real challenges when people from different cultures interact. As we'll see in this section, one way to combat those challenges is to be open-minded about similarities and differences. Being open-minded requires first being aware of potential differences and then avoiding the tendency to judge all differences negatively.

Be Mindful People from different cultures are often unaware of *how* they differ. An American college professor might think a Japanese student is being deceptive if the student doesn't look her in the eye when he speaks to her. In the United States, that behavior can suggest dishonesty, but in Japan, it can signal respect. If neither the professor nor the student is aware of how the other is likely to interpret the behavior, it's easy to see how a misunderstanding might arise.

Communicating effectively with people from other cultures requires **mindfulness**, which is awareness of how other people's behaviors and ways of thinking are likely to differ from our own. Unfortunately, being mindful is easier said than done. Many of us operate on what researchers call a *similarity assumption*—that is, we presume that most people think the same way we do, without asking ourselves whether that's true.

Mindfulness of different assumptions is often important when communicating across religious cultures as well. In today's global economy, you are likely to interact with students, customers, or friends whose religious assumptions and practices differ from your own. Being mindful means being sensitive to those differences. When communicating with people who practice Hinduism, for instance, you may want to remember that Hindus believe in a social system, called a *caste system*, in which some people are held in higher esteem than others. Marrying—or even eating with—someone of a different caste is avoided. Many Hindus also believe that after they die, their soul will return to live on Earth in a new body, human or otherwise. The quality of their next life depends on their actions in this one. Those cultural assumptions differ markedly from those of, say, Muslims. Muslims believe in the fundamental equality of all humans, meaning that no group is held in higher esteem than any other. They also believe they will be sent to Heaven or Hell after death, depending on their deeds in this life.

Questioning our cultural assumptions can be a real challenge because we're often unaware that we hold them in the first place. At the same time, however, it is one of the basic ways in which studying communication and learning about the influences of culture can make us more mindful and competent communicators.

Avoid Ethnocentrism It's one thing to be aware of how patterns of thought and behavior differ among cultures. It's another to avoid judging all other cultural practices as inferior to our own.

The first time she traveled through southern Africa, for instance, Gretchen was put off by some of the cultural practices she encountered. People would kiss her on the lips when they met her for the first time. Strangers sat uncomfortably near her

• **mindfulness**
Awareness—as in being aware of how other cultures' behaviors and ways of thinking are likely to differ from one's own.

Do you react ethnocentrically when you encounter cultural practices that are different from your own?

ymphotos/Shutterstock Images, LLC

• **ethnocentrism** The tendency to judge other cultures' practices as inferior to one's own.

on public buses, and their closeness bothered her even more because few of them used deodorant. Most of the men had multiple wives and took their children to witch doctors when they got sick.

Instead of accepting those characteristics as normal parts of the societies she visited, Gretchen found them backward and wrong. "What messed-up cultures!" she said on returning to the United States. In making that assessment, Gretchen was displaying **ethnocentrism**, the tendency to judge other cultures' practices as inferior to one's own. Had she been more open-minded, Gretchen might have learned why people behaved differently than she expected. She may even have come to appreciate that her own cultural practices aren't the only valid ways of interacting with others.

Particularly if you haven't had exposure to a broad range of cultures, it can be easy to believe that your values and traditions are the *right* values and traditions for everyone. If you think that way, consider how much your concept of culture depends merely on where you were raised. Had you been raised in the south of Africa, for instance, you would likely find it normal and right for a man to have several wives and for people to kiss on the lips when they meet, and you may think cultural values and traditions such as Gretchen's were abnormal and wrong. In other words, every cultural group—not just your own—considers its ways of living to be proper. When you communicate with people from other cultures, it is therefore valuable to resist ethnocentrism by remembering that being *different* does not necessarily mean being *wrong.* Perhaps you put a lot of stock in the use of deodorant and view consultations with witch doctors as primitive, but bear in mind that those are simply your cultural values. Although they may seem right to you, they aren't right to everyone.

Interacting with people whose cultural values and practices differ markedly from yours can be intriguing, but it can also make people uncomfortable. For tips on managing such a situation, check out the "Difficult Conversations" box.

Overcoming ethnocentrism takes practice. A first step is to recognize any tendencies you might have to judge other cultures' practices as inferior to your own. Check out "The Competent Communicator" to assess where you stand.

BE KNOWLEDGEABLE ABOUT DIFFERENT COMMUNICATION CODES

• **communication codes** Verbal and nonverbal behaviors whose meanings are often understood only by people from the same culture.

Another requirement for communicating with cultural awareness is to remember that cultures differ from one another in their use of **communication codes**, verbal and non-verbal behaviors whose meanings are often understood only by people from the same culture. Three kinds of communication codes—idioms, jargon, and gestures—differ significantly from society to society, and the variations can make communicating across cultures and co-cultures challenging. Being knowledgeable about those differences can boost the effectiveness of your intercultural communication.

Cultures Use Different Idioms An *idiom* is a phrase whose meaning is purely figurative; that is, we can't understand its meaning by interpreting the words literally. For example, most Americans know that the idiom "kicking the bucket" has nothing to do with kicking a bucket; it means to die. If you grew up in the United States, you can probably think of several other common idioms, including "a dime a dozen"

Difficult Conversations

Talking about Beliefs that Offend You

Imagine this: Your new suite mate is an exchange student from the Middle East, and you soon discover that his cultural background is strongly masculine. He believes, among other things, that women belong in the home, not the workforce. He is friendly enough, but he openly criticizes women who work outside the home, including faculty and staff at your school. You want to be welcoming of your suite mate, but you start to feel uncomfortable because your own ideas about women are substantially different.

Now, consider this: The two of you eat together in the dining hall from time to time, and you are concerned that the subject is bound to come up in conversation, perhaps when some of your other friends are around. You wonder about the pros and cons of expressing your own beliefs about women.

- Remember that you are entitled to have your ideas about gender and equality. The issue isn't whether you can take a different position than your suite mate takes, but whether and how to communicate about your position.

- Recall, too, that your position is likely informed by your cultural values, and be mindful that your suite mate's position is informed by his cultural values. You can certainly think your position is the *preferred* one, but avoid the ethnocentric tendency to think your position is the *only valid* one.

- If you choose to discuss your differing ideas about gender and equality with your suite mate, it may help to start by expressing curiosity rather than condemnation. Instead of simply telling him you disagree with his ideas, ask him how he came to believe as he does about women's roles. Rather than saying, "I think you're wrong," you might say, "I imagine you have encountered people who think differently than you do on this issue."

When we come across something that deviates from our strongly held values, our natural tendency may be to condemn it as wrong. Behaving politely and expressing curiosity may feel like implicitly endorsing your suite mate's ideas about women. Instead, however, this approach conveys *mindfulness* by acknowledging that his position is informed by his cultural values, just as yours is. You can hold different values without condemning your suite mate as wrong.

to mean something that's very common or nothing special, "having two left feet" to mean being a poor dancer, "shaking a leg" to mean hurrying, and "pulling your leg" to mean joking with you.

Every society has its own idioms whose meanings are not necessarily obvious to people from other cultures. In Armenia, for instance, people say "stop ironing my head" when they're annoyed with you. In Finland, if something "becomes ginger-bread," that means it goes completely wrong. If someone in Brazil says "Fish don't pull wagons," she is encouraging you to eat red meat. Likewise, if someone in Australia "lives out woop woop," he lives far away from everything else. When you interact with people from other cultures, it's very helpful to be aware that they may use phrases that are not familiar to you, and you may be using idioms that are unfamiliar to them.[40]

COMPETENT COMMUNICATOR

Who, Me? Being Aware of Ethnocentrism

What do you think about other cultures' values and traditions as compared to your own? On a scale of 1 to 7, indicate your level of agreement with each statement shown below. A score of 7 means you strongly agree; a score of 1 means you strongly disagree.

Design Pics/Don Hammond

1 _____ Most other cultures are backward compared with my culture.

2 _____ I see people who are similar to me as virtuous.

3 _____ The values and customs of other cultures have nothing to do with me.

4 _____ People in other cultures just don't know what's good for them.

5 _____ Most people would be happier if they lived like the people in my culture.

6 _____ Lifestyles in other cultures are not as valid as those in my culture.

7 _____ I do not trust people who are different.

8 _____ It is hard for me to respect the customs and traditions of other cultures.

9 _____ Other cultures should try to be more like my culture.

10 _____ People from other cultures act in strange and unusual ways when they come into my culture.

When you're finished, add up your score, which should range from 10 to 70. That is your general ethnocentrism score. If your score is 40 or below, you are relatively low on ethnocentrism. A score above 40 indicates relatively high ethnocentrism.

Ask Yourself

- Were you surprised by your score? Why or why not? What factors do you think your score reflects?

- How can learning about cultural influences on communication affect a tendency toward ethnocentrism?

SOURCE: Items adapted from Neuliep, J. W. (2002). Assessing the reliability and validity of the generalized ethnocentrism scale. *Journal of Intercultural Communication Research, 31*(4), 201–215. https://doi.org/10.13072/midss.507

Cultural differences in language use can also make it difficult to translate phrases and slogans from one culture to the next. As Table 3 illustrates, some humorous mistranslations can result.

Cultures Use Different Jargon A specific form of idiomatic communication—and one that often separates co-cultures in particular—is jargon. As we've seen, *jargon* is language whose technical meaning is understood by people within a given co-culture

TABLE 3

LOST IN TRANSLATION: SOME MISTRANSLATED SLOGANS

Sign in a Bangkok dry cleaner: *Drop your trousers here for best results!*

Sign in a Copenhagen airline ticket office: *We take your bags and send them in all directions.*

Sign in a Hong Kong tailor shop: *Ladies may have a fit upstairs.*

Sign in an Acapulco restaurant: *The manager has personally passed all the water served here.*

Sign in a Moscow hotel room: *If this is your first visit to Russia, you are welcome to it.*

but not necessarily by those outside it. Your doctor might inform her nurse, for instance, that you have "paroxysmal nocturnal dyspnoea," but she would probably tell you that you experience shortness of breath at night. Similarly, if your dentist orders a "periapical radiograph," he wants an X-ray of one of your teeth.

Not understanding jargon can make you feel like an outsider. You might even get the impression that doctors and dentists talk that way just to reinforce their in-group status. Jargon can serve an important function, however, by allowing people who use it to communicate with one another in ways that are very specific, efficient, and accurate. Just bear in mind that when you use jargon with people who don't belong to your in-group, they might have difficulty understanding your meaning. Culturally aware communicators know when they need to **code-switch**, or shift between jargon and plain language, in order to be understood by others.

Alexey Poprotsky/123RF

• **code-switch** To shift between jargon and plain language in order to be understood by others.

Cultures Use Different Gestures Cultures also differ a great deal in their use of *gestures*, which are movements, usually of the hand or the arm, that express ideas. The same gesture can have different meanings from society to society. For instance, American parents sometimes play the game "I've got your nose" with infants by putting a thumb between the index and middle finger. That gesture means good luck in Brazil, but it is an obscene expression in Russia and Indonesia. Similarly, holding up an index and pinky finger while holding down the middle and ring finger is a common gesture for University of Texas Longhorns fans. In Italy, however, people use that gesture to suggest that a man's wife has been unfaithful.[41] In some cultures, nodding the head—which Americans take to mean "yes"—actually means "no." Being aware of cultural differences in the meaning of such gestures can steer you away from unintentionally embarrassing yourself or insulting others.

SHARPEN Your Skills: *Gestures*

Select a gesture commonly used in the United States, such as the "OK" gesture or the "thumbs-up" gesture for good luck. Investigate which other cultures use that gesture and what meanings it has there. Write up your results in the form of advice for students planning to travel internationally.

BE FLEXIBLE AND RESPECTFUL WHEN INTERACTING WITH OTHERS

Finally, remember that cultures sometimes vary a good deal in how they communicate. When you interact with people from other cultures, expect some level of ambiguity, be aware of potential differences in access to communication technology, and adapt to the behavior patterns you observe.

Expect Ambiguity Communication experts have long recognized that many people value certainty in their interactions with others.[42] Most of us can recall being in social situations in which we were unsure of what to do or how to act. Such occasions present us with *ambiguity*, or a lack of certainty. Because cultures can differ so substantially in their communication patterns, such ambiguity is common when we interact cross-culturally. It's easy to feel uncomfortable and discouraged when we experience ambiguity and to long for the certainty of our own cultural practices. Good communicators remember, however, that ambiguity is normal when they interact with people from another culture. Instead of fearing the ambiguity, they use it as an opportunity to learn more about other ways of life.

Best friends Paul and Ethan discovered the value of expecting ambiguity when they traveled to Indonesia one summer. On the bus from the airport on the day they arrived, they were constantly pushed and shoved by other passengers. At their hotel, the guest checking in before them appeared to be haggling with the manager over the cost of the room, and the bargaining delayed Paul and Ethan's check-in. Once they finally reached the check-in desk, the manager refused to take Ethan's credit card when he offered it in his left hand. After completing their transaction, Paul and Ethan were told their luggage would be delivered to their room shortly, yet they waited nearly two hours before it arrived.

As experienced travelers, however, Paul and Ethan knew they should take the ambiguity of those interactions in stride. They soon discovered that Indonesians often push and shove while in crowds but consider such jostling to be normal, not an expression of anger or malice. They learned that bargaining over prices is expected in many business transactions and that it is polite to give and receive items only with the right hand, never the left. And because Indonesia is a highly polychronic society, people are far less concerned with punctuality than Paul and Ethan are used to—hence the delayed delivery of their luggage. Ambiguity comes with the territory in intercultural communication and offers a chance to learn about the values and traditions of culturally different people.

Appreciate Differences in Access to Communication Technology

An erroneous assumption many people make when interacting cross-culturally is that everyone has the same access to communication technology, such as the Internet. In fact, such access varies greatly around the world, particularly between countries that are economically *developed* (such as the United States, Germany, France, and Japan) and those that are economically *developing* (such as Bolivia, Angola, Pakistan, and Laos). Internet access even varies between U.S. households, depending on their economic resources.

Social scientists use the term *digital divide* to acknowledge the cultural gap between groups that do and do not have regular Internet access.[43] For instance, whereas electronically scanning a proposal and sending it as an e-mail attachment may be a simple task for you, a potential business client in a developing country may not have easy access to the equipment or the Internet service needed to retrieve it. If you know that ahead of time, you can make alternative arrangements to send your proposal, saving your client frustration—and possibly saving the business transaction.

Figure 1 charts the number of people, per 100 inhabitants, with reliable Internet access in the developed and developing world. Notice how the gap has widened—not shrunk—over the years.

Adapt to Others As you interact with people of other cultures and learn about their customs—particularly those related to communication behavior—it's advantageous to adapt to those customs. As mentioned in the introductory chapter, adapting means changing your behavior to accommodate what others are doing. If you find that people in a particular social setting are all speaking very quietly, for instance, then lowering your own speaking volume demonstrates adaptation. If others are bowing when they greet a leader or a learned person, you can adapt by doing the same. Good intercultural communicators adapt to the communicative behaviors of their conversational partners to emphasize similarity, convey respect, and promote unity.[44]

FIGURE 1
THE GLOBAL DIGITAL DIVIDE

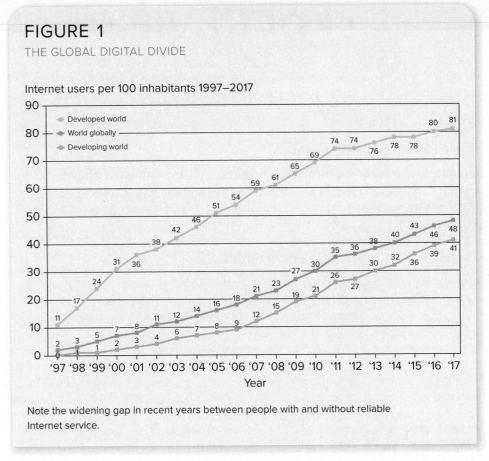

Internet users per 100 inhabitants 1997–2017

Note the widening gap in recent years between people with and without reliable Internet service.

SOURCE: Internet users per 100 inhabitants 1996-2017. International Telecommunications Union. Geneva, accessed August 2019.

During a trip to the Vatican in May 2017, for instance, First Lady Melania Trump made headlines when she wore a black, long-sleeved dress and a black lace veil to meet Pope Francis. Although such attire is not customary for U.S. women to wear during political events, it represented the First Lady's attempt to adapt to Vatican culture, where it signifies respect when meeting with a pope. Former first ladies, including Michelle Obama, Laura Bush, and Hillary Clinton, had all adopted the same specific dress code during meetings with Pope John Paul II and Pope Benedict XVI.[45]

Adaptation can help your intercultural communication flow smoothly, but only if others perceive the adaptation as respectful. If they think you are copying their behavior to mock them, you can cause offense. Whenever Margene speaks to someone with an accent, for example, she inadvertently adopts the same accent in her own speech. If the other speaker doesn't consciously notice, then Margene's adaptation likely helps to make the interaction positive. Researchers know that we like people who adapt to our vocal behavior, because we subconsciously think of them as similar to ourselves.[46] If the other speaker does notice that Margene has adopted his accent, however, he may feel she is making fun of his speech, even if Margene is unaware that she has adapted to his accent in the first place. When you do adapt to another person's behaviors, try not to exaggerate or draw attention to them. Adaptation is likely to be most effective when it appears natural, not forced.

When you adapt your behavior to others, do so in a way that conveys your interest in following their example and accommodating their traditions rather than in a way that mocks or disrespects them. The distinction can be a fine line, but being aware of the potential for conveying disrespect is a crucial first step.

For REVIEW

- **What is culture?**

  Culture is the totality of learned, shared symbols, language, values, and norms that distinguish one group of people from another.

- **How does culture influence communication behavior?**

  Culture influences communication behavior through variations in (1) the emphasis placed on individuals versus groups, (2) the communicative context, (3) power distance, (4) views about masculinity and femininity and about men's and women's roles, (5) orientation toward time, and (6) uncertainty avoidance.

- **In what ways can we improve our cultural communication skills?**

  We can be open-minded about cultural differences, knowledgeable about cultural communication codes, and flexible and respectful when communicating with people from other cultures.

KEY TERMS

culture 34	individualistic culture 44	monochronic culture 47
societies 34	collectivistic culture 44	polychronic culture 47
in-groups 35	low-context culture 45	uncertainty avoidance 48
out-groups 35	high-context culture 45	mindfulness 49
ethnicity 36	low-power-distance culture 46	ethnocentrism 50
nationality 36	high-power-distance culture 46	communication codes 50
enculturation 36	masculine culture 46	code-switch 53
co-cultures 38	feminine culture 46	

NOTES

1. Lavandera, E., & Hanna, J. (2019, August 9). El Paso shooting: Suspect told police he was targeting Mexicans, affidavit says. *CNN.* https://cnn.com/2019/08/09/us/el-paso-shooting-friday/index.html
2. Mezzofiore, G. (2019, July 30). Artists installed seesaws at the border so kids in the US and Mexico could play together. *CNN.* https://cnn.com/2019/07/30/us/seesaws-border-wall-us-mexico-trnd/index.html
3. Cazzato, V., Makris, S., Flavell, J. C., & Vicario, C. M. (2018). Group membership and racial bias modulate the temporal estimation of in-group/out-group body movements. *Experimental Brain Research, 236*(8), 2427–2437. https://doi.org/10.1007/s00221-018-5313-4
4. Santiago, C. D., Distel, L. M. L., Ros, A. M., Brewer, S. K., Torres, S. A., Papadakis, J. L., Fuller, A. K., & Bustos, Y. (2018). Mental health among Mexican-origin immigrant families: The roles of cumulative sociodemographic risk and immigrant-related stress. *Race and Social Problems, 10*(3), 235–247. https://doi.org/10.1007/s12552-018-9236-2

5. Buttelmann, D., & Böhm, R. (2014). The ontogeny of the motivation that underlies in-group bias. *Psychological Science, 25*(4), 921–927. https://doi.org/10.1177/0956797613516802

6. Abend, L. (2019, January 16). An island for "unwanted" migrants is Denmark's latest aggressive anti-immigrant policy. *Time.* https://time.com/5504331/denmark-migrants-lindholm-island/

7. ACLU. (2019). Family separation: By the numbers. https://www.aclu.org/issues/immigrants-rights/immigrants-rights-and-detention/family-separation

8. Human Rights Watch. (2019, July 11). US: Family separating harming children, families. https://www.hrw.org/news/2019/07/11/us-family-separation-harming-children-families

9. Moore, E. A., & Mertens, D. M. (2015). Deaf culture and youth resilience in diverse American communities. In L. C. Theron, L. Liebenberg, & M. Ungar (Eds.), *Youth resilience and culture: Commonalities and complexities* (pp. 143–155). Springer. https://doi.org/10.1007/978-94-017-9415-2_11

10. Nomeland, M. M., & Nomeland, R. E. (2012). *The deaf community in America: History in the making.* McFarland & Company.

11. Lennon, P. (2019, July 23). Rise and fall: The 110 year history of UNC's Confederate monument, Silent Sam. *The Daily Tar Heel.* https://www.dailytarheel.com/article/2019/07/silent-sam-print

12. Pew Research Center. (2011, April 8). Civil War at 150: Still relevant, still divisive. http://www.people-press.org/2011/04/08/civil-war-at-150-still-relevant-still-divisive/

13. Gordon, R. G. (Ed.). (2015). *Ethnologue: Languages of the world* (18th ed.). SIL International.

14. Ibid.

15. Office of the New York State Comptroller. https://www.osc.state.ny.us/

16. Foundation for Endangered Languages. http://www.ogmios.org/home.htm

17. See Campbell, N., & Kean, A. (2016). *American cultural studies: An introduction to American culture* (4th ed.). Routledge. https://doi.org/10.4324.9780203801994

18. Brosch, T., & Sander, D. (Eds.). (2016). *Handbook of value: Perspectives from economics, neuroscience, philosophy, psychology, and sociology.* Oxford University Press. https://doi.org/10.1093/acprof:oso/9780198716600.001.0001

19. Yin, L. (2009). Cultural difference of politeness in English and Chinese. *Asian Social Science, 5*(6). http://www.ccsenet.org/journal/index.php/ass/article/view/2492/2338

20. Brown, D. E. (2000). Human universals and their implications. In N. Roughley (Ed.), *Being humans: Anthropological universality and particularity in transdisciplinary perspectives* (pp. 156–174). Walter de Gruyter; Pinker, S. (2008, January 13). The moral instinct. *New York Times Magazine.* https://www.nytimes.com/2008/01/13/magazine/13Psychology-t.html

21. Becker, M., Vignoles, V. L., Owe, E., Brown, R., Smith, P. B., Easterbrook, M., Herman, G., de Sauvage, I., Bourguignon, D., Torres, A., Camino, L., Lemos, F. C. S., Ferreire, M. C., Koller, S. H., González, R., Carrasco, D., Cadena, M. P., Lay, S., Wang, Q., Bond, M. H., . . . Yamakoğlu, N. (2012). Culture and the distinctiveness motive: Constructing identity in individualistic and collectivistic contexts. *Journal of Personality and Social Psychology, 102*(4), 833–855. https://doi.org/10.1037/a0026853

22. Gorodnichenko, Y., & Roland, G. (2017). Culture, institutions, and the wealth of nations. *The Review of Economics and Statistics, 99*(3), 402–416. https://doi.org/10.1162/REST_a_00599

23. Piot, C. (1999). *Remotely global: Village modernity in West Africa.* University of Chicago Press.

24. The Independent. (2016, March 14). Is your name now "banned" in Saudi Arabia? https://www.independent.co.uk/news/world/middle-east/is-your-name-now-banned-in-saudi-arabia-9192298.html

25. Hofstede, G. (2019). *Geert Hofstede.* https://geerthofstede.com/culture-geert-hofstede-gert-jan-hofstede/6d-model-of-national-culture/

26. See LeFebvre, R., & Franke, V. (2013). Culture matters: Individualism vs. collectivism in conflict decision-making. *Societies, 3*(1), 128–146. https://doi.org/10.3390/soc3010128; Cai, D. A., & Fink, E. L. (2002). Conflict style differences between individualists and collectivists. *Communication Monographs, 69*(1), 67–87. https://doi.org/10.1080/03637750216536

27. Burgoon, J. K., Guerrero, L. K., & Floyd, K. (2010). *Nonverbal communication.* Pearson.

28. Martin, J., & Nakayama, T. (2017). *Intercultural communication in contexts* (7th ed.). McGraw-Hill.

29. Stahlin, W. A., Harris, P., & Kinkela, K. (2014, January). Increasing your cultural awareness. *Global Conference on Business & Finance Proceedings, 9,* 177–182.

30. Ramaswami, A., Huang, J.-C., & Dreher, G. (2014). Interaction of gender, mentoring, and power distance on career attainment: A cross-cultural comparison. *Human Relations, 67*(2), 153–173. https://doi.org/10.1177/0018726713490000

31. Hofstede, 2015.

32. Martin & Nakayama, 2017.

33. Yook, E. L., & Albert, R. D. (1998). Perceptions of the appropriateness of negotiation in educational settings: A cross-cultural comparison among Koreans and Americans. *Communication Education, 47*(1), 18–29. https://doi.org/10.1080/03634529809379107

34. Hofstede, G., Hofstede, G. J., & Minkov, M. (2010). *Cultures and organizations: Software of the mind* (3rd ed.). McGraw-Hill.

35. Ibid.

36. Kaufman-Scarborough, C. (2017). Monochronic and polychronic time. In K. Y. Yun (Ed.), *The international encyclopedia of intercultural communication.* Wiley-Blackwell. https://doi.org/10.1002/9781118783665.ieicc0110

37. Gesteland, R. R. (2012). *Cross-cultural business behavior: A guide for global management* (5th ed.). Copenhagen Business School Press.

38. van den Bos, K., & Lind, E. A. (2013). The social psychology of fairness and the regulation of personal uncertainty. In R. M. Arkin, K. C. Oleson, & P. J. Carroll (Eds.), *Handbook of the uncertain self* (pp. 122–141). Psychology Press. https://doi.org/10.4324/9780203848753

39. Seo, S., Kim, K., & Jang, J. (2018). Uncertainty avoidance as a moderator for influences on foreign resident dining out behaviors. *International Journal of Contemporary Hospitality Management, 30*(2), 900–918. https://doi.org/10.1108/IJCHM-03-2016-0152

40. Lustig, M. W., & Koester, J. (2017). *Intercultural competence: Interpersonal communication across cultures* (8th ed.). Pearson. https://doi.org/10.1080/14708477.2013.8556575

41. Pease, A., & Pease, B. (2006). *The definitive book of body language*. Bantam Books.

42. Antheunis, M. L., Schouten, A. P., Valkenburg, P. M., & Peter, J. (2012). Interactive uncertainty reduction strategies and verbal affection in computer-mediated communication. *Communication Research, 39*(6), 757–780. https://doi.org/10.1177/0093650211410420

43. Mihelj, S., Leguina, A., & Downey, J. (2019). Culture is digital: Cultural participation, diversity and the digital divide. *New Media & Society, 21*(7), 1465–1485. https://doi.org/10.1177/1461444818822816

44. See Goodwin, J. M. (2019). Communication accommodation theory: Finding the right approach. In M. A. Brown, & L. Hersey (Eds.), *Returning to interpersonal dialogue and understanding human communication in the digital age* (pp. 168–185). IGI Global. https://doi.org/10.4081/978-1-5225-4168-4.ch008

45. BBC. (2017, May 24). Melania Trump in black at the Vatican. Why? *BBC News*. https://www.bbc.com/news/world-europe-40030668

46. See, e.g., McGarva, A. R., & Warner, R. M. (2003). Attraction and social coordination: Mutual entrainment of vocal activity rhythms. *Journal of Psycholinguistic Research, 32*(3), 335–354. https://doi.org/10.1023/A:1023547703110

3

Nuccio DiNuzzo/Stringer/Getty images

PERCEIVING OURSELVES AND OTHERS

Villain or Victim: What's Your Perception?

When it comes to Jussie Smollett, people express a wide variety of opinions. The U.S. American actor and singer made headlines in 2019 after telling police he had been assaulted by two men wearing ski masks and shouting racial and homophobic slurs. Smollett reported that the attackers then doused him with an unknown liquid and put a noose around his neck. Less than a month after the alleged incident, Smollett was charged by a grand jury for filing a false police report, and he surrendered himself to authorities. Following a month of investigation, all charges against Smollett were dropped and the court file was sealed. Smollett's actions have drawn both strong support and sharp criticism, based on how others perceive him. Whereas some perceive Smollett as a victim of racial and homophobic persecution, others allege that he arranged the supposed attack in order to generate sympathy and support.

As You READ

- How do we form perceptions of others?
- What influences our perceptions?
- How do we manage our image?

Getting along in our social world depends on our ability to understand others and ourselves. Our minds, senses, and experiences help us to form perceptions about people that influence the way we communicate with them. We often hold well-informed perceptions of ourselves and others. Sometimes, however, we may form perceptions on the basis of very limited information, which may or may not be accurate. Your perception of Jussie Smollett, for instance, may be based only on the specific news items you pay attention to. The more we learn about the perception-making process, the better we will be at understanding and communicating appropriately with the people around us.

How We Perceive Others

Many people would call the selection of a romantic partner one of the most consequential social decisions a person can make, given that we could be choosing the person with whom we will spend the rest of our lives. Because it's such an important decision, you may think most of us would require lots of information to decide whether someone would be a suitable match.

Speed daters might disagree, however. In speed dating, groups of people get together so individuals can visit one another one-on-one for 3- to 8-minute "mini-dates" before moving on to the next person. Whenever two people both want to know more about each other, they each receive the other's contact information and take it from there. Although these mini-dates may seem too short for participants to make serious mate choices, much research has shown that people are surprisingly accurate at evaluating others after very brief periods of time.[1] In fact, our impressions and evaluations of others can be more accurate if we have less—rather than more—information to go on, as the "Fact or Fiction?" box explains.

We form our impressions and evaluations of others by engaging in **perception**, the process of making meaning from what we experience in the world around us. We notice physical experiences—such as fatigue, body aches, and congestion—and perceive that we are ill. We notice environmental experiences—such as cold air, wind, and rain—and perceive that a storm is underway. When we apply the same process to people and relationships, we engage in interpersonal perception, which helps us to make meaning about people from our own and others' behaviors.[2]

As social beings, we are constantly engaged in interpersonal perception. We form impressions and evaluations of others—accurate or not—on the basis of the information available to us. Although our perceptions may seem to take shape instantaneously, we will find in this section that they actually form in stages, though quickly. We will also see that several factors can influence the accuracy of our perceptions, including culture, stereotypes, primacy and recency effects, and perceptual sets.

• **perception** The process of making meaning from environmental experiences.

Speed dating relies on short conversations with multiple partners. Research shows that people are sometimes surprisingly accurate at evaluating others after very brief periods of time.

fizkes/Shutterstock

PERCEPTION IS A PROCESS

Our minds usually select, organize, and interpret information so quickly and so subconsciously that we think our perceptions are objective, factual reflections of the world. Suppose you had a conflict with your roommate before leaving for school or work this morning, and throughout the day he failed to respond to your text messages reminding him to pick up dinner. You might perceive that your roommate is ignoring you because he is not replying to you. In fact, however, you have created the perception that he's ignoring you based on the information you *selected* for

When Forming Perceptions, More Information Is Always Better

People sometimes criticize others for making snap judgments—that is, arriving at their perceptions on the basis of limited information. After listening to one speech, for example, you decide to vote for a political candidate without learning anything else about her. Or a customer comes into your store, and after taking one look at him, you perceive that he's trouble. It's easy to see how those on-the-spot judgments can be misleading and how your perceptions might have been more accurate if you'd had additional information.

In many cases, this observation is true: when forming perceptions of others, we should remember that first impressions can be misleading. That political candidate might sound good, but you may have a different perception of her when you learn that she has no experience in government. That customer might look suspicious, but you might think differently when you find out he's a youth minister on his way home from a long and tiring retreat. In many situations, the more information we can gather to check our perceptions, the more accurate our perceptions will be.

Research shows, however, that in certain cases our snap judgments are surprisingly accurate. Moreover, gathering additional information about someone *can* make our perceptions more accurate, but it doesn't always do so.

You might think, for instance, that you could get to know someone better by meeting him or her face-to-face rather than by simply chatting online. An interesting experiment proved otherwise, though. In the study, pairs of strangers communicated in one of three ways. Some conversed by Internet chat, where they had access only to each other's words. Others talked on the telephone, giving them access to their partners' words and voice. The rest met face-to-face, where they could hear and see each other in person. After short interactions, the participants reported their perceptions of each other's personalities, and the researchers compared those perceptions to the partners' reports of their own personalities.

The results showed some differences based on the "richness" of the communication channel. Participants' judgments of their partners' friendliness and moodiness were most accurate after face-to-face conversations and least accurate after Internet chats. In other words, the more information they had about each other, the more accurate their perceptions were. The opposite pattern was observed for perceptions of the partners' conscientiousness and openness, however. Those perceptions were most accurate after Internet chats and least accurate after face-to-face meetings. This experiment illustrates that having more information about a person—as you would if you had talked face-to-face instead of online—does not necessarily make your perceptions of him or her more accurate. More information is sometimes better, but not always.

ASK YOURSELF

- Why are snap judgments sometimes accurate? What clues might we be subconsciously noticing that help us interpret a situation quickly yet accurately?

- When have you made snap judgments that turned out to be inaccurate? What led you to form those perceptions?

SOURCES: Darbyshire, D., Kirk, C., Wall, H. J., & Kaye, L. K. (2016). Don't judge a (Face)book by its cover: Exploring judgment accuracy of others' personality on Facebook. *Computers in Human Behavior, 58,* 380–387. https://doi.org/:10.1016/j.chb.2016.01.021; Wall, H. J., Taylor, P. J., Dixon, J., Conchie, S. M., & Ellis, D. A. (2013). Rich contexts do not always enrich the accuracy of personality judgments. *Journal of Experimental Social Psychology, 49*(6), 1190–1195. https://doi.org/10.1016/j.jesp.2013.05.010

A loud conversation in a quiet place grabs your attention because it is unusual in that environment.

bernardbodo/123RF

• **selection** The process of paying attention to a certain stimulus.

attention (he doesn't respond to your text messages), the way you *organized* that information (he is deliberately being inconsiderate because he is angry about your conflict), and the way you *interpreted* it (he's ignoring you).[3] That isn't the only perception you could create, however. You might also perceive that he is having an extremely busy day or that he left his cell phone in his car. The perception you form depends on which pieces of information you attend to and which ones you ignore.

Selection, organization, and interpretation are the three basic stages of perception. Let's examine each in turn.

Selection Perception is initiated when one or more of your senses are stimulated. You enter a bagel store and hear a customer placing her order. You see a puppy chewing on an old tennis ball. You smell a coworker's cologne as he walks past. Those sensory experiences of hearing, seeing, and smelling can prompt you to form perceptions.

In truth, your senses are constantly stimulated by events in your environment. It's impossible, though, to pay attention to everything you are seeing, hearing, smelling, tasting, and feeling at any given moment.[4] When you're watching the puppy play with his tennis ball, you're probably not listening carefully to the news report on the television. Rather than paying attention to *all* the stimuli in your environment, you engage in **selection**, the process by which your mind and body help you isolate certain stimuli to pay attention to. For example, you notice that your partner didn't take out the garbage, but you overlook that he washed the dishes three nights in a row. Clearly, the information we attend to influences the perceptions we form. A key point is that we don't necessarily make conscious decisions about which stimuli to notice and which to ignore. How, then, does selection occur? Research indicates that three characteristics in particular make a given stimulus more likely to be selected for attention.

First, being unusual or unexpected makes a stimulus stand out.[5] You might not pay attention to people talking loudly in a restaurant, but if the same loud conversation were to take place in the library, it would grab your attention because it is unusual in that environment. Second, repetition, or how frequently you are exposed to a stimulus, makes it stand out.[6] For example, you're more likely to remember commercials you've seen repeatedly than ones you've seen only once. Similarly, you tend to notice more characteristics about the people you see frequently than about individuals you don't see often, such as their physical appearance and behavior patterns. Third, the intensity of a stimulus affects how much you take notice of it. You are more aware of strong odors than weak scents, and of bright and flashy colors than dull and muted hues.[7]

With so much sensory information available to you, how do you avoid becoming overwhelmed? A part of your brain called the *reticular formation* serves the important function of helping you focus on certain stimuli while ignoring others.[8] It is the primary reason why, when you are having a conversation with a friend in a crowded, noisy coffee shop, you can focus on what your friend is saying and tune out the many other sights and sounds that are bombarding your senses at the time.

• **organization** The process of categorizing information that has been selected for attention.

• **perceptual schema** A mental framework for organizing information.

Organization Once you have noticed a particular stimulus, the next step in the perception process is **organization**, the classification of information in some way. Organization helps you make sense of the information by allowing you to see its similarities to and differences from other things you know about. To classify a stimulus, your mind applies a **perceptual schema** to it, which is a mental framework for organizing information into categories we call *constructs*.

According to communication researcher Peter Andersen, we use four types of schema to classify information we notice about other people:[9]

1. *Physical constructs* emphasize people's appearance, causing us to notice objective characteristics such as height, age, ethnicity, and body shape, as well as subjective characteristics such as physical attractiveness.

2. *Role constructs* emphasize people's social or professional position, so we notice that a person is a teacher, a father, a military veteran, and so on.[10]

3. *Interaction constructs* emphasize people's behavior, so we notice that a person is outgoing, aggressive, shy, or considerate.

4. *Psychological constructs* emphasize people's thoughts and feelings, causing us to notice that a person is angry, self-assured, insecure, or carefree.

Whichever constructs we notice about people—and we may notice more than one at a time—the process of organization helps us determine the ways in which various pieces of information we select for attention are related to one another.[11] If you notice that your neighbor is a youth soccer coach and the mother of three children, for example, then those two pieces of information go together because they both relate to the roles she plays. Likewise, if you notice that she seems irritated or angry, those pieces of information go together as examples of her psychological state.

Which constructs would you use to describe these people?

Photomondo/Getty Images

Interpretation After noticing and classifying a stimulus, you have to assign it an **interpretation** to figure out its meaning for you. Let's say one of your coworkers has been acting especially friendly toward you since last week. She finds numerous occasions to run into you, brings you treats, and offers to run errands for you over her lunch break. Her behavior is definitely noticeable, and you've probably classified it as a psychological construct because it relates to her thoughts and feelings about you.

What is her behavior communicating? How should you interpret it? Is she being nice because she's getting ready to ask you for a big favor? Does she want to look good in front of her manager? Is she making a romantic gesture?

• **interpretation** The process of assigning meaning to information that has been selected for attention and organized.

Our interpretations of another person's behaviors rely on personal experience, knowledge, and the closeness of our relationship with that individual.

Glow Images/Alamy

To address those questions, you likely will pay attention to three factors: your *personal experience*, your *knowledge* of this coworker, and the *closeness of your relationship* with her. First, your personal experience helps you to assign meaning to behavior. If some coworkers have been nice to you in the past just to get favors from you later, then you might be suspicious of this person's behavior.[12] Second, your knowledge of the person helps you interpret her actions. If you know she's friendly and nice to everyone, you might interpret her behavior differently than if you notice she's being nice only to you.[13] Finally, the closeness of your relationship influences how you interpret a person's behavior. When your best friend does you an unexpected favor, you probably interpret it as a sincere sign of friendship. In contrast, when a coworker does you a favor, you may be more likely to wonder whether the person has an ulterior motive.[14]

The Circular Nature of Perception Although perception occurs in stages, the process is far from linear. Instead, the three stages of perception—selecting, organizing, and interpreting information—all overlap. How we interpret a communication behavior depends on what we notice about it, for example, but what we notice can also depend on the way we interpret it.

Let's assume, for example, that you are listening to a speech by a political candidate. If you find her ideas and proposals favorable, you might interpret her demeanor and speaking style as examples of her intelligence and confidence. If you oppose her ideas, however, you might believe her demeanor and speaking style reflect arrogance or incompetence. Either interpretation, in turn, might lead you to select for attention only those behaviors or characteristics that support your interpretation and to ignore those that do not. So, even though perception happens in stages, the stages don't always take place in the same order. We're constantly noticing, organizing, and interpreting things around us, including other people's behaviors.

As we consider next, perception, like other skills, takes practice. In addition, our perceptions are more accurate on some occasions than others.

WE COMMONLY MISPERCEIVE OTHERS' COMMUNICATION BEHAVIORS

Although we constantly form perceptions of others and of their communication behaviors, we are hardly experts at it. In fact, perceptual mistakes are easy to make. Let's say, for example, that on your overseas trip, you perceive that two adults you see in a restaurant are having a heated argument. As it turns out, you discover that they are not arguing but engaging in behaviors that, in their culture, communicate interest and involvement.

Our feelings about a politician's ideas often influence our interpretation of his or her behaviors.

MANDEL NGAN/Getty Images

Why do we commit such a perceptual error despite our accumulated experience? The reason is that each of us has multiple lenses through which we perceive the world. Those lenses include our cultural and co-cultural backgrounds, stereotypes, primacy and recency effects, and our perceptual sets. In each case, those lenses have the potential to influence not only our own communication behaviors but also our perceptions of the communication of others.

Cultures and Co-Cultures Influence Perceptions One powerful influence on the accuracy of our perceptions is the culture and co-cultures with which we identify. Recall from the chapter on communication and culture that culture is the learned, shared symbols, language, values, and norms that distinguish one group of people—such as Russians, Namibians, or Thais—from another. Co-cultures are smaller groups of people—such as single parents, bloggers, and history enthusiasts—who share values, customs, and norms related to mutual interests or characteristics besides their national citizenship.

Many characteristics of cultures can influence our perceptions and interpretations of other people's behaviors.[15] For instance, we saw in the chapter on communication and culture that people from individualistic cultures frequently engage in more direct, overt forms of conflict communication than do people from collectivistic cultures. In a conflict, then, an individualist might perceive a collectivist's communication behaviors as conveying weakness, passivity, or a lack of interest. Likewise, the collectivist may perceive the individualist's communication patterns as overly aggressive or self-centered. Those perceptions can arise even though each person is communicating in a way that is normal in his or her culture.

Co-cultural differences can also influence perceptions of communication. Teenagers might perceive their parents' advice as outdated or irrelevant, whereas parents may perceive their teenagers' indifference to their advice as naïve.[16] Liberals and conservatives may each see the other's communication messages as rooted in ignorance.[17]

Stereotypes Influence Perceptions A **stereotype** is a generalization about a group or category of people that can have a powerful influence on how we perceive others and their communication behavior.[18] Stereotyping is a three-part process:

- First, we identify a group to which we believe another person belongs ("you are a gay man").

- Second, we recall a generalization others often make about the people in that group ("gay men are emotionally sensitive").

• **stereotype** A generalization about a group or category of people that is applied to individual members of that group.

What stereotypes come to mind when you think of people such as these?

Ethan Miller/Getty Images; golero/Getty Images; Ron Chapple/Taxi/Getty Images

• Finally, we apply that generalization to the person ("therefore, you must be emotionally sensitive").

You can probably think of stereotypes for many groups.[19] What stereotypes come to mind for elderly people? How about people with physical or mental disabilities? Wealthy people? Homeless people? Science fiction fans? Immigrants? Athletes? What stereotypes come to mind when you think about yourself?

Making stereotypical judgments is common, and one reason why is that our brains react to cues about a person's race, sex, personality, social status, emotional state, and other characteristics at a subconscious level.[20] Such cues can shape our perceptions of other people even without our being aware that we hold those perceptions in the first place.[21] In fact, research by psychologist Jonathan Freeman has demonstrated that the brain evaluates how trustworthy other people's faces are, even before we realize we have even *seen* those faces.[22] That's how fast stereotypical judgments can form.

Many people find stereotyping distasteful or unethical, particularly when stereotypes have to do with characteristics such as sex, race, and sexual orientation.[23] Unquestionably, because it underestimates the differences among individuals in a group, stereotyping can lead to inaccurate, even offensive, perceptions of other people. It may be true, for instance, that gay men are more emotionally sensitive than straight men, but that doesn't mean *every* gay man is emotionally sensitive. Similarly, people of Asian descent may often be more studious than those from other ethnic groups, but not every Asian is a good student, and not all Asians do equally well in school.[24]

There is variation within almost every group, but stereotypes focus our attention only on the generalizations. In fact, we have a tendency to engage in *selective memory bias*—to remember information that supports our stereotypes while forgetting information that does not.[25] During conflict communication, for instance, both women and men tend to remember only their partners' stereotypical behaviors.[26] Men may recall that women nagged and criticized them but might forget that they also listened carefully. Likewise, women may recall that men tuned them out but might overlook their apologies and signs of remorse.

Although perceptions about an individual made on the basis of a stereotype are often inaccurate, they aren't necessarily so.[27] For example, consider the stereotype that women love taking care of children. If you met a woman and assumed (on the basis of that stereotype) that she enjoyed taking care of children, you might be

SHARPEN Your Skills: *Limitations of stereotypes*

Watch the TED talk *The Danger of a Single Story* by Nigerian novelist Chimamanda Adichie. Consider her claim that "the problem with stereotypes is not that they are untrue, but that they are incomplete." In a blog or journal entry, explain what this statement means to you and describe an occurrence in your own life when you have found this claim to be true.

Difficult Conversations

Disagreeing about Politics

Imagine this: While on your break at work, you and your coworker Karina are watching a television news reporter interview a political candidate about U.S. immigration practices. Karina's comments about the interview lead you to realize that the two of you have strongly opposing opinions about how the United States should manage undocumented immigrants. One of you feels that undocumented immigrants waste taxpayers' money by using social services without contributing to their cost. The other believes that everyone deserves to share in the "American dream" and points out that some U.S. industries, such as agriculture and construction, employ large numbers of undocumented workers.

Although you generally try to avoid arguing about politics, especially with people you like, you find Karina's opinions infuriating. You wonder aloud how she can possibly think the way she does—and she wonders that same about you. Soon, your conversation has turned into a genuine argument. You are each raising your voices, feeling distressed, and saying the other's beliefs are ignorant and dangerous. You both go back to work after your break feeling angry and frustrated with the other.

Now, consider this: Your conflict with Karina was based partly on your differing opinions about immigration. However, it likely was also influenced by your perceptions of each other. In particular, once you realized the difference in your positions, you may have stereotyped each other as a conservative or a liberal. Doing so may have led you to make inaccurate assumptions about the other and to consider yourself to be open-minded while dismissing the other person's arguments as uninformed.

- To keep stereotypes from influencing your perceptions, the first step is awareness. As you ponder Karina's opinions, pay attention to any assumptions you are making about her. Because her position differs from yours, do you assume she is narrow-minded or naïve? Do you presuppose anything about her background or experiences?

- If you do recognize assumptions you are making about Karina on the basis of her opinions, remind yourself that stereotypes are often inaccurate when applied to individuals. It may be true that people with liberal and conservative viewpoints have different backgrounds and life experiences, but that doesn't necessarily mean every conservative person is the same, nor every liberal person. Remember that what is true of a group is not automatically true of everyone in the group.

- Instead of dismissing Karina's arguments as wrong, ask her why she holds the opinions that she does, and then listen to her with an open mind. You may find that her positions are well informed and logical, even if you disagree with them.

Stereotypes can easily influence our perceptions of others, even outside of our awareness. The problem is that stereotyping leads us to think superficially about others and their ideas, which can make a difficult conversation—such as a political argument—even more challenging.

wrong—however, you also might be right. Not every woman enjoys taking care of children, but some do. By the same token, not every Asian person is a good student, but some are. The point is that just because your perception of someone is consistent with a stereotype, that perception isn't necessarily inaccurate. Just as we shouldn't assume that a stereotypical judgment is true, we should not assume that it's untrue.

FIGURE 1

PRIMACY EFFECT
AND RECENCY
EFFECT

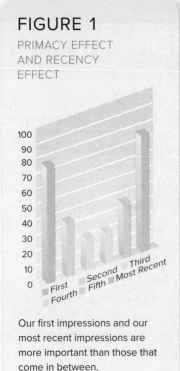

100
90
80
70
60
50
40
30
20
10
0
First
Second
Third
Fourth
Fifth
Most Recent

Our first impressions and our most recent impressions are more important than those that come in between.

• **primacy effect** The tendency to emphasize the first impression over later impressions when forming a perception.

• **recency effect** The tendency to emphasize the most recent impression over earlier impressions when forming a perception.

• **perceptual set** A person's predisposition to perceive only what he or she wants or expects to perceive.

Many successful comedians understand that the final impression they make on an audience is just as important as the first impression.

FilmMagic/Getty Images

Before assuming that your perceptions of others are correct, genuinely get to know those people, and let your perceptions be guided by what you learn about them as individuals. By communicating with them, you can begin to discover how well other people fit or don't fit the stereotypical perceptions you formed of them. This advice is especially useful when you find yourself in conflict with someone you disagree with, as the "Difficult Conversations" box explains.

Primacy and Recency Effects Influence Perceptions As the saying goes, you get only one chance to make a good first impression. There's no shortage of advice on how to accomplish that, from picking the right clothes to polishing your conversational skills. Have you ever noticed that no one talks about the importance of making a good *second* impression?

According to a principle called the **primacy effect**, first impressions are critical because they set the tone for all future interactions.[28] Our first impressions of someone's communication behaviors seem to stick in our mind more than our second, third, or fourth impressions do. In an early study of the primacy effect, psychologist Solomon Asch found that a person described as "intelligent, industrious, impulsive, critical, stubborn, and envious" was evaluated more favorably than one described as "envious, stubborn, critical, impulsive, industrious, and intelligent."[29]

Notice that most of those adjectives are negative, but when the description begins with a positive adjective (*intelligent*), the effects of the more negative ones that follow it are diminished.

Asch's study illustrates that the first information we learn about someone tends to have a stronger effect on how we perceive that person than information we receive later.[30] That finding explains why we work so hard to communicate competently during a job interview, on a date, or in other important situations. When people evaluate us favorably at first, they are more likely to perceive us in a positive light from then on.[31]

As most entertainers know, however, it's equally important to make a good *final* impression because that's what the audience will remember after leaving. Stand-up comedians will tell you that the two most important jokes in a show are the first and the last. That advice follows a principle known as the **recency effect**, which says that the most recent impression we have of a person's communication is more powerful than our earlier impressions.[32]

Which is most important, the first or the most recent impression? The answer is that *both* appear to be more important than any impressions we form in between.[33] To grasp this key point, think about the last movie you watched. You probably have a better recol-

lection of how the movie started and ended than you do of what occurred in between. Figure 1 illustrates the relationship between the primacy effect and the recency effect by showing how our first and most recent impressions overshadow our other perceptions.

Perceptual Sets Influence Perceptions "I'll believe it when I see it," people often say. However, our perception of reality is influenced by more than what we see. Our biases, expectations, and desires can create what psychologists call a **perceptual set**, or a predisposition to perceive only what we want or expect to perceive.[34] An equally valid motto might therefore be "I'll see it when I believe it."

For example, our perceptual set regarding gender guides the ways we perceive and interact with newborns. Without the help of a contextual cue such as the color or style of a baby's clothes, we sometimes have a hard time telling whether a dressed infant is male or female. However, research shows that if we're told an infant's name is David, we perceive that child to be stronger and bigger than if the same infant is called, say, Diana.[35] Our perceptual set tells us that male infants are usually bigger and stronger than female ones, so we "see" a bigger, stronger baby when believe it's a boy. Our perceptions can then affect our communication behavior: we may also hold and talk to the "female" baby in softer, quieter ways than we do with the "male" baby.

Our perceptual set also influences how we make sense of people, circumstances, and events. Deeply religious individuals may talk about healings as miracles or answers to prayer, whereas others may describe them as natural responses to medication.[36] Highly homophobic people are more likely than others to perceive affectionate communication between men as sexual in nature.[37]

In summary, perception is a complex process, susceptible to many different biases and patterns. As we will discover in the next section, we are vulnerable to mistakes not only when we form perceptions but also when we try to explain what we perceive.

How We Explain Our Perceptions

Actor Omari Hardwick has appeared in a long string of television shows and films, including *CSI: Miami*, *Being Mary Jane*, and Tyler Perry's *For Colored Girls*. He currently appears in the television crime drama *Power*. Despite his successes as an actor, it was his behavior at the 2019 NAACP Image Awards that turned heads. While greeting Beyoncé, who received the Entertainer of the Year award, Hardwick not only embraced the singer but kissed her twice on the cheek. The gesture, captured in a video that quickly went viral, struck many people as more intimate than would normally be expected for two people who are not romantically involved with each other. Hardwick drew immediate and widespread criticism from fans, who labeled his behavior as awkward, creepy, and an invasion of Beyoncé's personal space. How would you explain Hardwick's behavior?[38]

When we perceive social behavior, especially behavior we find surprising, our nearly automatic reaction is to try to make sense of it. We need to understand what is happening to know how to react to it. Think about it: if you perceive that someone is communicating with you out of anger or jealousy, you will likely react to that behavior differently than if you perceive it is motivated by humor or sarcasm. The ability to explain social behavior—including our own behavior—is therefore an important aspect of how we perceive our social world. In this section, we will see that we explain behaviors by forming attributions for them, and we will discover how to avoid two of the most common errors people make when formulating attributions for communication behavior.

WE EXPLAIN BEHAVIOR THROUGH ATTRIBUTIONS

An **attribution** is an explanation of an observed behavior, the answer to the question "why did this occur?"[39] We notice Omari Hardwick behaving in an unexpected manner toward Beyoncé, for instance, and we wonder what to attribute his actions to. Although we can generate countless attributions for a given behavior, our attributions vary along three important dimensions: locus, stability, and controllability.[40]

Locus Locus refers to where the cause of a behavior is "located," whether within or outside ourselves.[41] Some of our behaviors have *internal* loci (the plural of locus); they're caused by a particular characteristic of ourselves. Other behaviors have *external* loci, meaning they are caused by something outside ourselves. If your boss is late for your 9 A.M. performance review, an internal attribution you might make about her is that she has lost track of time or she's making you wait on purpose. An external attribution you might form about her is that the traffic is heavy that morning or an earlier meeting she is attending has run long.

• **attribution** An explanation for an observed behavior.

Paras Griffin/Getty Images

Stability A second dimension of attributions is whether the cause of a behavior is stable or unstable.[42] A *stable* cause is one that is permanent, semipermanent, or at least not easily changed. Why was your boss late? Rush hour traffic would be a stable cause for lateness, because it's a permanent feature of almost everyone's morning commute. The attribution that she is rarely punctual would likewise be stable, because it identifies an enduring aspect of her behavior. In contrast, a traffic accident or an overly long morning meeting would be an *unstable* cause of your boss's lateness, because those events occur only from time to time and are largely unpredictable.

Controllability Finally, causes for behavior vary in how controllable they are.[43] You make a *controllable* attribution for someone's behavior when you believe the cause of the behavior was under that person's control. In contrast, an *uncontrollable* attribution identifies a cause that was beyond the person's control. If you perceive that your boss is late for your appointment because she has spent too much time socializing with other coworkers beforehand, that is a controllable attribution because socializing is under her control. Alternatively, if you perceive she's late because she had a car accident on the way to work, that is an uncontrollable attribution because she couldn't help but be late if she wrecked her car.

AVOIDING TWO COMMON ATTRIBUTION ERRORS

Although most of us probably try to generate accurate attributions for other people's behaviors, we are still vulnerable to making attribution mistakes.[44] Those errors can create communication problems because, as noted above, our responses to other people's behaviors are often based on the attributions we make for those behaviors.

Let's say that Maggie and her stepson Craig argue one night about whether Craig can go on a school-sponsored overnight trip. After their argument, they both go to bed angry. When Maggie gets up the following morning, she finds that Craig hasn't done the dishes or taken out the trash, two chores he is responsible for doing every night before bed. It turns out that Craig was so upset by the argument that his chores slipped his mind. Maggie makes a different attribution, however: she perceives that Craig didn't do the chores because he was deliberately disobeying her. On the basis of her attribution, she tells Craig he's grounded for a week and is definitely not going on the trip. Her actions only prolong and intensify the conflict between them. Had Maggie correctly attributed Craig's behavior to an honest oversight, she might have been able to overlook it instead of making it the basis for additional conflict. In other words, recognizing a common attribution error might have equipped Maggie to avoid a mistake that made a bad situation worse.

We might think we always explain behavior objectively and rationally, but the truth is that we're all prone to taking mental shortcuts when generating attributions. As a result, our attributions are often less accurate than they should be. Two of the most common attribution errors—which we can better prepare ourselves to avoid by understanding them—are the self-serving bias and the fundamental attribution error.

Self-Serving Bias One of the most common attribution errors has to do with the way we explain our own behaviors. The **self-serving bias** refers to our tendency to attribute our successes to stable, internal causes while attributing our failures to unstable, external causes.[45] For

• **self-serving bias** The tendency to attribute one's successes to stable internal causes and one's failures to unstable external causes.

Many people have a self-serving bias when it comes to explaining their own behaviors.

Tetra Images/Getty Images

instance, if you gave a great informative speech in your class, you say it was great because you were well prepared, but if your speech went poorly, you say the assignment was unfair or other students were distracting you. Such attributions are self-serving, because they suggest that our successes are deserved but our failures are not our fault.

Although the self-serving bias deals primarily with attributions we make for our own behaviors, research shows that we often extend this tendency to important people in our lives.[46] In a happy relationship, for instance, people tend to attribute their partner's positive behaviors to internal causes ("She remembered my birthday because she's thoughtful") and negative behaviors to external causes ("He forgot my birthday because he's been very preoccupied by his job"). In a distressed relationship, the reverse is often true: people attribute negative behaviors to internal causes ("She forgot my birthday because she's completely self-absorbed") and positive behaviors to external causes ("He remembered my birthday only because I reminded him five times").

Fundamental Attribution Error Think about how you reacted the last time someone cut you off in traffic. What attribution did you make for the driver's behavior? You might have thought "She must be late for something important" or "He must have a car full of noisy children," but you probably didn't. "What a jerk!" may be closer to your reaction. Similarly, when listening to a student give a poor, disorganized presentation in class, you're more likely to think "he's just not a good speaker" than to think "he must have been tired from working late last night."

• **fundamental attribution error** The tendency to attribute others' behaviors to internal rather than external causes.

We can attribute a person's lateness to either internal or external causes. Was your boss late because she lost track of time—or because she got caught in heavy traffic?

Stockbyte/Getty Images

The reason for those responses is the human tendency to commit the **fundamental attribution error**, in which we attribute other people's behaviors to internal rather than external causes.[47] The high school student ran the pledge drive because he's a caring, giving person, not because he earned extra credit for doing so. The cashier gave you the wrong change because she doesn't know how to count properly, not because she was distracted by an announcement over the store's audio system.

As a student of communication, you should bear in mind that people's behaviors—including your own—are often responses to external forces. For instance, when the new doctor you are seeing spends only three minutes diagnosing your condition and prescribing a treatment before moving on to the next patient, you might perceive that she's not very caring. That would be an internal attribution for her communication behavior, which the fundamental attribution error makes more likely. To judge the merits of that attribution, however, ask yourself what external forces might have motivated the doctor's behavior. For example, might she have rushed through your consultation because another doctor's absence that day left her with twice as many patients as usual? Good communicators recognize the tendency to form internal attributions for people's behaviors, and they force themselves to consider external causes that might also be influential.

Like other forms of perception, attributions are important but prone to error. That observation doesn't imply that we *never* make accurate attributions for people's behaviors (including our own). It simply acknowledges that the self-serving bias and the fundamental attribution error are easy mistakes to commit.

SHARPEN Your Skills: *Attribution-making*

Working with a partner or in a small group, generate as many attributions as you can for Omari Hardwick's awkward hug and kiss with Beyoncé. Identify whether each attribution is internal or external, and note which type is easier to generate. Finally, narrow your list to the three attributions you believe are most plausible.

The more we know about those processes, therefore, the better we can base our communication behaviors on accurate perceptions of ourselves and others.

How We Perceive Ourselves

As much as your communication's effectiveness depends on your ability to perceive others, it also depends on your ability to perceive yourself. Ask yourself: Who am I? How do I relate to others? What is the *self* in *myself*? Grappling with those challenging questions will allow you to communicate and to form relationships with a sure understanding of who you are and what you have to offer.

In this section, we will discover that each of us perceives our self through our self-concept, and we will examine the characteristics of a self-concept. We will also learn how self-concept influences communication behavior and relates to self-esteem.

SELF-CONCEPT DEFINED

Let's say you are asked to come up with 10 ways to answer the question "Who am I?" What words will you pick? Which answers are most important? Each of us has a set of ideas about who we are that isn't influenced by moment-to-moment events (such as "I'm happy right now") but is fairly stable over the course of our lives (such as "I'm a happy person"). Your **self-concept**, also called your **identity**, is composed of your own stable perceptions about who you are. As we'll see in this section, self-concepts are multifaceted and partly subjective.

Self-Concept Is Multifaceted We define ourselves in many different ways. Some of these ways rely on our name: "I'm Sunita" or "I'm Darren." Some rely on physical or social categories: "I am a vegan" or "I am Australian." Others make use of our skills or interests: "I'm artistic" or "I'm a good cook." Still others are based on our relationships to other people: "I am an uncle" or "I do volunteer work with homeless children." Finally, some rely on our evaluations of ourselves: "I am honest" or "I am impatient." You can probably think of several other ways to describe who you are.

Which of those descriptions is the *real* you?

The answer is that your self-concept has several different parts, and each of your descriptions taps into one or more of those parts. What we call *the self* is, more accurately, a collection of smaller *selves*. If you're female, that's a part of who you are, but it isn't everything you are. Asian, athletic, agnostic, or asthmatic may all be parts of your self-concept, but none of those terms defines you completely. All the different ways you would describe yourself are pieces of your overall self-concept.

One way to think about your self-concept is to distinguish between aspects of yourself that are known to others and aspects that are known only to you. In 1955, U.S. psychologists Joseph Luft and Harry Ingham created the **Johari window**, a visual representation of the self as composed of four separate parts.[48] According to this model, which is illustrated in Figure 2:

- The *open area* consists of characteristics that are known both to the self and to others. Those probably include your name, sex, hobbies, academic major, and other aspects of your self-concept that you are aware of and freely share with others.

- The *hidden area* consists of characteristics that you know about yourself but choose not to reveal to others, such as emotional insecurities or traumas from your past that you elect to keep hidden.

- **self-concept** The set of stable perceptions a person has about who he or she is; also known as *identity*.

- **identity** The set of stable perceptions a person has about who he or she is; also known as *self-concept*.

- **Johari window** A visual representation of components of the self that are known or unknown to the self and to others.

FIGURE 2

JOHARI WINDOW

	Known to Self	Unknown to Self
Known to Others	**OPEN** What you know, and choose to reveal to others, about yourself.	**BLIND** What others know about you, but you don't recognize in yourself.
Unknown to Others	**HIDDEN** What you know about yourself, but choose not to reveal.	**UNKNOWN** The dimensions of yourself that no one knows.

- The *blind area* refers to aspects of ourselves that others see in us, but of which we are unaware. For instance, others might see us as impatient or moody even if we don't recognize these traits in ourselves.

- Finally, the *unknown area* comprises aspects of our self-concept that are not known either to us or to others. For example, no one—including you—knows what kind of parent you will be until you actually become one.

Self-Concept Is Partly Subjective Some of what we know about ourselves is based on objective facts. For instance, I'm 5'8" tall and have brown hair, I was born in Seattle but now live in Tucson, and I teach college for a living. Those aspects of my self-concept are objective—they are based on fact and not on someone's opinion. That doesn't mean I have no choice about them. I chose to move to Arizona and to take a teaching job, and although I was born with brown hair, I could change my hair color if I wanted to. Referring to those personal characteristics as "objective" simply means that they are factually true. Many aspects of our self-concept are subjective rather than objective, however. "Subjective" means that they are based on the impressions we have of ourselves rather than on objective facts.

It is often difficult for people to judge themselves accurately or objectively. Sometimes our self-assessments are unreasonably positive. For instance, you might know individuals who have unrealistic ideas about their intelligence, their talents, or their understanding of the world. In one study, the College Board (the company that administers the SAT college entrance examination) asked almost a million American high school seniors to rate their ability to get along with others. Every single student in the study responded that he or she was "above average"—a result that is mathematically impossible! Moreover, 60 percent claimed their ability to get along with others was in the top 10 percent, and a whopping 25 percent perceived themselves to be in the top 1 percent.[49]

In contrast, sometimes our judgments of ourselves are unreasonably negative. That is especially true for people with low self-esteem. Several studies have shown that such individuals tend to magnify the importance of their failures.[50] They often underestimate their abilities, and when they get negative feedback, such as a bad evaluation at work or a disrespectful remark from someone they know, they are likely to believe it accurately reflects their self-worth.

Several studies have also suggested that people with low self-esteem have a higher-than-average risk of major depressive disorder, a condition that impairs not only mental and emotional well-being but also physical health and the ways people communicate in their social relationships.[51] We return to self-esteem a little later in this chapter.

SHARPEN Your Skills: *Your Johari window*

Select three people who are important to you. Considering your relationship with each person separately, draw a Johari window that reflects your self-concept with that person, making the *open, hidden, blind,* and *unknown* portions of the window appropriately larger or smaller. Then write a short paragraph explaining why the panes of your Johari window differ in size for each relationship and how they reflect your communication behaviors with each of those people.

AWARENESS AND MANAGEMENT OF THE SELF-CONCEPT

Part of being a competent, skilled communicator is being aware of your self-concept and managing its influences on your communication with others. Two pathways by which self-concept can shape communicative behavior are self-monitoring and the self-fulfilling prophecy.

Self-Monitoring Recall from the introductory chapter that *self-monitoring* is an awareness of how you look and sound and how your behavior is affecting those around you. The tendency toward self-monitoring ranges along a continuum from high to low. People on the high end of the scale pay attention to how others are reacting to their own behaviors, and they have the ability to adjust their communication as needed. People on the low end express whatever they are thinking or feeling without paying attention to the impression they're creating.

To understand how self-monitoring operates, imagine that you've fixed up your friends Caleb and Keith to go out. As a high self-monitor, Caleb pays a great deal of attention to his clothes and grooming to make sure he looks and smells good. In contrast, as a low self-monitor, Keith doesn't spend much time thinking about those things. During their date, Caleb is aware of what he's saying, so he comes across as nice, easygoing, and funny. Keith, however, says whatever is on his mind, without considering what Caleb might think. Caleb notices if his behavior seems to make Keith uncomfortable, and he adjusts his actions accordingly. In contrast, Keith doesn't tune in to what he's doing and how he's affecting Caleb.

From that example, you might get the impression that it's best to be a high self-monitor. Self-monitoring certainly has its advantages. High self-monitors tend to be better at making whatever kind of impression they want to make, because they are aware of their communication behaviors and others' responses to them. They often find it easier than low self-monitors to put other people at ease in social situations. High self-monitors also tend to be good at figuring out what others are thinking and feeling, and that skill gives them a clear advantage in many social settings. High self-monitors also pay attention to how they are portrayed online. What would people learn about you if they Googled your name? Check out "The Competent Communicator" to find out.

Being a low self-monitor also has advantages, however. Low self-monitors spend less time and energy thinking about their appearance and behavior, so they are probably more relaxed than high self-monitors in many situations. In addition, because they are less aware of, or concerned with, the impressions they make, they are often more straightforward communicators. They may even be seen as more genuine and trustworthy than high self-monitors.

Some medical conditions can inhibit self-monitoring ability, including having an autism spectrum disorder, a developmental disorder that impairs a person's capability for social interaction. A 2018 report from the Autism and Developmental Disabilities Monitoring Network found that approximately 1 in 59 U.S. American 8-year-olds has

There are advantages and disadvantages associated with being either a high or low self-monitor.

Jozef Polc/123RF; Getty Images

Googling Yourself: Managing Your Online Image

Creditors, employers, and even prospective romantic partners use the Internet to learn about you. Will you like what they find? To assess your online image, type your name into google.com and explore the first dozen websites that the search identifies that are relevant to you (rather than to someone else with your name). Then respond with "true" or "false" to each of the following statements.

Design Pics/Don Hammond

1 _____ **Nearly everything I saw about myself was positive.**

2 _____ **I came across information I wouldn't necessarily want others to have about me.**

3 _____ **I would be fine knowing that a prospective romantic partner was looking at these websites.**

4 _____ **I found pictures of myself that I wouldn't be comfortable letting my employer see.**

5 _____ **Most people would have a positive impression of me after seeing the websites I found.**

6 _____ **Some of the information I found might make me look irresponsible.**

7 _____ **I'd feel comfortable letting my parents read the websites I came across.**

8 _____ **I wouldn't want someone coming across these websites before going out with me.**

9 _____ **All in all, I feel good about the information and photographs of myself that I found.**

10 _____ **At least some of what I found online about myself was troubling.**

It's best if you answered "true" to the odd-numbered statements and "false" to the even-numbered statements. If any of your answers were otherwise, consider taking steps to alter the online content. If the information or photos that concern you appear on websites over which you have some control—such as your Facebook page or a friend's personal web page—remove the material or make it viewable only by close acquaintances. This may be a particularly important consideration before you go on a job interview or set up a date.

some form of autism spectrum disorder.[52] Individuals with autism spectrum disorders are often unresponsive to others. They frequently avoid eye contact and have difficulty understanding other people's thoughts and feelings. That obstacle limits their ability to notice how others are reacting to them and to adjust their behaviors accordingly, two hallmarks of self-monitoring. Despite these challenges, however, it is possible for many people with autism spectrum disorders to lead independent, productive lives.

Self-Fulfilling Prophecy Imagine meeting a new coworker whom you've heard other people describe as painfully shy. Because you don't want to make her uncomfortable, you spend little time talking to her when you meet her, and you don't invite her to join you and your friends for lunch. Consequently, she says little to you all day and eats lunch alone at her desk. You think to yourself, "I guess everyone was right about her; she *is* really shy." Why did your expectation about a shy coworker come true? Most likely, the cause is a phenomenon called a **self-fulfilling prophecy**—a situation

• **self-fulfilling prophecy**
An expectation that gives rise to behaviors that cause the expectation to come true.

puttingcommunicationtowork

Search

Job Title >

Work Responsibilities >

Teacher, Kindergarten through Grade 12

Educators must know how to organize and present information in ways that will engage young people. But teaching involves far more than just relaying information—teachers must also be able to perceive and correct biases in their students and in themselves, and to understand and accurately evaluate student learning. Teachers must be able to modify their communication to interact effectively not only with students, but also with parents, administrators, and other stakeholders. They must also be keenly aware of the dangers of self-fulfilling prophecies in the classroom. The most effective teachers are also high-self monitors: they are constantly evaluating what is working (or not working) in the classroom, and they frequently share their best practices with colleagues.

in which a prediction leads people to act and communicate in ways that make that prediction come true.

How do self-fulfilling prophecies affect how we communicate? Sometimes our expectations influence our communication behavior, as when we're talking to someone we think is shy so we treat her as if she were shy. Similarly, when we expect our relationships to succeed, we behave in ways that strengthen them, and when we expect to be socially rejected, we perceive and react to rejection even when it isn't really there.[53]

There is one very important clarification here. For a prophecy to be self-fulfilling, it's not enough that you expect something to happen and then it does. Rather, it has to be the case that your expectation *causes* it to happen. To illustrate that point, let's say that yesterday morning you expected it to rain, and later it did rain. That isn't a self-fulfilling prophecy, because your expectation didn't cause the rain: it would have rained regardless of whether you thought it would. In other words, your expectation was fulfilled, but it was not *self*-fulfilled. A self-fulfilling prophecy is one in which the expectation itself causes the behaviors that make it come true.

The ability to watch out for self-fulfilling prophecies and other biases is useful in a wide range of careers. For one example, check out the "Putting Communication to Work" box.

VALUING THE SELF: SELF-ESTEEM

Knowing your self-concept and *being happy with* your self-concept are two different things. How do you feel about yourself? Are you satisfied with your looks? Your accomplishments? Your personality? Your relationships? Do you feel confident about and proud of who you are? Such questions concern your **self-esteem**, your subjective evaluation of your value and worth as a person.

Like self-monitoring, your level of self-esteem ranges along a continuum from high to low. If you evaluate yourself positively and feel happy about who you are, you

• **self-esteem** One's subjective evaluation of one's value and worth as a person.

probably have high self-esteem. In contrast, if you are pessimistic about your abilities and dissatisfied with your self-concept, you probably have low self-esteem.

Maintaining a positive image of ourselves does appear to have its advantages when it comes to communication behavior. Individuals with higher self-esteem are generally more outgoing and more willing to communicate and build relationships with others.[54] They are more comfortable initiating relationships, and they are more likely to believe that their partners' expressions of love and support are genuine.[55]

Despite its advantages, high self-esteem also has some drawbacks, particularly for adolescents and young adults. Although several researchers have speculated that having low self-esteem promotes aggressive and antisocial behavior, the opposite is true. Aggressive people tend to have higher self-esteem, not lower.[56] Adolescents with higher self-esteem are also more prone to be sexually active and to engage in risky sexual behaviors than teens with lower self-esteem.[57] Finally, when their relationships run into problems, people with high self-esteem are more likely than their low self-esteem counterparts to end those relationships and seek out new ones.[58]

In this section, we have considered that we perceive ourselves through our self-concepts, which are multifaceted and partly subjective. We have seen how we exercise awareness of our self-concepts through self-monitoring and self-fulfilling prophecies, and we have examined self-esteem and learned about its benefits and drawbacks. All those concepts help people to form and modify their perceptions of themselves. As we will discover in the next section, people use a variety of communication behaviors to express their desired self-perceptions to others.

Managing Our Image

Our self-concept is related to *the way we see ourselves*. When we communicate with other people, we are also interested in *the way we want them to see us*. In some situations, we might want others to regard us as friendly, outgoing, and fun. In other situations, we might want people to view us as reliable, competent, and serious. Our concern is the kind of **image** we want to project—that is, the personal "face" we want others to see.

The film *Love, Simon* (2018) tells the story of 17-year-old Simon Spier (played by Nick Robinson), a high school junior with a big secret. To his family and friends, he's a friendly, laid-back student who is active in musical theater. Only an anonymous pen pal knows he's gay. As the story progresses, Simon struggles to manage two separate images of himself, one public and one private. He eventually resolves his struggle by coming out to his loved ones and by exploring a romantic relationship after learning the identity of his online companion.

Spier found that he had to project an artificial image of himself at home and at school, and that he could be his true self only online. This is the process of image management, and this section describes research that has shed light on that process.

• **image** The way one wishes to be seen or perceived by others.

TCD/Prod.DB/Alamy Stock Photo

COMMUNICATION AND IMAGE MANAGEMENT

When it comes to communicating our image to others, few methods are more popular than the selfie—images that people take of themselves and post to social media. According to the technology manufacturer Samsung, fully one-half of all photos taken by those 18 to 24 years of age are selfies.[59] In various ways, the selfie allows you to exert a high degree of control over the way you present your image. For one, you can choose to photograph yourself in fun, exciting contexts, such as while attending a concert or sporting event, visiting a foreign

• **image management**
The process of projecting one's desired public image.

• **life story** A way of presenting oneself to others that is based on one's self-concept but is also influenced by other people.

city, or meeting your favorite celebrity. Moreover, you can choose to alter your images digitally—such as by fixing skin or hair problems or cropping out undesirable parts of the image—before posting them. In this way, you can make yourself appear more attractive or socially desirable to others. More than a third of social media users admit to altering their selfies before posting them, according to research.[60]

The process of behavioral adjustment to project a desired image is known as **image management**. In the following discussion, we consider that image management is collaborative, that we manage multiple identities, and that managing an image is complex.

Image Management Is Collaborative To some extent, managing your image is an individual process. After all, your image is yours. Yet you also get a lot of help managing your image from the people around you. As psychologist Dan McAdams has suggested, each of us develops a **life story**, a way of presenting ourselves to others that is based on our self-concept but is also influenced by other people.[61]

If others accept the image you portray, they will tend to behave in ways that encourage that image. Let's say you see yourself as a confident person, and you project that image when you interact with others. If other people see you as confident, they will treat you as though you are—and their behavior will strengthen that part of your identity in your own mind. If others don't accept the image of yourself that you portray, however, they may treat you as less credible or as untrustworthy.

Perhaps you have encountered people who seem as though they are trying to be someone they aren't, or who are portraying an image that you don't accept as genuine. In June 2015, for instance, civil rights activist Rachel Dolezal resigned as a chapter president of the National Association for the Advancement of Colored People (NAACP) amid controversy about her racial identity. After Dolezal reported to police and local news media that she had been a victim of several hate crimes, her parents—who are both Caucasian—said publicly that she is a white woman pretending to be African American. Investigations of that claim revealed that Dolezal had made public statements claiming to be black and had listed herself as black on at least one application, even though she had sued Howard University (a predominantly African American school) in 2002 for discriminating against her for being white. These and other discrepancies ignited a controversy about whether Dolezal had misrepresented who she was. Although the NAACP stated that racial identity is not a criterion for holding leadership positions in the organization, the credibility of Dolezal's identity may have harmed her ability to lead effectively.

We Manage Multiple Identities If you think of all the people who know you, you will probably realize that most of them know you only in certain contexts. You have your circle of friends, each of whom knows you as a friend. You have your family members, who might know you as a mother, a son, an aunt, a brother, a cousin, or a grandchild. Your boss and coworkers know you as an employee, and your landlord knows you as a tenant.

Each of those contexts carries its own distinctive role expectations, so you probably enact a somewhat different identity in each one. In fact, we all manage multiple identities. That is, we show different parts of ourselves to different people in our lives. You likely communicate differently at work than at home, and your friends probably know you differently than your professors do. You may

THE DARK SIDE OF COMMUNICATION

Mental Illness: Would You Tell?

paolo81/Getty Images

Experiencing a mental illness can be frightening, debilitating, and confusing. It can also cause patients and their families great shame because people so frequently misunderstand mental illness and stigmatize those who suffer from it.

Although mental illnesses vary substantially in their effects, many patients have difficulty deciding whether to disclose their condition to others. On the one hand, disclosing may help them acquire both medical and emotional support, and it may help others to become better educated about mental health. Disclosure can be risky, however. People suffering from mental illness may have several reasons for choosing not to disclose their condition:

- *Stigma:* They worry about others rejecting or even hurting them.
- *Privacy:* They are concerned that information about their illness will be shared without their consent.
- *Communication difficulties:* They don't know how to tell others about their condition.
- *Fear of discrimination:* They fear that employers, landlords, or others will discriminate against them.
- *Protection of others:* They don't want others to worry about them.

Despite those risks, talking about mental illness can be useful in many ways. Beyond helping individuals get the necessary medical attention and emotional support, disclosure can help to reduce the fear and stigma associated with mental disease. It may also strengthen relationships, particularly with others who also struggle with mental health issues.

also communicate differently in various online venues, such as Instagram, Snapchat, and Twitter. The point is that, just like Simon Spier, we all manage multiple identities; that is, we show different parts of ourselves to different people in our lives.

On occasion, people enact images of themselves that are inaccurate or dishonest. As noted above, for instance, some people post photos and stories on social media that portray their lives as far more exciting and glamorous than they actually are. This can actually have a negative effect, known as "Instagram envy," in which seeing other users' posts and photos makes people feel less happy with their own lives.[62]

The challenge of managing multiple identities is especially pronounced for individuals with "invisible" medical conditions—illnesses or disorders that are not necessarily apparent to others. Conditions such as Down syndrome, stuttering, developmental disabilities, and confinement to a wheelchair are relatively apparent, as most people will recognize these conditions when interacting with someone who has them. However, individuals can, to varying degrees, hide the fact that they have other kinds of conditions, such as cancer, diabetes, asthma, and depression, if they don't want others to know. Most people can't identify someone with diabetes or asthma, for example, simply by looking at the person.

People with invisible conditions have both the ability and the responsibility to determine how to incorporate their conditions into the image they project: they must continually decide whom to tell about their conditions, when to make those disclosures, and how to do so. That decision can be particularly agonizing for individuals suffering from invisible conditions that are also socially stigmatized, such as mental health disorders and HIV-positive status, because of the fear of how others will react to their disclosures. "The Dark Side of Communication" addresses this issue as it pertains to individuals who are mentally ill.

In the virtual world of the Internet, a person can create and maintain as many different identities as he or she chooses, simply by generating multiple e-mail addresses or web pages or participating in various virtual communities.[63] For instance, you might have one e-mail address associated with your college or university that indicates both

your name and the school (mine is koryfloyd@arizona.edu). You might have another address from a free e-mail server, such as iCloud or Gmail, containing no identifying information about yourself (for example, mybro4816@gmail.com). Perhaps you use such an anonymous address when you want to communicate online without revealing your identity. In virtual communities, such as chat rooms and Second Life, you can even manipulate your identity to appear as though you are of a different sex, different ethnicity, or even a different species.[64] Some people may create multiple online identities to protect themselves when interacting with strangers; others may do so for amusement or to explore various aspects of their personalities.

One online venue in which portraying multiple identities is surprisingly *un*common is the blog, a website that features running commentary, news, and/or personal thoughts about one or more topics. Although some blogs belong to companies or organizations, many are created and maintained by individuals—most frequently adolescents—who often use them as a type of online diary. One study of communication on personal blogs found that 67 percent of bloggers provided their real names on their blogs, whether their full names (31 percent) or just their first names (36 percent). In contrast, only 29 percent used a fake name, with the remainder providing no name whatsoever. Further, more than half the bloggers in the study provided explicit demographic information about themselves, such as their age, occupation, or geographic location.[65]

More recent research has found that male bloggers are more likely than their female counterparts to provide information about their location, to use emojis that indicate sadness or flirtatiousness, and to reveal their sexual identity as homosexual. In comparison, female bloggers are more likely to include links to their personal web pages.[66]

Image Management Is Complex Image management is often complicated and may generate competing goals for our interactions with others. Let's say you need to ask your parents to lend you money. You want them to think of you as a responsible adult who will pay them back in a timely manner. You therefore have to present your request in a way that projects your image as a mature person who makes good decisions. At the same time, though, you want to persuade them that you really need the money. That goal may prompt you to project the image that you need help. Thus, you may find your image needs in conflict: you want to appear responsible but also in need of assistance. Managing those competing image needs—while still persuading your parents to lend you money—can be complex.

Communication researcher Myra Goldschmidt found that when people ask others for favors, they often create narratives—ways of telling their stories—that help them to maintain their image while still being persuasive.[67] To your parents, you might make such statements as "I'll be able to pay you back as soon as I get my financial aid check" and "I'll even pay interest on the loan." Such strategies can help preserve your image as a responsible individual even in a situation in which that image might be threatened.

We've seen that managing your image is a collaborative process that often requires you to negotiate several identities in a complex way. How do we determine what our image needs are in the first place?

COMMUNICATION AND FACE NEEDS

Helping someone "save face" means helping that person to avoid embarrassment and preserve dignity at a time when that dignity is jeopardized. The very reason we hate getting embarrassed is that it threatens the image of ourselves we are trying to project, and that threat is a function of our need to save face. Sometimes we associate the concept of saving face with collectivistic cultures such as South Korea and Japan. In reality, saving face is important in many cultures.[68] Let's consider what happens when our desired public image is made vulnerable.

Face and Face Needs Each of us has a desired public image—a certain way that we want others to see and think of us—and we work to maintain that image through the ways we communicate. For instance, if you want others to see you as intelligent and competent, you will likely communicate in ways that nurture that impression and will try to avoid situations that would make you look uninformed or incompetent. Sociologist Erving Goffman coined the term **face** to describe our desired public image and the term **facework** to describe the behaviors we use to project that desired image to others.[69]

Researchers believe our face is made up of three different **face needs**, or important components of our desired public image.[70] You might find it easy to remember these face needs by noting that the first letters of their names—fellowship, autonomy, and competence—are also the first three letters in the word *face*.

Fellowship face refers to the need to have others like and accept us. That is the part of our identity that motivates us to make friends, join clubs and social groups, and communicate pleasantly with others. **Autonomy face** refers to our need to avoid being imposed on by others. It's our autonomy face that motivates us to be in control of our time and resources and to avoid having other people make decisions for us. Finally, **competence face** is our need to be respected—to have others acknowledge our abilities and intelligence. That need drives us to seek careers and hobbies in which we can excel and to avoid situations that will embarrass us.

Face Threats Each of us has a different desired public image, so our face needs vary. Some people have a very strong fellowship face need, meaning it is extremely important that others like them. Other people much prefer to be respected rather than liked. Similarly, one person may have a very high need for autonomy, whereas another person doesn't mind having decisions made for him or her. Those differences are part of what makes everyone's identity unique.

We often become consciously aware of our face needs only when they are jeopardized. Let's say you apply to join an honor society but are not accepted. The decision not to include you could threaten your fellowship face. It could also threaten your competence face by making you feel you aren't smart enough to get into the group. The rejection of your application, therefore, is a **face-threatening act** because it hinders the fulfillment of one or more of your face needs.

Face-threatening acts often lead people to behave in ways that help them restore their face. In the case of the honor society, you might say to others, "I didn't really want to be in that group anyway."[71] In truth, you probably *did* want to be in the honor society, or you wouldn't have applied. So, you would likely make such a statement as a way of managing your image with others—that is, you want it to *appear* that your face needs have not been threatened. Your statement is thus a type of *defense mechanism*—a response that minimizes the effects of a face-threatening act.

• **face** A person's desired public image.

• **facework** The behaviors people use to establish and maintain their desired public image with others.

• **face needs** Important components of one's desired public image.

• **fellowship face** The need to be liked and accepted by others.

• **autonomy face** The need to avoid being imposed on by others.

• **competence face** The need to be respected and viewed as competent and intelligent.

• **face-threatening act** Any behavior that threatens one or more face needs.

mettus/123RF

Face Threats in Socially Marginalized Groups Face threats are common in many socially marginalized populations. For example, many elderly people experience threats to their autonomy face as a result of physical and cognitive limitations associated with aging.[72] Similarly, people with certain disabilities may perceive threats to their autonomy face if they are unable to do activities that others can do, such as driving a car. Still other groups may feel their autonomy is jeopardized when they don't have the legal authority to make certain choices for themselves, as in the case of mentally ill adults who may not have final say over their own medical decisions.

Being marginalized also leads many people to feel disrespected and shamed. Such feelings can threaten both their fellowship face and their competence face. In U.S. society, for example, there are stigmas associated with being homeless, poor, unemployed, old, disabled, lesbian, gay, mentally ill, and (in some circles) divorced, even though a person may have no choice about belonging to any of these groups.[73] Stigmatized people might feel that they don't fit in with those around them, and those perceptions threaten their fellowship face by making them feel unaccepted. They may also perceive that others judge them not on the basis of their intelligence or abilities but because of their stigmatized condition. Such perceptions threaten their competence face by causing them to feel disrespected.

Whether we're aware of it or not, each of us is constantly managing our public image, hoping that others perceive us the way we want them to. Through communication behavior, we manage multiple identities in multiple ways, and we protect our face needs and respond to situations that threaten them.

SHARPEN Your Skills: *Minimizing face threats*

With others in your class, role-play a conversation in which you have to criticize someone else's work. Practice delivering your critiques to one another in ways that minimize face threats for the recipients.

For REVIEW

- **How do we form perceptions of others?**

  Perceiving others is a process whereby we select information for attention, organize that information according to a perceptual schema, and then interpret it to give it meaning.

- **What influences our perceptions?**

  Our cultural background, stereotypes, primacy and recency effects, and perceptual sets are among the most potent influences on our perceptions. Our attributions for behavior are also influenced by the self-serving bias and the fundamental attribution error.

- **How do we manage our image?**

  Over the course of life, we create and refine a self-concept. Our communication behavior reflects our self-concept through the way we manage our image, both in person and online.

KEY TERMS

NOTES

1. Murphy, N. A., Hall, J. A., Ruben, M. A., Frauendorfer, D., Mast, M. S., Johnson, K. E., & Nguyen, L. (2019). Predictive validity of thin-slice nonverbal behavior from social interactions. *Personality and Social Psychology Bulletin, 45*(7), 983–993. https://doi.org/10.1177/0146167218802834

2. Sadikaj, G., Moskowitz, D. S., & Zuroff, D. C. (2018). What's interpersonal in interpersonal perception? The role of target's attachment in the accuracy of perception. *Journal of Personality, 86*(4), 665–678. https://doi.org/10.1111/jopy.12343

3. Uhl-Bien, M., Schermerhorn, J. R., & Osborn, R. N. (2015). *Organizational behavior* (13th ed.). Wiley.

4. Goldstein, E. B., & Brockmole, J. R. (2017). *Sensation and perception* (10th ed.). Cengage.

5. Burgoon, J. K. (2015). Expectancy violations theory. In C. R. Berger, M. E. Roloff, S. R. Wilson, J. P. Dillard, J. Caughlin, & D. Solomon (Eds.), *The international encyclopedia of interpersonal communication*. John Wiley & Sons. https://doi.org/10.1002/9781117540190

6. Inoue, K., Yagi, Y., & Sato, N. (2018). The mere exposure effect for visual image. *Memory & Cognition, 46*(2), 181–190. https://doi.org/10.3758/s13421-017-0756-6

7. Goldstein & Brockmole, 2017.

8. Faraguna, U., Ferrucci, M., Giorgi, F. S., & Fornai, F. (2019). The functional anatomy of the reticular formation. *Frontiers in Neuroanatomy, 13*, 55. https://doi.org/10.3389/fnana.2019.00055

9. See Burgoon, J. K., Guerrero, L. K., & Floyd, K. (2010). *Nonverbal communication*. Pearson/Allyn & Bacon. https://doi.org/10.4324/9781315663425

10. Sowa, J. F. (2000). *Knowledge representation: Logical, philosophical, and computational foundations*. Brooks/Cole.

11. Krueger, J. (2014). The phenomenology of person perception. In M. J. Bruhn, & D. R. Wehrs (Eds.), *Cognition, literature, and history* (pp. 153–173). Routledge.

12. Coombs, W. T. (2012). Attribution theory in communication research. In N. M. Seel (Ed.), *Encyclopedia of the sciences of learning* (pp. 375–379). Springer. https://doi.org/10.1007/978-1-4419-1428-6; Weiner, B. (2012). An attribution theory of motivation. In P. A. M. Van Lange, A. W. Kruglanski, & T. E. Higgins (Eds.), *Handbook of theories of social psychology* (Vol. 1, pp. 135–155). Sage. https://doi.org/10.4135/9781446249215

13. Spitzberg, B. H., & Manusov, V. (2015). Attribution theory: Finding good cause in the search for theory. In D. O. Braithwaite, & P. Schrodt (Eds.), *Engaging theories in interpersonal communication: Multiple perspectives* (2nd ed., pp. 37–50). Sage. https://doi.org/10.4135/9781483329529

14. See, e.g., Manusov, V. (2009). Attribution and interpersonal communication: Out of our heads and into behavior. In D. R. Roskos-Ewoldsen, & J. L. Monahan (Eds.), *Communication and social cognition: Theories and methods* (pp. 141–170). Taylor & Francis. https://doi.org/10.4324/9780203936313

15. Kastanakis, M. N., & Voyer, B. G. (2014). The effect of culture on perception and cognition: A conceptual framework. *Journal of Business Research, 67*(4), 425–433. https://doi.org/10.1016/j.jbusres.2013.03.028

16. Kasabov, E., & Hain, T. (2014). Cross-generational perceptions and reactions during service recovery. *The Service Industries Journal, 34*(1), 71–87. https://doi.org/10.1080/02642069.2013.763347

17. Farwell, L., & Weiner, B. (2000). Bleeding hearts and the heartless: Popular perceptions of liberal and conservative ideologies. *Personality and Social Psychology Bulletin, 26*(7), 845–852. https://doi.org/10.1177/0146167200269009; Westfall, J., Van Boven, L., Chambers, J. R., & Judd, C. M. (2015). Perceiving political polarization in the United States: Party identity strength and attitude extremity exacerbate the perceived partisan divide. *Perspectives on Psychological Science, 10*(2), 145–158. https://doi.org/10.1177/1745691615569849

18. See Bordalo, P., Coffman, K., Gennaioli, N., & Shleifer, A. (2016). Stereotypes. *Quarterly Journal of Economics, 131*(4), 1753–1794. https://doi.org/10.1093/qje/qjw029

19. Lineweaver, T. T., Roy, A., & Horth, M. (2017). Children's stereotypes of older adults: Evaluating contributions of cognitive development and social learning. *Educational Gerontology, 43*(6), 300–312. https://doi.org/10.1080/03601277.2017.1296296

20. Macrae, C. N., & Bodenhausen, G. V. (2000). Social cognition: Thinking categorically about others. *Annual Review of Psychology, 51,* 93–120. https://doi.org/10.1146/annurev.psych.51.1.93

21. Freeman, J. B., & Johnson, K. L. (2016). More than meets the eye: Split-second social perception. *Trends in Cognitive Sciences, 20*(5), 362–374. https://doi.org/10.1016/j.tics.2016.03.003

22. Freeman, J. B., Stolier, R. M., Ingbretsen, Z. A., & Hehman, E. A. (2014). Amygdala responsivity to high-level social information from unseen faces. *Journal of Neuroscience, 34*(32), 10573–10581. https://doi.org/10.1523/JNEUROSCI.5063-13.2014

23. See, e.g., Madva, A., & Brownstein, M. (2018). Stereotypes, prejudice, and the taxonomy of the implicit social mind. *Noûs, 52*(3), 611–644. https://doi.org/10.1111/nous.12182

24. See Heng, T. T. (2018). Different is not deficient: Contradicting stereotypes of Chinese international students in US higher education. *Studies in Higher Education, 43*(1), 22–36. https://doi.org/10.1080/03075079.2016.1152466

25. Bäuml, K.-H. T., Aslap, A., & Abel, M. (2017). The two faces of selective memory retrieval—Cognitive, developmental, and social processes. *Psychology of Learning and Motivation, 66,* 167–209. https://doi.org/10.1016/bs.plm.2016.11.004

26. Allen, M., & Valde, K. S. (2006). The intersection of methodological and ethical concerns when researching a gendered world. In D. J. Canary, & K. Dindia (Eds.), *Handbook of sex differences and similarities in communication* (2nd ed., pp. 97–110). Lawrence Erlbaum Associates.

27. Hrebickova, M., & Graf, S. (2014). Method for self-report and age of stereotype rater can influence accuracy of national stereotype. *Personality and Individual Differences, 60,* Suppl, S61. https://doi.org/10.1016/j.paid.2013.07.264

28. Sullivan, J. (2019). The primacy effect in impression formation: Some replications and extensions. *Social Psychological and Personality Science, 10*(4), 432–439. https://doi.org/10.1177/1948550618771003

29. Asch, S. (1946). Forming impressions of personality. *Journal of Abnormal and Social Psychology, 41*(3), 258–290. https://doi.org/10.1037/h0055756

30. Finnerty, J., Haywood, C., Ellis, J., Turnbull, I., Jones, D., & Bennett, P. (2013). You don't get a second chance to make a first impression. *BMJ Supportive & Palliative Care, 3*(Suppl 1), A41. https://doi.org/10.1136/bmjspcare-2013-000591.111

31. Reis, J., Benevenuto, F., Olmo, P., Prates, R., Kwak, H., & An, J. (2015). Breaking the news: First impressions matter in online news. *Proceedings of the Ninth International AAAI Conference on Web and Social Media,* 357–366.

32. Fang, L., van Kleef, G. A., & Sauter, D. A. (2018). Person perception from changing emotional expressions: Primacy, recency, or averaging effect? *Cognition & Emotion, 32*(8), 1597–1610. https://doi.org/10.1080/02699931.2018.1432476

33. See, e.g., Garnefeld, I., & Steinhoff, L. (2013). Primacy versus recency effects in extended service encounters. *Journal of Service Management, 24*(1), 64–81. https://doi.org/10.1108/09564231311304198

34. Biggs, A. T., Adamo, S. H., Dowd, E. W., & Mitroff, S. R. (2015). Examining perceptual and conceptual set biases in multiple-target visual search. *Attention, Perception, & Psychophysics, 77*(3), 844–855. https://doi.org/10.3758/s13414-014-0822-0

35. Stern, M., & Karraker, K. H. (1989). Sex stereotyping of infants: A review of gender labeling studies. *Sex Roles, 20*(9-10), 501–522. https://doi.org/10.1007/BF00288198

36. Luhrmann, T. M. (2013). Making God real and making God good: Some mechanisms through which prayer may contribute to healing. *Transcultural Psychiatry, 50*(5), 707–725. https://doi.org/10.1177/1363461513487670; Oman, D. (2018). Clinical practice, religion, and spirituality. In D. Oman (Ed.), *Why religion and spirituality matter for public health* (pp. 245–260). Springer. https://doi.org/10.1007/978-3-319-73966-3

37. Floyd, K. (2019). *Affectionate communication in close relationships.* Cambridge University Press. https://doi.org/10.1017/9781108653510; Brantley-Hill, S. M., & Brinthaupt, T. M. (2014). Perceptions of affectionate communication among people with unfavorable and favorable attitudes toward homosexuality. *Journal of Homosexuality, 61*(2), 270–287. https://doi.org/10.1080/00918369.2013.839910

38. Gaynor, G. K. (2019, April 1). Actor Omari Hardwick draws fan outrage for kissing Beyoncé at NAACP Awards. *Fox News.* https://www.foxnews.com/entertainment/actor-omari-hardwick-draws-fan-outrage-for-kissing-beyonce-at-naacp-awards

39. Scherer, K. R., (2018). Attribution theory: A lively legacy. *Motivation Science, 4*(1), 15–16. https://doi.org/10.1037/mot0000092; Coombs, W. T. (2012). Attribution theory in communication research. In N. M. Seel (Ed.), *Encyclopedia of the sciences of learning* (pp. 375–379). Springer. https://doi.org/10.1007/978-1-4419-1428-6

40. Gonzalez, A. S. (2016). Attribution theory: Dimensions of causality, stability and controllability according to learners. In C. Gkonou, D. Tatzl, & S. Mercer (Eds.), *New directions in language learning psychology* (pp. 209–232). Springer. https://doi.org/10.1007/978-3-319-23491-5_1

41. Galvin, B. M., Randel, A. E., Collins, B. J., & Johnson, R. E. (2018). Changing the focus of locus (of control): A targeted review of the locus of control literature and agenda for future research. *Journal of Organizational Behavior, 39*(7), 820–833. https://doi.org/10.1002/job.2275

42. Gonzalez, 2016; Weiner, B. (2012). An attribution theory of motivation. In P. A. M. Van Lange, A. W. Kruglanski, & E. T. Higgins (Eds.), *Handbook of theories of social psychology* (pp. 135–155). Sage. https://doi.org/10.4135/9781446249215

43. Muschetto, T., & Siegel, J. T. (2019). Attribution theory and support for individuals with depression: The impact of controllability, stability, and interpersonal relationship. *Stigma and Health, 4*(2), 126–135. https://doi.org/10.1037/sah0000131

44. Barbee, A. P., Antle, B. F., Fallat, M. E., Forest, R., & McClure, M. E. (2017). EMS treatment of families in an ambiguous out-of-hospital child death: The role of attribution errors. *Journal of Loss and Trauma, 22*(7), 564–576. https://doi.org/10.1080/15325024.2017.1358572

45. Wang, X., Zheng, L., Li, L., Zheng, Y., Sun, P., Zhou, F. A., & Guo, Y. (2017). Immune to situation: The self-serving bias in unambiguous contexts. *Frontiers in Psychology, 8,* 822. https://doi.org/10.3389/fpsyg.2017.00822

46. Durtschi, J. A., Fincham F. D., Cui, M., Lorenz, F. O., & Conger, R. D. (2011). Dyadic processes in early marriage: Attributions, behavior, and marital quality. *Family Relations, 60*(4), 421–434. https://doi.org/10.1111/j.1741-3729.2011.00655.x

47. Ross, L. (2018). From the fundamental attribution error to the truly fundamental attribution error and beyond: My research journey. *Perspectives on Psychological Science, 13*(6), 750–769. https://doi.org/10.1177/1745691618769855

48. See Saxena, P. (2015). Johari window: An effective model for improving interpersonal communication and managerial effectiveness. *SIT Journal of Management, 5*(2), 134–146.

49. Reported in Myers, D. G. (1980). *The inflated self.* Seabury.

50. Brown, J. D. (2014). Self-esteem and self-evaluation: Feeling is believing. In J. Suls (Ed.), *Psychological perspectives on the self* (Vol. 4, pp. 27–58). Psychology Press. https://doi.org/10.4324/9781315806976

51. Rieger, S., Göllner, R., Trautwein, U., & Roberts, B. W. (2016). Low self-esteem prospectively predicts depression in the transition to young adulthood: A replication of Orth, Robins, and Roberts (2008). *Journal of Personality and Social Psychology, 110*(1), e16–e22. https://doi.org/10.1037/pspp0000037; Steiger, A. E., Allemand, M., Robins, R. W., & Fend, H. A. (2014). Low and decreasing self-esteem during adolescence predict adult depression two decades later. *Journal of Personality and Social Psychology, 106*(2), 325–338. https://doi.org/10.1037/a0035133

52. Baio, J., Wiggins, L., Christensen, D. L., Maenner, M. J., Daniels, J., Warren, Z., Kurzius-Spencer, M., Zahorodny, W., Rosenberg, C. R., White, T., Durkin, M. S., Imm, P., Nikolaou, L., Yeargin-Allsopp, M., Lee, L.-C., Harrington, R., Lopez, M., Fitzgerald, R. T., Hewitt, A., Pettygrove, S., . . . Dowling, N. F. (2018). Prevalence of autism spectrum disorder among children aged 8 years–Autism and Developmental Disabilities Monitoring Network, 11 sites, United States, 2014. *Morbidity and Mortality Weekly Report–Surveillance Summaries, 67*(6), 1–23. https://doi.org/10.15585/mmwr.ss6706a1

53. Clark, J. L., & Green, M. C. (2018). Self-fulfilling prophecies: Perceived reality of online interaction drives expected outcomes of online communication. *Personality and Individual Differences, 133,* 73–76. https://doi.org/10.1016/j.paid.2017.08.031; Zimmer-Gembeck, M. J., Trevaskis, S., Nesdale, D., & Downey, G. A. (2014). Relational victimization, loneliness and depressive symptoms: Indirect associations via self and peer reports of rejection sensitivity. *Journal of Youth and Adolescence, 43*(4), 568–582. https://doi.org/10.1007/s10964-013-9993-6

54. bin Bullare, F., Chang, C. H., Zhi, H., Chan, A., & Wider, W. (2017). Self-esteem, extraversion personality, and academic achievement among children from intact families and orphans. *Education Sciences & Psychology, 43,* 95–101.

55. Murray, S. L., Rose, P., Bellavia, G., Holmes, J. G., & Kusche, A. (2002). When rejection stings: How self-esteem constrains relationship-enhancement processes. *Journal of Personality and Social Psychology, 83*(3), 556–573. https://doi.org/10.1037/0022-3514.83.3.556

56. Baumeister, R. F. (2010). The self. In R. F. Baumeister, & E. J. Finkel (Eds.), *Advanced social psychology: The state of the science* (pp. 139–176). Oxford University Press.

57. Baumeister, R. F., Campbell, J. D., Krueger, J. I., & Vohs, K. D. (2003). Does high self-esteem cause better performance, interpersonal success, happiness, or healthier lifestyles? *Psychological Science in the Public Interest, 4*(1), 1–44. https://doi.org/10.1111/1529-1006.01431

58. Ibid.

59. Tobin, A. (2014, November 20). Millennial think tank: Self-expression, selfies, and personal branding. http://www.digitalistmag.com/lob/human-resources/millennial-self-expression-selfies-and-personal-branding-01771160

60. Ibid.

61. McAdams, D. P. (2020). Life-story approach to identity. In V. Zeigler-Hill, & T. Shackelford (Eds.), *Encyclopedia of personality and individual differences.* Springer. https://doi.org/10.1007/978-3-319-28099-8_2293-1

62. Lup, K., Trub, L., & Rosenthal, L. (2015). Instagram #instasad? Exploring associations among Instagram use, depressive symptoms, negative social comparison, and strangers followed. *Cyberpsychology, Behavior, and Social Networking, 18*(5), 247–252. https://doi.org/10.1089/cyber.2014.0560

63. Jordan, T. (2019). Does online anonymity undermine the sense of personal responsibility? *Media, Culture & Society, 41*(4), 572–577. https://doi.org/10.1177/0163443719842073

64. Tseng, F. C., Chang, C. T., Lee, H. C., & Teng, C. I. (2018). How does gender swapping impact online gamer loyalty? The perspective of interdependence theory. *Online Information Review, 42*(5), 647–662. https://doi.org/10.1108/OIR-08-2016-0230

65. Herring, S. C., Scheidt, L. A., Bonus, S., & Wright, E. (2004). Bridging the gap: A genre analysis of weblogs. *Proceedings of the 37th Hawaii International Conference on System Sciences (HICSS-37).* IEEE. http://csdl.computer.org/comp/proceedings/hicss/2004/2056/04/205640101b.pdf

66. Huffaker, D. A., & Calvert, S. L. (2005). Gender, identity, and language use in teenage blogs. *Journal of Computer-Mediated Communication, 10*(2), article 1. https://doi.org/10.1111/j.1083-6101.2005.tb00238.x

67. Goldschmidt, M. M. (2004). Good person stories: The favor narrative as a self-presentation strategy. *Qualitative Research Reports in Communication, 5,* 28–33.

68. Kwek, A., Wang, Y., & Weaver, D. B. (2019). Face and facework in ethnic Chinese shopping-intensive package tours: Dynamics and outcomes. *Tourism Management, 74,* 396–407. https://doi.org/10.1016/j.tourman.2019.04.021

69. Goffman, E. (1959). *The presentation of the self in everyday life.* Doubleday; see also Brown, P., & Levinson, S. C. (1987). *Politeness: Some universals in language usage.* Cambridge University Press. https://doi.org/10.1017/CBO9780511813085

70. Archer, D., & Jagodziński, P. (2018). Applying (im)politeness and facework research to professional settings: An introduction. *Journal of Politeness Research, 14*(2), 245–256. https://doi.org/10.1515/pr-2018-0015; Lim, T. S., & Bowers, J. W. (1991). Facework: Solidarity, approbation, and tact. *Human Communication Research, 17*(3), 415–449. https://doi.org/10.1111/j.1468-2958.1991.tb00239.x

71. Domenici, K., & Littlejohn, S. W. (2006). *Facework: Bridging theory and practice.* Sage. https://doi.org/10.4135/9781452204222

72. Perkins, M. M., Ball, M. M., Whittington, F. J., & Hollingsworth, C. (2012). Relational autonomy in assisted living: A focus on diverse care settings for older adults. *Journal of Aging Studies, 26*(2), 214–225. https://doi.org/10.1016/j.jaging.2012.01.001

73. See, e.g., Jensen, P. R. (2017). Undignified dignity: Using humor to manage the stigma of mental illness and homelessness. *Communication Quarterly, 66*(1), 20–37. https://doi.org/10.1080/01463373.2017.1325384

4

Josh Anderson/The New York Times/Redux

HOW WE USE LANGUAGE

What's in a Word?

"Hi. I'm Dr. Patti McCarver, and I'm your nurse." That's how McCarver, a registered nurse who has earned a doctorate degree, introduces herself to patients. Her words are fueling a national controversy over use of the word "doctor." Technically, a doctor is anyone who has a doctorate degree, including many college professors—yet physicians claim that most patients automatically equate "doctor" with "physician," and for decades only physicians used the title. As more nurses, pharmacists, physical therapists, and other health care providers gain doctorate degrees in their respective fields, however, they earn the right to use that title as well, which physicians claim will only confuse patients. Some states forbid nonphysicians to call themselves "doctor"—regardless of their education—unless they immediately specify their profession, as McCarver did. What do you think? Should nurses with doctorate degrees call themselves "doctor," or should that word be reserved for physicians?

······························► As You READ

- What are the defining characteristics of language?
- For what reasons do people use language?
- How can you use language more effectively?

Words can shape our lives in extraordinary ways. By announcing in 1776 that "all men are created equal," Thomas Jefferson and the Second Continental Congress declared to the world the emergence of a new sovereign nation founded on the principle of individual liberty. Nearly two centuries later, Martin Luther King Jr. described his vision for civil rights and racial equality by proclaiming, "I have a dream." In those and many other cases throughout history, powerful words have inspired women and men to enact dramatic social change.

Because language can be so consequential, we have to choose our words carefully in many situations. Using the right words in a job interview, a political campaign, and a marriage proposal may make the difference between failure and success. Being a competent communicator therefore requires us to use language in a deliberate and informed way.

The Nature of Language

Abraham Lincoln was reportedly fond of asking people, "How many legs does a dog have if you call its tail a leg?" Think about how you would respond to that question. Many replied that if you call the dog's tail a leg, then a dog has five legs. Lincoln answered that dogs have only four legs, because calling a tail a leg doesn't make it one.

Some would say the former U.S. president was correct and that simply changing the way we talk about an object doesn't change the nature of the object itself. Others, however, would claim that Lincoln's assessment was incorrect and that words have only the meanings we choose to assign them. Thus the term *leg* means what it does only because English language speakers give that meaning to it—so, if we call a tail a leg, it is therefore a leg. Lincoln's riddle illustrates one reason why it is so important for us to understand language: we use words to refer to objects, events, ideas, and other entities in the real world, but most words have only the meanings that we, as the users of a language, give them.

What is language in the first place? **Language** is a structured system of symbols used for communicating meaning. You can probably think of many behaviors and items that represent or symbolize some type of meaning. A smile often symbolizes happiness, for instance; a red traffic light symbolizes the need to stop. Many gestures also have symbolic meaning, in that they represent a particular concept or idea. For example, you might wave to say "hello" and shrug your shoulders to indicate "I don't know." Although facial expressions, traffic lights, and gestures all symbolize meaning, however, none qualifies as language. Why? The answer is that language is characterized by the use of a specific type of symbol: words.[1]

• **language** A structured system of symbols used for communicating meaning.

Words are the building blocks of language and verbal communication. As we will see in this chapter, we use them to represent ideas, observations, feelings, and thoughts. Words—whether we speak or write them—can have a profound influence on how we relate to others. In this section, we will see that language is symbolic, is usually arbitrary, is governed by rules, has layers of meaning, varies in clarity, and is bound by context and culture.

LANGUAGE IS SYMBOLIC

When we say language is symbolic, we mean that each word represents a particular object or idea, but it does not constitute the object or idea itself. For example, the word *textbook* represents a bound or online collection of published material to be read as a supplement for lectures and in-class activities in a course. The word itself is not the object, though; it merely symbolizes it. Similarly, the word *five* represents a specific quantity of something (one more than four, and one fewer than six), yet the word itself is not the quantity; it simply represents it.

One way to understand the symbolic nature of language is to remember that different languages often have different words for the same object. The English word *textbook*, for instance, is *läromedel* in Swedish, 教科書 in Japanese, **учебник** in Bulgarian, and *kitabu cha darasa* in Swahili. Those are different symbols, but they all represent the same entity, a textbook. If you were to invent your own language, you could create any term you wanted to represent the concept of a textbook.

We often acquire new words, and new meanings for older words, as technology advances. The widespread use of computer-mediated communication, for instance, has added new terms to our everyday conversations, such as *blog*, *e-mail*, and *instant messaging*. In addition, it has generated new meanings for existing words, such as *unplug*, *crash*, *tweet*, and *net*. As computer technology continues to develop, new words will likely be added to our vocabulary to help us communicate about it.

Words and phrases also acquire new significance in response to changing social conditions. In the wake of the worldwide coronavirus pandemic in 2020, for instance, the term *social distancing* entered widespread use to describe the maintenance of physical space between people to inhibit the spread of infection. Although the term was already in use among public health professionals, it became commonplace in the broader population as people managed social interaction during the pandemic.

The proliferation of new words has prompted efforts to catalog their meanings. One such effort is the online dictionary Wordnik.com, which aims to identify and define every word being used in the English language.[2]

Dictionary editors are constantly revising their products to account for newly developed words. In recent years, for instance, many people have vacationed near home to save on travel costs, an experience we now call a *staycation*.

Jasmin Merdan/123RF

LANGUAGE IS USUALLY ARBITRARY

Why do words symbolize the particular objects and ideas they do? For the most part, words have only an arbitrary connection to their meanings. Think of the word *car*. That word doesn't look or sound like a car, so why does it make us think of one? The only reason is that speakers of English have agreed to give the word *car* that particular meaning. They could just as easily have called cars "hanners" or "steeks" or "rayverts." Those words don't mean anything to speakers of English, but they would if we were to assign them a meaning. The point is that the meaning of almost all words is arbitrary: words literally mean whatever we, as users of a language, choose for them to mean.

Language can be arbitrary precisely *because* it is symbolic. As we saw earlier, words only symbolize their meanings; they don't constitute their meanings themselves. For that reason we can choose almost any word to symbolize a particular meaning, and so the connection between language and meaning is arbitrary.

In that sense, then, Abraham Lincoln was wrong when he said that calling a tail a leg doesn't make it one. It's true that calling a tail a leg doesn't change any of its physical properties, but because of the arbitrary nature of language, we can choose to make *leg* the appropriate term to describe a tail . . . or a rainbow, a fishing boat, a salt shaker, or any other object or idea we wish to describe.

Because the meaning of most words is arbitrary, the meaning of a word can change over time. For instance, the word "book"

Why do we call a car a car?

Tim OHara/Corbis

has traditionally referred only to a printed volume, but these days, it includes the digital versions we call e-books and the recorded versions we call audiobooks. In the same vein, "reading the newspaper" used to mean flipping through physical pages of news print, but now it includes reading about the news online.

LANGUAGE IS GOVERNED BY RULES

We have said that language is symbolic and that the meaning of most words is arbitrary. If those statements are both true, then how do we all understand one another? The answer is that language is not just a collection of symbols (words); it's also a system of rules for using those words.

You already know many of the rules that frame your native language. Even if you can't explain them, you usually take notice when they are violated. To a native speaker of English, for instance, the statement "I filled the bottle with water" sounds correct, but "I filled water into the bottle" does not. Even if you aren't quite sure *why* the second sentence sounds wrong, you probably still recognize that it does. Along the same lines, when you learn a new language, you don't learn just the words; you also learn the rules for how the words work together to convey meaning.

Researchers distinguish among four different types of language rules:

- **Phonological rules** deal with the correct pronunciation of a word, and they vary from language to language. If you speak French, for example, you know that the proper way to pronounce *travail* is "trah-VYE." According to English phonological rules, however, the word looks as though it should be pronounced "trah-VALE."

- **Syntactic rules** govern the order of words within phrases and clauses. The question, "What is your name?" makes sense to an English speaker because the words are in the proper order. To ask the same question in American Sign Language, a system of visual signs used by deaf people to communicate, we would sign "your – name – what?" Signing "what – your – name?" is incorrect because it violates the syntactic rules of American Sign Language.

- **Semantic rules** have to do with the meaning of individual words. Those meanings may be arbitrary, as we saw above, but speakers of a language agree on them. When you hear the word *lawyer*, for instance, you think of an attorney, not a paper mill or a cell phone or a Caribbean vacation. It is a semantic rule that connects *lawyer* with *attorney* and not with one of those other meanings.

- **Pragmatic rules** deal with the implications or interpretations of statements. "Nice to meet you" is a common greeting among speakers of English. Depending on the context and the speaker's tone of voice, you might think the speaker really is happy to meet you, or you might infer that he or she is just saying so to be polite. If there's a sarcastic tone in the speaker's voice, you might even infer that he or she is *unhappy* to meet you. In each instance, pragmatic rules lead you to your conclusion.

As children acquire a language, they gain an almost intuitive sense of its phonological, syntactic, semantic, and pragmatic rules. That knowledge allows native speakers of a language to speak and write fluently. In contrast, people who are less familiar with the language are more likely to violate those rules by mistake.[3]

The widespread use of electronically mediated forms of communication, such as texts and tweets, has led some to worry that students are no longer learning to use language properly. Is that concern valid? Check out the "Fact or Fiction?" box for insight into this question.

• phonological rules Rules that deal with the correct pronunciation of a word.

• syntactic rules Rules that govern the order of words within phrases and clauses.

• semantic rules Rules that specify the meanings of individual words.

• pragmatic rules Rules that specify the implications or interpretations of statements.

No matter how we communicate verbally, we observe phonological, syntactic, semantic, and pragmatic rules for language.

Wavebreak Media Ltd/123RF

Fact or *fiction?*

Texting Reduces the Ability to Use Language Properly

Many people have worried aloud that sending text messages impairs a person's ability to use grammatically correct language. One reason is that texting makes heavy use of abbreviations, such as *u* for *you* and *ppl* for *people*. Young Americans send and receive more than 3,300 texts per month, on average, raising concerns that they are losing their capacity for language in the process. Is that concern fact or fiction?

A 2014 study reports that there is no cause for alarm: text messaging does not have a negative effect on people's ability to use language properly. The study followed a group of students ranging in age from 8 to 30 years. The researchers collected all of the text messages participants wrote in a two-day period and coded them for improper uses of grammar and punctuation. They then compared participants' scores with their performance in standardized measures of grammar and intelligence.

The researchers reported that grammatical violations in text messages had no negative effects on the students' abilities to use language properly. In fact, omitting words and using ungrammatical word forms while texting were actually related to better spelling ability, especially for younger texters. If texting has any effect on language use, then, the effect appears to be a positive one.

ASK YOURSELF

- Do the findings of this study surprise you? Have you wondered whether texting reduces a person's language abilities?

- Do you feel comfortable switching back and forth between "texting language" and the language you use in other written communication?

SOURCES: Wood, C., Kemp, N., & Waldron, S. (2014). Exploring the longitudinal relationships between the use of grammar in text messaging and performance on grammatical tasks. *British Journal of Developmental Psychology, 32*(4), 415–429. https://doi.org/10.1111/bjdp.12049; Nielsen Co. (2010, October 14). U.S. teen mobile report calling yesterday, texting today, using apps tomorrow. www.nielsen.com/us/ en/insights/news/2010/u-s-teen-mobile-report-calling-yesterday-texting -today-using-apps-tomorrow.html

LANGUAGE HAS LAYERS OF MEANING

Many words imply certain ideas that are separate from their literal meanings. The literal meaning of a word—the way a dictionary defines it—is its **denotative meaning**. Think of the word *home*, for instance. Its denotative meaning is "one's place of residence." When you hear the word *home*, however, you may also think along the lines of "a place where I feel safe, accepted, and loved" or "a space where I am free to do whatever I want." Those are examples of the word's **connotative meaning**, the ideas or concepts the word suggests in addition to its literal definition.

• denotative meaning
The literal meaning of a word.

• connotative meaning
The ideas or concepts a word suggests in addition to its literal definition.

The Semantic Triangle To illustrate the relationship between words and their denotative and connotative meanings, psychologist Charles Ogden and English professor Ivor Richards developed the *semantic triangle* (Figure 1).[4] In its three corners, the semantic triangle portrays three necessary elements for identifying the meaning in language. The first element is the *symbol*, which is the word being communicated.

FIGURE 1

THE SEMANTIC
TRIANGLE

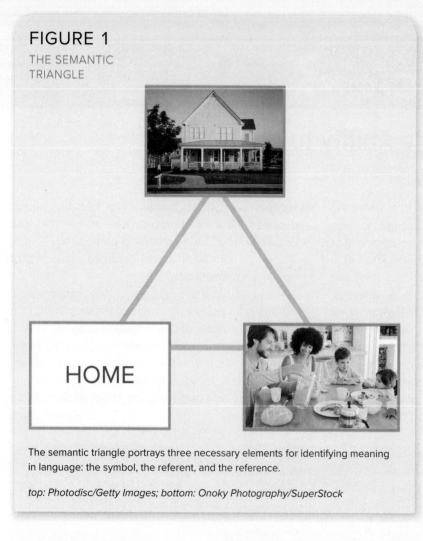

The semantic triangle portrays three necessary elements for identifying meaning in language: the symbol, the referent, and the reference.

top: Photodisc/Getty Images; bottom: Onoky Photography/SuperStock

In the second corner is the *reference*, which is the word's connotative meaning. Finally, there's the *referent*, which is the denotative meaning.

If several listeners hear the same word, they might attribute the same denotative meaning to it even if they have different connotative meanings. For instance, if I say the word *euthanasia*, the word itself is the symbol, and its referent is a medically assisted death. To one listener, the word evokes images of a merciful end to someone's pain and suffering. To another person, it evokes images of homicide. It makes other listeners think of an unfortunate but sometimes justified component of the death experience. Those are all differences in the word's reference, or connotative meaning, rather than in its denotative meaning. The semantic triangle therefore illustrates how people can hear the same words yet derive quite different meanings from them.

Loaded Language In the heated political battles over U.S. immigration policy, one of the most contentious issues concerns the practice of permanent residents, also known as Green Card holders, sponsoring relatives for immigration to the United States. Immigration rights advocates refer to the process as "family reunification," whereas opponents tend to call it "chain migration." Both those terms are examples of **loaded language**, words with strongly positive or negative connotations. Notice that "family reunification" sounds positive because it implies reuniting people with their loved ones. "Chain migration," however, seems to conjure images of unending chains of people pouring into the United States.

Loaded language reflects the fact that denotations and connotations represent different layers of meaning. At a denotative level, for instance, the word *cancer* simply refers to a malignant growth or tumor in the body. For many people, however, the term connotes any evil condition that spreads destructively. For instance, you might hear someone describe conditions such as poverty and bigotry as "cancers on society." That example illustrates that people can use the word *cancer* as a loaded term when they wish to evoke feelings of fear, disgust, or anger on the part of listeners. People can also use loaded words to evoke positive emotions. Terms such as *family* and *freedom* have emotionally positive connotations even if their denotative meanings are emotionally neutral.[5]

• loaded language
Words with strongly positive or negative connotations.

LANGUAGE VARIES IN CLARITY

Josh is driving his brother Jeremy to a doctor's appointment, and Jeremy has the directions. As they approach an intersection, they have the following conversation:

> **Josh:** *I need to turn left at this next light, don't I?*
>
> **Jeremy:** *Right.*

Which way should Josh turn? Was Jeremy saying that Josh was accurate in thinking that he should turn left, or was he correcting Josh by instructing him to turn right? We don't really know, because Jeremy has used **ambiguous language** by making a statement that we can interpret to have more than one meaning.

A certain amount of ambiguity is inherent in our language. In fact, according to the *Oxford English Dictionary*, the 500 most frequently used words in the English language have an average of 23 different meanings each. The word "set" has so many different meanings—nearly 200, more than any other English word—that it takes the *Oxford English Dictionary* 60,000 words to define it![6] One reason language varies in clarity is that some words are more *concrete* than others. A word that is concrete refers to a specific object in the physical world, such as a particular laptop computer, a specific restaurant, or an individual person. In contrast, a word that is *abstract* refers to a broader category or organizing concept of objects. According to English professor Samuel Hayakawa, words can be arrayed along a "ladder of abstraction" that shows their progression from more abstract to more concrete.[7]

Figure 2 gives an example of Hayakawa's ladder of abstraction. At the top of the ladder is a reference to all living beings, which is a broad, abstract category. Moving downward, the words become more and more concrete, referring to all animals, then all mammals, all primates, all *Homo sapiens*, and all males, before reaching the most concrete reference to a specific individual.

FIGURE 2
HAYAKAWA'S LADDER OF ABSTRACTION

Living being — More abstract

Animal

Mammal

Primate

Homo sapiens

Male

My brother Tim — More concrete

Note how the example begins at the top with a broad, abstract category and how, as we move down the ladder, the concepts become more and more concrete and specific.

LANGUAGE IS BOUND BY CONTEXT AND CULTURE

Finally, meaning in language is affected by the social and cultural context in which people use it. Societies and cultures differ in their degree of individualism and their use of communication codes. Many of those differences are evident in verbal messages. For instance, "I'm looking out for Number One" is a very individualistic message that would be relatively uncommon in a collectivistic society. In fact, a common saying in Japan, and one that reflects that nation's collectivistic culture, states, "It is the nail that sticks out that gets hammered down."[8]

In what became known as the **Sapir-Whorf hypothesis**, anthropologist Edward Sapir and linguist Benjamin Whorf proposed that language shapes our views of reality. Their notion was that language influences the ways members of a culture see the world—and that a society's attitudes and behaviors are reflected in its language.[9] The Sapir-Whorf hypothesis embodies two specific principles. The first, *linguistic determinism*, suggests that the structure of language determines how we think. In other words, we can conceive of something only if we have a term for it in our vocabulary.[10] Imagine a language that includes no term describing the emotion of envy. According to the principle of linguistic determinism, people who speak that language would not experience envy because they have no words to describe it.

The second principle, *linguistic relativity*, suggests that because language determines our perceptions of reality, people see the world differently depending on which language they speak. Whorf discovered, for instance, that the language of the Hopi Indians of the American Southwest makes no distinction between nouns and verbs. Whereas English uses nouns to refer to *things* and verbs to refer to *actions*, the Hopi

• **ambiguous language**
Words that can have more than one meaning.

• **Sapir-Whorf hypothesis**
A theory that language shapes a person's views of reality.

Our experiences can shape our use of language. A veteran fashion designer might have different terms for various shades of red, whereas you might use the term "red" to describe them all.

imagenavi/Getty Images

language describes just about everything as an action or a process. Compared to English speakers, then, the Hopi tend to see the world as being constantly in motion.[11]

The Sapir-Whorf hypothesis is provocative, but researchers have offered three criticisms that call it into question.[12] The first criticism centers on the cause-and-effect relationship between language and thought. The hypothesis proposes that language shapes and constrains how we think. It is equally possible, though, that our thoughts shape and constrain our language. For instance, an experienced fashion designer might look at four jackets and label their colors "scarlet," "ruby," "crimson," and "vermilion." You might look at the same jackets and call them all "red." Does the designer think of the four colors as different because she has more terms for them than you do, or does she have more terms because she has more experience thinking about differences among colors? It's difficult to know for sure, but either idea is possible.

Second, even if people don't have a word for a particular experience, that doesn't necessarily mean they don't have that experience. Perhaps you can recall a situation when you were embarrassed for someone else, for instance. That experience is called *fremdschämen* in German—and although there is no equivalent term in English, you may have had the experience nonetheless.

Finally, even people who don't acquire language, perhaps because of mental or cognitive deficiencies, are able to think, count, and interact with others. They wouldn't be able to do those things if language determined thought.

These criticisms don't necessarily mean that the Sapir-Whorf hypothesis is entirely wrong. They suggest, however, that language may not shape and constrain our ways of thinking quite to the extent that Sapir and Whorf believed.

Appreciating the Power of Words

English writer Rudyard Kipling, author of *The Jungle Book*, once called words "the most powerful drug used by mankind." To understand his point, think about how you feel when someone you love expresses affection to you, or when you listen to a speech by a politician you dislike, or when you comfort a friend who is grieving the loss of a family member. Words can literally change a person's day—or a person's life—in positive or negative ways.

You don't have to look very far to find examples of people whose words have affected both themselves and others. In May 2018, for instance, actress Roseanne Barr tweeted a racially insensitive message about Valerie Jarrett, a former senior advisor to the Obama administration. As a result of her tweet, Barr's television show was canceled and she was dropped as a client by her talent agency. Later that year, talk show host Megyn Kelly stirred controversy with remarks she made on air about Halloween costumes that include blackface, a form of makeup used by non-black performers to represent a caricature of a black person. Her remarks were widely condemned as a defense of racial stereotypes, and they resulted in the cancellation of her talk show. Other high-profile individuals have used their words for more constructive purposes, such as swimmer Michael Phelps, who has talked openly since 2018 about his struggles with depression, in the hopes of encouraging others with depression to seek treatment. What these and many other examples show is that our words can be powerful.

Entire books have been written about the power of language. Here we focus on four important functions that language serves in our daily lives. Specifically, we will discover that language expresses who we are, connects us to others, separates us from others, and motivates action.

LANGUAGE EXPRESSES WHO WE ARE

Think about playing a game in which you have to select one word to represent your identity. Should you pick an adjective, such as *adventurous, conservative*, or *shy*? Maybe you should choose a verb instead, such as *think, sing*, or *run*. That game is challenging because any word we choose might represent a part of who we are but may not represent us fully. As humans, we express our identities in many ways—by our clothes, jobs, preferred leisure activities, and the language we use to communicate with others.

Language expresses who we are in at least two ways: by naming and identifying us and by enhancing our credibility. Let's take a look at each.

Names Define and Differentiate Us What's something that belongs to you, yet is constantly used by others? The answer is *your name*. By itself, a name is simply a linguistic device that identifies something or someone. Your name does more, however, than differentiate you from others—it's also an important component of your sense of self. Naming is therefore one way you gain information about other people and represent yourself to the world.

A person's first name, for instance, can suggest information about the person's characteristics. One such characteristic is the person's sex. In Western societies, we usually assign names such as Jacob, Michael, and Caleb only to males and names such as Emma, Savannah, and Nicole only to females. Names can also provide clues about a person's ethnicity. You might infer that LaKeisha is African American, Huong is Asian, and Santiago is Latino, whereas names such as Brandon and Tina may not suggest any particular ethnicity. Because names go in and out of style over time, some names even suggest a person's age group, so you might assume that Chloe, Mia, and Addison are younger than Edna, Mildred, and Bertha.

In addition to demographic information, names can suggest information about our disposition and sense of self. For instance, we might perceive an adult man who goes by the name Richard differently from one who goes by Ricky, even though those are two forms of the same name. Indeed, research shows that we do make assumptions about people—accurately or not—on the basis of their names.[13] In one study, people made more positive evaluations of men named David, Jon, Joshua, and Gregory than they did of men named Oswald, Myron, Reginald, and Edmund, even though they were given no other information about the men.[14] Other studies have shown that people whose names strongly suggest a nonwhite ethnicity sometimes experience discrimination based only on their names.[15]

People can usually give their children any name they choose, but some countries restrict a parent's options. In North Korea, for instance, leader Kim Jong-un has prohibited anyone from sharing his name. In fact, citizens who were already called Jong-un have had to change their names.[16] Similarly, Saudi Arabia has prohibited parents from giving their children any of 50 different names—including Linda, Elaine, and Benjamin—thought to contradict the religion and culture of that country.[17]

Language Enhances or Diminishes Credibility A second way in which words express who we are is by reflecting our credibility. **Credibility** is the extent to which others perceive us to be competent and trustworthy. Some speakers have credibility on certain topics because of their training and expertise. You will probably have more confidence in medical advice if you hear it from a doctor, for instance, than from the barista at your local coffee shop. If the advice is about making a great latte, however, you'll probably trust your barista more than your doctor. In either case, you are assigning credibility on the basis of the speaker's specific expertise.

Language is intimately tied to issues of credibility. Irrespective of our training or credentials, our words can portray us as confident, trustworthy communicators, or they can make us appear unsure of ourselves. In either situation, our ability to get what we want is affected by the credibility our language use gives us. As we will see next, several specific forms of language have the potential to enhance or diminish our credibility.

• **credibility** The extent to which others perceive us to be competent and trustworthy.

A barista has credibility when it comes to making great coffee but not when it comes to giving medical advice.

Brand X/Getty Images

FIGURE 3

DIALECT
DIFFERENCES IN
NAMES FOR SOFT
DRINKS

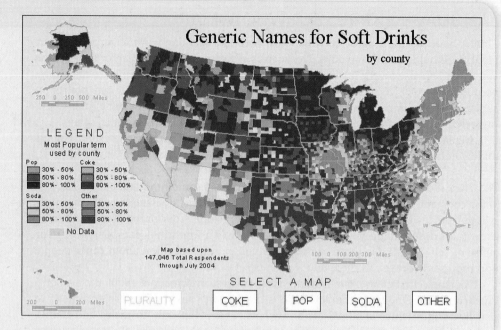

Soft drink map designed by Matthew T. Campbell under the direction of Dr. Gregory Plumb, Spatial
Graphics and Analysis Lab, Department of Cartography and Geography, East Central University
(Oklahoma). Used with permission.

Clichés *Clichés* are words or phrases that were novel at one time but have lost their
effect due to overuse. When politicians talk about "making a difference" or business
leaders refer to "thinking outside the box," they may lose credibility with their audiences; those phrases are clichés that can make speakers sound uninformed or out-of-
touch. Even if a cliché expresses the point you want to make, you will usually be more
persuasive if you use different words. Encouraging someone to "evaluate your situation from a new perspective" can be more powerful than telling the person to "think
outside the box" because the latter phrase is so overused.

Dialects We can also enhance or diminish our credibility by using *dialects*, language
variations shared by people of a certain region or social class. For instance, whether
you call a soft drink a "soda," a "pop," a "coke," or something else depends largely on
where you grew up. As Figure 3 shows, "pop" is the favored term in the U.S. northwest and midwest, whereas "coke" is used mostly in the south, and "soda" is favored
in the southwest and northeast. According to *communication accommodation theory*,
developed by communication scholars Howard Giles and John Wiemann, we may be
able to enhance our credibility by speaking in a dialect that is familiar to our audience.[18] In contrast, when we use a dialect different from that of our listeners, they may
see us as an outsider and question our credibility.

Equivocation Another form of language that sometimes influences a speaker's credibility is *equivocation*, language that disguises the speaker's true intentions through strategic ambiguity. We often choose to use equivocal language when we're in a dilemma,
a situation in which none of our options is a good one. Suppose, for example, that
you're asked to provide a reference for your friend Dylan, who is applying for a job on
your town's police force. One of the questions you're asked is how well Dylan handles
pressure. Even though Dylan is your friend, you can immediately think of several occasions when he hasn't dealt well with pressure. Now you're in a bind. On the one hand,
you want Dylan to get the job because he's your friend. On the other hand, you don't
want to lie to the police lieutenant who's phoning you for the reference.

Several studies have shown that when we're faced with two unappealing choices we
often use equivocal language.[19] You might tell the lieutenant, "Well, it depends; there
are different kinds of pressure." As you can probably tell, that statement doesn't give

the lieutenant much information at all. Instead, it might imply that you don't know how well Dylan deals with pressure, but you don't want to admit that you don't know. It might also imply that you do know how well Dylan handles pressure but don't want to say. In either case, you are likely to come across as less credible than if you had answered the question directly and honestly.[20] Researchers John Daly, Carol Diesel, and David Weber have suggested that those sorts of conversational dilemmas are common and that we frequently use equivocal language in them.[21]

Weasel Words A form of language related to equivocation is *weasel words*, terms or phrases intended to mislead listeners by implying something they don't actually say. Advertisers often use weasel words when making claims about their products. When you hear that "four out of five dentists prefer" a certain brand of toothpaste, the implication is that 80 percent of *all* dentists prefer that brand. That level of preference would be quite impressive—but the statement does not actually make that specific claim. For all we know, only five dentists were surveyed. If that were the case, the support of "four out of five" would appear much less notable.

One way people use weasel words is by making broad, unsupported generalizations. To make herself sound intelligent and informed, for instance, Eva is fond of starting statements with "People say that . . ." or "It's widely known that . . ." These phrases are weasel words because they imply a broad level of agreement with whatever Eva is saying, but they provide no evidence of that agreement. That is, Eva never specifies which people say or know whatever she is claiming, or how many people say or know it, or why we should trust their beliefs or knowledge in the first place.

Allness Statements One specific form of weasel words is an *allness statement*, a statement implying that a claim is true without exception. For instance, when you hear someone claim that "experts agree that corporal punishment is emotionally damaging to children," the implication is that *all* experts agree. Note, however, that the speaker provides no evidence to back up that implication. Likewise, when someone says, "There's no known cure for depression," the implication is that no cure exists. All the statement *actually* means, however, is that no cure is known to the speaker.

Naming and enhancing our credibility aren't the only ways language reflects who we are, but they are among the most noticeable. We also use language to form positive connections with others, as we'll consider next.

LANGUAGE CONNECTS US TO OTHERS

For many years, the telecommunications company AT&T ran an advertising campaign whose slogan was, "Reach out and touch someone." The phrase was meant to suggest that by calling someone on the telephone, we could establish or reinforce a personal bond with that person. Today, many of us use social networking apps for the same purposes: to meet new people and to stay connected with those we already know. Even texting and tweeting help us to reinforce relational bonds with others, as some of the abbreviations in Table 1 illustrate.

Language can help us to connect with others; it allows us to express affection, provide comfort and support, and share social information. Let's look at each of those primary social functions of language.

Language Expresses Affection
Think about the people in your life to whom you feel the closest. How do you convey your feelings of love and appreciation to them? Although you probably use some nonverbal behaviors—such as smiling, hugging, and kissing—chances are you also express your feelings verbally.

Language has a profound ability to communicate affection. Some statements express our fondness for another person, such as "I like you." Others reinforce the importance of our

TABLE 1
CONNECTING BY CHAT

When communicating via various forms of chat, many people use abbreviations for common phrases to connect to others efficiently. Here are some popular abbreviations and their meanings.

TL;DR	Too long; didn't read
SMH	Shaking my head
UG2BK	You've got to be kidding
TTYL	Talk to you later
IIRC	If I recall correctly
IME	In my experience
FWIW	For what it's worth
IMHO	In my humble opinion
TBH	To be honest
^5	High five

Research shows that communicating affection with our loved ones helps to keep us happy and healthy.

Cathy Yeulet/123RF

relationship with the person, such as "You're my best friend." Still others convey hopes or dreams for the future of the relationship, including "I can't wait until we get married." Finally, some statements express the value of the relationship by noting how we would feel without it, such as "My life would be empty without you." Statements such as those are characteristic of our closest personal relationships.

Research indicates that communicating affection is good both for relationships and for the people in them. Family studies researcher Ted Huston and his colleagues found that the more affection spouses communicated to each other during their first 2 years of marriage, the more likely they were to remain married 13 years later.[22] Other studies have found that expressing and receiving affection can produce several health benefits, including lower stress hormones,[23] better cardiovascular health,[24] stronger immunity,[25] an improved ability to recover from stress,[26] lower average blood sugar (a risk factor for diabetes),[27] better mental health,[28] and lesser risk of developing depression and anxiety.[29]

Language provides comfort to individuals in distress.

Victor R. Caivano/AP Images

Language Provides Comfort From time to time, you probably need to comfort someone in distress. Your spoken exchanges with the individual can be mundane, as when you soothe a child with a stubbed toe, or they can occur in extraordinary circumstances, as when you offer support to someone grieving the death of his or her romantic partner. Perhaps you can recall situations when you have been in distress yourself and another's comforting words calmed you.

We also use written messages to convey support to others. Consider that the U.S. greeting card industry is a $10 billion-a-year business. Although people send cards to acknowledge birthdays and communicate good wishes for holidays, they also use get-well and sympathy cards to extend verbal messages of comfort.[30] Cards can also express gratitude or convey hope. When someone has passed away, we may also comfort his or her loved ones by creating a tribute page on Facebook, where people can post fond memories of the deceased and words of support for his or her survivors.[31]

Perhaps you have tried to comfort someone during a difficult time but felt unsure about what to say. Check out the "Difficult Conversations" box for some useful tips.

Language Conveys Social Information A third way in which language connects people is by allowing us to share social information, which includes facts and opinions we have of others. We often do so by engaging in **gossip**, which is informal—and frequently judgmental—talk about people who are not present during the conversation. Gossip is a common communicative behavior in all sorts of social group settings, from neighborhoods to offices to churches and synagogues.[32]

• **gossip** Informal, and frequently judgmental, talk about people who are not present.

Many people frown on gossip—even those who engage in it themselves—because it frequently consists of spreading negative information about others. Although we sometimes gossip about people's positive qualities, such as talking about a coworker's new promotion, research shows that we are far more likely to gossip about a person's negative features or behaviors.[33] Moreover, studies indicate that most people enjoy hearing negative gossip more than positive gossip.[34] Mean-spirited gossip can

Difficult Conversations

Comforting a Grieving Friend

Imagine this: Your mom calls you to say that your high school friend Trevor was in a collision with a drunk driver. He had only minor injuries, but his younger brother Jayden was killed in the accident. Trevor attends a different college than you do, but you know you are likely to see him when you are home next week.

Now, consider this: You feel apprehensive about seeing Trevor because you aren't sure what to say to him. You want to provide comfort and help him deal with his grief. However, you're so worried about saying the wrong things that you consider not saying anything at all. Many people feel uncomfortable comforting others in times of loss—but you can use the following tips to craft an effective message.

- First, acknowledge the loss instead of ignoring it: "I'm so sorry to hear about Jayden. I know everyone will miss him greatly."

- Second, express sympathy for Trevor's feelings: "Words can't express how sorry I feel. Please know that my heartfelt sympathies are with you and your family."

- Third, offer a positive reflection of Jayden: "I will always remember Jayden's sense of humor and his infectious smile."

- Fourth, keep your comments focused on the deceased person and on the survivor. In an effort to express empathy, some people make statements such as "I know how you feel." Although that may sound helpful, it draws attention to you and away from the grieving friend you are trying to console.

- Finally, offer assistance: "Please remember I'm here for you, no matter what you need. I'll give you a call tomorrow to see if there's anything I can do for you."

Talking with someone who is grieving a significant loss is often difficult, but it is easier to do when you have an effective strategy. You may worry about making the "wrong" statements, but during times of grief, many people will appreciate any effort you make to comfort them.

---

embarrass people, however, by damaging their reputations and revealing personal, private information about them to others.

How, then, does engaging in gossip help us connect with others? The answer is that gossip serves to strengthen the social bonds between those who exchange it.[35] Like sharing secrets, sharing gossip with someone requires us to trust that person to handle the information sensitively. Thus, we don't typically share gossip with strangers or people we don't like; rather, we do so with people we trust and feel close to, reinforcing our personal relationships with them.

The utility of gossip has spurred a proliferation of gossip websites on the Internet, most of which provide gossip about celebrities and their lives and are extraordinarily popular. One such site—omg.yahoo.com—boasts 50 million unique visitors per month, a testament to how much people enjoy engaging in gossip about others.[36]

As we have seen, we can use language to express feelings of love and affection, provide comfort and support, and reinforce our social bonds through gossip. In these ways, language can serve to connect us to others. Language can also separate us from others by causing hurt, as the following discussion reveals.

Although gossip is frequently judgmental, sharing gossip can reinforce our social bonds to others.

Dave and Les Jacobs/Blend Images LLC

THE DARK SIDE OF COMMUNICATION

Crossing the Line: When Criticism Becomes Abuse

In personal relationships, when one person continually criticizes another in destructive rather than constructive ways, that behavior can qualify as *verbal abuse*. Verbal abuse can produce long-term psychological and emotional damage and can also be accompanied by physical aggression or violence.

"Laura" is a typical victim of verbal abuse. As she explains, she was constantly put down and demeaned by her ex-husband, even in front of others. She was made to feel inadequate, unimportant, and worthless. Unfortunately, those are common experiences for people who endure verbal abuse.

"I could never do anything right, in his opinion," she explains. "The food was never good enough, the house was never clean enough. I'm not thin enough. He calls me 'fat' and 'bitch' in front of our children and now my little boy has started calling me 'fat.' How am I supposed to react to that? He tells me I'm worthless. He won't give me money when I need it, says I don't pay the bills so why should he give me anything?"

Verbal abuse is especially damaging to children, who depend on their parents and loved ones for protection and who lack the ability to process criticism cognitively rather than emotionally.

J Walters/Shutterstock

According to the organization Prevent Child Abuse America, verbally abused children are likely to become depressed and socially withdrawn and to have difficulty making and keeping friends. That organization strongly encourages parents to seek help if they have difficulty managing stress so that they won't take their stress out on their children in the form of critical language.

LANGUAGE SEPARATES US FROM OTHERS

During election years, it is common for political candidates to run negative campaign advertisements that focus on the shortcomings of their opponent. Such ads often make misleading claims about the opponent's position on issues or derogatory statements about his or her character and values. Although viewers often perceive negative campaign ads as distasteful, these appeals can strongly influence voters by mobilizing them around their candidate of choice[37] and encouraging them to vote accordingly.[38] In these ways, the negative language in such advertisements is effective not in bringing people together but in separating them—ideologically, at least—from one another.

You may have grown up hearing that "sticks and stones might break my bones, but words can never hurt me." According to this common proverb, language has no power to cause people pain. Your own experiences, however, have probably taught you that the opposite is true: words can hurt us in profound and enduring ways. Two forms of language that can be especially harmful are criticisms and threats.

Criticisms **Criticism** consists of words that pass judgment on someone or something. When you say what you dislike about an organization's public relations campaign, a coworker's new reading glasses, or your grandmother's cooking, you're expressing criticism.

Criticism is often difficult to hear. Especially when it comes from people we respect or love, criticism can make us feel hurt, unappreciated, and incompetent. These reactions are magnified when we receive *destructive criticism*, which occurs when we feel that someone is criticizing us to put us down or destroy our self-confidence. As the "Dark Side" box describes, destructive criticism that is too frequent or harsh can constitute verbal abuse. Most of us would likely prefer to receive *constructive criticism*, as we do when we feel that someone is criticizing us to help us to improve.

Threats A second form of language that can cause hurt is a **threat**, a declaration of the intention to harm someone if the receiver does or doesn't do something specific

• **criticism** Words that pass judgment on someone or something.

• **threat** A declaration of the intention to harm someone.

("If you touch my car, I'll break your neck"). Statements such as those are intended to motivate or to prevent particular actions. Instead of using persuasion to accomplish those goals (a topic we'll take up later in this chapter), threats telegraph the promise of harm and cause fear. Threats of physical harm to another person, a person's family, or a person's property violate the law in most jurisdictions in the United States, even if the threatened harm is never enacted.

Criticisms and threats can separate us from others by causing emotional pain and fear. Those negative feelings are probably magnified when the person criticizing or threatening us is someone with whom we have close emotional ties, such as a family member, a good friend, or a romantic partner.

Thus far, we have seen how language can express who we are, connect us to others, and separate us from others. Words can also motivate us to behave in certain ways, a topic we explore next.

LANGUAGE MOTIVATES ACTION

One of marketing's most powerful tools for selling a product or a service is the *slogan*, a short and memorable phrase that will motivate people to become customers. Effective slogans become ingrained in our subconscious, causing us to recall them with minimal effort. How many times have you heard "Red Bull gives you wings," "L'Oréal—because you're worth it," and "Like a good neighbor, State Farm is there"? The purpose of an advertising slogan isn't just to be memorable, however: it's also to motivate you to buy the advertised product or service.

Just as advertisers use language in the form of slogans to motivate buying behavior, we can use various forms of language to motivate others to think or act in particular ways. Words can be powerfully persuasive if we choose them correctly. **Persuasion** is the process of convincing people that they should think or act in a certain way. Every time we watch a TV commercial, read a pop-up ad on the Internet or our smartphone, or listen to a political speech, someone is trying to influence what we believe or how we will behave.

Let's say you've decided to run in a 10-kilometer race to benefit the local children's hospital, and you're trying to persuade your relatives, friends, and coworkers to make pledges to sponsor you. What are some ways of asking for their sponsorship that would encourage them to agree?

Anchor and Contrast One strategy is to use what researchers call an **anchor-and-contrast approach**. First you draft a request so ambitious that few people will agree to do it. That sweeping request is the *anchor*. After people reject the anchor, you ask for what you actually want, the *contrast*, which will seem reasonable to most people by comparison to the anchor and thus encourage them to

• **persuasion** An attempt to motivate others, through communication, to adopt or to maintain a specific manner of thinking or doing.

• **anchor-and-contrast approach** A persuasion technique by which one precedes a desired request with a request that is much larger.

MichaelSvoboda/Getty Images

comply. To solicit sponsors for your 10K run, for instance, you could write a letter giving people the following sponsorship options:

- $40 per kilometer, or $400 in total
- $20 per kilometer, or $200 in total
- $10 per kilometer, or $100 in total
- $5 per kilometer, or $50 in total

If you simply asked people to pledge $50 or even $100, many probably would decline on the grounds that those amounts are too costly. But $50 doesn't seem like so much when it is contrasted with anchors of larger amounts, such as $200 and $400. In fact, it appears quite reasonable by comparison, and the fact that your potential sponsors will see it as such will likely increase the persuasive success of your appeal.[39]

Norm of Reciprocity You may have heard the old saying, "One good turn deserves another." This idea suggests that when someone gives you some type of gift or resource, you are expected to return the favor. Sociologist Alvin Gouldner called that expectation the **norm of reciprocity**.[40] Because of the norm of reciprocity, we should feel a sense of duty to help people who have helped us in the past.[41] Businesses and organizations appeal to reciprocity any time they offer you free samples of their products. You might employ that persuasive technique when soliciting sponsorships for your 10K race by reminding people of ways in which you have helped them in the past.

• norm of reciprocity The social expectation that favors should be reciprocated.

Social Validation A third persuasive strategy is to invoke the **social validation principle**, which maintains that people will comply with requests if they believe others are also complying.[42] Whenever advertisers say that "four out of five people preferred" a certain brand of car, refrigerator, or toilet bowl cleaner, they are hoping you will want to buy the same brand that most people are buying. The idea is that you gain social approval by acting the way others act. So, to the extent that social approval is important to you, the quest for approval can influence the decisions you make. When soliciting sponsors for your 10K race, you could invoke the social validation principle by pointing out how many others have already sponsored you.

• social validation principle The idea that people will comply with requests if they believe that others are also complying.

Expressing our identities, connecting us to others, separating us from others, and motivating action aren't the only functions that language serves. However, they are among the most relevant to our day-to-day lives as communicators.

Ways We Use and Abuse Language

We have seen that language serves a wide variety of functions. Now let's survey the ways in which language also varies in its form. Some forms, including humor, are generally positive and can produce good outcomes, such as entertaining others, strengthening relationships, and even contributing to healing. Other forms, such as hate speech, can cause devastating hurt. In this section, we explore several different forms of language—humor, euphemism, slang, defamation, profanity, and hate speech—and discover that many are neither entirely good nor entirely bad.

HUMOR: WHAT'S SO FUNNY?

A few years ago, psychologist Richard Wiseman designed a study with an ambitious goal: to discover the world's funniest joke. More than 2 million people from around the world visited his website and rated some 40,000 jokes for their level of humor. Here was the winning entry—the funniest joke in the world:

> *Two hunters are out in the woods when one of them collapses. He doesn't seem to be breathing, and his eyes are glazed. The other guy takes out his phone and calls the emergency services. He gasps: "My friend is dead! What can I do?" The operator says: "Calm down, I can help. First, let's make sure he's dead." There is a silence, then a gunshot is heard. Back on the phone, the guy says: "Okay, now what?"*

Not everyone finds that joke funny, and some may even find it offensive. Regardless, you can probably recognize the humor in it. The joke contains what researchers believe to be the most important aspect of humor: a violation of our expectations.[43] Most of us would interpret the operator's statement ("Let's make sure he's dead") as a suggestion to check the hunter's vital signs, not as a recommendation to shoot him. It's that twist on our expectations that makes the joke funny. In fact, researchers have discovered that specific parts of the brain process humor and that without the violation of expectations—the punch line—those neurological structures don't "light up" or provide the mental reward we associate with a good joke.[44]

Humor can enhance the closeness of our social and personal relationships. It can also demean or offend others if used inappropriately.

Nicolas McComber/Getty Images

Humor can enhance our communication and associations with others in many ways. It can bring us closer to people and make social interaction more pleasant and enjoyable.[45] It can defuse stress, such as the tension that occurs when people are in conflict with one another.[46] Within relationships, "inside jokes" can reinforce people's feelings of intimacy. Humor can provide so many personal and social benefits, in fact, that a good sense of humor is a strongly desired characteristic that both women and men seek in a romantic partner.[47]

Not all effects of humor are positive, however. Humor can also demean individuals and social or cultural groups, as in the case of racial jokes and gags about elderly people or persons with disabilities. Moreover, even when they are made without the intention to offend, jokes told at another's expense can cause embarrassment or distress and might even qualify as harassment.[48]

In 2017, comedian Steve Harvey stirred controversy after making jokes on his talk show that were widely interpreted as offensive to Asians. After the incident, he tweeted, "I offer my humblest apology for offending anyone, particularly those in the Asian community, last week. It was not my intention and the humor was not meant with any malice or disrespect whatsoever."[49] When using humor, it's therefore essential to take stock of your audience to make certain that your jokes will amuse rather than offend.

EUPHEMISMS: SUGAR COATING

Some topics are difficult or impolite to talk about directly. In those cases, we might use a **euphemism**, a vague, mild expression that symbolizes and substitutes for something that is more blunt or more harsh. Instead of saying that someone has died, for instance, we might say that he has "passed away," and rather than mentioning that she is pregnant, a woman might say that she's "expecting." You can probably think of many different euphemisms, including to "let go" (instead of to "fire") and to "sleep together" (instead of to "have sex"). After North Carolina governor Mark Sanford claimed to be hiking along the Appalachian Trail while he was actually visiting his mistress in Argentina in 2009, "hiking the Appalachian Trail" became a euphemism for having an extramarital affair.

• **euphemism** A vague, mild expression that symbolizes and substitutes for something blunter or harsher.

Typically, the euphemistic term sounds less harsh or less explicit than the term it stands for, and that's the point. We use euphemisms when we want to talk about sensitive topics without making others feel embarrassed or offended.[50] Yet euphemisms require more than just a technical understanding of the language (English, French, Japanese, and so on) in which they are made; they also require an understanding of cultural idioms. That understanding is necessary because euphemisms often have a literal meaning that differs from their euphemistic meaning. For example, at a literal level, the phrase "sleep together" simply means to engage in sleep while together. If you didn't realize that is a cultural euphemism for "have sex," then you wouldn't understand the meaning when it is used in that way.

SHARPEN Your Skills: *Slang*

Many groups of people have their own slang. Pair up with a classmate whose hobbies and interests are very different from yours, and learn some of the slang common to groups that pursue such interests. In a blog or journal entry, report on three such words.

Search

Job Title >

Work Responsibilities >

Grant Writer, Nonprofit Organization

Grant writers specialize in writing proposals or applications for funding for nonprofit organizations, such as educational and cultural institutions, community associations, research foundations, or special interest groups. Grant writers must have excellent communication skills and a particularly strong knowledge of language, policies, and industry-specific terminology and jargon. They also need to be able to research funding sources and cultivate a diversified network of funding sources.

SLANG: THE LANGUAGE OF CO-CULTURES

• **slang** Informal and unconventional words often understood only within a particular group.

Closely related to euphemism is **slang**, the use of informal and unconventional words that often are understood only by others in a particular group. Slang can serve an important social function by helping people to distinguish between those who do and don't belong to their particular social networks. If you grew up in Boston, for instance, you probably know that "Rhodie" is a slang term for people from nearby Rhode Island. In Australia, "snag" is slang for "sausage." If you don't know that "geggy" means "mouth," you're probably not from Scotland, and if you don't know whether you're in "T Town" (Texarkana) or "Big T" (Tucson), you're probably not a trucker.

• **jargon** Technical vocabulary of a certain occupation or profession.

A form of informal speech closely related to slang is **jargon**, the technical vocabulary of a certain occupation or profession. Jargon allows members of that occupation or profession to communicate with one another precisely and efficiently. For example, many law enforcement officers in North America talk to one another using *ten-codes*, or number combinations that represent common phrases. In that jargon, "10-4" means that you've received another person's message. Health care providers also use jargon specific to their profession—for instance, referring to a heart attack as a "myocardial infarction." Other occupations and professions that have their own jargon include attorneys, engineers, dancers, airplane pilots, television producers, and the military. You'll read about one career that benefits from a mastery of jargon in the "Putting Communication to Work" box.

Like humor and euphemisms, slang and jargon are neither inherently good nor inherently bad. As we have considered, those forms of language serve many positive purposes, among them reaffirming our membership in a particular social community. Whether you're into surfing or wine tasting, doing calligraphy or restoring vintage cars, learning and using the slang appropriate to those interests serves as a type of membership badge that connects you with others like you.

By the same token, however, using slang and jargon around people who don't understand it can make them feel like outsiders. If you're a police officer, saying that you're "10-7" instead of "done for the day" might make civilians around you feel excluded from the conversation, even if you're using that jargon for the sake of efficiency. For that reason you should consider how your use of slang and jargon might come across to others around you.

DEFAMATION: HARMFUL WORDS

In 2016, *Rolling Stone* magazine was sued by University of Virginia associate dean Nicole Eramo over a 2014 article about an alleged gang rape on campus. The article claimed that a female student had been sexually assaulted by several members of a fraternity and that Eramo had been indifferent to the student's suffering. Eramo's lawsuit ended in a $3 million verdict against the magazine and the journalist who wrote the article.

Eramo's claim was that *Rolling Stone* had engaged in **defamation**, language that harms a person's reputation or gives that person a negative image. Defamation comes in two forms. The first, *libel*, refers to defamatory statements made in print or some other fixed medium, such as a photograph or a motion picture. The second, *slander*, is a defamatory statement made aloud, within earshot of others.

For instance, let's say that Aliyah wants to open a day care center in a town where Toni also operates one. To discourage parents from using Aliyah's center, Toni circulates rumors that Aliyah has been charged with child molestation. That statement is defamatory because it harms Aliyah's reputation and could cause her financial damage in the form of lost business.

In 2016, a University of Virginia administrator sued *Rolling Stone* for defamation.

TheCoverVersion/Alamy Stock Photo

Does it matter whether Toni's accusation is true? Usually the answer is yes: under most legal systems, a statement must be false to be considered libel or slander. There are situations, however, when even a true statement can qualify as defamation. Those cases often involve public figures, such as politicians and celebrities, and they hinge on the importance of the information for the public. Disclosing in print that a senator has tested positive for HIV, for example, might qualify as libel even when it is true, *if* disclosing the information serves no prevailing public interest.

PROFANITY: OFFENSIVE LANGUAGE

Profanity is language that is considered vulgar, rude, or obscene in the context in which it is used. We sometimes call profane terms *swear words* or *curse words*, and they come in many forms. Some profane terms are meant to put down certain groups of people, as in calling a person a "bitch" or a "fag." (Many of those also qualify as instances of hate speech, our next topic.) Other terms attack religious beliefs or figures considered sacred by followers of a particular religion. Still others describe sexual acts or refer to people's sexual organs or bodily functions. Finally, some are general expressions of emotion, such as "Damn!"

Like other forms of language, profanity is context-specific: what makes a word profane is that it is considered rude or obscene in the language and context in which it is used. For instance, calling a woman a "bitch" might be profane, but using the same term to describe a female dog is not. In the United States, "fag" is a derogatory expression for a gay man, but to the British, it refers to a cigarette. Some swear words translate across languages; for example, the expression "Damn" in English is "Zut" in French and "Verflucht" in German and can be profane in all of them. Other words appear to be unique to certain languages; for instance, a Dutch speaker might say "Krijg de pest!" which translates to, "Go get infected with the plague!" Profanity has many different effects on social interaction. Often, it makes people feel uncomfortable or insulted. In recent years, some social groups have recognized that they can negate the effect of certain profane terms that refer to them by making the terms more commonplace, thus reducing or eliminating their shock value. That practice is called

• **defamation** Language that harms a person's reputation or image.

• **profanity** Language considered to be vulgar, rude, or obscene.

re-claiming the term. For instance, when homosexuals call one another "queers," their intent is not to offend but rather to remove the word's power to insult. Other social groups have supported efforts to eliminate certain insulting words from everyday speech. The movement "Spread the Word to End the Word," for example, encourages people never to call those with intellectual disabilities "retarded," because that term has derogatory implications.

Still, not all effects of profanity are negative. In certain contexts, the use of profanity can act as a social lubricant by maintaining an informal social atmosphere. Profanity is a common element in comedy, for instance, partly because it creates an expectation that nothing is taboo in that context and that ideas can flow freely. And, of course, many of us use profanity with close friends as a way not only to express ourselves, but to solidify social bonds through trust and honesty.

HATE SPEECH: PROFANITY WITH A HURTFUL PURPOSE

• **hate speech** Language used to degrade, intimidate, or dehumanize specific groups of people.

Hate speech is a specific form of profanity meant to degrade, intimidate, or dehumanize people based on their sex, national origin, sexual orientation, religion, race, disability status, or political or moral views.[51] Calling people derogatory names, intimidating them, making racist or homophobic taunts, and inciting violence against minorities might all qualify as hate speech.

Hate speech can occur in face-to-face contexts, and it is becoming increasingly common online.[52] In August 2019, a San Francisco–based web company dropped the website 8chan as a client after discovering that hate-filled rhetoric targeting immigrants was posted to that site shortly before a mass shooter killed 20 people at a shopping center in El Paso, Texas.[53] The site had previously posted racist material linked to a synagogue shooting in Poway, California, and two shootings in mosques in Christchurch, New Zealand. The company's CEO called 8chan "a cesspool of hate."[54] 8chan is only one of dozens of "hate websites" tracked by advocacy groups such the Southern Poverty Law Center.[55]

The rise of social media platforms such as Instagram, YouTube, and Twitter has provided additional avenues for the expression of hate speech. According to one report, 64 percent of U.S. teenagers have encountered racist, sexist, homophobic, or anti-religious hate speech on social media.[56] Social media platforms allow users to post images and messages that can easily reach thousands or even millions of viewers in a short period of time. Unfortunately, antisocial messages appear to multiply quickly. One study analyzed 21 million posts from 341,000 social media users and found that hate speech spreads faster, and to a much wider audience, than non-hateful speech.[57] Consequently, it is perhaps not surprising that most U.S. adults believe that hate speech is increasing, especially online, and that the major culprits are political divisiveness and the availability of social media for spreading hateful ideas.[58]

Social scientists recognize two broad ways in which hate speech is harmful.[59] For one, it traumatizes recipients—who are often already marginalized—by making them feel unwelcome, unvalued, and unsafe. Research shows that receiving or even witnessing hate speech can make people feel degraded,[60] erode trust in others,[61] and even make people more prejudiced toward others.[62] The negative effects aren't only psychological, though. One study even found that the negativity of racially motivated hate speech predicted suicide rates for ethnic immigrants.[63]

The second way in which hate speech is harmful is that it can incite physical violence. For example, hearing a hateful message about the LGTBQ community—such as those spread by members of the Westboro Baptist Church in Kansas[64]—may persuade people to enact violence against members of that community.[65] When hate speech is prevalent in an environment, such as in a town or workplace, it can also make prejudice and discrimination against minorities seem normal and acceptable, encouraging violence against those groups. One study found that racial minorities suffer an elevated risk of premature death simply from living in racially biased communities, whether they directly encounter hate speech or not.[66]

Hate speech is a controversial topic. Even though it is generally detested, efforts to curb it are often considered violations of the First Amendment of the U.S. Constitution, which protects the freedom of speech. Many U.S. states, colleges, and universities have instituted regulations prohibiting hate speech, but many of those regulations have been overturned when challenged in court. The U.S. Supreme Court has generally considered hate speech to be protected by the First Amendment unless it leads to imminent violence.[67]

As an alternative to outlawing hate speech, some have recently advocated a different approach. For instance, constitutional law professor Nadine Strossen argues that the solution to the problem of hate speech is not to censor it, but instead to counter it with *more* speech.[68] Her claim is that censoring offensive speech—such as disinviting college commencement speakers with whom students disagree—causes far more problems than it actually solves, even when it is done with positive intentions.[69] Strossen points out that engaging in *counterspeech*—messages that refute another person's ideas or claims—is far more effective at reducing hate speech than censoring or banning it.

In summary, language comes in many forms, including humor, euphemism, slang, libel and slander, profanity, and hate speech. Some, such as humor, generally have positive effects but can also produce unwanted negative outcomes. Other forms, such as profanity, are generally negative even though they can have positive effects on the people using them. Understanding the positive and negative aspects of these diverse forms of language helps us to appreciate the power and complexity of verbal communication.

Efforts to prohibit hate speech often conflict with the U.S. Constitution's protection of free speech.

Jim West/Alamy Stock Photo

Improving Your Use of Language

This section presents four pieces of advice for improving verbal communication. Some may be more relevant to one situation than another, but collectively they can serve as a useful road map for fine-tuning your language use. Specifically, we will explore how to separate opinions from factual claims, practice civil dialogue when discussing differences of opinion, speak at an appropriate level, and own your thoughts and feelings.

SEPARATE OPINIONS FROM FACTUAL CLAIMS

Many communicators have a tendency to confuse factual claims with personal opinions. In a 2018 Pew survey of U.S. American adults, for instance, participants were presented with 10 statements and were asked to classify each as either an opinion or a factual claim.[70] The statements, which were political in nature, included "Abortion should be legal in most cases," "Health care costs per person in the U.S. are the highest in the developed world," and "President Barack Obama was born in the United States." The Pew study reported discouraging findings: just 35 percent of adults correctly identified all of the opinions, and only 26 percent correctly identified all of the factual claims.

A factual claim makes an assertion that we can verify with evidence and show to be true or false ("I live in the United States"). An opinion expresses a personal judgment or preference that we could agree or disagree with but that is not true or false in an absolute sense ("I live in the greatest country on Earth"). Competent communicators know how to keep opinions and factual claims separate in verbal communication. Unfortunately, distinguishing factual claims from opinions is easier said than done, especially when we're dealing with strong opinions on emotionally heated issues. For example, correctly separating opinions from factual claims can be especially problematic when listening to a political speech or even a news report, because speakers may disguise opinions as factual claims. If we're unable to tell the difference, we risk supporting positions or voting for ideas based on faulty, untrustworthy data.

Let's say you and several friends are discussing an upcoming election in which you're choosing between two candidates. Half of you prefer Candidate C, the conservative, and the other half prefer Candidate L, the liberal. During your discussion, you hear various friends make the following statements:

- "Candidate C has more experience in government." That is a factual claim because we can show it to be true or false by looking at the candidates' records.

- "Candidate L is the better choice for our future." That is an opinion because it expresses a value judgment (this candidate is *better*) that we cannot objectively validate.

- "Candidate C is immoral." That is an opinion because the truth of the claim depends on the speaker's (in this case, your friend's) morals. Morals are subjective; therefore, the statement can't be proved true or false in an absolute sense.

- "Candidate L accepted bribes." That is a factual claim because it is possible to examine the evidence to discover whether it's true.

Opinions and factual claims require different types of responses. Suppose you tell me, "Candidate C has never held an elective office," and I reply by saying, "I disagree." That isn't a competent response. You have made a factual claim, which by definition is either true or false. Therefore, whether I agree with it is irrelevant. I can agree or disagree with an opinion, but a factual claim is either true or false no matter how I feel about it. If I had responded to your statement by saying "I think you're incorrect," that would be a competent reply because we would now be discussing the *truth* of your statement rather than my agreement with it.

How good are you at distinguishing opinions from factual claims? Check out "The Competent Communicator" box to find out.

As you develop that skill, keep these principles in mind.

- First, *opinions are opinions whether you agree with them or not*. The Pew study described above found that people tend to think statements they agree with are factual claims, whereas statements they disagree with are opinions. The truth is that your own agreement or disagreement with a statement is irrelevant as to whether the statement is an opinion or a factual claim. If you believe marijuana use should be legal in the United States, for instance, you might be inclined to call that statement a fact. It isn't, though. It is still a statement of opinion because it expresses an evaluation about what "should be."

- Second, *factual claims are factual claims whether they are true or not*. If you think it's untrue that men talk as much as women do, you might be inclined to call that statement an opinion, but it isn't. Even if it isn't true, it is still a factual claim because it expresses something that can be verified as either true or false by evidence.

- Third, *look for words that imply evaluation*. "Best," "worst," "greatest," and "most desirable" are clues that a statement is likely an opinion. For instance, the claim that "democracy is the best form of government" is an opinion, because that is a judgment call. In other words, people can genuinely disagree about which form of government is best. Be cautious, however, as the word "greatest" can also refer to quantities. Consider the claim "Defense spending accounts for the greatest portion of the federal budget." That is a factual claim, because it is either or true or false, regardless of differences in people's individual judgments.

- Finally, *watch for words that suggest action*. Terms such as "should" are often used to suggest a desirable course of action, as in the claim "Health care should be free for all." That is an opinion, because it is expressing an idea not about *what is* but *what should be*.

Although it's probably more difficult to separate opinions from facts when you feel strongly about an issue, that's often when it is most important to do so. Instead of telling others that their positions on sensitive issues are right or wrong, state that you agree or disagree with them. That language expresses your own position and acknowledges that different—even contradictory—opinions may also exist.

COMPETENT COMMUNICATOR

How Well Can You Distinguish Opinions from Factual Claims?

The ability to separate opinions from factual claims is an essential skill for effective verbal communication. How well can you spot the difference? Read each of the following statements. Assuming nothing more than what the statement tells you, indicate whether you think the statement is an opinion or a factual claim by placing a checkmark in the appropriate column.

Design Pics/Don Hammond

	opinion	factual claim
1. Lady Gaga is the best singer in the world.	____	____
2. Television was invented in the 1920s.	____	____
3. Religious people are happier than nonreligious people.	____	____
4. The United States is better off with a Republican as president.	____	____
5. Men talk as much as women do.	____	____
6. Same-sex couples should be allowed to adopt.	____	____
7. Children should be required to learn a foreign language.	____	____
8. Neil Armstrong was the first person to walk on the moon.	____	____
9. Dogs have a keener sense of smell than people do.	____	____
10. Recreational marijuana use should be legal in the United States.	____	____

Statements 1, 4, 6, 7, and 10 are all opinions. Statements 2, 3, 5, 8, and 9 are all factual claims. How well did you do? If you missed some of the answers, don't worry—distinguishing opinions from factual claims can be harder than it seems.

PRACTICE CIVIL DIALOGUE

Speaking of opinions, perhaps you've noticed that people often seem entrenched in their positions on controversial issues, from abortion, immigration, and gun control to climate change, vaccines, and the limits of privacy rights. Maybe you have also noticed that when you have a deeply held belief, it is harder to talk with those who think differently than you do, at least without arguing.

In 2018, for instance, the U.S. Supreme Court ruled in favor of Colorado baker Jack Phillips, who refused on religious grounds to bake a wedding cake for a same-sex couple.[71] The case hinged on whether business owners can refuse services based on their freedom of speech and freedom of religion, or whether they must abide by nondiscrimination laws that require equal treatment for all customers. In some ways, this case mirrored the conflict surrounding former Rowan County, Kentucky, clerk Kim Davis, who was jailed in 2015 for refusing to issue marriage licenses to same-sex couples in defiance of a federal court order.

Many Americans strongly believe that religious freedom is a bedrock of U.S. society and that individuals should never be forced to act in ways that are contrary to their religious convictions. Many others believe, instead, that religious freedom is never a valid excuse for discriminating against people in the provision of public services. That clash in beliefs makes it understandable why both the Supreme Court case[72] and the arrest of Kim Davis[73] prompted public protests.

Think about your own opinions on controversial issues such as these. When talking with others who think differently than you do—whether they are family members, friends, coworkers, or even strangers—it can be easy to experience opposing viewpoints as personal attacks. Many of us find that we quickly become angry and defensive when others disagree with our positions. Instead of listening in an open-minded manner to others' ideas, we impugn the other person's intelligence ("Only an idiot would think like you do") or morality ("You're a racist"). Even though such a reaction may make us feel better in the moment, it is easy to understand that arguing with and attacking others who believe differently than you is not particularly constructive. In fact, it can have the effect of creating a hostile environment or relationship and shutting down the possibility of further conversation.

A better approach is to practice **civil dialogue**, a process of engaging in honest, authentic, and respectful conversation with others, even about points of deep-seated disagreement. According to communication scholars John Genette, Clark Olson, and Jennifer Linde, Civil Dialogue® emerged as a structured procedure wherein people with differing viewpoints share their ideas with the help of a moderator.[74] However, many of the principles of civil dialogue can help you even in informal conversations with others.

Engaging in civil dialogue is not about being polite or "playing nice," and it isn't about creating safe spaces where people's ideas aren't questioned. Rather, civil dialogue encourages people to offer their opinions, listen earnestly to differing—even contradictory—viewpoints, and weigh the merits of what they hear. According to Genette, Olson, and Linde, civil communicators practice a number of specific skills. These include

- *Honesty.* Communicating in a civil manner requires us to be honest with ourselves and honest with others. Civil communicators don't modify the opinions they express simply because they know others will disagree; instead, they are clear about what they believe and why, and they welcome alternate points of view.

- *Care with language.* Civil communicators choose their words mindfully, so that they say precisely what they mean to say. In particular, they are careful not simply to copy catch-phrases or "talking points" they have heard from others, including from the media. Instead, they express their points of view in their own words.

- *Multipresence.* Although we may value "being in the moment," civil communicators remember that the present isn't all that matters. They are also mindful of the past and the future. When discussing an issue such as religious freedom versus discrimination, they would be cognizant of oppressions faced by minorities in the past, and they would also reflect on how their words and behaviors now could affect others in the future. In other words, they work to be "multipresent," or aware of the past, present, and future simultaneously.

- *Openness to change.* When we feel a strong sense of conviction in our positions, it can be easy to enter a conversation with the singular goal of changing other people's minds. Civil communicators also remain open to the possibility that their own minds can be changed. No matter how strongly they believe their own opinion is the right one, they remind themselves that alternate viewpoints can also have merit and that being open-minded is a strength, not a weakness.

- *Civil listening.* In a conversation about opposing points of view, many of us focus on what we plan to say and how we plan to say it. Civil dialogue is as much about what we don't say, however, as what we do. That is, it requires an ability and a willingness to listen to others, not simply to understand *how* they believe, but *why.* If you believe strongly that religious freedom protects people from acting

• **civil dialogue** A process of engaging in honest, authentic, and respectful conversation with others, even about points of deep-seated disagreement.

against their conscience, you might have a difficult time understanding how anyone could think that what Jack Phillips or Kim Davis did was wrong. Nonetheless, many people do. When you engage in civil listening with those who think differently than you, your goal is to understand why they think as they do. What values, experiences, belief systems, or other influences caused them to develop the opinions they have, and what leads them to remain committed to those positions?

The goal of civil dialogue is not to produce agreement or consensus. As you probably know from your own experience, changing a deeply held belief—whether your own or someone else's—sometimes feels impossible. Although they strive to be open to the possibility of change, civil communicators don't engage in conversation with change as a goal. They are willing to live with disagreement, even in their close relationships. Instead, they practice principles that help them express their viewpoints and consider opposing ideas in a constructive, mutually respectful manner.

* **I-statement** A statement that claims ownership of the communicator's feelings or thoughts.

* **you-statement** A statement that shifts responsibility for the communicator's feelings or thoughts to the other party in the communication.

USE CLEARLY UNDERSTANDABLE LANGUAGE

Another part of being an effective verbal communicator is knowing how simple or how complex your language should be for your audience. A competent instructor, for instance, knows to use simpler language when teaching an introductory course than when teaching an advanced course because students in each class will have different levels of understanding. When you use language that is too complex for your listeners, you are *talking over their heads*. If you have been in a situation when someone has talked over your head, you know how hard it can be to understand what the speaker is trying to say.

The opposite problem is *talking down* to people, or using language that is inappropriately simple. Talking down often happens by mistake. You might provide unnecessary detail when giving someone driving directions, for example, because you don't realize that he or she is familiar with the area. At other times, overly simple language is used on purpose. That behavior can make listeners feel patronized, disrespected, or even insulted.

SHARPEN Your Skills: *Speaking at an appropriate level*

Select a topic about which you know quite a bit, and imagine you were explaining that topic to two different groups. Write one paragraph representing how you would explain the topic to people who also have a sophisticated understanding of it. Write a second paragraph representing how you would explain it to people who know nothing about it. Then, in a blog or journal entry, describe how you used language differently in each paragraph.

Learning how to communicate better is an ongoing process.

arekmalang/123RF

OWN YOUR THOUGHTS AND FEELINGS

People often use language that shifts responsibility for their thoughts and feelings onto others. Perhaps, for example, when your academic adviser doesn't understand you, she typically says "You're not being clear," but when you don't understand her, she says "You're not paying attention." By using that language pattern, your adviser blames you for misunderstandings but takes no responsibility for her own role in the communication process. The real problem may be that she is not paying attention herself or is not using clearly understandable language.

Good communicators take responsibility for their thoughts and feelings by using I-statements rather than you-statements. An **I-statement** claims ownership of what a communicator is feeling or thinking, whereas a **you-statement** shifts that responsibility to the other person. Instead of saying, "You're not being clear," your adviser might say, "I'm having a hard time understanding you."

	You-Statement	I-Statement
TABLE 2 EXAMPLES OF YOU-STATEMENTS AND I-STATEMENTS	You're making me mad.	I'm mad right now.
	You're not listening to me.	I'm feeling ignored.
	You don't know what you're doing.	I don't think this task is getting done right.
	You hurt my feelings.	My feelings are hurt.
	You're not making any sense.	I'm having trouble understanding you.

Rather than saying, "You make me mad," you might say, "I'm angry right now." Table 2 provides examples of you-statements and I-statements.

I-statements don't ignore the problem; instead, they allow the communicator to claim ownership of his or her feelings. That ownership is important, because it acknowledges that the individual controls how he or she thinks and feels. Remember that other people can't control our thoughts and feelings unless we let them. Effective communicators therefore speak in ways that acknowledge responsibility for and ownership of the ways they feel and think.

You were not born using language. Rather, you had to learn how to use it. You can also *learn* to use it better. By distinguishing opinions from statements of fact, learning to engage in disagreement constructively, speaking at a level that is appropriate for your audience, and taking ownership of your thoughts and feelings, you will be empowered to express yourself effectively in a broad range of social and professional situations.

For REVIEW

- **What are the defining characteristics of language?**

  Language is a structured system of symbols used for communicating meaning. Language is symbolic, usually arbitrary, and rule-governed; it has layers of meaning and varies in clarity; and it is bound by context and culture.

- **For what reasons do people use language?**

  People use language to express who they are, to connect to others, to separate themselves from others, and to motivate action. Common uses and abuses of language include humor, euphemism, slang, defamation, profanity, and hate speech.

- **How can you use language more effectively?**

  You can improve your language skills by separating opinions from factual claims, engaging in civil dialogue, speaking at an appropriate level for your audience, and owning your thoughts and feelings.

KEY TERMS

NOTES

1. See Berwick, R. C., & Chomsky, N. (2016). *Why only us: Language and evolution.* MIT Press. https://doi.org/10.7551/mitpress/9780262034241.001.0001

2. Lehrer, B. (2015, October 26). Why all words deserve a spot in the dictionary. *The Brian Lehrer Show/WNYC radio.* http://www.wnyc.org/story/why-all-words-deserve-spot-dictionary/

3. Pinker, S. (2007). *The stuff of thought: Language as a window into human nature.* Viking.

4. Jones, M. N., Gruenenfelder, T. M., & Recchia, G. (2018). In defense of spatial models of semantic representation. *New Ideas in Psychology, 50,* 54–60. https://doi.org/10.1016/j.newideapsych.2017.08.001; Ogden, C. K., & Richards, I. A. (1927). *The meaning of meaning: A study of the influence of language upon thought and of the science of symbolism* (2nd ed.). Harcourt Brace. https://doi.org/10.17613.M6NN77

5. Faletto, J. (2017, December 7). These are the 70 most beautiful words in English, according to a survey. *Curiosity.com.* https://curiosity.com/topics/these-are-the-70-most-beautiful-words-in-english-according-to-a-survey-curiosity/

6. Oxford University Press. (2013). *Paperback Oxford English Dictionary.* Author.

7. See Leviton, L. C. (2015). Evaluation practice and theory: Up and down the ladder of abstraction. *American Journal of Evaluation, 36*(2), 238–242. https://doi.org/10.1177/1098214015573070; see also Hayakawa, S. I., & Hayakawa, A. R. (1991). *Language in thought and action.* Harcourt.

8. See Samovar, L. A., Porter, R. E., McDaniel, E. R., & Roy, C. S. (2015). *Intercultural communication: A reader* (14th ed.). Cengage.

9. Regier, T., & Xu, Y. (2017). The Sapir-Whorf hypothesis and inference under uncertainty. *Wires Cognitive Science, 8*(6), e1440. https://doi.org/10.1002/wcs.1440

10. Wolff, P., & Holmes, K. J. (2011). Linguistic relativity. *Wiley Inter-Disciplinary Reviews: Cognitive Science, 2*(3), 253–265. https://doi.org/10.1002/wcs.104

11. For more detail on the Sapir-Whorf hypothesis, see O'Neill, S. P. (2015). Sapir-Whorf hypothesis. In K. Tracy, C. Ilie, & T. Sandel (Eds.), *The international encyclopedia of language and social interaction.* Wiley-Blackwell. https://doi.org/10.1002/9781118611463

12. For more detail on criticisms of the Sapir-Whorf hypothesis, see McWhorter, J. H. (2014). *The language hoax: Why the world looks the same in any language.* Oxford University Press.

13. Alter, A. (2013, May 29). The power of names. *The New Yorker.* https://www.newyorker.com/tech/elements/the-power-of-names

14. Steele, K. M., & Smithwick, L. E. (1989). First names and first impressions: A fragile relationship. *Sex Roles, 21,* 517–523.

15. Rubinstein, Y., & Brenner, D. (2014). Pride and prejudice: Using ethnic-sounding names and inter-ethnic marriages to identify labour market discrimination. *Review of Economic Studies, 81*(1), 389–425. https://doi.org/10.1093/restud/rdt031; see also Bertrand, M., & Mullainathan, S. (2004). Are Emily and Greg more employable than Lakisha and Jamal? A field experiment on labor market discrimination. *American Economic Review, 94*(4), 991–1013. https://doi.org/10.1257/0002828042002561

16. Sang-hun, C. (2014, December 3). North Korea has room for only one Jong-un. *The New York Times.* http://www.nytimes.com/2014/12/04/world/asia/kim-jong-un-north-korea-name-ban.html?_r=0

17. Saul, H. (2016, March 14). Is your name now "banned" in Saudi Arabia? *The Independent.* http://www.independent.co.uk/news/world/middle-east/is-your-name-now-banned-in-saudi-arabia-9192298.html

18. Zhang, Y. B., & Giles, H. (2018). Communication accommodation theory. In Y. Y. Kim (Ed.), *The international encyclopedia of intercultural communication* (pp. 95–108). Wiley-Blackwell. https://doi.org/10.1002/9781118783665

19. Kline, S. L., Simunich, B., & Weber, H. (2009). The use of equivocal messages in responding to corporate challenges. *Journal of Applied Communication Research, 37*(1), 40–58. https://doi.org/10.1080/00909880802592623; Bull, P. (2008). "Slipperiness,

evasion, and ambiguity": Equivocation and facework in noncommittal political discourse. *Journal of Language and Social Psychology, 27*(4), 333–344. https://doi.org/10.1177/0261927X08322475

20. Bull, 2008.

21. Daly, J. A., Diesel, C. A., & Weber, D. (1994). Conversational dilemmas. In W. R. Cupach, & B. H. Spitzberg (Eds.), *The dark side of interpersonal communication* (pp. 127–156). Lawrence Erlbaum Associates. https://doi.org/10.4324/9780203936849

22. Huston, T. L., Caughlin, J. P., Houts, R. M., Smith, S. E., & George, L. J. (2001). The connubial crucible: Newlywed years as predictors of marital delight, distress, and divorce. *Journal of Personality and Social Psychology, 80*(2), 237–252. https://doi.org/10.1037/0022-3514.80.2.237

23. Pauley, P. M., Floyd, K., & Hesse, C. (2015). The stress-buffering effects of a brief dyadic interaction before an acute stressor. *Health Communication, 30*(7), 646–659. https://doi.org/10.1080/10410236.2014.888385; Floyd, K., & Riforgiate, S. (2008). Affectionate communication received from spouses predicts stress hormone levels in healthy adults. *Communication Monographs, 75*(4), 351–368. https://doi.org/10.1080/03637750802512371

24. Floyd, K., Mikkelson, A. C., Tafoya, M. A., Farinelli, L., La Valley, A. G., Judd, J., Davis, K. L., Haynes, M. T., & Wilson, J. (2007). Human affection exchange: XIV. Relational affection predicts resting heart rate and free cortisol secretion during acute stress. *Behavioral Medicine, 32*(4), 151–156. https://doi.org/10.3200/BMED.32.4.151-156

25. Floyd, K., Pauley, P. M., Hesse, C., Eden, J., Veksler, A. E., & Woo, N. T. (2018). Supportive communication is associated with markers of immunocompetence. *Southern Communication Journal, 83*(4), 229–244. https://doi.org/10.1080/1041794X.2018.1488270

26. Floyd, K., Mikkelson, A. C., Tafoya, M. A., Farinelli, L., La Valley, A. G., Judd, J., Haynes, M. T., Davis, K. L., & Wilson, J. (2007). Human affection exchange: XIII. Affectionate communication accelerates neuroendocrine stress recovery. *Health Communication, 22*(2), 123–132. https://doi.org/10.1080/10410230701454015

27. Floyd, K., Veksler, A. E., McEwan, B., Hesse, C., Boren, J. P., Dinsmore, D. R., & Pavlich, C A. (2017). Social inclusion predicts lower blood glucose and low-density lipoproteins in healthy adults. *Health Communication, 32*(8), 1039–1042. https://doi.org/10.1080/10410236.2016.1196423

28. Mansson, D. H. (2013). College students' mental health and their received affection from their grandparents. *Communication Research Reports, 30*(2), 157–168. https://doi.org/10.1080/08824096.2012.763028

29. Yamazaki, R., Christensen, L., Skov, K., Chang, C.-C., Damholdt, M. F., Sumioka, H., Nishio, S., & Ishiguro, H. (2016). Intimacy in phone conversations: Anxiety reduction for Danish seniors with Hugvie. *Frontiers in Psychology, 7*, article 537. https://doi.org/10.3389/fpsyg.2016.00537

30. Greeting Card Association. (2019). Industry information, trends and statistics. https://www.greetingcard.org/industry-resources/industry-information/; Paswan, A. K., & Subramanian, S. (2015). Communication of feelings and relationship: Greeting card buying behavior. In E. J. Wilson, & J. F. Hair (Eds.), *Proceedings of the 1996 Academy of Marketing Science (AMS) annual conference* (pp. 7–13). Springer International. https://doi.org/10.1007/978-3-319-13144-3

31. Blower, J., & Sharman, R. (2019). To grieve or not to grieve (online)? Interactions with deceased Facebook friends. *Death Studies.* Advance online publication. https://doi.org/10.1080/07481187.2019.162937

32. Dores, T. C., Beersma, B., Dijkstra, M. T., & Bechtoldt, M. N. (2019). The bright and dark side of gossip for cooperation in groups. *Frontiers in Psychology, 10*, 1374. https://doi.org/10.3389/fpsyg.2019.01374

33. McAndrew, F. T., Bell, E. K., & Garcia, C. M. (2007). Who do we tell and whom do we tell on? Gossip as a strategy for status enhancement. *Journal of Applied Social Psychology, 37*(7), 1562–1577. https://doi.org/10.1111/j.1559-1816.2007.00227.x

34. See De Backer, C. J. S., Nelissen, M., Vyncke, P., Braeckman, J., & McAndrew, F. T. (2007). Celebrities: From teachers to friends. A test of two hypotheses on the adaptiveness of celebrity gossip. *Human Nature, 18*(4), 334–354. https://doi.org/10.1007/s12110-007-9023-z

35. Wu, J., Balliet, D., & Van Lange, P. A. (2016). Reputation, gossip, and human cooperation. *Social and Personality Psychology Compass, 10*(6), 350–364. https://doi.org/10.1111/spc3.12255

36. eBizMBA. (2019, August). Top 15 most popular celebrity gossip websites. *eBizMBA Rank.* http://www.ebizmba.com/articles/gossip-websites

37. Song, H., Nyhuis, D., & Boomgaarden, H. (2019). A network model of negative campaigning: The structure and determinants of negative campaigning in multiparty systems. *Communication Research, 46*(2), 273–294. https://doi.org/10.1177/0093650217712596

38. Utych, S. M. (2018). Negative affective language in politics. *American Politics Research, 46*(1), 77–102. https://doi.org/10.1177/1532673X17693830

39. Loschelder, D. D., Friese, M., & Trötschel, R. (2017). How and why precise anchors distinctly affect anchor recipients and senders. *Journal of Experimental Social Psychology, 70*, 164–176. https://doi.org/10.1016/j.jesp.2016.11.001

40. Gouldner, A. W. (1960). The norm of reciprocity: A preliminary statement. *American Sociological Review, 25*(2), 161–178. https://doi.org/10.2307/2092623; see also Mahmoodi, A., Bahrami, B., & Mehring, C. (2018). Reciprocity of social influence. *Nature Communications, 9*, 2474. https://doi.org/10.1038/s41467-018-04925-y

41. Murnighan, J. K. (2015). Reciprocity. In C. Cooper (Ed.), *Wiley encyclopedia of management.* Wiley. https://doi.org/10.1002/9781118785317

42. Casiraghi, L., Faigenbaum, G., Chehtman, A., & Sigman, M. (2018). Social validation influences individuals' judgments about ownership. *Frontiers in Integrative Neuroscience, 12*, 2. https://doi.org/10.3389/fnint.2019.00002

43. Chen, H. C., Chan, Y. C., Dai, R. H., Liao, Y. J., & Tu, C. H. (2017). Neurolinguistics of humor. In S. Attardo (Ed.), *The Routledge handbook of language and humor* (pp. 282–294). Taylor & Francis. https://doi.org/10.4324/9781315731162

44. Campbell, D. W., Wallace, M. G., Modirrousta, M., Polimeni, J. O., McKeen, N. A., & Reiss, J. P. (2015). The neural basis of humour comprehension and humour appreciation: The roles of the temporoparietal junction and superior frontal gyrus. *Neuropsychologia, 79*(A), 10–20. https://doi.org/10.1016/j.neuropsychologia.2015.10.013; Mensen, A., Poryazova, R., Schwartz, S., & Khatami, R. (2014). Humor as a reward mechanism: Event-related potentials in the healthy and diseased brain. *PLoS One, 9*(1), e85978. https://doi.org/10.1371/journal.pone.0085978

45. Martin, R. A., & Ford, T. E. (2018). *The psychology of humor: An integrative approach* (2nd ed.). Academic Press.

46. Booth-Butterfield, M., & Wanzer, M. B. (2017). Humor, stress, and coping. In C. Robert (Ed.), *The psychology of humor at work* (pp. 76–95). Routledge. https://doi.org/10.4324/9781315671659

47. Hone, L. S., Hurwitz, W., & Lieberman, D. (2015). Sex differences in preferences for humor: A replication, modification, and extension. *Evolutionary Psychology, 13*(1), 167–181. https://doi.org/10.1177/147470491501300110

48. Knegtmans, J. J., Van, D. W., Mooijman, M., Van, L. N., Rintjema, S., & Wassink, A. (2018). The impact of social power on the evaluation of offensive jokes. *Humor, 31*(1), 85–104. https://doi.org/10.1515/humor-2017-0106

49. McDermott, M. (2017, January 17). Steve Harvey apologizes for racist jokes about Asians. *USA Today*. https://www.usatoday.com/story/life/people/2017/01/17/steve-harvey-apologizes-racist-jokes-about-asian-men/96668644/

50. Fernández, E. C. (2010). Euphemistic strategies in politeness and face concerns. *Pragmalingüística, 13*, 77–86. https://doi.org/10.25267/Pragmalinguistica.2017.i25

51. See, e.g., Malmasi, S., & Zampieri, M. (2018). Challenges in discriminating profanity from hate speech. *Journal of Experimental & Theoretical Artificial Intelligence, 30*(2), 187–202. https://doi.org/10.1080/0952813X.2017.1409284

52. Álvarez-Benjumea, A., & Winter, F. (2018). Normative change and culture of hate: An experiment in online environments. *European Sociological Review, 34*(3), 223–237. https://doi.org/10.1093/esr/jcy005; Guynn, J. (2019, February 13). If you've been harassed online, you're not alone. More than half of Americans say they've experienced hate. *USA Today*. https://www.usatoday.com/story/news/2019/02/13/study-most-americans-have-been-targeted-hateful-speech-online/2846987002/

53. Elfrink, T. (2019, August 5). "A cesspool of hate": U.S. web firm drops 8chan after El Paso shooting. *Washington Post*. https://www.washingtonpost.com/nation/2019/08/05/chan-dropped-cloudflare-el-paso-shooting-manifesto/

54. Ibid.

55. Southern Poverty Law Center. (2019). https://www.splcenter.org/fighting-hate/extremist-files/groups

56. Clement, J. (2018, December 4). Percentage of teenagers in the United States who have encountered hate speech on social media platforms as of April 2018, by type. *Statista*. https://www.statista.com/statistics/945392/teenagers-who-encounter-hate-speech-online-social-media-usa/

57. Mathew, B., Dutt, R., Goyal, P., & Mukherjee, A. (2019, June). Spread of hate speech in online social media. In *Proceedings of the 10th ACM Conference on Web Science* (pp. 173–182). ACM.

58. Research Releases in Culture & Media. (2019, July 16). U.S. adults believe hate speech has increased—mainly online. *Barna.com*. https://www.barna.com/research/hate-speech-increased/

59. Maitra, I., & McGowan, M. K. (2012). Introduction and overview. In I. Maitra, & M. K. McGowan (Eds.), *Speech and harm: Controversies over free speech* (pp. 1–23). Oxford University Press. https://doi.org/10.1093/acprof:oso/9780199236824.001.0001

60. Gelber, K., & McNamara, L. (2016). Evidencing the harms of hate speech. *Social Identities, 22*(3), 324–341. https://doi.org/10.1080/13504630.2015.1128810

61. Näsi, M., Räsänen, P., Hawdon, J., Holkeri, E., & Oksanen, A. (2015). Exposure to online hate material and social trust among Finnish youth. *Information Technology & People, 28*(3), 607–622. https://doi.org/10.1108/ITP-09-2104-0198

62. Soral, W., Bilewicz, M., & Winiewski, M. (2018). Exposure to hate speech increases prejudice through desensitization. *Aggressive Behavior, 44*(2), 136–146. https://doi.org/10.1002/ab.21737

63. Mullen, B., & Smyth, J. M. (2004). Immigrant suicide rates as a function of ethnophaulisms: Hate speech predicts death. *Psychosomatic Medicine, 66*(3), 343–348. https://doi.org/10.1097/01.psy.0000126197.59447.b3

64. Phelps-Roper, M. (2019). *Unfollow: A memoir of loving and leaving the Westboro Baptist Church*. Farrar, Straus and Giroux/Macmillan.

65. See *Chaplinsky v. State of New Hampshire*, 315 U.S. 568, for an example of speech that incited physical violence that was deemed unprotected by the U.S. First Amendment.

66. Leitner, J. B., Hehman, E., Ayduk, O., & Mendoza-Denton, R. (2016). Blacks' death rate due to circulatory diseases is positively related to whites' explicit racial bias: A nationwide investigation using Project Implicit. *Psychological Science, 27*(10), 1299–1311. https://doi.org/10.1177/0956797616658450

67. Tsesis, A. (2013, November 15). Inflammatory hate speech: Offense versus incitement. *Minnesota Law Review, 97*. http://papers.ssrn.com/sol3/papers.cfm?abstract_id=2234152

68. Strossen, N. (2018). *Hate: Why we should resist it with free speech, not censorship*. Oxford University Press.

69. Strossen, N. (2018, May 1). Don't silence graduation speakers: Fight hate speech with more speech. *USA Today*. https://www.usatoday.com/story/opinion/2018/05/01/censorship-hate-speech-freedom-first-amendment-column/564868002/

70. Mitchell, A., Gottfried, J., Barthel, M., & Sumida, N. (2018, June 18). *Distinguishing between factual and opinion statements in the news*. Pew Research Center. https://www.journalism.org/2018/06/18/distinguishing-between-factual-and-opinion-statements-in-the-news/

71. *Masterpiece Cakeshop, Ltd., et al. v. Colorado Civil Rights Commission, et al.*, 584 U.S. ___ (2018); 138 S. Ct. 1719.

72. Sherman, M., Hughes, R., & Aubert, A. (2017, December 5). Protesters gather as Supreme Court wrestles with case of wedding cake for same-sex couple. *WJLA*. https://wjla.com/news/local/protesters-outside-supreme-court-ahead-of-historic-case-on-wedding-cake-for-gay-couple

73. CBS News. (2015, September 8). Steadfast supporters boost efforts to free Kim Davis. https://www.cbsnews.com/news/kentucky-county-clerk-kim-davis-supporters-step-up-protest-efforts-outside-jail/

74. Genette, J., Olson, C. D., & Linde, J. (2018). *Hot topics, cool heads: A handbook for civil dialogue*. Kendall Hunt.

5

CNN/Handout/Getty Images

COMMUNICATING NONVERBALLY

Symbols of Resistance

Communication serves many purposes, including as a means of protesting perceived injustices. On June 5, 1989, an unidentified Chinese man became an icon of resistance by standing in front of a parade of tanks leaving Tiananmen Square in Beijing. The tanks had been used as part of the Chinese military's suppression of student-led pro-democracy protests the day before. As the lead tank attempted to pass the man on the street, he repeatedly changed his position to obstruct the tank's progress. Many other notable examples exist of people using nonverbal behaviors to protest social inequity. These include the Black Power movement's raised fist, quarterback Colin Kaepernick's taking a knee during the national anthem, and the "hands up, don't shoot" gesture used to protest police violence after the 2014 shooting of Michael Brown. In each instance, the gesture or stance has become a powerful visual symbol of resistance to injustice.

As You READ

- How do people communicate nonverbally?
- How do culture and sex influence nonverbal behavior?
- In what ways can you improve your nonverbal communication skills?

Nonverbal communication is powerful stuff. Sometimes the smallest action—a smile, a depressed vocal tone, a raised fist—can send unmistakable messages about ourselves to others. So much of what we learn about other people's thoughts and feelings comes not through listening to their words but through observing their body language—watching their facial expressions, seeing how they move and gesture, and taking note of their eye contact. Those and other behaviors can "speak" volumes about people in efficient and sometimes subtle ways.

The Nature and Functions of Nonverbal Communication

On the TV sitcom *Modern Family,* Gloria Pritchett (played by Sofía Vergara) is seldom shy about expressing frustration with her husband, Jay, or her sons, Manny and Joe. She frequently communicates her feelings through her facial expressions, posture, and tone of voice when she's annoyed. What makes nonverbal behavior such an effective form of communication? We'll find out in this section, first by differentiating nonverbal from verbal communication and then by examining six of its most important characteristics.

WHAT IS NONVERBAL COMMUNICATION?

Nonverbal means just what it sounds like—not verbal. Nonverbal communication requires neither words nor language. How do we communicate with others, if not with words and language?

The answer is, in many ways. We can tell a great deal about people by watching their facial expressions, for instance, or by listening to the tone of their voice. Think about it: when you listen to your doctor tell you the results of your recent blood tests, you might hear tension in her voice and determine that something is wrong, or you might see a pleasant look on her face and conclude that everything is fine. We also interpret people's gestures and the way they carry themselves: you see two teenage boys wrestling with each other and determine from their behaviors that they are playing rather than genuinely fighting.

Sometimes we even perceive others based on the way they use their time and the space around them. Perhaps you try talking with your boss about your recent evaluation and you feel ignored because she keeps looking at her iPhone. People routinely communicate more information through their nonverbal behaviors than they do through spoken language. So when it comes to communication, actions often do speak louder than words.

We can define **nonverbal communication** as those behaviors and characteristics that convey meaning without the use of words. Nonverbal communication behaviors sometimes *accompany* verbal messages, to clarify or reinforce them. For instance, if someone asks you which direction to go to find the bookstore, and you point and say, "It's that way," your nonverbal behavior (pointing) clarifies the meaning of your verbal message. If you just say, "It's that way" without pointing, your verbal message is ambiguous—and not especially helpful. At other times, however, nonverbal communication behaviors convey meaning on their own. If you ask me where the bookstore is and I shrug my shoulders, you will probably infer from my behavior that I don't know, even though I never actually said so.

Nonverbal behavior is a powerful way of communicating, and it comes naturally to many of us. In fact, we often engage in nonverbal behavior so effortlessly that you might wonder why you need to study it. The truth is, even though we frequently enact nonverbal behaviors and encounter them in others, there's a lot more to interpreting them than you might think.

• **nonverbal communication**
Behaviors and characteristics that convey meaning without the use of words.

On the basis of nonverbal behaviors, we interpret the actions of others as playful rather than aggressive.

Stephen Mullon/The Image Bank/Getty Images

SIX CHARACTERISTICS OF NONVERBAL COMMUNICATION

It's difficult to imagine life without nonverbal communication. The capacity to communicate without words is critical for those lacking in language ability. Such individuals include infants, who haven't yet learned how to speak, and people with certain neurological problems, like the effects of a stroke, that might limit their language use. But even people with language ability depend immensely on nonverbal communication. Because she had only a limited knowledge of Spanish, for instance, Bergitta relied heavily on nonverbal behaviors while traveling through Bolivia, Uruguay, and Argentina after graduation. She was frequently amazed at how well she could understand others simply by observing their gestures and facial expressions. Her communication was more challenging than it would have been if she had known the language, but she was still able to understand—and to be understood by others—through nonverbal behaviors.

Let's take a look at some of the most compelling reasons why nonverbal communication plays such an important role in human interaction.

Nonverbal Communication Is Present in Most Communication Contexts Whether you talk with people one-on-one or in a group, you have access not only to their spoken words, but also to several dimensions of nonverbal communication. For instance, you might tell from his facial expression that your supervisor is bored at a business lunch and eager to go home. At a party, you can judge from the tone of her voice when your host is being serious and when she's kidding. Even the way people dress and smell can send you information. Glancing around the auditorium at a large business event, you might be able to guess which people are managers and which are staff members by the formality of their clothing. We are flooded with nonverbal signals in many kinds of social situations.

In other communication contexts, such as talking on the telephone and sending e-mail, we don't have access to as many nonverbal cues as we do in face-to-face conversation. We still make use of what's available, however. Even if we haven't met those to whom we're speaking on a two-way radio, we can make judgments about them from certain qualities of their voices—noticing, for example, how fast they're talking, how loudly, with what tone, and with what type of accent. In electronically mediated communication—such as e-mail, instant messaging, and text messaging—we can introduce nonverbal cues through the use of **emoji**, cartoon depictions of faces and other objects that first became popular on Japanese cell phone services (Figure 1). Emojis have become so popular, in fact, that the *Oxford English Dictionary* named the "face with tears of joy" emoji as its 2015 Word of the Year.[1] Other cues that help us make judgments in electronic media are pauses and the use of all capital letters.

• **emoji** Cartoon depictions of faces and other objects.

Most human communication includes at least some form of nonverbal behavior, and when we have only a few nonverbal signals to go on, we pay extra attention to those cues. For example, vocal characteristics, such as the tone and sound of someone's voice, are important nonverbal cues in face-to-face conversation, but they are even more important on the telephone, where so many other nonverbal signals are unavailable. By the same token, when we lose the ability to use one of our senses in our communications, we typically compensate by relying more heavily on the remaining ones. People who are deaf pay extra attention to visual cues when communicating with others because they are unable to interpret vocal characteristics. Similarly, individuals with impaired vision often rely more heavily on hearing and touch to help them communicate, because they are unable to see gestures and facial expressions.

Nonverbal Communication Often Conveys More Information than Verbal Communication Go to the self-help section of almost any bookstore, and open up such titles as *How to Read a Person Like a Book* and *The Power of Nonverbal Communication: What You Do Is More Important Than What You Say*.[2] You'll probably get the

FIGURE 1
EMOJI

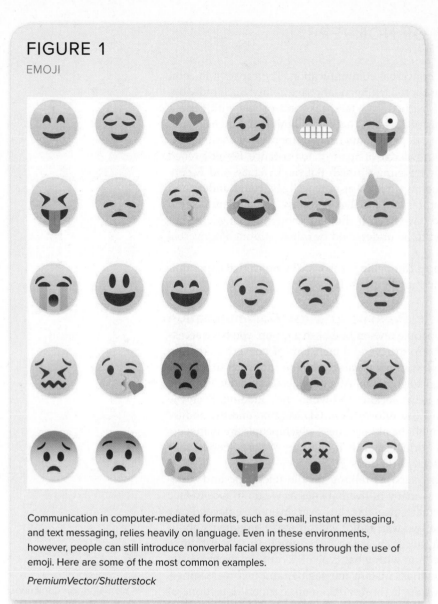

Communication in computer-mediated formats, such as e-mail, instant messaging, and text messaging, relies heavily on language. Even in these environments, however, people can still introduce nonverbal facial expressions through the use of emoji. Here are some of the most common examples.

PremiumVector/Shutterstock

impression that nearly all the information we get by communicating with others comes through nonverbal behavior. In fact, some unreliable but frequently cited studies have estimated that as much as 93 percent of meaning is transmitted nonverbally, leaving only 7 percent to be accounted for by the words we use.[3] Nonverbal communication isn't quite that powerful, however. More realistic estimates from nonverbal communication scholar Judee Burgoon suggest that 65 to 70 percent of meaning comes from nonverbal clues, with 30 to 35 percent coming from language.[4] In many situations, therefore, we do communicate more information through nonverbal behavior than we do through our words.

The most likely reason that nonverbal communication adds up to such a significant percentage is its use of many **nonverbal channels**, or behavioral forms of expression. The interpretation of some of those channels, including facial expressions, gestures, and personal appearance, relies on our sense of vision. Vocal characteristics—such as loudness, pitch, and tone of voice—engage our sense of hearing. We often express different messages with touch, such as a handshake and a hug, and we convey subtle messages about attraction to others through our use of smell.

• **nonverbal channels**
The various behavioral forms that nonverbal communication takes.

We sometimes rely on clues from nonverbal channels to make sense of a situation when talking isn't a good option. Rick has learned that his alcoholic mother, Claudia, has very unpredictable mood swings. When he gets home from school each day, he's never sure how she'll be feeling. Some days she's happy and outgoing; other days she's sullen and withdrawn. Occasionally, she'll start yelling at the slightest provocation. Over time, Rick has noticed that he can determine Claudia's mood without even talking to her: he needs only to look at her posture and facial expression to tell whether she's cheerful, depressed, or angry.

Nonverbal Communication Is Usually Believed over Verbal Communication It's not uncommon to get conflicting messages from what a person says and what he or she does. Most of the time, we believe the nonverbal clues.[5] Let's say you're waiting for your friend Joel at a coffee shop. When he walks in, Joel slumps into the seat next to you, rolls his eyes, and sighs heavily. You ask him how he's doing, and he says "Oh, it's been a *great* day." Joel's verbal behavior is sending you one message ("I'm having a great day"), but his nonverbal behavior is suggesting something quite different ("I'm having a terrible day"). Which of these contradictory messages do you believe? Most of us would put more stock in what Joel is *doing* than in what he is *saying*. In other words, we would believe his nonverbal message.

Why do we put our trust in nonverbal communication? Experts think we do so because most of us believe people have a harder time controlling nonverbal signals than verbal ones, so we think nonverbal behaviors more accurately reflect what a person is really thinking or feeling. It's easy for Joel to *say* he's having a great day, but if he feels frustrated or depressed, it's probably tougher for him to *act* as if his day is going well. When he slumps, rolls his eyes, and sighs, you probably conclude that his day is going poorly, despite what he says.

The human preference for believing nonverbal signals even when they conflict with words is especially critical for detecting **deception**—the act of leading someone to believe something one knows to be untrue—because people often have inconsistent verbal and nonverbal behaviors when they're lying. Imagine that Olivia spends the afternoon with her ex-boyfriend Greg but tells her current boyfriend Ethan that she spent the afternoon reading at Starbucks. Olivia might feel nervous telling such a lie, especially because she knows how upset Ethan would be if he found out she were lying. Chances are that her nervousness will affect her nonverbal behavior. She might perspire, get dry in the mouth, sound unusually tense, and appear especially rigid in her posture. If Olivia really had been at Starbucks as she said, there's probably no reason she would be nervous telling Ethan about it. She would be able to explain her afternoon's activities calmly. So, if she looks or sounds nervous, those nonverbal messages will contradict her verbal message and may give Ethan reason to think she's not telling the truth.

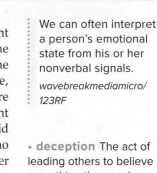

We can often interpret a person's emotional state from his or her nonverbal signals.

wavebreakmediamicro/ 123RF

• **deception** The act of leading others to believe something the speaker knows to be untrue.

Nonverbal Communication Is the Primary Means of Expressing Emotion

We have a large verbal vocabulary for describing our emotions, but our nonverbal behaviors do it much more efficiently. How many times have you been able to tell how someone is feeling just by looking at him or her? We might not always be right about the emotions we sense—and some of us are better than others at interpreting people's emotions—but research shows that humans are acutely sensitive to nonverbal emotion cues.[6] As we saw in the example above about Rick and his mother Claudia, Rick has developed the ability to interpret Claudia's emotional state accurately with just a glance, by paying attention to her facial expressions and posture.

Emotion is a powerful influence on our behavior, and our primary way of communicating how we feel is through our nonverbal behaviors. Two channels of nonverbal behavior that are particularly important in the communication of emotion are facial expressions and vocal behaviors.

Humans are highly visual beings, meaning that we tend to pay a lot of attention to people's facial expressions when we want to figure out their emotional state. We take close note of these expressions whether we're talking with them face to face, listening to them speak to a group, or even watching them on television. On reality TV shows such as *The Voice*, *The Amazing Race*, and *Chopped*, producers often shoot close-ups of people's faces during critical moments, to capture their facial expressions of emotion. Most of us can easily think of the type of facial expression that connotes happiness: the eyes tend to be wide and bright, and the person tends to be smiling. That look of happiness differs notably from the facial expressions we associate with anger, sadness, surprise, and disappointment. The distinctive patterns we perceive for each are keys to helping us interpret other people's emotions. In fact, several studies suggest that facial expressions of these basic emotions are interpreted similarly across cultures.[7] In a now-classic study, psychologist Paul Ekman took photographs of people communicating six basic emotions through their facial expressions: happiness, fear, disgust,

Reality television shows often capture images of intense emotional expressions.

CBS via Getty Images

anger, sadness, and surprise. He then showed the photos to participants in five different countries—Chile, Brazil, Argentina, Japan, and the United States—and asked them to match each photograph with the emotion they believed it displayed. When Ekman compared the responses from different countries, he found that the participants were equally accurate at matching emotions to the photographs.[8]

Similar studies have repeated those results using groups from a range of cultures—including Greek, Chinese, Turkish, Malaysian, Ethiopian, Swedish, Italian, Sumatran, Estonian, and Scottish[9]—and found that interpretations of emotional displays do differ somewhat from culture to culture. They also differ from emotion to emotion, with happiness, for instance, being interpreted more consistently than fear.[10] Overall, however, it appears that facial expressions of our most basic emotions are understood similarly around the world.

We also pay attention to vocal cues to understand a person's emotional state. When someone is yelling and using harsh vocal tones, we usually infer that the person is angry, whereas laughter and lots of pitch variation suggest happiness or excitement. It turns out that we may be even more accurate at interpreting emotions through vocal cues than through facial expressions.[11] That appears to be particularly true when the vocal channel is the only accessible channel, such as when we're speaking with someone on the phone. We don't necessarily get *more* information about individuals' emotional states from their voices than we do from their facial expressions, but we may get *more accurate* information.

Nonverbal Communication Metacommunicates As we discussed the introductory chapter, metacommunication is communication *about* communication, and we often metacommunicate verbally. When we use statements such as "Let me tell you what I think," "Don't take this the wrong way," and "I'm just kidding," we are sending messages related to our other messages—that is, we're communicating about our communication. Usually, we do so to avoid misunderstandings and to provide listeners with greater clarity about the meaning of our statements. Communicating clearly is a very important feature of social interaction, and several nonverbal behaviors also help us to achieve this goal.

Suppose, for example, that you're sitting at the dinner table with your brother and he leans over to you, lowers his voice to a whisper, and cups his mouth with his hand. That combination of nonverbal behaviors sends you the message "What I'm about to say is meant for only you to hear." In other words, your brother's nonverbal behavior metacommunicates his intentions to you. We often use nonverbal behaviors such as facial expressions and gestures to indicate how someone else should interpret our messages. For instance, we might smile and wink to indicate that we're being sarcastic, or raise our eyebrows to signal that what we're saying is very serious.

Nonverbal Communication Serves Multiple Functions Beyond its role in emotional expression, nonverbal communication serves several additional functions that help us interact

SHARPEN Your Skills: *Tone of voice*

Consider how tone of voice can influence meaning. Take a simple phrase such as "She made me do that." Say it as though you're angry, then surprised, and finally sarcastic. How does your voice change each time, even though the words are the same?

effectively with others. Let's take a quick look at some of them.

- *Nonverbal communication helps us manage conversations.* We can use nonverbal signals—such as raising a hand in class—to indicate that we wish to speak. We can also use eye contact to convey that we understand what a speaker is saying.[12]

- *Nonverbal communication helps us maintain relationships.* We reinforce many of our important relationships through the use of **immediacy behaviors**, nonverbal signals of affection and affiliation. In many relationships, such behaviors include smiling, engaging in affectionate touch, using warm vocal tones, and standing or sitting close to each other.[13]

- *Nonverbal communication helps us form impressions.* By observing how another person looks, sounds, dresses, and carries himself or herself, we can form impressions about that individual's personality, education level, cultural and ethnic background, economic status, political affiliation, and sexual orientation.[14] Our impressions may not always be accurate, but we rely heavily on nonverbal cues when we form them.

- *Nonverbal communication helps us influence other people.* When we attempt to cause others to think or act in a certain way, we might manipulate visual cues, such as our clothing, to appear more authoritative.[15] We can also use nonverbal immediacy behaviors to enhance our affiliation with others, leading them to be more open to our suggestions than they otherwise may be.[16]

- *Nonverbal communication helps us conceal information.* Several nonverbal behaviors coincide with our attempts to deceive other people. When we try to conceal the truth, we often speak in a higher voice than normal,[17] and our smile looks more fake or forced.[18] We also use fewer gestures and adopt a more rigid posture, probably because we're trying to control signs of nervousness.[19] Many people feel distressed when they think others are deceiving them. As you'll see in the "Difficult Conversations" box, however, spotting a liar is often more complicated than it seems.

• **immediacy behaviors** Nonverbal signals of affection and affiliation.

Ten Channels of Nonverbal Communication

Nonverbal communication engages nearly all our senses, so it's probably no surprise that we experience it in so many different forms, or channels. Those channels are facial displays, eye behaviors, movement and gestures, touch behaviors, vocal behaviors, the use of smell, the use of space, physical appearance, the use of time, and the use of artifacts.

FACIAL DISPLAYS

It's difficult to overstate the importance of **facial displays**, or facial expressions, in nonverbal communication. Indeed, according to the *principle of facial primacy*, the face communicates more information than any other channel of nonverbal behavior.[20] That communication power is especially evident in three important functions of facial displays: revealing identity, signaling attractiveness, and expressing emotion.

• **facial displays** Facial expressions that are an important source of information in nonverbal communication.

1. *Identity.* First, the face is the most important visual clue that humans use to identify one another.[21] After all, most of us don't display photos of our loved ones' hands, legs, or feet—we display pictures of their faces, because the appearance of the face is our most reliable clue to identity.

Difficult Conversations

When You Think Someone Is Lying

Imagine this: After you undergo a brief surgical procedure at the hospital, your doctor prescribes a round of powerful painkillers to help you during your recovery. Your pharmacist fills the prescription and sends you home with 30 tablets and instructions to take two tablets per day for 15 days. On the fourth day after surgery, however, you open the prescription container to find that some of your tablets are missing.

Now, consider this: You mention the missing painkillers to your roommate that morning. He says "that's weird" and "I wonder what happened to them," but his voice sounds higher and more stressed than normal, and he appears jittery and nervous. Although his words suggest that he knows nothing about the missing medication, his nonverbal communication leads you to think otherwise. The longer you talk, in fact, the more suspicious you become about whether he is telling you the truth—not because of what he says, but because of how he behaves nonverbally. Before simply accusing him of stealing your painkillers, however, consider the following:

- Just because you perceive that your roommate may be lying to you, that doesn't necessarily mean he is. According to research, the average person's ability to detect deception is quite poor, so it is easy to be wrong when trying a spot a lie.

- Even if your roommate is engaging in nonverbal behaviors that are consistent with deception—such as fidgeting and speaking in a higher voice—those aren't foolproof clues to deception. He may be feeling anxious or nervous for some other reason entirely.

- If you are convinced that your roommate is lying, raise your suspicion with him calmly. Instead of pointing your finger and saying "you're a liar," ask "are you telling me the truth?" and then explain why you believe he isn't. Give him a chance to admit his deception—and if he does, give him a chance to explain why he did what he did.

- If your roommate is adamant about his innocence, you may be unlikely to resolve the issue in that conversation. Rather than continue to accuse him, say that you hope he is telling you the truth because it will be hard to trust him again if you find out he lied.

Most of us feel very uncomfortable when we believe someone is lying to us, especially if we have a close relationship with that person. When that happens to you, remember that your suspicions may be unfounded and that it helps to give people the benefit of the doubt. If the other person truly has lied, that may harm your relationship in the short term—but over time, he or she may be able to regain your trust.

SOURCE: Burgoon, J. K., Guerrero, L. K., & Floyd, K. (2010). *Nonverbal communication*. Allyn & Bacon. https://doi.org/10.4324/9781315663425

• **symmetry** The similarity between the left and right sides of a face or body.

• **proportionality** The relative sizes of facial or body features.

2. *Attractiveness.* Second, the face plays a large role in attractiveness. Two properties that appear to be especially important are symmetry and proportionality. **Symmetry** is the similarity between the left and right sides of your face (Figure 2). **Proportionality** refers to the relative size of your facial features. It may seem odd to identify symmetry and proportionality as primary contributors to facial attractiveness because we so often think of attractiveness as a

FIGURE 2

ASYMMETRICAL AND SYMMETRICAL FACES

(a)   (b)

All else being equal, symmetrical faces are more attractive than asymmetrical faces. When researchers study facial symmetry, they often do so by taking a photograph of a face and modifying it with computer software to make it appear more symmetrical. For instance, the image in photo "a" is an original, unretouched photo of an adult man's face, and the image in photo "b" is a modified version of the same face that increases its symmetry. Research indicates that most people would find the face in photo "b" to be more attractive.

SensorSpot/Getty Images; SensorSpot/Getty Images

highly individual assessment. However, as you'll learn in the "Fact or Fiction?" box, we're much more similar than dissimilar when it comes to judging how attractive someone is.

3. *Emotion.* Finally, as noted above, facial behavior is our primary means of communicating emotion. Our facial muscles give us the ability to make hundreds of different expressions. We use those expressions to convey a host of emotions—from happiness, surprise, and determination to anger, fear, sadness, and contempt.

Facial expressions are also extremely useful for those who communicate through sign language. In sign language, facial expressions are sometimes called *nonmanual signals* because they work alongside hand signs to help express a particular meaning. For instance, when someone asks a yes or no question using sign language, the eyes are wide open, the eyebrows are raised, and the head and shoulders are pushed forward. Sometimes a person can change the entire meaning of a sign just by changing the facial expression that goes with it (Figure 3).[22]

EYE BEHAVIORS

Because the eyes are part of the face, it may strike you as odd that researchers study eye behavior separately from facial behavior. Just as facial behavior communicates more than any other nonverbal channel, however, the eyes communicate more than any other part of the face. Thus, we treat **oculesics**, the study of eye behavior, as a separate nonverbal channel.

• **oculesics** The study of eye behavior.

When many people think about eye behavior, eye contact first comes to mind, for good reason. Eye contact plays a role in several important types of relational interaction. We use eye contact to signal attraction to someone and to infer that someone is

FIGURE 3

FACIAL EXPRESSION IN AMERICAN SIGN LANGUAGE

(a)   (b)

Facial expression plays a vital role in communicating ideas in American Sign Language (ASL). In some instances, the same hand sign is associated with different meanings when it is accompanied by different facial expressions. Both photographs in the figure feature the hand sign for "you," but with different facial displays. The expression in photo "a" represents a question, such as "Are you?" or "Did you?" The expression in photo "b", however, is interpreted as an exclamation, such as "It's you!" Although the hand signal is the same in both photographs, the meaning differs because of the accompanying facial expression.

Kory Floyd; Kory Floyd

attracted to us. We use it to gain credibility and to come across as sincere or trustworthy. We use it to persuade others, as well as to signal that we are paying attention and understanding what others are saying. We can even use eye contact when we want to intimidate someone or take a dominant or an authoritative position in a conversation or a group discussion. Indeed, there are few times when we feel as connected to another person—in either positive or negative ways—as when we are looking each other in the eye. As we will see later in the chapter, however, those functions of eye contact often vary by culture.

Another eye behavior with communicative value is pupil size. The pupil is the dark spot right in the center of each eye, which you can see in a mirror. Your pupils control how much light enters your eyes; as a result, they continually change in size whenever your eyes are open. In darker environments, they dilate, or open wider, in order to take in all available light. In brighter environments, they contract, or become smaller, to avoid taking in too much light at once. What communication researchers find interesting, however, is that your pupils also dilate when you look at someone you find physically attractive and when you feel arousal, whether it is a positive response, such as excitement or sexual arousal, or a negative response, such as anxiety or fear. Watching how a person's pupils react to different social situations or conversational partners can therefore tell us something about the individual's interest and arousal.

MOVEMENT AND GESTURES

Think about the different ways you walk. When you're feeling confident, you may hold your head high and walk with smooth, consistent strides. When you're nervous, you probably walk more timidly, stealing frequent glances at the people around you. Your *gait*, or the way you walk, is one example of how your body movement can communicate

Fact or *fiction?*

In the Eye of Which Beholder?—Cultures Vary Widely in Perceptions of Beauty

Most of us have heard the cliché that "beauty is in the eye of the beholder," meaning that what one group finds attractive may not be appealing to another. Surprisingly, this idea dates back at least to the third century B.C., indicating that humans have long considered beauty to be subjective, a matter of individual taste. If that were the case, then we would expect to find little agreement from person to person, and from culture to culture, about what is physically attractive. Exactly how true is that idea, though?

Not very, according to research. In fact, a host of studies has shown just the opposite: people are remarkably consistent when it comes to judging attractiveness. Researcher Judith Langlois and her colleagues have reviewed 130 of those studies and found that within cultures, people showed 90 percent agreement with one another when judging someone's attractiveness. Moreover, people from different cultures agreed in their judgments of attractiveness 94 percent of the time. Thus, although we sometimes think of beauty as being culturally specific, Langlois and her team found that there was substantial agreement both *within* cultures and *across* cultures in assessing attractiveness.

These findings indicate that people are much more similar than different when it comes to judging looks. Therefore, people who are considered attractive by one social group are also likely to be considered attractive by other groups.

ASK YOURSELF

- Why does the idea that "beauty is in the eye of the beholder" persist?
- What do you find most physically attractive in members of another sex? How about in members of your own sex?

SOURCE: Langlois, J. H., Kalakanis, L. E., Rubenstein, A. J., Larson, A. D., Hallam, M. J., & Smoot, M. T. (2000). Maxims or myths of beauty: A meta-analytic and theoretical review. *Psychological Bulletin, 126*(3), 380–423. https://doi.org/10.1037/0033-2909.126.3.390

various messages about you to others, such as "I feel proud" or "I feel scared." The study of movement, including the movement of walking, is called **kinesics**.

Now consider how you use your arms and hands to communicate. Perhaps it's to wave at your neighbor when you see her at the grocery store. Maybe it's to hold up two fingers to signal that you want two hot dogs at the football game concession stand. The use of arm and hand movements to communicate is called **gesticulation**. Research indicates that most people—even those who are born blind—use gestures even before they begin speaking.[23]

Communication scholars divide gestures into several forms, including emblems, illustrators, affect displays, regulators, and adaptors.

- **Emblems** are any gestures that have a direct verbal translation. Whenever you see an emblematic gesture, you should be able to translate it into words. Examples include the wave for "hello" or "goodbye" and the upright extended palm for "stop."

- **Illustrators** are gestures that go along with a verbal message to clarify it. If you hold up your hands a certain distance apart when you say the fish you caught

• **kinesics** The study of movement.

• **gesticulation** The use of arm and hand movements to communicate.

• **emblems** Gestures that have a direct verbal translation.

• **illustrators** Gestures that go along with a verbal message to clarify it.

We often infer people's emotional state from the way they walk.

Erik Isakson/Blend Images/ Getty Images; Uwe Umstaetter/Getty Images

was "this big," your gesture serves as an illustrator to clarify what you mean by "this big."

• **affect displays** Gestures that communicate emotion.

- **Affect displays** are gestures that communicate emotion (*affect*). You probably know people who wring their hands when they are nervous or cover their mouth with their hands when they are surprised. Those are both affect displays because they coincide with particular emotions.

• **regulators** Gestures that control the flow of conversation.

- **Regulators** are gestures that control the flow of conversation. One regulator with which you're probably very familiar is raising your hand in class when you wish to speak. Gestures such as that help regulate who is speaking, and when, so communication can flow smoothly.

• **adaptors** Gestures used to satisfy a personal need.

- **Adaptors** are gestures you use to satisfy some personal need, such as scratching an itch or picking lint off your shirt. When we do those behaviors to ourselves, we call them *self-adaptors*. When adaptors are directed at other people (say, picking lint off someone else's shirt), they're called *other-adaptors*.

TOUCH BEHAVIORS

Touch is the first of our five senses to develop. Even before an infant can see, hear, taste, or smell, his or her skin can respond to stimuli in the environment. Touch is also the only sense without which we cannot survive. Consider that no matter how much we may cherish our other senses, it's entirely possible to survive without being able to see, hear, taste, or smell. Without touch, however, we would constantly be susceptible to burn, frostbite, and other potentially life-threatening forms of injury.

• **haptics** The study of the sense of touch.

Haptics is the study of how we use touch to communicate. In terms of human communication, there are five major areas in which touch plays a critical role in conveying meaning: affection, caregiving, power and control, aggression, and ritual.

- *Affectionate touch.* Behaviors such as hugging, kissing, and handholding communicate love, intimacy, commitment, and safety, and are commonplace in many romantic relationships, parent-child relationships, and friendships.[24] One reason affectionate touch is so important is that it contributes to our physical and mental well-being. Infants who are regularly cuddled, for instance, experience faster physical development than those who are not.[25] Affection is such an important need, in fact, that people suffer when they don't receive enough. To learn about the problems of affection deprivation, check out "The Dark Side of Communication."

- *Caregiving touch.* We often receive touch from others while receiving some form of care or service. When you get your hair cut, have your teeth cleaned, or work with a personal trainer, for instance, you are touched in ways that correspond to those activities. Caregiving touch is distinguished from affectionate touch because although it *can* reflect positive emotion for the person being touched, it does not necessarily do so.

- *Power and control touch.* Still other touches are used to exert control over people's behavior. We sometimes touch people merely to suggest a certain course of behavior, as when the host of a party puts his hand on a guest's back to guide her in a certain direction. In other cases, we touch people to control their behavior against their wishes, such as when police officers hold a suspect on the ground while applying handcuffs.

- *Aggressive touch.* Behaviors done to inflict physical harm—such as punching, pushing, kicking, slapping, and stabbing—are all forms of aggressive touch. Using touch behaviors to inflict physical harm on others almost always constitutes a criminal act. Despite the legal constraints on such behaviors, incidents of violence and abuse using aggressive touch are unfortunately still common in North America and many societies around the world.

- *Ritualistic touch.* Some touches are ritualistic, meaning that we do them as part of a custom or tradition. In North America, shaking hands is one such example; when we shake hands with people as part of a greeting ritual, we understand that the handshake does not convey any particular meaning about the relationship (the way that, say, holding hands would). That does not mean that shaking hands has no effect on social interaction, though. In fact, research shows that a quality handshake enhances positive affect[26] and can even make someone more likely to receive a job offer.[27]

Research indicates that physical affection—including affectionate touch—is essential for our physical and mental health.
Don Hammond/Design Pics

• **vocalics** Characteristics of the voice that communicate meaning.

• **paralanguage** Vocalic behaviors that communicate meaning along with verbal behavior.

Ritualistic touch does not necessarily convey relational meaning.
Ariel Skelley/Getty Images

VOCAL BEHAVIORS

Perhaps you have a high, breathy voice or a deep, booming voice. Maybe you usually talk very fast or quite loudly. Perhaps you have an accent that indicates to others where you grew up. And there are times when you speak with a particular tone in your voice, to suggest that you are irritated, amused, or bored. Those and other characteristics of the voice are referred to, collectively, as **vocalics**. We also refer to them as **paralanguage** (meaning "beside language") to indicate that they go along with the words we speak to convey meaning.

Some people are surprised to learn that the voice is a channel of nonverbal communication. After all, we speak with our voices, and spoken communication is verbal, right? That statement is true, but the only verbal aspect of spoken communication is *what we say*—the words themselves. Everything else about our voices, including the following characteristics, is nonverbal.

- *Pitch.* The pitch of your voice is an index of how high or deep your voice sounds. On average, women's voices have a higher pitch than men's voices, and adults have deeper voices than children.

THE DARK SIDE OF COMMUNICATION

Hungry for Affection: The Problem of Affection Deprivation

Affectionate touch is so important for maintaining physical and mental well-being that many communication scholars consider it to be a fundamental human need. According to research, however, a growing number of Americans now experience *affection deprivation*, which is a significant deficit in the amount of affectionate touch they receive.

Research has found that affection deprivation is associated with a wide range of problems for individuals and their relationships. When people don't receive enough affection, they are less happy in life and feel less satisfied and secure in their personal relationships. They feel more loneliness, depression, and stress, and less social support from others. In addition, they feel more chronic pain, experience lower quality sleep, and are more likely to

have been diagnosed with a mood disorder or an immune disorder. Affection-deprived people even have a harder time interpreting emotional expressions from others.

People respond to feelings of affection deprivation in a variety of ways. Some spend time in contexts that offer opportunities for contact, such as at church functions or neighborhood gatherings. Others visit pet shelters where they can share affection with four-legged friends. Another resource beginning to gather steam is the *cuddle party*, a group of individuals coming together under the guidance of a trained facilitator to share affectionate, nonsexual contact with each other. Whatever their approach, many people find the feeling of affection deprivation aversive and difficult to manage.

ASK YOURSELF

- When do you feel deprived of affectionate touch? What problems seem to go along with that experience?
- If the idea of cuddling with strangers at a party strikes you as odd, what else might you do to battle affection deprivation?

SOURCES: Floyd, K. (2014). Relational and health correlates of affection deprivation. *Western Journal of Communication, 78*(4), 383–403. https://doi.org/10.1080/10570314.2014.927071; Fortenbury, J. (2014, July 15). Fighting loneliness with cuddle parties: As Americans report feeling more isolated, some people turn to snuggling with strangers. *The Atlantic.* www.theatlantic.com/health/archive/2014/07/fighting-loneliness-with-cuddle-parties/373335/.

- *Inflection.* When we talk about the inflection in your voice, we are referring to your variation in pitch. Voices that have a lot of inflection are usually described as very expressive; those with little inflection are said to be monotone.[28]
- *Volume.* Volume is an index of how loud or quiet your voice is. Most of us alter our vocal volume as the social context demands, such as by speaking quietly in a library and more loudly at a crowded reception.
- *Rate.* Vocal rate refers to how fast or slowly you speak. The average adult speaks at a rate of approximately 150 words per minute,[29] but we might speak faster when we're excited or slower when we're unsure of ourselves.
- *Filler words.* Filler words are nonword sounds such as "umm" and "er" that people often use to fill the silence during pauses. If we have to pause while speaking—say, to remember the word we want to use—we can use filler words to indicate that we intend to continue speaking.
- *Pronunciation.* Pronunciation reflects how correctly you combine vowel and consonant sounds to say a word. For example, how would you pronounce the word *victuals*? Although it looks as though it should be pronounced "VIK-tules," its correct pronunciation is "VIT-tles."
- *Articulation.* Articulation, also known as enunciation, describes how clearly you speak. People who mumble their words or speak with their mouth full demonstrate poor articulation. In contrast, individuals whose words are clear and easily understandable are good articulators.

- *Accent.* An accent is a pattern of pronouncing vowel and consonant sounds that is representative of a particular language or geographic area. Everyone speaks with an accent—even you—although we typically notice only accents that are different from ours.
- *Silence.* Silence is the absence of sound. We frequently use silence to convey meaning in conversations.[30] For instance, we often become silent when we are unsure how to respond to a question or when we have said as much as we wish to about a topic. Research shows that culture makes a difference in how people tolerate conversational silence, with Japanese speakers able to withstand much longer silences than English speakers before feeling uncomfortable.[31]

THE USE OF SMELL

Of all the channels of nonverbal behavior, the hardest one to associate with human communication is smell. It turns out that your sense of smell, which we call **olfactics**, operates subtly but powerfully to influence your reactions to other people. In fact, two phenomena central to the human experience and to communication—memory and sexual attraction—are profoundly affected and regulated by smell.

Memory Smells can affect our communication behavior by influencing our memories and moods. Have you ever smelled a particular scent—maybe a certain food or cologne—and instantly remembered a particular person, event, or place? Maybe the aroma of banana bread makes you think of your grandmother's kitchen, or the smell of a particular cologne or perfume makes you think of a close friend. Those connections are examples of *olfactic association*, the tendency of odors to bring up specific memories. Why do olfactic associations matter for communication? It happens that memories often come with specific emotions, so when a smell reminds us of a particular person or place, it has the potential to affect our mood and behavior. For example, remembering your grandmother's kitchen might put you in a nostalgic mood or prompt you to call one of your relatives.

Sexual Attraction Smell also affects our communication by playing a role in determining to whom we are sexually attracted. That connection between smell and attraction may surprise you, because chances are you think of sexual attraction as being driven mostly by visual cues—whether you think an individual *looks* attractive. In fact, your judgments about a person's sexual attractiveness are strongly affected by the way he or she smells to you. More specifically, research tells us that when we are looking for other-sex romantic partners, we are drawn to people whose natural body scent is most different from our own. Why?

If two people have very similar scents, scientists have determined that their genes are also very similar, and this similarity can increase their probability of producing genetically abnormal children. People produce much healthier children when they mate with partners who are genetically dissimilar to them. A person's natural body scent sends a signal to your brain that tells you how similar his or her genes are to yours. The more similar a person's body odor is to yours, therefore, the less sexually attractive you will instinctively judge that individual to be. Of course, not all instances of sexual attraction coincide with the desire to reproduce. Nonetheless, nature has connected smell to sexual attraction to help motivate healthy mate choices when procreation is our goal. We don't sniff out a person's scent profile consciously, however; rather, our brain is adapted to pick up on those olfactic signals subconsciously.

THE USE OF SPACE

When we interact socially, we constantly negotiate our use of space. That negotiating process becomes particularly apparent when our personal space is limited; think of

Many smells evoke specific memories. The smell of freshly baked bread might make you think of your grandmother's kitchen.
Dougal Waters/Getty Images

• **olfactics** The study of the sense of smell.

We each prefer a certain amount of personal space. As a result, we often feel uncomfortable in crowded conditions.

Keith Brofsky/Getty Images

being in a crowded elevator or on a full airplane. Many of us find such situations uncomfortable, but why? The scientific study of spatial use, known as **proxemics**, tells us that we each have a preferred amount of personal space that we carry like an invisible bubble around us. How much personal space we prefer depends on our temperament, the situation we are in, and our level of familiarity with those around us.

Anthropologist Edward T. Hall discovered that in Western cultures, people use four different spatial zones, or levels of personal distance, when interacting with one another (see Figure 4):[32]

- **Intimate distance**, which ranges from 0 to approximately 1½ feet, is the zone we willingly occupy with only our closest and most intimate friends, family members, and romantic partners.

- **Personal distance**, which Hall defined as extending from 1½ to about 4 feet, is the distance we typically maintain with other friends and relatives.

- **Social distance**, which ranges from about 4 to 12 feet, is used with customers, casual acquaintances, and others whom we don't know very well to convey more formal, impersonal interaction.

- Finally, **public distance** typically applies when someone is giving a speech or performing in front of a large audience. The purpose is to keep the presenter far enough away from the group that he or she is safe and visible to everyone. Public distances are usually 12 to 25 feet or greater, depending on the circumstance.

PHYSICAL APPEARANCE

We place extraordinary importance on physical appearance. Whether we intend to or not, we make all sorts of judgments about people based on their looks. In particular, we have a strong predisposition to attribute positive qualities to physically attractive people, a tendency that researchers refer to as the **halo effect**. In other words, when a person *looks* good, most of us subconsciously assume he or she *is* good. Indeed, research has shown that we think attractive people are friendlier, more competent, and more socially skilled than less attractive people.[33]

Those perceptions translate into some real advantages for attractiveness. For instance, attractive people have higher self-esteem and more dating experience than less attractive people.[34] We are also nicer and more cooperative toward attractive people and more lenient toward attractive criminal defendants.[35] In fact, a video of South Carolina real estate agent Lauren Cutshaw went viral in 2018 when, during her arrest for driving while intoxicated, she told the arresting officer that she was too pretty to go to jail. Cutshaw's case made headlines again in 2019 when it was reported that, indeed, she received no jail time for her offense.[36] So if it seems at times that good-looking people get all the breaks, research tells us that is often the case. Much as we may like to claim otherwise, most of us are strongly influenced by physical appearance when making assessments about other people.

That preference for beauty has a dark side, however. Because physical attractiveness is so highly valued, some people go to dangerous extremes to achieve it. In particular, an alarming number of people suffer from eating disorders. Those with *anorexia nervosa* pursue thinness relentlessly, through excessive dieting and exercise, self-induced vomiting, and the abuse of laxatives or diuretics. *Bulimia nervosa* is characterized by bingeing on large quantities of food and then compensating for over-eating by vomiting or abusing laxatives. Finally, *binge eating disorder* causes people to experience episodes of excessive eating in which they feel a lack of self-control. All three disorders are associated with substantial health risks.[37]

Some aspects of personal appearance—such as your height and eye color—are relatively fixed. Others, however, are easily changeable, such as your clothing, cosmetics, hair style, and jewelry. Americans collectively spend billions of dollars annually to keep

- **proxemics** The study of the use of space.

- **intimate distance** The zone of space willingly occupied only with intimate friends, family members, and romantic partners.

- **personal distance** The zone of space occupied with close friends and relatives.

- **social distance** The zone of space occupied with casual acquaintances.

- **public distance** The zone of space maintained during a public presentation.

- **halo effect** A predisposition to attribute positive qualities to physically attractive people.

FIGURE 4

HALL'S FOUR SPATIAL ZONES

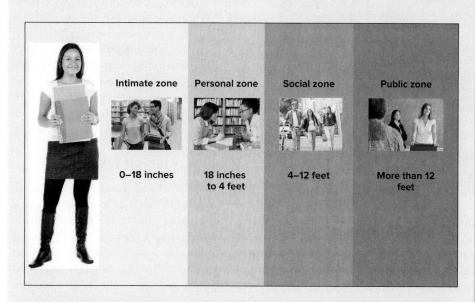

Edward T. Hall suggested that people observe four zones of space with each other: an intimate zone, a personal zone, a social zone, and a public zone.

Andres Rodriguez/Alamy; Sam Edwards/age fotostock; Image Source/Punchstock; Brzozowska/Getty Images; UpperCut Images/SuperStock

up with the latest styles and looks.[38] Far from being trivial, the attention people pay to their clothing and appearance makes a difference in how others perceive them. Decades of research have shown that the way people dress and present themselves influences how they are evaluated socially and how successful they are in their careers.[39] Even the color of clothing people choose makes a difference—one study found that female waitstaff received higher tips when wearing red clothing than when wearing any other color.[40]

As a nonverbal channel, personal appearance is influential not only in face-to-face interaction but also online. When interacting on the Internet, many people use avatars as representations of themselves. Although avatars are not "real" people, they signify real people, and so we become accustomed to perceiving them in many of the same ways we perceive the people around us. Including an avatar alongside an e-mail message or chat room posting can make our words seem more personal to others—but how does the appearance of an avatar matter? To find out, communication researchers Kristine Nowak and Christian Rauh had college students evaluate a series of avatars and report on their perceptions.[41] They discovered that

- Avatars should look as human as possible, rather than looking like animals or inanimate objects.

- Avatars should have a defined gender, rather than appearing androgynous.

- Communicators prefer avatars that look like themselves.

THE USE OF TIME

Chronemics is the way we use time. You might not immediately think of time usage as nonverbal behavior, but the way we give (or refuse to give) our time to others can send them important messages about how we feel about them. Because most of us spend our time on the people and activities that matter to us, for instance, the way we use time communicates messages about what we value. When we give our time to others, we imply that we value those people. On the contrary, when we spend our time

• **chronemics** The use of time.

How we spend our time sends a message about what is most important to us.

Dmitriy Shironosov/123RF

• **artifacts** Objects and visual features that reflect a person's identity and preferences.

looking at our smartphones instead of talking to the people we are with, we imply that our phones are more important than our friends.

Our use of time also sends messages about power.[42] When you go to see someone who is in a position of power over you, such as your supervisor, it is not uncommon to be kept waiting. However, you would probably consider it bad form to make a more powerful person wait for you. Indeed, the rule seems to be that the time of powerful people is more valuable than the time of less powerful people.

THE USE OF ARTIFACTS

Each of us inhabits and controls certain physical environments, such as a house or apartment, a dorm room, or an office. **Artifacts** are the objects and visual features within an environment that reflect who we are and what we like. One office you routinely visit, for instance, may be plush and opulent, with an oak desk, leather furniture, soft lighting, and expensive paintings on the walls. Another office may be plain and basic, featuring a metal desk and chairs, fluorescent lighting, and bare walls. What messages might those different artifacts send you about the occupants of those two offices?

In recent decades many corporations have specifically designed their work spaces to maximize collaboration and visibility among employees. These designs often take the form of large, open work areas with no walls or cubicles dividing one employee from another. Some people find such spaces intimidating, however—especially those with introverted personalities who prefer quiet over continuous interaction. To serve their needs—and those of employees who simply desire private spaces in which to conduct sensitive business—Michigan-based furniture company Steelcase designs office spaces intended to be cozy and to invite calm self-reflection. The company's designs are based on large-scale workplace surveys in which 95 percent of employees reporting wanting a greater sense of privacy at work.[43]

The 10 different channels by which we communicate with others nonverbally encompass almost all our senses, making nonverbal communication a truly engaging experience. Not everyone enacts nonverbal behavior in the same ways, however. As we will see in the next section, culture and sex are both powerful influences on our styles of communicating nonverbally.

Culture, Sex, and Nonverbal Communication

Suppose you've won an Olympic gold medal. Imagine the immense joy you feel as you stand atop the podium listening to your national anthem, with your friends and family beaming with pride from the stands. In that scenario, what nonverbal behaviors would you likely engage in? How would you stand? What expression would be on your face? What gestures might you make? If you can picture yourself in that situation, it's easy to imagine that everyone would behave the same way you would. Research tells us, however, that our ways of communicating nonverbally are affected not only by our individual emotions and the demands of the situation, but also by two major influences on nonverbal communication: culture and sex. We'll take a look at each in this section.

CULTURE INFLUENCES NONVERBAL COMMUNICATION

When they watch the Olympic Games on television, many U.S. American fans are surprised by some of the nonverbal behaviors of athletes from different cultures. They may greet each other differently than is the norm in the United States. They may stand closer to—or farther from—each other than is typical in U.S. culture. The reason is that these and many other nonverbal behaviors are shaped by the cultural practices with which people are raised. To learn about a career in which knowledge of cultural variation in nonverbal behavior is helpful, see "Putting Communication to Work."

Consider these many ways in which culture influences nonverbal communication:

- *Emblems:* The specific messages that an emblem symbolizes often vary by culture. The "come here" gesture commonly used in the United States means "goodbye" in China, Italy, and Columbia.[44] Gestures such as A-OK, thumbs up, and crossed fingers have sexual or obscene meanings in many parts of the world.[45]

- *Affect displays:* Some displays of affect (emotion) are specific to certain cultures. In China, for example, women express emotional satisfaction by holding their fingertips over their closed mouths. Similarly, men in Uruguay will hold their fists together and turn them in opposite directions, as if wringing out a wet cloth, to express anger.

- *Personal distance:* People from Arab countries generally converse with each other at closer distances than do people in the United States.[46] One classic study found that because of differences in their preferred conversational distance, Arab college students regarded those from the United States as aloof, whereas the U.S. students regarded the Arab students as overbearing.[47]

- *Eye contact:* In many Western cultures, direct eye contact signifies that someone is sincere, trustworthy, and authoritative, whereas the lack of eye contact elicits negative evaluations from others.[48] In comparison, some Asian, Latin American, and Middle Eastern cultures emphasize the lack of eye contact as a sign of deference or respect for authority.[49]

- *Facial displays of emotion:* As noted above, decades of research indicate that people around the world express emotions—particularly primary emotions such as happiness, sadness, fear, anger, surprise, and disgust—in highly similar ways.[50] What tends to differ across cultures is how expressive people are of emotion, with those in individualistic cultures routinely being more emotionally expressive than those in collectivistic cultures.[51]

- *Greeting behavior:* People in Western countries typically greet social acquaintances with a handshake, whereas people in Mediterranean countries usually kiss each other on both cheeks. In some Asian countries, it is common to greet others by bowing, with the longest and lowest bows reserved for the most respected individuals.[52]

- *Time orientations:* Recall from the culture chapter that some cultures—including those in the United States, Canada, Finland, Great Britain, and Germany—are *monochronic*, meaning that they see time as a tangible commodity, expect events to begin "on time," and dislike having their time wasted.[53] Other cultures—including those in France, Brazil, Mexico, and Saudi Arabia—are *polychronic*, meaning they see time as flexible and diffused and don't necessarily expect punctuality.[54]

- *Touch:* People in *high-contact cultures*, which include France, Mexico, and

Greeting behaviors vary significantly from culture to culture. Some people shake hands, some kiss each other on the cheek, and others bow when meeting someone new.

Lai Leng Lam/123RF

Job Title >

Work Responsibilities >

Overseas Teacher of English

Joe Raedle/Getty Images

Native English speakers with a bachelor's degree are often hired to teach English as a foreign language in other countries. Some work with young children, others with adolescents, and others with adult learners. In each case, the ability to adapt to the nonverbal customs of the host culture is an enormous advantage. For instance, those who teach in high-contact cultures, where people touch each other frequently, must learn to adapt to their lack of personal space. Those who teach in polychronic cultures must remember that their students may have quite different norms with respect to time. Although the teacher may be discussing U.S. traditions along with teaching the English language, he or she should also be ready to adapt to the local nonverbal norms.

Greece, touch each other significantly more often than do people in *low-contact cultures*, such as Japan, Sweden, and Finland.[55] Research indicates that the United States is most accurately classified as a *medium-contact culture*.[56]

- *Vocalics:* Besides their readily noticeable differences in accents, cultures also differ in their use of filler words.[57] Although "umm" and "er" are common filler words for English speakers, Chinese speakers often say "zhege zhege zhege"—which translates to "this this this"—as filler words.

Before we proceed, it's important to acknowledge that not *every* nonverbal behavior differs by culture. People around the world interpret a smile as an expression of joy.[58] Parents in every known culture speak *babytalk*—soft, high-pitched vocal tones and highly simplified language—to their infants.[59] The fact that two people come from different cultures doesn't mean they can't communicate with each other nonverbally. It simply means they should be aware of the many ways in which each of their cultural backgrounds is influencing the way they do so.

SEX INFLUENCES NONVERBAL COMMUNICATION

A second major influence on our nonverbal communication is our sex. Perhaps you have noticed that women and men sometimes react with different nonverbal behaviors—or to different degrees—to the same situation. The question of *why* sex influences nonverbal communication has intrigued researchers for decades.

One explanation is that beginning in early childhood, many boys and girls are socialized to communicate in gender-specific ways (masculine for boys, feminine for girls).[60] Another explanation is that anatomical and physiological differences between the sexes cause them to behave in different ways.[61] Both possibilities have received extensive support from research, but not always for the same behaviors. In other words, sex differences in some nonverbal behaviors appear to be more influenced by socialization than biology, whereas others are more affected by biology than socialization.

No matter what the reason, sex influences several forms of nonverbal communication, including the following:

- *Emotional expressiveness:* Several studies document that women are more expressive than men with respect to a variety of emotional states, including joy,[62] affection,[63] fear,[64] and shame.[65] Some research indicates that men are more expressive than women of anger,[66] although other studies have found no sex difference in anger expression.[67]

- *Vocalics:* On average, men's voices have a lower pitch than do women's. The primary reason is that men have a larger voice box and longer vocal cords—which produce the sound of the voice—than women do, as a result of physiological changes that occur during puberty.[68] Research indicates that men also use more filler words and pauses while speaking than do women.[69]

- *Touch:* Among adults, men are more likely to touch women than women are to touch men, unless the touch is occurring as part of a greeting (such as a handshake).[70] In same-sex pairs, however, women touch each other more than men do, although that sex difference is smaller in close friendships than among acquaintances.[71]

- *Appearance:* Women and men typically adorn themselves in notably different ways. In Western cultures, for example, cosmetic use is significantly more common for women than for men,[72] even though the use of cosmetics for men is substantially increasing.[73] Also, women and men usually wear different styles of clothing and jewelry and adopt different hairstyles, and those conventions further accentuate the differences in their appearance.

As with culture, it's important to note that not every nonverbal behavior differs by sex. Perhaps more important is to acknowledge that sex differences, even when they are present, aren't always substantial. Popular author John Gray, who wrote the highly successful book *Men Are from Mars, Women Are from Venus,*[74] has suggested that women and men communicate so differently that they might as well be from different planets. Although many communication behaviors do differ by sex, research tells us that those sex differences are often relatively small, not nearly as significant as Gray proposed. Indeed, communication scientist Kathryn Dindia has suggested a more modest metaphor for sex differences: "Men are from North Dakota, women are from South Dakota."[75]

Culture and sex aren't the only important influences on nonverbal communication. Another significant influence—and one in which our ability to communicate nonverbally is continually evolving—is computer-mediated communication. Table 1 highlights some of the ways in which changes in technology—and in our use of it—have influenced our nonverbal behavior.

TABLE 1
ELECTRONICALLY MEDIATED NONVERBAL COMMUNICATION

Although early computer-mediated communication relied exclusively on text, people eventually developed ways of expressing themselves nonverbally in electronic formats. These include

- **Emoji:** As we noted earlier in this chapter, textual and visual representations of facial expressions and objects can help to convey a person's emotional state :)

- **Capitalization:** When you type something in all capital letters, IT IS OFTEN INTERPRETED AS YELLING.

- **Random symbols:** Instead of using obscenities in an e-mail message, a series of random keyboard symbols will often do the %#@&* trick.

- **Images:** You can incorporate both still pictures and video clips in computer-mediated communication to add a visual dimension to your message.

- **Abbreviations:** You can use common abbreviations to indicate your nonverbal state, such as LOL for "laughing out loud" and SMH for "shaking my head."

Improving Your Nonverbal Communication Skills

In the CBS comedy series *The Big Bang Theory*, Sheldon Cooper was a theoretical physicist at Caltech who shared an apartment with his friend and colleague, Leonard Hofstadter. Despite having two doctoral degrees and being at the top of his professional field, Cooper was inept in most social situations. He did not understand many social conventions, such as the rules of politeness, and had little ability to interpret other people's emotions. Similarly, he showed near disdain for human contact. He maintained a social network, although even his closest friends found him annoying and complained that he was difficult to be around. In all, Cooper was not a particularly skilled nonverbal communicator.

Sheldon Cooper would be well advised to read this section, in which we will explore some ways of improving two particular types of nonverbal communication skills: interpreting nonverbal communication and expressing messages nonverbally.

Learning how to communicate better is an ongoing process.

CBS via Getty Images

INTERPRETING NONVERBAL COMMUNICATION

As we've seen in this chapter, people use nonverbal communication to express many types of messages, including those related to emotions and attitudes, power and dominance, persuasion, and deception. An important skill for communicators, therefore, is the ability to decode, or interpret, the nonverbal behaviors of others. That ability requires two separate but interrelated skills, as we will now consider.

Be Sensitive to Nonverbal Messages One skill useful in interpreting nonverbal communication is being sensitive to others' nonverbal messages. When your daughter grimaces after learning you're serving broccoli for dinner, or your son has an excited tone in his voice when talking about his last fencing match, do you notice those nonverbal emotion cues? When a competitor at work intentionally keeps you waiting for an appointment or seems unusually tense during your conversation, do you pick up on those potential signs of dominance or deception?

Sensitivity to nonverbal behaviors is essential because we can't interpret messages unless we first take note of them. Although research indicates that some of us are naturally more nonverbally sensitive than others, it is possible to increase our nonverbal sensitivity through mindful awareness—that is, by tuning in closely to what's happening around us.[76] When you're interacting with someone, try these approaches:

- Pay particular attention to facial expressions for signs of what the person is feeling. Remember that the face communicates more emotion than all other nonverbal channels.

- Take note of his or her tone of voice and body movements, because these are particularly relevant for signaling dominance and deception.

Decipher the Meaning of Nonverbal Messages Nonverbal messages sometimes carry multiple meanings. If you notice a young man smiling as he interacts with another person, it might mean he's happy. Alternatively, it might mean that he's persuading a customer to make a purchase, comforting a relative who has just shared bad news, or flirting.[77] If you hear him speaking loudly, it might mean he's excited, or it may mean he's angry, surprised, or talking with someone who's hard of hearing.

An essential part of interpretation, therefore, is deciphering the meaning of nonverbal behaviors that others enact. Accurately deciphering a nonverbal behavior means taking it to mean what the sender intended.[78] Suppose that while you are describing your grandmother's failing health, your friend Vanessa squeezes your hand to convey her support. If you take her behavior as a gesture of support, then you have accurately deciphered her nonverbal message. If you take it to mean she's trying to persuade you or is interested in you romantically, however, then you have deciphered her message inaccurately.

To improve your skill at deciphering nonverbal messages, try the following strategies:

Be Aware of the Situation Consider the social situation a person is in when interpreting his or her behaviors. If you notice a man crying, for instance, your first instinct might be to conclude that he's sad. Perhaps you also notice, however, that he is surrounded by smiling friends and relatives who are hugging him and patting him on the back. When you take these additional pieces of information into consideration, you might take his crying to mean that he is happy or relieved rather than sad.

Pay Attention to Groups of Nonverbal Behaviors When interpreting nonverbal behavior, it pays to consider all the behaviors you are observing, rather than just one. Besides noticing that the man in the previous example was crying, for instance, perhaps you also noticed that he was smiling, occasionally laughing, and carrying himself in a relaxed manner. When you consider all of those nonverbal cues simultaneously, you might conclude that he is feeling joyful or relieved rather than distressed.

Keep Culture in Mind Remember that cultural differences sometimes influence the meaning of a nonverbal message. That observation appears to be particularly true for gestures and eye behaviors. We've seen, for instance, that using the thumbs-up gesture or maintaining eye contact while talking with someone can have different meanings in different cultures. The more you learn about cultural variation in nonverbal behaviors, the more accurately you'll be able to decipher those behaviors.

Be Aware of What You Expect to See As you saw in the Perceiving Ourselves and Others chapter, we are often affected by a *perceptual set*, which is our tendency to perceive only what we want or expect to perceive. Your perceptual set can affect your ability to interpret nonverbal behavior accurately. Suppose you're observing a senator interact with young children at an urban day care center. You notice that she smiles at the children, hugs them, and gives them high-fives. If you like this politician, you may be predisposed to interpret these behaviors as signs that she truly cares about the children's well-being. If you dislike her, though, you may interpret the same behaviors as simply her showing off for the media. Neither interpretation may be fully accurate, yet your perceptual set caused you to "see" only what you expected to see.

Ask for Clarification When you're unsure of how accurately you've deciphered a person's nonverbal message, consider asking the person. Let's say you're describing a new product to a client, and her facial expression suggests confusion. Instead of assuming you've deciphered her expression accurately, you might ask her, "Did my description make sense?" If she replies that she found it confusing, then you can explain the product again using simpler language.

Remember that Interpreting Nonverbal Communication Is Challenging Accurately interpreting another person's nonverbal behavior can be difficult for a variety of reasons. First, not everyone is equally skilled. On average, for instance, women tend to be more accurate than men,[79] and extraverts are often more accurate than introverts.[80] Second, nonverbal behavior is often ambiguous, meaning that it can be interpreted in more than one way, and the correct interpretation of a behavior is not always clear.

When we communicate across cultures, we cannot assume that a nonverbal gesture has the same meaning to us as it does to other societies. In many cultures, the "thumbs-up" gesture is considered obscene.

U.S. Air Force photo by Staff Sgt. Marcus McDonald

Third, as this chapter has pointed out, people use multiple channels for sending nonverbal messages, which can make it difficult to pay attention to everything an individual is doing. Together, these facts can make interpreting nonverbal communication a challenge. The good news is that it is a skill that can be practiced and improved.

As you practice your sensitivity and deciphering skills, you should be able to improve your ability to interpret the meaning of nonverbal behaviors.[81]

EXPRESSING NONVERBAL MESSAGES

Some of us are good at interpreting the nonverbal behaviors of others but not particularly good at expressing ourselves nonverbally. Yet as we have seen, we communicate more information nonverbally than verbally. If you're skilled at expressing nonverbal messages, you'll therefore be able to communicate with others more effectively and more efficiently than someone who is less skilled.

Just as with interpretation skills, some people are naturally more expressive, charismatic, and outgoing than others.[82] To improve your own skill at expressing nonverbal messages, try the following ideas:

Work on Your Self-Awareness We learned in the introductory chapter that *self-monitoring* is your awareness of your own behavior and how it affects other people. Your skill at communicating nonverbally is enhanced when you are aware of the behaviors you are enacting. When talking with a customer at work, for instance, do you pay attention to the tone and quality of your voice? How about the way you are standing or what you're doing with your hands? We can't always control every nonverbal behavior, particularly when we're nervous or distracted, but self-awareness is the first step toward improving your ability to express yourself nonverbally.

Learn from Others Spend time with highly expressive people. Some researchers have suggested that we can learn how to become more nonverbally expressive by being around individuals who are extroverted and charismatic.[83] Research also suggests that certain professions attract highly expressive people. These professions include teachers and lecturers, actors and singers, politicians, salespeople, diplomats, customer service representatives, counselors and therapists, and members of the clergy.[84] To perform effectively in any of those professions, an individual must be able to communicate clearly and competently with others. Being nonverbally expressive is a key component of competent communication.

Practice Being Expressive Take part in games and activities that exercise your nonverbal expression skills. A good example is charades, a popular game in which you act out a word or a phrase without speaking while members of your team try to guess the word based on your depiction. Because success in charades depends on your ability to depict your word or phrase nonverbally, this game can be a good exercise of your expression skill. Another activity that can improve your nonverbal expression skills is role playing, which involves acting out the roles of characters in a specific situation the way you would if you were actually in that situation.

Pay Attention to How Others React to Your Behavior Even when you know what you intend to express nonverbally, others can still misunderstand you.

COMPETENT COMMUNICATOR

Nonverbal Know-How: Rate Your Interpretation and Expression Skills

How much do you agree with each of the following statements? On the line before each statement, record your level of agreement on a 1-to-7 scale. A higher number means you agree more; a lower number means you agree less.

Design Pics/Don Hammond

1. _____ When I feel depressed, I tend to bring down those around me.

2. _____ It is nearly impossible for people to hide their true feelings from me.

3. _____ I have been told that I have expressive eyes.

4. _____ In social settings, I can instantly tell when someone is interested in me.

5. _____ Quite often I tend to be the life of the party.

6. _____ People often tell me that I am a sensitive and understanding person.

When you're finished, add up your scores from items 1, 3, and 5. That is your score for expressiveness. Next add up your scores for items 2, 4, and 6. That is your score for interpretation. Both scores should range from 3 to 21.

If your scores on both scales are between 16 and 21, then you are already quite good at nonverbal interpretation and expressiveness. If your scores are between 9 and 15, you have a moderate ability to interpret and express nonverbal behavior, and the suggestions offered in this chapter may help you sharpen those abilities. If your scores are between 3 and 8, then you especially can benefit from the guidance provided in this chapter for improving your skills. You may also find that one of your scores is considerably higher than the other. If that's the case, then you know which skill you're already good at and which skill could benefit from more practice.

SOURCE: Riggio, R. E. (1986). Assessment of basic social skills. *Journal of Personality and Social Psychology, 51*(3), 649–660. https://doi.org/10.1037/0022-3514.51.3.649

That's because, as noted previously, many nonverbal behaviors are ambiguous, and not everyone is equally skilled at interpreting them. To check your effectiveness at nonverbal expression, observe how other people respond to what you do. Suppose you're giving a speech to a community group and you crack a joke in the middle of your presentation, but no one laughs. Although it's possible that your listeners didn't understand the joke or find it amusing, it may also be that your facial expressions and tone of voice suggested you were trying to be serious rather than funny. Skilled communicators pay attention to how others "read" their nonverbal behavior, and they adapt their behavior accordingly, in order to express themselves as clearly as possible.

You can take a first step toward improving your skills at nonverbal interpretation and expression by assessing how skilled you are now. Complete the exercise in "The Competent Communicator" to evaluate your current interpretation and expression abilities.

- How do people communicate nonverbally?

  Nonverbal communication comprises those behaviors and characteristics that convey meaning without the use of words. People communicate nonverbally via several channels, including facial displays, eye behaviors, movement and gestures, touch, vocal behaviors, smell, use of space, physical appearance, use of time, and use of artifacts.

- How do culture and sex influence nonverbal behavior?

  Culture and sex affect multiple nonverbal communication behaviors, including gestures, personal distance and touch, eye contact, time orientation, vocalics, and emotional expression.

- In what ways can you improve your nonverbal communication skills?

  You can improve your nonverbal communication skills by being sensitive to the nonverbal messages you encounter, learning to decipher their meanings accurately, and practicing your nonverbal expressiveness.

KEY TERMS

nonverbal communication 120
emoji 121
nonverbal channels 122
deception 123
immediacy behaviors 125
facial displays 125
symmetry 126
proportionality 126
oculesics 127
kinesics 129

gesticulation 129
emblems 129
illustrators 129
affect displays 130
regulators 130
adaptors 130
haptics 130
vocalics 131
paralanguage 131
olfactics 133

proxemics 134
intimate distance 134
personal distance 134
social distance 134
public distance 134
halo effect 134
chronemics 135
artifacts 136

NOTES

1. Brooks, R. (2015). Language is dead—An emoji is the "word" of the year. *GeekDad*. http://geekdad.com/2015/11/language -is-dead/?utm_campaign=coschedule&utm_source=twitter&utm_medium=GeekDads&utm_content=Language%20is%20Dead%20 -%20An%20Emoji%20is%20the%20%22Word%22%20of%20the%20Year

2. Nierenberg, G., Calero, H. H., & Grayson, G. (2011). *How to read a person like a book*. Rupa & Co.; Calero, H. H. (2005). *The power of non-verbal communication: What you do is more important than what you say*. Silver Lake.

3. Mehrabian, A. (1968). Communication without words. *Psychology Today, 2*(4), 51–52. https://doi.org/10.4324/9781315080918-15

4. Burgoon, J. K., Guerrero, L. K., & Manusov, V. (2011). Nonverbal signals. In M. L. Knapp, & J. A. Daly (Eds.), *Handbook of interpersonal communication* (4th ed., pp. 239–282). Sage.

5. Ibid.

6. See, e.g., Fischer, A. H., Kret, M. E., & Broekens, J. (2018). Gender differences in emotion perception and self-reported emotional intelligence: A test of the emotion sensitivity hypothesis. *PLoS One, 13*(1), e0190712. https://doi.org/10.1371/journal.pone.0190712

7. Ekman, P. (2015). *Emotion in the human face.* Malor Books. https://doi.org/10.1016/C2013-0-02458-9

8. Ekman, P. (1972). Universals and cultural differences in facial expressions of emotion. In J. Cole (Ed.), *Nebraska symposium on motivation, 1971* (vol. 19, pp. 207–282). University of Nebraska Press. https://doi.org/10.1037/0012043; see also Cordaro, D. T., Sun, R., Kamble, S., Hodder, N., Monroy, M., Cowen, A., Bai, Y., & Keltner, D. (2019). The recognition of 18 facial-bodily expressions across nine cultures. *Emotion.* Advance online publication. https://doi.org/10.1037/emo0000576

9. Boucher, J. D., & Carlson, G. E. (1980). Recognition of facial expression in three cultures. *Journal of Cross-Cultural Psychology, 11*(3), 263–280. https://doi.org/10.1177/0022022180113003; Ekman, P., Friesen, W. V., O'Sullivan, M., Chan, A., Diacoyanni-Tarlatzis, I., Heider, K., Krause, R., LeCompte, W. A., Pitcairn, T., & Ricci-Bitti, P. E. (1987). Universals and cultural differences in the judgments of facial expressions of emotion. *Journal of Personality and Social Psychology, 53*(4), 712–717. https://doi.org/10.1037/0022-3514.53.4.712

10. Laukka, P., Elfenbein, H. A., Söder, N., Nordstroöm, H., Althoff, J., Chui, W., Iraki, F. K., Rockstuhl, T., & Thingujam, N. S. (2013). Cross-cultural decoding of positive and negative non-linguistic emotion vocalizations. *Frontiers in Psychology, 4,* 353. https://doi.org/10.3389/fpsyg.2013.00353; Elfenbein, H. A., & Ambady, N. A. (2003). When familiarity breeds accuracy: Cultural exposure and facial emotion recognition. *Journal of Personality and Social Psychology, 85*(2), 276–290. https://doi.org/10.1037/0022-3514.85.2.276

11. Kappas, A., Hess, U., & Scherer, K. R. (1991). Voice and emotion. In R. S. Feldman, & B. Rimé (Eds.), *Fundamentals of nonverbal behavior* (pp. 200–237). Cambridge University Press. https://doi.org/10.1525/jlin.1994.4.1.82

12. Ho, S., Foulsham, T., & Kingstone, A. (2015). Speaking and listening with the eyes: Gaze signaling during dyadic interactions. *PLoS One, 10*(8), e0136905. https://doi.org/10.1371/journal.pone.0136905

13. Croes, E. A., Antheunis, M. L., Schouten, A. P., & Krahmer, E. J. (2019). Social attraction in video-mediated communication: The role of nonverbal affiliative behavior. *Journal of Social and Personal Relationships, 36*(4), 1210–1232. https://doi.org/10.1177/0265407518757382

14. See, e.g., Smith, E., Junger, J., Pauly, K., Kellermann, T., Neulen, J., Neuschaefer-Rube, C., Derntl, B., & Habel, U. (2018). Gender incongruence and the brain—Behavioral and neural correlates of voice gender perception in transgender people. *Hormones and Behavior, 105,* 11–21. https://doi.org/10.1016/j.yhbeh.2018.07.001

15. Shoulders, C. W., & Smith, L. (2018). Impact of teacher attire on students' views of teacher credibility, attitude homophily, and background homophily within school-based agricultural education programs. *Journal of Agricultural Education, 59*(2), 275–288. https://doi.org/10.5032/jae.2018.02275

16. Guadagno, R. E., Muscanell, N. L., Rice, L. M., & Roberts, N. (2013). Social influence online: The impact of social validation and likability on compliance. *Psychology of Popular Media Culture, 2*(1), 51–60. https://doi.org/10.1037/a0030592

17. Villar, G., Arciuli, J., & Paterson, H. (2013). Vocal pitch production during lying: Beliefs about deception matter. *Psychiatry, Psychology and Law, 20*(1), 123–132. https://doi.org/10.1080/13218719.2011.633320

18. See Levine, T. R. (Ed.). (2014). *Encyclopedia of deception.* Sage. https://doi.org/10.4135/9781483306902; Ekman, P., Friesen, W. V., & O'Sullivan, M. (1997). Smiles when lying. In P. Ekman, & E. L. Rosenberg (Eds.), *What the face reveals: Basic and applied studies of spontaneous expression using the facial affect coding system (FACS)* (pp. 201–214). Oxford University Press. https://doi.org/10.1093/acprof:oso/9780195179644.001.0001

19. Vrij, A., Semin, G. R., & Bull, R. (1996). Insight into behavior displayed during deception. *Human Communication Research, 22*(4), 544–562. https://doi.org/10.1111/j.1468-2958.1996.tb00378.x

20. Leitzke, B. T., & Pollak, S. D. (2016). Developmental changes in the primacy of facial cues for emotion recognition. *Developmental Psychology, 52*(4), 572–581. https://doi.org/10.1037/a0040067

21. Faerber, S., Kaufmann, J., & Schweinberger, S. (2015). Early temporal negativity is sensitive to perceived (rather than physical) facial identity. *Neuropsychologia, 75,* 132–142. https://doi.org/10.1016/j.neuropsychologia.2015.05.023

22. Guido, J. W. (2015). *Learn American Sign Language: Everything you need to start signing.* Wellfleet Press; Shaw, E. (2015). *A historical and etymological dictionary of American Sign Language: The origin and evolution of more than 400 signs.* Gallaudet University Press.

23. Bruce, S. M., Mann, A., Jones, C., & Gavin, M. (2007). Gestures expressed by children who are congenitally deaf-blind: Topography, rate, and function. *Journal of Visual Impairment & Blindness, 101*(10), 637–652. https://doi.org/10.1177/0145482X0710101010

24. Floyd, K. (2019). *Affectionate communication in close relationships.* Cambridge University Press. https://doi.org/10.1017/9781108653510

25. Field, T. M. (Ed.). (2014). *Touch in early development.* Psychology Press.

26. Dolcos, S., Sung, K., Argo, J. J., Flor-Henry, S., & Dolcos, F. (2012). The power of a handshake: Neural correlates of evaluative judgments in observed social interactions. *Journal of Cognitive Neuroscience, 24*(12), 2292–2305. https://doi.org/10.1162/jocn_a_00295

27. Stewart, G. L., Dustin, S. L., Barrick, M. R., & Darnold, T. C. (2008). Exploring the handshake in employment interviews. *Journal of Applied Psychology, 93*(5), 1139–1146. https://doi.org/10.1037/0021-9010.93.5.1139

28. Babel, M., McGuire, G., & King, J. (2014). Towards a more nuanced view of vocal attractiveness. *PLoS One, 9*(2), e88616. https://doi.org/10.1371/journal.pone.0088616

29. Wolvin, A. (Ed.). (2010). *Listening and human communication in the 21st century.* Blackwell. https://doi.org/10.1002/9781444314908

30. Knutson, H. V., & Kristiansen, A. (2015). Varieties of silence: Understanding different forms and functions of silence in a psychotherapeutic setting. *Contemporary Psychoanalysis, 51*(1), 1–30. https://doi.org/10.1080/00107530.2015.954218

31. Yamada, H. (2015). Yappari, as I thought: Listener talk in Japanese communication. *Global Advances in Business Communication, 4*(1), 3.

32. See Matsumoto, D., Frank, M. G., & Hwang, H. S. (Eds.). (2013). *Nonverbal communication: Science and applications.* Sage. https://doi.org/10.4135/9781452244037; see also Hall, E. T. (1963). A system for the notation of proxemic behavior. *American Anthropologist, 65*(5), 1003–1026. https://doi.org/10.1525/aa.1963.65.5.02a00020

33. Zebrowitz, L. A., & Franklin, R. G. (2014). The attractiveness halo effect and the babyface stereotype in older and younger adults: Similarities, own-age accentuation, and older adult positivity effects. *Experimental Aging Research, 40*(3), 375–393. https://doi.org/10.1080/0361073X.2014.897151

34. Bale, C., & Archer, J. (2013). Self-perceived attractiveness, romantic desirability and self-esteem: A mating sociometer perspective. *Evolutionary Psychology, 11*(1), 68–84. https://doi.org/10.1177/147470491301100107

35. Devine, D. J., & Caughlin, D. E. (2014). Do they matter? A meta-analytic investigation of individual characteristics and guilt judgments. *Psychology, Public Policy, and Law, 20*(2), 109–134. https://doi.org/10.1037/law0000006

36. MSN. (2019, September 18). Woman who said she was too pretty for jail gets no time. *MSN.com.* https://www.msn.com/en-us/video/viral/woman-who-said-she-was-too-pretty-for-jail-gets-no-time/vi-AAHuKwI?ocid=mailsignout

37. Jahraus, J. (2018). Medical complications of eating disorders. *Psychiatric Annals, 48*(10), 463–467. https://doi.org/10.3928/00485713-20180912-04

38. Fashion United. (2019). Global fashion industry statistics. https://fashionunited.com/global-fashion-industry-statistics/

39. See, e.g., Gurung, R. A., Punke, E., Brickner, M., & Badalamenti, V. (2018). Power and provocativeness: The effects of subtle changes in clothing on perceptions of working women. *Journal of Social Psychology, 158*(2), 252–255. https://doi.org/10.1080/00224545.2017.1331991

40. Gueguen, N., & Jacob, C. (2014). Clothing color and tipping: Gentlemen patrons give more tips to waitresses with red clothes. *Journal of Hospitality & Tourism Research, 38*(2), 275–280. https://doi.org/10.1177/1096348012442546

41. Nowak, K. L., & Rauh, C. (2006). The influence of the avatar on online perceptions of anthropomorphism, androgyny, credibility, homophily, and attraction. *Journal of Computer-Mediated Communication, 11*(1), 153–178. https://doi.org/10.1111/j.1083-6101.2006.tb00308.x

42. MacLellan, L. (2017, October 10). Time is a strong but rarely recognized power construct in the workplace. *Quartz at Work.* https://qz.com/work/1096844/managing-time-is-a-power-construct-that-we-play-out-at-work/

43. Zeiger, M. (2014, June 3). Steelcase and Susan Cain design offices for introverts. http://www.fastcodesign.com/3031341/steelcase-and-susan-cain-design-offices-for-introverts.

44. Jandt, F. E. (2015). *An introduction to intercultural communication: Identities in a global community* (8th ed.). Sage. https://doi.org/10.1016/j.ijintrel.2007.07.001

45. See Matsumoto, D. (2006). Culture and nonverbal behavior. In V. L. Manusov, & M. L. Patterson (Eds.), *The Sage handbook of nonverbal communication* (pp. 219–236). Sage. https://doi.org/10.4135/9781412976152

46. Feghali, E. K. (1997). Arab cultural communication patterns. *International Journal of Intercultural Relations, 21*(3), 345–378. https://doi.org/10.1016/S0147-1767(97)00005-9

47. Watson, O. M. (1970). *Proxemic behavior: A cross-cultural study.* Mouton.

48. Schulze, L., Renneberg, R., & Lobmaier, J. S. (2013). Gaze perception in social anxiety and social anxiety disorder. *Frontiers in Human Neuroscience, 7,* 872. https://doi.org/10.3389/fnhum.2013.00872; Larsen, R. J., & Shackelford, T. K. (1996). Gaze avoidance: Personality and social judgments of people who avoid direct face-to-face contact. *Personality and Individual Differences, 21*(6), 907–917. https://doi.org/10.1016/S0191-8869(96)00148-1

49. Matsumoto, D. (2006). Culture and nonverbal behavior. In V. Manusov, & M. L. Patterson (Eds.), *The Sage handbook of nonverbal communication* (pp. 219–236). Sage. https://doi.org/10.4135/9781412976152

50. Ekman, P. (1993). Facial expression and emotion. *American Psychologist, 48*(4), 384–392. https://doi.org/10.1037/0003-066X.48.4.384; Ekman, P., & Friesen, W. V. (1986). A new pan-cultural facial expression of emotion. *Motivation and Emotion, 10*(2), 159–168. https://doi.org/10.1007/BF00992253; Scherer, K. R., & Wallbott, H. G. (1994). Evidence for universality and cultural variation of differential emotion response patterning. *Journal of Personality and Social Psychology, 66*(2), 310–328. https://doi.org/10.1037/0022-3514.66.2.310

51. Matsumoto, D., Yoo, S. H., & Fontaine, J. (2008). Mapping expressive differences around the world: The relationship between emotional display rules and individualism versus collectivism. *Journal of Cross-Cultural Psychology, 39*(1), 55–74. https://doi.org/10.1177/0022022107311854

52. Malott, K. M. (2008). Achieving cultural competency: Assessment of US-based counselor educators instructing internationally. *International Journal for the Advancement of Counseling, 30*(1), 67–77. https://doi.org/10.1007/s10447-007-9045-6

53. Kaufman-Scarborough, C. (2017). Monochronic and polychronic time. In Y. Y. Kim (Ed.), *International encyclopedia of intercultural communication.* Wiley-Blackwell. https://doi.org/10.1002/9781118783665

54. Xu-Priour, D.-L., Truong, Y., & Klink, R. R. (2014). The effects of collectivism and polychronic time orientation on online social interaction and shopping behavior: A comparative study between China and France. *Technological Forecasting and Social Change, 88,* 265–275. https://doi.org/10.1016/j.techfore.2014.07.010

55. Andersen, P. A. (2011). Tactile traditions: Cultural differences and similarities in haptic communication. In M. Hertenstein, & S. J. Weiss (Eds.), *The handbook of touch: Neuroscience, behavioral, and health perspectives* (pp. 351–372). Springer. https://doi.org/10.1080/09602011.2012.711659

56. Andersen, P. A. (2012). The basis of cultural differences in nonverbal communication. In L. A. Samovar, R. E. Porter, & E. R. McDaniel (Eds.), *Intercultural communication: A reader* (11th ed., pp. 293–312). Wadsworth.

57. Kramsch, C. (1998). *Language and culture.* Oxford University Press.

58. Sauter, D. A., Eisner, F., Ekman, P., & Scott, S. K. (2010). Cross-cultural recognition of basic emotions through nonverbal emotional vocalizations. *Proceedings of the National Academy of Sciences, 107*(6), 2408–2412. https://doi.org/10.1073/pnas.0908239106

59. Kalashnikova, M., Carignan, C., & Burnham, D. (2017). The origins of babytalk: Smiling, teaching, or social convergence? *Royal Society Open Science, 4*(8), 170306. https://doi.org/10.1098/rsos.170306

60. Wood, J. T. (2016). *Gendered lives: Communication, culture, and gender* (12th ed.). Cengage.

61. Floyd, K., & Weber, R. (Eds.). (2020). *The handbook of communication science and biology.* Routledge.

62. Burgoon, J. K., & Bacue, A. (2003). Nonverbal communication skills. In B. R. Burleson, & J. O. Greene (Eds.), *Handbook of communication and social interaction skills* (pp. 179–219). Lawrence Erlbaum Associates.

63. Floyd, K. (2019). *Affectionate communication in close relationships.* Cambridge University Press. https://doi.org/10.1017/9781108653510

64. Kring, A. M., & Gordon, A. H. (1998). Sex differences in emotion: Expression, experience, and physiology. *Journal of Personality and Social Psychology, 74*(3), 686–703. https://doi.org/10.1037/0022-3514.74.3.686

65. Else-Quest, N. M., Higgins, A., Allison, C., & Morton, L. C. (2012). Gender differences in self-conscious emotional experience: A meta-analysis. *Psychological Bulletin, 138*(5), 947–981. https://doi.org/10.1037/a0027930

66. Simpson, P. A., & Stroh, L. K. (2004). Gender differences: Emotional expression and feelings of personal inauthenticity. *Journal of Applied Psychology, 89*(4), 715–721. https://doi.org/10.1037/0021-9010.89.4.715

67. Campbell, A., & Muncer, S. (2008). Intent to harm or injure: Gender and the expression of anger. *Aggressive Behavior, 34*(3), 282–293. https://doi.org/10.1002/ab.20228

68. Marieb, E. N., & Keller, S. M. (2018). *Essentials of human anatomy and physiology* (12th ed.). Pearson.

69. Bortfield, H., Leon, S. D., Bloom, J. E., Schober, M. F., & Brennan, S. E. (2001). Disfluency rates in conversation: Effects of age, relationship, topic, role, and gender. *Language and Speech, 44*(2), 123–147. https://doi.org/10.1177/00238309010440020101

70. Major, B., Schmidlin, A. M., & Williams, L. (1990). Gender patterns in social touch: The impact of setting and age. *Journal of Personality and Social Psychology, 58*(4), 634–643. https://doi.org/10.1037/0022-3514.58.4.634

71. Ibid.

72. See Dortch, S. (1997). Women at the cosmetics counter. *American Demographics, 19,* 4.

73. North, A. (2018, September 24). What the rise of men's makeup means for masculinity. *Vox.* https://www.vox.com/the-goods/2018/9/24/17851190/makeup-chanel-queer-eye-maybelline-men

74. Gray, J. (1992). *Men are from Mars, women are from Venus: A practical guide to improving communication and getting what you want in your relationships.* HarperCollins.

75. Dindia, K. (2006). Men are from North Dakota, women are from South Dakota. In K. Dindia, & D. J. Canary (Eds.), *Sex differences and similarities in communication* (2nd ed., pp. 3–20). Lawrence Erlbaum Associates.

76. Bäzinger, T., Scherer, K. R., Hall, J. A., & Rosenthal, R. (2011). Introducing the MiniPONS: A short multichannel version of the Profile of Nonverbal Sensitivity (PONS). *Journal of Nonverbal Behavior, 35*(3), 189–204. https://doi.org/10.1007/s10919-001-0108-3

77. See, e.g., Bartlett, M. S., Littlewort, G. C., Frank, M. G., & Lee, K. (2014). Automatic decoding of facial movements reveals deceptive pain expressions. *Current Biology, 24*(7), 738–743. https://doi.org/10.1016/j.cub.2014.02.009

78. Riggio, R. E. (2005). The Social Skills Inventory (SSI): Measuring nonverbal and social skills. In V. Manusov (Ed.), *The sourcebook of nonverbal measures: Going beyond words* (pp. 25–34). Lawrence Erlbaum Associates. https://doi.org/10.4324/9781410611703

79. Baez, S., Flichtentrei, D., Prats, M., Mastanduendo, R., Garcia, A. M., Cetkovich, M., & Ibáñez, A. (2017). Men, women... who cares? A population-based study on sex differences and gender roles in empathy and moral cognition. *PLoS One, 12,* e0179336. https://doi.org/10.1371/journal.pone.0179336

80. Davis, M. H., & Kraus, L. A. (1997). Personality and empathic accuracy. In W. Ickes (Ed.), *Empathic accuracy* (pp. 144-168). Guilford.

81. Riggio, R. E. (2006). Nonverbal skills and abilities. In V. Manusov, & M. L. Patterson (Eds.), *The Sage handbook of nonverbal communication* (pp. 79–96). Sage. https://doi.org/10.4135/9781412976152

82. Ilies, R., Curşeu, P. L., Dimotakis, N., & Spitzmuller, M. (2013). Leaders' emotional expressiveness and their behavioural and relational authenticity: Effects on followers. *European Journal of Work and Organizational Psychology, 22*(1), 4–14. https://doi.org/10.1080/1359432X.2011.626199

83. Kramer, A. D. I., Guillory, J. E., & Hancock, J. T. (2014). Experimental evidence of massive-scale emotional contagion through social networks. *Proceedings of the National Academy of Sciences, 111*(24), 8788–8790. https://doi.org/10.1073/pnas.1320040111

84. Liu, M. W., & Guan, Y. (2014). Consumer compliance in face-to-face interactions: The role of sensitivity and expressiveness. *Advances in Consumer Research, 42,* 584–585.

6

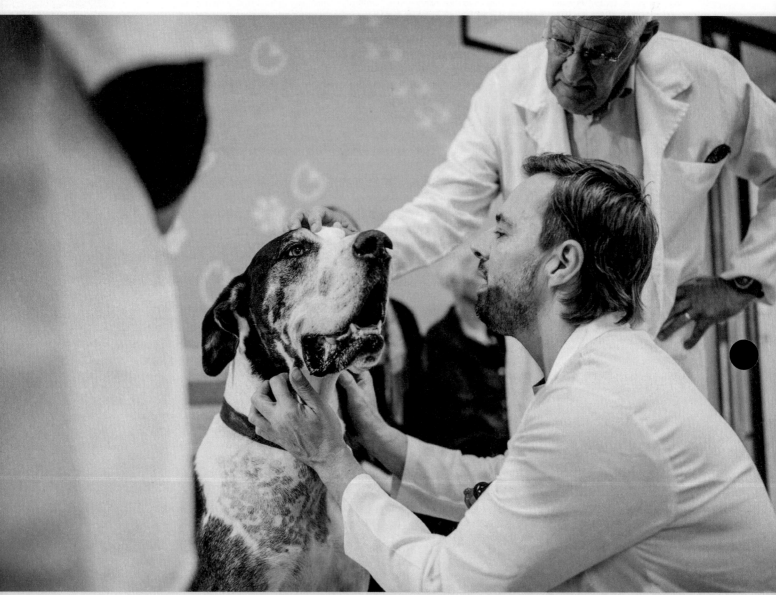

Westend61/Getty images

LISTENING EFFECTIVELY

Uniquely Qualified to Listen

When you think about professions that have a high risk of suicide, veterinary medicine may not immediately come to mind. In reality, however, veterinarians are up to 3.5 times as likely to die by suicide as the general population.[1] The emotional strain of having to euthanize animals—including those that are treatable—takes a toll on vets, along with the financial pressures of high debt loads from veterinary training. According to research, one in six vets considers suicide,[2] and that alarming statistic led veterinarian Nicole McArthur to found the online support group Not One More Vet. The group offers both telephone-based and online support services for veterinary professionals who are feeling overwhelmed and in need of help. Those in need can talk for free to other veterinarians who are uniquely qualified to listen and provide empathy and support to their colleagues in crisis.

Anyone in suicidal crisis or emotional distress can call the National Suicide Prevention Lifeline at 1-800-273-8255. The lifeline is free to call and is available 24 hours a day, 7 days a week.

▶ As You READ

- What does it mean to listen effectively?
- Why is listening effectively so challenging?
- How can you improve your listening skills?

You've probably had the frustrating experience of feeling as though someone was *hearing* you but not really *listening*. If so, you know that effective communication involves more than understanding the words that another person is speaking. You must also make sense of the speaker's intended message.

As you might imagine, problems with listening are fairly common in many types of relationships, from marriages and families to relationships in the workplace.[3] In addition, students often struggle to listen effectively to lectures and class presentations. Why? The reason is that proficient listening is a challenging skill you have to learn and practice. When you do it properly, listening adds much to the quality of your learning and your relationships. It can even help those in need, as it does for veterinarians who are struggling. When you don't listen effectively, however, your communication, relationships, and learning suffer.

What It Means to Listen

You probably don't give much thought to how well you listen. You can take classes to become a better speaker or a better writer, but few schools offer courses on improving listening skills. Yet if you are like most people, you spend much more time listening than you do speaking, writing, or engaging in other communicative behaviors. That's one reason why listening effectively is such a valuable skill.

WHAT IS LISTENING?

Listening is one of the most important concepts in human communication, yet many people find effective listening hard to define. When someone says, "You're not listening to me!" what exactly does that statement mean?

We can think of **listening** as the active process of making meaning from another person's spoken message.[4] Several details about that definition are important to note. First, listening isn't just about **hearing**, which is the sensory process of receiving and perceiving sounds—listening is about creating meaning from what you hear. It is also about **attending** to someone's words, or paying attention well enough to understand what that person is trying to communicate. Second, listening is an active process. That means it isn't automatic; you have to *make* yourself listen to someone.

Even if people are hearing the same message, they may construct different meanings for it, an indicator that they are listening differently. For instance, you might listen to your brother's description of his new officemate and conclude that he finds her competent and likable. After listening to the same description, however, your mother might conclude that your brother feels threatened by his officemate's intelligence and self-confidence. You and your mother both heard the same description, but you listened to it differently.

Finally, listening deals with spoken messages. We certainly pay attention to written messages, as well as to nonverbal messages, which influence our interpretation of people's behaviors. But we can engage in listening only when someone is speaking.

Listening Styles People listen for various reasons—sometimes to learn, sometimes to evaluate, and sometimes to provide empathy. Researchers have identified four distinct styles, each consisting of a different set of attitudes and beliefs about listening. However, most of us have one primary style that we use the most often. Here is a brief overview of each style.

- **listening** The active process of making meaning out of another person's spoken message.

- **hearing** The sensory process of receiving and perceiving sounds.

- **attending** Paying attention to someone's words well enough to understand what that person is trying to communicate.

Effective listening is important in a wide range of personal and professional relationships.

Andersen Ross/Digital Vision/Getty Images

- *Relational style:* This style emphasizes concern for other people's emotions and interests. As the name suggests, someone with a relational style listens to understand people's emotions and connect with others. For instance, when Palik listens to his middle school students, he tries to understand what they are thinking and feeling so that he can relate to them effectively.

- *Task-oriented style:* Someone with this style sees listening as part of a transaction. A task-oriented listener likes neat, concise, error-free presentations and gets impatient with disorganized communication. For example, Monica approves when her interns fill her in on the week's activities in a clear, straightforward way, and gets frustrated when she can't understand them.

- *Critical style:* This style emphasizes intellectual challenges. Someone with a critical style listens to identify inconsistencies and logical errors while others speak. Emma really enjoys listening to political commentators, for instance, because she likes noticing when they contradict themselves.

- *Analytical style:* People with this style withhold judgment while listening and consider all sides of an issue before responding. As an emergency room physician, for example, Ben listens carefully to everything his patients say before making up his mind about their symptoms or treatment.

Each style has its distinctive strengths and weaknesses, so none is inherently better than the others. If you're primarily a relational listener, for example, you're likely to get to know other people well, but you might not be able to work as efficiently as a task-oriented listener. Critical listeners might do best in majors that emphasize clarity and precision, such as engineering and computer science, whereas analytical listeners might prefer majors that involve greater room for debate, such as art and political science.

Regardless of your primary listening style, research demonstrates that we adopt different styles for different situations. For instance, you might prefer a task-oriented style when you're in a rush but a relational style when you're visiting loved ones. Similarly, you might adopt an analytical style when listening to your professor give a lecture but a critical style when listening to the evening news.[5] What's your listening style? Check out the "Competent Communicator" box to find out.

Listening Effectively Listening to someone doesn't automatically mean listening *effectively*. Effective listening requires listening with the conscious and explicit goal of understanding what the speaker intends to communicate. You might never know for certain whether you have understood a speaker's meaning *exactly* as he or she intended. If you're listening with the goal of understanding the speaker's meaning as best you can, however, you're listening effectively.

As we consider in this chapter, several barriers exist that make effective listening difficult, and different situations call for different types of listening. Understanding those dimensions of listening can help each of us to improve our ability to listen effectively. That's a worthwhile goal, as we'll now see.

THE IMPORTANCE OF LISTENING EFFECTIVELY

How much of your day do you think you spend listening? In one study, researchers Richard Emanuel and colleagues found that college students spent more time listening than doing any other communication activity. As depicted in Figure 1, participants spent 54 percent of their waking hours listening.[6] In contrast, they spent only 17 percent of their time reading, 16 percent speaking, and 11 percent writing. Other studies have found similar results, at least with college students, suggesting that most of us spend a similar percentage of our communication time listening.[7]

The ability to listen effectively is important to our success in a variety of contexts. Good listening skills are essential in the workplace. Suppose, for instance, that your employees don't listen when you tell them the alarm they will soon be hearing signals a fire drill, not a real fire. Some might panic at the sound of the alarm, and some might

Relational, Task, Critical, Analytical: What's Your Listening Style?

Design Pics/Don Hammond

We have seen that people listen for different reasons—sometimes to learn, sometimes to evaluate, and sometimes to provide empathy to others. Did you know that each of us also has a primary listening style?

A *listening style* is a set of attitudes and beliefs about listening, and researchers have identified four distinct styles. We can adopt any of these styles as the situation dictates, but research suggests that most of us have one style that we use most often. Which one best describes yours? After each of the following statements indicate how much you agree or disagree by writing a number from 1 (strongly disagree) to 7 (strongly agree).

1 _____When listening to others, it is important to understand the feelings of the speaker.

2 _____I am impatient with people who ramble on during conversations.

3 _____I often catch errors in other speakers' logic.

4 _____I wait until all the facts are presented before forming judgments and opinions.

5 _____I listen primarily to build and maintain relationships with others.

6 _____I prefer speakers who quickly get to the point.

7 _____When listening to others, I notice contradictions in what they say.

8 _____When listening to others, I consider all sides of an issue before responding.

When you're finished, add your scores in this manner:

- Add your scores for questions 1 and 5. This is your *relational style* score.
- Add your scores for questions 2 and 6. This is your *task-oriented style* score.
- Add your scores for questions 3 and 7. This is your *critical style* score.
- Add your scores for questions 4 and 8. This is your *analytical style* score.

Note which of your four scores is highest. This indicates which listening style describes you best. If two scores tie for highest, this suggests that you identify equally with two separate styles.

SOURCE: Bodie, G. E., Worthington, D. L., & Gearhart, C. C. (2013). The Listening Styles Profile-Revised (LSP-R): A scale revision and evidence for validity. *Communication Quarterly, 61*(1), 72–90. https://doi.org/10.1080/1463373.2012.720343

injure themselves as they rush frantically from their workspaces. Now suppose your manager at work doesn't listen to the staff's warnings about problems with the company's equipment. As a result, a critical production line breaks down, stalling operations for a week.

Those examples illustrate how consequential effective listening can be in the workplace. After analyzing 625 business and professional publications to see which

FIGURE 1
BREAKDOWN OF COMMUNICATION ACTIVITIES

Speaking **16%**

Listening **54%**

Reading **17%**

Writing **11%**

Other **2%**

College students spend more time listening than communicating in other ways.

Corbis/VCG/Getty Images

SOURCE: Emanuel, R., Adams, J., Baker, K., Daufin, E. K., Ellington, C., Fitts, E., & Okeowo, D. (2008). How college students spend their time communicating. *International Journal of Listening, 22*(1), 13–28. https://doi .org/10.1080/10904010701802139

communication skills businesses value most, researchers found that listening was among the most important.[8] In other research, listening also topped the list of the most important communication skills in families and personal relationships.[9] Being a good listener is vital to just about every social and personal bond we have.[10]

Despite the importance of listening skills, many of us nevertheless overestimate our listening abilities. In one study, 94 percent of corporate managers rated themselves as "good" or "very good" at listening, whereas not a single one rated himself or herself as "poor" or "very poor." Their employees told quite a different story, however; several rated their managers' listening skills as weak.[11] There appears to be very little association, in other words, between how good *we* think we are at listening and how good *others* think we are.[12]

As we'll soon see, many obstacles can get in the way of our ability to listen well. The good news, though, is that listening is a skill we can improve, and in this chapter we look at some ways to do just that.[13]

MISCONCEPTIONS ABOUT LISTENING

Are you surprised to learn that people often overestimate their listening abilities? Here are some other misunderstandings about the listening process.

How good a listener are you?

Peopleimages/E+/Getty Images

Myth: Hearing Is the Same as Listening Some people use the terms *hearing* and *listening* interchangeably, but they aren't the same activity. Hearing is merely the perception of sound. Most people hear sounds almost continuously—you hear your roommate's music, the neighbor's dogs barking, the car alarm that wakes you in the middle of the night. Hearing is a passive process that occurs when sound waves cause the bones in your inner ear to vibrate and send signals to your brain.

Unlike hearing, listening is an active process of paying attention to a sound, assigning meaning to it, and responding to it. Hearing is a part of that process, but listening requires much more than just perceiving the sounds around you.

By the same token, we can have the relatively infrequent experience of listening without hearing, and our understanding can be impaired as a result. Imagine, for instance, that you call your parents with the exciting news that you have been approved for a summer study abroad experience. After sharing the details, however, all you hear from your parents is silence. You might interpret their silence as meaning that they don't support your plans or that they're worried about the extra tuition costs. In fact, they simply hit the mute button on their phone by accident, so you were unable to hear what they were saying. Even though you were *listening*, that is, you weren't *hearing*. As that example illustrates, listening and hearing are related but separate processes.

Myth: Listening Is Natural and Effortless It's easy to think of listening as a completely natural, mindless process, much like breathing. In reality, listening is a *learned skill*, not an innate ability. We have to acquire our listening abilities. Just as we are taught to speak, we have to be taught to listen—and to listen effectively.

We learn from our experiences. Perhaps, for example, you can recall instances when you didn't listen effectively to a supervisor's instructions about how to accomplish a work project and you made poor decisions as a result. Maybe you have been in a situation with a romantic partner when you didn't listen as effectively as you could have, and the consequence was an unnecessary argument. Those types of unhappy experiences have probably taught you about the importance of effective listening, because good communicators learn from their mistakes. We also learn through instruction, such as the instruction you are receiving in your introductory communication course. The more you learn about what makes listening effective and what barriers to watch out for, the better equipped you'll be to listen effectively to others.

The fact that listening is a skill also means that people vary in their listening abilities. Just as some people are better than others at drawing or singing or writing, some are better listeners than others. Finally, like most other skills, your listening ability can improve with education and training.[14] Counselors and social workers, for instance, are trained to listen effectively to clients, a skill that improves the quality of their work. In recent years, medical schools around the United States have added course work on effective listening and other interpersonal skills to their curricula for training new physicians. People in many professions, from education and ministry to customer service and politics, can benefit from training in effective listening.

Myth: All Listeners Hear the Same Message We might assume that when several people are listening to the same message, they are all hearing and understanding the message in the same way. The truth is, however, that our perceptions of what we see and hear are always limited. Our experiences, our biases, and even our gender and culture all influence how we create meaning from the information we take in.

Effective listening is an essential skill for health workers. Many medical schools now teach new physicians how to listen effectively to patients.

JGI/Blend Images LLC

The safer assumption is that all listeners are hearing something slightly different, because each of us is filtering the message through our own unique experiences and biases. As communication scholar Ben Broome points out, even the most skilled listener can't "step outside" himself or herself entirely.[15] Broome is not implying that no one can ever understand another person's meaning. Rather, he is encouraging us to be aware of how people might interpret and understand the same message differently.

HOW CULTURE AFFECTS LISTENING BEHAVIOR

Cultural messages shape many communication behaviors, and listening is no exception. Research indicates that culture affects listening behavior in at least three ways: expectations for directness, nonverbal listening responses, and understanding of language.

Culture Affects Listeners' Expectations for Directness Listening behavior is influenced by how people in a given culture think about the importance of time. Reflecting their monochronic culture, American speakers commonly say that "time is money" and conceive of time as something that can be saved, spent, and wasted. Listeners in a monochronic culture therefore value direct, straightforward communication and become impatient with speakers who don't get to the point.[16] In contrast, people in polychronic cultures such as China and Korea emphasize social harmony over efficiency. These listeners often pay close attention to nonverbal behaviors and contextual cues to determine the meaning of a speaker's message.[17]

Culture Affects Nonverbal Listening Responses Cultural expectations can also influence what individuals consider to be appropriate listening responses, particularly with respect to nonverbal behavior. For instance, people in U.S. culture typically expect listeners to maintain eye contact with them while they're speaking. Listeners who look down or away usually seem as though they aren't listening. Within Native American culture, however, looking down or away while listening is a sign of respect rather than a signal that someone is not listening.[18]

Culture Affects Understanding of Language When people speak a language in which listeners aren't fluent, listeners can have a hard time understanding what is being said for at least two reasons. One reason, which we examined in the chapter on language, is that many languages include idioms—phrases often understandable only to native speakers of that language. For instance, you might tell an overseas visitor that you're "on Cloud 9" about your upcoming graduation, but if English isn't her first language, she may not understand that you mean you're very happy. Consequently, she would have difficulty listening effectively to you.

The second reason language differences can lead to listening challenges is that listeners may not comprehend the words being spoken. When I have foreign exchange students in my classes, I try to be aware of terms and phrases they may be unable to interpret because of their limited knowledge of English, and I provide an explanation for those words. That approach is especially helpful when I'm using highly technical terms with which non-native listeners may be unfamiliar.

Ways of Listening

Until now, we've been talking about listening as though it were a single activity. In truth, listening *effectively* has several stages, all of which are equally important.

STAGES OF EFFECTIVE LISTENING

Judi Brownell, an expert on listening, developed the **HURIER model** to describe the six stages of effective listening, outlined in Table 1.[19] The six stages, from whose first letters the model is named, are hearing, understanding, remembering, interpreting, evaluating, and responding. We don't necessarily have to enact those stages in order;

• **HURIER model** A model describing the stages of effective listening as hearing, understanding, remembering, interpreting, evaluating, and responding.

TABLE 1	HURIER MODEL OF EFFECTIVE LISTENING

Brownell's model suggests that effective listening has six elements, represented by the acronym HURIER.

Hearing	Physically perceiving sound
Understanding	Comprehending the words we have heard
Remembering	Storing ideas in memory
Interpreting	Assigning meaning to what we've heard
Evaluating	Judging the speaker's believability and intentions
Responding	Indicating that we are listening

sometimes listening effectively requires us to go back and forth among them. Nonetheless, when we listen effectively, those are the behaviors we adopt.

Hearing Hearing, the physical process of perceiving sound, is where listening begins. Yet, as we've seen, we can certainly hear someone without listening to that person. Hearing without listening is common when we're tired or uninterested in what a person is saying, or when we're hearing multiple voices at once, as in a crowded restaurant. However, we can't really listen effectively to someone unless we can first hear the person.

The sensory task of hearing may be difficult for individuals with hearing impairments. Some read lips, and others use sign language to communicate. For individuals without hearing problems, though, hearing is the first step in effective listening.

Understanding It's not enough simply to hear what someone is saying—you also have to understand it. That means comprehending the meanings of the words and phrases.[20] If someone is speaking in a language you don't comprehend, you might be able to hear, but you won't be able to listen effectively. The same is true when you hear technical language or jargon with which you're unfamiliar: even if the speaker is speaking your language, you can't effectively listen if you do not understand the words. If you're uncertain whether you understand what a speaker is saying, the most effective course of action is usually to ask the person questions so you can check your understanding.

SHARPEN Your Skills: *Visualization*

Electronically record someone in your family telling you a story about his or her childhood. As you listen to your relative speak, visualize as much of the story as you can, using all your senses. Create a mental representation of the sights, sounds, tastes, smells, and feelings the speaker describes. A week later, retell the story to yourself, and then play your recording of the original story to see how many details you correctly recalled.

Remembering The third stage of the HURIER model of effective listening is remembering, or being able to store something in your memory and retrieve it when needed.[21] Remembering what you hear is often important for interpersonal communication, because it can help you to avoid awkward situations with others. For instance, you might have had the embarrassing experience of running into someone whose name you can't remember, even though you have met the person before. In such an encounter, the ability to remember what you heard previously—the person's name in this instance—can help you communicate more effectively.

As a student, you probably have your memory skills tested on an ongoing basis. If you're particularly good at remembering the details of a conversation, you're in the minority. Research shows that most people can recall a mere 25 percent of what they hear—and even then, they remember only about 20 percent of it accurately.[22] The average person is therefore not especially good at remembering. Fortunately, short-term memory is a skill you can practice and improve.

Mnemonics are tricks that can aid our short- and long-term memory. Such devices come in several forms. If you've ever studied music, for instance, perhaps you learned to recall the lines of the treble staff—EGBDF—by treating the letters as an acronym for a phrase such as "Every good boy does fine." You might also develop rhymes to help you remember certain rules, such as the spelling convention "*I* before *E,* except after *C.*" In another mnemonic device, you might treat an acronym as if it were a word. For instance, if you remember the elements of Brownell's effective listening model by learning the word HURIER, you are employing that type of mnemonic device. Research suggests that using mnemonic devices can significantly enhance our memory of what we hear.[23]

Comstock/Stockbyte/Getty Images

Interpreting Besides hearing, understanding, and remembering, an effective listener must interpret the information he or she receives. As you'll recall from the perception chapter, **interpretation** is the process of assigning meaning to information that has been selected for attention and organized. This process has two parts. The first part is paying attention to all the speaker's verbal and nonverbal behaviors so you can assign meaning to the person's message. Suppose your friend Maya says, "It's a beautiful day outside!" Based on her facial expressions and tone of voice, you might interpret her message as sincere—meaning that Maya thinks today's weather *is* beautiful—or as sarcastic—meaning she thinks the weather is bad. Those are very different interpretations of Maya's message, even though her words are the same.

The second part of interpreting is signaling your interpretation of the message to the speaker. If you interpret Maya's statement as sincere, you might smile and say you're looking forward to getting outside to enjoy the great weather. If you interpret her statement as sarcastic, however, you might laugh or respond with a cynical remark of your own. Signaling, in other words, not only lets the speaker know we're following along with the message, but also allows us to check our interpretations. Suppose, for instance, that Maya intended her comment to be sarcastic but you interpreted it as sincere. If you smiled and said you were looking forward to getting outside, you would probably be signaling to Maya that you have misinterpreted the intent of her statement. She might then say "I was just kidding" to correct your interpretation.

Evaluating The next step in the HURIER process involves assessing the value of the information we've received, a process called **evaluation**. Several things happen at the evaluation stage, another crucial step for effective listening. For one thing, you're judging whether the speaker's statements are accurate and true. You might base those judgments on what you already know, or you might seek out information that verifies or challenges their accuracy. Second, you're separating factual claims from opinions. As explained in the language chapter, opinions assert *what should be,* whereas factual claims assert *what is,* and each statement calls for a different type of response. Finally, you're considering the speaker's words in the context of other information you have from that speaker, such as his or her actions or previous statements. You might note, for instance, that the speaker is making a different claim today than he or she made last week, which would call the accuracy of the claim into question. All those processes help you to be an active, engaged listener rather than a passive recipient of information.

- **mnemonics** Devices that can aid short- and long-term memory.

- **interpretation** The process of assigning meaning to information that has been selected for attention and organized.

- **evaluation** Assessing the value of information we have received.

Responding to a speaker with silence and a lack of expression is known as stonewalling.

Eric Audras/Getty Images

• stonewalling Responding to another person's words with silence and lack of expression.

• backchanneling Using facial expressions, nods, vocalizations, and verbal statements to let a speaker know you are paying attention.

• paraphrasing Restating in your own words what a speaker has said, to show that you understand.

• empathizing Conveying to a speaker that you understand and share his or her feelings.

• supporting Expressing your agreement with a speaker's opinion or point of view.

• analyzing Providing your own perspective on what a speaker has said, such as by explaining your opinion or describing your experience.

• advising Communicating advice to a speaker about what he or she should think, feel, or do.

Responding The last stage of effective listening is responding, or indicating to a speaker that we are listening. We sometimes refer to that process as "giving feedback." We respond both verbally and nonverbally using a variety of strategies.[24]

Below are seven types of listening responses you might use, arranged in order from the most passive to the most active strategies:

- **Stonewalling:** Responding with silence and a lack of expression on your face. Stonewalling often signals a lack of interest in what the speaker is saying.
- **Backchanneling:** Using facial expressions, nods, vocalizations such as "uh-huh," and verbal statements such as "I understand" and "that's very interesting" to let the speaker know you're paying attention.
- **Paraphrasing:** Restating in your own words what the speaker has said, to show that you understand.
- **Empathizing:** Conveying to the speaker that you understand and share his or her feelings on the topic being discussed.
- **Supporting:** Expressing your agreement with the speaker's opinion or point of view.
- **Analyzing:** Providing your own perspective on what the speaker has said, such as by explaining your opinion or describing your experience.
- **Advising:** Communicating advice to the speaker about what he or she should think, feel, or do.

Depending on the situation, some of those responses may be more useful or appropriate than others. For instance, if you are listening to a friend who has just lost her favorite uncle to cancer, empathizing and supporting responses are probably the most fitting. Stonewalling, backchanneling, or paraphrasing might make it seem as though you don't care about your friend, whereas analyzing or advising might seem insensitive. In contrast, if you're listening to a client who is wondering how she can make the most of her stock portfolio, then analyzing and advising are probably called for. Figure 2 displays the responding strategies along a continuum from most passive to most active.

To summarize, the stages of effective listening are hearing, understanding, remembering, interpreting, evaluating, and responding. (Keep in mind that mnemonic word *HURIER.*) According to Brownell's model, those stages characterize effective listening no matter why we are listening in the first place. As you probably know, we listen to others for several different reasons. We'll take a close look at three of the most common types of listening next.

TYPES OF LISTENING

When we talk about different *types* of listening, we're referring to the different *goals* we have when we listen to other people. Sometimes we listen to learn, sometimes to

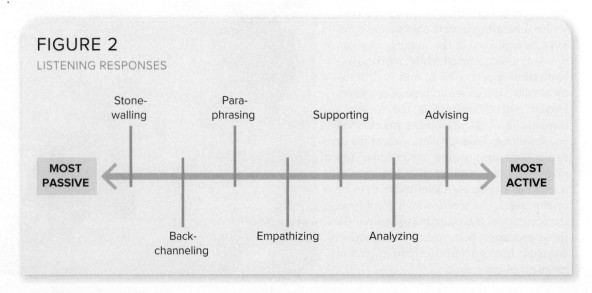

FIGURE 2
LISTENING RESPONSES

MOST PASSIVE ← → MOST ACTIVE

Stonewalling · Paraphrasing · Supporting · Advising

Backchanneling · Empathizing · Analyzing

evaluate, and sometimes to empathize. Those goals aren't necessarily exclusive; sometimes we listen with more than one goal in mind. When we distinguish among types of listening, we are considering what our *primary* listening goal is at a given time.

Informational Listening
Much of the listening you do in class or at work is **informational listening**, or listening to learn. Whenever you watch the news or listen to driving directions or pay attention to a professor's lecture, you're engaged in informational listening.

Informational listening is one of the most important ways we learn. It is also a relatively passive process. When we engage in informational listening, we're simply taking in information. That is, although we may be listening effectively and even taking notes, we are listening primarily to learn something new rather than to critique what we're hearing or to support the person saying it.

Critical Listening
When our goal is to evaluate or analyze what we're hearing, we are engaged in **critical listening**. You listen carefully to a television commercial to see whether you want to buy the product being advertised. You listen to a sales presentation or a political speech and evaluate the merits of what you're hearing. You listen critically to your mother's description of her recent medical appointment to determine how worried she is about the results of her blood test.

Critical listening doesn't necessarily mean criticizing what you're hearing. Instead, it means analyzing and evaluating the merits of a speaker's words. Compared to informational listening, critical listening is therefore a more active, engaging process. It requires not only taking in information but also evaluating and judging it. As you will see at the end of this chapter, practicing critical listening skills is one of the best ways of becoming a better listener.

Empathic Listening
The most challenging form of listening is often **empathic listening**, which occurs when you are trying to identify with the speaker by understanding and experiencing what he or she is thinking or feeling.[25] When talking to a friend who has just lost a beloved pet, you can use empathic listening to give comfort and support.

Effective empathic listening requires two separate skills. The first, *perspective taking*, is the ability to understand a situation from another's point of view.[26] The second skill, *empathic concern*, is the ability to identify how someone else is feeling and to experience those feelings yourself.[27] When listening to a coworker describing his recent diabetes diagnosis, for instance, you can practice perspective taking by trying to think about the situation as he would think about it. You can practice empathic concern by imagining how he must feel and by sharing in those emotions.

Empathic listening is different from *sympathetic listening*, which involves feeling sorry for another person. If your neighbors lost their young grandson to leukemia, for instance, you might be able to sympathize with them even if you can't truly understand their grief. With empathic listening, however, the goal is to understand a situation from the speaker's perspective and to feel what he or she is feeling. You might be listening to a friend who didn't get into her first-choice graduate school and trying to convey that you feel and share her disappointment. Listening empathically can be a challenge, because our own perceptions can cause

• **informational listening** Listening to learn.

• **critical listening** Listening to evaluate or analyze.

• **empathic listening** Listening to experience what the speaker thinks or feels.

When you listen to an instructor for the purpose of learning something, you are engaged in informational listening.
Ariel Skelley/Getty Images

us to focus on how *we* would be feeling in the same situation, when our goal is to understand the *speaker's* feelings.

Other Types of Listening Informational, critical, and empathic listening aren't the only types of listening. For example, sometimes we engage in *inspirational listening*, which is listening to be inspired by what someone is saying. That type of listening is common when we're taking in a sermon or a motivational speech. Other times, we engage in *appreciative listening*, which is listening for pure enjoyment. We adopt that style when listening to someone telling a funny story or singing one of our favorite songs. When it comes to interacting with others, however, informational, critical, and empathic listening are among the most common and most important types.

Common Barriers to Effective Listening

In an episode of the sitcom *It's Always Sunny in Philadelphia*, Frank reads about an at-large serial killer who has been murdering attractive young blonde women. After noticing that Mac hasn't been to the bar recently—and after noticing scratches on his neck—Frank announces to Dennis and Dee that he thinks Mac is the serial killer. Dennis then responds, "You know what? I just realized something . . . I know who the killer is . . . Oh my God, Dee, the real serial killer is Mac." "That's what I just said," replies Frank. Frank then announces that he has a plan to get Mac's confession, after which Dennis announces that he has just come up with the same plan. In this conversation, Dennis isn't listening to Frank, but is instead offering the same ideas that Frank has already offered.*

This scene raises the question, Why are so few of us good listeners? One answer is that several problems get in our way, acting as barriers to our ability to listen well. In this section, we examine several obstacles to effective listening.

NOISE

• **noise** Anything that distracts people from listening to what they wish to listen to.

Frazer Harrison/Staff/ Getty Images

How many different stimuli are competing for your attention right now—or perhaps at work, where your boss, customers, and coworkers may all be trying to talk to you at once? As you will recall from the introductory chapter, anything that interferes with encoding or decoding a message is called **noise**. In the context of listening, noise is anything that distracts you from listening to what you wish to listen to. That distraction could be *physical noise*, which consists of actual sound, or *psychological noise*, which is anything else we find distracting.

Most of us find it tougher to listen to a conversational partner when there are other sounds in the environment, such as a TV or loud music.[28] These are examples of physical noise. However, it isn't just sound that can distract us. If we're hungry or tired, or if we're in an especially hot or cold environment, those influences qualify as psychological noise because they distract us and thus reduce our ability to listen effectively.[29]

When faced with such distractions, focus your attention on your conversational partner and listen intently to what he or she is saying. That strategy requires being conscious of noise in your environment and identifying the factors that are drawing your attention

Dialogue from the TV Series "It's Always Sunny in Philadelphia" by FX Networks, LLC.

away from your conversation. If you can eliminate or ignore these, such as by turning off your car radio or disregarding your ringing cell phone, you will better focus attention on your partner. If you're being distracted by noise you can't ignore or reduce, it may be best to reschedule your conversation for a time when fewer stimuli are competing for your attention.

PSEUDOLISTENING AND SELECTIVE ATTENTION

At one time or another, you've probably pretended to pay attention to someone when you weren't really listening, a behavior called **pseudolistening**. When you are pseudolistening, you use feedback behaviors that make it *seem* as though you're paying attention, even though your mind is elsewhere. A variation of pseudolistening is **selective attention**, which means listening only to what you want to hear and ignoring the rest.[30] With selective attention, you are actually listening to some parts of a person's message but pseudolistening to other parts. In her job as an insurance adjustor, for instance, Sue-Ann receives an evaluation from her supervisor every January. Most of her supervisor's comments are usually positive, but some suggest ways in which Sue-Ann could improve. The problem is, Sue-Ann doesn't listen to those suggestions. Instead, she listens selectively, paying close attention to her supervisor's praise but only pretending to listen to his critiques.

People engage in pseudolistening and selective attention for many different reasons. Think about your own experiences. Maybe you're bored with what a speaker is saying, but you don't want to seem rude. Maybe you don't understand what you're hearing, but you're embarrassed to say so. Maybe you're paying attention to something else while someone is talking to you, or maybe you simply don't like what is being said. Whatever the reason, pseudolistening and selective attention are not only barriers to effective listening; they can also be a source of frustration for those you're pretending to listen to, because (as you probably know from your own experience) people are often aware when others aren't listening to what they're saying.

INFORMATION OVERLOAD

A third barrier to effective listening is **information overload**, the state of being overwhelmed by the huge amount of information each of us takes in every day. We talk to people, watch television, listen to the radio, surf the Internet, get text messages, thumb through magazines, read newspapers and college textbooks, and observe a variety of advertisements. At times, the sheer volume of information we have to attend to can seem overwhelming. When it is, we find it hard to listen effectively to new information.

Sources and Effects of Information Overload As just one example of information overload, consider how many advertising messages you see or hear on a daily basis. These might include ads on television, in magazines and newspapers, on billboards, on people's clothing, and during movie previews. You might receive ads in the mail, hear them on the radio, and find them in product inserts. You perhaps see them at gas pumps, at automated teller machines, on banners flying behind airplanes, and on the stickers you peel off fruit. You might also receive ads in the form of e-mail spam and pop-up announcements on the Internet. Researchers have estimated that the average U.S. American is exposed to as many as 4,000 advertising messages each day.[31]

It might seem as though information overload is a product of the digital age, as massive amounts of information have become so easily and immediately available at the touch of a key. In fact, the term *information overload* was coined in 1970 by sociologist Alvin Toffler, in a book discussing the downsides of rapid technological change.[32] Thus, people were experiencing the distracting effects of information overload long before computer-mediated communication was widely used.

One of the biggest problems with information overload is that it can interrupt our attention. If you're e-mailing with an important client, for instance, your ability to pay attention to her messages can be compromised repeatedly by each new radio advertisement

> • **pseudolistening** Pretending to listen.

> • **selective attention** Listening only to what one wants to hear and ignoring the rest.

> • **information overload** The state of being overwhelmed by the enormous amount of information encountered each day.

Children diagnosed with attention-deficit hyperactivity disorder find information overload significantly problematic.

racorn/123RF

you hear, each new faxed announcement you receive, and each new pop-up ad you see. Those interruptions might seem small and inconsequential when considered individually, but when you think about their effects on the entire population over time, they become a significant distraction. An analysis by database management firm BaseX estimated the annual cost to U.S. companies of unnecessary interruptions from information overload to be a staggering $997 billion.[33]

Information overload can be particularly troubling for people with *attention-deficit hyperactivity disorder (ADHD)*, a developmental disorder. Individuals with ADHD are often easily distracted and have trouble focusing their attention for very long at a time. They are often also overly active and restless.[34] Although ADHD symptoms usually appear during childhood, a majority of children diagnosed with ADHD will continue to suffer from it as adults.[35] Because of their impaired ability to focus and susceptibility to distraction, individuals with ADHD may have an especially difficult time coping with the volume of information most of us encounter every day.

Managing Information Overload Online Between Snapchat, Twitter, Facebook, and YouTube, keeping up with the people in your life can seem like a full-time job. Texting alone can overwhelm: young adults in the United States send or receive an average of almost 3,900 text message per month.[36] You've learned in this chapter that information overload hampers your ability to listen effectively in face-to-face conversations. Scientists have discovered that the same effect occurs in electronically mediated communication.

When you're swamped with texts, tags, and tweets, you experience what researchers call *conversational overload*, which reduces your ability to attend to those messages adequately.[37] In particular, research has found that

- *People are more likely to attend to—and respond to—simple messages than complex ones.* Paying attention to a message requires cognitive energy, and each person has only so much to spend. When their attention is already stretched thin, people attend to messages that are simple and direct.

- *When people feel overloaded, they end or reduce their communication.* People experience overload when the energy required to attend to their communication tasks exceeds what they are willing or able to invest. In those situations, a very common strategy is to reduce the number of incoming messages, such as by unfriending Facebook users or opting out of listservs.

Good listening skills are as important in electronically mediated communication as they are in face-to-face interaction. The better you can prevent barriers to effective listening—including information overload and conversational overload—the more effective an interpersonal communicator you'll be.

GLAZING OVER

A fourth reason effective listening is challenging is that the mind thinks much faster than most people talk. Most of us are capable of understanding up to 600 words per minute, but the average person speaks fewer than 150 words per minute.[38] That gap leaves a lot of spare time for the mind to wander, during which we can engage in what researchers call **glazing over**, or daydreaming.

For instance, Rochelle picks up her 6-year-old daughter and 9-year-old son every afternoon, and during the drive home the children describe what they did in school that day. Although she listens to what they say, Rochelle allows her mind to wander

• **glazing over** Daydreaming or allowing the mind to wander while another person is speaking.

as they talk. She thinks about the novel she's reading and ponders her grocery list. Because her children speak more slowly than she can listen, and because the reports of their school activities are similar every day, Rochelle often glazes over when listening to them.

Glazing over is different from pseudolistening, which, as you'll recall, means only pretending to listen. When you're glazing over, you actually *are* listening to the speaker. It's just that you're allowing your mind to drift while doing so.

Glazing over can lead to at least three different problems. First, it can cause you to miss important details in what you're hearing. If you're glazing over while listening to a lecture in your communication course, for instance, you might fail to hear a critical piece of information about the term paper assignment. Second, glazing over might lead you to listen less critically than you normally would. For example, if your mind is wandering while you're listening to a salesperson describe the terms of a car loan, you might not realize that the deal isn't as good as it seems. Finally, glazing over can make it appear to a speaker that you aren't listening to what he or she is saying, even though you are. In those instances, you can come across as inattentive or dismissive. An effective listener will work to keep his or her focus on what the speaker is saying, instead of daydreaming or thinking about other topics.

We glaze over when we go back and forth between listening to someone and allowing our mind to wander with other thoughts.
Wavebreakmedia Ltd/Getty Images

REBUTTAL TENDENCY

Regan has recently started work as a customer service representative for an electronics retailer, but his first two weeks on the job have not gone well. He knows he should listen nonjudgmentally to customers as they describe their frustrations with the products they bought and then offer them his assistance and advice. Instead, Regan begins arguing with customers in his mind while they're still speaking. Rather than listening carefully to their concerns, he jumps to conclusions about what they have done wrong, and he formulates his response even before they have stopped talking.

Regan is enacting a **rebuttal tendency**, the propensity to debate a speaker's point and formulate a reply while that person is still speaking.[39] According to research by business professor Steven Golen, the tendency to think of how you're going to respond to a speaker, arguing with the speaker in your mind, and jumping to conclusions before the speaker has finished talking are all barriers to effective listening.[40] There are two reasons why.

First, the rebuttal tendency requires mental energy that should be spent paying attention to the speaker. That is, it's difficult to listen effectively when all you're thinking about is how to respond. The second reason is closely related: because you're not paying close attention to the speaker, you can easily miss some of the details that might change your response in the first place. Regan had that very experience when a woman returned a wireless Internet router she was having trouble installing. Regan concluded too quickly that she hadn't followed the instructions, and he got sidetracked thinking about what he was going to say in response. Consequently, he didn't hear the customer say that she'd already had a technician guide her through the installation procedure and advise her that the router was defective. If Regan had heard that important detail, he could have exchanged the product efficiently and sent the customer on her way. Instead, he spent 10 minutes telling the customer to do what she had already done, leaving her feeling frustrated.

• **rebuttal tendency** The propensity to debate a speaker's point and formulate a reply while that person is still speaking.

CLOSED-MINDEDNESS

Another barrier to effective listening is **closed-mindedness**, the tendency not to listen to anything with which we disagree.[41] Perhaps you know people whom you would

• **closed-mindedness** The tendency not to listen to anything with which one disagrees.

describe as closed-minded: they typically refuse to consider the merits of a speaker's point if it conflicts with their own views. They also tend to overreact to certain forms of language, such as slang and profanity, and stop listening to speakers who use them.[42]

Many people are closed-minded only about particular issues, not about everything. For example, as an educator, Bella prides herself in being open to diverse opinions on a range of topics. When it comes to her own religious beliefs, however, she is so thoroughly convinced of their merits that she refuses even to listen to religious ideas that she doesn't already accept. It's as if Bella is shutting her mind to the possibility that any religious ideas besides her own can have value. Many of her teaching colleagues find this reaction off-putting. It prevents Bella not only from learning more about their religious traditions but also from teaching others about her beliefs, because she refuses to talk about religion with anyone who doesn't already share her views.

Bella should remember that we can listen effectively to people even if we disagree with them. As the Greek philosopher Aristotle (384–322 B.C.) wrote: "It is the mark of an educated mind to be able to entertain a thought without accepting it." When we refuse even to listen to ideas with which we disagree, we limit our ability to learn from other people and their experiences. If you find yourself feeling closed-minded toward particular ideas, remind yourself that listening to an idea doesn't necessarily mean accepting it.

Most of us probably prefer to think of ourselves as open-minded. When others call us closed-minded, therefore, it is easy to take offense, as the "Difficult Conversations" box addresses.

COMPETITIVE INTERRUPTING

Normal conversation is a series of speaking "turns." You speak for a while, and then you allow another person to have a turn, and thus the conversation goes back and forth. Occasionally, though, people talk when it isn't their turn. We call that behavior *interrupting,* and there are many reasons people do it. Sometimes they interrupt to express support or enthusiasm for what the other person is saying ("Yeah, I agree!"); sometimes they do so to stop the speaker and ask for clarification ("Wait, I'm not sure what you mean"); and sometimes they talk out of turn to warn the speaker of an impending danger ("Stop! You're spilling your coffee!").

• **competitive interrupting** The practice of using interruptions to take control of the conversation.

Photodisc Collection/Getty Images

For some people, however, interrupting can be a way to dominate a conversation. Researchers use the term **competitive interrupting** to describe the practice of using interruptions to take control of the conversation. The goal in competitive interrupting is to make sure that you get to speak more than the other person does and that your ideas and perspectives take priority. You can probably think of people who engage in that behavior—individuals with whom you feel you "can't get a word in edgewise."

Although research shows that most interruptions *aren't* competitive, talking with a competitive interrupter can be frustrating.[43] Some people respond by becoming competitive themselves, turning the conversation into a battle of wits; others simply withdraw from the interaction. Some studies suggest that on average, men interrupt more often than women, although other studies have found no sex difference in the use of interruptions.[44]

How else do women and men differ in their listening behaviors? Check out the "Fact or Fiction?" box to find out.

Difficult Conversations

Being Called "Closed-Minded"

Imagine this: Your oldest cousin Judy gives birth to fraternal twins, one girl and one boy. Quite naturally, she posts many photos of the newborns on social media and shares stories of their daily activities and development. You usually enjoy seeing her postings, but you are surprised when you read her announcement that she has decided not to vaccinate her children.

Now, consider this: You decide to ask Judy about her choice, and she explains that she is worried about the link between vaccines and autism. She says she has read several magazine articles on the topic and has watched a three-part series about autism on her favorite talk show, and she is convinced that vaccines are harmful. You recall from your public health class last spring that there is no scientific evidence to support a link between autism and vaccines, and you offer to let Judy read about the issue in your course material before making up her mind. She angrily declines and calls you closed-minded for refusing to believe how dangerous vaccines are, given that "everyone knows they cause autism." As you consider how to respond, bear the following in mind:

- Remember that when people say "you're being closed-minded," all they often mean is "you should agree with me." Most of us like to believe we make sound, well informed decisions, so when other people disagree with us, it is easier to call them closed-minded than to consider their reasons for thinking differently. Judy may simply be frustrated that you hold a different position on the issue of vaccination than she does.

- If Judy really does think you have closed your mind to the evidence, ask her where she is finding her own information. Doing so may cause her to realize that she is listening only to sources that support her belief, just as she is accusing you of doing.

- Even if you believe you are being open-minded about the issue, ask yourself honestly if *you* are open to all sides of the debate. You may feel that the strongest evidence supports your position, but are you open to being persuaded? Being open-minded doesn't mean you should take a position that you don't believe to be well supported. It does mean that you recognize the possibility that your position may be wrong, and you are open to changing your mind if better evidence comes along.

- Judy may be so strongly committed to her belief that no possible evidence could lead her to reconsider. If that is the case, then you may have to agree to disagree if you want to maintain your relationship with each other.

Few of us enjoy being called closed-minded, and even fewer of us recognize closed-mindedness in ourselves. People often use that term as an insult to ridicule beliefs that are different from their own. It is always worth considering honestly whether we are open to the possibility of changing our minds about an important issue. When two people are closed-minded about each other's ideas, however, that can easily lead to some difficult conversations.

Fact or *fiction?*

Sex Matters: Men and Women Listen Differently

In this text we examine several stereotypes about how women and men communicate. Some are outright false, others are true, and some are true but highly exaggerated. One idea that relates to listening is that women and men have different listening styles: women are more interested in people, whereas men are more interested in facts. Are those distinctions fact or fiction?

Research suggests these assumed differences are true. In a study of adults' listening styles, researchers Stephanie Sargent and James Weaver found that women rated themselves higher on people-oriented listening than men did, suggesting that women use their listening skills to learn about people and make connections with others. In contrast, men rated themselves higher on content-oriented listening, an outcome suggesting that men use their listening skills to take in content and solve intellectual challenges. Those findings do not mean women don't engage in content-oriented listening and men don't engage in people-oriented listening—they certainly do in both cases. Rather, the study results show that women and men—overall—have different approaches to listening, just as the stereotype suggests.

You might recall reading earlier in this chapter that people often overestimate their listening abilities, so you may wonder how you can have confidence in the result of a study that relies on self-reports. Because virtually every study of listening styles uses a self-report method for collecting data, that's a critical question. The answer is that reporting on *how* you listen is different from reporting on *how well* you listen. Many of us do have a tendency to exaggerate how well we listen, but research suggests that we are much more accurate at reporting the style of listening we use.

Research shows that women and men have different styles of listening. Women are more likely than men are to say they use their listening skills to learn about people and make personal connections. Men are more likely to say they use their listening skills to solve intellectual challenges.

Lifesize/Getty Images

How can we apply the information about sex differences in listening styles to improve our communication abilities? When communicating with members of the other sex, we can consider their listening tendencies and formulate our messages accordingly. Let's say you're describing to different friends a recent conflict you had with your romantic partner. Because you know that men tend to focus on the content of what they're hearing, you might tailor your description to male friends to highlight what the conflict was about and what each person's position was. Because you know that women tend to focus on the interpersonal aspects of what they're hearing, you might adapt your description to female friends to focus on what the conflict taught you about your relational partner and yourself. Although sex differences in listening preferences are just tendencies, they can still give you clues for communicating effectively with members of each sex.

ASK YOURSELF

- How do the general sex differences described above compare to the listening behavior of women and men you know?

- Is one style of listening better than another, in your opinion? How might men's and women's styles of listening be appropriate in different situations?

SOURCE: Sargent, S. L., & Weaver, J. B. (2003). Listening styles: Sex differences in perceptions of self and others. *International Journal of Listening, 17(1),* 5–18. https://doi.org/10.1080/10904018.2003.10499052

Table 2 summarizes the barriers to effective listening. Bear in mind that each of them can be overcome. Specifically, with training and practice, most of us can improve our abilities to listen well, as we'll now consider.

Honing Your Listening Skills

We've looked at several examples of ineffective listening in this chapter. Regan doesn't listen effectively to his customers' complaints, and Rochelle glazes over when listening to her children describe their school day. Clearly, listening effectively can be a challenge. Fortunately, effective listening is a skill that can be developed through education and practice. Author Mary Lou Casey once wrote that "what people really need is a good listening to," and her sentiment suggests that we can do much good in our interpersonal relationships if we sharpen our listening abilities. In this section, we'll look at strategies you can use to improve your skills in informational, critical, and empathic listening. We will also look at ways to improve your listening experience online.

BECOME A BETTER INFORMATIONAL LISTENER

When you engage in informational listening, your goal is to understand and learn from the speaker's message. For instance, you might be participating in a videoconference about saving for retirement or asking a nurse practitioner over the phone about your medications. How can you make the most of those opportunities?

Separate What Is and Isn't Said One important strategy for improving your informational listening skills is to beware of the tendency to "hear" words or statements that aren't actually said. Think about the last time you saw a TV commercial for a pain reliever, for instance. A common tactic for advertisers is to claim that "nothing is more effective" than their product. What do you learn from hearing that statement? In other words, how would you restate the message in your own words?

The advertisers are hoping you learn that their particular pain reliever is the strongest one available—but that's not really what they said, is it? All they said is that nothing is more effective, a statement that could mean that there are several other products *just as effective* as theirs. It may also mean that all the products are equally ineffective! If you listened to that type of ad and concluded that the product was the most effective one available, you arrived at that conclusion on your own. When you are engaged in informational listening, practice being aware of what is actually being said versus what you are simply inferring.

Perhaps the most effective way to determine whether you have understood a speaker's message is to paraphrase it. As we saw earlier in the chapter, paraphrasing means restating a speaker's message in your own words in order to clarify its meaning. If you paraphrase a statement in a way that accurately reflects its meaning, the speaker will usually confirm your understanding.

noise—Anything that distracts you from listening to what you wish to listen to	**TABLE 2** BARRIERS TO EFFECTIVE LISTENING
pseudolistening—Using feedback behaviors to give the false impression that you are listening	
selective attention—Listening only to points you want to hear, while ignoring all other points	
information overload—Being overwhelmed with the large amount of information you must take in every day	
glazing over—Daydreaming when you aren't speaking or listening during a conversation	
rebuttal tendency—Propensity to argue inwardly with a speaker and formulate your conclusions and responses prematurely	
closed-mindedness—Refusal even to listen to ideas or positions with which you disagree	
competitive interrupting—Interrupting others to gain control of a conversation	

Let's suppose that while leaving a theater after a movie, your roommate Dean and you have the following exchange:

> **Dean:** *I think we should swing by that new barbecue place on the way home.*
>
> **You:** *You want to pick up some dinner?*
>
> **Dean:** *Yeah, I'm starving.*

You conclude that Dean is implying he's hungry and wants to get some food, but that isn't actually what he said. To check your understanding, you therefore paraphrase his statement by putting it into your own words. Because you understood his statement correctly, he replies by confirming your interpretation.

If you paraphrase a statement in a way that changes its meaning, many speakers will reply by correcting your understanding. Let's say the exchange with Dean goes like this:

> **Dean:** *I think we should swing by that new barbecue place on the way home.*
>
> **You:** *You want to pick up some dinner?*
>
> **Dean:** *No, I want to see if my friend Blake is working tonight.*

In that instance, your interpretation of Dean's statement was inaccurate. By paraphrasing his statement, you invited him to correct your understanding, and he did. Paraphrasing is a simple but very efficient way to determine whether you have correctly separated what a speaker has and has not said.

Avoid the Confirmation Bias The **confirmation bias** is the tendency to pay attention only to information that supports our values and beliefs, while discounting or ignoring information that doesn't.[45] This tendency becomes a problem for listening when it causes us to make up our minds about an issue without paying attention to all sides.

Suppose you're turning to talk radio for perspective on U.S. immigration policies. If you favor a conservative approach to immigration laws, including deportation of undocumented immigrants, then you may consider Ben Shapiro a more credible source than Rachel Maddow. If your preference is for a more liberal immigration policy, including a guest-worker program, then you'll probably listen more to what Maddow has to say. In either case, by seeking a perspective that already aligns with your point of view, you avoid exposing yourself to alternative viewpoints.

Good informational listeners are aware, however, that their beliefs are not necessarily accurate. Thus, another strategy for improving your informational listening skills is to ask yourself whether you have listened to all sides of an issue before you form a conclusion—or whether, instead, you are simply avoiding information that would lead you to question your beliefs.

Listen for Substance More Than Style The psychological principle called the **vividness effect** is the tendency of dramatic, shocking events to distort our perceptions of reality.[46] We watch news coverage of a mass shooting, for instance, and we worry more about being victimized. A 2019 Reuters poll found, for instance, that 59 percent of Americans believe mass shootings pose the biggest safety threat to them.[47] A similar poll conducted by the American Psychological Association found that a third of American adults avoid going to certain places or attending certain events because they fear mass shootings.[48] There is no question that mass shootings are tragic events that can shatter the lives of victims. However, the average American's probability of dying in a mass shooting is 1 in 11,125, according to statistics compiled by the National Safety Council.[49] That likelihood is smaller than the odds of dying from the flu, from choking on food, from drowning, and from having a motorcycle accident *combined*. This observation in no way diminishes the pain and terror that mass shootings have caused, but it can help us avoid falling victim to the vividness effect by believing we are at a higher risk than we actually are.

• **confirmation bias** The tendency to pay attention only to information that supports one's values and beliefs, while discounting or ignoring information that does not.

• **vividness effect** The tendency of dramatic, shocking events to distort one's perceptions of reality.

The vividness effect can also occur in relationships. If your parents went through a traumatic divorce when you were a child, that experience might make you think marriage is more likely to fail than it actually is. The reason for all these mistaken conclusions is that dramatic events are more vivid and memorable than everyday events, so we pay more attention to them.

We can experience much the same problem during informational listening if we focus only on what's most vivid. Let's say that your history class yesterday included dramatic stories and flashy PowerPoint slides you found highly entertaining, but in today's class the lecture was comparatively dry and lacked those bells and whistles. You shouldn't conclude that the flashy presentation contained better information than the dry one did, or that you necessarily learned more from it. Similarly, you might love being in classes with engaging, humorous teachers, but that doesn't necessarily mean you'll learn more from them than from more serious teachers. Being a good informational listener means being able to look past what is dramatic and vivid to focus on the *substance* of what you're hearing. That skill starts with being aware of the vividness effect and remembering that vivid experiences can distort your perceptions. The next time you go through a dramatic event or listen to a particularly engaging speaker, ask yourself whether you are listening and paying attention to accurate information instead of being swayed by the event's drama or the speaker's charisma.

Listening for substance more than style is critical in many career fields. For one example, check out "Putting Communication to Work."

BECOME A BETTER CRITICAL LISTENER

Many interpersonal situations require you to assess the reliability and trustworthiness of what you're hearing. Here are three ways to hone that ability.

• skepticism A method of
questioning that involves
evaluating evidence for a
stated claim.

Be a Skeptic Being a good critical listener starts with being skeptical of what
you hear. **Skepticism**—a method of questioning that involves evaluating evidence
for a stated claim—isn't about being cynical or finding fault; it's about questioning
whether a claim is well supported. As we noted above with respect to the confirmation
bias, some people pay attention only to evidence that supports what they
already believe. Being skeptical means setting aside your biases and being willing to
be persuaded by the merits of the argument and the quality of the evidence. A good
critical listener doesn't accept claims blindly but questions them to see whether they
are valid.[50]

Suppose your coworker Fahid has come up with a business opportunity, tells you
about his plan, and asks you to consider investing in it. Poor critical listeners might
make their decision based on how they feel about Fahid or how excited they are at the
prospect of making money. If you're a good critical listener, though, you'll set aside
your feelings and focus on the merits of Fahid's idea. Does he have a sound business
plan? Is there a genuine market for his product? Has he budgeted for advertising? Did
he explain how he would use your investment? Being a critical listener doesn't mean
criticizing his plans—it means evaluating them to see whether they make sense.

Evaluate a Speaker's Credibility Besides analyzing the merits of an argument,
a good critical listener pays attention to the credibility of the speaker. As we've
seen, *credibility* refers to the reliability and trustworthiness of someone or something.
All other things being equal, you can generally presume that information from a credible
source is more believable than information from a noncredible source.

Several qualities make a speaker more or less credible. One is expertise. It makes
more sense for us to trust medical advice we receive from a physician than from a professional
athlete, for instance, because the doctor is a medical expert and the athlete is
not. At the same time, it doesn't make sense to trust a physician for legal or financial
advice, because he or she isn't an expert in those realms.

It's sometimes easy to confuse *expertise* with *experience*. Having experience with
something may give a person credibility in that area, but it doesn't necessarily make
the individual an expert. Consider Hannah, the mother of six children. In the course
of raising her kids, Hannah has become a very experienced parent, so she has sufficient
credibility to give advice to other moms insofar as she can draw on her many
experiences. Yet Hannah isn't an expert on parenting because her only source of credibility
is her individual experience. For example, she isn't a recognized authority on
parenting issues, nor does she have a degree in child development.

Good critical listeners
set aside their feelings
and biases and focus on
the merits of the idea.

Image Source/Getty Images

Conversely, people can be experts on topics and areas with which they have no direct personal experience. As a board-certified obstetrician and gynecologist, Tyrell is an expert on pregnancy and women's health, even though, as a man, he has not personally experienced a pregnancy or a disease to which only women are vulnerable. Similarly, Young Li is an outstanding marital therapist who has helped countless couples even though she has never married. How can a man be a good obstetrician and a single person be a good marital therapist? The answer is that they draw on their training and expertise to help others, not on their individual experiences.

Another characteristic that affects a speaker's credibility is bias. If a speaker has a special interest in making you believe some idea or claim, that bias tends to reduce his or her credibility. For instance, if a tobacco company executive claimed publicly that smoking has health benefits, a good critical listener would be highly skeptical because the executive is a biased source. That bias might seem obvious, because we know the executive makes a living from the sale of tobacco products—but sometimes you have to dig below the surface to evaluate someone's credibility. For example, you might be intrigued to hear about a research report claiming that using your cell phone while driving does not increase your risk of being in a collision. You might assume the study was conducted by a reputable source, such as a research team at a major university, and that assumption would enhance the report's credibility in your mind. You decide to investigate further, however, and you discover that the study was funded by a group that lobbies on behalf of the telecommunications industry. Given its purpose, such a group would have a vested interest in research results favorable to cell phone use. That doesn't necessarily mean the study's conclusions are wrong. It does mean, though, that you should be more skeptical when thinking about the results.

Understand Probability Evaluating the merits of a claim means speculating about the likelihood that the claim is true. Such speculation can be tricky, however, because we sometimes confuse what's possible with what's probable and what's probable with what's certain. A claim is *possible* if there's even the slightest chance, however small, that it might be true. In contrast, to be *probable*, a statement has to have greater than a 50 percent chance of being true. Finally, a statement is *certain* only if its likelihood of being true is 100 percent and nothing less.

Consider a claim such as "I can survive without water for a month." There's a possibility that assertion could be true, but the likelihood is pretty small. The claim certainly isn't probable, and a good critical listener wouldn't treat it as though it were. The statement "I will get married someday" is not only possible, it's also probable, because a very large majority of people marry at least once in their lives. Is that claim therefore certain? No, because there's a chance, however small, that it might not happen. For a claim to be certain, there can be *absolutely no chance* that it isn't true. A claim such as "I will die someday" is certain, because every living being eventually dies. Good critical listeners understand the differences among possibility, probability, and certainty. They bear in mind that a claim that is possible isn't necessarily one that is worth believing.

BECOME A BETTER EMPATHIC LISTENER

Within our relationships, a common goal for listening is to provide empathy and support. Being a good empathic listener can be challenging at times, but it's not impossible.

Good empathic listeners listen in a nonjudgmental way.

Don Hammond/Design Pics

Listen Nonjudgmentally When we listen to learn, and especially when we listen to evaluate, we often make judgments about the information we're taking in. But good empathic listening is about being open-minded and nonjudgmental.

Two strategies are particularly helpful here. First, listen without interrupting. Being empathic means letting the other person say what he or she needs to say without jumping into the middle of the message. Fight the urge to interrupt, and simply listen to the other person. Second, think twice before offering unsolicited advice. When other people tell us their problems, our tendency is often to respond with advice on solving those problems.[51] A good empathic listener remembers that people aren't always looking for advice—they often just want someone to listen to them.

According to the program Mental Health First Aid, which teaches skills for helping those with psychological and emotional difficulties, these suggestions can assist in listening nonjudgmentally:[52]

- *Recognize your current emotions.* Before you can listen effectively to someone else, it helps to make sure you are feeling calm, open, and ready to help.
- *Choose to be open to what the speaker is saying.* Be mindful about accepting the other person's values, feelings, and experiences as valid, even if you disagree with them.
- *Respond verbally.* Ask questions, give cues such as "I understand," and pay attention to your tone of voice—all of which can encourage the other person to communicate with you honestly.
- *Use body language to encourage the speaker to continue to talk.* Sit or stand facing the other person, keep an open body position, and maintain a comfortable level of eye contact—not too much and not too little.
- *Consider the speaker's background.* If you are listening to someone whose cultural background is different from yours, remember that you may need to adjust certain behaviors—such as eye contact and personal space—to help that person feel more comfortable.

Acknowledge Feelings Empathizing is about understanding how someone else is feeling and trying to relate to those feelings. It's *not* the same as sympathizing, which is feeling sorry for the other person. An important strategy for good empathic listening, therefore, is to acknowledge a speaker's feelings and allow him or her to continue expressing them.

We do so by responding to speakers with *continuer statements*, phrases that identify the emotions a person is experiencing and allow him or her to communicate them further. In contrast, it is important to avoid *terminator statements*, phrases that fail to acknowledge a speaker's emotions, shutting down his or her opportunity to express them. After listening to a patient describe her concerns about the progress of her illness, for instance, empathic physicians can use continuer statements such as "That must make you feel very uncertain" and "I can imagine how scary this must be" to convey to the patient that they understand and appreciate her feelings. Physicians with less empathic ability will be more likely to use terminator statements such as "We're doing everything we can" and "You just need to give this some time." Those types of responses imply to the patient that her feelings are unimportant.

In a 2007 study, researchers, with permission, recorded nearly 400 conversations between advanced cancer patients and their oncologists[53] and listened for times when patients expressed negative emotions such as sadness, fear, and anxiety. When those moments arose, doctors replied with continuer statements only 22 percent of the time. Younger physicians were more likely than older ones to use continuers, and female physicians were more likely than male doctors to do so. That doesn't mean oncologists lack empathy. Rather, it illustrates that they may have trouble communicating their empathy through emotionally supportive listening responses, which are particularly important for individuals struggling with a terminal illness such as advanced cancer.

Communicate Support Nonverbally One of the most important aspects of being a good empathic listener is communicating your support nonverbally. When you're listening rather than speaking, your nonverbal behaviors convey your interest, understanding, and empathy to the speaker.

Perhaps the most important nonverbal behavior in this situation is eye contact. Others often watch your eye behaviors to see whether you're paying attention to what they're saying. If you allow yourself to be distracted by your environment, you can convey the message that you aren't really listening. Other important empathic behaviors are your use of facial expressions and touch. A reassuring smile and a warm touch can make people feel as though you understand, support, and empathize with them.[54]

EFFECTIVE LISTENING ONLINE

We may think of listening as being primarily a face-to-face activity, and it often is. But effective listening isn't limited to face-to-face interaction: given how much of our communication takes place online, it pays to consider how people can listen effectively in that context as well. In this section, we'll examine some strategies for finding an effective listener online and for being an effective listener yourself.

Finding an Effective Listener Online Where do you turn when you need someone to listen to you? These days, many people go online, whether it's to communicate with existing friends and loved ones or to make new connections with people who understand what they're going through. In either case, it's possible to find good listeners in online venues.

One of the most common online sources for listening—especially empathic listening—is the online support group. Support groups give people a context for sharing their challenges and being heard by others who can empathize—usually because they have faced similar challenges themselves. Research shows that communicating with others who have endured the same situations can give people a sense of safety and community, reducing feelings of loneliness and isolation.[55]

Many support groups meet in face-to-face settings. Millions of others are hosted online, for issues ranging from eating disorders, Parkinson's disease, and infertility to child rearing, debt relief, and suicide prevention. One study found that Facebook alone hosted over 600 support groups, containing more than a million members total, devoted specifically to the topic of breast cancer.[56] Even Alcoholics Anonymous—which offers thousands of support groups for people struggling with alcoholism—hosts more than a hundred online meetings in a variety of languages.[57]

For many participants, one of the biggest benefits of online support groups is the opportunity to have others listen actively and empathically to what they say. If you're

Need Someone to Listen? Just Click

From time to time, we all need someone to listen to us. We often turn to close friends and relatives, but they aren't always available and they may not be particularly skilled at listening. Sometimes it's easier to talk to a stranger, but seeing a licensed counselor can be expensive and can make people feel stigmatized. As a solution to those problems, psychologist Glen Moriarty started the website 7cupsoftea.com. The site brings together hundreds of individuals from around the world who are trained to listen with compassion, empathy, and respect. Users are able to chat—anonymously and for free—with trained listeners about any topic they wish to discuss. Moriarty got the idea for the site while sitting at his kitchen table talking to his wife about a problem. He acknowledged that he was fortunate to have someone to listen to him, and he realized that many people don't.

Users of the site seek listeners for a wide variety of reasons, including feeling lonely, trying to get over a breakup, and simply wanting to "vent" to someone. Others look for listeners whom they can talk to about more serious issues, such as feeling depressed or having suicidal thoughts. All conversations are encrypted to maintain security, and users can evaluate listeners' abilities to be supportive, empathic, and kind. Moriarty stresses the value of his listeners' nonjudgmental approach. As the website explains, "Unlike talking to family or friends, a 7 Cups of Tea listener doesn't judge or try to solve problems and say what to do. Our listeners just listen. They understand."*

When you're dealing with a problem and just want someone to listen, it may not occur to you to turn to the Internet. There is certainly value in talking with your close friends, relatives, and peers. Their advice and perspective can be useful, especially because they know you and understand your priorities. Don't overlook the value of talking to a stranger who will do nothing but listen, however. When we share our problems with others, we don't always want or need advice on what to do—sometimes, simply having someone listen is enough.

*www.7cupsoftea.com

SOURCE: www.7cupsoftea.com

grieving over the loss of a parent, for instance, it helps to be listened to by others who have endured the same experience. Research shows that when people in online support groups feel heard and understood, they experience improvements in their well-being as a result.[58]

A key characteristic of many online support groups is that they allow participants to talk and listen anonymously, by using fake user names instead of their real names. That anonymity can be therapeutic, especially when people are discussing sensitive topics. According to research, people are more likely to seek support online—rather than in person—if they feel stigmatized by the issue for which they are seeking support.[59] Suffering from a mental illness, being significantly in debt, and dealing with suicide are examples of issues that can invite judgment from others, which may encourage people to look for support in environments where they can be heard anonymously.

We all go through times when we need someone to listen to us empathically. Perhaps we have problems we don't want to share with friends or relatives, however, yet seeing a therapist is too expensive or inconvenient. The "Dark Side of Communication" box suggests an alternative for times when we need an empathic ear.

Being an Effective Listener Online Having discussed ways to find a good listener online, let's now consider what it means to be an effective online listener yourself. Whether your listening is informational, critical, or empathic, you can benefit by remembering these tips.

- *Be attentive.* When you interact with someone online, it's sometimes easy to become distracted by other stimuli in your environment. Perhaps you're watching a television program or checking your e-mail at the same time, for instance, so you are dividing your attention between multiple tasks. Just as those behaviors would impair your ability to listen in a face-to-face conversation, they diminish your ability to listen effectively online. Instead, stay attuned to what the other person is saying. That's especially important when you're communicating with someone in real time—such as in an online chat or via instant messaging—because it will be more evident if you aren't responding to the person's words in a timely manner.

- *Remember that words can be misinterpreted.* When you listen to someone in a face-to-face conversation, you can use nonverbal behaviors—such as facial expressions and tone of voice—to help you interpret the meaning of his or her words. As we discussed in the nonverbal communication chapter, however, many computer-mediated messages rely heavily on words, and words can have more than one meaning. Without nonverbal cues to guide you, therefore, it can be easier to misinterpret what someone else is saying. Good online listeners remind themselves that words in an e-mail message, instant message, or text can have multiple meanings, and they ask for clarification when they're not sure how to interpret someone's statements.

- *Don't be a lurker.* In support groups and other online communities, a *lurker* is someone who regularly reads other people's words but rarely if ever contributes to the conversation. Because lurkers pay attention to the words of others, it may seem as though lurking is all about listening. Remember, however, that listening is an active process of making meaning out of another person's message. Lurking, on the other hand, is a passive process that requires no engagement in the conversation. According to research, 90 percent of users in most online communities are lurkers who never contribute to the discussion.[60] When people lurk, they simply benefit from others' contributions without adding anything to the interaction.[61] Moreover, if too many people in an online community are merely lurking, then the knowledge shared in that community may not be representative of everyone there.[62] Lurking isn't as big of a problem when you aren't particularly interested or invested in the topic of conversation. When you do care about what others are saying, however, take a more active role by interpreting, evaluating, and responding to other people's comments.

As you discover more about good listening behaviors in this course, practice what you learn in both your online and offline environments.

For REVIEW

- ### What does it mean to listen effectively?

  We listen effectively when we hear, understand, remember, interpret, evaluate, and respond to what someone has said. Cultural messages shape listening, just as they influence many communication behaviors.

- ### Why is listening effectively so challenging?

  Many barriers exist to effective listening, including noise, pseudolistening, selective attention, information overload, glazing over, rebuttal tendency, closed-mindedness, and competitive interrupting.

- ### How can you improve your listening skills?

  You can be a better informational listener by separating what is and isn't said, avoiding the confirmation bias, and listening for substance. You can improve your critical listening skills by being skeptical, evaluating credibility, and understanding probability. You can become better at empathic listening by listening nonjudgmentally, acknowledging a speaker's feelings, and communicating support nonverbally.

KEY TERMS

NOTES

1. Tomasi, S. E., Fechter-Leggett, E. D., Edwards, N. T., Reddish, A. D., Crosby, A. E., & Nett, R. J. (2019). Suicide among veterinarians in the United States from 1979 through 2015. *Journal of the American Veterinary Medical Association, 254*(1), 104–112. https://doi.org/10.2460/javma.254.1.104

2. Nett, R. J., Witte, T. K., Holzbauer, S. M., Elchos, B. L., Campagnolo, E. R., Musgrave, K. J., Carter, K. K., Kurkjian, K. M., Vanicek, C., O'Leary, D. R., Pride, K. R., & Funk, R. H. (2015, February 13). Notes from the field: Prevalence of risk factors for suicide among veterinarians—United States, 2014. *Centers for Disease Control and Prevention Morbidity and Mortality Weekly Report, 64*(5), 131–132.

3. See, e.g., Fertitta, T. (2019). *Shut up and listen! Hard business truths that will help you succeed.* HarperCollins.

4. Worthington, D. L., & Bodie, G. D. (2017). Defining listening: A historical, theoretical and pragmatic assessment. In D. L. Worthington, & G. D. Bodie (Eds.), *The sourcebook of listening research: Methodology and measures* (pp. 1–18). Wiley-Blackwell. https://doi.org/10.1002/9781119102991

5. Bodie, G. D., & Worthington, D. L. (2017). Listening Styles Profile-Revised (LSP-R) (Bodie, Worthington, & Gearhart, 2013; Watson, Barker, & Weaver, 1995). In D. L. Worthington, & G. D. Bodie (Eds.), *The sourcebook of listening research: Methodology and measures* (pp. 402–409). Wiley-Blackwell. https://doi.org/10.1002/9781119102991

6. Emanuel, R., Adams, J., Baker, K., Daufin, E. K., Ellington, C., Fitts, E., Holladay, L., & Okeowo, D. (2008). How college students spend their time communicating. *International Journal of Listening, 22*(1), 13–28. https://doi.org/10.1080/10904010701802139

7. Dindia, K., & Kennedy, B. L. (2004, November). *Communication in everyday life: A descriptive study using mobile electronic data collection.* Paper presented at the annual conference of the National Communication Association, Chicago, IL; Janusik, L. A., & Wolvin, A. D. (2009). 24 hours in a day: A listening update to the time studies. *International Journal of Listening, 23*(2), 104–120. https://doi.org/10.1080/10904010903014442

8. Waldeck, J., Durante, C., Helmuth, B., & Marcia, B. (2012). Communication in a changing world: Contemporary perspectives on business communication competence. *Journal of Education for Business, 87*(4), 230–240. https://doi.org/10.1080/08832323.2011.608388

9. Manusov, V., Stofleth, D., Harvey, J. A., & Crowley, J. P. (2019). Conditions and consequences of listening well for interpersonal relationships: Modeling active-empathic listening, social-emotional skills, trait mindfulness, and relational quality. *International Journal of Listening, 34*(2), 110–126. https://doi.org/10.1080/10904018.2018.1507745

10. See, e.g., Kee, J. W. Y., Khoo, H. W., Lim, I., & Koh, M. Y. H. (2018). Communication skills in patient-doctor interactions: Learning from patient complaints. *Health Professions Education, 4*(2), 97–106. https://doi.org/10.1016/j.hpe.2017.03.006; Park, J.-K., Chung, T.-L., Gunn, F., & Rutherford, B. (2015). The role of listening in e-contact center customer relationship management. *Journal of Services Marketing, 29*(1), 49–58. https://doi.org/10.1108/JSM-02-2014-0063

11. Brownell, J. (1990). Perceptions of effective listeners: A management study. *Journal of Business Communication, 27*(4), 401–415. https://doi.org/10.1177/002194369002700405

12. See, e.g., Floyd, K., Generous, M. A., Clark, L., Simon, A., & McLeod, I. (2015). Empathic communication by physician assistant students: Evidence of an inflation bias. *Journal of Physician Assistant Education, 26*(2), 94–98. https://doi.org/10.1097/JPA.0000000000000016

13. See Krashen, S., Renandya, W. A., Mason, B., & Bose, P. (2018). Paths to competence in listening comprehension. *Beyond Words, 6*(1), 1–3. https://doi.org/10.33508/bw.v6i1.1671

14. King, G., & Servais, M. (2017). Effective Listening and Interactive Communication Scale (ELICS) (King, Servais, Bolack, Shepherd, & Willoughby, 2012). In D. L. Worthington, & G. D. Bodie (Eds.), *The sourcebook of listening research: Methodology and measures* (pp. 252–258). Wiley-Blackwell. https://doi.org/10.1002/9781119102991

15. Broome, B. J. (1991). Building shared meaning: Implications of a relational approach to empathy for teaching intercultural communication. *Communication Education, 40*(3), 235–249. https://doi.org/10.1080/03634529109378847

16. See Kaufman-Scarborough, C. (2017). Monochronic and polychronic time. In Y. Y. Kim (Ed.), *The international encyclopedia of intercultural communication*. Wiley-Blackwell. https://doi.org/10.1002/978117873665.ieicc0110

17. Kang, H. S. (2018). Traits of high-context culture in Koreans' communication. *Discourse and Cognition, 25*(2), 1–24.

18. Egan, G., & Reese, R. J. (2019). *The skilled helper: A problem-management & opportunity-development approach to helping* (11th ed.). Cengage.

19. Brownell, J. (2018). *Listening attitudes, principles, and skills* (6th ed.). Routledge. https://doi.org/10.4324/9781315441764

20. See, e.g., Kuperberg, G. R., & Jaeger, T. F. (2016). What do we mean by prediction in language comprehension? *Language, Cognition, and Neuroscience, 31*(1), 32–59. https://doi.org/10.1080/23273798.2015.1102299

21. St. Clair-Thompson, H. L. (2010). Backwards digit recall: A measure of short-term memory or working memory? *European Journal of Cognitive Psychology, 22*(2), 286–296. https://doi.org/10.1080/09541440902771299

22. Benoit, S. S., & Lee, J. W. (1986). Listening: It can be taught! *Journal of Education for Business, 63*(5), 229–232. https://doi.org/10.1080/08832323.1988.10117315

23. Gross, A. L., Parisi, J. M., Spira, A. P., Kuelder, A. M., Ko, J. Y., Sacynski, J. S., Samus, Q. M., & Rebok, G. W. (2012). Memory training interventions for older adults: A meta-analysis. *Aging & Mental Health, 16*(6), 722–734. https://doi.org/10.1080/13607863.2012.667783

24. Stave, M., & Pederson, E. (2015). Is the listener really listening? Exploring the effect of verbal and gestural speaker cues on backchanneling. In D. C. Noelle, R. Dale, A. S. Warlaumont, J. Yoshimi, T. Matlock, C. D. Jennings, & P. P. Maglio (Eds.), *Proceedings of the 37th annual meeting of the cognitive science society* (p. 3088). Cognitive Science Society.

25. Keaton, S. A. (2017). Active-Empathic Listening Scale (AELS) (Drollinger, Comer, & Warrington, 2006; also Bodie, 2011). In D. L. Worthington, & G. D. Bodie (Eds.), *The sourcebook of listening research: Methodology and measures* (pp. 161–166). Wiley-Blackwell. https://doi.org/10.1002/9781119102991

26. Brown-Schmidt, S., & Heller, D. (2018). Perspective-taking during conversation. In S.-A. Rueschemeyer, & G. Gaskell (Eds.), *The Oxford handbook of psycholinguistics* (2nd ed., pp. 549–572). Oxford University Press. https://doi.org/10.1093/oxfordhb/9780198568971.001.0001

27. Chopik, W. J., O'Brien, E., & Konrath, S. H. (2017). Differences in empathic concern and perspective taking across 63 countries. *Journal of Cross-Cultural Psychology, 48*(1), 23–38. https://doi.org/10.1177/0022022116673910.

28. Haapakangas, A., Hongisto, V., Varjo, J., & Lahtinen, M. (2018). Benefits of quiet workspaces in open-plan offices—Evidence from two office relocations. *Journal of Environmental Psychology, 56*, 63–75. https://doi.org/10.1016/j.jenvp.2018.03.003

29. Kekäläinen, P., Niemelä, R., Tuomainen, M., Kemppilä, S., Palonen, J., Riuttala, H., Nykyri, E., Seppänen, O., & Reijula, K. (2010). Effect of reduced summer indoor temperature on symptoms, perceived work environment and productivity in office work: An intervention study. *Intelligent Buildings International, 2*(4), 251–266.

30. Brosowsky, N. P., & Crump, M. J. C. (2018). Memory-guided selective attention: Single experiences with conflict have long-lasting effects on cognitive control. *Journal of Experimental Psychology, 147*(8), 1134–1153. https://doi.org/10.1037/xge0000431

31. Simpson, J. (2017, August 25). Finding brand success in the digital world. *Forbes.* https://www.forbes.com/sites/forbesagencycouncil/2017/08/25/finding-brand-success-in-the-digital-world/#2c2b8748626e

32. Toffler, A. (1970). *Future shock.* Random House.

33. Spira, J. B. (2011). *Overload! How too much information is hazardous to your organization.* Wiley; see also Bhasin, K. (2012). This is how information overload destroys your productivity. www.businessinsider.com/infographic-how-information-overload-affects-you-in-the-workplace-2012-2

34. Bergey, M. R., Filipe, A. M., Conrad, P., & Singh, I. (Eds.). (2019). *Global perspectives on ADHD: Social dimensions of diagnosis and treatment in sixteen countries.* Johns Hopkins University Press. https://doi.org/10.1353/book.56717

35. See, e.g., Owens, E. B., Zalecki, C., Gillette, P., & Hinshaw, S. P. (2017). Girls with childhood ADHD as adults: Cross-domain outcomes by diagnostic persistence. *Journal of Consulting and Clinical Psychology, 85*(7), 723–736. https://doi.org/10.1037/ccp0000217

36. Rufferty, I. (2017, September 20). 50 texting statistics that can quench everyone's curiosity, even mine. *BSG SMS.* https://medium.com/bsg-sms/50-texting-statistics-that-can-quench-everyones-curiosity-even-mine-7591b61031f5

37. Lenhart, A. (2010, September). *Cell phones and American adults.* Pew Research Center; Jones, Q., Ravid, G., & Rafaeli, S. (2004). Information overload and the message dynamics of online interaction spaces: A theoretical model and empirical exploration. *Information Systems Research, 15*(2), 194–210. https://doi.org/10.1287/isre.1040.0023

38. Wolvin, A. (2011). *Listening and human communication in the 21st century.* Wiley-Blackwell. https://doi.org/10.1002/978144314908

39. Neal, K. L. (2014). *Six key communication skills for records and information managers.* Elsevier. https://doi.org/10.1016/C2013-0-18364-X

40. Golen, S. (1990). A factor analysis of barriers to effective listening. *International Journal of Business Communication, 27*(1), 25–36. https://doi.org/10.1177/002194369002700103

41. Kashimi, E. S., Greiner, T., Sadewo, G., Ampuni, S., Helou, L., Nguyen, V. A., Lam, B. C. P., & Kaspar, K. (2017). Open- and closed-mindedness in cross-cultural adaptation: The roles of mindfulness and need for cognitive closure. *International Journal of Intercultural Relations, 59*, 31–42. https://doi.org/10.1016/j.ijintrel.2017.05.001; Masicampo, E. J., & Baumeister, R. F. (2012). Committed but closed-minded: When making a specific plan for a goal hinders success. *Social Cognition, 30*(1), 37–55. https://doi.org/10.1521/soco.2012.30.1.37

42. Profetto-McGrath, J. (2005). Critical thinking and evidence-based practice. *Journal of Professional Nursing, 21*(6), 364–371. https://doi.org/10.1016/j.profnurs.2005.10.002

43. Farley, S. D., Ashcraft, A. M., Stasson, M. F., & Nussbaum, R. L. (2010). Nonverbal reactions to conversational interruption: A test of complementarity theory and the status/gender parallel. *Journal of Nonverbal Behavior, 34*(4), 193–206. https://doi.org/10.1007/s10919-010-0091-0; Nelson, A., & Brown, C. D. (2012). *The gender communication handbook: Conquering conversational collisions between men and women.* Wiley.

44. Redeker, G., & Maes, A. (1996). Gender differences in interruptions. In D. I. Slobin, J. Gerhardt, A. Kyratzis, & J. Guo (Eds.), *Social interaction, social context, and language* (pp. 579–612). Lawrence Erlbaum Associates. https://doi.org/10.4324/9781315806525

45. Knoblock-Westerwick, S., Mothes, C., & Polavin, N. (2017). Confirmation bias, ingroup bias, and negativity bias in selective exposure to political information. *Communication Research, 47*(1), 104–124. https://doi.org/10.1177/0093650217719596

46. Myers, J. (2014). Stalking the "vividness effect" in the preventive health message: The moderating role of argument quality on the effectiveness of message vividness. *Journal of Promotion Management, 20*(5), 628–646. https://doi.org/10.1080/10496491.2014.946199

47. See Chan, M. (2019, August 16). How likely is the risk of being shot in America? It depends. *Time*. https://time.com/5476998/risk-of-guns-america/

48. Ducharme, J. (2016, August 15). A third of Americans avoid certain places because they fear mass shootings. *Time*. https://time.com/5653218/mass-shootings-stress/

49. Mosher, D., & Gould, S. (2018, October 29). The odds that a gun will kill the average American may surprise you. *Business Insider*. https://www.businessinsider.com/us-gun-death-murder-risk-statistics-2018-3

50. Snyder, L. G., & Snyder, M. J. (2008). Teaching critical thinking and problem solving skills. *Journal of Research in Business Education, 50*(2), 90–99.

51. Tannen, D. (1990). *You just don't understand: Women and men in conversation*. Ballantine.

52. Kapil, R. (2019, August 15). Five tips for nonjudgmental listening. *Mental Health First Aid*. https://www.mentalhealthfirstaid.org/2019/08/five-tips-for-nonjudgmental-listening/

53. Pollak, K. I., Arnold, R. M., Jeffreys, A. S., Alexander, S. C., Olsen, M. K., Abernethy, A. P., Sugg Skinner, C., Rodriguez, K. L., & Tulsky, J. A. (2007). Oncologist communication about emotion during visits with patients with advanced cancer. *Journal of Clinical Oncology, 25*(36), 5748–5752. https://doi.org/10.1200/JCO.2007.12.4180

54. Floyd, K. (2019). *Affectionate communication in close relationships*. Cambridge University Press. https://doi.org/10.1017/9781108653510

55. See Deckx, L., van den Akker, M., Buntinx, F., & van Driel, M. (2018). A systematic literature review on the association between loneliness and coping strategies. *Psychology, Health & Medicine, 23*(8), 899–916. https://doi.org/10.1080/13548506.2019.1446096

56. Bender, J. L., Jimenez-Marroquin, M.-C., & Jadad, A. R. (2011). Seeking support on Facebook: A content analysis of breast cancer groups. *Journal of Medical Internet Research, 13*(1), e16. https://doi.org/10.2196/jmir.1560

57. Alcoholics Anonymous Online Intergroup. (2018). Online meetings directory. https://www.aa-intergroup.org/directory.php

58. Han, J. Y., Shah, D. V., Kim, E., Namkoong, K., Lee, S.-Y., Moon, T. J., Cleland, R., Bu, Q. L., McTavish, F. M., & Gustafson, D. H. (2011). Empathic exchanges in online cancer support groups: Distinguishing message expression and reception effects. *Health Communication, 26*(2), 185–197. https://doi.org/10.1080/10410236.2010.544283

59. DeAndrea, D. C. (2015). Testing the proclaimed affordances of online support groups in a nationally representative sample of adults seeking mental health assistance. *Journal of Health Communication, 20*(2), 147–156. https://doi.org/10.1080/10810730.2104.914606

60. Sun, N., Rau, P. P.-L., & Ma, L. (2014). Understanding lurkers in online communities: A literature review. *Computers in Human Behavior, 38*, 110–117. https://doi.org/10.1016/j.chb.2014.05.022; see also Tobin, S. J., Vanman, E. J., Verreynne, M., & Saeri, A. K. (2015). Threats to belonging on Facebook: Lurking and ostracism. *Social Influence, 10*(1), 31-42. https://doi.org/10.1080/15534510.2014.893924

61. Tagarelli, A. (2017). Exploring lurking behaviors in online social networks. *Proceedings of the 7th international conference on web intelligence, mining and semantics*. Article 4. https://doi.org/10.1145/3102254.3102258; van Mierlo, T. (2014). The 1% rule in four digital health social networks: An observational study. *Journal of Medical Internet Research, 16*(2), e33. https://doi.org/10.2196/jmir.2966

62. Nielsen, J. (2006, October 9). The 90-9-1 rule for participation inequality in social media and online communities. *Nielsen Norman Group*. https://www.nngroup.com/articles/participation-inequality/

7

AP Photo/Chuck Burton

COMMUNICATING IN SOCIAL AND PROFESSIONAL RELATIONSHIPS

A Most Unlikely Friendship

Jennifer Thompson and Ronald Cotton were never destined to become friends. In 1984, when Thompson was attending college, a man broke into her home, threatened her with a knife, and raped her. At the police station later that day, she identified Cotton from a photo as her assailant and subsequently picked him out of a line-up. Based on her identifications and her testimony at trial, Cotton was convicted and sentenced to life in prison. Eleven years later, DNA analysis of evidence from the crime scene proved conclusively that Cotton had not committed the crime. After Cotton was released from prison and cleared of all charges, Thompson felt overwhelming guilt at having identified him as her attacker. The two met shortly after Cotton's release. "I physically couldn't stand up," Thompson recalls. "I just started to sob. I looked at him and I said, 'If I spent every minute of every hour of every day for the rest of my life telling you that I'm sorry, can you ever forgive me?'" Cotton, who was also crying, replied, "Jennifer, I forgave you years ago."[1] The two have since become good friends who travel the United States speaking about the dangers of eyewitness identifications and wrongful convictions.

As You READ

- Why do social relationships matter so much to us?
- Which characteristics of friendships make them vital to our social experience and well-being?
- How do we manage social relationships in the workplace?

Imagine what life would be like without friends. Families and romantic relationships are important to us, but our friends and acquaintances also contribute significantly to our well-being. Sometimes we look to friends for social and emotional support. Sometimes we seek out our friends when we just want to hang out and relax, and sometimes we do so when we need help making a decision or talking through a problem. Just as Jennifer Thompson and Ronald Cotton have done for each other, friends support us, lift our spirits, and remind us we're not alone in the world.

This chapter probes the importance of social and professional relationships, such as those with our friends and coworkers, and focuses on how we use interpersonal communication to manage them. All relationships are social to some extent. Because romantic and familial relationships often meet different social needs than friendships and workplace relationships do, we examine them in the next chapter.

Why Social Relationships Matter

Each of us can probably think of many friends who support us through life's ups and downs. Having strong social ties with friends, neighbors, coworkers, and others improves the quality of our life in multiple ways. In this opening section, we'll see that we form social relationships because we have a strong need to belong. We'll also examine some benefits of our social relationships, as well as certain costs we incur by maintaining them.

WE FORM RELATIONSHIPS BECAUSE WE NEED TO BELONG

• **need to belong theory** A psychological theory proposing a fundamental human inclination to bond with others.

In his book *Personal Relationships and Personal Networks* (2007), communication scholar Mac Parks wrote: "We humans are social animals down to our very cells. Nature did not make us noble loners."[2] He's right. One reason social relationships matter is that it's in our nature to form them. In fact, evolutionary psychologists argue that our motivation toward social relationships is innate rather than learned.[3]

That fundamental human inclination to bond with others is the idea behind psychologist Roy Baumeister's **need to belong theory**.[4] This theory says each of us is born with a drive to seek, form, maintain, and protect strong social relationships. To fulfill that drive, we use communication to form social bonds with others at work, at school, in our neighborhoods, in community and religious organizations, on sports teams, in online communities, and in other social contexts. According to the theory, each of those relationships helps us feel we aren't alone because we belong to a social community.

Strong social relationships improve the quality of our life in many ways.
Glow Images

What We Need from Social Relationships The need to belong theory suggests that for us to satisfy our drive for relationships, we need social bonds that are both interactive and emotionally close. For example, most of us wouldn't be satisfied if we had emotionally close relationships with people with whom we never got to communicate. Being cut off from social interaction can be physically and psychologically devastating. That's one of the reasons solitary confinement is considered such a harsh punishment for prisoners.[5] Women and men who are deployed for military service,[6] and many elderly individuals who live alone,[7] also experience loneliness when they don't see their families or friends for extended periods.

By the same token, interacting only with people for whom we have no real feelings is unrewarding as well. Imagine moving to a large city where you don't know anyone. Even though you'd have plenty of interactions with people—taxi drivers, grocery store clerks, an eye doctor, the neighborhood dry cleaner—you might not initially encounter anyone to whom you feel close. Although task-oriented relationships help you to

People don't just *enjoy* social interaction—they truly *need* it.

Image Source/Getty Images

accomplish various needs, such as getting from one place to another and having your vision checked, they don't fulfill your need to belong because they usually aren't emotionally close.

In a study of active Instagram users from around the world, researchers found that the frequency of participants' use of Instagram was strongly predicted by their need to belong and their desire for socially supportive relationships.[8] Table 1 lists the top five reasons for using Snapchat, as identified by a separate study. Notice that the primary reason related to friends.

Only a decade or so ago, people who developed relationships online were stigmatized as lacking the self-confidence and social skills to form face-to-face bonds.[9] Today, online relationships are so common that it is difficult to distinguish people who form them from those who don't. Research finds no differences in self-esteem, social skills, loneliness, anxiety, or number of face-to-face relationships between college students who have and have not formed social relationships online.[10]

These days, relationships that start online don't necessarily stay online. Similarly, people might meet face-to-face but then communicate primarily online. Communication

Top Five Reasons for Using Snapchat	**TABLE 1**
1. I use it because my friends are on it.	RELATING BY SNAP
2. I use it because it's fun.	
3. I use it because it's easy and free.	
4. I use it to satisfy my curiosity.	
5. I use it to communicate with others.	

SOURCE: Piwek, L., & Joinson, A. (2016). "What do they Snapchat about?" Patterns of use in time-limited instant messaging service. *Computers in Human Behavior, 54,* 358–367. https://doi.org/10.1016/j.chb.2015.08.026

GoodStudio/Shutterstock

scholar Michael Rabby has identified four specific relationship types based on the differences between face-to-face and electronic communication:[11]

- People in a *virtual relationship* have never met each other face to face. Their relationship starts online and stays online.

- Those in a *Pinocchio relationship* also met each other online but have since met in the "real world." They tend to use a combination of online and face-to-face communication to maintain their relationship.

- People in a *cyber emigrant relationship* initially met each other face to face but have since begun to maintain their relationship primarily or exclusively online.

- Finally, *real worlders* started their relationship face to face and continue to maintain it primarily in that manner.

Despite being common, social relationships formed online differ from face-to-face relationships in some important ways. One study found that offline friendships were perceived to be of higher quality than online friendships and friendships maintained through a mix of on- and offline interaction.[12] Over time, however, the differences between offline and "mixed-mode" friendships decreased. A separate study found that, for adolescents and young adults, romantic relationships formed online were less satisfying than those initiated offline.[13]

Just as the Internet provides multiple opportunities for forming positive social relationships, it unfortunately also allows people to violate the privacy of others. As "The Dark Side of Communication" explains, such behavior can have devastating effects on its victims.

Whether formed online or in person, many social relationships fulfill our needs for interaction and emotional closeness and can help us feel connected to others in meaningful and significant ways. The natural "need to belong" is not the only reason social relationships matter to human beings, but Baumeister's need to belong theory suggests it's one of the biggest.

SOCIAL RELATIONSHIPS BRING REWARDS

Besides fulfilling our need to belong, social relationships matter because they bring us rewards. We'll now look at three types of rewards—emotional, material, and health—and find they are often intertwined in our social relationships.

Social Relationships Bring Emotional Rewards Friends provide at least two types of emotional rewards. One is emotional support, or encouragement during times of emotional turmoil. Whether you're going through a serious crisis or just having a bad day, friends can provide comfort and empathy to help you make it through.[14] When Jennifer Thompson and Ronald Cotton worked through their traumatic history, they supported and listened to each other. Although their struggles were challenging, their strong friendship helped them cope.

The second emotional reward of having friends is happiness. We enjoy interacting with friends because it's fun and relaxing and because our friends entertain us. One of Erin's favorite ways to spend a Friday night, for example, is to invite her good friends over to cook dinner, watch movies on Netflix, and talk about what's going on in their lives. Hanging out with her close friends always makes Erin feel good. Indeed, many of our happiest times are spent with our close friends around us.[15]

Social Relationships Bring Material Rewards A second way social relationships benefit us is by helping to meet our material needs, such as our needs for money, food, shelter, and transportation. People tend to share those types of resources with others to whom they feel close. When you need help moving, or a place to stay for the weekend, or a few extra dollars to tide you over until payday, you're more likely to have those material needs met if you have strong social relationships to draw on than if you don't. You are also more likely to offer those material rewards to your close

THE DARK SIDE OF COMMUNICATION

Invasions of Privacy Online

Erik Pendzich/Alamy Stock Photo

Actress Bella Thorne was understandably outraged in 2019 when she discovered that a hacker allegedly stole topless photos of her from her Twitter account and threatened to post them on publicly accessible websites. In recent years, many public figures, including entertainers, politicians, and professional athletes, have been victimized by hackers who stole their photos and other personal information and posted them online. Not only are such violations of privacy embarrassing; they can also damage victims' reputations and threaten their livelihoods.

How can you protect your own photos and personal information? Experts offer the following tips:

- Make sure any device containing private material—including phones and tablets—is protected by a password. Use a complex set of letters and numbers in your password, and change your password on a regular basis.

- On smartphones, tablets, and computers, disable the auto-upload feature. This feature automatically saves photos and documents to online storage systems such as iCloud and Dropbox, which can end up preserving sensitive images or documents that you don't want saved or accidentally shared with your contacts.

- Think twice about giving other people or companies access to your online information.

- Delete sensitive materials on a regular basis.

- Encrypt your computer's hard drive to make it more difficult for hackers to access your personal materials.

SOURCES: Andone, D. (2019, June 16). Bella Thorne shares nude photos on Twitter after a hacker threatened to release them. *CNN*. https://www.cnn.com /2019/06/15/entertainment/bella-thorne-nude-photos-hack/index.html; Skipworth, H. (2014, September 1). How to keep your photos safe: Top tips to stop images and data leaking. *Digital Spy*. http://www.digitalspy.com/tech/internet/feature/a593741/how-to-keep-your-photos-safe-top-tips-to-stop-images-and -data-leaking/.

friends than to strangers or people you don't know well. Researchers use the term *social capital* to refer to the resources we have as a result of our social relationships.[16]

Social Relationships Bring Health Rewards Positive social relationships also promote good health. A study by psychologist Sheldon Cohen and his colleagues found, for instance, that the more social relationships people had, the better able they were to fight off the common cold.[17] Another study reported that people with a strong social network were twice as likely as others to survive a heart attack.[18] In fact, after reviewing 70 published studies on the topic, psychologist Julianne Holt-Lunstad and her colleagues concluded that a lack of strong, positive relationships is as big a risk to our health as smoking 15 cigarettes per day.[19] Research suggests that close relationships help people to manage the negative effects of stress[20] and maintain a healthy lifestyle.[21]

SOCIAL RELATIONSHIPS CARRY COSTS AS WELL AS BENEFITS

It's relatively easy to think of the benefits of social relationships—they bring us emotional support, help us during times of need, and even make us healthier. However, friendships and other social relationships carry costs as

Alexander Walter/Getty Images

well as rewards. Think about what it "costs" you to be friends with someone. A friendship takes time that you might spend doing something rewarding by yourself. It requires an emotional investment, particularly when your friend is in need of your support. There can be material costs associated with doing things together, such as the expenses you incur in taking road trips and going out to dinner. Friendships often require physical investments as well—you may not *want* to help your friend move into her new apartment, but you do it anyway because she's your friend.

Much of the time, we decide that the benefits of friendship are well worth the costs. Some social relationships, however, eventually reach the point where the costs of staying in the relationship outweigh the benefits. As we'll see in the next section, a social exchange orientation suggests that being in that kind of "under-benefited" state can motivate people to end relationships—or at least make them feel unsatisfied in them.

- **attraction theory** A theory that explains why individuals are drawn to others.

- **interpersonal attraction** The force that draws people together.

- **physical attraction** Attraction to someone's appearance.

- **social attraction** Attraction to someone's personality.

- **task attraction** Attraction to someone's abilities or dependability.

Paul Bradbury/age fotostock

Forming and Maintaining Social Bonds

We've examined why social relationships matter and how we are rewarded by them. In this section, we look at several theories that explain the various interpersonal forces at work in the formation and development of social relationships. Some of those theories help us to understand with whom we choose to form social relationships, and other theories explain why and how we maintain social relationships once we form them.

WHY WE FORM RELATIONSHIPS: ATTRACTION THEORY

Attraction theory explains why individuals are drawn to others. The process of forming most relationships begins with **interpersonal attraction**, the force that draws people together.

Interpersonal attraction comes in three different forms. You are probably already familiar with the concept of **physical attraction**, or being drawn to someone because of his or her looks, but there are at least two other ways to be attracted to another person. A second type of interpersonal attraction is **social attraction**, which means being attracted to someone's personality. For example, you might like your new officemate at work because of her positive attitude or great sense of humor. A third kind of interpersonal attraction is **task attraction**, or being attracted to someone's abilities and dependability.[22] You might feel positive toward your new carpool partner because he shows up on time every day, rain or shine, or toward your suitemate because of her excellent karaoke technique. Any or all of those types of attraction can draw you to others and make you want to get to know them.

To consider how physical, social, and task attraction play a role in your own social relationships, think of your closest friend and then respond to the items in "The Competent Communicator."

What Draws You? Attraction in Your Closest Friendship

Close friendships always include one or more forms of interpersonal attraction. We might be attracted to someone's personality. We might find the person physically attractive. We might also be drawn to someone as a work partner. Think about your current closest friendship, and note how much you agree or disagree with each of the following statements, using a scale of 1 (strongly disagree) to 7 (strongly agree).

Design Pics/Don Hammond

Social Attraction

_____ I find this person easy to be around.

_____ I really enjoy his or her personality.

_____ We get along very well with each other.

_____ He or she is the kind of person I like to spend time with.

Physical Attraction

_____ I think this person is good looking.

_____ He or she has a nice appearance.

_____ Most people would find this person physically attractive.

_____ This person has a nice look.

Task Attraction

_____ This person would be fun to work with.

_____ I can always count on this person.

_____ I would enjoy studying with this person.

_____ This person is very dependable.

Add up your scores for each scale. For each type of attraction, a score of 4–12 indicates that you don't perceive that type of attraction very strongly for your friend. A score of 13–20 suggests you have a moderate level of that form of attraction. A score of 21–28 indicates that you perceive a good deal of that form of attraction for your friend.

Your scores for each scale might differ quite a bit. If so, that simply means your friendship is based more heavily on some forms of attraction than on others. In any event, this exercise will give you a chance to reflect on what you find most attractive about your closest friendship.

SOURCE: Items adapted from McCroskey, J. C., & McCain, T. A. (1974). The measurement of interpersonal attraction. *Speech Monographs, 41*(3), 261–266. https://doi.org/10.1080/03637757409375845

A variety of qualities in a new acquaintance can spark interpersonal attraction, but four are especially powerful: personal appearance, proximity, similarity, and complementarity. Let's look at each and then consider the role culture plays in what we find attractive about others.

We Are Attracted by Appearance

When we say a person is attractive, we often mean that he or she *looks* attractive. Humans are very visually oriented, so finding someone physically attractive often motivates us to get to know that person better. There are at least two reasons for this attraction. One is that we value and appreciate physical attractiveness, so we want to be around people we think are attractive.[23] Another reason is that throughout history, humans have sought others who are physically attractive as mates.[24] Because attractive people often have very healthy genes, their children are likely to have especially good health because they will inherit those genes.[25]

We Are Attracted by Proximity

Another important predictor of attraction is **proximity**, or closeness, including how closely together people live or work and thus how often they interact. We're more likely to form attraction—particularly social and task attraction—with people we see often than with those we rarely see.[26] For example, we tend to know our next-door neighbors better than the neighbors down the road, and we're more likely to become friends and maintain friendships with classmates and coworkers than with people we seldom see, such as other students at school or other employees at work.

We Are Attracted by Similarity

We've all had the experience of getting to know someone and marveling at how much we have in common with that person. When we meet people with backgrounds, experiences, beliefs, and interests that are similar to our own, we find them to be comfortable and familiar. Sometimes it's almost as if we already know them.

We find similarity to be very attractive, particularly with respect to social attraction. Research shows we're more likely to form social relationships with people who are similar to us.[27] We often find social validation in those who are familiar. In other words, being attracted to people who are similar to us is, in a way, like being attracted to ourselves. We might be especially drawn to individuals who share our hobbies, sense of humor, or worldview, because those people make us feel good about who we are.[28] We don't necessarily think about that effect at a conscious level, but it may nonetheless be one of the reasons we find similarity attractive.

The preference for similarity affects how people form relationships online as well as in person. Some popular dating sites, such as Match.com, Zoosk.com, and OkCupid. com, are designed to appeal to a wide variety of individuals. Other sites allow people to search for daters who are similar to them in specific ways. These include TeacherFriendsDate.com for educators, FarmersOnly.com for farmers, and ClownDating. com for amateur or professional clowns. There are even sites specifically for supporters of President Donald Trump, including Trump.Dating.com and TrumpSingles.com. The number and popularity of these niche dating sites are understandable from the perspective of attraction theory because these sites appeal to our fondness for similar others. Some other examples of niche dating sites and the populations to which they appeal appear in Table 2.

We Are Attracted by Complementarity

As the "Fact or Fiction?" box confirms, similarity is often more attractive than difference. Still, opposites can sometimes attract. Specifically, we can be attracted to those who are unlike us if we see their differences as providing **complementarity**—a beneficial supplement by another person of something we lack in ourselves. Many people also benefit from the diversity of their friends' experiences. Thus, we might enjoy having friends whose religious, political, economic, or sexual orientations differ from our own, because they bring us new ideas and help us learn to communicate with a wider range of people.

Fact or *fiction?*

When Forming Friendships, Opposites Attract

You've probably heard the expression "opposites attract." It suggests that we find differences attractive and will be drawn most strongly to people who are different from us. Is that idea fact or fiction?

According to research, it is largely fiction. When we're forming friendships, difference *can* be attractive to us, but only if we see the difference as complementary—that is, if it benefits us in some way, such as by reflecting a positive personality trait that we lack. Study after study has shown, however, that we find similarity to be much more attractive.

In one study, researchers paired up college students at the beginning of a semester with strangers of their same sex and ethnicity. Both people in each pair reported on their individual attitudes, personalities, and ways of seeing the world. Over the next eight weeks, they also reported how much they liked each other. The researchers found that having similar attitudes was the strongest predictor of initial attraction. If their attitudes were highly dissimilar, the students tended not to like each other. The study also found that having similar personalities and ways of seeing the world was the strongest predictor of whether students remained friends after being initially drawn to each other. The results of this and dozens of other studies suggest that when it comes to forming friendships, the more accurate statement would be "similars attract."

ASK YOURSELF

- Have you tended to believe that opposites attract? Why do you suppose that idea persists?
- Why do we find similarity to be rewarding in a friend?

SOURCES: Cemalcilar, Z., Baruh, L., Kezer, M., Kamiloglu, R. G., & Nigdeli, B. (2018). Role of personality traits in first impressions: An investigation of actual and perceived personality similarity effects on interpersonal attraction across communication modalities. *Journal of Research in Personality, 76,* 139–149. https://doi.org/10.1016/j.jrp.2018.07.009; Neimeyer, R. A., & Mitchell, K. A. (1988). Similarity and attraction: A longitudinal study. *Journal of Social and Personal Relationships, 5*(2), 131–148. https://doi.org/10.1177/026540758800500201

Culture Sometimes Influences Our Perceptions of Attractiveness

Culture influences so many of the ways we interact with others that it shouldn't be a surprise to learn it influences our perceptions of attractiveness as well. We see the effects of culture most directly on perceptions of physical attractiveness. Consider

		TABLE 2
VeggieConnection.com	Vegetarians and vegans	NICHE DATING SITES
TallFriends.com	Tall daters	
DateBritishGuys.com	Daters seeking British men	
AmishDating.com	Amish adults	
GlutenFreeSingles.com	Adults who follow a gluten-free diet	
SaladMatch.com	Salad lovers	
Bristlr.com	Daters who love beards	

Cultures vary significantly in how they manipulate or mutilate the body to make it physically attractive.

Barry Barker/McGraw-Hill Education

weight, for example. In North America and Western Europe, a thin, physically fit body type is generally considered most attractive. In many African and Australian tribal cultures, however, a fuller figure is viewed as most attractive, at least for women.[29]

Cultural diversity also exists in the ways people manipulate or mutilate the body to achieve physical attractiveness. Girls in the Mursi ethnic group of southern Ethiopia and among the Mebêngôkre Indians of Brazil have their lips pierced at a young age, and a large wooden or clay plate is inserted into the hole. As the girls grow older, their lip plates are increased in size, and individuals with the largest plates are considered the most desirable as mates.[30] In a different kind of body manipulation, women in the Padaung tribe of Myanmar often wear metal rings around their necks to make their necks appear longer than they are. The longest-necked women are considered the most attractive and most desirable as mates.[31]

Other perceptions of attractiveness are largely cross-cultural. For instance, people around the world prefer bodies and faces that are symmetrical and proportional (two concepts we reviewed in the communicating nonverbally chapter). Across cultures, men are also attracted to women who appear healthy and young, because those characteristics signal their ability to produce healthy off-spring.[32] Similarly, women across cultures are attracted to men who look powerful and appear to have resources, because those characteristics signal their ability to provide for a family.[33] We may not consider these factors at a conscious level when we're assessing another person's attractiveness, but research demonstrates that people around the world are nonetheless attracted to such qualities in others.[34]

WHY WE FORM RELATIONSHIPS: UNCERTAINTY REDUCTION THEORY

A second major theory about why we form relationships focuses not on attraction but on the uncertainty we feel when we don't know others very well. Let's say you meet someone and want to get to know the person better. What does it *mean* to get to know that individual? According to communication scholars Charles Berger and Richard Calabrese, it means you're reducing your level of uncertainty about the person.[35]

When you first meet a new coworker, for instance, you don't know much about her, so your uncertainty about her personality and her likes and dislikes is high. Berger and Calabrese's **uncertainty reduction theory** suggests that you will find uncertainty to be unpleasant, so you'll be motivated to reduce it by using communication behaviors to get to know your new coworker. At first, you probably talk about basic information, such as where she lives and what she does outside work. As you get to know her better, she will probably disclose more personal information about herself. You might also learn about her by paying attention to nonverbal cues, such as her personal appearance, the sound of her voice, and her use of gestures. Communication researcher Dale Brashers found that people routinely use a variety of sources when collecting information to reduce their uncertainty.[36] Each new piece of information you gain further reduces your uncertainty.

Uncertainty reduction theory also proposes that the less uncertain we are, the more we will like a new acquaintance. The relationship between liking and uncertainty, as reflected in uncertainty reduction theory, is shown in Figure 1.

But does reducing your uncertainty about a person *guarantee* that you'll like him or her? Theories developed since uncertainty reduction theory say no. In his *predicted outcome value theory*, Michael Sunnafrank explained that we consider the merits of what we learn about other people when forming opinions of them.[37] In contrast to uncertainty reduction theory, Sunnafrank's theory suggests that when we dislike the information we learn about others, that information can cause us to like them less, not more.[38]

• **uncertainty reduction theory** Theory suggesting that people find uncertainty to be unpleasant, so they are motivated to reduce their uncertainty by getting to know others.

Research has also revealed cultural diversity in the way people deal with uncertainty. Recall from the communication and culture chapter that some cultures accept uncertainty as a normal part of life, whereas others tend to avoid it whenever possible. Some studies have compared participants from Japan—an uncertainty-avoiding society—and the United States—an uncertainty-accepting society. Compared to U.S. adults, Japanese adults are less engaged and less likely to reveal information about themselves when they know little about the person with whom they're interacting. That cultural difference emerges whether people are communicating online[39] or in simulated face-to-face conversations.[40]

Even if we do form a social relationship with someone, that doesn't guarantee that we'll want to maintain it. For instance, some friendships grow and flourish, whereas others start strong but fade over time. We'll look next at two sets of ideas that help us understand why and how we maintain the social relationships we have formed: theories of cost/benefit calculations and theories of relational maintenance behaviors.

WHY WE MAINTAIN RELATIONSHIPS: SOCIAL EXCHANGE AND EQUITY THEORIES

Suppose you're drawn to someone, you get to know that person, and now the two of you are friends. You've formed a social relationship—but how will you decide whether you want to stay in it? One way to understand why we maintain certain friendships while letting others fizzle out is to examine the give-and-take of relational costs and benefits.

Earlier in this chapter, we saw that relationships carry costs as well as rewards. We give certain things to a friendship, such as our time, attention, and money, and we get certain benefits from it, such as emotional support, entertainment, and help. Two specific theories help us understand how those costs and benefits influence which relationships we are most likely to maintain: social exchange theory and equity theory.

Social Exchange Theory The guiding principle of **social exchange theory** is that people seek to maintain relationships in which their benefits outweigh their costs.[41] Think of your relationship with a friend. There are costs involved in being someone's friend: you have to be willing to help when needed, and sharing activities with your friend might cost money and time that you could spend in other ways. Being in a friendship also has benefits, including having someone to talk to and spend time with. The question, according to social exchange theory, is whether you think the benefits of a particular friendship outweigh the costs. If you do, then you're likely to stay in that relationship; if not, then you're less inclined to maintain it.

An important concept in social exchange theory is **comparison level**, which is the set of expectations we have regarding the costs and benefits of a relationship. Our comparison level should reflect realistic expectations, based on our experiences with other social relationships and on cultural norms for such relationships. For example, perhaps you think neighbors should be friendly and should offer help when you need it but should otherwise mind their own business. Those ideas—based on your experience with your neighbors growing up and on the norms of your neighborhood—form part of your comparison level for your own neighborly relationships.

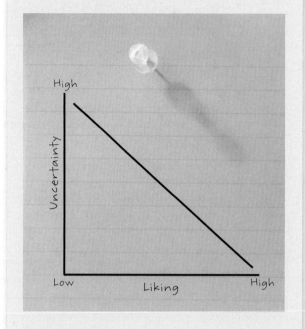

FIGURE 1

THE RELATIONSHIP BETWEEN LIKING AND UNCERTAINTY ACCORDING TO UNCERTAINTY REDUCTION THEORY

This theory says that as uncertainty about a person goes down, liking for that person goes up.

• **social exchange theory** Theory suggesting that people seek to maintain relationships in which their benefits outweigh their costs.

• **comparison level** A realistic expectation of what one wants and thinks one deserves from a relationship.

FIGURE 2

COMPARISON LEVEL AND COMPARISON LEVEL FOR ALTERNATIVES IN SOCIAL EXCHANGE THEORY

	Comparison Level	
	High	*Low*
Comparison Level for Alternatives — *High*	Your relationship is satisfying, but you may be inclined to end it if an even more satisfying relationship looks probable.	You're likely to be dissatisfied with this relationship and will probably look for opportunities to end it.
Comparison Level for Alternatives — *Low*	You'll probably be satisfied with this relationship and won't be likely to end it.	Although you won't find your relationship satisfying, you are unlikely to end it.

Social exchange theory says that four outcomes are possible when we cross our comparison level with our comparison level for alternatives.

• **comparison level for alternatives** An assessment of how much better or worse one's current relationship is than one's other options.

• **equity theory** Theory suggesting that a good relationship is one in which one's ratio of costs and benefits is equal to the partner's.

Relationships entail both costs and benefits. According to social exchange theory, we prefer relationships in which the benefits outweigh the costs.

Paul Burns/Corbis

Are you satisfied with your neighborly relationships, or do you think you could find better neighbors if you moved? Social exchange theory suggests that we maintain relationships when we think doing so is better than our alternatives, such as ending them and developing new ones. According to the theory, we pay attention to our **comparison level for alternatives**, which is our perception of how much better or worse our current relationship is than our other options. When we perceive that we could do better than the relationships we're in, we are likely to end that relationship and pursue a new one.

In some relationships, our comparison level for a particular relationship strongly influences *how satisfied we are in that relationship*.[42] Significantly, though, our comparison level for alternatives more strongly influences *whether that relationship will last*. Even satisfying friendships can end if the alternatives are more appealing. However, sometimes unsatisfying friendships endure. The association between the comparison level and the comparison level for alternatives is depicted in Figure 2.

Social exchange theory therefore provides a rationale for why people maintain relationships that appear to be costly, such as an abusive friendship. Any type of abuse—whether physical, psychological, or emotional—represents a cost rather than a benefit of being in a relationship. For the person being abused, however, the choice between maintaining and ending the abusive relationship is rarely as simple as it seems to outsiders. Some victims of abuse perceive that an abusive friend's positive qualities make up for his or her negative characteristics; thus, they have a favorable comparison level. Others believe the costs of ending the relationship—which might include loneliness, loss of other friends, or even the threat of violence—exceed the costs of staying in the relationship. In that case, their comparison level exceeds their comparison level for alternatives because they believe that even if the relationship is bad, ending it would be worse.

Equity Theory If we think of social relationships as having costs and rewards, then it's easy to see that both people in a given relationship might not benefit equally. **Equity theory** borrows the concepts of cost and benefit from social exchange theory and extends them, stating that a good relationship is one in which our ratio of costs and benefits is equal to our partner's. Imagine that your friend Chandra is always texting you about her problems but never seems to have time to listen to you communicate about yours. She's getting the benefit of your time and attention without the cost of giving her own time and attention to you. You, however, are putting more into the friendship than you're getting from it.

In that situation, Chandra is **over-benefited** and you are **under-benefited**. According to equity theory, such inequality will lead to trouble.[43] It's fine if you're working harder on your relationship than your friend is, as long as you're getting more out of it than she does. For example, if you're doing all the cooking every night but Chandra is letting you share her apartment for free, you're probably getting more out of the friendship than Chandra is, even though you might also be putting more effort into it.

However, if both partners get the same level of benefit but one partner's costs are greater than the other's, equity theory predicts that the partner with the greater costs won't want to maintain that relationship. That doesn't mean relationships have to be equitable every moment or in every instance—just in the long run. In many long-term friendships each friend may be over-benefited at some points and under-benefited at others, but as long as they experience equal costs and rewards in the long term, equity theory predicts that their friendship will be stable.

Our costs and benefits in friendships aren't just a matter of tangible goods. We also invest time, attention, and care in our friends; in an equitable relationship, we reap those rewards back from them. In some situations, however, we may go through prolonged periods when our investments far outweigh our returns, such as when we provide substantial care for someone suffering a significant health problem.

When you feel you're getting less out of a relationship than you're putting into it, you are likely to find that relationship dissatisfying.
Image Source/Getty Images

HOW WE MAINTAIN RELATIONSHIPS: RELATIONAL MAINTENANCE BEHAVIORS THEORY

Social exchange theory and equity theory both explain *why* we choose to maintain relationships. In contrast, **relational maintenance behaviors theory** explains *how* we maintain them—specifically, it focuses on the primary behaviors we use to do so.

Let's imagine you've made friends with someone, and you're both satisfied with the costs and benefits of your friendship. You'll therefore want to maintain your relationship so it grows and thrives. How do you do so? Communication researchers Laura Stafford and Dan Canary have found that people use five primary relational maintenance behaviors.[44] You can remember them by noting that their first letters spell the word SOAPS:

- **S**ocial networks
- **O**penness
- **A**ssurances
- **P**ositivity
- **S**haring tasks

1. *Social networks* include all the friendships and family relationships you have, whether those relationships are maintained online or face to face. An important relational maintenance behavior is to share your social networks with another. You and a close friend, for instance, are likely to know each other's family, coworkers, and other friends. When you do, we say that your and your friend's social networks have converged. Convergence is an important way to keep relationships stable and strong.[45]

2. *Openness* describes a person's willingness to discuss his or her relationship with a friend or other relational partner. People who use this relational maintenance strategy are likely to disclose their thoughts and feelings, to ask how their friend feels about the relationship, and to confide in their friend. Although it's certainly possible to have too much openness in a relationship, an optimal amount will help maintain the relationship and keep it strong.[46]

- **over-benefited** A state in which one's relational benefits outweigh one's costs.

- **under-benefited** A state in which one's relational costs outweigh one's benefits.

- **relational maintenance behaviors theory** Theory specifying the primary behaviors people use to maintain their relationships.

• **self-disclosure** Act of intentionally giving others information about oneself that one believes is true but thinks others don't already have.

3. *Assurances* are verbal and nonverbal behaviors that people use to stress their faithfulness and commitment to others. A statement such as "Of course I'll help you; you're my best friend" sends the message that someone is committed to the relationship, and it reassures the friend or partner that the relationship has a future.[47]

4. *Positivity* includes behaviors such as acting friendly and cheerful, being courteous to others, and refraining from criticism. Individuals who engage in positivity behaviors smile a lot, express affection and appreciation for others, and don't complain—in other words, they're pleasant and fun to be around. Those types of behaviors tend to make people well liked.[48]

5. *Sharing tasks* means performing your fair share of the work in a friendship. If your friend gives you a ride to the airport whenever you need it, for example, then it's only fair that you help her paint her apartment when she asks. As we've seen, being in a social relationship requires investments of energy and effort—so, one way of maintaining a relationship is to make sure you're both contributing equally.[49]

You may have additional ways of maintaining your social relationships, such as doing favors for a friend and always asking about his or her day. Many friends also maintain their relationships by participating in their shared interests, such as watching sporting events, going to movies, and trying out new recipes.[50] In various ways, each of those behaviors conveys the message that you appreciate and value your friend and enjoy his or her company. Because friendships are largely voluntary, feeling appreciated and valued can motivate you to stay in them.

SHARPEN Your Skills: *Relational maintenance behaviors*

Choose one of your friendships and make a point of practicing positivity, openness, and assurances with that friend over the next few weeks. Keep track of how you adapted your behavior, and when, on your calendar or notepad. What changes in your friendship do you notice in that time?

Self-disclosure is one of the primary ways we reveal who we are to others.

Rubberball/Getty Images

Revealing Ourselves in Relationships

Now that we've explored why and how we form social relationships, let's examine how we communicate about ourselves in those relationships. **Self-disclosure** is the act of intentionally giving others information about ourselves that we believe is true but that we think they don't already have. From intimate conversations about our hopes and dreams to mundane chats about our favorite restaurants, self-disclosure reveals a part of us to someone else through communication. In this section, we'll first look at several characteristics of self-disclosure and review some of the benefits it can bring to us and our relationships. We'll then survey some risks of self-disclosure—and thereby gain insight into avoiding them.

CHARACTERISTICS OF SELF-DISCLOSURE

Most of us engage in some form of self-disclosure on an ongoing basis. It has at least five key characteristics.

Self-Disclosure Is Intentional and Truthful For an act of communication to qualify as self-disclosure, it must meet two conditions. First, we must deliberately share the information about ourselves. Second, we must believe the information is true.

FIGURE 3
SOCIAL PENETRATION THEORY

Social penetration

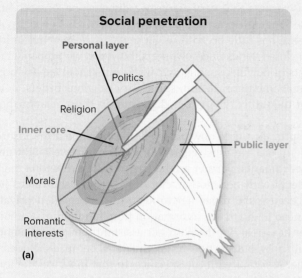

(a)

Depth but no breadth

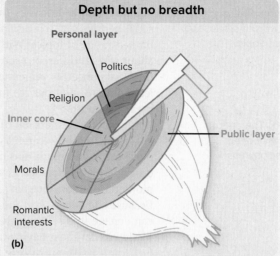

(b)

Breadth but no depth

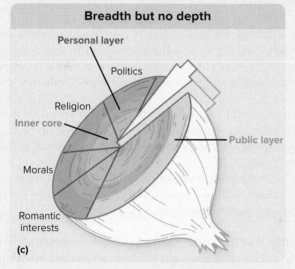

(c)

Breadth and depth

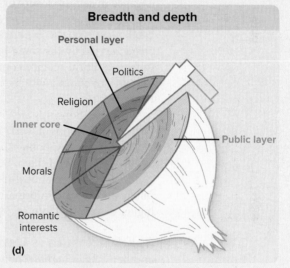

(d)

Researchers use the image of a multilayered onion to represent the process of social penetration in a relationship. The outer layer represents breadth of self-disclosure, and the inner layers reflect depth of self-disclosure. Our close relationships are usually characterized by both breadth and depth.

Let's say that through a momentary lapse in attention, your friend Dean accidentally mentions his financial problems to you. That incident would not constitute an act of self-disclosure according to the definition provided above, because Dean did not share the information deliberately. This is an example of what is called verbal "leakage"—information unintentionally shared with others.

Now let's say you tell a coworker you've never traveled outside your home country. That statement qualifies as self-disclosure if you believe it to be true. It's your belief in the truth of the information that matters, not the absolute truth of the statement. Perhaps you traveled outside the country when you were too young to remember. If you believe the information you're providing is true, however, then it qualifies as self-disclosure.

Self-Disclosure Varies in Breadth and Depth **Social penetration theory**, developed by researchers Irwin Altman and Dalmas Taylor and depicted in Figure 3,

• **social penetration theory** Theory suggesting that the depth and breadth of self-disclosure help us learn about a person we're getting to know.

illustrates how self-disclosing over time is like peeling away the layers of an onion: each self-disclosure helps us learn more and more about a person we're getting to know.[51]

According to social penetration theory, peeling away the layers to get to know someone requires sharing disclosures that vary along two dimensions: breadth and depth. **Breadth** describes the range of topics we discuss with various people. With some people, our self-disclosure has little breadth, because we disclose about only a limited range of topics. With close friends and coworkers, however, we probably talk about several different aspects of our life, such as our work and school experiences, financial concerns, professional ambitions, health, spiritual or religious beliefs, political opinions, and desires for the future, giving our disclosure in those relationships greater breadth.

The second dimension, **depth**, measures how personal or intimate our disclosures are, reflecting how carefully we feel we must guard the information we might give out. Let's say Ramona and her romantic partner are having problems. Ramona might describe her difficulties in detail with her mother, not only because she values her mother's opinion, but also because she trusts her to keep the information private. Because she doesn't feel the need to guard the information from her mother, Ramona can engage in disclosure that has great depth. With her assistant, however, Ramona discloses that she is having difficulty, but she doesn't go into detail because she doesn't feel comfortable entrusting her assistant with the specifics. In that instance, Ramona engages in self-disclosure of less depth.

Self-Disclosure Varies among Relationships Not every relationship is characterized by the same breadth and depth of self-disclosure. With your classmate in your political science course, for instance, you might disclose in depth about politics but not about anything else. See the representation of this type of relationship in Figure 3b.

Other relationships are characterized by breadth of disclosure but very little depth. With casual friends at work, for example, you might disclose a little about several areas of your life—family, hobbies, political ideas, career ambitions—but not provide intimate details about any of them. See Figure 3c.

In still other relationships, such as close friendships, people typically share both public and private information about multiple aspects of their lives. You can see that higher degree of depth and breadth depicted in Figure 3d.

Self-Disclosure Is Usually Reciprocal The adage "One good turn deserves another" suggests that when someone gives you a gift or shares a resource, you should return the favor. Sociologist Alvin Gouldner called that expectation the **norm of reciprocity**.[52] In North American cultures, among others, the norm of reciprocity usually extends to self-disclosure; that is, when we disclose to other people, we typically expect them to disclose to us in return.[53]

There are exceptions, such as when we disclose to a physician or counselor. We don't usually expect that individual to disclose back to us. In our friendships and other personal relationships, however, we generally expect that others will share information with us as we share it with them.

Self-Disclosure Is Influenced by Cultural and Gender Roles Many factors affect how much information we are willing to disclose to other people, such as the type of relationship we have with them and how long we've known them. Self-disclosure is also affected by the norms for our sex and culture.[54]

People often believe that women self-disclose more than men because disclosure and emotional expressiveness are a bigger part of the feminine gender role than the masculine gender role, especially in North America.[55] Is that generalization true? The evidence does suggest that women, on average, self-disclose more than men, although the difference is smaller than many believe.[56]

Diversity in cultural norms can also affect self-disclosure. In some cultures, such as those in North America and northern Europe, people are often encouraged to

• **breadth** The range of topics we self-disclose to various people.

• **depth** The degree of intimacy of our self-disclosures.

• **norm of reciprocity** The social expectation that favors should be reciprocated.

express themselves and to self-disclose to their friends and family. Other cultures, such as most Asian and Middle Eastern cultures, value discretion and encourage people to disclose only under more limited circumstances. For instance, people in those cultures may be inclined to disclose personal information only within their families or romantic relationships, rather than with social or professional acquaintances.[57]

BENEFITS OF SELF-DISCLOSURE

Self-disclosure can be good for us and for our relationships. Here we take a brief look at four key benefits of self-disclosure: enhancement of relationships and trust; reciprocity; emotional release; and assistance to others.

Whereas people in North America and northern Europe are often encouraged to express themselves, people in Asian and Middle Eastern cultures are frequently taught to value discretion.

Cathy Yeulet/123RF

1. *Enhancement of relationships and trust.* One benefit of self-disclosure is that it often helps us maintain high-quality relationships. We tend to disclose the most to people we like—and we also tend to like people who disclose to us.[58] Sharing appropriate self-disclosure in close relationships helps us to maintain those relationships and to reinforce the trust we share with those individuals.[59]

2. *Reciprocity.* As noted above, many of us follow a norm of reciprocity when it comes to self-disclosure: when others disclose to us, we tend to disclose back to them.[60] Thus, one way to get to know other people is to tell them about ourselves, so they feel more comfortable doing the same in return.

3. *Emotional release.* Sometimes the best part of self-disclosing is the feeling of getting something "off your chest." Perhaps you've had the experience of holding on to a secret of yours that you felt you just had to talk to someone about. Appropriate self-disclosures can often bring emotional release.[61] Also, as several studies have shown, self-disclosures can reduce the stress of holding on to a secret. That stress reduction is an important benefit because it can improve our mental and physical health.[62]

4. *Assistance to others.* We can also self-disclose in ways that help other people, such as when we are consoling individuals who are going through hard times. If your friend is in distress due to the challenges she is facing in her life, you might disclose how you managed traumatic situations in your own life. That disclosure can provide comfort and signal to your friend that she's not alone (see the "Difficult Conversations" box for one such situation). Many self-help programs, including Alcoholics Anonymous, encourage such disclosures to help their members realize they are all going through a similar struggle.[63] We can also help others by offering encouragement, such as when a coach self-discloses to a basketball team to help the players feel supported and energized before a big game. Although enhanced relationships, reciprocity, emotional release, and assistance to others are not the only benefits provided by self-disclosure, they're among the most important for social relationships.

Self-disclosure can help us console others during difficult times.

elenathewise/123RF

Difficult Conversations

Responding to a Friend in Need

Imagine this: Your friend Erica stops by your apartment late one night. You can tell immediately that she has been drinking heavily. She seems unusually sad and depressed, and in the course of your conversation she confides in you that she has been thinking recently about committing suicide.

Now, consider this: Erica has never seemed suicidal to you before, so you wonder whether she is exaggerating, owing to her intoxication. Given that her threat of suicide may be real, however, you feel obliged to help in some way. You worry about saying the wrong thing, though, and you don't want to upset her further if she is already suicidal. Here are some tips that can help you navigate this difficult conversation:

- Don't be afraid to talk to Erica about her thoughts of suicide. Some people worry that if they mention suicide to a distressed person, they are putting that thought in the person's head, so they avoid the subject altogether. Erica has already said she is thinking about suicide, so it's best if you don't ignore her statement.

- Ask questions about what is happening in her life to make her feel depressed and suicidal, and listen to her answers without judgment. You might ask when she started feeling this way, or whether something occurred to make her contemplate suicide.

- As Erica describes her problems and feelings, resist the urge to jump in with advice unless she asks you for your perspective. Focus on listening in a patient and empathic manner, and ask her how you can be helpful to her during this difficult time. If you have gone through problems similar to Erica's, disclosing that fact can help Erica feel that she is not alone.

- Especially if you sense that her suicidal intentions are serious, dial 911, call a suicide hotline (such as 1-800-SUICIDE), or take her to a hospital emergency room.

Talking to someone who is depressed and potentially suicidal can be scary. It's easy to worry that you will say the wrong thing and make the person even more upset. If you find yourself in such a situation, remember that the most constructive approach often involves listening non-judgmentally and helping your friend feel understood and accepted.

RISKS OF SELF-DISCLOSURE

Like many communication behaviors, self-disclosure isn't always a positive action; it has both good and bad aspects. Here we'll look at four potential risks of self-disclosure: being rejected, obligating others, hurting others, and violating privacy.

1. *Rejection.* What if the people to whom we're disclosing don't like what we tell them? Let's say your coworker decides to confide to you that he's gay. His disclosure might bring you closer together. If his sexuality is a problem for you, however, his disclosure could lead you to reject him. Often, the way a person reacts to a disclosure will determine whether its outcome is positive or negative.

2. *Obligations in others.* The reciprocity of self-disclosure can be a very good thing if we are trying to get to know someone better. However, it can make the other person feel put on the spot and uncomfortable about disclosing something back. Even worse, it could encourage the person to avoid us in the future.

3. *Hurt to others.* It's possible to hurt others with disclosures that are too critical or too personal. Despite the idea that honesty is the best policy, uncensored candor can lead to wounded feelings and resentment. Especially when sharing highly sensitive disclosures, consider how receivers will react to the information. If necessary, preface your statement by saying "I know this is a sensitive topic" or "I understand this may be hard to hear." By doing so, you help to prepare your listener for a critical or personal disclosure, reducing the chances that he or she will feel harmed.

4. *Violation of other people's privacy.* Inappropriate disclosures can even hurt people who aren't participating in the conversation. People in many relationships—including families, friendships, and workplace relationships—disclose private information that is not meant to be shared, sometimes unintentionally by forwarding an e-mail or text without permission. When we do so, we risk hurting our loved ones and damaging their trust in us.

Although these poor outcomes *can* occur when we self-disclose, they aren't inevitable. When managed with care and sensitivity, self-disclosure can reinforce the most positive aspects of our social and professional relationships.

Characteristics of Friendships

Our friendships with others are likely as different and individual as the friends themselves. Some are probably long-term friendships that seem almost like family ties. Others might be specific to a certain context, such as work, school, the gym where we work out, or the organization where we volunteer. Yet nearly all friendships have certain qualities in common. As we'll see in this section, a typical friendship is a voluntary, usually platonic relationship between peers that is governed by rules and differs by sex. Although a particular friendship might be an exception to any of those characteristics, most friendships reflect them all.

• **parasocial relationship** A one-sided friendship with someone who isn't aware of your existence.

Brand X Pictures/PunchStock

FRIENDSHIPS ARE VOLUNTARY

One of the defining characteristics of friendship is that it is *voluntary.*[64] We choose our friends and they choose us; we don't *have to* be friends with anyone. Part of what makes a friendship so special is that both friends are in the relationship by choice.

When we meet someone we want to be friends with, initiating a friendship requires communication behaviors. Not only do we need to interact with that person to form the friendship in the first place, we also must use relationship maintenance behaviors such as positivity, openness, assurances, network convergence, and sharing tasks to maintain our friendship.

One exception to the voluntary nature of friendship involves parasocial relationships. A **parasocial relationship** is a one-sided friendship with someone who isn't aware of your existence. When you repeatedly see a favorite singer, movie star, or television personality, you can come to feel as though you *know* that person and consider him or her a friend. Like genuine friendships, parasocial relationships can help us explore our personalities[65] and feel better about ourselves.[66] Because the other person hasn't agreed to become your friend, however, the relationship is not fully voluntary.

FRIENDSHIPS ARE USUALLY PLATONIC

Although many people count their romantic partners among their closest friends, one characteristic that generally distinguishes friendship from other close relationships is that it is platonic. A **platonic relationship** is one that is nonromantic and nonsexual. Platonic friendships, whether between people of the same sex or people of different sexes, allow people to give and receive support without having to manage the complications of romantic or sexual attraction.

An exception to the platonic nature of friendship occurs when people form **friends-with-benefits (FWB) relationships**. In an FWB relationship, friends engage in sexual activity with each other, even though they don't consider their relationship to be romantic.[67] Communication scholar Paul Mongeau and his colleagues have studied the nature of FWB relationships for many years. They have discovered that not all FWB relationships are the same; instead, the relationship comes in at least seven different types.[68] These include

- *True friends:* those who consider themselves to be close friends who share sexual activity.
- *Just sex partners:* those who interact almost exclusively for the purpose of sexual interaction.
- *Network opportunists:* casual friends who engage in sexual activity if neither finds a more desirable partner.
- *Successful transition pairs:* friends with benefits who eventually form a romantic relationship with each other.
- *Unintentional transition pairs:* friends with benefits who end up falling in love with each other, even though that wasn't their intention.
- *Failed transition pairs:* friends with benefits who tried unsuccessfully to become romantic partners.
- *Transition out pairs:* former romantic partners who now have an FWB relationship.

Research indicates that between 42 and 60 percent of U.S. college students have at least one FWB relationship.[69] Some scholars have even suggested that FWB relationships are replacing more traditional romantic dating and courtship.[70]

FRIENDSHIPS USUALLY DEVELOP BETWEEN PEERS

A second important characteristic of friendship is that it is usually a relationship between equals. A **peer** is someone similar to us in power or status. We aren't a peer of our professors, boss, or parents, because they all exercise some measure of control over us, at least temporarily. Most of us conceive of friendship as a relationship between peers—people who are our equals, no more or less powerful than we are.

We *can* have satisfying friendships with others who have some type of power over us. Those relationships can be complicated, however, because people in power sometimes have to make decisions that conflict with the friendship. A supervisor might want to share news about an upcoming layoff with a friend who works for her, for instance, but may feel she cannot because of her supervisory position. In such friendships, it is often best to discuss these competing expectations directly and agree on ground rules for addressing them.

FRIENDSHIPS ARE GOVERNED BY RULES

In some ways, a friendship is like a social contract to which both parties agree. By being someone's friend, we acknowledge—at least implicitly—that we expect certain things from that person and that he or she can expect certain things from us. Those expectations are possible because friendships follow rules. Even if the rules aren't explicitly stated, most people within a given society usually know and understand them.[71]

As Table 2 shows, researchers have studied many of the rules of friendship. Some relate to a specific behavior, such as practicing self-disclosure or including friends in your

TABLE 2

FRIENDSHIP RULES

One way to understand a relationship is to think about the rules or expectations that govern it. Various studies have examined people's expectations for friendship. Here are some of the most important rules those studies have found. What rules would *you* add to this list?

- Stand up for your friend in his or her absence.
- Provide support when needed.
- Trust each other.
- Keep your friend's secrets.
- Include friends in your activities.
- Make time to spend together.
- Offer money or other resources when needed.

SOURCES: Argyle, M., & Henderson, M. (1984). The rules of friendship. *Journal of Social and Personal Relationships, 1*(2), 211–237. https://doi.org/10.1177/0265407584012005; Hall, J. A. (2011). Sex differences in friendship expectations: A meta-analysis. *Journal of Social and Personal Relationships, 28*(6), 723–747. https://doi.org/10.1177/0265407510386192

activities. Others relate to the qualities we should exhibit in our friendships, such as loyalty and authenticity. Perhaps you've been in a friendship in which one or more of those implicit rules were broken. For example, maybe you have a friend who rarely makes time for you or often excludes you from his plans. Most people agree there are ways to treat our friends that are simply right or wrong.[72] Like communication rules in general, these friendship rules often become explicit only when somebody violates them.

FRIENDSHIPS DIFFER BY SEX

You have probably noticed differences between your friendships with women and those with men. Researchers have written volumes about sex differences and similarities in friendships and friendship behaviors.[73] Let's examine those separately for same- and other-sex friendships.

SHARPEN Your Skills: *Friendship rules*

Survey some of your closest friends to determine what rules they follow in their friendships. Ask specifically about any differences in their rules for same- and other-sex friendships. Document your findings in a blog or journal entry.

Men and women value different aspects of their same-sex friendships.

Yellow Dog Productions/The Image Bank/Getty Images

Same-Sex Friends One of the most consistent findings in research is that women and men value different aspects of their same-sex friendships. Friendships between women often emphasize conversational and emotional expressiveness more than do friendships between men.[74] Best friends Juanita and Lindsay, for instance, frequently get together just to talk and catch up. Their visits often include sharing their feelings about what's going on in their lives. They would say their ability to share, disclose, and express feelings with each other is what makes their friendship so close.

Men's friendships tend to place a heavier emphasis on shared activities and common interests.[75] For instance, the time Alex spends with his best friend Jake almost always revolves around some activity. It might be playing a round of golf and then having nachos and beer at a sports bar, or playing video games and comparing their picks for fantasy football. For Alex and Jake, it's the *doing*, not the *talking*, that makes their friendship close.

Two aspects of those sex differences are important to note. First, like nearly all sex differences in behavior, differences in same-sex friendships are just averages. They don't characterize all friendships. Some women's friendships focus more on shared activities than conversation, and some men routinely share personal conversations with their male friends even if they aren't engaged in an activity together. Second, those differences don't mean friendships are any more important to one sex than the other. Some people believe women's friendships are closer and more satisfying than men's because women self-disclose more to each other than men do. Instead, research has long shown that women and men report equal levels of closeness in their same-sex friendships.[76] What differs between the sexes is simply the characteristics that make those friendships close. For women, it's often shared conversation; for men, it's frequently shared activity.

Many lesbian, gay, bisexual, and transgender adults form important same-sex friendships with heterosexuals.[77] As communication professor Lisa Tillmann-Healy describes in her book, *Between Gay and Straight: Understanding Friendship across Sexual Orientation*, such friendships can be both inherently challenging and richly rewarding.[78] One study of gay male–straight male friendships found that some friends embrace and celebrate the differences in their sexual orientation. Others struggle with those differences, and still others ignore them completely.[79] A similar study of women found that sexual tension and discomfort with self-disclosure are common barriers to same-sex friendships between straight women and lesbians.[80] Despite their challenges, however, same-sex friendships between heterosexuals and nonheterosexuals can promote understanding and sensitivity, provide emotional support, and discourage harmful stereotypes.[81]

Other-Sex Friends What about other-sex friendships, then? Research suggests that both men and women value them as a chance to see things from each other's perspective.[82] Other-sex friendships can provide opportunities for men to be emotionally expressive and for women to enjoy shared activities that their same-sex friendships may not.[83] In addition, many other-sex friends feel some degree of physical or romantic attraction toward each other,[84] and they often communicate in ways that resemble romantic relationships, such as flirting with each other and sharing sexual humor or even sexual interaction.[85]

In fact, a study of American college students conducted by communication scientists Melissa Bisson and Timothy Levine found that 60 percent of the students reported having engaged in sexual activity with a nonromantic other-sex friend.[86] Although some research has suggested that sexual activity changes the fundamental nature of an other-sex friendship from platonic to romantic,[87] participants in Bisson and Levine's study reported avoiding such problems by not talking explicitly about the status of their relationship. Research by communication scholars Mikayla Hughes, Kelly Morrison, and Kelli Jean Asada suggests that such relationships are more positive if the friends observe certain rules, such as not getting emotionally attached and always practicing safe sex.[88]

Whether they are attracted to each other or not, many other-sex friends have specific reasons for not wanting their friendship to evolve into a romantic relationship. In surveys of more than 600 U.S. college students, communication scholars Susan

Messman, Dan Canary, and Kimberly Hause discovered that people avoid romance in their other-sex friendships for six primary reasons:[89]

1. They aren't physically attracted to their friend.
2. Their relatives and other friends wouldn't approve of a romantic relationship with the friend.
3. They aren't ready to be in a romantic relationship.
4. They want to protect their existing friendship.
5. They fear being disappointed or hurt.
6. They are concerned about a third party, such as a sibling who is romantically interested in the friend.

Many other-sex friends communicate in ways that resemble romantic relationships, such as by flirting with each other and sharing sexual humor.

rawpixel/123RF

Less research has examined the qualities of other-sex friendships in which one of the friends is lesbian, gay, bisexual, or transgender. One study examined the friendships of gay men and straight women that formed through workplace contact. The researcher found that gay men and straight women had rewarding but complex friendships.[90] Many participants in that study said they felt there were few "models" for such friendships, so they made up their own friendship rules. Other research has found that straight women who maintain friendships with gay men often feel stigmatized by other straight women.[91]

Studies show that same- and other-sex friendships offer unique rewards. Both women and men report that their same-sex friends are more loyal and helpful than their other-sex counterparts.[92] Other-sex friendships, however, allow women and men to enjoy those aspects of friendship most valued by another sex.

Social Relationships in the Workplace

Nearly all of us will be employed at some point in life, and many jobs will require us to interact with other people. It's therefore realistic to assume that we will have to relate to and communicate with people we know from work, whether they are coworkers, superiors, subordinates, or customers. Further, many public agencies and private corporations expect specific behaviors from their employees, which likely include communicating honestly, treating people with dignity, listening attentively, and being open to others' opinions. All those communication behaviors contribute to a civil and respectful work environment, and they can also facilitate the formation of workplace friendships.[93]

Friendships at work can be a dual-edged sword. On the one hand, having friends at work can make the workday fun and pleasant and provide us with help and support when we need it. On the other hand, friendship roles and work roles sometimes conflict. For instance, your friends may want to visit with you at work, but if you have tasks to complete by a deadline, you may not have time to socialize.

Workplace friendships may also be more challenging to control than regular friendships. If you have an argument with a regular friend, you can choose to avoid him or her until you both cool down. Because of your work obligations, however, you may not have that option with workplace friends.

For all the foregoing reasons, it is particularly useful to understand the dynamics of workplace friendships, so we can deal with the challenges they present. Let's examine those dynamics in three specific workplace relationships: between coworkers, between superiors and subordinates, and with clients.

SOCIAL RELATIONSHIPS WITH COWORKERS

In the workplace, you are probably most likely to form close relationships with your immediate coworkers. One reason is that coworkers are usually peers rather than superiors or subordinates, so they tend to have levels of power and responsibility similar to ours.[94] Another reason is that by virtue of being coworkers, they share some

common experiences with us, such as working in the same organizational culture and perhaps for the same department and supervisor. On top of that, we typically spend a great deal of time with our coworkers, perhaps even more than we spend with friends outside work. Thus, there is a ready-made basis for relationships with coworkers.[95] To understand social bonds between coworkers, it is instructive to examine both friendships and romantic relationships.

Friendships among Coworkers Having close friends in the workplace can benefit people both personally and professionally. Research shows that the quality of people's friendships with their coworkers affects their job satisfaction.[96] All other things being equal, the closer you are to your coworkers, the happier you are at work. Perhaps as a result, research finds that managers in a wide variety of organizations generally welcome and promote the development of workplace friendships.[97]

Friendships in the workplace provide many benefits. For one, they can be a rich source of information. Coworkers commonly share information about the work organization, its activities, and its people; in fact, employees rely more on their coworkers for information than any other source.[98] When coworkers are also friends, however, they may be especially inclined to share. Research confirms, in fact, that exchanging information in an organization contributes to the development of close workplace friendships.[99] Another benefit of workplace friends is that they are often a reliable source of emotional support.[100] Because they understand the specific demands of their shared work environment, workplace friends can empathize with each other and provide support even in ways that relatives and external friends cannot.[101]

Like regular friendships, workplace friendships follow a developmental path. One study found that workplace friendships go through three distinct phases: (1) acquaintance to friend, (2) friend to close friend, and (3) close friend to "almost best" friend.[102] Once formed, workplace friendships tend also to be managed in much the same way as regular relationships. Communication scholars Patricia Sias and her colleagues have discovered that coworkers use several communicative strategies to maintain close friendships with each other.[103] These include, among others

- Helping each other.
- Asking about each other's lives.
- Being direct and open in their communication with each other.
- Avoiding messages that would embarrass or offend each other.
- Displaying a positive mood around each other.

puttingcommunicationtowork

Search

Job Title >

Work Responsibilities >

Equal Employment Opportunity Officer

Equal employment opportunity officers usually work for the human resources division of a company, organization, or institution. They help to recruit and retain a diverse workforce that includes women, ethnic minorities, and persons with disabilities. They also advise executives, administrators, or government officials of their responsibilities toward employees, and they may help to mediate disputes between supervisors and employees. The position requires not only a thorough understanding of employment laws but also an ability to communicate sensitively with a wide variety of people.

As beneficial as friendships with coworkers are, however, they can also be challenging. This is because the relationship has both a *social dimension* and a *task dimension*, and those different aspects of the friendship frequently come into conflict. The social dimension is your personal relationship with the coworker, whereas the task dimension is your professional relationship. Let's say, for example, that you're friends with your coworker Kellie, who's up for a promotion. As her friend, you want her to have the promotion, but as her coworker, you don't believe she has really earned it. It's easy to see how those mixed feelings could be troublesome for your friendship.

Clearly, then, to maintain friendships with your coworkers, you need to balance the personal and professional sides of the relationships at all times. For instance, you might decide it's important to tell Kellie you support her, to voice enthusiasm if she receives the promotion, and to express disappointment if she doesn't, because she's your friend. Even though you don't feel she has earned the promotion, your friendship with Kellie may motivate you to be supportive of her anyway.

Alternatively, you might remind Kellie that the promotion is very competitive, that she is competing with employees who have more experience and seniority than she does, and that she shouldn't be surprised if she doesn't get it. You might even say "I'm telling you this as your coworker" to make it clear that you are speaking from the perspective of your professional relationship rather than your personal one. Which approach you choose will probably depend on how close your friendship is and on what your experiences have been in similar situations.

One career requiring the ability to manage social relationships in the workplace is equal employment opportunity officer. Check out "Putting Communication to Work" to learn more about that job.

Romantic Relationships between Coworkers If you watched the television show *The Office*, you might have been amused by the on-again/off-again romance between coworkers Ryan Howard and Kelly Kapoor. But you may not have realized that the two actors who played those parts, B. J. Novak and Mindy Kaling, vacillated from friends and coworkers to romantic partners and back again several times before settling into a long-term, working friendship. Because people spend so much time at work, it is not surprising that some form romantic relationships with colleagues. According to one survey, 38 percent of people have dated a coworker at least once, and a third of those workplace romances led to marriage.[104]

People can derive several benefits from working with their romantic partners. For instance, the positive feelings associated with attraction can energize employees. Research shows that positive emotion—such as the emotion of being in love—can boost people's creativity and help them be more innovative, which can be useful in a range of careers.[105] When romantic partners work in different departments of an organization, their relationship can encourage greater communication and cooperation within the workplace and improve people's ability to work as a team.[106] Experiencing love can also lead people to be more open and cooperative with others, which can ease personality conflicts in the workplace.[107]

Like friendships, workplace romances also have both social and task dimensions, and these dimensions can sometimes conflict, leading to relationship problems. For instance, suppose Tina works in the human resources department of a credit union where her boyfriend Erik works as a teller. Due to her role, Tina frequently encounters sensitive information about employees, and one day she learns that Erik's manager is unhappy with his performance and wants to transfer him to another branch. As a human resources professional, Tina feels obligated to keep such sensitive information private—but as Erik's girlfriend, she also feels a strong desire to share the information with him, especially because it affects him directly. This leads Tina to experience a *conflict of interest*, in which her personal and professional motivations contradict each other.

Another downside of workplace romances is that, when they end, the breakup can cause turbulence for the organization. In a regular romantic relationship, partners who break up might choose never to see or communicate with each other again. That isn't always an option when the partners work together, however. Because of their work roles, they may have to continue communicating and cooperating for the good of their employer, even if they feel hurt by the demise of their relationship. According to research, seeing each other in the workplace after a failed relationship can stir resentment as well as remind people of their own shortcomings as a romantic partner.[108]

These potential problems have led some employers to prohibit their employees from becoming romantically involved with each other. Not all romances are bad for the workplace, however. What determines whether a workplace romance will have positive or negative effects on an organization? According to research, three factors are especially influential: (1) the perceived fairness with which the organization treats its employees, (2) the evaluations that others in an organization make of a couple's relationship, and (3) the adjustment of organizational norms to support a couple's involvement.[109] Specifically, when workplace couples believe that their organization supports them, treats them fairly, and evaluates them positively, their relationships are more likely to benefit the organization rather than cause it problems.

SOCIAL RELATIONSHIPS BETWEEN SUPERIORS AND SUBORDINATES

As challenging as relationships among coworkers can be, those between superiors and subordinates are considerably more complicated, because they include a power difference that coworker relationships generally do not have. If a supervisor and an employee become friends—and particularly if they become romantic partners—the power difference between them introduces a task dimension that can complicate their communication.

As with coworkers, many people enjoy becoming friends with their boss. Indeed, research shows that having a positive, friendly relationship with your supervisor

usually adds to your job satisfaction.[110] That makes sense: if you like your supervisor, you'll probably enjoy working for him or her.

Genuine friendships between superiors and subordinates certainly aren't impossible to form or maintain. The challenge arises because what's best for the superior–subordinate relationship isn't always what's best for the friendship. If you're the employee, you might dislike or disagree with your boss's decisions concerning the company's policies or future direction, particularly when those decisions affect you. Conversely, if you're the supervisor, you may agonize about such decisions because you realize that what's best for the company is not always what's best for each individual employee.

To understand those stresses, imagine that your supervisor announces that the company will reduce the clerical staff on whom you depend to get your work done. Now imagine that to accommodate a new business strategy, your boss cancels a promotional campaign you've been developing, including a photo shoot you were looking forward to. In such cases, it can be hard not to take your boss's actions personally, and that kind of response can strain your friendship. In a study of superior–subordinate friendships, communication scholar Theodore Zorn found that superiors commonly experienced those types of tensions between their work responsibilities and their friendships with subordinates.[111]

Superiors and subordinates can find it challenging to be friends. Becoming romantically involved is even more fraught with difficulty, however, because of the conflict of interest inherent in supervising one's romantic partner. Suppose Liam is a unit manager at a software company where his partner, Chad, is a designer. If Liam oversees and evaluates Chad's work, he may feel that it is in his own interest to give Chad positive marks. Because they are romantically involved, what benefits Chad—such as a glowing performance review and the possibility of a raise—benefits both of them. That could motivate Liam to evaluate Chad's work more positively than he should, which would be unfair to his other employees. Many organizations specifically prohibit such an arrangement by not allowing employees to report directly to their spouses or romantic partners.

One situation that makes superior–subordinate relationships particularly problematic is when the subordinate feels bullied. *Workplace bullying* occurs when a superior engages repeatedly in aggressive and antisocial behavior directed at a subordinate.[112] Bullying behaviors can include engaging in hurtful teasing or tormenting, singling out the subordinate for punishment, neglecting or ignoring the subordinate's needs, intimidating the subordinate physically, and other similarly cruel actions. Research shows that employees who are subjected to workplace bullying suffer a range of health detriments, including post-traumatic stress disorder,[113] impaired sleep,[114] and even suicide ideation.[115]

Often it's best if both parties in a power-imbalanced friendship acknowledge that their personal relationship and their work relationship might conflict and if they agree to keep those relationships separate. It's helpful, too, if the two can discuss the potential for conflicts directly, particularly if they started their relationship as peers and one of them was later promoted. By acknowledging the possibility of conflicts and establishing their expectations for how to address clashes of interests *before they occur*, a supervisor and an employee can lay the groundwork for a successful relationship. Although doing so doesn't mean they'll avoid all the tensions that often accompany that type of relationship, they will be better able to handle them when they arise.

SOCIAL RELATIONSHIPS BETWEEN CLIENTS AND PROFESSIONALS

In most professions, you'll also interact with customers. For instance, you might work for a financial or technology firm that offers ongoing consulting services to a number of long-term business clients. Depending on the nature of your job, you may have clients you see or talk to on a regular basis, so it's reasonable to expect that you may form social relationships with some of them.[116] Those relationships can be highly rewarding personally, and they can also benefit your organization because they may be a large part of the reason your customers continue to buy from you or your company.[117] After all, most of us prefer dealing with a service provider or a salesperson with whom we can develop a comfortable and trusting relationship.

Tyler Olson/123RF

Friendships between professionals and customers can run into some of the same task-versus-social tensions that occur in friendships between coworkers and between superiors and subordinates. You may be friends with the person who cuts your hair, for instance, but you still expect that person to do a professional job, and he or she still expects you to provide full payment. If either of you doesn't uphold your end of the bargain, the customer–provider relationship can be disrupted and the friendship can suffer.

Perhaps to avoid those tensions, some companies discourage their employees from developing personal friendships with customers. Although *friend-liness* is critical in customer relations, many businesses recognize that the feelings of loyalty and favor we often have for friends can interfere with the professional relationship. When he took a position as a sales representative for a cable television company, for instance, Deion started giving his friends discounts on their cable service that other customers didn't receive. In turn, his friends consistently gave him the highest possible scores on customer satisfaction surveys. Those special deals and preferential treatments continued for almost a year before Deion's regional manager realized what was happening. She reprimanded Deion for allowing his friendships to compromise his professional relationships.

The separation of personal and professional relationships is particularly important in the health care setting. In the United States, ethical guidelines of the American College of Physicians discourage doctors from treating friends, relatives, intimate partners, or others with whom they have close personal relationships.[118] A doctor's professional judgment and objectivity could be compromised by his or her personal feelings for the patient. If objectivity is lost, then the doctor might not make proper decisions about the patient's condition or treatment and might put the patient's health at risk.

If you do become friends with customers, be especially clear with them about the boundaries between your personal and professional relationships. While conducting business, treat them as you would treat any other customer, and ask them to treat you as they would any other provider. A personal friendship with customers can be successful if the friends agree that their professional relationship is separate and should be treated professionally.

In both our professional and our personal lives, having friends and other social relationships enriches us. English poet Samuel Taylor Coleridge once called friendship a "sheltering tree" to point out how friends can shield and protect us from many of the stresses of life. Friends make our life safer, happier, and more meaningful.

For REVIEW

- **Why do social relationships matter so much to us?**

  We have a natural need to belong that motivates us to seek, form, and maintain social relationships. Those relationships in turn provide us with emotional, material, and health rewards.

- **Which characteristics of friendships make them vital to our social experience and well-being?**

  Friendships are voluntary, usually platonic relationships, most often among peers, that are governed by rules and differ by sex.

- **How do we manage social relationships in the workplace?**

  In relationships with coworkers, superiors, subordinates, and clients, it is important to separate the social dimension of the relationship from its task dimension and to be aware of power differences.

KEY TERMS

need to belong theory 182

attraction theory 186

interpersonal attraction 186

physical attraction 186

social attraction 186

task attraction 186

proximity 188

complementarity 188

uncertainty reduction theory 190

social exchange theory 191

comparison level 191

comparison level for
alternatives 192

equity theory 192

over-benefited 193

under-benefited 193

relational maintenance
behaviors theory 193

self-disclosure 194

social penetration theory 195

breadth 196

depth 196

norm of reciprocity 196

parasocial relationships 199

platonic relationships 200

friends-with-benefits (FWB)
friendships 200

peer 200

NOTES

1. American Public Media. (2013, November 20). The story: Jennifer Thompson. http://www.thestory.org/stories/2013-11/jennifer-thompson

2. Parks, M. R. (2007). *Personal relationships and personal networks.* Lawrence Erlbaum Associates, 1. https://doi.org/10.4324/9781315089911

3. See Keshavan, M. S. (2015). The evolution, structure, and functioning of the social brain. In R. K. Schutt, L. J., Seidman, & M. S. Keshavan (Eds.), *Social neuroscience: Brain, mind, and society* (pp. 29–40). Harvard University Press.

4. Maunder, R. E. (2018). Students' peer relationships and their contribution to university adjustment: The need to belong in the university community. *Journal of Further and Higher Education, 42*(6), 756–768. https://doi.org/10.1080/0309877X.2017.1311996; Baumeister, R. F., & Leary, M. R. (1995). The need to belong: Desire for interpersonal attachments as a fundamental human motivation. *Psychological Bulletin, 117*(3), 497–529. https://doi.org/10.1037/0033-2909.117.3.497

5. Haney, C. (2018). The psychological effects of solitary confinement: A systematic critique. *Crime and Justice, 47*(1), 365–416. https://doi.org/10.1086/696041

6. Merolla, A. J. (2010). Relational maintenance during military deployment: Perspectives of wives of deployed U.S. soldiers. *Journal of Applied Communication Research, 38*(1), 4–26. https://doi.org/10.1080/00909880903483557

7. Domènech-Abella, J., Lara, E., Rubio-Valera, M., Olaya, B., Moneta, M. V., Rico-Uribe, L. A., Ayuso-Mateos, J. L., & Haro, J. M. (2017). Loneliness and depression in the elderly: The role of social network. *Social Psychiatry and Psychiatric Epidemiology, 52*(4), 381–390. https://doi.org/10.1007/s00127-017-1339-3

8. Wong, D., Amon, K. L., & Keep M. (2019). Desire to belong affects Instagram behavior and perceived social support. *Cyberpsychology, Behavior, and Social Networking, 22*(7), 465–471. https://doi.org/10.1080/cyber.2018.0533

9. Whitty, M. (2001). Age/sex/location: Uncovering the social cues in the development of online relationships. *CyberPsychology & Behavior, 4*(5), 623–630. https://doi.org/10.1089/109493101753235223

10. Schiffrin, H., Edelman, A., Falkenstern, M., & Stewart, C. (2010). The associations among computer-mediated communication, relationships, and well-being. *Cyberpsychology, Behavior, and Social Networking, 13*(3), 299–306. https://doi.org/10.1089/cyber.2009.0173

11. Rabby, M. (2007). Relational maintenance and the influence of commitment in online and offline relationships. *Communication Studies, 58*(3), 315–337. https://doi.org/10.1080/10510970701518405

12. Antheunis, M. L., Valkenburg, P. M., & Peter, J. (2012). The quality of online, offline, and mixed-mode friendships among users of a social networking site. *Cyberpsychology: Journal of Psychosocial Research on Cyberspace, 6*(3), article 6. https://doi.org/10.5817/CP2012-3-6

13. Blunt-Vinti, H. D., Wheldon, C., McFarlane, M., Brogan, N., & Walsh-Buhi, E. R. (2016). Assessing relationship and sexual satisfaction in adolescent relationships formed online and offline. *Journal of Adolescent Health, 58*(1), 11–16. https://doi.org/10.1016/j.adohealth.2015.09.027

14. Lee, S., Chung, J. E., & Park, N. (2018). Network environments and well-being: An examination of personal network structure, social capital, and perceived social support. *Health Communication, 33*(1), 22–31. https://doi.org/10.1080/10410236.2016.1242032

15. Demir, M., Orthel-Clark, H., Özdemir, M., & Bayram Özdemir, S. B. (2015). Friendship and happiness among young adults. In M. Demir (Ed.), *Friendship and happiness* (pp. 117–135). Springer. https://doi.org/10.1007/978-94-017-9603-3

16. Bian, M., & Leung, L. (2015). Linking loneliness, shyness, smartphone addiction symptoms, and patterns of smartphone use to social capital. *Social Science Computer Review, 33*(1), 61–79. https://doi.org/10.1177/0894439314528779

17. Cohen, S., Doyle, W. J., Turner, R., Alper, C. M., & Skoner, D. P. (2003). Sociability and susceptibility to the common cold. *Psychological Science, 14*(5), 389–395. https://doi.org/10.1111.1467-9280.01452

18. Menéndez-Villalva, C., Gamarra-Mondelo, M. T., Alonso-Fachado, A., Naveira-Castelo, A., & Montes-Martínez, A. (2015). Social network, presence of cardiovascular events and mortality in hypertensive patients. *Journal of Human Hypertension, 29*(7), 417–423. https://doi.org/10.1038/jhh.2014.116

19. Holt-Lunstad, J., Smith, T. B., Baker, M., Harris, T., & Stephenson, D. (2015). Loneliness and social isolation as risk factors for mortality: A meta-analytic review. *Perspectives on Psychological Science, 10*(2), 227–237. https://doi.org/10.1177/1745691614568352

20. Lee, C. Y. S., & Goldstein, S. E. (2016). Loneliness, stress, and social support in young adulthood: Does the source of support matter? *Journal of Youth and Adolescence, 45*(3), 568–580. https://doi.org/10.1007/s10964-015-0395-9

21. Scarapicchia, T. M. F., Amireault, S., Faulkner, G., & Sabiston, C. M. (2017). Social support and physical activity participation among healthy adults: A systematic review of prospective studies. *International Review of Sport and Exercise Psychology, 10*(1), 50–83. https://doi.org/10.1080/1750984X.2016.1183222

22. Schaffer, B. S., & Manegold, J. G. (2018). Investigating antecedents of task commitment and task attraction in service learning team projects. *Journal of Education for Business, 93*(5), 222–232. https://doi.org/10.1080/08832323.2018.1457620

23. Fugère, M. A., Chabot, C., Doucette, K., & Cousins, A. J. (2017). The importance of physical attractiveness to the mate choices of women and their mothers. *Evolutionary Psychological Science, 3*(3), 243–252. https://doi.org/10.1007/s40806-017-0092-x

24. See Perilloux, C., Cloud, J. M., & Buss, D. M. (2013). Women's physical attractiveness and short-term mating strategies. *Personality and Individual Differences, 54*(4), 490–495. https://doi.org/10.1016/j.paid.2012.10.028

25. Ibid.

26. See Finkel, E. J., & Eastwick, P. W. (2015). Interpersonal attraction: In search of a theoretical Rosetta Stone. In M. Mikulincer, P. R. Shaver, J. A. Simpson, & J. F. Dovidio (Eds.), *APA handbook of personality and social psychology, Vol. 3. Interpersonal relations* (pp. 179–210). American Psychological Association. https://doi.org/10.1037/14344-007

27. Singh, R., Tay, Y. Y., & Sankaran, K. (2017). Causal role of trust in interpersonal attraction from attitude similarity. *Journal of Social and Personal Relationships, 34*(5), 717–731. https://doi.org/10.1177/0265407516656826

28. Montoya, R. M., & Horton, R. S. (2013). A meta-analytic investigation of the processes underlying the similarity-attraction effect. *Journal of Social and Personal Relationships, 30*(1), 64–94. https://doi.org/10.1177/0265407512452989

29. For an extended discussion, see Guerrero, L. K., & Floyd, K. (2006). *Nonverbal communication in close relationships.* Lawrence Erlbaum Associates. https://doi.org/10.4324/9781410617064

30. Tao, H., & Li, W.-J. (2017). Female body damage and decorative behaviour from the perspective of semiotics. *Advances in Social Science, Education and Humanities Research, 83,* 703–708. https://doi.org/10.2991/hss-172017.121

31. Morrison, E. R. (2015). Beauty or physical attractiveness. In P. Whelehan, & A. Bolin (Eds.), *The international encyclopedia of human sexuality.* Wiley. https://doi.org/10.1002/9781118896877.wbiehs.044

32. Buss, D. M., & Schmitt, D. P. (2019). Mate preferences and their behavioral manifestations. *Annual Review of Psychology, 70,* 77–110. https://doi.org/10.1146/annurev-psych-010418-103408

33. Conroy-Beam, D., Buss, D. M., Pham, M. N., & Shackelford, T. K. (2015). How sexually dimorphic are human mate preferences? *Personality and Social Psychology Bulletin, 41*(8), 1082–1093. https://doi.org/10.1177/0146167215590987

34. Ibid.

35. Knobloch, L. K. (2015). Uncertainty reduction theory. In C. R. Berger, & M. E. Roloff (Eds.), *International encyclopedia of interpersonal communication.* Wiley-Blackwell. https://doi.org/10.1002/9781118540190

36. Brashers, D. E. (2007). A theory of communication and uncertainty management. In B. Whaley, & W. Samter (Eds.), *Explaining communication theory: Contemporary theories and exemplars* (pp. 201–218). Lawrence Erlbaum Associates. https://doi.org/10.4324/9781410614308

37. Horan, S. M., & Houser, M. L. (2012). Understanding the communicative implications of initial impressions: A longitudinal test of predicted outcome value theory. *Communication Education, 61*(3), 234–252. https://doi.org/10.1080/03634523.2012.671950; Ramirez, A., Sunnafrank, M., & Goei, R. (2010). Predicted outcome value theory in ongoing relationships. *Communication Monographs, 77*(1), 27–50. https://doi.org/10.1080/03637750903514276

38. Ramirez, A., Walther, J. B., Burgoon, J. K., & Sunnafrank, M. (2002). Information-seeking strategies, uncertainty, and computer-mediated communication: Toward a conceptual model. *Human Communication Research, 28*(2), 213–228. https://doi.org/10.1111/j.1468-2958.2002.tb00804.x

39. See Keaten, J. A., Kelly, L., Pribyl, C. B., & Sakamoto, M. (2009). Fear and competence in Japan and the U.S.: Fear of negative evaluation, affect for communication channels, channel competence and use of computer mediated communication. *Journal of Intercultural Communication Research, 38*(1), 23–39. https://doi.org/10.1080/17475750903381606

40. Derlega, V. J., Winstead, B. A., & Greene, K. (2008). Self-disclosure and starting a close relationship. In S. Sprecher, A. Wenzel, & J. Harvey (Eds.), *Handbook of relationship initiation* (pp. 153–174). Psychology Press. https://doi.org/10.4324/9780429020513

41. Cropanzano, R., Anthony, E. L., Daniels, S. R., & Hall, A. V. (2017). Social exchange theory: A critical review with theoretical remedies. *Academy of Management Annals, 11*(1), 479–516. https://doi.org/10.5465/annals.2015.0099; Stafford, L. (2015). Social exchange theories: Calculating the rewards and costs of personal relationships. In D. O. Braithwaite, & P. Schrodt (Eds.), *Engaging theories in interpersonal communication: Multiple perspectives* (2nd ed., pp. 403–415). Sage. https://doi.org/10.4135/9781483329529

42. Nakonezny, P. A., & Denton, W. H. (2008). Marital relationships: A social exchange theory perspective. *American Journal of Family Therapy, 36*(5), 402–412. https://doi.org/10.1080/0192618070647264

43. Arvanitis, A., & Hantzi, A. (2016). Equity theory ratios as causal schemas. *Frontiers in Psychology, 7,* 1257. https://doi.org/10.3389/fpsyg.2016.01257

44. Stafford, L. (2016). Marital sanctity, relationship maintenance, and marital quality. *Journal of Family Issues, 37*(1), 119–131. https://doi.org/10.1177/0192513X13515884

45. See Tong, S. T., Kashian, N., & Walther, J. B. (2011). Relational maintenance and CMC. In K. B. Wright, & L. M. Webb (Eds.), *Computer-mediated communication in personal relationships* (pp. 98–118). Peter Lang. https://doi.org/10.3726/b12772

46. Schrodt, P., & Phillips, K. E. (2016). Self-disclosure and relational uncertainty as mediators of family communication patterns and relational outcomes in sibling relationships. *Communication Monographs, 83*(4), 486–504. https://doi.org/10.1080/0363775 1.2016.1146406

47. Goodboy, A. K., & Myers, S. A. (2008). Relational maintenance behaviors of friends with benefits: Investigating equity and relational characteristics. *Human Communication, 11*(1), 71–85.

48. Ogolsky, B. G., & Bowers, J. R. (2013). A meta-analytic review of relationship maintenance and its correlates. *Journal of Social and Personal Relationships, 30*(3), 343–367. https://doi.org/10.1177/0265407512463338

49. Barstad, A. (2014). Equality is bliss? Relationship quality and the gender division of household labor. *Journal of Family Issues, 35*(7), 972–992. https://doi.org/10.1177/0192513X14522246

50. See, e.g., Daniels, S., Glorieux, I., Minnen, J., & van Tienoven, T. P. (2012). More than preparing a meal? Concerning the meanings of home cooking. *Appetite, 58*(3), 1050–1056. https://doi.org/10.1016/j.appet.2012.02.040

51. Altman, I., & Taylor, D. (1973). *Social penetration: The development of interpersonal relationships.* Holt; see also Hwang, J., Han, H., & Kim, S. (2015). How can employees engage customers? Application of social penetration theory to the full-service restaurant industry by gender. *International Journal of Contemporary Hospitality Management, 27*(6), 1117–1134. https://doi .org/10.1108/IJCHM-03-2014-0154

52. Gouldner, A. W. (1960). The norm of reciprocity: A preliminary statement. *American Sociological Review, 25*(2), 161–178. https://doi.org/10.2307/2092623

53. Levinson, S. C. (2016). Turn-taking in human communication–Origins and implications for language processing. *Trends in Cognitive Sciences, 20*(1), 6–14. https://doi.org/10.1016/j.tics.2015.10.010

54. De Choudhury, M., Sharma, S. S., Logar, T., Eekhout, W., & Nielsen, R. C. (2017, February). Gender and cross-cultural differences in social media disclosures of mental illness. In *Proceedings of the 2017 ACM conference on computer supported cooperative work and social computing* (pp. 353–369). ACM. https://doi.org/10.1145/2998181.2998330

55. See, e.g., Morman, M. T., Schrodt, P., & Tornes, M. J. (2013). Self-disclosure mediates the effects of gender orientation and homophobia on the relationship quality of male same-sex friendships. *Journal of Social and Personal Relationships, 30*(5), 582–605. https://doi.org/10.1177/0265407512463991

56. Dindia, K., & Allen, M. (1992). Sex differences in self-disclosure: A meta-analysis. *Psychological Bulletin, 112*(1), 106–124. https://doi.org/10.1037/0033-2909.112.1.106

57. Wu, J., & Lu, H. (2013). Cultural and gender differences in self-disclosure on social networking sites. In J. Petley (Ed.), *Media and public shaming: Drawing the boundaries of disclosure* (pp. 97–114). I. B. Tauris & Co.

58. Tardy, C. H., & Smithson, J. (2018). Self-disclosure: Strategic revelation of information in personal and professional relationships. In O. Hargie (Ed.), *The handbook of communication skills* (4th ed., pp. 217–258). Routledge. https://doi.org/10.4324 /9781315436135

59. Lin, R., & Utz, S. (2017). Self-disclosure on SNS: Do disclosure intimacy and narrativity influence interpersonal closeness and social attraction? *Computers in Human Behavior, 70*, 426–436. https://doi.org/10.1016/j.chb.2017.01.012

60. Wuyts, D., Soenens, B., Vansteenkiste, M., & Van Petegem, S. (2018). The role of observed autonomy support, reciprocity, and need satisfaction in adolescent disclosure about friends. *Journal of Adolescence, 65*, 141–154. https://doi.org/10.1016 /adolescence.2018.03.012

61. Rimé, B., Bouchat, P., Paquot, L., & Giglio, L. (2019). Intrapersonal, interpersonal and social outcomes of the social sharing of emotion. *Current Opinion in Psychology, 31*, 127–134. https://doi.org/10.1016/j.copsyc.2019.08.024

62. Zhang, R. (2017). The stress-buffering effect of self-disclosure on Facebook: An examination of stressful life events, social support, and mental health among college students. *Computers in Human Behavior, 75*, 527–537. https://doi.org/10.1016/j .chb.2017.05.043

63. Stone, D. A., Conteh, J. A., & Francis, J. D. (2017). Therapeutic factors and psychological concepts in Alcoholics Anonymous. *Journal of Counselor Practice, 8*(2), 120–135. https://doi.org/10.22229/nav074629

64. Cheung, S. K., & McBride-Chang, C. (2014). Friendship satisfaction. In A. C. Michalos (Ed.), *Encyclopedia of quality of life and well-being research* (pp. 2364–2366). Springer. https://doi.org/10.1007/978-94-007-0753-5

65. Derrick, J. L., Gabriel, S., & Tippin, B. (2008). Parasocial relationships and self-discrepancies: Faux relationships have benefits for low self-esteem individuals. *Personal Relationships, 15*(2), 261–280. https://doi.org/10.1111/j.1475-6811.2008.00197.x

66. Young, A. F., Gabriel, S., & Hollar, J. L. (2013). Batman to the rescue! The protective effects of parasocial relationships with muscular superheroes on men's body image. *Journal of Experimental Social Psychology, 49*(1), 173–177. https://doi.org /10.1016/j.jesp.2012.08.003

67. Wentland, J. J., & Reissing, E. (2014). Casual sexual relationships: Identifying definitions for one night stands, booty calls, fuck buddies, and friends with benefits. *Canadian Journal of Human Sexuality, 23*(3), 167–177. https://doi.org/10.3138/cjhs.2744

68. Mongeau, P. A., Knight, K., Williams, J., Eden, J., & Shaw, C. (2013). Identifying and explicating variation among friends with benefits relationships. *Journal of Sex Research, 50*(1), 37–47. https://doi.org/10.1080/00224499.2011.623797

69. Letcher, A., & Carmona, J. (2015). Friends with benefits: Dating practices of rural high school and college students. *Journal of Community Health, 40*(3), 522–529. https://doi.org/10.1007/s10900-014-9966-z

70. Paik, A. (2010). "Hookups," dating, and relationship quality: Does the type of sexual involvement matter? *Social Science Research, 39*(5), 739–753. https://doi.org/10.1016/j.ssresearch.2010.03.011

71. Suttles, G. D. (2017). Friendship as a social institution. In G. J. McCall, M. M. McCall, N. K. Denzin, G. D. Suttles, & S. B. Kurth (Eds.), *Friendship as a social institution* (pp. 95–135). Routledge. https://doi.org/10.4324/9780203791493

72. See Wilson, R. E., Harris, K., & Vazire, S. (2015). Personality and friendship satisfaction in daily life: Do everyday social interactions account for individual differences in friendship satisfaction? *European Journal of Personality, 29*(2), 173–186. https:// doi.org/10.1002/per.1996

73. See, e.g., Dunbar, R. I. M. (2018). The anatomy of friendship. *Trends in Cognitive Sciences, 22*(1), 32–51. https://doi.org/10.1016/j.tics.2017.10.004

74. Hall, J. A. (2011). Sex differences in friendship expectations: A meta-analysis. *Journal of Social and Personal Relationships, 28*(6), 723–747. https://doi.org/10.1177/0265407510386192; Parks, M. R., & Floyd, K. (1996). Meanings for closeness and intimacy in friendship. *Journal of Social and Personal Relationships, 15*(1), 517–537. https://doi.org/10.1177/0265407596131005

75. Wood, J. T., & Inman, C. C. (1993). In a different mode: Masculine styles of communicating closeness. *Journal of Applied Communication Research, 21*(3), 279–295. https://doi.org/10.1080/00909889309365372

76. Floyd, K. (1995). Gender and closeness among friends and siblings. *Journal of Psychology, 129*(2), 193–202. https://doi.org/10.1080/00223980.1995.9914958; see also Morman, M. T., & Floyd, K. (1998). "I love you, man": Overt expressions of affection in male-male interaction. *Sex Roles, 38*(9-10), 871–881. https://doi.org/10.1023/A:1018885417249

77. Gillespie, B. J., Frederick, D., Harari, L., & Grov, C. (2015). Homophily, close friendship, and life satisfaction among gay, lesbian, heterosexual, and bisexual men and women. *PLoS One, 10*(6), e0128900. https://doi.org/10.1371/journal.pone.0128900

78. Tillmann-Healy, L. M. (2001). *Between gay and straight: Understanding friendship across sexual orientation.* AltaMira Press.

79. Price, J. (1999). *Navigating differences: Friendships between gay and straight men.* Harrington Press. https://doi.org/10.4324/9780203047637

80. O'Boyle, C. G., & Thomas, M. D. (1996). Friendships between lesbian and heterosexual women. In J. S. Weinstock, & E. D. Rothblum (Eds.), *Lesbian friendships* (pp. 240–248). New York University Press.

81. See, e.g., Galupo, M. P. (2009). Cross-category friendship patterns: Comparison of heterosexual and sexual minority adults. *Journal of Social and Personal Relationships, 26*(6–7), 811–831. https://doi.org/10.1177/0265407509345651

82. Procsal, A. D., Demir, M., Doğan, A., Özen, A., & Sümer, N. (2015). Cross-sex friendship and happiness. In M. Demir (Ed.) *Friendship and happiness* (pp. 171–185). Springer. https://doi.org/10.1007/978-94-017-9603-3

83. Reeder, H. (2017). "He's like a brother": The social construction of satisfying cross-sex friendship roles. *Sexuality & Culture, 21*(1), 142–162. https://doi.org/10.1007/s12119-016-9387-5

84. Bleske-Rechek, A., Joseph, W. E., Williquette, H., & Donovan, B. (2016). Sex differences in young adults' attraction to opposite-sex friends: Natural sampling versus mental concepts. *Evolutionary Psychological Science, 2*(3), 214–219. https://doi.org/10.1007/s40806-016-0056-6; Bleske-Rechek, A., Somers, E., Micke, C., Erickson, L., Matteson, L., Stocco, C., Schumacher, B., & Richie, L. (2012). Benefit or burden? Attraction in cross-sex friendship. *Journal of Social and Personal Relationships, 29*(5), 569–596. https://doi.org/10.1177/0265407512443611

85. See Lemay, E. P., & Wolf, N. R. (2016). Projection of romantic and sexual desire in opposite-sex friendships: How wishful thinking creates a self-fulfilling prophecy. *Personality and Social Psychology Bulletin, 42*(7), 864–878. https://doi.org/10.1177/0146167216646077

86. Bisson, M. A., & Levine, T. R. (2009). Negotiating a friends with benefits relationship. *Archives of Sexual Behavior, 38*(1), 66–73. https://doi.org/10.1007/s10508-007-9211-2

87. Owen, J., Fincham, F. D., & Manthos, M. (2013). Friendship after a friends with benefits relationship: Deception, psychological functioning, and social connectedness. *Archives of Sexual Behavior, 42*(8), 1443–1449. https://doi.org/10.1007/s10508-013-0160-7

88. Hughes, M., Morrison, K., & Asada, K. J. K. (2005). What's love got to do with it? Exploring the impact of maintenance rules, love attitudes, and network support on friends with benefits relationships. *Western Journal of Communication, 69*(1), 49–66. https://doi.org/10.1080/10570310500034154

89. Messman, S. J., Canary, D. J., & Hause, K. S. (2000). Motives to remain platonic, equity, and the use of maintenance strategies in opposite-sex friendships. *Journal of Social and Personal Relationships, 17*(1), 67–94. https://doi.org/10.1177/0265407500171004

90. Rumens, N. (2008). The complexities of friendship: Exploring how gay men make sense of their workplace friendships with straight women. *Culture and Organization, 14*(1), 79–95. https://doi.org/10.1080/14759550701864918; see also Rumens, N. (2010). Firm friends: Exploring the supportive components in gay men's workplace friendships. *Psychological Review, 58*(1), 135–155. https://doi.org/10.1111/j.1467-954X.2009.01879.x

91. Moon, D. (1995). Insult and inclusion: The term *fag hag* and gay male "community." *Social Forces, 74*(2), 487–510. https://doi.org/10.1093/sf/74.2.487

92. Rose, S. M. (1985). Same- and cross-sex friendships and the psychology of homosociality. *Sex Roles, 12*(1-2) 63–74. https://doi.org/10.1007/BF00288037

93. Myers, K. K., Siebold, D. R., & Park, H. S. (2011). Interpersonal communication in the workplace. In M. L. Knapp, & J. A. Daly (Eds.), *The Sage handbook of interpersonal communication* (4th ed., pp. 527–562). Sage.

94. Sias, P. M. (2014). Workplace relationships. In L. L. Putnam, & D. K. Mumby (Eds.), *The Sage handbook of organizational communication: Advances in theory, research, and methods* (pp. 375–400). Sage.

95. McBain, R., & Parkinson, A. (2017). Placing relationships in the foreground: The role of workplace friendships in engagement. In W. J. Zerbe, C. E. J. Hartel, N. M. Ashkanasy, & L. Petitta (Eds.), *Emotions and identity: Research on emotions in organizations* (pp. 199–221). Emerald Publishing Limited. https://doi.org/10.1108/reom

96. Mao, H.-Y., Hsieh, A.-T., & Chen, C.-Y. (2013). The relationship between workplace friendship and perceived job significance. *Journal of Management & Organization, 18*(2), 247–262. https://doi.org/10.1017/S1833367200000985

97. See Colbert, A. E., Bono, J. E., & Purvanova, R. K. (2016). Flourishing via workplace relationships: Moving beyond instrumental support. *Academy of Management Journal, 59*(4), 1199–1223. https://doi.org/10.5465/amj.2014.0506

98. Sias, P. M. (2014). Workplace relationships. In L. L. Putnam, & D. K. Mumby (Eds.), *The Sage handbook of organizational communication: Advances in theory, research, and methods* (3rd ed., pp. 375–400). Sage.

99. Ellwardt, L., Steglich, C., & Wittek, R. (2012). The co-evolution of gossip and friendship in workplace social networks. *Social Networks, 34*(4), 623–633. https://doi.org/10.1016/j.socnet.2012.07.002

100. Colbert et al., 2016; Ptacek, J. (2014). *I get by with a little help from my friends: A qualitative study of nurse close work friendship and social support.* Unpublished masters thesis, Department of Communication, Western Michigan University.

101. Sias, 2014.

102. Sias, P. M., & Cahill, D. J. (1998). From coworkers to friends: The development of peer friendships in the workplace. *Western Journal of Communication, 62*(3), 273–299. https://doi.org/10.1080/10570319809374611

103. Sias, P. M., Gallagher, E. B., Kopaneva, I., & Pedersen, H. (2012). Maintaining workplace friendships: Perceived politeness and predictors of maintenance tactic choice. *Communication Research, 39*(2), 239–268. https://doi.org/10.1177/0093650210396869

104. CareerBuilder. (2012, February 9). Nearly one-third of workers who had office romances married their co-worker, finds annual CareerBuilder Valentine's Day survey. http://www.careerbuilder.com/share/aboutus/pressreleasesdetail.aspx?sd=2%2F9%2F2012&id=pr678&ed=12%2F31%2F2012

105. Isgett, S. F., & Fredrickson, B. L. (2015). Broaden-and-build theory of positive emotions. In J. D. Wright (Ed.), *International encyclopedia of the social & behavioral sciences* (2nd ed., pp. 864–869). Elsevier. https://doi.org/10.1016/B978-0-08-097086-8.10548-3

106. Cowan, R. L., & Horan, S. M. (2014). Love at the office? Understanding workplace romance disclosures and reactions from the coworker perspective. *Western Journal of Communication, 78*(2), 238–253. https://doi.org/10.1080/10570314.2013.866688; Mainiero, L. A. (1989). *Office romance: Love, power, and sex in the workplace.* Rawson Associates.

107. Mainiero, 1989.

108. Pierce, C., & Aguinis, H. (2000). Effects of a dissolved workplace romance and rater characteristics on responses to a sexual harassment accusation. *Academy of Management Journal, 43*(5), 869–880. https://doi.org/10.5465/1556415

109. See, e.g., Alder, G. S., & Quist, D. M. (2014). Rethinking love at the office: Antecedents and consequences of coworker evaluations of workplace romances. *Human Resource Management, 53*(3), 329–351. https://doi.org/10.1002/hrm.21572

110. Alegre, I., Mas-Machuca, M., & Berbegal-Mirabent, J. (2016). Antecedents of employee job satisfaction: Do they matter? *Journal of Business Research, 69*(4), 1390–1395. https://doi.org/10.1016/j.jbusres.2015.10.113

111. Zorn, T. E. (1995). Bosses and buddies: Constructing and performing simultaneously hierarchical and close friendship relationships. In J. T. Wood, & S. Duck (Eds.), *Under-studied relationships: Off the beaten track* (pp. 122–147). Sage.

112. Glambek, M., Skogstad, A., & Einarsen, S. (2015). Take it or leave: A five-year prospective study of workplace bullying and indicators of expulsion in working life. *Industrial Health, 53*(2), 160–170. https://doi.org/10.2486/indhealth.2014-0195

113. Spence Laschinger, H. K., & Nosko, A. (2015). Exposure to workplace bullying and post-traumatic stress disorder symptomology: The role of protective psychological resources. *Journal of Nursing Management, 23*(2), 252–262. https://doi.org/10.1111/jonm.12122

114. Hansen, Å. M., Hogh, A., Garde, A. H., & Persson, R. (2014). Workplace bullying and sleep difficulties: A 2-year follow-up study. *International Archives of Occupational and Environmental Health, 87*(3), 285–294. https://doi.org/10.1007/s00420-013-0860-2

115. Leach, L. S., Poyser, C., & Butterworth, P. (2017). Workplace bullying and the association with suicidal ideation/thoughts and behaviour: A systematic review. *Occupational and Environmental Medicine, 74*(1), 72–79. https://doi.org/10.1136/oemed-2016-103726

116. Adelman, M. B., Ahuvia, A., & Goodwin, C. (1994). Beyond smiling. In R. T. Rust, & R. L. Oliver (Eds.), *Service quality: New directions in theory and practice* (pp. 139–171). Sage. https://doi.org/10.4135/9781452229102

117. Gwinner, K. P., Gremler, D. D., & Bitner, M. J. (1998). Relational benefits in service industries: The customer's perspective. *Journal of the Academy of Marketing Science, 26*(2), 101–114. https://doi.org/10.1177/0092070398262002

118. American College of Physicians. (2012). *Ethics manual* (6th ed.). Author. https://doi.org/10.7326/0003-4819-156-1-201201031-00001

8

Everett Collection Inc/Alamy Stock Photo

COMMUNICATING IN INTIMATE RELATIONSHIPS

Close Friends Who Are "Chosen Family"

Tina Fey and Amy Poehler understand that family isn't always based on bloodlines. The pair met in 1993 when both were enrolled in an improvisation class at Chicago's famous ImprovOlympic theater. More than a quarter century later, Fey and Poehler have appeared in multiple movies together, including *Sisters* (2015), *Baby Mama* (2008), and *Mean Girls* (2004). In 2001, Fey persuaded Poehler to join her on the cast of *Saturday Night Live*, and three years later, the two became the first female co-anchors of the show's popular skit "Weekend Update." The actors aren't simply productive coworkers, however; they are also best friends. Although they don't always work together, they have supported each other in both their careers and their personal lives. They even joke about their plan to have Poehler's two sons eventually marry Fey's two daughters. Their friendship is so close, in fact, that the two actors feel like siblings. Poehler explains: "I think that Tina and I are chosen sisters. I think we are chosen family."[1]

As You READ

- What makes some relationships intimate?
- How do we form, maintain, and dissolve romantic relationships?
- What makes a family, and how do we communicate in families?

It's difficult to overstate the importance of our close relationships. We may have many good friends, coworkers, and other acquaintances, but our relationships with romantic partners and family members are special. Those are the people whose lives affect us the most and with whom we share our deepest sorrows and greatest joys. Most of us invest more in, and feel more committed to, those relationships than any others. The significant relationships we develop with our families and romantic partners truly shape our lives in unique and important ways.

Family life and romantic relationships also influence each other. Growing up in a family gives most of us our first exposure to the concept of personal relationships and our first examples of romantic unions. Moreover, when we form romantic relationships in adulthood, those often provide the basis for starting new families. Thus, although romantic and familial relationships are different in some notable respects, there is often an intimate connection between the two.

The Nature of Intimate Relationships

Many people think specifically of romantic relationships when they hear the word *intimate*, but intimacy is about more than just romance. **Intimacy** means significant emotional closeness that we experience in a relationship, whether romantic or not. As we'll see in this section, intimate relationships require deep commitment, foster interdependence, require continuous investment, and spark dialectical tensions.

INTIMATE RELATIONSHIPS REQUIRE DEEP COMMITMENT

When Rachelle Friedman imagined her wedding, she never dreamed of coming down the aisle in a wheelchair. At her bachelorette party, however, she was pushed into a swimming pool by one of her bridesmaids as a joke. After hitting her head on the bottom of the pool, Friedman suffered a spinal cord injury that left her unable to talk or to feel any sensation below her collarbone. Despite the physical and emotional trauma of the accident, Friedman's fiancé—and now husband—Chris Chapman never wavered in his commitment to his bride. Despite Friedman's long and challenging ordeal, Chapman adapted to her changing physical and emotional needs without ever once hinting a desire to call off their wedding.

Like Chapman, most of us are more committed to our intimate relationships than we are to other relationships in our lives. For instance, we may be more willing to put aside minor differences and make compromises to preserve our intimate relationships. **Commitment** is our desire to stay in a relationship no matter what happens. When people are committed to each other, they assume they have a future together. That assumption is important because most intimate relationships—such as families and romantic relationships—experience conflict and distress from time to time. What allows us to deal with those difficult times is the belief that our relationship will survive them.

How do we commit ourselves to others? Intimate relationships usually include some level of *emotional commitment,* or a sense of responsibility for each other's feelings and emotional well-being. For example, it's your emotional commitment to your sibling that leads you to listen to his or her problems, even if they seem trivial to you. Our intimate relationships also include a level of *social commitment*, which motivates us to spend time together, to compromise, to be generous with praise, and to avoid petty conflict. In some romantic relationships, social commitment takes the form of spending time with a partner's friends or family members even if we don't enjoy their company. Finally, some intimate relationships are bound by *legal*

• **intimacy** Significant emotional closeness experienced in a relationship, whether romantic or not.

• **commitment** The desire to stay in a relationship no matter what happens.

Parents often provide the social, emotional, and financial commitments that help their children succeed.

kali9/E+/Getty images

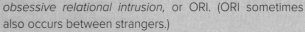

THE DARK SIDE OF COMMUNICATION

When a Desire for Commitment Turns to Obsession

Although deep commitment is necessary in intimate relationships, an excessive level can turn into an unhealthy obsession with another person. According to communication scholars William Cupach and Brian Spitzberg, intimate relationships are healthy and satisfying only if both partners desire approximately the same level of connection and interaction with each other. When one expresses a substantially higher level of interest in the relationship than the other, the result can be what Cupach and Spitzberg call

obsessive relational intrusion, or ORI. (ORI sometimes also occurs between strangers.)

ORI can prompt an individual to enact several specific behaviors aimed at increasing intimacy with the target of his or her affections. Those include spying on the target or invading his or her privacy, sending the person unwelcome expressions of attraction or love, and engaging in sexually harassing behaviors. They can also include demanding that the target curtail communication with others and commit to an exclusive relationship with the obsessed person.

Although relational intrusion can occur in face-to-face contexts, it is also becoming increasingly common online. Using the Internet, e-mail, or other electronic means to intrude on another person's life is called cyberstalking. Intrusive behaviors can have various negative effects on the recipients, including physical and psychological stress, disruptions in everyday routines, loss of sleep or appetite, and diminished trust in others.

SOURCES: Spitzberg, B. H., Cupach, W. R., Hannawa, A. F., & Crowley, J. P. (2014). A preliminary test of a relational goal pursuit theory of obsessive relational intrusion and stalking. *Studies in Communication Sciences, 14*(1), 29–36. https://doi.org/10.1016/j.scoms.2014.03.007; Cupach, W. R., & Spitzberg, B. H. (2014). *The dark side of relationship pursuit: From attraction to obsession and stalking* (2nd ed.). Routledge.

and *financial commitments*, which are more formal expressions of people's obligations to each other. Parents have a legal responsibility to provide housing, food, clothing, health care, and education for their children who are minors, and family members often take on financial obligations to care for relatives who are aging or who have specific physical or mental needs. No matter what form it takes, commitment is one of the foundations of intimate relationships.

Although deep commitment is important for many relationships, people can take it too far. At an extreme level, one person's commitment can turn into obsession, a topic explored in "The Dark Side of Communication."

INTIMATE RELATIONSHIPS FOSTER INTERDEPENDENCE

Another hallmark of intimate relationships is that they include high degrees of **interdependence**. Because people in families and romantic relationships depend on one another, what happens to one person, or what one person does, affects everyone else in the relationship. For instance, the way parents use their time and money depends not only on themselves but also on their children's needs. Likewise, how children perform in school and the way they treat their siblings also affect their parents.

Interdependence means that an event or a decision that affects one person in a relationship—such as taking a job or moving—affects everyone else in the relationship.

Parents and children are therefore interdependent. So are romantic partners: if a woman is offered a job promotion that requires her to relocate, for example, her decision will affect her romantic partner as much as it will affect her. The essence of interdependence is the idea that our actions influence other people's lives as much as they influence our own.

Almost all relationships have some measure of interdependence; what distinguishes intimate relationships is their *degree* of interdependence. You might feel very close to your best friend, but you probably wouldn't sell your house and move if his job were relocated. If your supervisor at work broke her leg, you might send flowers or visit her in the hospital, but you probably wouldn't offer her round-the-clock care.

Like most social relationships, friendships and professional relationships are interdependent to a degree. What typically sets our romantic and familial relationships apart, however, is their *higher* level of interdependence. That often motivates us to engage in greater relational maintenance behaviors than we do with friends or coworkers.

Ryan McVay/Getty Images

- **interdependence** The state in which what happens to one person affects everyone else in the relationship.

- **investment** The commitment of one's energies and resources to a relationship.

- **dialectical tensions** Conflicts between two important but opposing relational needs or desires.

INTIMATE RELATIONSHIPS REQUIRE CONTINUOUS INVESTMENT

Compared to other relationships, intimate relationships usually also exhibit a higher degree of **investment**—that is, the commitment of our energies and other resources. We also expect to benefit from our investment—think of our expectations from financial investments, for instance—but we know we cannot retrieve the resources we've dedicated to the relationship if it comes to an end. For example, if we drift apart from our siblings during adulthood, we may retain memories of our relationships, but we cannot get back the time, attention, and material resources we invested in them.

People in romantic relationships are often especially aware of how much—and how equitably—they are each investing in the relationship. Research shows that romantic partners are happiest when they feel they are both investing in their relationship to the same degree.[2] If you think you are putting more into your relationship than your partner is, it's easy to feel resentful. The most satisfying intimate relationships appear to be those in which both parties are investing equally.

INTIMATE RELATIONSHIPS SPARK DIALECTICAL TENSIONS

Have you ever felt as though you wanted to be closer to someone but also wanted to maintain your individuality? In your relationships, have you wished to have more self-disclosure but still desired to keep some thoughts private? Maybe you enjoy novelty and surprise in your relationships but you also like them to be stable and predictable. If you can relate to any of those feelings, you have experienced what relationship researchers call **dialectical tensions**—conflicts between two important but opposing needs or desires. Dialectical tensions are common in intimate relationships.[3] Within families, romantic relationships, and even friendships, three dialectical tensions in particular often arise.

©Jozef Polc/123RF

Autonomy versus Connection A common tension in intimate relations is between *autonomy*—the desire to be your own person—and *connection*—the desire to be close to others. People often observe that tension in their children, especially entering adolescence. After all, adolescence is a period of life when teenagers begin to develop independent identities and make decisions for themselves.[4] Many, however, still want to be emotionally close to their parents. They continue to need and crave the security of family closeness even as they are learning to behave like adults. In fact, it's not uncommon for parents and children to experience that dialectical tension for some time, even as the children grow into adulthood.

Openness versus Closedness A second dialectical tension in intimate relationships is the conflict between *openness*—the desire for disclosure and honesty—and *closedness*—the desire to keep certain facts, thoughts, or ideas to yourself. Suppose your mother asks you how your new relationship is going. On the one hand, you might want to confide in her as a way of reinforcing your closeness to her. On the other hand, you may feel it's best to keep some of the details to yourself, out of respect for your partner's privacy. In other words, part of you desires openness, and another part desires closedness.

Chris Noble/Stone/Getty Images

Predictability versus Novelty Finally, many intimate relationships experience conflict between *predictability*—the desire for consistency and stability—and *novelty*—the desire for fresh new experiences. After nearly 20 years of marriage, for instance, Pauline and Victor were so settled in their routines that their relationship had become highly predictable. Such predictability can be comforting, but at times it made their marriage feel stale and left them longing for something new. They found that trying new activities—such as taking a foreign language class together and volunteering at a soup kitchen—provided a refreshing change from the predictability of their married life. By the same token, however, they recognized that predictability gave their relationship an orderliness and certainty they both appreciated.

Researchers believe that dialectical tensions are a normal part of any close, interdependent relationship and that they become problematic only when people fail to manage them constructively. At the end of this chapter we'll look at several strategies relational partners use to manage dialectical tensions.

Characteristics of Romantic Relationships

The most intimate of intimate relationships is often with a romantic partner. Forming romantic relationships is a nearly universal human experience. Some 95 percent of us will marry at least once in our lifetime, and many who don't will have at least one significant, marriage-like romantic relationship.[5]

Marriages and long-term relationships are very important to our health and well-being. Multiple studies have shown, for instance, that married people live longer[6] and healthier[7] lives than those who never marry. One reason is that being married reduces a person's likelihood of engaging in risky health behaviors. Married people drink less[8] and are less likely to use an illicit drug such as marijuana than their unmarried counterparts.[9] They are also less likely to suffer from a mental disorder such as depression.[10] Several studies have shown that the health benefits of marriage are greater for men than for women.[11] Women are also healthier if married than if single, however, particularly if they are unemployed and lack the social support and financial resources employment provides.[12]

People in every known society form romantic unions, and although many romantic relationships share certain characteristics, there is also diversity among them. Let's look at variations in the extent to which romantic relationships are exclusive, voluntary, based on love, composed of other-sex partners, and permanent.

ROMANTIC RELATIONSHIPS AND EXCLUSIVITY

One common expectation for romantic relationships is that they are exclusive. Usually, exclusivity takes the form of **monogamy**, which means being in only one romantic relationship at a time and avoiding romantic or sexual involvement with others outside that relationship. Exclusivity is an expression of commitment and faithfulness that romantic partners share and trust each other to uphold. As a result, relational **infidelity**, which means having romantic or sexual interaction with someone outside the romantic relationship, is often an emotionally traumatic experience for the partner who is wronged.

Not all romantic partners expect their relationship to be exclusive, however. Instead, some choose to have "open" relationships in which romantic and/or sexual involvement with people outside the relationship is accepted.[13] Although it's difficult to know how common open relationships are, research indicates that they are observed between heterosexuals,[14] bisexuals,[15] gay men,[16] and lesbians alike.[17]

ROMANTIC RELATIONSHIPS AND VOLUNTARINESS

Another common expectation for romantic relationships—although one that varies by culture, as we'll see below—is that they are voluntary. This means that people choose for themselves whether to be romantically involved—and if they decide to, they get to select their romantic partner. That expectation presumes that a relationship is satisfying only if both partners have freely chosen to participate in it. One indicator of this belief in the United States is the abundance of online and in-person dating services, which allow customers to browse the profiles of prospective partners and choose the ones with whom they want to make contact. One such service—Match.com—boasts over 35 million unique monthly users.[18]

Even if people enter into romantic relationships voluntarily, they do not always stay in them voluntarily. Indeed, research shows that many people are unhappy in their relationships but stay in them anyway.[19] According to relationship scholars Denise Previti and Paul Amato, the most common reasons people stay in relationships involuntarily are

- They want to provide stability for their children.
- Their religious beliefs disallow separation or divorce.
- They are concerned about the financial implications of separating.
- They see no positive alternatives to their current relationship.[20]

Individuals may also have their own reasons for staying in relationships they find dissatisfying. As this research makes clear, relationship stability does not necessarily imply relationship satisfaction.

ROMANTIC RELATIONSHIPS AND LOVE

In much of the Western world, people think of marriage and other romantic relationships as being based on love. In individualistic societies such as the United States and Canada, that is, people tend to believe not only that they should get to choose their romantic partner but that their choice should be based on love and attraction.[21] According to one survey, 88 percent of U.S. American adults cited love as the most important reason to marry.[22] Indeed, the typical U.S. wedding ceremony (whether religious or civil) emphasizes the importance of love in the marital relationship, whereas a lack of love is frequently cited as a reason relationships fail.[23]

Whether or not they love each other, however, some people enter into romantic relationships for other reasons. Some do so for financial stability.[24] Others form relationships to gain, consolidate, or protect power,[25] such as when members of royal or politically powerful families intermarry.

Some cultures endorse the practice of arranged marriage, in which individuals are expected to marry the partner their parents select for them.

Photo Japan/Alamy stock photo

ROMANTIC RELATIONSHIPS AND SEXUALITY

In many ways, people communicate similarly in same- and other-sex romantic relationships.[26] Both kinds of relationships value intimacy and equality between relational partners.[27] They both experience conflict,[28] and over similar topics.[29] They both seek emotional support from family members and friends.[30] Further, they divorce at the same rate, and for similar reasons.[31] People in same-sex romantic relationships report levels of relationship satisfaction equal to those of other-sex dating, engaged, and married couples.[32]

Despite those similarities, same- and other-sex romantic relationships in most parts of the world differ with respect to their legal recognition. In the United States and abroad, the question of whether same-sex romantic partners should be allowed to marry has been socially and politically controversial for decades. Supporters of same-sex marriage argue that people should be permitted to marry whomever they love and that it is discriminatory to deny marriage rights to people based on their sex. Opponents say that marriage is inherently a reproductive relationship and that allowing same-sex couples to marry threatens the sanctity of marriage and the family. In June 2015, the Supreme Court of the United States ruled that denying same-sex couples the ability to marry violated the U.S. Constitution, thereby guaranteeing same-sex couples the right to marry in all 50 states. With this decision, the United States joined more than 20 other nations that have legalized same-sex marriage since 2000.

A growing number of countries around the world, including the United States, recognize the legal right of same-sex couples to marry.

CREATISTA/Shutterstock

ROMANTIC RELATIONSHIPS AND PERMANENCE

People often conceive of marriage and other long-term romantic relationships as permanent. That expectation is reflected in the fact that traditional wedding vows in many parts of the world emphasize the permanence of marriage. The vow "till death do us part" captures this sentiment by suggesting that once spouses are married, they will stay together for life. One survey of 300 marriage license applicants illustrates this idea. Even though respondents correctly noted that a large percentage of new marriages end in divorce, every single respondent said the likelihood that his or her own marriage would end in divorce was zero![33]

Many marriages do last for many years, thanks in part to the large number of ways in which societies promote, protect, and reward marriages. In the United States, for instance, federal law provides spouses a number of benefits that are often denied to couples who are not legally married. Many of those benefits relate to communication and the maintenance of marriage and family relationships.[34] Here are just a few:

- *Spousal privilege:* Communication between spouses is privileged and protected, just like doctor–patient and attorney–client communication.

- *Visitation:* Marriage gives spouses rights of visitation if one spouse is hospitalized or imprisoned.

- *Stepchildren:* Stepparents have legal status with stepchildren only if they are legally married to the children's parent.

- *Cohabitation on controlled properties:* Marriage allows spouses to live together on military bases and other controlled properties.

- *Inheritance and property rights:* Unless a person's will specifies otherwise, a spouse is entitled to receive a person's estate when he or she passes away.

- *Medical and burial decisions:* Spouses have the ability to make medical decisions for each other and to make burial or cremation decisions when one of them dies.

- *Domestic violence protection:* If one spouse is abusive or violent, the other spouse can request domestic violence protection orders from a court.

Many marriages and romantic relationships don't last, however. After a period of time together, romantic partners often find that they no longer share the same goals or feel the same level of attraction toward each other. They may also have developed romantic feelings for someone else and may choose to end their current relationship to develop a relationship with that person. No matter the cause, many romantic relationships end.

ROMANTIC RELATIONSHIPS AROUND THE WORLD

As we've seen, many common expectations for romantic relationships have exceptions. Some are also subject to cultural diversity, as we'll discover next.

Culture Affects Expectations for Exclusivity Although exclusivity is often expected for romantic relationships in the Western world, people in many other cultures don't share that expectation. In fact, many countries—primarily in Africa and southern Asia—allow the practice of **polygamy**, in which one person has two or more spouses at a time. Some people in a polygamous relationship report that they appreciate the closeness and intimacy they share with multiple partners. Others indicate that feelings of jealousy and resentment can lead to increased conflict in such relationships.[35] Some cultures are also more accepting than the United States of marital infidelity. In a study by the Pew Research Center, adults in France, Italy, Spain, South Africa, and at least 20 other countries were more likely than Americans to say that having an extramarital affair is morally acceptable.[36]

Similarly, some romantic couples engage in **polyamory**, which means having more than one consensual romantic or sexual relationship at once.[37] Some people refer to that arrangement as having an "open relationship," or a relationship in which monogamy is not expected. According to two studies, more than 20 percent of U.S. American adults have engaged in a polyamorous relationship at some point in their lives.[38] That research found that polyamory was more common for men than for women and more common for lesbian, gay, and bisexual adults than for those who identify as heterosexual.

A commonly voiced concern about polyamorous relationships is that they contribute to high levels of jealousy. If one's romantic partner is sexually involved with others, that is, one might feel especially protective of the relationship. Research finds just the opposite, however. According to a 2017 study involving over 2,000 adults, people in polyamorous relationships reported significantly less jealousy and significantly more trust with their romantic partner than those in monogamous relationships.[39] It may be the case that when partners agree to allow romantic or sexual involvement with others, they don't see such involvement as a threat to their relationship.

Culture Affects Expectations for Voluntariness People in Western cultures usually expect to be able to choose their own romantic partners. In much of the world, however, it is common for other people—usually one person's parents—to choose that individual's romantic partner. In fact, according to the practice of *arranged marriage* (which is most common in the Middle East, Asia, and Africa), many people are expected to marry the partner their parents select for them.

Sometimes, children can reject their parents' selection of a spouse, in which case the parents look for someone else. In other cases, children may be pressured to marry the person their parents have chosen for them. In either situation, an arranged marriage is not entirely voluntary.[40]

The fact that arranged marriages aren't voluntary doesn't necessarily mean that spouses in such marriages are dissatisfied with the relationship. Indeed, people who expect their marriages to be arranged may prefer this practice to the task of choosing a spouse on their own.[41] For people who expect to choose their own romantic partner, however, the practice of arranged marriage would likely decrease their satisfaction with their relationships.

Culture Affects Expectations for Love Would you marry someone you didn't love? Although many people in individualistic Western cultures would say no,

• **polygamy** The state of having two or more spouses at once.

• **polyamory** Having more than one consensual romantic or sexual relationship at once.

many in collectivistic societies would say yes. For example, in China and India, the choice of a spouse often has more to do with the wishes and preferences of family and social groups than it does with love, even if the marriage isn't arranged. One study found that only half the participants in India and Pakistan felt love was necessary for marriage, whereas 96 percent of the U.S. participants did.[42] Sociologist Frances Hsu explained that when considering marriage "an American asks 'How does my heart feel?' A Chinese [person] asks, 'What will other people say?'"[43] As family studies scholar Stephanie Coontz points out, the connection between love and marriage is a historically recent trend, even in Western cultures.[44] She explains that although romantic love has existed throughout the ages, societies began thinking of love as a basis for marriage only within the last three centuries. Coontz indicates that before that time, some societies believed that love should develop after marriage, and many others thought love had no place at all in marriage. Thinking of marriage primarily as a romantic relationship is therefore a recent development.

Culture Affects Expectations for Sexuality Social and legal acceptance of same-sex romantic relationships varies dramatically among different cultures. At present, same-sex partners can marry with full legal recognition in Argentina, Australia, Belgium, Brazil, Canada, Colombia, Denmark, Ecuador, Finland, France, Germany, Iceland, Ireland, Luxembourg, Malta, Mexico, the Netherlands, Norway, Portugal, South Africa, Spain, Sweden, Taiwan, the United Kingdom, the United States, and Uruguay. Several other countries, including Slovenia and Switzerland, recognize civil unions or domestic partnerships, and still other countries, such as Bulgaria and Israel, recognize same-sex marriages initiated overseas. Same-sex relationships exist in many other nations, as well, even if they do not receive legal recognition.

In sharp contrast, many other nations prohibit people of the same sex from being romantically or sexually involved at all. In some countries—such as Guyana, Bangladesh, Sierra Leone, and Tanzania—people convicted of engaging in same-sex relations face life in prison. Other nations—including Iran, Nigeria, Sudan, Somalia, Mauritania, Yemen, and Saudi Arabia—impose the death penalty on those who violate laws banning same-sex relations.[45]

Whatever their form, romantic relationships are clearly among the most significant of all human relationships. To examine your own expectations for romantic relationships, see "The Competent Communicator."

Forming and Communicating in Romantic Relationships

Romantic relationships don't form overnight. Instead, like many important relationships, they evolve. In this section, we'll see that people follow some fairly consistent steps when they develop a romantic relationship. They also vary in how they handle several common communication tasks, and when they end, they tend to do so in predictable stages.

GETTING IN: STAGES OF RELATIONSHIP DEVELOPMENT

Communication scholar Mark Knapp has suggested that relationship formation has five separate stages: initiating, experimenting, intensifying, integrating, and bonding.[46] Let's first take a brief look at each stage:

1. *Initiating.* The **initiating stage** occurs when people meet and interact for the first time. For instance, you might make eye contact with someone on the first day of class and decide to introduce yourself, or you might find yourself sitting next to someone on an airplane and strike up a conversation. "What's your name?" and "Where are you from?" are common questions people ask at this initial stage.

2. *Experimenting.* When you meet someone in whom you're initially interested, you might move to the **experimenting stage**, during which you have conversations

• **initiating stage** The stage of relationship development at which people meet and interact for the first time.

• **experimenting stage** The stage of relationship development at which people converse to learn more about each other.

So, What Do You Expect? Your Expectations for Romantic Relationships

People come into romantic relationships with a variety of expectations. What are yours? Read the statements below and circle the numbers for each statement with which you agree. You can take this quiz whether you are currently in a romantic relationship or not.

rawpixel/123RF

1. **I expect my romantic partner to be my best friend.**

2. **I expect my romantic relationship to be only one of several important relationships in my life.**

3. **I expect my romantic relationship to be problem-free.**

4. **I expect any romantic relationship to have its share of problems.**

5. **I think the most important aspects of a good romantic relationship are love and attraction.**

6. **I think a romantic relationship can be successful and satisfying even without high degrees of love and attraction.**

7. **I expect that once I get married or enter into a significant relationship, I will remain in that relationship until one of us dies.**

8. **I don't necessarily expect to spend the rest of my life with the same romantic partner.**

9. **I think living together before marriage sets up the marriage to fail.**

10. **I think living together before marriage is realistic and wise.**

When you're finished, count how many odd-numbered statements you circled. Then count how many even-numbered statements you circled. Which number is greater? If you circled more odd-numbered statements, your expectations for romantic relationships are mostly *idealistic*. You believe in the ideal version of romantic relationships and want that for yourself. If you circled more even-numbered statements, your expectations are mostly *pragmatic*. You may want a good romantic relationship for yourself, but you don't necessarily expect it to be perfect or permanent.

to learn more about that person. Individuals in the experimenting stage might ask questions such as "What movies do you like?" and "What do you do for fun?" to gain basic information about a potential partner. This stage helps individuals decide whether they have enough in common to move the relationship forward.

• **intensifying stage** The stage of relationship development at which people move from being acquaintances to being close friends.

3. *Intensifying.* During the **intensifying stage**, people move from being acquaintances to being close friends. They spend more time together and might begin to meet each other's friends. They start to share more intimate information with each other, such as their fears, future goals, and secrets about the past. They also increase their commitment to the relationship and may express it verbally through statements such as "You're really important to me."

4. *Integrating.* The **integrating stage** occurs when a deep commitment has formed, and the partners share a strong sense that the relationship has its own identity. At that stage, the partners' lives become integrated, and they also begin to think of themselves as a pair—not just "you" and "I" but "we." Others start expecting to see the two individuals together and begin referring to them as a couple.

5. *Bonding.* The final stage in Knapp's model of relationship development is the **bonding stage**, in which the partners make a public announcement of their commitment to each other. That might include moving in together, getting engaged, or having a wedding. Beyond serving as a public expression of a couple's commitment, bonding also allows individuals to gain the support and approval of people in their social networks.

The integrating stage occurs when the relationship begins to form its own identity.
monkeybusinessimages/ Getty Images

Individual and Cultural Variations in Relationship Formation

Not every couple goes through the stages of relationship development in the same way. Some may stay at the experimenting stage for a long time before moving into the intensifying stage. Others may progress through the stages very quickly. Still others may go as far as the integrating stage but put off the bonding stage. Furthermore, research shows the stages of relational development to be similar in same-sex and other-sex relationships.[47]

Relationship formation is not necessarily the same in all cultures. In countries that practice arranged marriage, for instance, the process of forming a marital relationship would look much different and include negotiation and decision making by the parents, with less input (if any) from the children. In countries where polygamy is common, the integration and bonding stages would also look different, because one person may have multiple spouses at once. As we noted earlier in this chapter, cultures vary in their expectations about romantic relationships—and as their expectations differ, so do their ways of forming relationships.

Forming Relationships Online

The Internet provides a wide range of options for meeting people and developing relationships, including dating sites, social networking sites, chat rooms, bulletin boards, and the variety of social media platforms. In fact, as Table 1 shows, building or maintaining relationships are among the top 10 reasons people report for using social media in the first place.

• **integrating stage** The stage of relationship development at which a deep commitment has formed, and the partners share a strong sense that the relationship has its own identity.

• **bonding stage** The stage of relationship development at which partners make a public announcement of their commitment to each other.

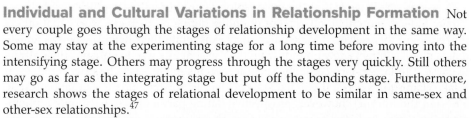

TABLE 1

WHY DO PEOPLE USE SOCIAL MEDIA?

1. To stay in touch with what my friends are doing
2. To stay up-to-date with news and current events
3. To fill up spare time
4. To find funny or entertaining content
5. General networking with other people
6. Because a lot of my friends are on them
7. To share photos or videos with others
8. To share my opinion
9. To research/find products to buy
10. To meet new people

SOURCE: Valentine, O. (2018, January 11). Top 10 reasons for using social media. *Global Web Index.* https://blog.globalwebindex.com/chart-of-the-day/social-media/

As a result, online communication has become one of the primary means of establishing romantic relationships.[48] Because communication capabilities on the Internet differ from those in face-to-face interaction, we might expect that relationships would develop quite differently online than in real life. Yet several studies indicate that individuals follow largely the same steps whether forming relationships online or in face-to-face contexts.[49]

Many forms of computer-mediated communication pose particular challenges for communicating with potential dating partners, however. Suppose, for instance, that Jake has posted a profile on a dating website. He browses the profiles of other users to see whether anyone sparks his interest, and other users do the same with his profile. One challenge is that Jake's pool of prospective dating partners is limited to those with Internet access. Although Internet availability is relatively high in middle-class urban areas, it remains low in many poorer rural areas and among ethnic minority populations.[50] In the United States today, 10 percent of adults don't use the Internet at all.[51] Online access is lower still in much of the developing world, a phenomenon known as the *digital divide*.[52] How significant a challenge that will likely pose for Jake therefore depends largely on where he lives.

A second challenge is that the information offered in online profiles may be inaccurate. Indeed, more than 80 percent of online dating participants worry that others misrepresent themselves.[53] Male daters may exaggerate their height, whereas female daters might subtract a few pounds from their weight as a way to enhance their attractiveness.[54] In face-to-face contexts, such deceptions might easily be discovered; even if Jake claims to be 5'11", it will likely be evident to any date he meets that he is only 5'8". On the Internet, however, prospective dating partners may have only a photograph by which to judge a person's claims about appearance—and photographs are easy to alter. Communication researchers Jeffrey Hancock and Catalina Toma found that approximately a third of photographs in online dating profiles are inaccurate representations of the person's appearance.[55] Women's photographs were judged to be less accurate than men's photographs because women's photographs were more likely to be older and retouched.

• **catfishing** Using false information, including stolen or edited photos, to create a fake online persona.

A more extreme form of online deception involves people who misrepresent who they are and what they want. The term **catfishing** refers to using false information, including stolen or edited photos, to create a fake online persona. People who engage in catfishing, called *catfish*, then use their deceptive profiles to develop online relationships with others. According to one poll, a primary reason people engage in catfishing is loneliness; those who struggle with social connection may catfish as a way to develop new relationships, even under false pretenses. Others in the same poll said they use catfishing to escape their insecurities, overcome dissatisfaction with their personal appearance, and explore their sexuality or gender identity.[56]

Despite these and other challenges, the Internet continues to grow as a venue for relationship formation. In 1999, only around 2 million single U.S. adults had used some form of online dating service,[57] whereas by 2019, the top 10 online dating sites alone had nearly 28 million combined users.[58] It appears, therefore, that many individuals are able to overcome the limitations of online communication and to follow similar trajectories for relationships formed online and offline.[59]

Romantic relationships are as individual as the people in them. Several of the ways people differ are related to their communication behaviors within the relationship, as we consider next.

COMMUNICATING IN ROMANTIC RELATIONSHIPS

We can learn a lot about the quality of romantic relationships by looking at the way the partners communicate with each other. Although couples engage in many forms of communication, four communication behaviors have

Tithi Luadthong/Alamy Stock Photo

particular influence on their satisfaction with their relationship: conflict, privacy, emotional communication, and instrumental communication.

Romantic Relationships Vary in How They Handle Conflict Conflict is a common characteristic of many romantic relationships. Communication scholars Joyce Hocker and William Wilmot define **conflict** as "an expressed struggle between at least two interdependent parties who perceive incompatible goals, scarce resources, and interference from the other party in achieving their goals."[60] Partners in a romantic relationship can have conflicts about many issues, including how they spend their time and money, raise their children, manage their personal and professional obligations, and enact their sex life. Although conflict isn't fun, it isn't necessarily bad for a relationship. The way couples handle it—rather than the amount of conflict they have—is what influences the success of their relationship.

> • **conflict** An expressed struggle between at least two interdependent parties who perceive incompatible goals, scarce resources, and interference from the other party in achieving their goals.

Much of what we know about how romantic partners handle conflict comes from research on marriage. For instance, social psychologist and marital therapist John Gottman has spent many years studying how spouses communicate during conflict episodes.[61] His work suggests marital couples can be classified into four groups, depending on how they handle conflict:[62]

1. *Validating couples* talk about their disagreements openly and cooperatively and communicate respect for each other's opinions even when they disagree with them. They stay calm when discussing hotly contested topics. They also use humor and expressions of positive emotion to defuse the tension that conflict can create.

2. *Volatile couples* also talk about their disagreements openly, but in a way that is competitive rather than cooperative. Each spouse tries to persuade the other to adopt his or her point of view, and their conflicts tend to be marked with expressions of negative rather than positive emotion. Those conflicts, however, are often followed by intense periods of affection and "making up."

3. *Conflict-avoiding couples* tend to avoid open discussion of issues about which they disagree. To avoid the discomfort of engaging in conflict directly, they try to defuse negative emotion and focus on their similarities, believing that most problems will resolve themselves. They often "agree to disagree," a position that can side-step conflict but can also leave their points of disagreement unresolved.

4. *Hostile couples* have frequent and intense conflict. They use negative emotion displays, such as harsh tones of voice and facial expressions of anger or frustration. They also engage in personal attacks, insults, sarcasm, name calling, blaming, and other forms of criticism with each other.

Hostile couples argue in an intensely negative manner.
Dean Drobot/123RF

Research by scholars Thomas Holman and Mark Jarvis has indicated that the same categories also apply to unmarried heterosexual couples.[63]

Less research has examined the conflict communication of lesbian and gay couples, but Gottman's studies have identified some differences between the conflict styles of homosexual and heterosexual couples.[64] Specifically, gay and lesbian couples

- Use more humor and positive emotion during conflict conversations.
- Are less likely to become hostile after a conflict.
- Use fewer displays of dominance and power during a conflict episode.
- Are less likely to take conflict personally.
- Stay calmer emotionally and physiologically during conflict.

For many romantic relationships, conflict is an unpleasant but unavoidable fact of life. We will learn more about strategies for managing conflict later in this chapter.

Romantic Relationships Vary in How They Handle Privacy In every romantic relationship, the partners must choose for themselves how to manage information they consider to be private. When Kali and Neal were having difficulty conceiving a child, for instance, they carefully considered whom they were going to tell. Neal felt the information was no one's business but theirs and preferred to keep it private. Kali wanted to tell her family and close friends because she needed their emotional support. Their problems conceiving were causing enough stress in their relationship already; disagreeing about whether to keep the problems private was only making matters more stressful.

Communication scientist Sandra Petronio believes we all experience tensions between disclosing certain information and keeping it private. She developed **communication privacy management (CPM) theory** to explain how individuals and couples manage those tensions.[65] CPM theory would say Kali and Neal *jointly own* the information about their problems. The information belongs to both of them, so they must decide together whether to keep it to themselves or share it with others.

Individuals and couples vary in their approach to privacy. Some of us are "open books"—that is, uninhibited about disclosing private information to others. Others are discreet, sharing private information with only a select few. Research indicates that some of us are simply more inclined than others to disclose private information. In most cases, however, we adapt our disclosure to the people to whom we are disclosing, to how much we trust them, and how much they have disclosed to us.[66] No matter what our reasons for disclosing to others, we should always be aware of information that a romantic partner expects us to keep private.

Romantic Relationships Vary in How They Handle Emotional Communication

Emotional communication is an important part of most romantic relationships. The way romantic partners express emotion to each other can say a lot about the quality of their relationship.[67] Specifically, it reflects how satisfied the partners are with each other.[68]

Suppose Anita and her husband Jonah have been together for 8 years. They co-own a home where they run a small pottery studio and raise Jonah's twin girls from a previous marriage. They have their challenges just like any couple, but they are both highly satisfied with their relationship. Now suppose Brad and Lynne live across the street from Anita and Jonah. They have been together almost 10 years but have separated twice in that time. Their most recent separation lasted 7 months and would have ended their relationship permanently were it not for pressure from Lynne's family for the couple to work out their difficulties. Both Brad and Lynne would describe their relationship as very unsatisfying.

According to research, one of the most noticeable differences between the communication patterns of those two couples will be in their expression of emotion. Over the course of several studies, social psychologists John Gottman and Robert Levenson have identified two patterns of emotional communication that differentiate happy from unhappy couples.

First, happy partners such as Anita and Jonah communicate more positive emotion and less negative emotion with each other than do unhappy partners such as Brad and Lynne.[69] In particular, people in satisfying relationships express more affection, use more humor, and communicate more assurances (i.e., verbal expressions of their commitment to the relationship). In comparison, people in unsatisfying relationships express more negative emotion in the form of anger, contempt, sadness, and hostility.[70] Gottman's work has found, specifically, that people in satisfied couples maintain a ratio of approximately five positive behaviors for every one negative behavior.[71]

The second pattern of emotional communication Gottman and Levenson identified is that unhappy couples are

Dmytro Zinkevych/Shutterstock

• **communication privacy management (CPM) theory** A theory explaining how people in relationships negotiate the tension between disclosing information and keeping it private.

more likely than happy couples to reciprocate expressions of negative emotion.[72] When Lynne criticizes or expresses anger toward Brad, for example, he often reciprocates her behavior by expressing criticism or anger back at her. That type of response escalates the negativity in their conversation. As a result, they often find it difficult to address the issues underlying their conflict because they are so focused on the negative emotion they're each communicating. In comparison, people in happy couples are more likely to respond to negative expressions with positive or neutral ones. When Jonah expresses anger toward Anita, for instance, Anita responds calmly in order to keep Jonah's anger from escalating into conflict.

Romantic Relationships Vary in How They Handle Instrumental Communication People in most romantic relationships communicate with each other using **instrumental communication**, which is communication about day-to-day topics and tasks such as who's making dinner and who's taking the children to soccer practice.[73] The fact that instrumental communication addresses the necessary daily tasks couples face explains why it is one of the most common forms of communication among romantic partners.[74] It can also be one of the most contentious issues couples face because romantic partners often disagree over the division of responsibilities for instrumental tasks.[75]

People in unhappy relationships tend to reciprocate expressions of negative emotion.

John Burke/Jupiterimages

• **instrumental communication**
Communication about day-to-day topics and tasks.

The way partners negotiate the division of everyday tasks matters for their relationship for at least two reasons. First, day-to-day tasks such as cleaning, cooking, and childcare *need* to be completed, so most couples cannot leave decisions about who will do them to chance. Second, the way in which partners divide mundane, everyday tasks often reflects the balance of power in their relationship.[76] If one partner assumes greater power and control than the other, that partner is in a greater position to dictate how tasks will be divided. If instead both partners see themselves as equally powerful, the division of instrumental tasks can be more equitable.[77]

Romantic relationships vary greatly in how the partners communicate about the division of day-to-day tasks. In other-sex relationships, partners who believe in traditional gender role behaviors will often divide instrumental tasks along stereotypical gender lines.[78] Thus, men perform tasks such as yard maintenance and auto repair, whereas women take responsibility for meal preparation and childcare. In contrast, partners who do not necessarily adopt traditional gender role behaviors frequently have a conflict over how instrumental tasks should be divided.[79] Specifically, women often wish their partners would take greater responsibility for household tasks and childcare than they actually do.[80] Compared to men, women are more likely to feel that the division of instrumental tasks is unfair, and those feelings reduce their relational satisfaction.[81]

With regard to same-sex relationships, recent research has speculated that homosexual partners may divide instrumental tasks more equally than other-sex couples do, with each partner sharing in both stereotypically masculine and stereotypically feminine responsibilities. In a survey of 113 same-sex romantic couples from around the United States, communication researcher Justin Boren discovered that a pattern of sharing was common, particularly among those who were highly satisfied with their relationships.[82]

How partners divide mundane tasks such as childcare often reflects the balance of power in their relationship.

moodboard/Getty Images

GETTING OUT: ENDING ROMANTIC RELATIONSHIPS

Romantic relationships develop over time, and when they come apart, they also come apart over time. Communication researcher Mark Knapp has described five stages

Ryan McVay/Getty Images

relationships go through when they end: differentiating, circumscribing, stagnating, avoiding, and terminating.[83]

1. *Differentiating.* Partners in any romantic relationship are similar to each other in some ways and different in other ways. In happy, stable relationships, partners see their differences as complementary. However, when partners begin to view their differences as undesirable or annoying, they are entering the **differentiating stage**, which is often the first stage in relationship dissolution.

2. *Circumscribing.* When romantic partners enter the **circumscribing stage**, they begin to decrease the quality and quantity of their communication with each other. Their purpose in doing so is to avoid dealing with conflicts.[84] They start spending more time apart,[85] and when they're together, they usually don't talk about problems, disagreements, or sensitive issues in their relationship. Instead they focus on "safe" topics and issues about which they agree.

3. *Stagnating.* If circumscribing progresses to the point where the partners are barely speaking to each other, the relationship enters the **stagnating stage**, in which it stops growing and the partners feel as if they are just "going through the motions." Partners avoid communicating about anything important because they fear it will only lead to conflict. Many relationships stay stagnant for long periods of time.

4. *Avoiding.* When partners decide they are no longer willing to live in a stagnant relationship, they enter the **avoiding stage**, during which they create physical and emotional distance from each other. Some partners take a direct route to creating distance, such as by moving out of the house or saying "I can't be around you right now." Others create distance indirectly, for example by making up excuses for being apart ("I have company in town all next week, so I won't be able to see you") and curtailing their availability by screening phone calls or not responding to texts or messages. People sometimes engage in the avoidance stage through the process of ghosting. **Ghosting** occurs when someone you have been seeing suddenly and unexpectedly stops all contact with you on social media. For instance, one partner might unfriend the other on Facebook, unfollow the other on Instagram or Twitter, and stop liking or commenting on social media posts. According to one poll, women and men are equally likely to have been ghosted and equally likely to have ghosted others.[86] A less-severe form of avoidance is called orbiting. **Orbiting** occurs when someone who has ghosted you continues to interact with you on social media, such as by watching your stories or liking your posts. Experts suggests that people might engage in orbiting to preserve the possibility of a later relationship, to avoid missing out on news about your life, or even because they don't realize you can still see that they are viewing your posts.[87]

5. *Terminating.* The last stage in Knapp's model of relationship dissolution is the **terminating stage**, at which point the relationship is officially judged to be over. In nonmarital relationships, that usually means that one or both partners moves out if the couple shared a residence. It also includes dividing property, announcing to friends and family that the relationship has ended, and negotiating the rules of any future contact between the partners. For legally married partners, relational termination means getting a **divorce**, which is the legal discontinuation of the marriage. In the United States today, approximately 39 percent of all marriages end in divorce.[88]

For many couples, the decision to terminate their romantic relationship is a significant one. It often requires a

• **differentiating stage** The stage of relationship dissolution at which partners begin to view their differences as undesirable or annoying.

• **circumscribing stage** The stage of relationship dissolution at which partners begin to decrease the quality and quantity of their communication with each other.

• **stagnating stage** The stage of relationship dissolution at which the relationship stops growing and the partners feel as if they are just "going through the motions."

SHARPEN Your Skills: *Changes in communication*

Identify a couple in which the partners have been together for at least 10 years, and ask them (together or separately) how their communication patterns have changed in the time they've been together. Also, ask them what advice they would give to others about communicating successfully in relationships. Document your findings in a blog or journal entry.

substantial reorganization of the family, and it can take an enormous mental and emotional toll, particularly on children of the couple. Children can be negatively affected by divorce or relationship dissolution well into their own adulthood.[89] That isn't always the case, though. When the romantic relationship is highly conflicted, neglectful, or abusive, children and their parents are often better off after the relationship ends.[90]

Communicating in Families

In 2018, president Donald Trump drew bipartisan criticism for allowing immigration officials to separate the children of migrants from their parents at the U.S.–Mexico border. At least 2,700 children were housed in detention centers while their parents' immigration status was sorted out.[91] Critics argued that dividing families is inhumane and that separating children from their parents would cause those children irreparable psychological trauma, because of the importance of the parent–child bond.

Indeed, it's hard to overestimate the importance of families in our lives. For most of us, our first relationships are with our family members. Familial relationships can provide us with a feeling of belonging, a sense of our own history, and a measure of unconditional love and support we cannot find anywhere else. Growing up in a family also introduces us to the concept of relationships and can help us form mental models for how to engage in friendships and romantic relationships in adolescence and adulthood. Yet families can also be a source of great frustration and heartache—and many family relationships experience both peace and conflict. The depth of our engagement with families, and the fact that they can be both so positive *and* so negative, make families one of our most important intimate relationships.

In this section, we'll examine what makes a family a family and which characteristics familial relationships often share. We'll also survey types of family structures and discover what communication issues are common in family relationships.

WHAT MAKES A FAMILY?

If you were asked to draw a picture of your family, whom would you choose to include? Some people might be obvious options, such as your parents, spouse, siblings, and children. How about your grandparents? Nieces and nephews? In-laws? What about your stepsiblings? Maybe there are close friends or longtime neighbors you think of as family—would you include them?

Even researchers have difficulty defining exactly what makes a family a family, yet many scholars agree that most family relationships have one or more of three important characteristics: genetic ties, legal obligations, and role behaviors. Let's briefly examine each.

©Ariel Skelly/Blend Images LLC

Genetic Ties Many family members are related "by blood," meaning they share a specified proportion of their genetic material. For instance, you share about 50 percent of your genes with your biological mother, biological father, and each full biological sibling (or 100 percent with an identical twin or triplet). With your grandparents, aunts and uncles, and any half-siblings, you share about 25 percent of your genes, and with cousins, about 12.5 percent.

However, a genetic link isn't the only characteristic that defines family relationships. Consider that we typically share zero percent of our genes with our spouses, steprelatives, and adopted relatives, yet we usually consider them to be family. Moreover,

- **avoiding stage** The stage of relationship dissolution at which partners create physical and emotional distance from each other.

- **ghosting** Suddenly and unexpectedly stopping all contact with someone on social media.

- **orbiting** Continuing to interact with someone on social media after having ghosted that person.

- **terminating stage** The stage of relationship dissolution at which the relationship is officially deemed to be over.

- **divorce** The legal discontinuation of a marriage.

Identical twins are called "identical" because they share 100 percent of their genetic material with each other. Fraternal twins share only 50 percent of their genes—the same as other full biological siblings.

Sean Justice/Corbis

• **role** A pattern of behavior that defines a person's function within a group, such as a family.

although sharing a genetic tie makes two people biological relatives, it does not necessarily mean they share a social or an emotional relationship.

Legal Obligations Another aspect of many family relationships is that they include legal bonds. For example, parents have many legal obligations toward their minor children; neglecting to house, feed, educate, and care for them is a crime.[92] Furthermore, marriage is the most heavily regulated family relationship from a legal perspective—in the United States, well over a thousand different federal laws govern some aspect of marriage.[93]

The law also regulates adoptive relationships, domestic partnerships, and even some aspects of stepfamilies. The existence of a legal familial bond is therefore another characteristic of many family relationships. Family members may feel they have responsibilities to one another even without the law's saying so, but laws formalize those responsibilities and help ensure they are met.

Role Behaviors Regardless of whether a relationship is bound by genetic or legal ties, many people believe the most important characteristic that defines a family is that the people in it *act* like family. According to that idea, family members are expected to enact **roles**, patterns of behavior that define a person's function in a group. These may include living together, taking care of and loving one another, and representing themselves as a family to outsiders. People who enact such behaviors and who think of themselves as family therefore *are* family, according to that definition.

These elements—genetic, legal, and role—are not mutually exclusive. Rather, they are characteristics that often help to define a relationship as familial, and some relationships, such as parental relationships, often include all three. How researchers define family is important because that determines, in part, which relationships family scholars study and which they do not. How *you* define family is also important because that can influence whom you invite to significant occasions in your life, with whom you share resources, and to whom you entrust secrets or sensitive information.

The ability to communicate effectively with people in a variety of family relationships is valuable in many careers. For one example, check out the "Putting Communication to Work" box.

TYPES OF FAMILIES

The ABC television series *Modern Family* depicts a large and diverse family structure headed by Jay Pritchett (played by Ed O'Neill). Pritchett lives with his second (and much younger) wife Gloria, their son Joe, and Gloria's son Manny. His daughter Claire and her husband Phil have three biological children, whereas his son Mitchell is raising an adopted Vietnamese daughter with his partner Cameron. The diversity of relationships in Pritchett's extended family illustrates the point that families come in many forms.

We examine some of the diversity of family types in this section. Let's begin by distinguishing between what researchers call family of origin and family of procreation. **Family of origin** is the family we grew up in, so it typically consists of our parents or stepparents and any siblings we have. **Family of procreation** is the family we start as an adult, and it consists of our spouse or romantic partner and/or any children we raise as our own. Most adults would say they belong to both a family of origin and a family of procreation; others, however, may identify with only one type of family or with neither.

Families of origin and families of procreation develop in many forms. Historically, the most traditional profile has consisted of a married woman and man and their biological children. Researchers often call that configuration a *nuclear family,* and although

• **family of origin** The family in which one grows up, usually consisting of parents and siblings.

• **family of procreation** The family one starts as an adult, usually consisting of a spouse or romantic partner and children.

putting**communication**to**work**

[   ] Search

Job Title >

Work Responsibilities >

Financial Planner

Personal finance is not only about saving and investing; financial planners must also help their clients make important decisions that will affect their family members. Effective financial planners will help clients to prioritize savings (retirement or the kids' college funds?) and to make difficult decisions about uncomfortable topics, such as dividing their estates in their wills and determining who will make their health care decisions for them if they cannot make them for themselves. Navigating these issues requires strong listening skills and an ability to understand the nature of—and expectations for—each client's most intimate relationships.

it has been the most common family form in the United States, is that still the case today? See the "Fact or Fiction?" box to find out.[94] One family type that is becoming increasingly common is the *blended family*, with two adult partners (who may be married or cohabiting and of the same or another sex) raising children who are not the biological offspring of both partners. The children might be adopted, or they might be the biological offspring of one of the parents and the stepchildren of the other.

Jason Merritt/TERM/Staff/ Getty images

Fact or *fiction?*

Still Going Nuclear: The Average American Family Remains a Nuclear Family

In the 1950s TV show *Leave It to Beaver*, the Cleaver family was like most American families at the time: a legally married husband and wife and their biological children living together in the same household. For decades, people have referred to that arrangement as the "average American family," and in the 1950s, almost two-thirds of families in the United States fit that description. The Simpsons, from the much later animated series of the same name, represent the same family configuration. Is the average American family of today still nuclear in form?

The answer is no. According to the U.S. Census Bureau, fewer than half of households in the United States are now headed by a married couple. That statistic doesn't mean fewer people are marrying—rather, it means more U.S. families are now headed by single adults, cohabiting other-sex couples, and cohabiting same-sex couples than at any point in the country's history.

Furthermore, typical family arrangements vary around the country. According to the Census Bureau's American Community Survey, the highest percentage of families headed by a married couple is in Utah County, Utah, at nearly 70 percent. The lowest, at just 26 percent, is in Manhattan, New York.

Families come in many forms.

FluxFactory/iStock/Getty images

ASK YOURSELF

- Do you consider your family of origin to be average or typical? If so, in what ways?
- How do you think changes in the family structure affect the ways family members communicate?

SOURCE: U.S. Census Bureau. (2013, August). *America's families and living arrangements: 2012.* https://www.census.gov/prod/2013pubs/p20-570.pdf

A third family form is the *single-parent family*, in which one adult raises one or more children. As in blended families, the children may be the parent's biological offspring or they may be adopted or stepchildren. There are nearly 14 million single-parent families in the United States, and more than 80 percent of those are headed by a single mother.[95] Finally, many families represent *co-parenting families*, in which children divide their time between two parents who are no longer romantic partners but who share custody and financial obligations for the children.

COMMUNICATION ISSUES IN FAMILIES

As in all significant relationships, communication plays a big part in making or breaking family relationships. We'll examine four communication issues families commonly encounter: roles, rituals, stories, and secrets.

Family Roles Family roles embody the functions people serve in the family system. Roles are different from family positions, so we wouldn't talk about the "role of the father," for instance, or the "role of the daughter." *Positions* such as father and daughter are based on the structure of our relationships with others, but *roles* are based on the social and emotional functions our behavior serves within the family. One person might be the problem solver; another might act as the jokester or the peacemaker. One sibling may be the troublemaker, whereas another is the caregiver or the helpless victim.

Family roles often become particularly relevant when the family is in conflict. Family therapist Virginia Satir has suggested that four roles are especially common during conflict episodes.[96] The first is the *blamer*, who holds others responsible for whatever goes wrong but accepts no responsibility for his or her own behaviors. A second role is the *placater*, the peacemaker who will go to any lengths to reduce conflict. That person may simply agree with whatever anyone says to keep others from getting angry. A third role is the *computer*, who attempts to use logic and reason—rather than emotion—to defuse the situation. Finally, there's the *distracter*, who changes the subject by making random, irrelevant comments so the rest of the family will forget about the conflict. Each role leads people to communicate in different ways. Some role behaviors, such as computing and placating, can be useful for resolving conflict or at least preventing it from escalating. The behavior of blamers and distracters, on the other hand, might make conflict worse by taking attention away from the topic of the conflict.

Family Rituals Many families have their own important traditions. One family's tradition might be to spend every Thanksgiving serving turkey dinners at a shelter for homeless veterans. Another's might be to attend drag races together every summer. We call those behaviors **family rituals**, or repetitive activities that have special meaning for a family. Rituals serve a variety of functions in family interactions, among them reinforcing a family's values and providing a sense of belonging. A family ritual such as an annual road trip isn't just about the trip; it's also about spending time together, creating memories, and emphasizing the importance of family relationships.

According to communication scholars Dawn Braithwaite, Leslie Baxter, and Anneliese Harper, rituals can be especially important in blended families of stepparents and stepchildren. These researchers found that people often "import" into their blended family rituals from their original family[97] that are sometimes retained or adapted. For instance, Braithwaite and her colleagues described one family in which a widowed mother and her children would have a pizza "picnic" in the living room on a regular basis. The children would cuddle with the mother on the couch, eat pizza, and talk, and all considered it to be a special time. When the mother remarried and acquired stepchildren, however, the ritual stopped, perhaps because the stepchildren would have been uncomfortable taking part. Braithwaite and colleagues also found that it's important for blended families to develop their own rituals. In one such family, a young man described how his new stepfather began a ritual of watching the Super Bowl with his brother and him. According to this young man, that ritual served as a means of promoting communication with his stepfather.[98]

McGraw Hill.

• **family rituals** Repetitive activities that have special meaning for a family.

Family Stories Many of us can think of particular stories we've heard over and over again from members of our family. Maybe your grandparents were fond of describing how they overcame hardships when they were first married, and your

Sharon Mccutcheon/EyeEm /
Getty images

parents have a favorite story about your childhood antics. Even events that were stressful or unpleasant at the time but turned out well, such as fixing a flat tire while on vacation, can serve a reassuring or cautionary function when they become part of the family lore. Stories are common in families, and communication scholars Jody Koenig Kellas and Haley Kranstuber Horstman suggest that they do more than provide entertainment. Family stories, they explain, give families a sense of their history, express what family members expect of one another, and reinforce connections across different generations.[99]

Family stories are as varied as families are, but they all tend to have at least two characteristics in common. First, they're told and retold, often over long periods of time. In that way, they become part of a family's collective knowledge: after a while, most everyone in the family has heard each story over and over. Second, family stories convey an underlying message about the family, such as "We are proud," "We overcome adversity," or "We stick together no matter what."

Family Secrets Many families have secrets they intentionally keep hidden from others. These often contain information the family considers private and inappropriate for sharing with outsiders, such as details of religious practices, health or legal issues, family conflicts, or financial information. When you were growing up, you may remember your parents telling you not to talk about such issues with people outside your family. Keeping family secrets doesn't just protect private family information, though; it also reinforces the family's identity and exclusivity, because only family members are allowed to know the secrets.[100]

Secrets can also be kept *within* families. For instance, Marco may not want his parents to know that he has moved in with his girlfriend, so he swears his sister to secrecy. Erin and Tammy may not want their kids to know that Tammy has breast cancer, so they agree to keep it secret. People might choose to keep secrets from other family members for many reasons, such as avoiding embarrassment or conflict, protecting another's feelings, and maintaining a sense of autonomy and privacy.

Improving Communication in Intimate Relationships

Sharing exciting, exhilarating activities helps partners feel happier in their relationships.

Westend61/Getty images

Because romantic and familial relationships are so important to us, it's in our best interests to communicate within them as competently as we can. In this section, we look at six strategies for improving communication within your intimate relationships: emphasizing excitement, focusing on positivity, handling conflict constructively, having realistic expectations, repairing damaged relationships, and managing dialectical tensions.

GO FOR FUN: EMPHASIZE EXCITEMENT

You might have heard the saying "The family that plays together, stays together." That bit of folk wisdom has some truth to it. Research by relationships scholar Art Aron and his colleagues has shown that partners who engage together in exciting or exhilarating forms of play—such as rollerblading, riding a roller coaster, and going to a suspenseful movie—increase their level of relationship satisfaction.[101] Less exhilarating activities such as playing cards and going out to dinner, even if they are pleasant, don't have the same effect. Why? Aron suggests that when partners engage in activities that elevate their physical arousal—the way riding a roller coaster or watching a thriller movie can—they may attribute their elevated arousal to each other instead of to the activity. Subconsciously, that is, people may notice their physical arousal and conclude that their partner, rather than the activity, is causing it. Sharing exhilarating play activities together can therefore help partners keep a level of positivity and freshness in their relationship that might otherwise fade with time.

You can use the knowledge gained from the Aron research to improve your own relationships. With your romantic partner, family members, and even your friends, make opportunities to share exciting and novel experiences. You may well find that your relationships become closer as a result.

STAY POSITIVE: USE CONFIRMING MESSAGES

Another important way to emphasize positivity in family relationships is to use **confirming messages**, behaviors that indicate how much we value another person.[102] Those are the opposite of **disconfirming messages**, behaviors that imply a lack of respect or value for others. Several decades ago, researcher Jack Gibb observed that people can communicate confirming messages in at least six ways:[103]

- *Descriptive:* messages that communicate support clearly and specifically, without judgmental words, such as "There are a few opportunities for improvement in the yardwork you've done."

- *Inquiry orientation:* messages that invite others to work cooperatively to solve problems or understand issues, such as "Why don't we see if there's a way we can both go to Stephanie's soccer match?"

- *Spontaneity:* messages that are unplanned and free of hidden motives: "I'm planning a birthday party for Derrick; want to come?"

- *Empathy:* messages that express understanding of, and interest in, another's thoughts and feelings, such as "I'm sorry you didn't get the promotion you wanted at work; you must be so disappointed."

- *Equality:* messages that seek others' viewpoints and express value for others' ideas: "You have a very nice way of responding to solicitors who come to our door; I've never thought of taking the approach you do."

- *Provisional:* messages that convey points of view but invite alternative views: "What leads you to the opinion that Proposition 40 is unfair to families like ours? Is it possible that the source of your information is wrong?"

Gibb also believed that at least six types of disconfirming messages create a defensive, unsupportive climate in relationships:

- *Evaluative:* messages that convey judgments of what's right and wrong, good and bad: "That was the worst job of cutting the lawn you've ever done."

- *Control:* messages that attempt to impose ideas on others and coerce others to agree, such as "You can't use the laptop right now; I'm using it."

- *Strategy:* messages that suggest the speaker is trying to direct other people's behaviors, such as "Are you busy tomorrow?"

- *Neutrality:* messages that imply indifference or a lack of interest in others: "Life's unfair sometimes; you'd better get used to it."

- *Superiority:* messages that imply the speaker is superior to his or her listeners, such as "I can't imagine why you organized our family vacation this way; you don't know what you're doing."

- *Certainty:* messages that convey that the speaker's ideas are absolutely true and no other viewpoints are valid: "You're wrong."

Research shows that confirming messages are particularly important in marital relationships. Psychologist John Gottman has spent much of his career looking at why marriages succeed or fail. As we considered earlier in this chapter, stable, satisfied

• confirming messages Behaviors that convey how much another person is valued.

• disconfirming messages Behaviors that imply a lack of respect or value for others.

couples have a 5-to-1 ratio of positive to negative communication. That doesn't mean that people in happy marriages never communicate negatively; rather, it means they enact at least five positive behaviors (such as confirming messages) for every negative one. Gottman has found that couples with lower positive-to-negative ratios have an elevated risk of divorce.[104]

DEAL WITH THE DARK SIDE: HANDLE CONFLICT CONSTRUCTIVELY

Even the happiest, most stable relationships experience conflict from time to time when partners have competing goals. How can we manage conflict in a constructive way?

It turns out that handling conflict constructively is more about what we *don't do* than what we *do.* That is, couples who manage conflict in a positive manner do so by avoiding certain problematic behaviors. To identify those behaviors, Gottman has spent years studying how romantic partners interact with each other during conflict episodes. We might expect that couples who fight frequently are most likely to split up. In fact, Gottman's research has found otherwise: The *way* couples argue, not how frequently, predicts their chances of staying together.[105] Gottman identified four specific warning signs for separation or relational dissolution: criticism, contempt, defensiveness, and stonewalling. He refers to them as the "Four Horsemen of the Apocalypse" to indicate that they signal distress.[106] Let's take a close look at each.

Criticism According to Gottman, the first warning sign occurs when partners engage in **criticism** or complaints that focus on the other person's personality or character rather than on his or her problematic behaviors. Statements such as "You always have to be right" and "You never care about my feelings" focus on attacking the person and assigning blame, which makes these criticisms problematic for conflict. In contrast, a statement such as "I wish you would put your cell phone away when we sit down to dinner" focuses on a specific action that one partner wishes the other would change, and are less problematic.

Some criticisms also express global opinions about a person's value or virtue instead of offering specific critiques about the topic of the conflict. For example, a distressed partner might say, "You never think of anyone but yourself" rather than, "You should be more attentive when I describe my feelings to you." Because such criticisms can come across as personal attacks instead of accurate descriptions of the sources of conflict, they tend to inflame conflict situations. At that point, criticism becomes a sign of a distressed relationship.

Contempt A second warning sign occurs when partners show **contempt** for each other, which means showing a lack of respect for the other person. That behavior can include calling names ("You stupid idiot!"), using sarcasm or mockery to make fun of the other person, and engaging in nonverbal behaviors that suggest a low opinion of the partner, such as sneering and eye rolling. It can also include ridiculing the person in front of others and encouraging others to do the same. Contempt functions to put down and degrade the other person. Responding to conflict with contempt often increases the partners' stress, and elevated stress in turn can impair physical health as well as relational satisfaction.[107]

Defensiveness A third danger sign is that partners become defensive during their conflict. **Defensiveness** means seeing yourself as a victim and denying responsibility for your behaviors. Instead of listening to their partners' concerns and acknowledging that they need to change certain behaviors, defensive people whine ("It's not fair"), make excuses ("It's not my fault"), and respond to complaints with additional complaints ("Maybe I spend too much money, but you never make time for the kids and me"). People are particularly prone to defensiveness when they recognize that the criticisms have merit but they don't want to accept the responsibility of changing their behavior.

Stonewalling The last of Gottman's "Four Horsemen" is **stonewalling**, or withdrawing from the conversation. People who engage in stonewalling often act as though

- **criticism** Words that pass judgment on someone or something.

- **contempt** Hostile behavior in which people show a lack of respect for each other.

- **defensiveness** Seeing oneself as a victim and denying responsibility for one's behaviors.

- **stonewalling** Withdrawing from a conversation.

they are "shutting down." They stop looking at their partners, stop speaking, and stop responding to what their partners are saying. In some cases, they physically leave the room to end the conversation. The reason for their departure isn't to calm down, which might be an effective strategy. Rather, it is to shut down the conversation entirely.

Gottman's research has suggested that people stonewall when they feel emotionally and psychologically "flooded," or incapable of engaging in the conversation any longer. Unfortunately, when one partner stonewalls, it becomes almost impossible for the couple to resolve its disagreements. Research has also shown that when men stonewall during a conflict, women often experience significant increases in stress hormones.[108]

Gottman's research therefore tells us that *constructive* conflicts are characterized not just by the behaviors that are present but also by those that are absent. When we are able to engage in conflict without criticizing, showing contempt, becoming defensive, and stonewalling, we stand a much better chance of preserving the quality of our relationship even as we work with our partner to resolve our differences. You can read more about the constructive use of conflict in the "Difficult Conversations" box.

Exactostock/Superstock

GET REAL: HAVE REALISTIC EXPECTATIONS

Another way to improve communication in intimate relationships is to make sure that *everyone* in those relationships has realistic expectations for them. When expectations are unrealistic, relationships are likely to fail, causing the individuals to feel disappointed, hurt, or betrayed. Only through open communication can everyone's expectations come to light and the partners reach agreement on how realistic they are.

Six months after marrying Carla, for instance, Gregory stopped spending time with his parents, brother, and even his close friends. He wanted to spend all his time with Carla and began feeling anxious when they were apart. Carla started to feel smothered, and she explained to Gregory that they both needed other people in their lives besides each other. She encouraged him to reconnect with his family and friends. Gregory in turn explained that spending time with Carla helped him feel secure about their relationship. Eventually, they agreed on a new expectation for spending time together that seemed more reasonable to both of them. By communicating about their different expectations for their marriage and coming to an agreement on what they both considered realistic, Carla and Gregory were able to strengthen their feelings of satisfaction with each other.

As in Gregory's case, it's common to want to spend a lot of time with a romantic partner. However, it is important to be realistic about what we expect from our relationships. No one person—not even a spouse—can meet *all* our social and emotional needs. Expecting someone to do so places an unfair burden on that person and may lead to disappointment.

A better approach is to appreciate each relationship individually and to remember that the important people in our lives are important for different reasons. For example, you might talk to your romantic partner about most issues, but maybe you feel more comfortable discussing your dad's health or your daughter's financial difficulties with your sibling. Further, just as no single person can meet all *your* needs, you cannot meet someone else's every need. Being realistic about your expectations helps you appreciate the most positive aspects of each of your relationships.

REPAIR DAMAGED RELATIONSHIPS

When a relationship encounters problems, it is useful to engage in **relational repair,** which comprises your efforts to fix those problems so that the relationship can continue. Relational repair behaviors often follow some type of **relational transgression**, which is any behavior that violates an important expectation in the relationship. Transgressions can include lying to a relational partner, being romantically or sexually unfaithful, failing to keep a promise, and communicating in ways that hurt the partner emotionally.

When we have caused harm to a relational partner, most of us are more motivated to engage in relational repair if we are committed to that relationship than if we are not. According to the **investment model of commitment processes**, developed by

• relational repair Efforts to fix problems in a relationship so that the relationship can continue.

• relational transgression A behavior that violates an important expectation in a relationship.

• investment model of commitment processes A theoretic model proposing that relationship commitment is a function of satisfaction, resources (or investments), and the perceived quality of relational alternatives.

Difficult Conversations

Real Life and Romance: Handling Conflict Constructively

Imagine this: Your romantic partner and you moved into an apartment together eight months ago, and you have experienced frequent conflict during that time. It seems you can never agree on who has responsibility for which household chores. This afternoon, you came home from school to a sink full of dirty dishes, even though you *thought* your partner had agreed to wash them . . . and you now feel that another argument is likely.

Now, consider this: Even though you're angry—and feel you have a right to be—you also want your conflict to be constructive, not destructive. You already know there are certain behaviors that are best avoided during an argument, including criticism, contempt, defensiveness, and stonewalling. Beyond avoiding those problematic behaviors, consider the following tips:

- Try to think of conflict as an opportunity rather than as a problem. Conflict doesn't often feel good, but that doesn't mean it can't produce positive results. Use conflict conversations as a chance to understand your partner's feelings and expectations better and to identify solutions to your problems that you may not have thought of before.

- Hold yourself and your partner accountable for staying calm and respectful. If your partner interrupts you while you're speaking, say "Please don't interrupt me" . . . and then make sure you don't interrupt him or her, either.

- Clearly describe the focus of your dissatisfaction, which in this case is the dirty dishes that should have been washed but weren't. Then, try to keep your conversation focused on that particular problem until you come to a resolution. Avoid bringing up past offenses that are unrelated to the present problem.

- Pick your battles. Remember that not every problem is worth arguing about. Even if you're angry at your partner's behavior, it may be best to let little problems go and save conflict conversations for issues that are more important.

Even though it makes many people uncomfortable, conflict is a normal part of most close relationships. Rather than using conflict as an opportunity to criticize, express contempt, become defensive, or engage in stonewalling, see it as a chance for your partner and you to understand each other better and work together toward resolving your problems.

psychologist Caryl Rusbult, commitment to a relationship is a function of three factors.[109] Specifically, we are more committed to a relationship if we feel more satisfied in it; if we receive resources from it; and if we believe our alternatives to being in that relationship are undesirable.

How do people attempt to repair a relationship in the wake of a transgression? Research indicates that several communication strategies are common.[110]

- *Apologies:* Perhaps the most common relational repair strategy is to apologize for the transgression. Effective apologies include an admission of responsibility ("It was my fault that I let you down"), an expression of regret ("I'm sorry for what I did"), a commitment not to repeat the offense ("I'll never do it again"), and a request for forgiveness ("I hope you can forgive me").

- *Explanations:* Apologies are often accompanied by explanations, which are accounts of why an offending behavior occurred. Explanations such as "I didn't know," "I never wanted this to happen," and "I wasn't trying to upset you" work to minimize someone's responsibility for a transgression.

- *Denials:* A denial occurs when, instead of explaining or apologizing for our behavior, we claim we have done nothing wrong. Some denials assert that an alleged offense never occurred ("I did not have lunch with my ex-girlfriend yesterday"). Others admit the behavior but claim it was not a violation of relationship expectations ("I'm allowed to see my ex-girlfriend if I want to").

- *Appeasements:* Appeasements are forms of compensation that we offer someone to make up for a transgression. To make up for missing her son's school play, for instance, a mother might buy her son a video game, take him out for ice cream, show him extra attention at home, or promise not to miss the next play.

- *Avoidance:* Avoidance means making a conscious effort to ignore the transgression and to prevent discussion about it. If an apology has been offered and accepted, avoidance can allow people to move forward in their relationship without dwelling on the hurt that was caused. Some people avoid talking about transgressions altogether, however, which can leave hurt feelings to fester.

Two observations about these communication strategies are worth making. First, they can be enacted separately or together. As mentioned, for instance, apologies may be accompanied by explanations and then by avoidance. Transgressors may also engage in appeasements along with apologies, or denials along with avoidance.

Second, even though these strategies are common, they are not necessarily equally effective. For instance, people may engage in denial or avoidance when they don't believe they are at fault or when they are unwilling to admit responsibility for a transgression, but those behaviors can be dissatisfying and even hurtful to the partners who feel they have been wronged. Similarly, apologies and appeasements are often more effective at repairing a relationship if they are perceived to be genuine and voluntary, rather than insincere and coerced.

The intended outcome of successful relational repair behaviors is usually **forgiveness**, the process by which a wronged person stops feeling angry or resentful about an offense. Communication scholars Vincent Waldron and Doug Kelley have proposed that forgiveness requires (1) acknowledging the other person's hurtful conduct, (2) extending that person undeserved mercy, (3) transforming one's own emotions to let go of anger and hurt, and (4) renegotiating the relationship to clarify future rules and expectations.[111] When forgiveness occurs, therefore, it opens the door for relational repair.

- **forgiveness** The process by which a wronged person stops feeling angry or resentful about an offense.

PUSH AND PULL: MANAGE DIALECTICAL TENSIONS

As we saw earlier in this chapter, people in romantic and familial relationships often experience dialectical tensions—conflicts between two opposing needs. Managing dialectical tensions can help improve communication in intimate relationships. Researchers have identified eight different strategies to manage dialectical tensions.[112] None of these is inherently positive or negative. Whether they work depends on our goals for the relationship and the context in which we are using them.

Let's suppose Moira is engaged to Albee and has been spending a lot of time with him. She is experiencing the tension between autonomy and connection. She strongly desires to retain her own individuality and autonomy but also passionately wants to be connected to Albee. Different strategies she might use to manage that tension include

- **Denial**, which entails responding to only one side of the tension and ignoring the other. Were Moira to adopt this strategy, she might deny her desire for autonomy and focus all her attention on being connected with Albee.

- **denial** A strategy for managing dialectical tensions that entails responding to only one side of a tension and ignoring the other side.

• disorientation A strategy for managing dialectical tensions that entails ending the relationship in which the tension exists.

• alternation A strategy for managing dialectical tensions that entails going back and forth between the two sides of a tension.

• segmentation A strategy for managing dialectical tensions that entails dealing with one side of a tension in some aspects of a relationship and with the other side of the tension in other aspects of the relationship.

• balance A strategy for managing dialectical tensions that entails trying to compromise, or find a middle ground, between the two opposing forces of a tension.

• integration A strategy for managing dialectical tensions that entails developing behaviors that will satisfy both sides of a tension simultaneously.

• recalibration A strategy for managing dialectical tensions that entails reframing a tension so the contradiction between opposing needs disappears.

- **Disorientation**, which means ending the relationship in which the tension exists. Moira may feel so disoriented by the tension between her desires for autonomy and connection that she calls off her engagement to avoid it.

- **Alternation**, which means going back and forth between the two sides of the tension. On some days, Moira might act in ways that enhance her autonomy and individuality. On other days, she might act in ways that strengthen her connection to Albee.

- **Segmentation**, which means dealing with one side of a tension in some aspects of a relationship and with the other side of the tension in other aspects of that relationships. Moira might emphasize her connection to Albee by sharing intimate disclosures, but she might stress her autonomy by keeping her finances separate from his. Rather than going back and forth between the two sides of the tension, as in alternation, she addresses one side of the tension in some ways and the other side in other ways.

- **Balance**, which means trying to compromise, or find a middle ground, between the two opposing forces of a tension. For instance, Moira may disclose most but not all of her feelings to Albee. She may not feel as autonomous as she wants *or* as connected as she wants, but she may feel she is satisfying each desire to some degree.

- **Integration**, which entails developing behaviors that will satisfy both sides of a tension simultaneously. Moira feels connected to Albee when they spend their evenings together, but she also likes to choose how she spends her time. To integrate those needs, she reads or does crossword puzzles while Albee watches television in the same room, an option that allows her to feel autonomous and connected at the same time. Unlike the balance strategy, which focuses on compromising each desire, integration finds ways to satisfy both without compromising either.

- **Recalibration**, which means reframing a tension so the contradiction between opposing needs disappears. By communicating about their needs and expectations for their relationship, Moira and Albee might realize that autonomy and connection are both desirable. As a result, they may come to see autonomy and connection as complementary rather than opposing needs.

- **Reaffirmation**, which means simply embracing dialectical tensions as a normal part of life. Moira may come to realize that she will always feel torn between being autonomous and being connected. Instead of fighting the tension or struggling to resolve it, she accepts it as a normal feature of her relationship. Whereas recalibration means eliminating the tension by seeing the opposing needs as complementary, reaffirmation means accepting the tension as normal.

Individuals in families and romantic relationships commonly try several of those strategies, and they may find some more effective than others. Improving your communication in intimate relationships doesn't require you to adopt specific strategies and ignore others. Rather, if you're aware of the options for managing dialectical tensions, you can use the ones that work best for you.

SHARPEN Your Skills: *Dialectical tensions*

Identify a dialectical tension you are currently experiencing in a romantic or familial relationship. Have a conversation with the other person in which you describe how those two needs oppose each other, and he or she describes how they complement each other. In your conversation, work to recalibrate the dialectical tension by discussing how both sides of the tension are useful for your relationship.

• reaffirmation A strategy for managing dialectical tensions that entails embracing dialectical tensions as a normal part of life.

- What makes some relationships intimate?

Intimate relationships require deep commitment, foster interdependence, require continuous investment, and spark dialectical tensions.

- How do we form, maintain, and dissolve romantic relationships?

Forming romantic relationships involves initiating, experimenting, intensifying, integrating, and bonding. We maintain our relationships by the way we handle conflict, privacy, emotional communication, and instrumental communication. Ending romantic relationships involves differentiating, circumscribing, stagnating, avoiding, and terminating.

- What makes a family, and how do we communicate in families?

Family relationships typically involve some combination of genetic ties, legal obligations, and role behaviors. We use family roles, rituals, stories, and secrets to maintain communication in our familial relationships.

KEY TERMS

intimacy 218
commitment 218
interdependence 220
investment 220
dialectical tensions 220
monogamy 222
infidelity 222
polygamy 224
polyamory 224
initiating stage 225
experimenting stage 225
intensifying stage 226
integrating stage 227
bonding stage 227
catfishing 228
conflict 229
communication privacy management (CPM) theory 230

instrumental communication 231
differentiating stage 232
circumscribing stage 232
stagnating stage 232
avoiding stage 233
ghosting 233
orbiting 233
terminating stage 233
divorce 233
role 234
family of origin 234
family of procreation 234
family rituals 237
confirming messages 239
disconfirming messages 239
criticism 240

contempt 240
defensiveness 240
stonewalling 240
relational repair 241
relational transgression 241
investment model of commitment processes 241
forgiveness 243
denial 243
disorientation 244
alternation 244
segmentation 244
balance 244
integration 244
recalibration 244
reaffirmation 244

NOTES

1. Robson, S. V. (2015, December 15). Tina Fey and Amy Poehler talk about being "chosen sisters." *Popsugar.* www.popsugar.com/entertainment/Tina-Fey-Amy-Poehler-Interview-Sisters -39012049

2. See Oshio, T., Nozaki, K., & Kobayashi, M. (2013). Division of household labor and marital satisfaction in China, Japan, and Korea. *Journal of Family and Economic Issues, 34*(2), 211–223. https://doi.org /10.1007/s10834-012-9321-4

3. Suter, E. A., & Norwood, K. M. (2017). Critical theorizing in family communication studies: (Re)reading relational dialectics theory 2.0. *Communication Theory, 27*(3), 290–308. https://doi.org/10.1111 /comt.12117

4. Oudekerk, B. A., Allen, J. P., Hessel, E. T., & Molloy, L. E. (2015). The cascading development of autonomy and relatedness from adolescence to adulthood. *Child Development, 86*(2), 472–485. https://doi.org/10.1111/cdev.12313

5. Yau, N. (2017). Percentage of people who married, given your age. *FlowingData.com.* https://flowingdata.com/2017/11/01 /who-is-married-by-now/

6. Tatangelo, G., McCabe, M., Campbell, S., & Szoeke, C. (2017). Gender, marital status and longevity. *Maturitas, 100*, 64–69. https://doi.org/10.1016/j.maturitas.2017.03.002

7. Umberson, D., & Kroeger, R. (2016). Gender, marriage, and health for same-sex and different-sex couples: The future keeps arriving. In S. McHale, V. King, J. Van Hook, & A. Booth (Eds.), *Gender and couple relationships* (pp. 189–213). Springer. https://doi.org/10.1007/978-3-319-21635-5_12

8. Dinescu, D., Turkheimer, E., Beam, C. R., Horn, E. E., Duncan, G., & Emery, R. E. (2016). Is marriage a buzzkill? A twin study of marital status and alcohol consumption. *Journal of Family Psychology, 30*(6), 698–707. https://doi.org/10.1037 /fam0000221

9. Scott, K. M., Wells, J. E., Angermeyer, M., Brugha, T. S., Bromet, E., Demyttenaere, K., de Girolamo, G., Gureje, O., Haro, J. M., Jin, R., Karam, A. N., Kovess, V., Lara, C., Levinson, D., Ormel, J., Posada-Villa, J., Sampson, N., Takeshima, T., Zhang, M., & Kessler, R. C. (2010). Gender and the relationship between marital status and first onset of mood, anxiety and substance use disorders. *Psychological Medicine, 40*(9), 1495–1505. https://doi.org/10.1017/S0033291709991942

10. See Marcussen, K. (2005). Explaining differences in mental health between married and cohabiting individuals. *Social Psychology Quarterly, 68*(3), 239–257. https://doi.org/10.1177/019027250506800304

11. Umberson & Kroeger, 2016.

12. Rendall, M. S., Weden, M. M., Favreault, M. M., & Waldron, H. (2011). The protective effect of marriage for survival: A review and update. *Demography, 48*(2), 481–506. https://doi.org/10.1007/s13524-011-0032-5

13. Klesse, C. (2018). Theorizing multi-partner relationships and sexualities—Recent work on non-monogamy and polyamory. *Sexualities, 21*(7), 1109–1124. https://doi.org/10.1177/1363460717701691

14. Cohen, M. T. (2016). An exploratory study of individuals in non-traditional, alternative relationships: How "open" are we? *Sexuality & Culture, 20*(2), 295–315. https://doi.org/10.1007/s12119-015-9324-z

15. Gusmano, B. (2018). Coming out through an intersectional perspective: Narratives of bisexuality and polyamory in Italy. *Journal of Bisexuality, 18*(1), 15–34. https://doi.org/10.1080/15299716.2017.1416510

16. Haupert, M. L., Gesselman, A. N., Moors, A. C., Fisher, H. E., & Garcia, J. R. (2017). Prevalence of experiences with consensual nonmonogamous relationships: Findings from two national samples of single Americans. *Journal of Sex & Marital Therapy, 43*(5), 424–440. https://doi.org/10.1080/0092623X.2016.1178675

17. Munson, M., & Stelboum, J. P. (2013). *The lesbian polyamory reader: Open relationships, non-monogamy, and casual sex.* Routledge. https://doi.org/10.1300/J155v03n01_01

18. eBiz/MBA. (2019, September). Top 15 most popular dating websites, September 2019. http://www .ebizmba.com/articles/dating-websites

19. See Spiker, D. A., Hammer, J. H., & Parnell, K. J. (2019). Men in unhappy relationships: Perceptions of couple therapy. *Journal of Social and Personal Relationships, 36*(7), 2015–2035. https://doi.org /10.1177/0265407518775537

20. Previti, D., & Amato, P. R. (2003). Why stay married? Rewards, barriers, and marital stability. *Journal of Marriage and Family, 65*(3), 561–573. https://doi.org/10.1111/j.1741-3737.2003.00561.x

21. Sprecher, S., & Hatfield, E. (2017). The importance of love as a basis of marriage: Revisiting Kephart (1967). *Journal of Family Issues, 38*(3), 312–335. https://doi.org/10.1177/0192513X15576197

22. Pew Research Center. (2018, February 13). 8 facts about love and marriage in America. http://www .pewresearch.org/fact-tank/2018/02/13/8-facts-about-love-and-marriage/

23. See Hawkins, A. J., Willoughby, B. J., & Doherty, W. J. (2012). Reasons for divorce and openness to marital reconciliation. *Journal of Divorce & Remarriage, 53*(6), 453–463. https://doi.org/10.1080/10502556.2012.682898

24. LeBaron, A. B., Kelley, H. H., & Carroll, J. S. (2018). Money over marriage: Marriage importance as a mediator between materialism and marital satisfaction. *Journal of Family and Economic Issues, 39*(2), 337–347. https://doi.org/10.1007 /s10834-017-9563-2

25. Simon, C. J. (2019). Migration and career attainment of power couples: The roles of city size and human capital composition. *Journal of Economic Geography, 19*(2), 505–534. https://doi.org/10.1093/jeg/lby009

26. Ellis, L., & Davis, M. (2017). Intimate partner support: A comparison of gay, lesbian, and heterosexual relationships. *Personal Relationships, 24*(2), 350–369. https://doi.org/10.1111/pere.12196

27. Peplau, L. A., Fingerhut, A. W., & Beals, K. P. (2004). Sexuality in the relationships of lesbians and gay men. In J. Harvey, A. Wenzel, & S. Sprecher (Eds.), *Handbook of sexuality in close relationships* (pp. 350–369). Lawrence Erlbaum Associates.

28. Ogolsky, B. G., & Gray, C. R. (2016). Conflict, negative emotion, and reports of partners' relationship maintenance in same-sex couples. *Journal of Family Psychology, 30*(2), 171–180. https://doi.org/10.1037/fam0000248

29. Kurdek, L. A. (2006). Differences between partners from heterosexual, gay, and lesbian cohabiting couples. *Journal of Marriage and Family, 68*(2), 509–528. https://doi.org/10.1111/j.1741-3737.2006.00268.x

30. Graham, J. M., & Barnow, Z. B. (2013). Stress and social support in gay, lesbian, and heterosexual couples: Direct effects and buffering models. *Journal of Family Psychology, 27*(4), 569–578. https://doi.org/10.1037/a0033420

31. Goldberg, A. E., & Garcia, R. (2015). Predictors of relationship dissolution in lesbian, gay, and heterosexual adoptive parents. *Journal of Family Psychology, 29*(3), 394–404. https://doi.org/10.1037/fam0000095

32. See, e.g., Rodrigues, D. L., Lopes, D., & Prada, M. (2019). Cohabitation and romantic relationship quality among Portuguese lesbian, gay, and heterosexual individuals. *Sexuality Research and Social Policy, 16*(1), 100–111. https://doi.org/10.1007/s13178-018-0343-z

33. Barker, L. A., & Emery, R. E. (1993). When every relationship is above average: Perceptions and expectations of divorce at the time of marriage. *Law and Human Behavior, 17*(4), 439–450.

34. Nolo.com. (2016, May 11). Marriage rights and benefits. https://www.nolo.com/legal-encyclopedia/marriage-rights-benefits-30190.html

35. See Esmaili, G., Sadrpushan, N., & Gorji, Y. (2012). Comparison of life quality for men in monogamy and polygamy families. *Journal of Sociological Research, 3*(2), 428–439. https://doi.org/10.5296/jsr.v3i2.2669

36. Wike, R. (2014, January 14). French more accepting of infidelity than people in other countries. *Pew Research Center.* http://www.pewresearch.org/fact-tank/2014/01/14/french-more-accepting-of-infidelity-than-people-in-other-countries/

37. Balzarini, R. N., Campbell, L., Kohut, T., Holmes, B. M., Lehmiller, J. J., Harman, J. J., & Atkins, N. (2017). Perceptions of primary and secondary relationships in polyamory. *PLoS One, 12*(5), e0177841. https://doi.org/10.1371/journal.pone.0177841

38. Haupert, M. L., Gesselman, A. N., Moors, A. C., Fisher, H. E., & Garcia, J. R. (2017). Prevalence of experiences with consensual nonmonogamous relationships: Findings from two national samples of single Americans. *Journal of Sex & Marital Therapy, 43*(5), 424–440. https://doi.org/10.1080/0092623X.2016.1178675

39. Conley, T. D., Matsick, J. L., Moors, A. C., & Ziegler, A. (2017). Investigation of consensually nonmonogamous relationships: Theories, methods, and new directions. *Perspectives on Psychological Science, 12*(2), 205–232. https://doi.org/10.1177/1745691616667925

40. Khurshid, A. (2020). Love marriage or arranged marriage? Choice, rights, and empowerment for educated Muslim women from rural and low-income Pakistani communities. *Compare: A Journal of Comparative and International Education, 50*(1), 90–106. https://doi.org/10.1080/03057925.2018.1507726

41. Sandhya, S. (2009). The social context of marital happiness in urban Indian couples: Interplay of intimacy and conflict. *Journal of Marital and Family Therapy, 35*(1), 74–96. https://doi.org/10.1111/j.1752-0606.2008.00103.x

42. Levine, R. B. (1993). Is love a luxury? *American Demographics, 15,* 27–28.

43. Hsu, F. L. K. (1981). The self in cross-cultural perspective. In A. J. Marsella, B. De Vos, & F. L. K. Hsu (Eds.), *Culture and self* (pp. 24–55). Tavistock. Quote is from p. 50.

44. Coontz, S. (2016, April). Marriage is not what it seems. In *Phi Kappa Phi Forum, 96*(1), 22; Coontz, S. (2006). *Marriage, a history: How love conquered marriage.* Penguin.

45. OutLife. (2019). Which countries criminalise homosexuality? https://www.outlife.org.uk/which-countries-criminalise-homosexuality?

46. See Kauffman, J., & Kornberg, J. (2018). Creating greeting cards to understand and to evaluate Knapp's Staircase Model of relationships. *Communication Teacher, 32*(4), 198–202. https://doi.org/10.1080/17404622.2017.1372601

47. Peplau, L. A. (2003). Lesbian and gay relationships. In L. Garnets, & D. Kimmel (Eds.), *Psychological perspectives on lesbian, gay, and bisexual experiences* (pp. 395–419). Columbia University Press.

48. LeFebvre, L. E. (2018). Swiping me off my feet: Explicating relationship initiation on Tinder. *Journal of Social and Personal Relationships, 35*(9), 1205–1229. https://doi.org/10.1177/0265407517706419

49. See, e.g., Donn, J. A., & Sherman, R. C. (2002). Attitudes and practices regarding the formation of romantic relationships on the Internet. *CyberPsychology & Behavior, 5*(2), 107–123. https://doi.org/10.1089/109493102753770499

50. See Perrin, A. (2019, May 31). Digital gap between rural and nonrural America persists. Pew Research Center. https://www.pewresearch.org/fact-tank/2019/05/31/digital-gap-between-rural-and-nonrural-america-persists/

51. Anderson, M., Perrin, A., Jiang, J., & Kumar, M. (2019, April 22). 10% of Americans don't use the internet. Who are they? Pew Research Center. https://www.pewresearch.org/fact-tank/2019/04/22/some-americans-dont-use-the-internet-who-are-they/

52. Van Dijk, J. A. G. M. (2017). Digital divide: Impact of access. In P. Rössler (Ed.), *The international encyclopedia of media effects.* Wiley-Blackwell. https://doi.org/10.1002/9781118783764

53. Gibbs, J. L., Ellison, N. B., & Heino, R. D. (2006). Self-presentation in online personals: The role of anticipated future interaction, self-disclosure, and perceived success in Internet dating. *Communication Research, 33*(2), 1–26. https://doi.org/10.1177/0093650205285368

54. Guadagno, R. E., Okdie, B. M., & Kruse, S. A. (2012). Dating deception: Gender, online dating, and exaggerated self-presentation. *Computers in Human Behavior, 28*(2), 642–647. https://doi.org/10.1016/j.chb.2011.11.010

55. Hancock, J. T., & Toma, C. L. (2009). Putting your best face forward: The accuracy of online dating photography. *Journal of Communication, 59*(2), 367–386. https://doi.org/10.1111/j.1460-2466.2009.01420.x

56. Vanman, E. (2018, July 25). It's not about money: We asked catfish why they trick people online. *The Conversation.* http://theconversation.com/its-not-about-money-we-asked-catfish-why-they-trick-people-online-100381

57. Sautter, J. M., Tippett, R. M., & Morgan, S. P. (2010). The social demography of Internet dating in the United States. *Social Science Quarterly, 91*(2), 554–575. https://doi.org/10.1111/j.1540-6237.2010.00707.x

58. Statista.com. (2019). *Most popular online dating apps in the United States as of June 2019, by audience size (in millions)*. https://www.statista.com/statistics/826778/most-popular-dating-apps-by-audience-size-usa/

59. See Walther, J. B. (2010). Computer-mediated communication. In C. R. Berger, M. E. Roloff, & D. R. Roskos-Ewoldsen (Eds.), *Handbook of communication science* (2nd ed., pp. 489–505). Sage. https://doi.org/10.4135/9781412982818

60. Hocker, J. L., & Wilmot, W. W. (2017). *Interpersonal conflict* (10th ed.). McGraw-Hill. Quote is from p. 40.

61. Gottman, J. M., & Tabares, A. (2018). The effects of briefly interrupting marital conflict. *Journal of Marital and Family Therapy, 44*(1), 61–72. https://doi.org/10.1111/jmft.12243

62. Gottman, J. M. (2015). *Principia amoris: The new science of love*. Routledge. https://doi.org/10.4324/9780203081785

63. Holman, T. B., & Jarvis, M. O. (2003). Hostile, volatile, avoiding, and validating couple-conflict types: An investigation of Gottman's couple-conflict types. *Personal Relationships, 10*(2), 267–282. https://doi.org/10.1111/1475-6811.00049

64. See Gottman, J. M., Levenson, R. W., Swanson, C., Swanson, K., Tyson, R., & Yoshimoto, D. (2003). Observing gay, lesbian, and heterosexual couples' relationships: Mathematical modeling of conflict interaction. *Journal of Homosexuality, 45*(1), 65–91. https://doi.org/10.1300/J082v45n01_04; Garanzini, S., Yee, A., Gottman, J., Gottman, J., Cole, C., Preciado, M., & Jasculca, C. (2017). Results of Gottman method couples therapy with gay and lesbian couples. *Journal of Marital and Family Therapy, 43*(4), 674–684. https://doi.org/10.1111/jmft.12276

65. Petronio, S. (2017). Communication privacy management theory: Understanding families. In D. O. Braithwaite, E. A. Suter, & K. Floyd (Eds.), *Engaging theories in family communication* (2nd ed., pp. 107–117). Routledge. https://doi.org/10.4324/9781315204321

66. See Sprecher, S., & Treger, S. (2015). The benefits of turn-taking reciprocal self-disclosure in get-acquainted interactions. *Personal Relationships, 22*(3), 460–475. https://doi.org/10.1111/pere.12090

67. Lavner, J. A., Karney, B. R., & Bradbury, T. N. (2016). Does couples' communication predict marital satisfaction, or does marital satisfaction predict communication? *Journal of Marriage and Family, 78*(3), 680–694. https://doi.org/10.1111/jomf.12301

68. Bloch, L., Haase, C. M., & Levenson, R. W. (2014). Emotion regulation predicts marital satisfaction: More than a wives' tale. *Emotion, 14*(1), 130–144. https://doi.org/10.1037/a0034272

69. See, e.g., Fredrickson, B. L. (2013). Updated thinking on positivity ratios. *American Psychologist, 68*(9), 814–822. https://doi.org/10.1037/a0033584

70. Gottman, J. M. (2011). *The science of trust: Emotional attunement for couples*. W. W. Norton.

71. See Kim, H. K., Capaldi, D. M., & Crosby, L. (2007). Generalizability of Gottman and colleagues' affective process models of couples' relationship outcomes. *Journal of Marriage and Family, 69*(1), 55–72. https://doi.org/10.1111/j.1741-3737.2006.00343.x

72. Gottman, 2011.

73. Newkirk, K., Perry-Jenkins, M., & Sayer, A. G. (2017). Division of household and childcare labor and relationship conflict among low-income new parents. *Sex Roles, 76*(5-6), 319–333. https://doi.org/10.1007/s1199-016-0604-3

74. Alberts, J. K., Yoshimura, C. G., Rabby, M., & Loschiavo, R. (2005). Mapping the topography of couples' daily conversation. *Journal of Social and Personal Relationships, 22*(3), 299–322. https://doi.org/10.1177/0265407505050941

75. Dillon, L. M., Nowak, N., Weisfeld, G. E., Weisfeld, C. C., Shattuck, K. S., Imamoğlu, O. E., Butovskaya, M., & Shen, J. (2015). Sources of marital conflict in five cultures. *Evolutionary Psychology, 13*(1), 1–15. https://doi.org/10.1177/147470491501300101

76. Barstad, A. (2014). Equality is bliss? Relationship quality and the gender division of household labor. *Journal of Family Issues, 35*(7), 972–992. https://doi.org/10.1177/0192513X14522246

77. Forste, R., & Fox, K. (2012). Household labor, gender roles, and family satisfaction: A cross-national comparison. *Journal of Comparative Family Studies, 43*(5), 613–631. https://doi.org/10.3138/jcfs.43.5.613

78. Yavorsky, J. E., Kamp Dush, C. M., & Schoppe-Sullivan, S. J. (2015). The production of inequality: The gender division of labor across the transition to parenthood. *Journal of Marriage and Family, 77*(3), 662–679. https://doi.org/10.1111/jomf.12189

79. Mannino, C. A., & Deutch, F. M. (2007). Changing the division of household labor: A negotiated process between partners. *Sex Roles, 56*(5-6), 309–324. https://doi.org/10.1007/s11199-006-9181-1

80. Kluwer, E. S., Heesink, J. A. M., & Van de Vliert, E. (2000). The division of labor in close relationships: An asymmetrical conflict issue. *Personal Relationships, 7*(3), 263–282. https://doi.org/10.1111/j.1475-6811.2000.tb00016.x

81. Kawamura, S., & Brown, S. L. (2010). Mattering and wives' perceived fairness of the division of household labor. *Social Science Research, 39*(6), 976–986. https://doi.org/10.1016/j.ssresearch.2010.04.004

82. Boren, J. P. (2007, November). *Negotiating the division of household labor in same-sex romantic partnerships* [Paper presentation]. National Communication Association, Chicago, IL, United States; see also Goldberg, A. E. (2013). "Doing" and "undoing" gender: The meaning and division of housework in same-sex couples. *Journal of Family Theory & Review, 5*(2), 85–104. https://doi.org/10.1111/jftr.12009

83. Mongeau, P. M., & Henningsen, M. L. M. (2015). Stage theories of relationship development: Charting the course of interpersonal communication. In D. O. Braithwaite, & P. Schrodt (Eds.), *Engaging theories in interpersonal communication: Multiple perspectives* (2nd ed., pp. 389–402). Sage. https://doi.org/10.4315/9781483329529

84. Welch, S.-A., & Rubin, R. B. (2002). Development of relationship stage measures. *Communication Quarterly, 50*(1), 24–40. https://doi.org/10.1080/1463370209385644

85. Avtgis, T. A., West, D. V., & Anderson, T. L. (1998). Relationship stages: An inductive analysis identifying cognitive, affective, and behavioral dimensions of Knapp's relational stages model. *Communication Research Reports, 15*(3), 280–287. https://doi.org/10.1080/08824099809362124

86. Crotty, N. (2014, July 11). *Generation ghost: The facts behind the slow fade*. https://www.elle.com/life-love/sex-relationships/advice/a12787/girls-ghosting-relationships/

87. Nagesh, A. (2018, April 27). Forget ghosting—Orbiting is the new trend that will ruin your love life in 2018. *BBC*. https://www.bbc.co.uk/bbcthree/article/e98e8f01-c01b-445d-8a67-2ed3228b540f

88. Luscombe, B. (2018, November 26). The divorce rate is dropping. That may not actually be good news. *Time*. https://time.com/5434949/divorce-rate-children-marriage-benefits/

89. Thuen, F., Breivik, K., Wold, B., & Ulveseter, G. (2015). Growing up with one or both parents: The effects on physical health and health-related behavior through adolescence and into early adulthood. *Journal of Divorce & Remarriage, 56*(6), 451–474. https://doi.org/10.1080/10502556.2015.1058659

90. See Duerr, H. P., Duerr-Aguilar, Y. A., Andritzky, W., Camps, A., Deegener G., Dum, C., Godinho, B., Li, L., Rudolph, J., Schlottke, P. F., & Hautzinger, M. (2014). Loss of child well-being: A concept for the metrics of neglect and abuse under separation and divorce. *Child Indicators Research, 8*(4), 867–885. https://doi.org/10.1007/s12187-014-9280-4

91. Lind, D. (2018, June 15). The Trump administration's separation of families at the border, explained. *Vox.* https://www.vox.com/2018/6/11/17443198/children-immigrant-families-separated-parents

92. Statsky, W. P. (2014). *Family law: The essentials* (3rd ed.). Cengage.

93. General Accounting Office. (1997). Memo B-275860. www.gao.gov/archive/1997/og97016.pdf

94. U.S. Census Bureau. (2009). *American community survey.* www.census.gov/acs/www/

95. Wolf, J. (2018, May 22). The single parent statistics based on Census data. *VeryWell Family.* https://www.verywellfamily.com/single-parent-census-data-2997668

96. Satir, V., Banmen, J., Gerber, J., & Gomori, M. (2006). *The Satir model: Family therapy and beyond.* Science and Behavior Books.

97. Braithwaite, D. O., Baxter, L. A., & Harper, A. M. (1998). The role of rituals in the management of the dialectical tension of "old" and "new" in blended families. *Communication Studies, 49*(2), 105–120. https://doi.org/10.1080/10510979809368523

98. Ibid. Quote is from page 113.

99. Koenig Kellas, J., & Horstman, H. K. (2015). Communicated narrative sense-making: Understanding family narratives, storytelling, and the construction of meaning through a communicative lens. In L. H. Turner, & R. West (Eds.), *The Sage handbook of family communication* (pp. 76–90). Sage. https://doi.org/10.4135/9781483375336

100. Afifi, T. D., Merrill, A., & Davis, S. M. (2015). Examining family secrets from a communication perspective. In L. H. Turner, & R. West (Eds.), *The Sage handbook of family communication* (pp. 169–183). Sage. https://doi.org/10.4135/9781483375336

101. Tomlinson, J. M., Hughes, E. K., Lewandowski Jr., G. W., Aron, A., & Geyer, R. (2019). Do shared self-expanding activities have to be physically arousing? *Journal of Social and Personal Relationships, 36*(9), 2781–2801. https://doi.org/10.1177/0265407518801095

102. Johnson, Z. D., & LaBelle, S. (2016). Student-to-student confirmation in the college classroom: An initial investigation of the dimensions and outcomes of students' confirming messages. *Communication Education, 65*(1), 44–63. https://doi.org/10.1080/03634523.2015.1058961

103. Gibb, J. R. (1961). Defensive communications. *Journal of Communication, 11*(3), 141–148. https://doi.org/10.1111/j.1460-2466.1961.tb00344.x

104. Gottman, J. (2003). Why marriages fail. In K. M. Galvin, & P. J. Cooper (Eds.), *Making connections: Readings in relational communication* (pp. 258–266). Roxbury.

105. Gottman, J. M. (2014). *Principia amoris: The new science of love.* Routledge. https://doi.org/10.4324/9780203081785

106. Ibid

107. See, e.g., Kiecolt-Glaser, J. K., & Wilson, S. J. (2017). Lovesick: How couples' relationships influence health. *Annual Review of Clinical Psychology, 13*, 421–443. https://doi.org/10.1146/annurev-clinpsy.032816-045111

108. Kiecolt-Glaser, J. K., Loving, T. J., Stowell, J. R., Malarkey, W. B., Lemeshow, S., Dickinson, S. L., & Glaser, R. (2005). Hostile marital interactions, proinflammatory cytokine production, and wound healing. *Archives of General Psychiatry, 62*(12), 1377–1384. https://doi.org/10.1001/archpsyc.62.12.1377

109. Rusbult, C. E., Agnew, C. R., & Arriaga, X. B. (2012). The investment model of commitment processes. In P. A. M. Van Lange, A. W. Kruglanski, & E. T. Higgins (Eds.), *The handbook of theories of social psychology* (vol. 2, pp. 218–231). Sage. https://doi.org/10.4135/9781446249215

110. See, e.g., Merolla, A. J., & Zhang, S. (2011). In the wake of transgressions: Examining forgiveness communication in personal relationships. *Personal Relationships, 18*(1), 79–95. https://doi.org/10.1111/j.1475-6811.2010.01323.x

111. Waldron, V. R., & Kelley, D. L. (2008). *Communicating forgiveness.* Sage. https://doi.org/10.4135/9781483329536

112. Baxter, L. A., & Braithwaite, D. O. (2009). Relational dialectics theory, applied. In S. W. Smith, & S. R. Wilson (Eds.), *New directions in interpersonal communication research* (pp. 48–68). Sage. https://doi.org/10.4135/9781483349619

9

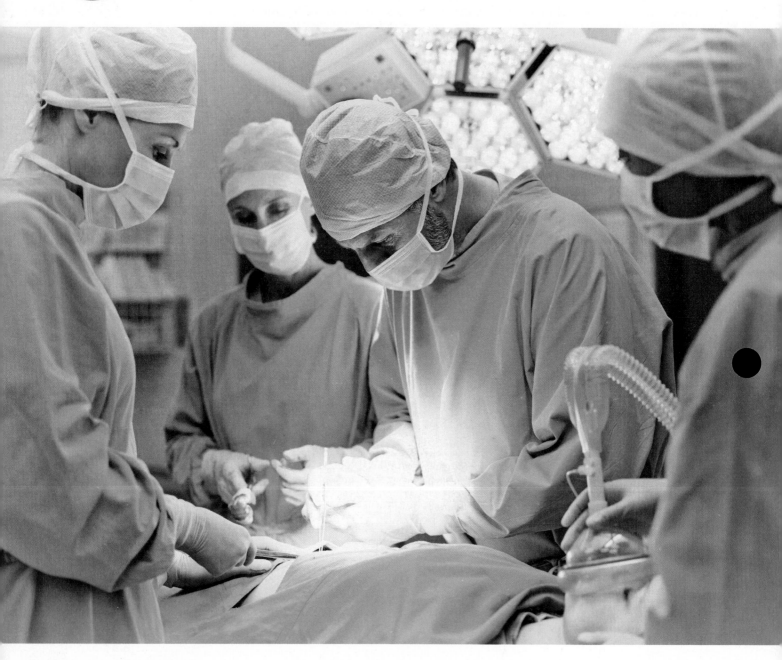

Morsa Images/Getty Images

COMMUNICATING IN SMALL GROUPS

Communicating for Life

We may not think of effective communication in small groups as having life-or-death consequences, but that is often the case on a surgical team. According to research, communication failures among surgical team members substantially increase the odds of complications or death for patients.[1] For instance, poor communication can result in specimens being mislabeled, equipment going missing, the wrong implants being used, and even the wrong surgical procedures being conducted.[2] To improve communication skills in the high-pressure environment of the operating room, some hospital systems have created briefing cards that lay out communication tasks to be accomplished before every surgery, such as confirming the surgical site, describing the anesthetic plan, identifying the medications, and asking all team members to share any concerns during the procedure.[3] By helping surgical teams communicate more systematically, the briefing cards guard against poor-quality team communication, reducing complications and increasing survival rates for patients.[4]

··▶ As You READ

- What are small groups, and what do they do?
- Why and how do people join small groups?
- How can you communicate better in a small group?

We humans have lived, worked, and communicated in small groups for thousands of years. Archeologists tell us our prehistoric ancestors lived in small groups of hunters and gatherers and may have interacted with only a couple of dozen people over their entire lives.[5] Although the world is considerably different today, our tendency to interact in small groups endures.

Communicating in small groups can be difficult, however. People often have strikingly different ideas about what decisions a group should make and how they should be implemented. Coming together over ideas can therefore be a challenging process. For that reason, it's beneficial to know how small group communication operates and how we can excel at it. We can apply that knowledge to almost any small group to which we belong.

What Is a Small Group?

In 1942, a small group of farmers near Americus, Georgia, began discussing a concept they called "partnership housing." Their idea was that people in need of safe, adequate shelter would work alongside volunteers to build simple, affordable houses. The homes would be sold—at no interest and for no profit—to those who needed them. As the group communicated its ideas with others, it received the help and capital it required to launch its mission. What began nearly eight decades ago as a small group of farmers grew into today's Habitat for Humanity, an international charitable organization with more than 2 million annual volunteers that has provided affordable shelter for more than 22 million people around the world.[6]

In this and countless other instances, people communicating in a small group have had a positive influence on the lives of others. That success doesn't mean small group communication is without its problems. Indeed, working in small groups can be frustrating and even stressful. Further, as we'll see, small groups don't always make the smartest, most informed decisions, despite their best efforts. If we know how to conduct small group communication effectively, however, and we learn what problems to avoid, we stand a better chance of making our small group experiences positive and productive.

We can define a **small group** as a collection of three or more people working cooperatively and interdependently to accomplish a task. Small groups address a broad range of tasks, whether it's creating a dramatic presentation, organizing a fundraiser,

• **small group** A collection of people working interdependently to accomplish a task; small groups typically include 3 to 20 members.

Habitat for Humanity, which has provided affordable housing for nearly 22 million people, began as a small group.

Mark Wilson/Getty Images

Stockbroker/MBI/Alamy Stock Photo

making a policy recommendation, or providing affordable housing. Although small groups have diverse missions, they share important similarities that distinguish them from other social units. In this section, we'll see that

- Small groups are distinguished by their size.
- Small groups are interdependent.
- Small groups are cohesive.
- Small groups enforce rules and norms.
- Small groups include individual roles.
- Small groups have their own identities.
- Small groups have distinctive communication practices.
- Small groups often interact online.

SMALL GROUPS ARE DISTINGUISHED BY THEIR SIZE

An important part of what distinguishes a small group is its size. A 1,500-person church, a 90-piece orchestra, and the 435-member U.S. House of Representatives are all groups, but most researchers wouldn't classify any of them as a small group. Rather, communication scholars consider small groups to include at least 3 members (as noted in the formal definition above) but no more than about 15 or 20.[7]

The size of a small group matters because most of us communicate differently in larger and smaller collections of people. When we interact with only one other person, we are engaged in interpersonal rather than small group communication. Interpersonal communication usually focuses on the development and maintenance of a personal relationship, whereas small group communication is often concerned with the performance of tasks. When we interact with *larger* groups of people, our communication can become impersonal because we may not know the other group members very well. Indeed, if the group is too large, we might feel as though our input won't be heard. However, interpersonal communication and large group communication each have their functions.

Many of us form and maintain interpersonal relationships *within* groups. We use our understanding of interpersonal communication in those relationships. Yet communicating effectively with a small group utilizes a distinct set of skills.[8]

Source: National
Aeronautics and Space
Administration (NASA)

• **interdependence** The
state in which what hap-
pens to one person affects
everyone else in the
relationship.

A small group's size depends on its purposes. If the small group is a barbershop quartet, it needs exactly four people. If it's a jury, it will usually have 12 members plus a couple of alternates. Focus groups, committees, support groups, sports teams, and other small groups vary in size according to the tasks they have to accomplish. If there are too few members, the group may not have sufficient help to complete its goals. Likewise, if there are too many members, scheduling and coordinating the group's activities can be cumbersome. For those reasons, each small group must evaluate for itself what the best number of members will be.[9]

SMALL GROUPS ARE INTERDEPENDENT

When professional chefs create new recipes, they keep in mind that each ingredient will affect, and be affected by, each of the others. Too little salt leaves a soup tasting bland, but too much salt overpowers the individual flavors of the chicken and the vegetables. The appropriate amount of water—essential for a good broth—depends on the volume of the soup's ingredients. Because each ingredient influences and is influenced by every other in the composition of a tasty finished product, we say the ingredients are interdependent.

According to *systems theory*, members of a small group also demonstrate **interdependence** in the sense that each one affects and is affected by every other member in some way.[10] Whenever the National Aeronautics and Space Administration (NASA) launches a mission into space, for instance, a group of 16 flight controllers monitors every aspect. Each individual controller oversees specific dimensions, such as communication with the crew, deployment and retrieval of the spacecraft's payload, flight navigation, electrical generation, and the execution of spacewalks. To ensure the success of the mission and the safety of the crew, the flight controllers have to work interdependently. Although each person's responsibilities are different, everyone's actions influence, and are influenced by, everyone else's. For instance, communication with the crew is impaired if electrical generation malfunctions. Spacewalks are safe only if the flight navigation is accurate. In this interdependent group of flight controllers, the members have to communicate to understand how their behaviors and decisions affect the others.

Similarly, many families are highly interdependent. If Jennifer chooses to practice her electric guitar in her room during the evening, her decision affects everyone else in the family who has to listen to her. If her mom decides to pursue a new job out of state, her action affects the others in the family, who will either have to move to follow her or adjust to her frequent absences from home.

Interdependence doesn't necessarily mean that each member's influence on all other members is always positive. Perhaps you can recall attending small group gatherings in which two or three people expressed a disagreement that soon escalated into a full-scale argument within the group. In that instance, group members were influencing one another in a *negative* way by letting a conflict get out of hand. They were still demonstrating interdependence, however, because the moods and behaviors of some members affected, and were affected by, those of others.

SMALL GROUPS ARE COHESIVE

If you've ever studied music, you know that a song's melody is its primary tune and that other pitches are added to the melody to create harmonies. Most melodies aren't quite as beautiful without harmonies, and most harmonies are incomplete without the melodies. When melodies and harmonies work together, though, they can produce something truly special. The same principle applies in small groups. To be effective, small groups must have **cohesion**, which means the members work together—as melodies and harmonies do—in the service of a common goal.[11] Cohesion takes

• **cohesion** The force by
which the members of a
group work together in the
service of a common goal.

Working at Odds: Dysfunctional Groups

Darren Klimek/Getty Images

A cohesive group is effective because everyone is contributing to the group's collective goals. When cohesion breaks down and some members behave in ways that inhibit the group's goals, the group becomes *dysfunctional* because it is no longer operating to pursue a collective purpose. According to researchers who study small groups, four behaviors in particular can cause a group to become dysfunctional.

The first dysfunctional behavior, *parasitism,* occurs when some group members persuade or coerce others to do their work for them.

The second behavior, *interpersonal aggression,* refers to actions that undermine the physical or psychological well-being of others, such as bullying and intimidation. Third, *boastfulness* exaggerates the value of your own contributions in relation to those of other group members. Finally, *misuse of resources* occurs when group members waste important materials or misuse equipment, reducing their availability for the rest of the group.

Dysfunction does not just cause groups to become unproductive. It also increases stress and impairs the psychological well-being of the individuals in the group. As you communicate within small groups, it is therefore helpful to watch out for parasitism, interpersonal aggression, boastfulness, and misuse of resources. If everyone is aware that those behaviors are problematic, your group stands a better chance of avoiding dysfunction.

SOURCE: Aubé, C., Rousseau, V., Mama, C., & Morin, E. M. (2009). Counterproductive behaviors and psychological well-being: The moderating effect of task interdependence. *Journal of Business and Psychology, 24*(3), 351–361. https://doi.org/10.1007/s10869-009-9113-5

interdependence a step further: Groups are interdependent if the members all influence one another, but they are cohesive only if the members work together toward the same goal.[12]

Two types of cohesion are particularly important for small groups. The first is what researchers call *task cohesion,* the extent to which everyone in the group is working together toward the same objectives.[13] Task cohesion is high when all the group members know their specific tasks and follow through on them. If only some members do so while others neglect their responsibilities, then task cohesion is low. If you've taken part in small groups in which only a few members did the majority of the work, you know that being in such groups is often unsatisfying.

Musical groups require cohesion to be able to make music together.

MIXA/Glow Images

The second important type of cohesion is *social cohesion,* which refers to the level of positive regard group members have for one another.[14] In groups with high social cohesion, the members generally get along well and maintain positive relationships among themselves. They trust and listen to one another, they adapt their communication behaviors to one another, and they respect one another's opinions even when they disagree. In contrast, members of groups with low social cohesion are often distrustful of the other members. They disregard one another's opinions and don't seem to care much about one another. In some groups, low social cohesion causes members to argue frequently; in others, it causes them to ignore one another. Not surprisingly, most people are more satisfied participating in groups with high social cohesion than in those with low social cohesion.[15]

When members act contrarily to a group's goals, the group can become dysfunctional and counterproductive. Take a closer look at group dysfunction in "The Dark Side of Communication."

Like other small groups, SWAT teams must enforce specific rules and norms in order to accomplish their missions.

Aaron Roeth Photography

SMALL GROUPS ENFORCE RULES AND NORMS

In many communities, a team of specially trained police officers—known as a SWAT team—conducts high-risk operations such as apprehending fugitives, serving search warrants for illegal drugs, and responding to hostage situations. Many large police departments have their own SWAT teams, but in smaller populations, the teams are often composed of officers from several agencies.

As is common in small groups, SWAT teams enforce specific rules and norms. Suppose that Chad has joined the SWAT team in his county. He will quickly learn the group's formal rules, which include (1) always arrive on time and with the right gear, (2) prioritize safety in every situation, and (3) be professional at all times. These and other rules are communicated to all new team members during training and are explicitly described in the team's policy manual.

Other principles for how team members should behave are never officially stated, however, but seem to be understood implicitly within the group. Those are called the group's *norms,* and even though they aren't expressly communicated, they still affect the group's behavior. In his dealings with other team members, for instance, Chad comes to understand that he is expected to keep all communication within the team confidential, even though no one has given him that instruction explicitly. He also realizes that, as a rookie, he is expected to carry the team's gear and drive the safety vehicles whenever the team is responding to an incident. Although Chad is a lieutenant in his own police department, he recognizes that this does not automatically give him a leadership role on the SWAT team. Again, no one explicitly described this group norm to Chad; rather, he infers it by observing how others on the team behave.

Nearly every small group has both rules and norms that its members are expected to follow. Some govern how group members should interact with one another, such as "we stick together no matter what." Others dictate how the group should function, such as "we always take a vote on important decisions." Still other rules and norms focus on the nature of the group's mission, such as "everything we do must be done with the utmost professionalism." Table 1 gives additional examples of small group rules and norms. As we'll see later in this section, introducing new members to the rules and norms is an important part of socializing them into the group.

TABLE 1

EXAMPLES OF RULES AND NORMS IN A SMALL GROUP

Behavior in most small groups is influenced by explicit rules and implicit norms. Here are some that a college study group might use.

Rules
Study sessions always start at 8 p.m.
Members always share study materials.
Everyone produces a weekly reading outline.
One person brings snacks each week.
No music is played during meetings.

Norms
Send a text message if you're going to be late.
Don't discuss the group with others.
Come to each meeting prepared.
Always cooperate with one another.
If one person falls behind, help that person to catch up.

SMALL GROUPS INCLUDE INDIVIDUAL ROLES

As a captain of the U.S. women's soccer team, Megan Rapinoe fulfilled a formal role.

Alika Jenner/Getty Images

Most small groups have one or more collective goals or purposes. Tennis teams exist to compete with other teams in tennis matches. Jazz bands exist to create and perform music. In each case, everyone is expected to work together toward the group's collective mission, but that doesn't mean everyone contributes in the same way. Rather, individual members of the group often take on specific roles, patterns of behavior that define a person's function within a group or a larger organization.[16]

Some roles in small groups are *formal roles,* meaning they are specifically assigned to people to help the group to fulfill its mission. On a tennis team, for instance, one person usually plays the role of captain, the individual in charge of organizing team meetings and boosting players' morale. Because they are specifically assigned, formal roles usually receive official recognition both inside and outside the group. For example, all the players on a team know who the captain is because someone selected him or her and officially bestowed that title.

Other roles are better described as *informal roles,* meaning they are not formally assigned and anyone in the group can choose to take them on.[17] Unlike formal roles, which often ensure that important group assignments get fulfilled, informal roles more frequently relate to how well or poorly the group functions while carrying out its mission, and members take on whichever one fits their personality. In a jazz band, for instance, one member might play the role of humorist, always making funny observations to lighten the mood. Another might enact the role of mediator, helping members to find common ground when conflicts arise. A third might play the nurturer, attending to everyone else's emotional and physical needs. An individual member might have more than one informal role, and a specific informal role might be fulfilled by more than one member at a time.

Because formal roles are assigned and officially recognized, it's tempting to conclude that they're more important to a group's success than informal roles. That's not always the case, however. Although a team captain can keep a group organized and on task, members who enact helpful informal roles might make equally important contributions to a satisfying and productive group atmosphere.[18] Formal and informal roles can therefore complement each other, together creating a positive small group experience.

SMALL GROUPS HAVE THEIR OWN IDENTITIES

When two people get married or enter a committed relationship, it's often as if their relationship takes on a life of its own. They may say to each other: "There used to be you and me, but now there's you, me, and *us.*" That sentiment reflects the idea that the relationship has become an entity unto itself, one with its own identity. Many small groups have the same experience: once people come together to form a small group, the group takes on its own identity. When that happens, people begin referring to "the group" as well as to individual members, and they start to think about the group's needs and desires, reflecting the idea that the group has become an entity of its own.

One reason group identities are important is that they set boundaries around a group's membership by defining who belongs and who does not. Some groups establish and maintain their boundaries in elaborate ways. For instance, members of the Freemasons, an international fraternal organization, are thought to use secret knocks, hand signals, passwords, and other covert signs to differentiate true members from individuals posing as members.[19] These rituals enhance communication within individual chapters of the group and create a shared identity among members around the world. Likewise, individual fraternities and sororities often put new pledges through highly involved initiation rituals, during which they may teach them secret handshakes or code words by which they can signify their membership.[20] Similarly, many gangs require new members to get specific tattoos to signify their affiliation with and allegiance to the gang.[21]

Other groups establish and maintain their boundaries in less dramatic ways. For example, the Red Hat Society is a social organization for women over 50 whose members wear red hats and purple clothing whenever they meet in small groups.[22] Their attire therefore serves as a marker of membership, distinguishing those who belong to the group from those who do not. In the same vein, Alcoholics Anonymous members attending individual small group meetings recite the "serenity prayer," which symbolizes their inclusion in the group. Membership cards, lapel pins, member jackets, and similar tokens also signify who belongs to a group and who does not. In each of these ways, groups express and reinforce their identity both to those in the group and to outsiders.

SMALL GROUPS HAVE DISTINCTIVE COMMUNICATION PRACTICES

Central to accomplishing any group's mission is the practice of communication.[23] Can you imagine any small group that could meet its goals if its members couldn't communicate with one another? They wouldn't be able to share ideas, encourage one another, make collective decisions, assign individual tasks, or stay informed about what other members are doing.

Researchers have discovered four specific types of communication that characterize small groups.[24] The first type, *problem-solving communication,* focuses on the details of how a small group can accomplish its tasks. *Role communication,* the second type, relates to the formal and informal roles each member plays within the group. *Consciousness-raising communication,* the third type, strengthens the group's identity and the morale of its members. Finally, *encounter communication* describes the interpersonal interactions among group members.

To illustrate each type of communication, let's say you're on an advisory board charged with reviewing the policies of the student health center on your campus. At your first meeting, you and the other board members will probably identify each of your specific tasks, discuss how often you need to meet, and determine how you'll communicate with one another about your progress between meetings. Those are all examples of problem-solving communication because they relate to your goals and your strategies for meeting them. You might also talk about who's going to be in charge of your board, who's going to keep the records of your meetings, and who will be responsible for communicating with the health center administrators. That conversation is an example of role communication because it concerns the individual roles that board members will play.

Suppose the advisory board experiences several challenges while attempting to complete its mission, and you and the other board members are feeling overwhelmed and discouraged. Perhaps the leader of your group gives everyone a pep talk about the importance of your task, stressing that you'll be successful if you all stick together and work as a team. That is an example of consciousness-raising communication because it is meant to raise morale and reinforce your identity as a group. Let's say you've been particularly discouraged lately because of the stresses of school and your part-time job, and you confide in another group member about your feelings. That is an example of encounter communication because it is an interpersonal conversation that occurs within the group.

SMALL GROUPS OFTEN INTERACT ONLINE

An increasing number of small groups interact either primarily or exclusively online. Some do so because their members are located in different cities or countries, so face-to-face communication is impractical.[25] Other groups interact online because computer-mediated communication can be more efficient than face-to-face conversation. Technologies such as e-mail, instant messaging, message boards, group texting, and videoconferencing allow group members to send and respond to messages whenever—and wherever—they choose.

Nonetheless, online groups pose challenges. Compared to people in face-to-face groups, individuals who interact with other group members online report being less committed to the group and less happy while working with it. Small group researchers Stefanie Johnson, Kenneth Bettenhausen, and Ellie Gibbons found negative outcomes are particularly likely in groups that interact via computer-mediated communication more than 90 percent of the time.[26] Other research has found that regardless of their culture, people feel less confident in their ability to be productive in virtual groups compared to face-to-face groups.[27]

As we've seen in this section, several characteristics define the small group experience: group size, interdependence, cohesion, rules and norms, individual roles, unique identities, and communication practices. In addition, people in many small groups interact—either primarily or exclusively—online. Why might someone choose to take part in the small group experience at all? We'll probe some of the most important reasons in the next section.

Functions of Small Groups

Once a month, community members in towns and cities across the United States come together for a dinner in which they eat locally grown foods and discuss ways to make food production more sustainable. They are members of the Slow Food movement, an organization that began in Italy in 1986 to promote long, leisurely dining experiences that encourage conversation and an appreciation of the food being eaten. The movement, which opposes the quick consumption of mass-produced food, now has 100,000 worldwide members. Yet despite the organization's size, Slow Food members meet in small groups to enjoy and celebrate their good meals. Whether we're talking about a Slow Food group, a service organization, a committee, or a sports team, we'll discover in this section that small groups can serve several different functions.

Groups don't come together by accident. Rather, we form them when we believe they'll help us in some way. In this section, we'll see that small groups can

- Focus on discrete tasks.
- Evaluate and advise.
- Create art and ideas.
- Provide service and support.
- Promote social networking.
- Compete.
- Help us to learn.

Figure 1 illustrates the functions small groups can serve. As you read and examine these functions, bear in mind that they aren't mutually exclusive. Any given group can serve multiple functions at once.

Members of the Slow Food movement meet in small groups to enjoy leisurely dining experiences.
Jozef Polc/123RF

FIGURE 1
SOME FUNCTIONS OF SMALL GROUPS

Focus on discrete tasks: Tim Pannell/Corbis; Evaluate and advise: El Nariz/Shutterstock; Provide service and support: The Ames Tribune/Jon Britton/AP Photo; Help us learn: Alberto Pomares/Getty Images; Create art and ideas: Mike Watson/Glow Images; Promote social networking: Prostock-studio/Shutterstock; Compete: Don Hammond/Design Pics

SOME SMALL GROUPS FOCUS ON DISCRETE TASKS

One function of some groups is to accomplish specific assigned tasks. Following allegations that the Russian government had manipulated social media to sow social discord and influence the outcome of the 2016 U.S. presidential election, for instance, the bipartisan U.S. Senate Intelligence Committee came together to investigate the evidence. In 2019, the group completed its assigned task by releasing a written report criticizing the Russian government for spreading false reports and

Difficult Conversations

Motivating Action for a Group Assignment

Imagine this: You have a group paper due in your communication course in two weeks. Your group is far behind on its progress because of disagreements over what to do. Some members feel their ideas have been ignored, and everyone seems to lack enthusiasm about working together.

Now, consider this: If you don't complete the paper on time, you and the rest of your group are likely to fail the course. You've already mentioned your concerns about your group to your instructor, but she expects you and your fellow students to resolve your problems on your own. Before giving up on your group and writing the entire paper yourself, consider trying the following suggestions:

- Remind all group members that their contributions matter. People are often unenthusiastic about contributing to a group project if they don't believe their efforts are valued. Reminding everyone in the group that his or her part is important and valuable can make members feel more invested in the outcome.

- Try to figure out how your work process is holding back your progress, and make efforts to address those problems. Perhaps members aren't completing their tasks because they're unsure of what their tasks are. That uncertainty can easily impede your progress, so identifying it and then addressing it— such as by making each member's task more concrete—is an important step toward improvement.

- Set specific deadlines for moving forward. Consider the time you have left to finish your paper, and then establish dates by which each part of the paper is due to the rest of the group. Then, communicate those deadlines clearly to everyone, and remind members as each deadline approaches.

Many students don't enjoy doing group projects because such projects require them to rely on others. Group work is common in a wide variety of careers, however, so learning how to motivate action— especially in a group that is stalling or stagnating—is valuable.

conspiracy theories on social media platforms such as Twitter and Facebook and recommending several specific actions to protect American voters from such influence in the future.[28]

Similarly, whenever a jury is assembled for a criminal or civil trial, it hears evidence, takes part in deliberation, and then fulfills its mission by communicating a verdict. Some small groups that focus on discrete tasks, such as a jury, disband after their tasks have been completed. Other groups, such as the Senate Intelligence Committee, remain in operation and simply turn their attention to the next assigned task.

Suppose you're part of a small group that is organized to complete a group paper for one of your classes. What can you do if members become disorganized and unenthusiastic about their task? Check out the "Difficult Conversations" box for tips on handling this common conundrum.

SOME SMALL GROUPS EVALUATE AND ADVISE

The purpose of some small groups is to discuss and evaluate particular issues and give advice on how they should be addressed. The president of the United States, for instance, appoints a cabinet of 15 individuals who head major governmental agencies, such as the departments of State, Justice, Defense, Homeland Security, Education, and Commerce. The cabinet meets regularly to advise the president on issues related to domestic and foreign policy.[29] Although its individual members change, the cabinet has been a permanent group since the presidency of George Washington in the late eighteenth century.

Other small groups evaluate and advise on an as-needed basis. To evaluate the merits of a new product and how best to market it, for instance, many companies turn to *focus groups*. Focus groups are usually composed of 6 to 10 typical consumers who may use and provide their feedback on a new product before it is available to the public. They may also give input on the new product's name or packaging. Other small groups that evaluate and advise are an award selection committee, an advisory board, and an employee performance evaluation committee.

SOME SMALL GROUPS CREATE ART AND IDEAS

Coldplay is a small group whose purpose is to create, perform, and record rock music. Composed of four musicians, the Grammy Award–winning band has sold over 75 million albums worldwide and is one of the most successful creative small groups in history.[30]

Like Coldplay, many small groups exist primarily to create forms of art. A string quartet, a sculpting class, and the cast of *Saturday Night Live* are all small groups that produce artistic expressions. Other groups are charged with creating ideas instead of art. Many companies and organizations, for instance, use *brainstorming groups*, small groups of people assembled to generate innovative ways of thinking. When a county hospital needed a more efficient way of processing patients in the emergency room, it brought together a small group of nurses, medical technicians, paramedics, and volunteers to compile a list of suggestions. After listening to one another's experiences and concerns, the members of the brainstorming group were able to generate ideas for improving efficiency that hospital administrators had not previously considered.

SOME SMALL GROUPS PROVIDE SERVICE AND SUPPORT

Many small groups focus on providing community service to those who need it. For instance, local chapters of Kiwanis International serve their communities through such activities as building playgrounds, running food drives, and raising money for pediatric medical research.[31]

Similarly, local chapters of the Lions Club raise funds to aid victims of natural disasters and to support screening for blindness and hearing loss.[32] Although Kiwanis and the Lions Club are international organizations, their members frequently work in small groups to accomplish community service missions. Many colleges, universities, and religious organizations also sponsor groups whose purpose is to provide community services.

Other small groups provide social and emotional support for people dealing with difficult circumstances. Some *support groups* aid those battling health concerns, such as diabetes, alcoholism, depression, and eating disorders. Others help people to cope with the prejudice and discrimination they experience because they are mentally or physically disabled or sexual minorities. People in support groups often benefit by communicating with others whose circumstances are similar to theirs.[33] A woman addicted to gambling, for instance, may feel the only people who understand her are others battling the same addiction. Listening to others' stories in a support group may help the individual feel less alone and better able to control the problem behavior. Research has shown, in fact, that taking part in support groups for health conditions can improve physical and mental wellness.[34] Although some support groups meet in person, many meet online, providing encouragement and support to members worldwide.[35]

SOME SMALL GROUPS PROMOTE SOCIAL NETWORKING

At one point or another, many of us have joined small groups simply to meet other people. Groups with this purpose, known as *social networking groups,* allow people to meet, communicate, and get to know each other.[36] On the day she moved into her new residence hall, for instance, Lindsay and her fellow residents were divided into groups of 10 and given time to get to know one another. Taking part in that type of social networking group ensured that Lindsay knew at least 9 other people when she began the year in her new campus home.

Although social networking groups sometimes meet in person, as in Lindsay's case, they are particularly common on the Internet. For instance, chat rooms allow people to communicate online in real time, via text or webcams. Chat rooms often focus on a particular shared interest (such as pop culture or video gaming) or appeal to a specific demographic (such as single fathers or women over 40). Their primary purpose, however, is typically to allow people to communicate and to get to know one another.[37] In addition, social media platforms such as YouTube, Instagram, Twitter, Facebook, Tumblr, Flickr, and Reddit help people fulfill their need to belong by sharing their lives in a variety of individual and group interactions online.[38] According to research, 3.48 billion people—or 45 percent of the total world population—use social media, giving them an ability to connect with others that is truly unprecedented in human history.[39]

SOME SMALL GROUPS COMPETE

Many small groups are organized to take part in team competitions. For instance, colleges and universities around the United States sponsor groups of 8 to 12 students who compete in Quiz Bowl.[40] Quiz Bowl is an academic competition in which students respond to questions posed by a moderator about a wide range of subjects. The team that correctly answers the most questions in the shortest time wins the match, so members of a Quiz Bowl team must work interdependently to accomplish their mission.

Comstock/JupiterImages

Similarly, the teams organized for many athletic competitions are small groups. Your school may have a wrestling, diving, or crew team, for example, that has 20 or fewer members and therefore functions as a small group. The purpose of competitive groups is to train and practice a particular set of skills and then to compete with similar groups to win material prizes (such as trophies) or recognition.

SOME SMALL GROUPS HELP US TO LEARN

Finally, we join some small groups because they help us to learn. You may have taken part in *study groups,* which usually include a small number of students who help one another to understand the material and prepare for the exams in a specific course. Workshops and Bible studies are also small groups that help us to learn. Participating in learning groups enhances critical thinking skills, such as the ability to analyze and evaluate ideas,[41] and lets us contribute our own understanding of the material for the benefit of others as well as take advantage of what others can teach us. Similarly, participating in a wine tasting group, a quilting circle, or a computer coding club can help us learn specific skills relevant to those interests.

As we've seen, small groups can enact several different functions, including accomplishing discrete tasks, evaluating and advising, creating, providing service and support, promoting social networking, competing, and helping us to learn. These functions are not mutually exclusive; many groups focus on more than one of them at once. A nonprofit organization might form a committee to evaluate its public relations efforts, for instance, but the committee might also create new ideas, implement those ideas in the form of a new public relations campaign, and provide an opportunity for social networking among its members. A support group might provide encouragement for people suffering from arthritis, but in the process its members might learn more about their condition and the options available for treatment. As these examples illustrate, participating in small groups often helps people in many different ways.

Joining Small Groups

The first group to which most of us belong is a family—and because we're either born or adopted into our family, we have little say over its membership. Over the course of our life, however, we may join and leave a wide variety of small groups. Although each one is different, we can understand the process of joining them by considering why and how we do so. We begin this section by exploring some of the major reasons people have for joining small groups. We then look at the process by which people become socialized into groups.

WE JOIN SMALL GROUPS FOR MANY REASONS

Thinking back on your own small group experiences, you'll likely realize that you joined different groups for different reasons. Perhaps you joined some enthusiastically, primarily for social reasons, whereas you might have taken part in others because you felt compelled to. People join because they need to belong, because groups provide protection, because group membership can improve their performance, and because they feel pressure to join.

We Join Small Groups because We Need to Belong Humans are highly social beings. We don't just *want* to belong to social networks; we *need* to. Friendships and families can meet many of our social needs, but small groups can also give us a sense of social belonging. Especially in situations when we feel out of place or unsure of ourselves—such as you might if you were new to a school and didn't have many friends—finding a group to belong to and identify with (such as a club, a fraternity or sorority, or a church group) can be comforting.

Small groups can serve a wide variety of purposes.

SDI Productions/E+/Getty images

We Join Small Groups for Protection The expression "There's safety in numbers" suggests we are better protected against threats or problems when we're part of a group than when we're alone. The reason is that group members can take care of one another, and those who are stronger can protect those who are weaker.

In some instances, the protection we gain from groups is physical. You and your immediate neighbors might form a neighborhood watch group, for example, in which you agree to look out for one another's safety and property. Belonging to the group provides you the

Fact or *fiction?*

Quitting Cigarettes Is Easier in Groups

Individuals who want to stop smoking often take part in group therapy. Many believe the support and accountability they receive from the group will help them to quit more effectively than they could on their own. Is that belief fact or fiction?

According to research, taking part in a smoking-cessation group is more effective than trying to quit individually. In one study, researchers reviewed the results of dozens of studies comparing group therapy for smoking cessation to alternatives such as self-help programs and brief support from health care providers. After looking across the studies, which collectively involved thousands of smokers, the researchers concluded that people were more effective at quitting smoking when they took part in a group than when they tried to quit on their own.

Other studies have produced similar results. For instance, people are more successful at giving up cocaine and at losing weight when they take part in small groups designed to help them than when they try to accomplish those goals by themselves.

ASK YOURSELF

- Why do you suppose working in small groups helps people to improve their health more than working alone?
- What health problems, if any, do you think most people would resolve more effectively alone than in groups?

SOURCES: Stead, L. F., Carroll, A. J., & Lancaster, T. (2017). Group behaviour therapy programmes for smoking cessation. *Cochrane Database of Systematic Reviews, 18,* CD001007. https://doi.org/:10.1002/14651858.CD001007.pub3; Befort, C. A., Donnelly, J. E., Sullivan, D. K., Ellerbeck, E. F., & Perri, M. G. (2010). Group versus individual phone-based obesity treatment for rural women. *Eating Behaviors, 11*(1), 11–17. https://doi.org/10.1016/j.eatbeh.2009.08.002; Schmitz, J. M., Oswald, L. M., Jacks, S. D., Rustin, T., Rhoades, H. M., & Grabowski, J. (1997). Relapse prevention treatment for cocaine dependence: Group vs. individual format. *Addictive Behaviors, 22*(3), 405–418. https://doi.org/10.1016/S0306-4603(96)00047-0

assurance of knowing that if something goes wrong, neighbors will seek help on your behalf. Religious and community groups may also come together to provide aid when a member is sick and unable to care for himself or herself. In those cases, being in a small group gives some measure of protection for someone's physical health and well-being.

We can also gain social or emotional protection from groups. Many people battling addictions to alcohol, drugs, or gambling, for instance, gain emotional sustenance from others experiencing the same trials by participating in a recovery group. Members of such groups are routinely assigned a sponsor to whom they are accountable for their behavior. When they feel the urge to gamble or use alcohol or drugs, they can call on their sponsor for the support necessary to resist those behaviors.

We Join Small Groups to Improve Our Effectiveness A third reason people join small groups is to improve their skills or to become more effective at some task.[42] For instance, many people struggling with their weight find benefit in joining a weight loss team. Team members may work out together, offer mutual encouragement, and hold one another accountable for maintaining their diet and exercise regimens. Participating in their small groups often makes people much more effective at losing weight than they could be alone. Similarly, many individuals trying to quit smoking seek support and encouragement from small groups precisely because they believe a team-based approach will be effective. Will it? Check out the "Fact or Fiction?" box to find out.

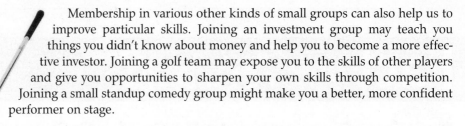

Membership in various other kinds of small groups can also help us to improve particular skills. Joining an investment group may teach you things you didn't know about money and help you to become a more effective investor. Joining a golf team may expose you to the skills of other players and give you opportunities to sharpen your own skills through competition. Joining a small standup comedy group might make you a better, more confident performer on stage.

We Join Small Groups because We Feel Pressure to Join Although we often join small groups by choice, we sometimes join because we feel pressured into doing so. Perhaps you've been enrolled in college courses that required you to participate in a group project. In such cases, your group participation wasn't voluntary. Similarly, if many of your friends at work are joining a small group to support a certain political candidate, you might feel pressured to do the same, even if that wouldn't have been your choice.

Feeling pressure to join a small group doesn't necessarily mean your experience in it will be negative. After being assigned to a group for a class project, for example, you might develop a friendship with some of the other members. Whether you join a group by choice or for another reason, your experience will be as positive or negative as you make it.

Now that we've identified some of the reasons we join small groups, let's take a look at how we become socialized into them.

George Doyle/StockByte/Getty Images

WE ARE SOCIALIZED INTO SMALL GROUPS

Think back to your first day of college. You can likely remember the anticipation, some uncertainty about your courses, and the excitement about being part of a campus community. You probably found these feelings faded as you learned what to expect and became accustomed to your college routine. The process by which you gained greater certainty about the college experience is called *socialization*, and the same occurs when you join a small group.

Researchers believe we are socialized into small groups in five phases—the antecedent phase, the anticipatory phase, the encounter phase, the assimilation phase, and the exit phase (Figure 2). Let's review each.

Before You Join: The Antecedent Phase The first phase of socialization begins before we even enter a new group, when we develop certain beliefs, attitudes, and expectations about it in the **antecedent phase**.

Let's say that in the last three classes in which you've worked on a group project, you ended up doing the bulk of the work while other members shirked their responsibilities. As a result, you've come to believe that group work is never fair. You've developed a negative attitude about small groups and the expectation that you will always have to do more than your share. The next time you decide to join a small group, you therefore approach it less optimistically than you might if your previous experiences had been more positive.[43]

• **antecedent phase**
Phase of group socialization in which people develop certain beliefs, attitudes, and expectations about a group.

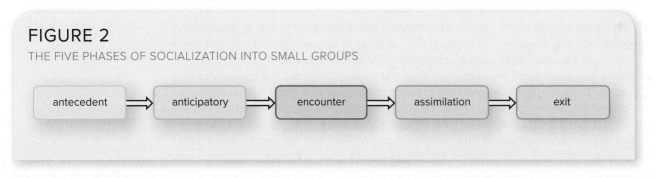

FIGURE 2
THE FIVE PHASES OF SOCIALIZATION INTO SMALL GROUPS

antecedent → anticipatory → encounter → assimilation → exit

Deciding to Join: The Anticipatory Phase When we first decide to join a group, we make judgments about what we expect from that group and its members. The process of forming those judgments is called the **anticipatory phase**. Some of our judgments might be based on the beliefs, attitudes, and expectations we formed from previous experiences with small groups. Others may be influenced by what we've heard about the particular group's objectives or traditions.

The anticipatory phase can be stressful if our expectations for a group are unrealistic.[44] For instance, you might join a study group expecting it will help you to understand the course material, only to discover that the group's primary purpose is social, not academic. You may then alter your expectations for the group or you may decide to join a different group instead.

Joining a Group: The Encounter Phase The **encounter phase** occurs the first time we meet with others as a group. For some groups, that meeting will occur face-to-face. For others, it may occur in electronically mediated formats, such as via Zoom or Microsoft Teams.

At least three important tasks are typically addressed during the encounter phase. First, groups often use their initial meeting to establish their mission and define their goals. A committee might identify its specific tasks, whereas a support group might discuss its members' needs. Second, groups often assign roles and responsibilities during the encounter phase, such as leader or record keeper for the group. Finally, groups may use the encounter phase to remind members of expectations for their behavior. Those expectations form part of the group's culture, and they often take the form of statements such as "Everyone in this group is expected to do his or her fair share of the work" and "In this group, no one is more important than anyone else."

Accepting a Group's Culture: The Assimilation Phase Once the expectations for a group's culture are known, individual members must decide whether to accept them. If they do, they enter the **assimilation phase**. It's at this stage of socialization that the group acquires its own identity. Members begin to identify with the group and to think of themselves not as "you and I" but as "we."

During the assimilation phase, group members may begin enacting specific rituals or communication behaviors that signify their membership in the group. Those might include wearing specific signs of membership, such as matching shirts or lapel pins, or conforming to the group's traditions by greeting other members with a secret handshake or reciting a specific pledge at every group meeting. Some members may accept a group's culture outright; others may accept it but attempt to change it over time.[45] Members who do not accept a group's culture or who find themselves at odds with a group's purpose often enter the final stage of group socialization by leaving.

Leaving a Group: The Exit Phase Membership in most small groups has a life span. Individual members may leave voluntarily or involuntarily in the final stage of socialization, the **exit phase**. For instance, you might grow dissatisfied with the advisory board you're on at work after its new leader changes the group's mission significantly, so you may choose to leave it voluntarily. If instead you were to be laid off from your job, you would have to leave the advisory board whether you wanted to or not.

• **anticipatory phase**
Phase of group socialization in which people decide to join a group and make judgments about what they expect from that group and its members.

• **encounter phase**
Phase of group socialization in which the group meets for the first time.

• **assimilation phase**
Phase of group socialization in which members decide to accept the group's culture and the group acquires its own identity.

In a small group such as a Little League team, new members are socialized into the group's norms and expectations.
Ariel Skelley/Getty Images/ Blend Images

• **exit phase** Phase of group socialization in which people leave a group.

Members also exit groups when the groups themselves cease to exist.[46] Many small groups meet only long enough to accomplish a specific task, such as studying for exams in a college course, painting a mural in a neighborhood park, or drafting a policy on yard maintenance for a homeowners' association. When they have completed the task, they disband. Other small groups stop meeting because members lose interest or because they can no longer count on the resources they require. Whatever the reason, most small groups disband at some point, causing their members to exit.[47]

In this section, we've seen that people join small groups for various reasons and that becoming socialized into a small group has many phases. Next we explore some of the advantages and challenges of communicating in small group settings.

Advantages and Challenges of Small Group Communication

In the fantastic world of Marvel comics and films, an elite team of super heroes called The Avengers joins together to protect the planet from all threats. Although the entire team is committed to the mission and is protective of one another, the different personalities, competing egos, and unique powers of each team member can prompt conflict and cause them to wear on one another's nerves. The Avengers might not be real, but the communication challenges they face within their small group are. In this section, we explore some of the benefits we can accrue and some of the tribulations we can encounter when participating in a small group.

COMMUNICATING IN SMALL GROUPS HAS ADVANTAGES

Participating in small groups confers some specific benefits. In this section, we examine three: small groups provide resources, they experience synergy, and they expose us to diversity.

Small Groups Provide Resources Accomplishing almost any task requires the availability of **resources**, or assets that enable us to be productive. Some resources are tangible, such as money, space, materials, and equipment. Others are intangible, such as time, information, talent, and expertise. Each of us has different resources at our disposal. When we come together with people in a small group, we gain access to the resources of others.[48]

• **resources** Assets that enable a group to be productive.

Suppose you're on a committee to raise funds for a renovation of your local high school's computer facilities. As a busy college student, you don't have much free time to go door to door or make phone calls soliciting donations, but your training in communication allows you to draft good persuasive messages for others to use. Other committee members can provide materials for making signs, cars to use for canvassing neighborhoods, or money to cover expenses. In this small group, as in many small groups, each of you can take advantage of the resources of other members.

Small Groups Experience Synergy In many small groups, members can accomplish more by working together than they could by working individually. When they do, researchers say they are experiencing **synergy**, a collaboration that produces more than the sum of its parts. For example, when The Avengers assemble, they form a small group with a diverse set of unique resources. Those resources are more powerful together than they would be if each team member worked separately—that's the meaning of synergy.

• **synergy** A collaboration that produces more than the sum of its parts.

Let's say you and two friends are each running for separate seats on your county's board of supervisors. By campaigning as individuals, each of you might generate approximately 25,000 votes, for a total of 75,000 votes. Instead, however, you decide to campaign as a group by publicly endorsing one another, representing yourselves as three running mates, and encouraging people to vote for all three of you. By adopting that strategy, you are able to pool your money to buy more advertising time and post more campaign signs around your county than your individual opponents can afford. As a result, each of you generates 40,000 votes. That's a total of 120,000 votes, or 45,000 more than you would have generated by working individually. Can you think of occasions when you have taken part in a small group that experienced synergy?

Small Groups Expose Us to Diversity The expression, "Two heads are better than one" reflects the idea that getting input from others can help us to make better, more informed decisions than we would make on our own. The reason is that each person brings a different set of ideas, experiences, insights, and values to bear on the choice. Listening to the perspectives of other people often makes us consider aspects of a decision that hadn't occurred to us before. Thus, one important advantage of participating in a small group is exposure to ways of thinking that are different from our own.[49]

Suppose two "juries" were to hear the same fictitious criminal case in a law school's mock trial exercise. Jury A is composed of 12 people with highly diverse work experience, cultural background, educational level, and socioeconomic status. Jury B consists of 12 people with highly similar characteristics. After hearing the case, Jury B quickly arrives at a unanimous verdict. Because the members of this jury are so similar, they paid attention to the same pieces of evidence, were persuaded by the same arguments, and brought similar biases and prejudices to bear on their decision. In contrast, Jury A takes much longer to arrive at a unanimous verdict. Because of their diversity, the members each paid attention to different aspects of the case. Whereas some found the physical evidence persuasive, others listened more carefully to the eyewitness accounts or watched the defendant's facial expressions while testimony was being presented.

When it came time to reach a verdict, the members of Jury A drew from a much more diverse set of ideas, arguments, and biases. Even though arriving at a unanimous decision was a long and difficult process for this group, its verdict was better informed because it was fully considered from many different points of view. Although working in diverse groups can present challenges, it can also help us to think in more open-minded ways—and thereby to come to better decisions.

The super heroes who make up The Avengers are subject to both the advantages and the challenges of small group communication.

Charles Eshelman/ FilmMagic/Getty Images

COMMUNICATING IN SMALL GROUPS POSES CHALLENGES

Taking part in small groups can be extremely rewarding, but it isn't always easy. At least three challenges are common to small groups: they require sacrifices, they can experience conflict, and they can be difficult to coordinate.

Small Groups Require Sacrifices Belonging to a small group sometimes requires making sacrifices for the benefit of the group. Let's say you're on a committee at work that is charged with drafting a new strategic plan. Your deadline is fast approaching, so the group decides to hold a meeting on Sunday afternoon, a time you usually spend with your family. As a result, you may have to sacrifice your family time for the sake of the group's mission.

Besides sacrificing time, group members sometimes find they have to do more work than their fellow members to make sure tasks get completed. The reason is that some group members may engage in **social loafing**, meaning they contribute less to the group than the average member, which is particularly easy as the group grows in size.[50] Perhaps you've been in small groups at school in which one or two people did the bulk of the work and others hardly did any. If so, you know that can be a frustrating experience for those who take responsibility for the group's productivity.[51] In effect,

• **social loafing** The tendency of some members of a group to contribute less to the group than the average member does, particularly as the group grows in size.

TABLE 2	When group members engage in social loafing, the group's productivity suffers and other members can become resentful. Here are some strategies for reducing social loafing.
WAYS TO REDUCE SOCIAL LOAFING	• *Name names.* Make every member's individual contributions to the group known to the rest of the group, so that if a specific person is being unproductive, others will know. Research shows that naming reduces social loafing by up to 29 percent. • *Be specific about goals.* Social loafing is easier when the group's goals are ambiguous; make sure each person knows exactly what he or she is meant to do. • *Make the consequences clear.* People are less likely to engage in social loafing if they understand how their individual behaviors contribute to the group's goal.

SOURCE: Høigaard, R., Säfvenbom, R., & Tønnessen, F. E. (2006). The relationship between group cohesion, group norms, and perceived social loafing in soccer teams. *Small Group Research, 37*(3), 217–232. https://doi.org/10.1177/1046496406287311

members who do more than their share of work are sacrificing their time and effort so the group can accomplish its goals. Table 2 presents some strategies for reducing social loafing in small groups.

Small Groups Can Experience Conflict Whenever small groups have to make decisions, they are likely to experience some measure of conflict. As we considered in the chapter on communicating in intimate relationships, conflict arises when two or more parties perceive that their goals are incompatible and their resources are limited. This situation is probable in many group decision-making contexts.

Suppose you and some close friends are trying to decide on a graduation gift for another friend in the group. You intend to pool your money to purchase one item on behalf of the group, but you're undecided about what to buy and how much to spend. One person thinks you should get your friend an Amazon Echo. Another thinks a gift card for her favorite Mexican restaurant would be a better idea. Two people in the group think you should just give your friend money, and you think it would be best to buy her some work clothes for the job she is about to begin.

Because you have a finite amount of money to spend, your group has to choose just one gift, and because different people prefer different outcomes, members may experience conflict in the process of making a decision. As we saw in the chapter on intimate relationships, conflict is a normal part of human communication, and it isn't necessarily problematic. What matters is how groups handle conflict when it

Many small groups experience conflict. As a normal part of human communication, conflict isn't necessarily problematic. What matters is how groups handle it.

inesbazdar/123RF

arises. If it is managed inappropriately, conflict can be a destructive force in a group, leading to resentment and hurt feelings and a general lack of productivity for the group. If managed constructively, however, it can lead groups to make more informed and more creative decisions than they otherwise would. We'll examine strategies for managing group conflict appropriately in the chapter on decision making and leadership in groups.

Small Groups Can Be Difficult to Coordinate If you've ever been in charge of coordinating a group's meetings or activities, you know how challenging that task can be. Even in groups with only three or four members, finding dates and times to meet that fit everyone's schedule can be difficult. That challenge is even more pronounced in groups with 15 or more members. Electronic communication tools, such as scheduling apps and integrated e-mail and calendar platforms, can facilitate the coordination of people's schedules. Some groups may even find it necessary to divide their work, assigning specific tasks to pairs of people who can more easily coordinate their schedules rather than trying to get the entire group together.

Scheduling isn't the only challenge for small groups. Particularly as groups grow in size, members often find it increasingly difficult to communicate efficiently with one another. As a result, larger groups tend to communicate less about their tasks than do smaller groups.[52] People in larger groups also encounter more challenges when trying to maintain their relationships with one another.[53]

Although small groups require sacrifice, can experience conflict, and can be tough to coordinate, those realities don't mean that participating in them isn't worth the effort. On the contrary, belonging to a small group can be a positive and rewarding experience. That outcome is all the more likely if we are aware of the challenges of small group communication and can manage them productively.

Becoming a Better Small Group Communicator

If you've participated in many small groups, some of your experiences were probably more favorable than others. Although your future experiences in groups will also vary, you can use your knowledge of small group communication to make them positive. In this section, we'll examine key steps you can take to improve communication in both new and established groups.

SOCIALIZE NEW MEMBERS CONSTRUCTIVELY

Becoming part of a small group requires more than signing your name to a membership roster. New members must also be socialized into the group. They must be informed about the group's expectations, roles, ways of working, and culture. New members who are not properly socialized may feel unwelcome or unenthusiastic about having joined the group. They may also unintentionally disrupt activities because they aren't aware of the group's norms and expectations. Part of communicating competently in small groups, therefore, is helping to socialize new members.

Experts point out that two sets of skills are necessary for proper socialization.[54] As we'll now consider, the first set consists of skills the group must have, and the second set encompasses skills of the new member.

Adding New Members to a Group When new members join a group, it is important to welcome them. Four behaviors in particular help to socialize new members positively and constructively:

- *Recruit good members.* Seek out potential members who will contribute to the group's mission. Be on the lookout for individuals who fit the group's personality, and encourage them to consider joining.

- *Create a group orientation.* Spend time with new members and teach them about the group's history, norms, expectations, and procedures. Knowing about these aspects of the group will aid them in being positive contributors.[55]

- *Include new members in activities.* Ensure that new members are included in group functions and activities. If, for example, the work team meets every Wednesday morning for breakfast, invite the new members. They will feel welcomed and encouraged to participate when they are included.

- *Be a mentor.* An experienced group member can be a mentor for a new member.[56] A *mentor* is someone who serves as a trusted friend, counselor, or teacher for another person. Even if new members are properly initiated when they first join a group, they may benefit from having a seasoned mentor. How good are you at mentoring? Take the quiz in "The Competent Communicator" to find out.

These behaviors are useful ways of socializing new members into groups to which you already belong. What if *you* are the new member, however? Let's look at four ways you can help to ensure successful socialization for yourself.

When the New Member Is You When you join a new group, you can aid your own process of socialization by following four steps:

- *Embrace the group's culture.* If you've made the effort to join a small group, you probably already support that group's goals, norms, values, and behaviors. Thus, part of socializing yourself into a new group is communicating in ways that reflect the group's culture.

- *Acquire appropriate skills.* If you are to become an active member of a group, you'll need to develop the skills to carry out your roles and responsibilities. If you've joined a community outreach group, for instance, you may need to brush up on your conversational skills so you can interact with the public. Think about the skills you'll need to contribute to the group's mission, and look for ways to acquire or improve them.

Your experience in a work group—or in most any group—is enhanced if you are able to build and maintain positive group relationships.

Blend Images/SuperStock

COMPETENT COMMUNICATOR

One on One: Mentoring a New Group Member

One of the most important skills for socializing new members to groups is mentoring. How good a mentor are you already? Indicate how well each of the following statements describes you by assigning it a number between 1 ("not at all") and 7 ("very well").

rawpixel/123RF

_____ **I enjoy helping people.**

_____ **People frequently turn to me for advice.**

_____ **I like to take someone "under my wing" and help him or her to succeed.**

_____ **I feel bad if a new person in my group seems uncomfortable.**

_____ **I am a good listener.**

_____ **Supporting people intellectually and emotionally makes me feel good.**

_____ **People tell me I am good at giving guidance.**

_____ **I like to "show people the ropes" when they are new to a group or situation.**

_____ **I try to be the kind of person that others can trust.**

_____ **I take my responsibilities toward other people seriously.**

When you're finished, add up your scores. A score of 10–25 suggests that mentoring is a skill you can build, and learning about small group communication is one way to do so. If you scored between 26 and 55, you are fairly good at mentoring, and as you have more opportunities to be a mentor, you can improve that skill. If you scored above 55, you are probably an experienced mentor. You are well poised to help socialize new members into the small groups to which you belong.

- *Learn what matters.* Groups often have multiple goals that require members to juggle several demands on their time and attention. Usually, however, some of these goals are more important than others. Learn how the group prioritizes competing demands. If you understand what matters most, you will be well positioned to work toward the group's most valued goals.

- *Contribute to the group.* Like most people, as a new member you probably require a period of adjustment during which you learn about the group's mission and culture. Once you are socialized into the group, take responsibility for contributing to it and its members.[57]

Joining a group can be intimidating for anyone. Whether you're helping to socialize a new member into your group or attempting to join a new group yourself, you can contribute to a more positive socialization experience by following the steps we've examined.

MAINTAIN POSITIVE GROUP RELATIONSHIPS

Your experiences in almost any small group will be more productive and meaningful if you develop and maintain positive relationships within the group. That doesn't necessarily mean you have to become a friend with every member. Indeed, you can establish positive relationships in two other specific ways: by contributing to the creation of a constructive group environment and by helping to build group cohesion.

Contribute to a Constructive Group Environment Maintaining positive relationships within a group is easiest if an optimistic, constructive attitude prevails. When group members believe they have the resources to achieve their tasks and deal successfully with challenges, they feel better about themselves and others. Here are a few tips to help you to contribute to a constructive group environment:

- *Celebrate success.* When someone in the group receives good news or achieves success in a task, ask that person if you can share the news with the group. Many people are uncomfortable telling others of their own good fortune for fear they will be seen as bragging, but they appreciate when others relate their good news for them. That way, everyone can celebrate members' successes.

- *Take advantage of diversity.* Especially when they communicate electronically, groups can find it difficult to ensure that everyone's input is heard when a decision must be made. By actively seeking and considering divergent opinions, online groups can make decisions that better reflect their members' needs.[58]

- *Defuse stress.* It's normal for groups to experience stress from time to time. When interactions among group members become tense, try to defuse the stress. Suggest a group outing, such as going on a hike or taking in a movie. Use humor to reduce tensions and help people relax. When group members feel less stressed, they will likely get along better and be more productive.

- *Respect others.* In almost any group, there are people whose perspectives are at odds. Creating a positive group environment doesn't mean everyone has to agree or individuals have to give up their own viewpoints. Rather, group members show respect for others by listening to different perspectives. Acknowledge the positive aspects of others' ideas and then present your own. When group members treat one another respectfully, their diversity can benefit them by helping them to consider all the possibilities in a given situation.

The ability to build and maintain positive relationships in groups is a particular asset in the workplace. To explore one career in which small group communication skills are especially useful, check out "Putting Communication to Work."

Help to Build Group Cohesion Recall from earlier in this chapter that group cohesion is the extent to which everyone in the group works together toward a common goal. Cohesive groups are more productive and have happier, more satisfied members than groups lacking cohesion. Contributing to group cohesion is therefore an important way to build positive group relationships. You can promote cohesion in the groups to which you belong in the following ways:

- *Emphasize collective goals.* Encourage the group to identify its shared goals clearly. Some goals will be broad, such as "Support economic development in the

putting**communication**to**work**

Search

Job Title >

Work Responsibilities >

Jury Coordinator for Superior Court

Jury coordinators are responsible for organizing small groups of citizens who report to the superior court each day for jury duty. They welcome and conduct briefings for jurors to help to prepare them for service. They work with judges to administer jury selection questionnaires. Most important, whenever a new jury is paneled, they orient the jurors to their responsibilities and help them select a leader. This career requires excellent small group communication skills and the ability to help people from very different backgrounds to work together.

community." Others will be specific, such as "Plan a rally for next Thursday evening." Whatever the group's goals, cohesion suffers when members lose sight of their collective purpose. Take opportunities to remind others in the group of the common goals. When members concentrate on their shared objectives, group cohesiveness often increases.

• *Keep track of progress.* When a goal takes longer to achieve than a group planned, or when members encounter unanticipated problems along the way, those who are working toward a common goal can get discouraged. You can help by acknowledging your group's progress so far. Stress what members have already accomplished, not what they haven't yet achieved. When they are raising funds, for instance, some groups create a large drawing of a thermometer, which they post in a visible place and fill in with color to indicate how much money they have collected. When group members pay attention to what they have achieved, they may focus more on their collective goals than on the challenges of meeting those goals.

• *Remind others of their value to the group.* Almost everyone has a need to belong and appreciates feeling valued. Therefore, another way you can contribute to group cohesion is to point out the reasons you value others in the group. Some reasons might directly relate to the group's task; for instance, you might value one member because of her skill at generating publicity or her knack for organizing efficient workspaces. More generally, you might value a member's empathy or sense of humor. In either case, people are often more committed to groups or causes if they feel valued than if they don't, so reminding people of the ways in which you appreciate them can increase the cohesiveness of the group.

For REVIEW

- **What are small groups, and what do they do?**

  Small groups are collections of 3 to 20 people who focus on discrete tasks, evaluate and advise, create art and ideas, provide services and support, promote social networking, compete, and/or help their members to learn.

- **Why and how do people join small groups?**

  People join small groups because they need to belong, they seek protection, they want to improve their effectiveness at a skill, and/or they are pressured into joining. Whatever the reason, people are socialized into small groups in several stages.

- **How can you communicate better in a small group?**

  You can contribute to a positive socialization experience for new members, and you can maintain good group relationships by contributing to a constructive environment and helping to build group cohesion.

KEY TERMS

small group 252

interdependence 254

cohesion 254

antecedent phase 266

anticipatory phase 267

encounter phase 267

assimilation phase 267

exit phase 267

resources 268

synergy 268

social loafing 269

NOTES

1. Relethford, J. H. (2003). *Reflections of our past: How human history is revealed in our genes.* Basic.
2. Habitat for Humanity International. (2015). *Annual report.* http://www.habitat.org/sites/default/files/annual-report-2015.pdf
3. Beebe, S. A., & Masterson, J. T. (2014). *Communicating in small groups: Principles and practices* (11th ed.). Pearson.
4. Adams, K. L., & Galanes, G. J. (2014). *Communicating in groups: Applications and skills* (9th ed.). McGraw-Hill.
5. Rothwell, J. D. (2012). *In mixed company: Communicating in small groups* (8th ed.). Wadsworth.
6. Ibid.
7. Henman, L. D. (2003). Groups as systems. In R. Y. Hirokawa, R. S. Cathcart, L. A. Samovar, & L. D. Henman (Eds.), *Small group communication theory & practice: An anthology* (8th ed., pp. 3–7). Roxbury.
8. Drescher, S., Burlingame, G., & Fuhriman, A. (2012). Cohesion: An odyssey in empirical understanding. *Small Group Research, 43*(6), 662–689. https://doi.org/10.1177/1046496412468073

9. See Rovio, E., Esokla, J., Kozub, S. A., Duda, J. L., & Lintunen, T. (2009). Can high group cohesion be harmful? A case study of a junior ice-hockey team. *Small Group Research, 40*(4), 421–435. https://doi.org/10.1177/1046496409334359

10. Kjormo, O., & Halvari, H. (2002). Two ways related to performance in elite sport: The path of self-confidence and competitive anxiety and the path of group cohesion and group goal-clarity. *Perceptual and Motor Skills, 94*(3), 950–966. https://doi.org/10.2466/pms.2002.94.3.950

11. Friedkin, N. E. (2004). Social cohesion. *Annual Review of Psychology, 30,* 409–425. https://doi.org/10.1146/annurev.soc .30.012703.110625

12. Fujishin, R. (2013). *Creating effective groups: The art of small group communication* (3rd ed.). Rowman & Littlefield.

13. Stahl, G., Law, N., Cress, U., & Ludvigsen, S. (2014). Analyzing roles of individuals in small-group collaboration processes. *International Journal of Computer-Supported Collaborative Learning, 9*(4), 365–370. https://doi.org/10.1007/s11412-014-9204-9

14. Wittenbaum, G. M., Hollingshead, A. B., Paulus, P. B., Hirokawa, R. Y., Ancona, D. G., Peterson, R. S., Jehn, K. A., & Yoon, K. (2004). The functional perspective as a lens for understanding groups. *Small Group Research, 35*(1), 17–43. https://doi .org/10.1177/1046496403259459

15. Tropman, J. E. (2014). *Effective meetings: Improving group decision making* (3rd ed.). Sage.

16. Southwell, D., & Twist, S. (2007). *Secret societies.* Rosen; see also Bond, M. (2007). The dining Freemasons (security protocols for secret societies). *Lecture Notes in Computer Science, 4631,* 266–275. https://doi.org/10.1007/978-3-540-77156-2_33

17. See, e.g., Newer, H. (1999). *From wrongs of passage: Fraternities, sororities, hazing, and binge drinking.* Indiana University Press.

18. Totten, M. (2014). *Gang life: 10 of the toughest tell their stories.* James Lorimer & Company.

19. www.redhatsociety.com

20. Frey, L. R., & Sunwolf. (2005). The communication perspective on group life. In S. A. Whelan (Ed.), *The handbook of group research and practice* (pp. 158–186). Sage.

21. Harris, T. E., & Sherblom, J. C. (2010). *Small group and team communication* (5th ed.). Allyn & Bacon.

22. Kairam, S. R., Wang, D. J., & Leskovec, J. (2012). The life and death of online groups: Predicting group growth and longevity. *Proceedings of the Fifth ACM International Conference on Web Search and Data Mining,* 673–682. https://doi.org /10.1145/2124295.2124374

23. Schiller, S. Z., & Mandviwalla, M. (2007). Virtual team research: An analysis of theory use and a framework for theory appro- priation. *Small Group Research, 38*(1), 12–59. https://doi.org/10.1177/1046496406297035

24. Johnson, S. K., Bettenhausen, K., & Gibbons, E. (2009). Realities of working in virtual teams: Affective and attitudinal outcomes of using computer-mediated communication. *Small Group Research, 40*(6), 623–649. https://doi.org /10.1177/1046496409346448

25. Hardin, A. M., Fuller, M. A., & Davison, R. M. (2007). I know I can, but can we? Culture and efficiency beliefs in global vir- tual teams. *Small Group Research, 38*(1), 130–155. https://doi.org/10.1177/1046496406297041

26. U.S. Committee on Finance. (2015, August 5). Finance committee releases bipartisan IRS report. http://www.finance.senate .gov/newsroom/chairman/release/?id=11f4db1f-9986-4ecb-ba61-f3a8abeb2672

27. Grossman, M. (2010). *Encyclopedia of the United States cabinet, 1789–2010* (2nd ed.). Grey House Publishing.

28. Krueger, R. A., & Casey, M. A. (2014). *Focus groups: A practical guide for applied research* (5th ed.). Sage.

29. Coldplaying.com. (2014, May 18). Coldplay album sales: New album predictions and past figures. http://www.coldplaying .com/coldplay-album-sales/

30. www.kiwanis.org.

31. www.lionsclubs.org.

32. Davison, K. P., Pennebaker, J. W., & Dickerson, S. S. (2000). Who talks? The social psychology of illness support groups. *American Psychologist, 55*(2), 205–217. https://doi.org/10.1037/0003-066X.55.2.205

33. Goodwin, P. J., Leszcz, M., Ennis, M., Koopmans, J., Vincent, L., Guther, H., Drysdale, E., Hundleby, M., Chochinov, H. M., Navarro, M., Speca, M., Masterson, J., Dohan, L., Sela, R., Warren, B., Paterson, A., Pritchard, K. I., Arnold, A., Doll, R., O'Reilly, S. E., . . . Hunter, J. (2001). The effect of group psychosocial support on survival in metastatic breast cancer. *New England Journal of Medicine, 345*(24), 1719–1726. https://doi.org/10.1056/NCJMoa001871; see also Gilden, J. C., Hendryx, M. S., Clar, S., & Singh, S. P. (1992). Diabetes support groups improve health care of older diabetic patients. *Journal of the American Geriatrics Society, 40*(2), 147–150. https://doi.org/10.1111/j.1532-5415.1992.tb01935.x

34. Wang, Y.-C., Kraut, R., & Levine, J. M. (2012). To stay or leave? The relationship of emotional and informational support to commitment in online health support groups. *Proceedings of the ACM 2012 Conference on Computer Supported Cooperative Work,* 833–842. https://doi.org/10.1145/2145204.2145329

35. Muscanell, N. L., & Guadagno, R. E. (2012). Make new friends or keep the old: Gender and personality differences in social networking use. *Computers in Human Behavior, 28*(1), 107–112. https://doi.org/10.1016/j.chb.2011.09.016

36. Reich, S. M., Subrahmanyam, K., & Espinoza, G. (2012). Friending, IMing, and hanging out face-to-face: Overlap in adoles- cents' online and offline social networks. *Developmental Psychology, 48*(2), 356–368. https://doi.org/10.1037/a0026980

37. For discussion, see Ellison, N. B., Steinfield, C., & Lampe, C. (2007). The benefits of Facebook "friends": Social capital and college students' use of online social network sites. *Journal of Computer-Mediated Communication, 12*(4), 1143–1168. https://doi.org/10.1111/j.1083-6101.2007.00367.x

38. www.collegequizbowl.org

39. O'Donnell, A. M., Hmelo-Silver, C. E., & Erkens, G. (Eds.). (2011). *Collaborative learning, reasoning, and technology.* Routledge.

40. See Young, C. B., & Henquinet, J. A. (2000). A conceptual framework for designing group projects. *Journal of Education for Business, 76*(1), 56–60. https://doi.org/10.1080/08832320009599051

41. Keyton, J., Harmon, N., & Frey, L. R. (1996, November). *Grouphate: Implications for teaching small group communication* [Paper presentation]. Speech Communication Association, San Diego, CA, United States.

42. Bauer, T. N., Bodner, T., Erdogan, B., Truxillo, D. M., & Tucker, J. S. (2007). Newcomer adjustment during organizational socialization: A meta-analytic review of antecedents, outcomes, and methods. *Journal of Applied Psychology, 92*(3), 707–721. https://doi.org/10.1037/0021-9010.92.3.707

43. Hehman, E., Gaertner, S. L., Dovidio, J. F., Mania, E. W., Guerra, R., Wilson, D. C., & Friel, B. M. (2011). Group status drives majority and minority integration preferences. *Psychological Science, 23*(1), 46–52. https://doi.org/10.1177/0956797611423547

44. Sinclair-James, L., & Stohl, C. (1997). Group endings and new beginnings. In L. R. Frey, & J. K. Barge (Eds.), *Managing group life: Communicating in decision-making groups* (pp. 308–334). Houghton Mifflin.

45. Keyton, J. (1993). Group termination: Completing the study of group development. *Small Group Research, 24*(1), 84–100. https://doi.org/10.1177/1046496493241006

46. Baker, D. F., & Campbell, C. M. (2004). When is there strength in numbers? A study of undergraduate task groups. *College Teaching, 53*(1), 14–18. https://doi.org/10.3200/CTCH.53.1.14-19

47. Sunwolf. (2002). Getting to "groupaha!": Provoking creating processes in task groups. In L. R. Frey (Ed.), *New directions in group communication* (pp. 203–217). Sage.

48. Williams, K., Harkins, S., & Latané, B. (1981). Identifiability as a deterrent to social loafing: Two cheering experiments. *Journal of Personality and Social Psychology, 40*(2), 303–311. https://doi.org/10.1037/0022-3514.40.2.303

49. Lount, R. B., & Wilk, S. L. (2014). Working harder or hardly working? Posting performance eliminates social loafing and promotes social laboring in workgroups. *Management Science, 60*(5), 1098–1106. https://doi.org/10.1287/mnsc.2013.1820

50. Høigaard, R., Säfvenbom, R., & Tønnessen, F. E. (2006). The relationship between group cohesion, group norms, and perceived social loafing in soccer teams. *Small Group Research, 37*(3), 217–232. https://doi.org/10.1177/1046496406287311

51. Myers, S. A., & Anderson, C. M. (2008). *The fundamentals of small group communication.* Sage.

52. Ibid.

53. Ibid.

54. Song, Z., Chon, K., Ding, G., & Gu, C. (2015). Impact of organizational socialization tactics on newcomer job satisfaction and engagement: Core self-evaluations as moderators. *International Journal of Hospitality Management, 46,* 180–189. https://doi.org/10.1016/j.ijhm.2015.02.006

55. Carvin, B. N. (2011). The hows and whys of group mentoring. *Industrial and Commercial Training, 43*(1), 49–52. https://doi.org/10.1108/00197851111098162

56. Keyton, J. (2000). Introduction: The relational side of groups. *Small Group Research, 31*(4), 387–396. https://doi.org/10.1177/104649640003100401

57. Majchrzak, A., Malhotra, A., Stamps. J., & Lipnack, J. (2004). Can absence make a team grow stronger? *Harvard Business Review, 82*(5), 131–137, 152.

58. Evans, C. R., & Dion, K. L. (2012). Group cohesion and performance: A meta-analysis. *Small Group Research, 43*(6), 690–701. https://doi.org/10.1177/1046496412468074

10

Chip Somodevilla/Getty Images

DECISION MAKING AND LEADERSHIP IN GROUPS

Making Critical Decisions Requires Communication

For the nine justices of the U.S. Supreme Court, making difficult decisions is a way of life. The Supreme Court serves as the highest judicial body in the nation, handing down final decisions on controversial cases that often require interpretation of the U.S. Constitution. Because their cases can be so hotly contested and have such far-reaching effects on the country, Supreme Court justices, who are appointed for life, must learn to work together productively despite frequent differences of opinion. They do so by communicating with one another regularly, both in writing and in face-to-face conferences. When they meet to discuss the merits of a case, they follow rules and traditions that protect everyone's right to be heard. Those procedures help the Court to make decisions even when the justices' positions are strongly divided, as they were in a 2020 case, *South Bay United v. Gavin Newsom*. In that case the Court ruled that states could restrict church attendance to limit the spread of COVID-19. Then, as in many other controversial cases, the justices were narrowly divided by a vote of 5 to 4.

•••► As You READ

- How do groups generate ideas and make decisions?
- How do leaders enact leadership and exercise power?
- What communication skills improve group decision making?

No matter what its primary functions are, almost every group makes decisions. A criminal jury decides whether a defendant is guilty. A faculty committee may have decided to select this textbook for your class. From time to time, the justices of the U.S. Supreme Court decide on a case with far-reaching implications for Americans. Those decisions are all very different, but as you'll discover in this chapter, they have more in common than you might think.

Whether groups make good or bad decisions often depends on how their members interact. The quality of a group's choices can also be influenced by who leads the group and how that leader exercises power. Because so many groups make decisions that affect the lives of others—often in significant ways—learning about leadership and decision making can help you contribute more productively in the groups to which you belong.

Generating Ideas and Making Decisions

Centerville, Iowa, is like a lot of small towns that have recently seen an uptick in the need for mental health services. Without many resources available in this community of 5,500, however, residents in distress either had to visit the local 25-bed hospital or find a sheriff's deputy willing to drive them to a psychiatric facility, which was often in another state. A four-month wait to see a psychiatrist was the norm. The situation improved dramatically when a group of mental health leaders, organized by physician assistant Dewey McConville, came together to create the Appanoose County Mental Health Coalition. The community organization marshals on-call therapists who can help clients struggling with mental health challenges ranging from schizophrenia and substance abuse to depression and suicidal thoughts. The Coalition's efforts have paid off for the community by reducing both the number of psychiatric hospitalizations and the costs of transferring people to out-of-state facilities.[1]

For many groups—such as the Centerville mental health providers—the ability to make wise decisions is essential to the quality of life of those they serve. Fortunately, groups have several good options for generating and choosing among ideas, as we'll see in this section. We also consider that several cultural and social characteristics can influence which decision-making options are best.

A musical group can use a variety of decision-making methods to choose its repertoire of songs for an upcoming performance.

Izzet Keribar/The Image Bank Unreleased/Getty Images

GROUPS GENERATE IDEAS THROUGH VARIOUS METHODS

A human resources committee may need to decide how to advertise the three new positions it must fill. A musical group may need to choose a repertoire of songs to perform for an upcoming concert series. In both cases, generating a list of possible options is an important first step in the decision-making process. Here we'll examine three of the most common methods groups use to generate ideas: brainstorming, the nominal group technique, and ideawriting.

Brainstorming can be a very effective method of generating ideas.

Inti St Clair LLC/Blend Images

Groups Can Brainstorm A technique popularized in the 1950s to stimulate creative decision making,[2] **brainstorming** allows group members to freely offer any ideas they wish and create a list of all the proposed ideas before any are evaluated. The concept behind brainstorming is that if people feel free to think in unorthodox ways without fear of being ridiculed, they may generate better and more creative ideas.[3]

Groups usually begin a brainstorming session by identifying the question to be answered or the problem to be solved. During the session, group members are encouraged to pose ideas, no matter how outlandish they might seem at first. All ideas are added to a master list, and the process continues until no one expresses any new thoughts. At that point, the group considers the merits of each idea, discarding some and possibly combining others, with the goal of selecting the best one or more. Finally, the group may decide which idea or ideas to adopt. We will consider various methods of group decision making later in this chapter.

To brainstorm productively, groups should agree to some ground rules that are clearly communicated to group members before the brainstorming session begins. That way, everyone knows what to expect. Those rules could include

- *Be creative:* Encourage all ideas, even ones that seem unusual or outrageous. Ideas may have merit even if they sound unworkable or crazy at first.

- *Urge everyone to contribute:* Don't allow one or two group members to run the show. Make sure everyone gets a chance to add ideas to the list.

- *Allow piggybacking:* Encourage group members to "piggyback" on one another's ideas by adding to what each other has said.

Researchers suggest that brainstorming sessions last no longer than about 30 minutes so the group's energy and creativity don't wane.[4] When done properly, brainstorming can lead a group to generate useful and innovative ideas. Brainstorming works well when all members of the group feel comfortable offering thoughts and sharing opinions. Members who are shy or who fear being ridiculed may be unlikely to participate, however, and good ideas might be stifled. In that instance, the nominal group technique might be a more productive option.

Groups Can Use the Nominal Group Technique For some group members, brainstorming can be intimidating. The **nominal group technique (NGT)** calls for group members to generate their initial ideas silently and independently, which can be more comfortable for those in the group who are shy. NGT then encourages group members to combine their ideas and consider them as a group.[5]

Like brainstorming, NGT begins with the identification of a question to be answered or a problem to be solved. Instead of contributing their initial ideas aloud in front of the group, however, members each make a list of ideas on their own, working silently.

• **brainstorming** An idea-generating process in which group members offer whatever ideas they wish before any are debated.

• **nominal group technique (NGT)** An idea-generating process in which group members generate their initial ideas silently and independently and then combine them and consider them as a group.

Afterward, a group facilitator asks each member to read his or her ideas aloud, one at a time, while the facilitator writes them on a master list. The facilitator can also collect the ideas and compile the master list on his or her own so no one knows who came up with each idea.[6]

Once the master list is in place, NGT follows essentially the same process as brainstorming. The group considers the merits of each idea on the list, discarding some and debating or modifying others. Finally, the group selects whichever idea it believes to be the best. The major advantage of NGT over brainstorming is that it can encourage participation from members who might be uncomfortable contributing their ideas aloud.[7]

Groups Can Ideawrite One disadvantage of brainstorming and the nominal group technique is that their collaborative nature can make some group members intimidated about offering their own ideas or critiquing the ideas of others. A third method for generating ideas, called **ideawriting**, encourages members to propose and evaluate ideas more independently, which can help each idea receive proper consideration.[8]

• **ideawriting** An idea generating process in which members independently list their own ideas and then systematically evaluate one another's ideas before they are considered by the group.

Like brainstorming and NGT, ideawriting starts with the description of a specific question to be answered or problem to be solved. The ideawriting process then proceeds in four steps.

1. In the first step, each member creates a list of three to four ideas including the reasons each idea has merit. Members put their individual lists in a pile.

2. In the second step, each member chooses a list from the pile that is not his or hers. Working alone, members read all the ideas and reasons shown on the list they select and add their own comments about the strengths and weaknesses of each idea. When they're done, they return the list to the pile, select another list, and do the same. The second step continues until every member has read and commented on every other member's ideas.

3. In the third step, members retrieve the list of ideas they originally created, which now contains written comments from everyone else in the group. Each member reads and responds in writing to the comments made about his or her ideas, which allows everyone to react to feedback and potential criticism of their ideas in a nonthreatening way.

4. Finally, in the fourth step, group members come together to create a master list of ideas they think are worthy of additional discussion. They then work toward selecting the best idea, as they would in brainstorming and NGT.

Of the three idea-generation methods we've surveyed, ideawriting is the least collaborative, because group members accomplish most of the steps individually rather than as a group. The major advantage of ideawriting is that it allows each member to offer ideas, respond to others' ideas, and react to criticisms of his or her own ideas privately and independently.[9] Privacy can help to shield group members from the feelings of resentment or defensiveness that might arise in a public process, and independence can inspire some members to produce more innovative ideas than they might in a more collaborative setting.

Having used a technique such as brainstorming, NGT, or ideawriting to generate ideas, groups usually must choose the best idea from among the various options. That process requires them to use a decision-making method, our next point of focus.

SHARPEN Your Skills: *Brainstorming*

With a small group of students from your class, spend 15 minutes brainstorming to generate a list of actions you could take to address a social problem in your community. First, identify the problem you want to address—such as homelessness, unequal access to health care, hunger, inadequate childcare, or low adult literacy. Next, follow the principles of brainstorming to list various actions your group could take to improve the lives of those affected. Afterward, spend a few minutes discussing what you found most enjoyable and most challenging about brainstorming. Present your final list of ideas to the rest of the class as a way to encourage community involvement.

GROUPS MAKE DECISIONS IN MANY WAYS

To illustrate the various methods by which groups can make decisions, let's imagine you're an employee of Star Bank. You are assigned to a team charged with choosing a marketing slogan for the bank's new account options, which were designed to meet the needs of senior citizens. Your team has generated several ideas for slogans and has narrowed the list to three:

- *Star Bank: Where Seniors Reach for the Stars*
- *Star Bank: The Right Choice for Your Active Lifestyle*
- *Protect Your Golden Years with Star Bank*

dcdebs/iStock/Getty Images

Your team must select one slogan from this list. Let's examine five methods by which the team members might arrive at their decision: consensus, majority rule, minority rule, expert opinion, and authority rule.

Some Groups Decide by Unanimous Consensus
One option for making a decision is to try to get everyone to agree about which slogan is best. Once you begin discussion, for instance, you might find that all the members of your team prefer the first marketing slogan to the other two. If everyone in the group prefers the same slogan, then the group has **unanimous consensus**, which is uncontested support for a decision. In some instances, unanimous consensus is the only option for group decision making. A jury hearing a criminal case, for example, often must arrive at a unanimous verdict about the defendant's innocence or guilt. Verdicts on which not all jurors agree are considered invalid. Even if it isn't required, however, unanimous consensus can be advantageous because group members are likely to support more enthusiastically a decision on which they all agree.

- **unanimous consensus** Uncontested support for a decision—sometimes the only option in a group's decision-making process.

Achieving unanimous consensus isn't always easy, though. Particularly if the decision is controversial, group members may vary dramatically in the outcomes they prefer. In that case, arriving at a decision may require the group to engage in long, often frustrating discussions. Even so, such discussions may end in a **stalemate**, an outcome in which members' opinions are so sharply divided that unanimity is impossible to achieve. In the event of a stalemate, a group may have to resort to one of the other forms of decision making *if* it has the option of doing so.

- **stalemate** An outcome where members' opinions are so sharply divided that consensus is impossible to achieve.

When trying to decide by unanimous consensus, groups must also be careful not to achieve **false consensus**, which occurs when some members say they support the decision even though they do not. These members may feel pressure to support the majority's wishes so unanimity can be reached, but the resulting false consensus reduces the chance that everyone will be enthusiastic about the decision. Groups often discover false consensus after the fact, when members who felt pressured to vote with the majority begin voicing their concerns about the decision. The likelihood of false consensus is diminished if group members feel safe expressing their opinions, even those that contradict the views of their fellow members.

- **false consensus** An outcome where some members of a group say they support the unanimous decision even though they do not.

Some Groups Decide by Majority Rule
Instead of choosing a marketing slogan by unanimous consensus, your team might reach its decision by **majority rule**, a decision-making process that follows the will of the majority. If someone says, "Let's take a vote" when a group decision is looming, he or she is probably recommending majority rule. To select among your marketing slogans, therefore, each member of your team might cast a vote for one of the slogans. The slogan receiving the fewest votes will be discarded, and each member will then vote for one of the remaining two. The slogan that now receives more votes has been chosen by majority rule.

- **majority rule** A decision-making process that follows the will of the majority.

Majority rule operates on the democratic principle that decisions should reflect what most people want, not what a smaller number of more powerful people prefers.

The primary advantage of majority rule is that, by definition, it ensures that most people in the group support the decision being made. People raised in democratic societies are used to majority rule as a form of decision making, and under most circumstances, they accept that the will of the majority should be followed even if they themselves voted with the minority.

When a vote is particularly close, however, the minority can feel the decision was arbitrary. For instance, if one marketing slogan received eight votes from your team and the other received seven, those who favored the second slogan might feel the decision was unfair because the margin of victory was so small. They may then be less inclined to support the team's decision than if the winning slogan had won by more votes. When using majority rule to make decisions on controversial issues, everyone in the group should remember the importance of supporting the majority decision, whatever it is.

Majority rule can be problematic in groups that have an even number of members, because of the possibility of a tied vote. If each marketing slogan wins 50 percent of the vote, neither has received a majority. Whenever an even number of votes will be cast, groups should determine ahead of time what procedures to follow in the event of a tie. For example, perhaps the leader will cast a vote only if it is necessary to break a tie. To prevent the possibility of a tied vote, some groups—including the U.S. Supreme Court—decide ahead of time to have an odd number of members.

Some Groups Decide by Minority Rule A third form of decision making is **minority rule**, a process in which a small number of members makes a decision on behalf of the group. Decision makers often use minority rule for the sake of efficiency.

Let's say your Star Bank team wants to host a reception to unveil its new marketing slogan. Instead of having the entire team discuss where and when to hold the event, the leader might delegate that responsibility to two or three team members. Those members then have the ability to make decisions about the reception on the team's behalf. The minority rule strategy saves the team's time for discussing more important decisions, such as which marketing slogan to adopt.

By definition, minority rule excludes the input of most members of the group. For that reason, it is rarely a good option for making decisions that are controversial or consequential.

Some Groups Decide by Expert Opinion Some groups include people whose training or experience makes them experts on the type of decision the groups are making. Such groups may reach their decisions by deferring to **expert opinion**, or the recommendations of individuals with expertise in a particular area. Let's assume your Star Bank team includes someone with a master's degree in marketing. Because of that person's expertise, your team might ask his or her advice on which marketing slogan to adopt, instead of taking a vote or trying to achieve unanimous consensus.

Expert opinion works on the principle that certain people have better judgment or more informed opinions on specific topics that enable them to make better decisions than nonexperts. Bear in mind, however, that expertise is always specific to particular topics or matters. No one is an expert on everything. If the group is going to rely on expert opinion, members should make certain they're listening to someone with appropriate expertise.

Some Groups Decide by Authority Rule Suppose that instead of building unanimous consensus, taking a vote, assigning the decision to a minority, or consulting an expert, your team at Star Bank leaves the choice of a slogan to the team leader. That approach is an example of **authority rule**, a process by which the leader of the group makes the decisions. Authority rule is a common method of decision making in some groups. In a class or workshop, for instance, a teacher usually makes decisions

• minority rule
A decision-making process in which a small number of members makes a decision on behalf of the group.

• expert opinion
Recommendations of individuals who have expertise in a particular area that are sometimes the basis of a group's decision-making process.

• authority rule
A decision-making process in which the leader of the group makes the decisions.

Authority rule is best if one person has the experience and responsibility to make decisions for everyone else in the group.

PhanuwatNandee/iStock/ Getty Images

about the group's activities, and others adapt to those decisions. In a group of firefighters responding to a blaze, the senior commander makes the decisions and issues the orders.

Authority rule is best when someone in the group has legitimate authority over other members. Teachers and fire commanders make decisions on behalf of their groups because it's their responsibility and their prerogative to do so. Authority rule is also very efficient. If firefighters had to meet to consider and vote on all possible approaches to dealing with an emergency, lives would be lost in the time their discussions took. If the commander makes the decisions, however, the group can act more quickly, and this consideration is critical when time is short.[10]

Authority rule can be problematic, however, when exercised in groups that have no legitimate authority figure. If someone on your work team were to say "I've decided we should choose the second slogan," the other members may resent that person's attempt to exercise authority over the team. When no one in the group is a legitimate authority figure, other methods of decision making are likely to be more effective.

Finding the Best Decision-Making Method The method of making decisions that is best depends on several factors that vary from decision to decision. One factor is the importance of the decision itself. Relatively unimportant decisions may be best made by authority or minority rule because those methods are efficient. More important decisions—those that will affect many people or require a great deal of money to implement—might be better made by unanimous consensus, majority rule, or expert opinion, because those methods often entail a closer, more critical consideration of the options.

A second factor in determining the right decision-making method is whether the decision requires expert knowledge. Expert opinion is often the most effective method of making decisions that require specialized knowledge not shared by everyone in the group. Authority rule can also be effective in such situations if the leader has authority *because of his or her expertise*, as, for example, a fire commander usually does.

A third factor influencing the choice of decision-making method is how quickly the decision must be made. Authority rule is often the fastest way of making decisions, whereas building unanimous consensus is frequently the most time-intensive. When selecting its method of decision making, a group might consider the time constraints on the decision.

CULTURAL CONTEXT AFFECTS DECISION MAKING

Diversity in the cultural and social characteristics of its members also can influence the decision-making method a group prefers. These characteristics include individualism, power distance, and time orientation. We examined them in the communication and culture chapter; now let's see how they can affect group decision making.

Individualism Affects Decision Making People in individualistic cultures are taught that their primary responsibility is to themselves. Competition, self-reliance, and individual achievement are valued in highly individualistic cultures. In contrast, people in collectivistic cultures believe their primary responsibility is to their families, their communities, and their employers. Collectivistic cultures value collaboration, harmony, and solidarity rather than competition and individual achievement.

Whether a group hails from an individualistic or a collectivistic culture can influence how that group makes decisions. Groups in collectivistic cultures, for instance, may place great emphasis on reaching group consensus. Because collectivistic cultures stress collaboration, group members value what's best for the group, even if that means having to compromise on their individual preferences. In contrast, groups in individualistic cultures are more likely to encourage members to voice their opinions on decisions, even if those opinions differ. Because individualistic cultures emphasize competition, group members may be less interested in reaching consensus than in persuading others to agree with their position.

Power Distance Affects Decision Making Recall that cultures vary in how they expect power to be distributed within a society. In high-power-distance cultures, certain groups of people have great power and the average citizen has much less. In low-power-distance cultures, people value equality and believe no one person or group should have excessive power over others.

A culture's power distance can influence how groups within that culture arrive at decisions. Groups in high-power-distance cultures may be particularly deferential to authority, for instance. Consequently, they may prefer to make decisions by authority rule or by following expert opinion. In contrast, groups in low-power-distance cultures are more likely to prefer majority rule as a decision-making method, given that majority rule treats everyone's vote as equal to everyone else's.

Time Orientation Affects Decision Making Cultures differ with respect to their norms and expectations concerning the use of time. Monochronic cultures view time as a tangible commodity. As a result, people in monochronic cultures, such as the United States, enjoy "saving" time and try to avoid "wasting" it. In contrast, polychronic cultures, including Japan and South Korea, conceive of time as more fluid. People don't prioritize efficiency and punctuality to the same extent that people do in monochronic cultures. Instead, they attach greater value to the quality of their lives and their relationships with others.

A group's preferred decision-making method may depend on whether its culture is monochronic or polychronic. Groups from monochronic cultures may opt for majority rule, minority rule, or authority rule because those methods often use time efficiently. However, groups from polychronic cultures, which have less incentive to make decisions quickly, may be more likely to try achieving unanimous consensus if they believe that method will produce a better decision.

In summary, groups have many options for making decisions. Individualism, power distance, and time orientation can each influence the decision-making methods a group *prefers,* but they do not necessarily determine the methods that group will *use.* As we've seen, a group's method of decision making is also affected by the nature of the decision to be made. Nonetheless, cultural influences can be powerful, shaping not only how groups make decisions but also how satisfied they are with them. For one example of a job that requires good decision-making skills, check out the "Putting Communication to Work" box.

Job Title >

Work Responsibilities >

Editor, Print or Online Magazine

Just about every story you read in a magazine or on your favorite website started as simply one idea of many pitched to an editor. Editors work with writers, photographers, and graphic artists to cultivate stories and designs that will engage readers and lure advertisers. Communication skills are crucial for editorial staff at every level, from fresh-out-of-college editorial assistants tasked with research and support roles; to copyeditors who check writing for spelling, grammar, and style; to managing editors who ensure that the workflow among staff is efficient and produces optimal results. All of these employees are overseen by the executive editor or editor-in-chief, who determines the overall vision for the product, evaluates ideas from staff and freelance writers, and makes key decisions on content and design.

Being a Leader

Mary Ellen Diaz knows about effective leadership. A world-class chef who trained at the famed Le Cordon Bleu in Paris, Diaz has worked in exclusive restaurants, including at the Ritz-Carlton hotel in Chicago. Although she prepared gourmet meals for her restaurants' clients, she felt personally drawn to the cause of providing food for the hungry. She didn't want to feed people leftover scraps or second-rate food but the same high-quality meals she prepared in Chicago's restaurants. With a small group of staff members, Diaz founded First Slice, an organization that distributes fresh, expertly prepared food to the needy. Because of her leadership and the decisions her group has made, First Slice delivers more than 1,400 meals each month to the hungry, homeless, and disenfranchised in Chicago.

With effective leadership and constructive decision-making techniques, groups of people can achieve great things. What does it mean to be a leader, however? In this section, we'll discover that effective leaders often share specific physical and psychosocial traits and enact distinct behavioral styles of leadership.

Jackson Vereen/Cole Group/ Getty Images

LEADERS OFTEN SHARE SPECIFIC TRAITS

One way to understand leadership is to look at some common traits of leaders. **Traits** are distinguishing personal characteristics that are often relatively enduring and not easily changeable. Each of us has certain physical traits, such as our eye color, sex, and height. We also have psychosocial traits, such as our self-esteem, temperament, and level of anxiety when faced with a communication task. Physical traits tend to be more enduring than psychosocial traits.

• **traits** Defining characteristics of a person that are often relatively enduring and not easily changeable.

Most U.S. presidents—including Barack Obama, Bill Clinton, and George W. Bush—have been taller than the average U.S. man.

Saul Loeb/AFP/Getty Images

• **physical traits**
The body's physical attributes.

None of these traits, however, necessarily determines who's going to be a good leader and who isn't. Rather, most of us can learn to be an effective leader no matter what physical and psychosocial traits we possess. In fact, sometimes the responsibilities of leadership are assigned to us whether or not we want them. Still, researchers have discovered that leaders often share particular traits, as we'll now consider.

Physical Traits The body's attributes are referred to as its **physical traits**. Three physical traits in particular can influence who is likely to become leaders and how effective they are perceived to be.

One such trait is sex. Some studies have reported that people perceive women less favorably than men as potential leaders and that they evaluate the work of female leaders less positively than the work of male leaders.[11] That doesn't mean that men actually *are* more effective leaders, only that they are sometimes perceived to be. Other research has found that people in groups express more negative nonverbal reactions, such as facial expressions and gestures, toward female leaders than male leaders,[12] particularly when female leaders enact stereotypically masculine behaviors such as dominance and aggression.[13] Other studies have not found that difference.[14] Although people may respond to male and female leaders differently, however, they appear to judge female and male leaders as being equally competent.[15]

A second physical trait that can affect leadership is height.[16] In Western cultures, people often associate height with dominance, competence, and power.[17] It therefore may not surprise you to learn that taller people are more likely than shorter people to be nominated or elected to leadership positions.[18] For example, two-thirds of U.S. presidents have been taller than the average U.S. adult man, and since 1990, the taller candidate for president has won the popular vote 67 percent of the time.[19] Perhaps because the average adult man is taller than the average adult woman, however, height is a stronger predictor of leadership success for men than it is for women.[20]

Finally, physical appearance influences leadership. Studies have shown, for instance, that leaders with masculine-looking faces are judged as more competent than are leaders with feminine-looking faces.[21] Masculine faces typically feature a wide, square jaw and small eyes, whereas feminine faces feature large eyes and a small, rounded jaw. Researchers speculate that people associate masculine faces with competent leadership because they think of men as being more dominant and powerful than women.[22]

Regardless of whether they appear masculine or feminine, however, leaders are more likely to be physically attractive than unattractive.[23] As you might know from your own experience, people associate physical attractiveness with a range of positive qualities, including intelligence, honesty, and competence. It should therefore come as no surprise that physically attractive people are *perceived* to be better leaders than less attractive individuals.

It's worth repeating that although sex, height, and physical appearance are *related to* leadership, none of those traits determines who will be a good leader and who will not. Leadership is a skill you can develop and nurture over time, regardless of your physical traits.

• **psychosocial traits**
Characteristics of one's personality and ways of relating to others.

Psychosocial Traits Many effective leaders share particular **psychosocial traits**, which are characteristics of their personality and ways of relating to others. Like physical traits, psychosocial traits are relatively enduring and not easily changed, although experience and education can help leaders hone their useful traits. Much of the research has focused on three particular traits: self-esteem, self-monitoring, and expressiveness.

Recall from the chapter on perception that self-esteem is a person's subjective evaluation of his or her value and worth. Because having self-esteem gives us confidence in ourselves, it seems likely that people are better leaders if their self-esteem is higher rather than lower. In line with that idea, research tells us that people with high self-esteem rate themselves as better leaders than do those with low self-esteem.[24] Surprisingly, though, a leader's self-esteem doesn't predict how *other people* rate his or her leadership abilities.[25] Although having high self-esteem improves how leaders perceive themselves, it doesn't improve how others perceive them.

A second psychosocial trait that has been studied with reference to leadership is self-monitoring. Recall that self-monitoring is our awareness of our own behavior and its effects on others. Some researchers have suggested that people who are high self-monitors are able to perceive the needs of others in a group and adapt their own behavior to meet those needs. In line with that idea, several studies have found that self-monitoring is strongly related to leadership emergence in groups.[26] Curiously, some research has shown that self-monitoring predicts leadership only for men,[27] but most research indicates that both female and male leaders are likely to be high self-monitors.

Finally, several studies have indicated that leaders are more likely to be outgoing and expressive rather than shy and withdrawn. One project examined the findings of 73 different studies and found that people are more apt to become leaders—and more apt to be *effective* leaders—if they are extroverted rather than introverted.[28] **Extroversion** is a personality trait shared by people who are friendly, assertive, and outgoing with others. Leadership is inherently social, so extroverts tend to excel at leadership because they are comfortable interacting socially with others. How extroverted are you? Take the quiz in "The Competent Communicator" to find out.

In contrast, **introversion** characterizes people who are shy, reserved, and aloof. Because of their more reserved nature, introverts can experience **communication apprehension**, anxiety or fear about communicating with others. Apprehensive communicators often have difficulty leading. One study found that people who scored high on a test of communication apprehension perceived themselves—and were perceived by others—as less likely to be good leaders than were people who scored low on communication apprehension.[29]

Those observations don't mean that introverted people cannot be effective leaders. On the contrary, they often benefit from skills and perspectives that improve their ability to lead and inspire others.[30] For one, they often excel at listening and developing meaningful connections with employees and customers. Research suggests that introverts may make better decisions because they are less impulsive and more self-reflective.[31] They may also be more open to receiving and implementing suggestions from others and building consensus, all of which can enhance their effectiveness as leaders.[32]

Just as not every effective leader is male, tall, and physically attractive, not every effective leader scores high on self-esteem, self-monitoring, and extroversion. Examining traits that many leaders share tells us only part of the story about effective leadership. To understand leadership more fully, we must look not only at *who leaders are* but also at *how leaders behave*, our next topic.

LEADERS ENACT DISTINCT STYLES

Think about the leaders of groups to which you've belonged. How would you describe their leadership styles? Regardless of his or her physical or psychosocial traits, chances are each leader had a specific way of enacting leadership responsibilities. Many years ago, a team of social psychologists determined that most leaders enact one of three distinct styles in the way they lead others—democratic, autocratic, and laissez-faire. Let's take a quick look at each.

Some Leaders Are Democratic One of the underlying principles of a democracy is that every citizen has the right to participate in decision making. Group leaders who enact a **democratic style** reflect that principle in their leadership.[33]

• **extroversion** A personality trait shared by people who are friendly, assertive, and outgoing with others.

• **introversion** A personality trait shared by people who are shy, reserved, and aloof.

• **communication apprehension** Anxiety or fear about communicating with others.

• **democratic style** A leadership style in which every member of a group has the right to participate in decision making.

Your Extroversion—High, Low, or No?

Extroversion is a personality trait reflecting how assertive, friendly, and outgoing you are. How extroverted are you? Read each of the following statements and indicate whether you think it is true or false with respect to yourself. There are no right or wrong answers. Simply respond to each statement in whatever way seems to best represent you.

rawpixel/123RF

	True	False
1. I see myself as someone who is talkative.	____	____
2. I see myself as someone who is unreserved.	____	____
3. I see myself as someone who is full of energy.	____	____
4. I see myself as someone who generates a lot of enthusiasm.	____	____
5. I see myself as someone who doesn't tend to be quiet.	____	____
6. I see myself as someone with an assertive personality.	____	____
7. I see myself as someone who is rarely shy or inhibited.	____	____
8. I see myself as someone who is outgoing and sociable.	____	____

When you're finished, add up the number of statements you marked as true. If your total was 7 or above, you are highly extroverted. You are generally outgoing and sociable, and rarely inhibited or shy. If your total was between 4 and 6, you are moderately extroverted. You're outgoing and assertive, but not to a substantial degree. If your total was 3 or lower, you are not particularly extroverted. You tend to be more reserved and shy in social interaction.

SOURCE: Items adapted from John, O. P., & Srivastava, S. (1999). The Big-Five trait taxonomy: History, measurement, and theoretical perspectives. In L. A. Pervin, & O. P. John (Eds.), *Handbook of personality: Theory and research* (Vol. 2, pp. 102–138). Guilford.

Let's say Taylor chairs the committee overseeing the adult literacy outreach program at her community center. When the committee needs to generate ideas about how to raise community awareness, Taylor strives to get everyone's input. She cultivates a nonjudgmental environment in which committee members feel free to express their ideas. She makes sure the committee considers every opinion, even ideas that may conflict with her own views. When it's time for the committee to make a decision, she counts everyone's vote equally, and she supports the will of the majority even if it doesn't reflect her own preferences. As a leader with a democratic style, Taylor sees herself as a facilitator for the group's mission.

• autocratic style
A leadership style in which leaders see themselves as having both the authority and the responsibility to take action on a group's behalf.

Some Leaders Are Autocratic As the organizer of his calculus study group, Adya believes it's his responsibility to make decisions on behalf of his group. He sets the schedule for group meetings and decides where each one will be held. Whenever the group gets together, Adya takes charge and controls how the study session proceeds. Adya is enacting an **autocratic style** of leadership.[34] That is, he sees himself as having both the authority and the responsibility to take action on his group's behalf. When decisions need to be made, he makes them, usually without asking others in the group what they want. When tasks need to be done, he assigns them to individuals in the group instead of soliciting volunteers. Unlike Taylor, Adya considers himself to be the most important member of his group.

Some Leaders Are Laissez-Faire Meghan has just been promoted to lieutenant in charge of eight patrol officers in her police precinct. Her philosophy is that patrol officers should work independently, with little direction or personal involvement from her. She rarely interacts with her officers, and she gives them little feedback on their job performance. When she is forced to oversee decisions or mediate conflicts, she involves herself only as long as is necessary. Afterward, she resumes her general lack of engagement in the operations of her division. All these characteristics reflect Meghan's **laissez-faire style** of leadership.[35] It's not that she doesn't care about her patrol officers; she simply thinks they function at their best with minimal supervision. Thus, unlike Taylor and Adya, Meghan often sees herself as the person who is least important to the success of her group.

• **laissez-faire style** A leadership style in which leaders offer minimal supervision.

Each Leadership Style Has Its Strengths Which type of leader—democratic, autocratic, or laissez-faire—would you prefer? If you were raised in a country with a democratic style of government, such as the United States, you might be inclined to say democratic leaders are best because they value everyone's input equally. You might also like laissez-faire leaders because they allow you to work autonomously. If you value equality and autonomy, you might say that autocratic leaders are least preferable because they give you neither equality nor autonomy.

Preferences aside, each style of leadership is best under certain circumstances. When it's important that everyone in a group believes that he or she has an equal voice in decision making, the democratic style of leadership is the most likely to accomplish that goal.[36] Even if everyone doesn't agree with the group's decision, the democratic style helps ensure that no one feels neglected or unimportant.

If the group's priority is to accomplish its tasks quickly, however, the autocratic style is best because only one person needs to make the decisions. The autocratic style is also the most effective when the leader has knowledge or expertise that the group members at large lack. If a senior physician is leading a group of interns in a complicated surgery, for instance, it's best for everyone if the physician takes charge and gives orders rather than taking a vote about how to proceed with the surgery because the surgeon's experience confers knowledge the interns don't yet have.

In groups composed of people who are proficient at working on their own, the laissez-faire style can be best because it provides group members with the greatest autonomy to do their work. Although most leaders need to provide some level of oversight, a laissez-faire leader lets his or her group members work independently, giving direction only when absolutely necessary. That approach backfires when group members lack the skills or training to work autonomously, but it can be very effective when group members are proficient at working on their own.

> **SHARPEN Your Skills:** *Leadership styles*
>
> In a small group, discuss and identify the primary leadership styles of several leaders with whom you're familiar, such as the U.S. president, the governor of your state, the mayor of your city, the president of your college, and your student body president. Identify the behaviors and characteristics that lead you to make each assessment. Afterward, compare your assessments with those of other groups in your class.

Exercising Power

Regardless of which styles of leadership they enact, leaders rely on the exercise of power to achieve their goals. **Power** is the ability to influence or control people or events.[37] Being an effective leader requires having some form of power.

• **power** The ability to influence or control people or events.

Leaders can exercise many different forms of power over others.

savas keskiner/Getty Images

People exercise influence or control over others in many ways. In this section, we explore the various forms of power that leaders can possess. We will observe that power resides not in leaders themselves but in their relationships with the people they lead.

LEADERS EXERCISE MANY FORMS OF POWER

Exercising power over people may seem relatively straightforward: a leader tells people what to do and they do it. The important question, however, is *why* they do it. Some people might follow instructions because they are being paid to do so. Others might follow along because they want to please the leader or because they fear the consequences of disobeying.

In their now classic studies, social psychologists John French and Bertram Raven determined that the reason *why* a leader is followed constitutes the form of power that leader has. French and Raven proposed that power comes in six specific forms: reward, coercive, referent, legitimate, expert, and informational.[38] As we take a close look at these forms, keep in mind that they aren't mutually exclusive. Rather, one person may exercise multiple forms of power in different situations or even within the same situation.

• **reward power** A form of power based on the leader's ability to reward another for doing what the leader says.

Leaders Exercise Reward Power As its name implies, **reward power** operates when a leader has the ability to reward another for doing what the leader says. The supervisor of your work team has power over you, for instance, because she pays you and can promote you for following her instructions. In this case, your pay and the possibility of advancement are the rewards. If your supervisor loses the ability to pay or promote you (say, if your company goes bankrupt or she leaves her job), she also loses her power over you.

Having reward power requires you not only to provide a reward to those who follow your instructions but to provide a *sufficient* reward. People who feel they are not rewarded adequately for following someone are likely to eventually stop. When employees perceive that they are not receiving fair wages in exchange for their work, for instance, their willingness to follow the company leadership decreases.[39]

• **coercive power** A form of power that comes from the ability to punish.

Leaders Exercise Coercive Power The opposite of reward power is **coercive power**, or power that comes from the ability to punish. When you go to court, for example, the judge has power over you because he or she can punish you with fines or imprisonment for not doing what you must. Throughout history, dictators have exercised coercive power over their populations by ordering imprisonment or even death for those who don't follow their orders.

Just as reward power requires the ability to provide a *sufficient* reward, coercive power requires the ability to issue a *sufficient* punishment. For instance, most of us would follow the directions of a university administrator who had the power to expel us. If the worst punishment that administrator could dole out were a memo of reprimand that would get buried in some file drawer, however, we might feel less obligated to follow his or her directions.

Although exercising coercive power can be an effective way of achieving our goals, it entails certain disadvantages. One study, for example, found that the more often a manufacturing company exercised coercive power over its dealers, the fewer other forms of power the dealers perceived it to have.[40] So the company's ability to control its dealers through those other forms was diminished. As "The Dark Side of Communication" explains, excessive use of coercive power can also constitute emotional abuse.

Leaders Exercise Referent Power French and Raven used the term **referent power** to refer to the power of attraction, the idea being that we tend to comply with requests made by people we like, admire, or find attractive in some way. It's human nature to desire their approval. In contrast, gaining the approval of people we don't like or admire is usually not a high priority. In a volunteer group, for instance, you might work harder for a group leader you like than for one you dislike.

From an early age, many of us try to be like the people we admire. This grants those people a form of power called referent power.
Stephanie Bajak Photography/Moment/Getty Images

In a similar vein, many of us are persuaded to buy products or services endorsed by celebrities we like or find attractive.[42] Because we usually don't know the celebrities personally, we aren't trying to gain their approval when we follow their recommendations. Instead, we are trying to *be* like them. Researchers have shown that we have a strong tendency to try to identify with people we find attractive.[43] Therefore, when a handsome singer or a glamorous actress endorses a particular brand of shampoo, protein bar, or cable TV service, we are often persuaded to buy those brands by our desire to be like that individual.

Leaders Exercise Legitimate Power People exercise **legitimate power** when their status or position gives them the right to make requests with which others must comply. When the president of the United States meets with the cabinet, for instance, members of that group follow the president's directives because the president is in a position of legitimate authority.

Because legitimate power is granted by people's status or position, it is no longer effective when they lose their status or leave their position. Suppose you have been promoted to interim department head at your company to fill in for someone who is on maternity leave. During the time you fill that position, you have legitimate power

- **referent power** A form of power that derives from attraction to the leader.

- **legitimate power** A form of power in which leaders' status or position gives them the right to make requests with which others must comply.

OJO Images Ltd/Alamy Stock Photo

• **expert power** A form of power that stems from having expertise in a particular area.

• **informational power** A form of power that stems from the ability to control access to information.

to issue instructions, make purchasing decisions, conduct employee evaluations, and hire and fire at your discretion. Each of those abilities is a legitimate exercise of the position you hold. When the permanent department head returns from maternity leave, however, you will return to your previous position. At that point, you will no longer have the powers you exercised as the interim department head because you will no longer have legitimate claim to them.

Leaders Exercise Expert Power The fifth form of power on French and Raven's list is **expert power**, power that stems from having expertise in a particular area. In a chamber orchestra, for instance, the musicians follow the instructions of the conductor because he or she has the musical expertise to make the orchestra sound as good as possible. In many cases, we perceive that it is in our best interests to comply with the directions of experts, because their experience or training gives them specialized knowledge we lack.

It can be tricky to identify exactly what constitutes expertise. For the most part, we recognize expertise through agreement. That is, a person is an expert if the right people consider him or her to be so. For instance, a physician is considered a medical expert because he or she graduated from medical school, completed a residency, and was certified to practice medicine by other medical professionals. That individual's doctoral degree and medical license indicate a consensus about his or her qualifications as an expert. Other people may have the same level of medical knowledge as the doctor but may not exercise expert power because their expertise is not formally recognized. Later in this section, we will further discuss the importance of recognizing power.

Leaders Exercise Informational Power A final form of power is **informational power**, power that stems from the ability to control access to information. Many socialist and communist governments exercise informational power over their populations, for example, by controlling all the media in their countries. Citizens in those societies are exposed only to news their governments want them to know, and thus they become dependent on their government leaders for information.

A similar situation can occur in smaller groups if one person has news or information that others want. This person has power over the others until he or she releases the information. Informational power is usually greatest when the information is valuable and cannot be obtained elsewhere.

Table 1 summarizes the six forms of power leaders can exercise.

POWER RESIDES IN RELATIONSHIPS, NOT IN PEOPLE

As we saw in the last section, people wield many forms of power in many different situations. Because some people seem to have more power than others, we might think of them as being *powerful people*, as though their power resides within

TABLE 1 FORMS OF POWER	According to French and Raven, leaders exercise six forms of power in their relationships with others.
	1 Reward Power based on the ability to reward for compliance
	2 Coercive Power based on the ability to punish for noncompliance
	3 Referent Power based on liking, admiring, and being attracted to the leader
	4 Legitimate Power based on rightfully granted status or position
	5 Expert Power based on knowledge, training, experience, and/or expertise
	6 Informational Power based on access to valued information

them. In truth, however, power doesn't exist within people—it exists within relationships. As we'll see in this section, we have power only over particular people and only when our power is recognized. In other words, power is an inherently social experience.

Power Is Relative One characteristic of power is that it is *relative*, meaning that people have power only *in relation to* other people. No person has absolute power. Regardless of what forms of power we possess, each of us exercises power only over particular people in particular situations. Your manager may have some power over you, but that doesn't mean she also has power over your friends and neighbors. She is powerful only relative to the people who work for her.

We often acknowledge the relative nature of power when people overstep their boundaries by attempting to exert power they don't have, as when a child rejects direction from an older sibling with the response "You're not the boss of me!" Similarly, adults may feel defensive when they receive direction from people who have no reward, coercive, referent, legitimate, expert, or informational power over them.[44]

Power Requires Recognition In groups and organizations, powerful people have only the power their followers recognize in them. A charismatic religious leader may exercise referent power over her followers, but she does not have that power over others who don't share her followers' desire to please her and gain her approval.

Recognizing that someone has power does not necessarily mean we give our consent to be governed. If a police officer stops you while you're driving, for instance, you would likely recognize the power he has over you even if you don't want to be subject to that power. In other words, we don't always enjoy having others tell us what to do, even though we may still recognize their right to do so. We can therefore say that a person can have power over others only if others recognize that power.

We've seen that leaders can exercise many different forms of power, that all power is relative, and that power requires recognition. To end this section, let's also acknowledge that power itself is neither positive nor negative. Rather, it's the way we *use* power that makes it good or bad. When we abuse the power we have over others or exercise it unwisely, we can cause harm and heartache; in such instances, we may not hold on to power for long. As former U.S. senator Elizabeth Dole observed, however: "Power is a positive force if it is used for positive purposes."[45] Using power in a positive way can improve the lives of those who follow us.

> **SHARPEN Your Skills:** *Applying referent power*
>
> Suppose you are the most senior staff member at the restaurant where you wait tables. You need to schedule extra wait staff to work over a holiday weekend, when many employees had already asked for time off. With another student, brainstorm ways you could use referent power to influence wait staff to sign up for holiday weekend shifts. Offer your ideas in a journal entry or short presentation to your class.

Leadership and Decision-Making Skills

Effective leadership and decision making are not always easy to achieve or sustain. Many factors can inhibit the ability of leaders and groups to function at their best. The more we understand about leadership and decision-making skills, the better equipped we are to contribute positively to the groups to which we belong. As we'll see in this section, three particular skills that are useful for groups and their leaders are their ability to

- Manage conflict constructively.
- Avoid groupthink.
- Listen carefully.

FIGURE 1

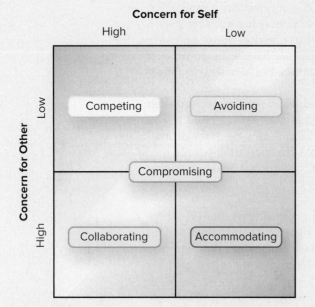

Our options for dealing with conflict rest on two underlying factors: concern for *our own* needs and desires, and concern for *the other party's* needs and desires. These factors give rise to five main strategies for engaging in conflict: competing, avoiding, accommodating, compromising, and collaborating.

Adapted from Blake, R. R., & Mouton, J. S. (1984). The Managerial Grid III (3rd ed.). Houston, TX: Gulf.

• competing style A style for managing conflict that represents a high concern for the self but a low concern for the other party.

• avoiding style A style for managing conflict that represents a low concern for both the self and the other party.

• accommodating style A style for managing conflict that represents a high concern for the other party but a low concern for the self.

MANAGE CONFLICT CONSTRUCTIVELY

Because the members of a group are interdependent, they are bound to experience conflict from time to time. Recall that conflict occurs when two or more interdependent parties enact a struggle over goals they perceive to be incompatible. Especially when groups are faced with making decisions, conflict can arise because of perceived differences in the goals of individual members. Conflict is not necessarily problematic. In fact, it can motivate groups to make more creative decisions than they otherwise might. What matters is the way groups manage conflict when it arises.

According to researchers Robert Blake and Jane Mouton, our options for dealing with conflict are based on two underlying dimensions: our concern for our own needs and desires, and our concern for the other party's needs and desires.[46] When plotted on a graph (Figure 1), these dimensions give rise to five major strategies for engaging in conflict: competing, avoiding, accommodating, compromising, and collaborating. These strategies are behaviors rather than personality types, so we can learn to use any of them. Some may seem more appropriate or more desirable than others. As we examine them, however, consider that each may be best under certain circumstances.

Competing The **competing style** represents a high concern for our own needs and desires and a low concern for those of the other party. The goal is to win the conflict while the other party loses. Engaging in conflict in this style is much like playing football. There are no tied games—rather, one team's win is the other team's loss.

Competing might be appropriate when there is a concrete outcome that cannot be shared, such as when two people are vying for the same job. People may also see ongoing competition as a positive aspect of their relationship if it motivates each to perform at his or her best.[47] The competing style of managing conflict becomes problematic, however, when it leads to resentment or a desire to get even with people who win.[48]

Avoiding A very different approach to conflict is the **avoiding style**, which demonstrates low concern for both the self and the other party. Adopting this style means ignoring the conflict and hoping it will go away on its own. Some people choose avoidance because they are uncomfortable engaging in conflict. Others choose it because they don't care enough about the outcome of the conflict to bother. Avoiding conflict isn't always the wrong choice; many people in groups opt to ignore or avoid certain points of contention among themselves to maintain harmony.[49] When avoidance becomes a group's primary way of managing conflict, however, it often leaves important matters unresolved. In this situation, the result can be dissatisfying relationships within the group.[50]

Accommodating The **accommodating style** is the opposite of competing and reflects a high concern for the other party but a low concern for the self. The goal of accommodating is to sacrifice so the other party wins. People in a group sometimes accommodate to keep the peace, which may work well in the short term. In the long run, however, continually accommodating the other party can lead to resentment.

Cultural ideas play an important role in the use of accommodation. In collectivistic societies, accommodating in response to conflict is often expected and is viewed as respectful or noble.[51] In contrast, in individualistic societies, people may be seen as weak or spineless if they consistently accommodate others.

Compromising The **compromising style** reflects a moderate concern for everyone's needs and desires. In this strategy, both parties in the conflict give up something in order to gain something. No one gets exactly what he or she wants, but everyone leaves the conflict having gained something valuable.

Let's say you're negotiating a job offer with a new work group, and you want a higher salary than the group leader wants to pay. Through your negotiation, you agree to accept a lower salary than you originally wanted, and the group leader agrees to give you an extra week of vacation in return. Neither of you got exactly what you wanted, but you each got something you valued in return for giving up something else. Compromising takes time and patience, but it often leads to more satisfying outcomes than do competing, avoiding, or accommodating.

Collaborating The **collaborating style** represents a high concern for the needs of both sides in a conflict. The goal is to arrive at a win–win situation that maximizes both parties' gains.

After they unexpectedly had a third child, for example, Mick and Laura felt the strain of paying for day care while Mick worked and Laura went to school. Their other children, Tara and Tana, were excited about having a younger sibling but upset about the reduced attention they would get. Soon, the tensions gave rise to conflict within the family. After collaborating on a solution, the family decided that Mick would cut his work hours and Laura would enroll in online courses so that at least one of them would be home every day. The money they saved in day care expenses more than made up for Mick's reduced income. Moreover, both Laura and Mick felt better because they were able to care for their new child themselves, and Tara and Tana got to spend more time with their parents than they had before.

• **compromising style**
A style for managing conflict that represents a moderate concern for everyone's needs and desires.

• **collaborating style**
A style for managing conflict that represents a high concern for the self and for the other.

SHARPEN Your Skills: *Conflict resolution*

With two or three other people, generate a topic of conflict and then role-play resolving it using each of Blake and Mouton's conflict styles. Afterward, discuss which style or styles seemed most appropriate for the conflict you were having, and consider how other styles might have been more appropriate for a different type of conflict.

Work at It: Groups Can Resolve Any Conflict if They Try Hard Enough

The fact that there are many ways to manage conflict in groups might suggest that if you have the right skills and try hard enough, your group can eventually resolve any conflict it might encounter. That outcome would be great, but the truth is that some conflicts are simply irresolvable.

Let's say you're part of a jury hearing a lawsuit brought against a pharmaceutical company. The plaintiff has alleged the company was negligent when it failed to warn consumers that its prescription pain relievers should not be given to animals. During your deliberations, you discover that some jurors steadfastly believe the company is negligent. Others believe just as strongly that reasonable people should know not to give animals medications prescribed for humans. The longer your deliberations go, the more entrenched jurors become in their opposing viewpoints. As a result, you report to the judge that the jury is hopelessly deadlocked, and the case is dismissed.

This scenario illustrates that when people hold diametrically opposed opinions they are unwilling or unable to change, they are unlikely to resolve their conflicts no matter how hard they try. In such cases, the only real option is to avoid the conflict, agree to disagree, or try to minimize the effects of the conflict on other aspects of the group's relationship.

ASK YOURSELF

- What conflicts have you experienced that seemed impossible to resolve?
- When should a group give up trying to resolve a conflict? When should a group continue trying to resolve a conflict, even if it seems irresolvable?

In many situations, collaborating is the best way for groups to handle conflict. Yet collaborating can require a great deal of energy, patience, and imagination. Even when it is the ideal approach to managing conflict, it can therefore also be the most time-consuming and laborious solution.

Managing conflict appropriately can be very beneficial for groups, but can *every* conflict be resolved? Take a look at the "Fact or Fiction?" box to find out.

AVOID GROUPTHINK

Let's suppose you're part of a group of engineers designing a new toy for children. The toy is colorful and fun to play with, and the manufacturer is pressuring your group to approve the toy's design so it can go into production in time for the holiday shopping season. Although you like the toy, you are concerned that the paint on its exterior could be unsafe for children. When the group meets to consider approving the design, however, you feel pressured to keep your concerns to yourself. You sense that some other engineers are also concerned about safety, but most don't speak up. When someone asks whether the paint is safe for children, the group leader says, "Yes, it's safe; now let's move on." Soon, you hear people say it's important that the group approve the toy's design unanimously so the company will have confidence in the product. Although you have serious doubts about the toy's safety, you feel pressured to ignore your misgivings—and, along with everyone else in the group, you vote to approve the design.

That example illustrates the problem of **groupthink**, which occurs when group members seek unanimous agreement despite their individual doubts.[52] According to psychologist Irving Janis, a pioneer of groupthink research, there are eight major warning signs that a group has fallen victim to groupthink:[53]

- *Illusion of invulnerability.* Group members are overly confident in their position, ignoring obvious problems.

- *Collective rationalization.* Members "explain away" any ideas that are contrary to the group's position.

- *Illusion of morality.* Members believe the decisions they make are morally correct, ignoring any arguments to the contrary.

- *Excessive stereotyping.* Members construct negative stereotypes of anyone who disagrees with them.

- *Pressure for conformity.* Members feel pressure to conform to the group's decision and are branded as disloyal if they do not.

- *Self-censorship.* Members don't speak up if they have dissenting viewpoints.

- *Illusion of unanimity.* Members falsely perceive that everyone agrees with the group's decision, because they don't hear anyone offering counterarguments.

- *Mindguards.* Some members actively prevent the group from hearing about arguments or evidence against the group's position.

Groupthink is particularly likely to occur when a group has a strong, authoritarian leader, is composed of members with similar backgrounds, and is isolated from outside influence.[54] Under those conditions, groups can produce decisions that appear both unanimous and well informed but are actually neither. Indeed, decisions produced by groupthink tend to be problematic because they have not been subjected to critical thought. In fact, group members are nearly 200 percent more likely to voice disagreement if groupthink is not occurring than if it is.[55] Groupthink discourages all attempts to consider a decision critically, because critical analysis might prevent members from reaching consensus.

Decisions reached by groupthink can have disastrous effects, such as exposing thousands of children to potentially unsafe paint on a new toy. In fact, groupthink has been identified as a contributing factor in several national disasters, including the

Groupthink may have played a role in the 2008 collapse of the U.S. banking system.

Henrik5000/iStock/Getty Images

1941 attack on Pearl Harbor, the 1972 Watergate scandal, the 1986 explosion of the space shuttle *Challenger*, and the 2008 collapse of the banking industry.[56] What is most troubling about those examples is that some of them might have been avoided if the groups in charge had thought critically about their decisions instead of falling victim to groupthink.

Avoiding groupthink is therefore an important aspect of communicating competently in groups.[57] Group members can take several specific steps to prevent groupthink from occurring:

- *Be aware of the potential for groupthink.* Teach others in the group about what groupthink is, why it is so problematic, and what its warning signs are. If you detect any of the warning signs, speak up and remind others how important it is to avoid groupthink.

- *Make sure the group has sufficient time to make decisions.* Groupthink can occur when members feel pressured to arrive at a decision quickly. If your group is making an important decision, remind members to allow sufficient time for discussion. If the process feels rushed, say "It might be better to put off making this decision until we have more time."

- *Encourage dissenting viewpoints.* When it appears that most members have the same position on an issue, ask, "What are some alternate ideas?" Encourage members to play devil's advocate by questioning the merits of one another's positions. Remind the group to examine each idea critically and not accept any idea at face value.

- *Seek input from outside the group.* Suggest that group members consult with people outside the group who might offer useful input on the group's decision. Look up relevant research and bring it to the group's attention.

- *Give important decisions a second chance.* Even after the group has made its decision, recommend that members meet once more to reconsider it. Encourage members to express any doubts or second thoughts they have about the decision. Listen to all arguments, whether they are for the decision or against it. Then ask the group to vote on its decision again.

It might seem that these recommendations will discourage a group from reaching any decision at all. Their purpose, however, is to help the group to make a *good* decision by avoiding the problems of groupthink.

LISTEN CAREFULLY

When we interact with others, our ability to communicate effectively relies heavily on how well we listen. That observation is especially true when we interact within groups, a setting where multiple ideas or positions are often discussed at the same time. One way to become a better group communicator is to build listening competence. Particularly useful strategies are knowing how to recognize barriers to effective listening and practicing listening skills.

Recognize Barriers to Effective Listening in Groups A starting point for honing your listening skills is to acknowledge factors that might be inhibiting your ability to listen attentively. Barriers to effective listening that are common in many groups include these:

- *Noise.* Noise is anything in the physical environment (such as sound) or in your individual experience (such as hunger) that distracts you from listening effectively. Try to identify what is causing the noise and do what you can to reduce its effect.

- *Boredom.* When you're bored, effective listening becomes difficult because your mind wanders. If you find that boredom is preventing you from listening effectively, suggest to the group that members take a break and come back to the

Boredom makes it diffi-
cult to listen effectively.
Royalty-Free/Corbis

discussion later. If a break isn't possible, try to identify some aspect of what's being said that you find interesting, and focus on that. Doing so may help you overcome your boredom and allow you to listen more actively.

• *Information overload.* Many of us have difficulty listening effectively when we feel we're being bombarded with information. If a member of your group is overloading you with information, politely suggest that he or she identify the most critical pieces of information and focus specifically on those.

• *Rebuttal tendency.* We saw in the listening that the rebuttal tendency is the propensity to debate a speaker's point and formulate your reply while the person is still speaking. The rebuttal impulse can be a particularly common barrier to effective listening in groups that evaluate or analyze—such as juries, focus groups, and advisory boards—because members of such groups may disagree on the merits of the various ideas they're discussing. If you notice the rebuttal tendency in yourself, remember to listen to everything a speaker says *before* you formulate your response.

Practice Listening Listening is a skill, not an innate ability. Thus, you can hone your ability to listen through practice. Perhaps you're unsure about how you can *practice* listening. If so, remember that people listen with various goals in mind. As we considered in the listening chapter, people sometimes engage in informational listening, which is listening to learn. At other times, they engage in critical listening, which is listening to evaluate and analyze what they hear. Individuals also engage in empathic listening, when the goal is to experience what another person is thinking or feeling. These goals are quite different from one another. You can therefore practice your listening skills by paying attention to the specific listening goals that are most useful to you in a given situation.

Informational listening skills are particularly important when you need to understand and retain what you're hearing, such as when you take part in a study group. To ensure you have understood what you've heard, try paraphrasing the speaker's message. Paraphrasing is restating the speaker's message in your own words to clarify its meaning. If you paraphrase a statement in a way that accurately reflects its meaning, the speaker will usually reply by confirming your understanding. If you paraphrase in

Difficult Conversations

Managing High-Stakes Decisions

Imagine this: You have been selected to listen to a criminal trial in your home town as a member of the jury. The defendant in the case is a young woman who was accused of child abuse when her six-year-old son arrived at school with bruises on his back and legs. You feel terrible about the child's injuries, yet you are not entirely convinced that the mother was at fault.

Now, consider this: When the jury begins its deliberations, you discover that jurors are sharply divided on the question of guilt. Some are convinced that the mother abused her son, whereas others are convinced she is innocent. Productive discussion is difficult because jurors on both sides are adamant in their positions, but you are undecided and want to hear what each person has to say. How can the other jurors and you listen respectfully to everyone's arguments, even those with which you disagree? Consider recommending the following strategies:

JGI/Blend Images LCC

- Before continuing deliberations, ask each juror to state his or her position and the primary reason for that position. Alternate between jurors convinced of the defendant's guilt, those convinced of her innocence, and those who are undecided.

- As jurors begin their speaking turns, ask each one to start by paraphrasing the previous speaker's argument, before stating his or her own position. Being required to paraphrase others' comments will encourage jurors to listen more carefully to one another and avoid letting their minds wander.

- During this exercise, and throughout your deliberations, enforce a ban on interruptions. Even if they strongly disagree with what someone else is saying, encourage all jurors to respect one another by listening without interrupting.

Making high-stakes decisions—such as evaluating someone's guilt or innocence—is substantially more difficult when group members don't listen respectfully to one another. Encouraging jurors to listen fairly to everyone's positions, to paraphrase other people's ideas, and not to interrupt won't guarantee that the group will come to a unanimous decision, but these actions can help all members feel that their voices were heard in the process.

a way that changes the meaning of a statement, however, the speaker will generally correct your misunderstanding. Paraphrasing can therefore help you to understand a speaker's message more accurately.

Critical listening skills are especially important in groups that have to make important decisions, such as a state legislature and a corporate board of directors. To improve your critical listening skills, remind yourself not to accept what you hear at face value. Instead, question what you hear. Start by considering the credibility of the speakers. Are they experts on the topic about which they're speaking? Are they biased toward one point of view? If you find the speakers to be credible, ask yourself whether their statements have merit. Are their assertions logical and well thought out, or do they seem inconsistent? Do the speakers make claims that are improbable? Keep in mind, too, that it's relatively easy to listen critically when you are hearing ideas or claims you don't like, because you may already be inclined to discredit such information. It's when you *approve* of the speakers or their message that it is most important to listen critically. Doing so will help to ensure you accept ideas on their merits rather than at face value.

Finally, empathic listening skills are most important in groups that provide comfort, such as support groups. In such groups, people often listen to understand how others are thinking or feeling. If that's your goal, practice listening without interrupting. As you probably know from your own experience, being interrupted while you're speaking is frustrating. Particularly when people are sharing personal or sensitive information—as they often do in a support group—they appreciate being able to speak without interruption. Also, practice listening without offering advice. Unless they specifically ask for your advice, many people would prefer that you simply listen to what they have to say.

Effective listening is challenging when group members disagree, especially about critical decisions. Check out the "Difficult Conversations" box for advice on encouraging respectful listening during group deliberations.

The effectiveness of communication in many groups depends on members' ability to listen to one another. By acknowledging the barriers to effective listening and practicing the listening skills appropriate to the situation, you can improve your own ability to communicate effectively in groups.

For REVIEW

- ### How do groups generate ideas and make decisions?

  Groups can use brainstorming, nominal group technique, and ideawriting to generate ideas, and they can make decisions by unanimous consensus, majority rule, minority rule, expert opinion, and authority rule. The preferred decision-making technique depends on the nature of the decision and on the cultural context of the group.

- ### How do leaders enact leadership and exercise power?

  Leaders can enact democratic, autocratic, or laissez-faire leadership styles, each of which has its strengths. Leaders exercise several forms of power—including reward, coercive, referent, legitimate, expert, and informational power—over the people they lead.

- ### What communication skills improve group decision making?

  Group members should learn to manage conflict appropriately, avoid groupthink, and listen carefully to contribute positively to group decision making.

KEY TERMS

brainstorming 283

nominal group technique (NGT) 283

ideawriting 284

unanimous consensus 285

stalemate 285

false consensus 285

majority rule 285

minority rule 286

expert opinion 286

authority rule 286

traits 289

physical traits 290

psychosocial traits 290

extroversion 291

introversion 291

communication apprehension 291

democratic style 291

autocratic style 292

laissez-faire style 293

power 293

reward power 294

coercive power 294

referent power 295

legitimate power 295

expert power 296

informational power 296

competing style 298

avoiding style 298

accommodating style 298

compromising style 299

collaborating style 299

groupthink 301

NOTES

1. Ben, C. (2017, May 1). Community health survey kick-starts rural mental health treatment options. *Naco.org.* https://www.naco.org/articles/community-health-survey-kick-starts-rural-mental-health-treatment-options

2. Al-Samarraie, H., & Hurmuzan, S. (2018). A review of brainstorming techniques in higher education. *Thinking Skills and Creativity, 27,* 78–91. https://doi.org/10.1016/j.tsc.2017.12.002

3. See Yagolkovskiy, S. R. (2016). Stimulation of individual creativity in electronic brainstorming: Cognitive and social aspects. *Social Behavior and Personality, 44*(5), 761–766. https://doi.org/10.2224/sbp.2016.44.5.761

4. Gautschi, T. F. (1990). How to improve group decisions. *Design News, 47*(17), 188.

5. For an applied example, see Hanson, C. S., Chapman, J. R., Gill, J. S., Kanellis, J., Wong, G., Craig, J. C., Teixeira-Pinto, A., Chadban, S. J., Garg, A. X., Ralph, A. F., Pinter, J., Lewis, J. R., & Tong, A. (2018). Identifying outcomes that are important to living kidney donors: A nominal group technique study. *Clinical Journal of the American Society of Nephrology, 13*(6), 916–926. https://doi.org/10.2215/CJN.13441217

6. Peña, A., Estrada, C. A., Soniat, D., Taylor, B., & Burton, M. (2012). Nominal group technique: A brainstorming tool for identifying areas to improve pain management in hospitalized patients. *Journal of Hospital Medicine, 7*(5), 416–420. https://doi.org/10.1002/jhm.1900

7. McMillan, S. S., King, M., & Tully, M. P. (2016). How to use the nominal group and Delphi techniques. *International Journal of Clinical Pharmacy, 38*(3), 655–662. https://doi.org/10.1007/s11096-016-0257-x

8. Watkins, P. J. (2005). Idea writing: Generating solutions for effective change. *Planning and Changing, 36*(1-2), 40–46.

9. Saaty, T. L., & Peniwati, K. (2013). *Group decision making: Drawing out and reconciling differences.* RWS Publications. https://doi.org/10.13033.ijahp.v9i3.533

10. See Adler, R. B., Maresh-Fuehrer, M., Elmhorst, J., & Lucas, K. (2019). *Communicating at work: Principles and practices for business and the professions* (12th ed.). McGraw-Hill.

11. Rudman, L. A., Moss-Racusin, C. A., Phelan, J. E., & Nauts, S. (2012). Status incongruity and backlash effects: Defending the gender hierarchy motivates prejudice against female leaders. *Journal of Experimental Social Psychology, 48*(1), 165–179. https://doi.org/10.1016/j.jesp.2011.10.008

12. Williams, M. J., & Tiedens, L. Z. (2016). The subtle suspension of backlash: A meta-analysis of penalties for women's implicit and explicit dominance behavior. *Psychological Bulletin, 142*(2), 165–197. https://doi.org/10.1037/bul0000039

13. See Rudman, L. A., & Phelan, J. E. (2008). Backlash effects for disconfirming gender stereotypes in organizations. *Research in Organizational Behavior, 28,* 61–79. https://doi.org/10.1016/j.riob.2008.04.003

14. See Roth, P. L., Purvis, K. L., & Bobko, P. (2012). A meta-analysis of gender group differences for measures of job performance in field studies. *Journal of Management, 38*(2), 719–739. https://doi.org/10.1177/0149206310374774

15. Koch, S. C. (2005). Evaluative affect display toward male and female leaders of task-oriented groups. *Small Group Research, 36*(6), 678–703. https://doi.org/10.1177/1046496405281786

16. Cohen, A.(2009). *The tall book.* Bloomsbury.

17. Stulp, G., Buunk, A. P., Verhulst, S., & Pollet, T. V. (2015). Human height is positively related to interpersonal dominance in dyadic interactions. *PLoS One, 10*(2), e0117860. https://doi.org/10.1371/journal.pone.0117860

18. Blaker, N. M., Rompa, I., Dessing, I. H., Vriend, A. F., Herschberg, C., & Van Vugt, M. (2013). The height leadership advantage in men and women: Testing evolutionary psychology predictions about the perceptions of tall leaders. *Group Processes & Intergroup Relations, 16*(1), 17–27. https://doi.org/10.1177/1368430212437211

19. Stulp, G., Buunk, A. P., Verhulst, S., & Pollet, T. V. (2013). Tall claims? Sense and nonsense about the importance of height of US presidents. *The Leadership Quarterly, 24*(1), 159–171. https://doi.org/10.1016/j.leaqua.2012.09.002

20. Blaker et al., 2013.

21. Oh, D., Buck, E. A., & Todorov, A. (2019). Revealing hidden gender biases in competence impressions of faces. *Psychological Science, 30*(1), 65–79. https://doi.org/10.1177/0956797618813092

22. Sczesny, S., & Kühnen, U. (2004). Meta-cognition about biological sex and gender stereotypic physical appearance: Consequences for the assessment of leadership competence. *Personality and Social Psychology Bulletin, 30*(1), 13–21. https://doi.org/10.1177/0146167203258831

23. Re, D. E., & Perrett, D. I. (2014). The effects of facial adiposity on attractiveness and perceived leadership ability. *Quarterly Journal of Experimental Psychology, 67*(4), 676–686. https://doi.org/10.1080/17470218.2013.825635; Cherulnik, P. D., Turns, L. C., & Wilderman, S. K. (2006). Physical appearance and leadership: Exploring the role of appearance-based attribution in leader emergence. *Journal of Applied Social Psychology, 20*(18), 1530–1539. https://doi.org/10.1111/j.1559-1816.1990.tb01491.x

24. Paglis, L. L., & Green, S. G. (2002). Leadership self-efficacy and managers' motivation for leading change. *Journal of Organizational Behavior, 23*(2), 215–235. https://doi.org/10.1002/job.137

25. Chemers, M. M., Watson, C. B., & May, S. T. (2000). Dispositional affect and leadership effectiveness: A comparison of self-esteem, optimism, and efficacy. *Personality and Social Psychology Bulletin, 26*(3), 267–277. https://doi.org/10.1177/0146167200265001

26. See, e.g., Wilmot, M. P. (2011). *Self-monitoring personality at work revisited: A comparative meta-analysis.* Unpublished masters thesis, University of Nebraska-Lincoln.

27. Ellis, R. J. (1988). Self-monitoring and leadership emergence in groups. *Personality and Social Psychology Bulletin, 14*(4), 681–693. https://doi.org/10.1177/0146167288144004

28. Judge, T. A., Bono, J. E., Ilies, R., & Gerhardt, M. W. (2002). Personality and leadership: A qualitative and quantitative review. *Journal of Applied Psychology, 87*(4), 765–780. https://doi.org/10.1037/0021-9010.87.4.765; see also Zopiatis, A., & Constanti, P. (2012). Extraversion, openness and conscientiousness: The route to transformational leadership in the hotel industry. *Leadership & Organizational Development Journal, 33*(1), 86–104. https://doi.org/10.1108/01437731211193133

29. Hawkins, K., & Stewart, R. A. (1991). Effects of communication apprehension on perceptions of leadership and intragroup attraction in small task-oriented groups. *Southern Communication Journal, 57*(1), 1–10. https://doi.org/10.1080/10417949109372846; but see Farrell, M. (2017). Leadership reflections: Extrovert and introvert leaders. *Journal of Library Administration, 57*(4), 436–443. https://doi.org/10.1080/01930826.2017.1300455

30. Vien, C. L. (2016). Leadership tips for introverts: Introverts' reflective, relationship-centered approach to leadership can be as effective as the more outgoing style favored by extroverts. *Journal of Accountancy, 221*(4), 46.

31. Khalil, R. (2016). Influence of extroversion and introversion on decision making ability. *International Journal of Research in Medical Sciences, 4*(5), 1534–1538. https://doi.org/10.18203/2320-6012.ijrms20161224

32. Farrell, M. (2017). Leadership reflections: Extrovert and introvert leaders. *Journal of Library Administration, 57*(4), 436–443. https://doi.org/10.1080/01930826.2017.1300455

33. Khan, M. S., Khan, I., Qureshi, Q. A., Ismail, H. M., Rauf, H., Latif, A., & Tahir, M. (2015). The styles of leadership: A critical review. *Public Policy and Administration Research, 5*(3), 87–92.

34. De Hoogh, A. H., Greer, L. L., & Den Hartog, D. N. (2015). Diabolical dictators or capable commanders? An investigation of the differential effects of autocratic leadership on team performance. *The Leadership Quarterly, 26*(5), 687–701. https://doi.org/10.1016/j.leaqua.2015.01.001

35. Wong, S. I., & Giessner, S. R. (2018). The thin line between empowering and laissez-faire leadership: An expectancy-match perspective. *Journal of Management, 44*(2), 757–783. https://doi.org/10.1177/0149206315574597

36. Foels, R., Driskell, J. E., Mullen, B., & Salas, E. (2000). The effects of democratic leadership on group member satisfaction: An integration. *Small Group Research, 31*(6), 676–701. https://doi.org/10.1177/104649640003100603; see also Al-Ababneh, M. (2013). Leadership style of managers in five-star hotels and its relationship with employees job satisfaction. *Journal of Occupational and Organizational Psychology, 3*(2), 93–98.

37. Dunbar, N. E., Lane, B. L., & Abra, G. (2017). Power in close relationships: A dyadic power theory perspective. In J. A. Samp (Ed.), *Communicating interpersonal conflict in close relationships: Contexts, challenges, and opportunities* (pp. 75–92). Routledge. https://doi.org/10.4324/9781315774237

38. Raven, B. H. (2017). The comparative analysis of power and power preference. In J. T. Tedeschi (Ed.), *Social power and political influence* (pp. 172–198). Routledge. https://doi.org/10.4324/9781315129693

39. See Montero, R., & Vásquez, D. (2015). Job satisfaction and reference wages: Evidence for a developing country. *Journal of Happiness Studies, 16*(6), 1493–1507. https://doi.org/10.1007/s10902-014-9571-y

40. Baron, J. N., & Pfeffer, J. (1994). The social psychology of organizations and inequality. *Social Psychology Quarterly, 57*, 190–209. https://doi.org/10.2307/2786876

41. Elk, M., & Bolaños, C. (2019, February 20). Denver: Immigrant teachers threatened with deportation if they join strikes. *The Guardian*. https://www.theguardian.com/us-news/2019/feb/20/denver-teachers-strikes-immigrants-work-visas-jeopardized

42. Bergkvist, L., Hjalmarson, H., & Mägi, A. W. (2016). A new model of how celebrity endorsements work: Attitude toward the endorsement as a mediator of celebrity source and endorsement effects. *International Journal of Advertising, 35*(2), 171–184. https://doi.org/10.1080/02650487.2015.1024384

43. Patel, P., & Basil, M. (2017). The effects of celebrity attractiveness and identification on advertising interest. In N. Krey, & P. Rossi (Eds.), *Academy of Marketing Science annual conference* (pp. 579–589). Springer.

44. See, e.g., Passini, S., & Morselli, D. (2010). Disobeying an illegitimate request in a democratic or authoritarian system. *Political Psychology, 31*(3), 341–355. https://doi.org/10.1111/j.1467-9221.2010.00761

45. Elizabeth Dole, speech to the 300 Group, London, November 15, 1989.

46. See Garg, K., Mishra, M., & Wadhawan, C. (2018). Assessing leadership styles of higher education students through Blake and Mouton's managerial grid. *Indian Journal of Public Health Research & Development, 9*(12), 1754–1857. https://doi.org/10.5958/0976-5506.2018.02244.1

47. Blake, R. R., & Mouton, J. S.(1984). *The managerial grid III* (3rd ed.). Gulf.

48. Urban, E. (2005). Competition and interpersonal conflict in same-sex platonic friendships. *The Hilltop Review, 1*(1), article 3.

49. Roloff, M. E., & Wright, C. N. (2009). Conflict avoidance: A functional analysis. In T. D. Afifi, & W. A. Afifi (Eds.), *Uncertainty, information management, and disclosure decisions: Theories and applications* (pp. 320–340). Routledge. https://doi .org/10.4324/9780203933046

50. Zhang, Z. X., & Wei, X. (2017). Superficial harmony and conflict avoidance resulting from negative anticipation in the workplace. *Management and Organization Review, 13*(4), 795–820. https://doi.org/10.1017/mor.2017.48

51. Wilmot, W. W., & Hocker, J. L. (2018). *Interpersonal conflict* (10th ed.). McGraw-Hill.

52. Russell, J. S., Hawthorne, J., & Buchak, L. (2015). Groupthink. *Philosophical Studies, 172*(5), 1287–1309. https://doi .org/10.1007/s11098-014-0350-8

53. Janis, I. L. (1972). *Victims of groupthink.* Houghton Mifflin.

54. See Solomon, M. (2006). Groupthink versus the wisdom of crowds: The social epistemology of deliberation and dissent. *Southern Journal of Philosophy, 44*(S1), 28–42. https://doi.org/10.1111/j.2041-6962.2006.tb00028.x

55. See McCauley, C. (1998). Group dynamics in Janis's theory of groupthink: Backward and forward. *Organizational Behavior and Human Decision Processes, 73*(2-3), 142–162. https://doi.org/10.1006/obhd.1998.2759

56. Schafer, M., & Crichlow, S. (1996). Antecedents of groupthink: A quantitative study. *Journal of Conflict Resolution, 40*(3), 415–435. https://doi.org/10.1177.0022002796040003002; Vaughan, D. (1996). *The Challenger launch decision: Risky technology, culture, and deviance at NASA.* University of Chicago Press. https://doi.org/10.1093/sf/75.4.1491

57. Macleod, L. (2011). Avoiding "groupthink": A manager's challenge. *Nursing Management, 42*(10), 44–48. https://doi .org/10.1097/01.NUMA.0000394953.94337.b4

11

Pablo Blazquez Dominguez/Getty Images

CHOOSING, DEVELOPING, AND RESEARCHING A TOPIC

An Unstoppable Voice for Progress

Greta Thunberg didn't set out to become famous. As a young child in Sweden, she learned about climate change and couldn't understand why people weren't more alarmed about it. After convincing her own parents to reduce their carbon footprint, Thunberg began missing school to protest climate change at the Swedish national parliament. Her strikes were followed in 2019 by a trip to the Americas, where Thunberg attended the United Nations Climate Action Summit in New York and led a climate change rally in Montreal, Canada. In what has been described as "The Greta effect," Thunberg's outspoken criticism has prompted renewed urgency over climate policies. As a result of her high-profile efforts, Thunberg was nominated for the Nobel Peace Prize and was named *Time* magazine's Person of the Year in 2019.

As You READ

- For what reasons might you plan a speech?
- How can you select a topic that is right for you and your audience?
- Where can you find supporting information?

At the end of the World War II, the nation of Germany was divided into two states: West Germany, which was democratically governed, and East Germany, which was under communist rule. In the German capital of Berlin, a concrete wall nearly a hundred miles long divided the city, preventing people from crossing from one side to the other. For over a quarter century, the Berlin Wall stood as a symbol of the ongoing tension between communism and democracy. In 1987, in one of the most memorable speeches of his U.S. presidency, Ronald Reagan stood at the Berlin Wall and exhorted communist leader Mikhail Gorbachev, "Tear down this wall!" East and West Germany lifted their travel restrictions two years later, and by 1990, the wall was gone. Spurred by Reagan's persuasive and memorable speech, a nation torn apart by war eventually reunited.

Even if you find that story inspiring, you may think it has little to do with you. Perhaps you find public speaking to be a chore, one of those necessary evils of studying communication that won't matter to your life. The thought of speaking before a group may even bring on pangs of anxiety. If you feel that way, you're in good company. Research indicates that most of us would rather do almost anything other than get up in front of others and give a speech—particularly if we feel our words won't accomplish much.

Obviously, not every speech will reunite a country or promote changes in climate policy around the world. As you'll see in this chapter, however, you don't have to be a U.S. president or a Nobel Peace Prize nominee to give competent, effective public presentations that can help your listeners. Whether your purpose is to inform, to entertain, or to persuade, you can learn to develop speeches that will meet your goals and connect with your audience.

Know Why You're Speaking

When Matt and Jessica Flannery attended a lecture at Stanford Business School one day in 2003, they had no way of knowing how many people they would eventually help as a result. The speaker was Muhammad Yunus, a Bangladeshi economist who would later win the Nobel Peace Prize for combating poverty and advancing social and financial development in some of the world's neediest countries. Yunus spoke that day about lending small amounts of money to help struggling entrepreneurs to set up businesses and become self-sufficient. His speech inspired the Flannerys to establish Kiva, a nonprofit organization allowing people to lend money online to help poor entrepreneurs around the world. Many recipients of Kiva's microloans require only a few hundred dollars to purchase supplies or equipment for family farms, bakeries, laundromats, clothing stores, and other small enterprises. As recipients pay back their loans over time, Kiva is able to fund other applicants. As of 2020, Kiva has made over $1.4 billion in loans to help people across the globe to gain economic security.[1]

Yunus's speech had profoundly influenced the Flannerys. Indeed, his words motivated them to take actions that would change many lives for the better. Like Yunus, you can learn to create successful speeches by carefully identifying your goals.

Acting students are taught to ask themselves "What's my motivation?" when practicing for a performance. That question leads them to consider why their character should be saying or doing what's described in the scene. If the script calls for a character to appear aggressive toward others, for instance, a performer must know *why* the character is being aggressive to make his or her portrayal believable. Because characters can have several different motivations, it's useful for performers to consider which motivations are relevant to the scenes they are practicing.

Preparing a public presentation is no different. To be effective, you must begin by asking about your *own* motivation. Good public speakers carefully consider the goals of

Muhammad Yunus's speech had a profound influence on Matt and Jessica Flannery—and on the millions they have helped through Kiva.
Timothy A. Clary/AFP/ Getty Images

the speeches they prepare. As we'll see in this section, we can speak with many different goals in mind, such as to inform, to persuade, to entertain, to introduce, and to give honor. Those goals are not necessarily mutually exclusive; sometimes a speaker has more than one goal for the same speech. Just like actors who consider their characters' motivations, you can improve your performance as a speaker by identifying the goal or goals you want to accomplish in your speech.

WE SPEAK TO INFORM

Anthony Sullivan knows about informative speaking. Having appeared in television advertisements for nearly two dozen household products, Sullivan is an expert at teaching audiences how a product works in 20 seconds or less. In one commercial, for instance, he informs viewers about a cordless sweeping device called the Swivel Sweeper by explaining how it works and demonstrating its effectiveness on dirty floors. Regardless of whether they eventually buy the product, viewers learn what the Swivel Sweeper can do by watching and listening to Sullivan's informative speech.

When we speak to inform, our goal is to teach listeners something they don't already know. Teaching a seminar for lifeguards, leading a workshop for senior citizens, and demonstrating a product at a trade fair are all examples of informative speaking. In each case, the speaker has knowledge on a particular topic that he or she wishes to impart to the audience. To do so successfully, the speaker must make the material interesting, clear, and easy for listeners to follow. We further examine informative speaking in the chapter on speaking informatively.

Millions of Swivel Sweepers have been sold on television thanks to informative speaking by pitchmen such as Anthony Sullivan.
Stan Honda/AFP/ Getty Images

WE SPEAK TO PERSUADE

On the reality TV series *Big Brother*, contestants live together for three months in a house isolated from the outside world but under constant video surveillance. Each week, two contestants are nominated for eviction, and the others vote to decide which one will stay. Immediately before the voting, the nominated contestants have a few minutes to persuade their housemates not to evict them.

As we saw in the chapter on language, persuasion is the process of guiding people to adopt a specific attitude or enact a particular behavior. When we speak to persuade, we are therefore appealing to our listeners to think or act in a certain way. During a motivational halftime speech in the locker room, a basketball coach can persuade her team to play more effectively in the game's second half. During an inspiring commencement address, a celebrity or political figure can persuade new graduates to believe in themselves. For decades, social scientists have studied the most effective ways to persuade others. We explore the components of a good persuasive speech more fully in the chapter on speaking persuasively.

WE SPEAK TO ENTERTAIN

Whenever Kevin Hart, Jim Gaffigan, and Amy Schumer take the stage to do standup comedy, they speak for the purpose of entertaining their listeners. Similarly, many motivational speakers seek to entertain their audiences with fun, inspirational stories. When we speak to entertain, our goal usually isn't to teach new information or to persuade our audience to adopt certain attitudes or behaviors. Rather, we seek to amuse our listeners and help them to have an enjoyable time.

Although speaking to entertain may sound like more fun than speaking to inform or to persuade, it isn't necessarily easier. To be effective, speakers who entertain must be keenly aware of who their listeners are and what their audience is likely to find amusing. Inner-city schoolchildren probably differ from retired nurses in this regard, and computer sales reps from religious missionaries. Many a comedian has had the experience of bombing on stage by telling jokes the audience found inappropriate, incomprehensible, or simply not funny. Speaking to entertain therefore requires the ability to fit your material to the characteristics and interests of your listeners.

WE SPEAK TO INTRODUCE

In April 2019, Texas senator Ted Cruz introduced Justice Ada Brown to the Senate Committee on the Judiciary as a nominee to be a United States District Judge. During his speech, Cruz spoke of Brown's previous successes and her future potential with the federal court, noting, "Justice Brown's experience as a prosecutor, a trial advocate, a trial court judge, and an appellate court justice make her a very well qualified nominee to be a judge on the Northern District of Texas."*

Like Cruz, many of us will give public presentations to introduce other people. When we do so, our aim is often to inform listeners of the person's background and notable characteristics. Suppose you were introducing a new colleague to your project team at work. In your presentation, you might say a few words about the person's hometown, education, previous work experience, and hobbies or interests. Good speeches of introduction are usually short and focused on information listeners will find interesting.

We also speak to introduce ourselves. Perhaps you've been called on to introduce yourself to your classmates on the first day of the academic term. If so, you may have informed your audience of your major, career goals, and reasons for taking that particular course. Just as when we introduce others, we want to select a few pieces of information our listeners will find interesting when we introduce ourselves.

WE SPEAK TO GIVE HONOR

On many occasions, we speak to give honor. Speaking at the 2019 funeral of 14-term Congressman and civil rights advocate Elijah Cummings, former president Barack Obama said "His life validates the things we tell ourselves about what is possible in this country."[2] His remarks were part of a *eulogy,* a speech made to honor the memory of people after their death. We use eulogies and many other types of presentations to give honor to people, places, or significant points in history.

A eulogy is one of the most common types of speeches that give honor, yet many people find them intimidating to prepare. Take a look at the "Difficult Conversations" box for suggestions on putting together memorable remarks that are appropriate for the situation.

At a social gathering such as a wedding reception or graduation party, it's common for particular guests to give a *toast,* a short speech of tribute to the person or people being celebrated. Most toasts offer comments on the honoree's positive qualities and congratulations on his or her accomplishments. Similarly, we might deliver a *speech of recognition* to honor someone who is receiving an award. Such presentations usually explain the criteria for the award and then identify the recipient by describing his or her achievements.

SHARPEN Your Skills: *Identifying speaking goals*

Identify an important political figure and search online for the text of one of his or her most notable speeches. Read the text and identify the speaking goal or goals you see reflected in the speech. Enumerate the goals in a blog post or journal entry.

*https://www.cruz.senate.gov/?p=press_release&id=4445

Difficult Conversations

Writing a Memorable and Respectful Eulogy

Imagine this: Your childhood friend Brooke has passed away after a year-long battle with cancer. Her parents are planning her memorial service and have asked you to deliver one of the eulogies.

Now, consider this: You have never written a eulogy before, so you are nervous about doing so. Nonetheless, Brooke was a good friend and you want to do the best job you can for her and her family. In addition, several of your other childhood friends will be in attendance, so you want to deliver the best speech possible. How do you write a eulogy that is both memorable and respectful? Here are some strategies you can follow:

- Think about the emotional tone you want your remarks to have. Do you want your comments to be serious, lighthearted, or both? Many successful eulogies combine serious commentary on the person's death with positive, even humorous memories from his or her life. Consider what you think will work best for the audience you expect to have. Remember that a eulogy doesn't have to be somber, just appropriate for the situation.

- Introduce yourself at the start of your eulogy, and describe the relationship you had with the deceased. In this case, you could share the story of how you and Brooke met, perhaps indicating what drew you to each other as friends.

- Think about the person who has died, and focus your remarks on his or her most positive qualities. Maybe you appreciated Brooke's loyalty to her family, her ambition and drive, and her love for animals. Recall these in your eulogy, and include a brief story or two to illustrate what you most valued and enjoyed about Brooke.

- Although your comments may focus on the person who has passed away, remember that the purpose of a eulogy is to comfort those who remain. As you discuss Brooke's life, remind listeners how much they meant to her and encourage them to share their fondest memories of her with one other.

- Keep your remarks brief. Many memorial services feature more than one eulogy, so if you are one of several speakers, plan to speak for no more than five minutes.

Writing a eulogy can be challenging—the audience is often emotional, you may be distraught over the person's death yourself, and you generally have a short period of time in which to prepare. Despite those obstacles, you can craft memorable and appropriate remarks by paying attention to these tactics.

Speakers also give speeches to honor important places. In 2019, for instance, U.S. Supreme Court associate justice Clarence Thomas delivered a *speech of dedication* to honor the opening of a new chapel at Hillsdale College in Hillsdale, Michigan. As is common during speeches of dedication, the jurist spoke of the importance of the institution and the educational purposes it serves. Perhaps the most famous speech of dedication in U.S. history was President Abraham Lincoln's Gettysburg Address,

delivered in November 1863, during the Civil War, to dedicate a new national cemetery for soldiers. Finally, we can use speeches to honor significant points in history. On the 18th anniversary of the September 11 terrorist attacks on the United States, Vice President Mike Pence gave a *speech of commemoration*. He honored the memory of the victims and rescue workers who had lost their lives, and he reemphasized the United States' commitment to prosperity and peace.

In summary, informing, persuading, entertaining, introducing, and honoring are not the only reasons we give public presentations, but they are among the most common. Table 1 describes those reasons. In addition, many presentations have multiple goals. For instance, salespeople often attempt to persuade customers to buy a product by informing them of the item's positive features. The best man at a wedding might give a toast to honor the couple but also to entertain the guests with funny stories about the new spouses. Even if a speech has one primary goal, it can also have one or more secondary goals.

Once you have identified the goal or goals for your presentation, you should think about an appropriate topic on which to speak. We'll examine that key step next.

Choose an Appropriate Topic

When you are invited to give a speech, you may be assigned a topic based on your specific knowledge—whether it's your cultural experiences and adventures from your extensive travel or your expertise in retirement planning, Pilates, or deep-sea fishing.

TABLE 1 FIVE REASONS WHY WE SPEAK	
	To inform—Teaching listeners about something they don't already know
	To persuade—Affecting listeners' attitudes or behaviors
	To entertain—Causing listeners enjoyment
	To introduce—Informing listeners of someone's background
	To give honor—Giving recognition or commemoration to a person, place, or event

At other times, however, you may select the topic for your speech. When you're in that situation, you can identify appropriate topics by following four steps:

1. Brainstorm to identify potential topics.
2. Identify topics that are right for you.
3. Identify topics that are right for your audience.
4. Identify topics that are right for the occasion.

BRAINSTORM TO IDENTIFY POTENTIAL TOPICS

When no speech topic has been assigned, start by brainstorming to generate a list of potential topics. As you may recall from the chapter on decision making and leadership in groups, brainstorming encourages you to identify as many ideas as possible without stopping to evaluate them. You can use two questions to guide your brainstorming: what topics do you care about, and what topics are in the news?

What Topics Do You Care About? One way to identify potential topics is to consider what interests you. What experiences, hobbies, beliefs, attitudes, values, and skills do you have? How do you enjoy spending your time? What issues do you care about? Jot down as many topics as you can think of. Some of your topics might be questions; others might be statements. Don't stop to evaluate your ideas just yet; for now, your goal is to generate as many ideas as possible. Your list might look something like this:

History of hip-hop music

Five reasons to learn a foreign language

What is the twin paradox?

Common financial mistakes

How to make perfect lasagna

Preventing school violence

How to make money blogging

Caring for someone with dementia

What do Muslims believe?

Social media etiquette

Latin American pottery

Has political correctness outlived its usefulness?

Why the Titanic sank

Can anyone really multitask?

Tips for taking digital photos

What does the secretary of state do?

How sign language works

Surviving a hurricane

The Emancipation Proclamation

Child labor laws around the world

What is autism spectrum disorder?

Managing student loan debt

Could you live in a tiny house?

Why be ethical?

Considering what you already care about is a good first step toward generating a list of potential speech topics. "The Competent Communicator" provides hints for

One way to choose a speech topic is to consider issues that are currently in the local, national, or international news.

Uppercut/Getty Images

What Moves You? Selecting Your Speech Topic

A good first step in selecting a speech topic is to create a list of issues that are important to you or about which you already have some knowledge. If you need inspiration in selecting your speech topic, try the following exercise. Read each question in the left column. Write down the first three answers that come to mind in the middle column.

Hill Street Studios/Blend Images/Getty Images

Afterward, consider a few ways you might talk about each answer and write them in the third column. When you're done, you will have a list of potential topics.

Questions	Your Answers	Your Topics
What do you talk about the most with your friends and family?		
What do you find intriguing, confusing, or bewildering?		
What are your favorite websites?		
What is your fantasy career?		
What are your favorite ways to spend free time?		
With which people, living or dead, would you most like to have a conversation?		

creating an inventory of topics that interest you. As we consider next, you can also identify potential speech topics by looking at issues in the news.

What Topics Are in the News? A second way to brainstorm potential topics is to consider issues in the local, national, or international news. Fortunately, most of us have multiple sources of news available at all hours of the day and night. We can watch news broadcasts on network and cable television. We can pick up any of the hundreds of newspapers or news magazines published every day. Perhaps most conveniently, we can log onto websites that highlight contemporary news stories. A list of contemporary topics might look like this:

Pros and cons of stem cell research	Opioid addiction
Animal rights	Private space exploration
Identity theft	The Black Lives Matter movement
The Apple Watch	European refugee crisis
The death of George Floyd	School shootings
North Korea's nuclear program	COVID-19
Global climate change	2020 U.S. presidential election
#MeToo	Brexit
Gun violence and the Second Amendment	Effectiveness of airport security screening
Rising costs of higher education	U.S. women's soccer team

You can combine the list of topics you care about with the list of topics in the news to create a master list of potential topics. You'll then need to select one topic as the focus of your speech, being sure that it is appropriate for you, for your audience, and for the occasion.

IDENTIFY TOPICS THAT ARE RIGHT FOR YOU

When you are homing in on your presentation topic, first consider whether the topic is right for you. Ask:

- *What do I already know about this topic?* If you choose to speak about an issue with which you're already familiar, you will speak with credibility and confidence.

- *What do I need to learn about this topic?* Even if you're already familiar with your topic, you should still be willing to invest some time to ensure that your knowledge is up to date.

- *How much do I care about this topic?* Choosing a topic you care about will make preparing your speech more enjoyable, and your presentation will be more engaging for your listeners.

- *How valuable is the topic?* If you're going to the trouble of researching and preparing a speech, don't waste your energy on a trivial topic. Select something that is meaningful and valuable to you.

Answering those four questions won't always lead you toward the same topic. For instance, you might know a great deal about Impressionist paintings, cell mitosis, or the Electoral College, but you may care more about classic car restoration, martial arts, or the international space station. Some speakers may be drawn to topics such as sustainable agriculture, homeschooling, and online banking, whereas others might find the same topics trivial or boring.

Even if your answers to those questions don't lead you to a specific topic, they ought to narrow the field of potential topics. Once they do, there's another key question to consider: whether the topic is appropriate for your audience.

SHARPEN Your Skills: *Brainstorming speech topics*

Suppose your community group is sponsoring a charity auction to benefit juvenile diabetes research, and you have been asked to speak at the event. You anticipate that your audience will consist of businesspeople and community leaders, parents of juvenile diabetics, and local media representatives. Go through the four steps described in this section to identify at least two possible topics for your speech. Create your own version of Figure 1 by brainstorming to generate a list of potential topics and then narrowing down that list by considering what's right for you, your audience, and the occasion.

IDENTIFY TOPICS THAT ARE RIGHT FOR YOUR AUDIENCE

To give an effective speech, you need to select a topic that is right not only for yourself but also for your listeners. Once you have a potential topic in mind, ask:

- *How appropriate is this topic for my audience?* Consider whether your topic will be suitable for your listeners. Topics that are appropriate for adults, for instance, may not be appropriate for children.
- *How much will my audience care about this topic?* Consider whether your listeners will likely care about your topic. If the answer is yes, they will be more attentive to your speech and more likely to remember what you say.

We will return to this discussion of ways to analyze your audience later in this chapter. For now, though, if you narrowed your list of potential topics by considering which are right for you, then you should have narrowed it even further by considering which are right for your audience. However, before settling on a specific topic, ask yourself what kind of topics would be appropriate for the speaking occasion.

IDENTIFY TOPICS THAT ARE RIGHT FOR THE OCCASION

To give an effective speech, you need a topic that is appropriate for the situation. With your potential topic in mind, ask:

- *Why am I speaking?* Is your goal to inform, or persuade, or entertain? Are you introducing or honoring someone? Select a topic that will fit the primary goal of your speech.
- *What is the emotional tone of the event?* Is the occasion joyous and celebratory, such as a wedding or commencement? Is it somber, such as a memorial service? Is it formal but emotionally neutral, such as a stockholders' meeting? You want to make sure your topic fits the tone of the occasion.

If you start with a broad list of potential topics, you can narrow it by considering first which topics are right for you, then which topics are right for your audience, and finally which topics are right for the occasion. That process should leave you with a "short list" of excellent options from which to make your final selection.

As an illustration, let's suppose Jarnell has been asked to speak at the commencement ceremony at a local high school. The ceremony's coordinator says the choice of topic is up to Jarnell, who is an associate editor for a literary magazine. Having never before given such a speech, Jarnell first brainstorms to identify potential topics. He then evaluates which topics are right for him, his audience, and the occasion. That process leads him to two excellent potential topics. Figure 1 illustrates Jarnell's steps to identify his speech topics.

FIGURE 1

SELECTING A
SPEECH TOPIC

Step 1: Brainstorm. Jarnell begins by generating a list of potential topics. At this point, his priority is to generate ideas, not to evaluate them. Here's his first list:

Military history	Human cloning
Bird flu	Welfare reform
Nelson Mandela	Amnesty
Celebrating milestones	Air Force One
How to swing a golf club	Eyewitness testimony
French feminism	Clinical depression
National parks	Amelia Earhart
Condoms in schools	Personal responsibility
Samuel Beckett	The Latin language
Gone With the Wind	Aromatherapy

Step 2: What's Right for Him? Using his first list, Jarnell considers the topics he knows and cares about, and he eliminates the others. Here's his revised list:

Celebrating milestones	Amnesty
Nelson Mandela	Air Force One
How to swing a golf club	Clinical depression
Samuel Beckett	Personal responsibility
Gone With the Wind	The Latin language

Step 3: What's Right for His Audience? Jarnell knows his listeners are high school students, most of whom plan to go to college. Considering his listeners, he identifies what he thinks are appropriate topics and eliminates the others. Here's his revised list:

Celebrating milestones	Personal responsibility
Samuel Beckett	The Latin language

Step 4: What's Right for the Occasion? Because he's speaking at a commencement ceremony Jarnell knows the occasion will be celebratory. Thus, he considers which topics will fit the occasion, and he eliminates the others. Here's his final list:

Celebrating milestones	Personal responsibility

Analyze Your Audience

Since capturing seven Olympic medals, swimmer Amanda Beard has been spending much of her time making public appearances. One day, she may be speaking to a group of advertising executives. The next day, her audience might be a group of underprivileged children at an after-school swimming program or several dozen reporters at a press conference. Like other celebrities who give frequent public appearances, Beard knows she must tailor each presentation to the audience if she is to speak effectively. Doing so requires her to know who her listeners are and to understand the situation they are in.

CONSIDER WHO YOUR LISTENERS ARE

Good public speakers engage in **audience analysis**, which means thinking carefully about the characteristics of their listeners so they can address their audience in the most effective way. An important part of audience analysis is taking account of listeners' *demographic characteristics*, which include their age and facility with computer-mediated communication, sex and sexual orientation, culture, socioeconomic status,

• **audience analysis**
Carefully considering the characteristics of one's listeners when preparing a speech.

A frequent public speaker, Olympic medalist Amanda Beard understands the importance of adapting to her audience.

Ethan Miller/Getty Images

physical and mental characteristics, and political orientation. If you don't know much about your listeners before your speech, ask the person hosting your speech or someone who is familiar with your audience. Knowledge about audience characteristics can help you draft your presentation for maximum effect, because you can use what you know to determine which issues, examples, opinions, and forms of evidence will be most relevant to your listeners.

Age To know your listeners, consider their age, which can influence their attitudes on a number of topics. Indeed, researchers find important differences in attitudes depending on year of birth. Sociologists often distinguish between Generation Z (born after 1996), Millennials (born between 1981 and 1996), Generation X (born between 1965 and 1980), Baby Boomers (born between 1946 and 1964), and The Silent Generation (born before 1946). Considering these differences can help you to predict how receptive to your remarks your audience will be. Take a look at Table 2 for examples of issues on which the generations often have different attitudes.

Age matters as well when a talk includes references to popular culture. Consider that musical acts such as twentieth-century greats Count Basie, Glenn Miller, and Benny Goodman may not be familiar to young adults, just as Ed Sheeran, Taylor Swift, and Maroon 5 may be unfamiliar to seniors.

Your listeners' age can also influence their facility with computer-mediated communication. Suppose you're speaking on communicating with family and friends while traveling abroad. If your listeners are teens or young adults, they may follow along easily as you describe texting friends and relatives, IMing through Facebook, talking online through Zoom or FaceTime, and blogging about your travel experiences, because people in those age groups have grown up communicating in those ways. If your audience is composed of senior citizens, however, some listeners will not understand your references, given that computer-mediated communication has been in widespread use only since the early 1990s.

Similarly, listeners' age can affect which forms of presentation will best grab and hold their attention. Children, adolescents, and young adults often appreciate presentations that use multiple forms of media. When speaking to such groups, you may thus choose to incorporate music, Prezi slides, and video clips into your speech. Some older adults or seniors, however, may find the use of such media distracting and prefer a no-frills presentation style.

Sex and Sexual Orientation Effective speakers also consider the audience's sex composition, particularly if their topic will be of greater interest to one sex than another.

TABLE 2 GENERATION GAPS: AGE AFFECTS ATTITUDES	Issue	Generation Z	Millennials	Generation X	Boomers	Silents
	Approve of President Trump's job performance	30%	29%	38%	43%	54%
	Believe the government should do more to solve problems	70%	64%	53%	49%	39%
	Believe increasing racial/ethnic diversity is good for society	62%	61%	52%	48%	42%
	Know someone who prefers gender-neutral pronouns	35%	25%	16%	12%	7%
	Believe in human-caused climate change	54%	56%	48%	45%	38%

SOURCE: Parker, K., Graf, N., & Igielnik, R. (2019, January 17). *Generation Z looks a lot like Millennials on key social and political issues.* Pew Research Center.

On average, women and men differ from each other in their attitudes about particular topics. Studies show that although there are individual variations, men are often more interested in issues such as finance, national security, athletics, and career achievement. Women, in contrast, are often more interested in issues such as health care, education, social justice, and personal relationships.[3] If your audience is composed primarily of one sex or another, it may be best to tailor your presentation to appeal to their interests.

Especially when speaking to large, diverse audiences, effective presenters also bear in mind that listeners may vary in their sexual orientation. That matters because some forms of language reflect only the experiences of heterosexual people. Suppose a community business leader, while delivering the commencement address at a local college, encourages graduates to thank their "spouses and families" for their support. To heterosexual people, such a statement may sound like an important reminder to acknowledge the sacrifices their relatives have made while they went to school. To gay and lesbian listeners, however, the statement may sound dismissive, because the word *spouses* might imply legally recognized marriages, which were only recently made available to same-sex couples throughout the United States. Were the commencement speaker simply to encourage graduates to thank their "families" instead of their "spouses and families," that statement would include both legally recognized marriages and other committed romantic relationships.

Listeners' sex and sexual orientation can both influence how they respond to a public presentation.

Glowimages/Getty Images

Culture The United States is among the most culturally diverse countries in the world.[4] As you may recall from the chapter on communication and culture, cultural groups can vary significantly in their perceptions of communication behaviors. Consequently, effective speakers must take into account the cultural makeup of their audiences and speak in culturally sensitive ways.

Culturally sensitive speakers recognize that many cultural minorities have histories of social, economic, or political oppression. To avoid perpetuating such oppression, they are careful to avoid using words or phrases that insult, mock, or belittle cultural groups. Speakers who aren't culturally sensitive can cause offense even if they don't intend to do so. In July 2018, for instance, Papa John's Pizza founder John Schnatter resigned from the company's board of directors after reports that he had used a racial slur during a training session.

In a statement released after the incident, Schnatter explained that he had simply repeated what someone else had said and that his comment was not intended to cause offense.[5] Often, however, what matters is how comments are *interpreted* rather than how they are *intended*. Communicators who are insensitive to the way listeners or readers might interpret their remarks risk offending or alienating cultural groups in their audiences, even if their intentions are honorable. The risk of causing unintended offense is often heightened when speakers use humor inappropriately, as "The Dark Side of Communication" box details.

SHARPEN Your Skills: *Audience analysis*

Select three very different audiences to whom you might speak, such as a group of immigrants studying for citizenship, the board of trustees of a nonprofit organization, and a fourth-grade class. Working with a few other classmates, discuss the probable characteristics of each audience and articulate three ways you could adapt your speech to them.

A Joke Gone South: Offending Your Listeners

When used appropriately, humor can help us connect emotionally with others, so even if they aren't speaking to entertain, good speakers often inject humor into their remarks. Unfortunately, some jokes can backfire, causing the audience to take offense at the speaker's remarks. A notable example occurred during the 2015 Academy Awards ceremony. While announcing the Best Picture award for the film *Birdman*, actor Sean Penn wondered aloud who gave the movie's Mexican-born director, Alejandro G. Iñárritu, a green card, the document used to prove lawful permanent residence in the United States.

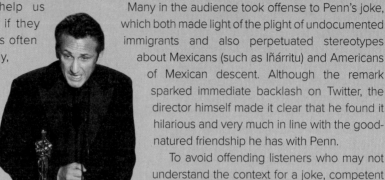

Gabriel Bouys/AFP/Getty Images

Many in the audience took offense to Penn's joke, which both made light of the plight of undocumented immigrants and also perpetuated stereotypes about Mexicans (such as Iñárritu) and Americans of Mexican descent. Although the remark sparked immediate backlash on Twitter, the director himself made it clear that he found it hilarious and very much in line with the good-natured friendship he has with Penn.

To avoid offending listeners who may not understand the context for a joke, competent speakers must exercise caution when using humor—particularly humor directed at a specific group of people, such as immigrants—to ensure that it won't seem offensive or derogatory.

Economic Status The United States is diverse not only culturally but also economically. According to the U.S. Census Bureau, approximately the same percentage of U.S. households earn below $10,000 per year as earn more than $150,000 per year.[6] Considering the economic status of your listeners can help you to tailor your message to their priorities and experiences. For instance, wealthy listeners are often older, more educated, and more widely traveled than are less wealthy listeners. As a result, they may be more likely to take for granted certain expectations, such as home ownership and health insurance coverage. Wealthy audiences are often conservative as well, so they may be more resistant to change. In contrast, low-income audiences are often more liberal and more open to new ways of thinking. You can bear such differences in mind when choosing a speech topic. For instance, a speech on high-level investment strategies may not be well suited to a less wealthy audience, whereas a speech describing coupon-clipping strategies might not appeal to a wealthier one.

svengine/iStock/Getty Images

Physical and Mental Capabilities Many audiences include people with differing physical and mental capabilities. Some may have a sensory impairment, such as being deaf or blind. Some may use a walker or a wheelchair to get around, and others may cope with physical disfigurements or deformities. Still others may face cognitive limitations, such as those associated with autism, a psychological disorder characterized by impaired communication and social skills, and dyslexia, a learning disability that affects reading and writing.

Although many people function well despite physical or mental challenges, a speaker still must sensitively accommodate listeners' needs. If you're speaking at a senior center, for instance, many of your listeners are likely to have impaired hearing and vision. To accommodate them, you need to speak clearly and at an appropriate volume, and your visual aids must be large enough to be easily seen. You may even need to describe your visual aids verbally for the benefit of those who cannot see them. In addition, if several of your listeners use wheelchairs or have limited mobility, you should avoid asking them to take part in activities that require standing or moving about. You can appear insensitive if you don't consider your listeners' particular needs.

Jose Alfonso De Tomas Gargantilla/123RF

Political Orientation During the 2000 U.S. presidential election, journalist Tim Russert devised the method of dividing the country into "red states" and "blue states." Red states—such as Kansas, Texas, Utah, and Georgia—tend to support political candidates from the Republican Party because their populations are politically more conservative. Blue states—such as California, Illinois, Pennsylvania, and New York—usually support political candidates from the Democratic Party because their populations tend to be more liberal. More recently, states such as Arizona, Florida, and Maine have been called "purple states" (a mix of red and blue) because their populations support both conservative and liberal political candidates. Knowing whether your audience is primarily conservative, primarily liberal, or a mix of the two can help you to tailor your message accordingly.

Being aware of listeners' political orientation is particularly important if you are speaking on a politically contentious topic such as gun control, immigration, or universal health care. Conservative audiences will feel quite differently about those issues than will liberal ones. Your listeners' political leanings will also affect how persuasive they judge evidence to be. Liberal listeners are more persuaded by arguments from liberal sources than conservative ones, whereas conservative listeners follow the opposite pattern.[7] If you know something about your listeners' political orientation, you can consider which types of statements and which forms of evidence they are most likely to accept.

The politics of audience members is one of the many characteristics to which a political communication professional must be sensitive. To explore a career in which political savvy is advantageous, check out the "Putting Communication to Work" box.

You may not know much about your listeners' age, experience with computer-mediated communication, sex and sexual orientation, culture, socioeconomic status, physical and mental capabilities, or political orientation before your speech. If, however, you are able to gather at least some of that information beforehand, you can use it to make your presentation more appropriate and more effective. Figure 2 provides guidance for learning about your listeners in advance of your speech.

To relate effectively to your listeners, it's helpful to understand as much as you can about who they are, what they know, and what they care about. When you're planning a speech, try to uncover the following information about your listeners:

- How old are they? How much variation in age do they have?

- How familiar are they with computer-mediated communication and popular culture?

- What percentage is male and what percentage is female?

- What are their cultural backgrounds?

- What is their economic status?

- What mental or physical impairments do they have, if any?

- How do they feel about politics?

SW Productions/Photodisc/ PunchStock

FIGURE 2
WHO'S LISTENING? LEARNING ABOUT YOUR AUDIENCE

Job Title >

Work Responsibilities >

Public Policy Consultant

A public policy consultant usually works on behalf of a political candidate or a political action committee. His or her job is to strategize with the campaign or committee about the most effective ways of making its policy positions known to the public and then to draft messages that communicate those positions. Some consultants might specialize in writing press releases and working with news media, whereas others might focus on designing public message campaigns or writing speeches for a political candidate. The job requires excellent verbal skills and a keen understanding of how to develop and research a message.

CONSIDER THE SPEAKING CONTEXT

As useful as it is to know the composition of your audience, it's equally helpful to consider the context of your speaking engagement. To do so, you need to think about several issues: the purpose of your audience, its size, the time available for your speech, the demands competing for your listeners' attention, and your audience's existing knowledge about your topic.

Purpose To maximize your effectiveness as a speaker, consider *why* your audience will come together to hear you. Will your listeners be required to attend, or will they assemble by choice? Will they anticipate being taught? Persuaded? Entertained? Is the context formal or informal? Is it joyous or somber? Those issues matter because they influence the behaviors your audience will expect from you.

Suppose you're leading a fire safety course that all new employees at your company are required to complete. In this situation, your listeners are probably expecting you to teach them what they need to know as efficiently as possible. Because they are not attending the workshop by choice, their motivation to pay attention is likely to be low. You can speak effectively to them by being clear, concise, and informative and by incorporating humor to lighten their experience. The most effective speakers think carefully about what their audience expects and requires of them in each specific situation, and they adapt their presentations accordingly.

Size A second factor to consider is the size of your audience. In general, the larger the group, the more formally structured you should make your presentation. If you're speaking to a youth group with only a dozen members, for instance, you might be most effective by behaving somewhat informally. You might choose to sit instead of stand, ask your listeners to introduce themselves, request audience participation in an activity, speak in an informal and conversational tone, and encourage your listeners to interrupt you with questions. None of those behaviors would be effective with an audience of 300, however. With that many listeners, activities and audience participation could easily become unmanageable, and an informal style of speaking would be inappropriate. Consider how you would feel, for example, if you were one of 300 people in the audience and the speaker asked each of you to introduce yourself. You would probably find such a request unreasonable (if not bizarre) for an audience of that size, and you would likely lose respect for the speaker as a result. To be effective, the speaker should adapt his or her presentation style to fit the size of the audience.

Available Time Have you had the frustrating experience of taking a course in which the time allotted for class runs out but the speaker continues speaking anyway? If so, you can appreciate that listeners have only a finite amount of time to spend listening to a speaker. To be effective, speakers must be aware of how long their presentations are supposed to last, and they must be realistic about how much material they can cover.

When you are giving a speech, make sure to stay within your allotted time. Listeners quickly become frustrated with speeches that run long. *Copyright 2007, Mike Watson Images Limited/ Glow Images*

Suppose you're preparing a speech about gun safety. If you have 45 minutes to speak, you might choose to discuss the 10 most dangerous mistakes gun owners make. If you have only 15 minutes to speak, however, then trying to cover the 10 most dangerous mistakes is probably a mistake itself. In that context, you'll give a more effective speech by covering, say, the *three* most dangerous mistakes. Whatever the situation, your listeners are likely aware of how long your speech is supposed to last, and they may get restless and lose interest if you speak longer than you should. In contrast, if you speak for slightly less than your allotted time, your audience is likely to be appreciative.

Distractions You probably know from your own experience that it's difficult to give your undivided attention to anyone for very long. No matter who's listening to your speech, other factors are almost always competing for their attention. Perhaps your speech is right before lunch, and your listeners are distracted by hunger. Perhaps it's Friday afternoon, and they're eager to leave for the weekend. Maybe your microphone is faltering, and your listeners can't hear you clearly. These and many other issues can make it challenging for your audience to pay close attention to your words.

You can address most such factors if you're aware of what they are. If your speech is right before lunch, for instance, you can try to reschedule it for a time when your audience will be less distracted. If rescheduling isn't an option, then you can say to your listeners: "I know we're all eager to get to lunch, so if you'll give me your attention, I'll make my remarks as briefly as I can." Audiences will understand that certain factors, such as the time of your speech, may be beyond your control. They often will appreciate it, however, if you acknowledge their situation ("I know we're all eager to get to lunch") and pledge to do what you can to minimize it ("I'll make my remarks as briefly as I can").

Prior Knowledge of Your Topic Finally, consider what your audience already knows about the topic of your speech. Armed with this information, you can avoid two mistakes: talking down to your listeners and talking over their heads. *Talking down* means telling people what they already know as if they didn't already know it. *Talking over people's heads* means assuming they have information or an understanding they don't actually have.

Let's say you're leading a workshop to teach adolescents about personal finance. If your listeners are members of their school's accounting club, they probably know the basics of how credit works, what a profit margin is, and how to reconcile a checking account statement. They may feel annoyed if you stopped to define a term such as *annual interest rate* because they probably already know what that term means. You can cover more advanced topics with such an audience than you could with a group of students who lack training in the basics of finance. Many students without such training would feel frustrated if you used a term such as *annual interest rate* without defining it, because unlike the accounting club members, they may not know what it means.

Public speakers are most effective when they tailor their presentations to meet their listeners' needs and expectations. Doing so requires considering not just who their listeners are but also their listeners' situation. Analyzing the audience and adapting your presentation to it can help you to speak effectively and memorably.

Know Where to Find Information

When planning a speech, you'll often find it helpful to consult various sources for information or guidance. You may already have used some or all of these sources to prepare papers or other class assignments, and they can be just as valuable when you are developing a speech. In this section, we'll look at several potential sources of good supporting material.

WEBSITES

The Internet puts a wealth of information at your fingertips, and it can be an invaluable source of supporting material if you use it responsibly. One of the Internet's greatest assets as a source of supporting material is also its greatest liability, and that is the sheer volume of information it can provide. Having an enormous amount of information at your disposal can be a great advantage when you're searching for supporting material. Indeed, you can use the Internet to find material on almost any topic imaginable, so it's unlikely you would fail to discover something useful for your speech. The disadvantage is that the breadth of information available can seem overwhelming. Particularly if you are searching for material on a popular topic, such as pop music or environmental activism, you could easily identify hundreds or even thousands of websites after just a few moments of searching. Because it would be nearly impossible to read and evaluate all those sources, you might find Internet searches to be more

You can use the resources of your college or public library to find multiple materials relevant for your speech.

rawpixel/123RFWebsites

trouble than they're worth. As we'll see, however, it's easy to narrow the parameters of an Internet search so that you identify only specific types of information.

Many public speakers use one or more of three kinds of websites when searching online for supporting material: general search engines, research search engines, and website-specific searches. The broadest of these, the **general search engine**, is a website that allows you to search for other websites containing information on a topic that you specify. On those sites, you can enter words or phrases, and the search engine will produce a list of other websites on which those words or phrases appear. For instance, if you type "Yellowstone National Park" into google.com, that search engine will produce a list of over 22 million other websites offering information about the park. You can then scroll through the list to identify those sites you want to read.

Typing "Yellowstone National Park" into google.com will identify over 22 million websites offering information about the park and its residents.

W. Wayne Lockwood/ Corbis/VCG/Getty Images

In most cases, using a general search engine will identify a wide range of sources. Some may be helpful to you and others may not. Among the 22 million websites about Yellowstone National Park, for instance, are bound to be thousands that advertise the park's services or describe family vacations taken there. Those may not be particularly useful sources of supporting material for the claims you want to make in your speech. You can reduce the number of websites identified in a search by submitting more terms to the search engine. For instance, if you type "Yellowstone National Park future volcanic eruptions" into google.com, the search will identify approximately 300,000 websites. That's still a large number—and, once again, many sites are likely not to be useful to your search—but it is considerably less than the 22 million sites your original search identified.

Because of the overwhelming amount of information a general search engine can produce, it's essential to evaluate the usefulness of what you find, as "Fact or Fiction?" explains. If you know ahead of time that you want to look specifically for published research on your topic, you may prefer to use a research search engine such as scholar. google.com.

• **general search engine** A website on which one can search for other websites containing information on a specified topic.

A **research search engine** doesn't scan the Internet as broadly as general search engines do but rather looks only for research that has been published in books, academic journals, and other periodicals. If you type "Yellowstone National Park" into scholar.google.com, the search will identify approximately 76,000 sources reporting published research on the park. In many instances, the publications are available to read online.

• **research search engine** A website on which one can search for research published in books, academic journals, and other periodicals.

Finally, you can do a website-specific search, which means confining your search to specific websites that you know will contain the information you're seeking. To find information about Yellowstone National Park, for instance, you could consult the website for the U.S. National Park service, www.nps.gov. That page provides information about Yellowstone's history, location, geographic characteristics, climate, and visitor hours. Similarly, you could use websites for various organizations to search for information relevant to those groups. For example, you might consult the website for the American Medical Association if you were interested in health or the website for the United Nations if you were interested in international politics.

Table 3 gives examples of general search engines, research search engines, and specific websites. You may find these handy when doing research for a speech.

Websites are extraordinary research tools, but they aren't your only option. Books, archives, conference papers, databases, personal observations, and surveys can also provide many useful resources that can help you to prepare a speech.

BOOKS

Books are another invaluable resource for research. Books include both fictional and nonfictional works, as well as reference volumes such as dictionaries and encyclopedias.

Fact or *fiction*?

All Information Found Online Is Equally Valuable

When people do online research for a speech, they sometimes believe any information they find will be valuable. As you prepare your own speeches, be careful not to fall victim to that false idea. There's no question that the Internet provides access to a wide range of information, but not all the information is equally trustworthy.

Suppose you were researching the effectiveness of acupuncture for treating migraine headaches. You would undoubtedly come across hundreds of websites offering people's personal testimonies of how effective—or ineffective—acupuncture was for them. Some of their comments might be on blogs, others on bulletin boards, and others on their Facebook pages. To find out whether acupuncture has genuine value for treating migraines, however, you need to look at reports of research, not personal accounts.

Indeed, although they may be convincing, personal reports can be invalid for at least two reasons. First, the people making them might be exceptional. For example, the fact that acupuncture works for some people doesn't necessarily mean it works for most people. Second, people don't always know what affects their health. Even if individuals' migraines improved after having acupuncture, that doesn't automatically mean that the acupuncture treatments caused their improvement. Researchers design studies to overcome both those types of problems, so the findings from research studies are more valid than people's reports of their personal experiences. That point is essential to keep in mind when you search online for information.

To evaluate the merit of information you find online, investigate the ABCs: Accuracy, Balance, and Credibility.

- *Accuracy.* What documentation does the website provide for the accuracy of its information? Are there references to research studies, experts, or other published research? How current is the information?

- *Balance.* Is the website promoting the particular viewpoint of an organization or cause? If an issue is contentious, are all sides of the issue presented and equally discussed?

- *Credibility.* Who created the information, and what is that person's expertise? What evidence is offered for that person's credentials?

Answering these questions about information you find online may take some time and effort, but it will help you to ensure that you use only quality, trustworthy information. Websites that are accurate, balanced, and credible tend to provide these details readily. If these details are difficult to find, consider that you may be looking at a website with less trustworthy information.

ASK YOURSELF

- How do you know whether someone's personal testimony is valid for other people besides that individual?
- Are you generally more persuaded by research findings or reports of personal experiences? Why?

With a bit of searching, you are likely to find books containing information about almost any speech topic you could choose.

In a library, each book has a unique catalog number—its "call number"—that helps you to locate the book on the library shelf. Most libraries allow you to search for books by author, subject, title, and/or publisher so you can easily find what you want.

TABLE 3

FIND IT ONLINE:
EXAMPLES OF
INTERNET SEARCH
TOOLS

These examples of general search engines, research search engines, and specific websites might be useful when you conduct research on a particular speech topic, such as medicine, psychology, art, or the environment.

General Search Engines	Research Search Engines	Website Searches (organization in parentheses)
google.com	scholar.google.com	ama-assn.org (American Medical Association)
yahoo.com	scirus.com	apa.org (American Psychological Association)
about.com	highbeam.com	arts.gov (National Endowment for the Arts)
bing.com	doaj.org	doi.gov (U.S. Department of the Interior)
lycos.com	pubmed.gov	epa.gov (U.S. Environmental Protection Agency)

You can also find and read many books online. The website books.google.com allows you to search books by title, author, or subject and lets you survey a book's content online. Thus far, more than 25 million books had been scanned into the system's database, making it a valuable resource for finding books relevant to your topic.

Most books can also be purchased online, through vendors such as amazon.com and barnesandnoble.com. In many cases, books are available in either print or digital formats, allowing you to read the material in whichever manner suits you best.

PERIODICALS AND NONPRINT MATERIALS

Periodicals are materials that are published on a regular basis, such as magazines, newspapers, and scientific journals. Newspapers are often published daily, whereas magazines might be published weekly or monthly and journals are typically published quarterly. Because they are produced on a recurring basis, periodicals generally provide more current information than books do. Thus, if you're preparing a speech about the economy, you will find more recent information in *The Wall Street Journal*, a daily financial newspaper, than in a book published several months ago.

Nonprint materials are audiovisual resources such as sound recordings, movies, and photographs. Many libraries have extensive collections of records, videotapes, CDs, DVDs, and photographs that patrons can check out. You can use nonprint materials both as sources of research and as audiovisual aids to enhance your presentation.

Finally, for making their older resources available to users, most libraries also have collections of electronic print materials, such as microfilm, a medium that stores reproductions of books and periodicals on film at a greatly reduced font size. Libraries often transfer printed materials to microfilm both to preserve the materials and to conserve space. With a special viewer, you can read materials on microfilm and even print them in their original font size.

CONFERENCE PAPERS

Most academic disciplines have scholarly associations made up of professors, graduate and undergraduate students, and industry professionals. In the field of communication, these include the National Communication Association and the International Communication Association, among others. Scholarly associations often hold academic conferences on a yearly or semi-yearly basis, and it is common at such conferences for scholars to share their latest research in the form of a conference paper.

FIGURE 3

EXAMPLES OF
SOURCES FOR
RESEARCH ON
VAPING

Source	Example
Government website	Centers for Disease Control and Prevention. (2019). Outbreak of lung injury associated with the use of e-cigarette, or vaping, products. https://www.cdc.gov/tobacco/basic_information/e-cigarettes/severe-lung-disease.html
Industry website	JUUL. (2019). The alternative for adult smokers: Designed for smokers, by smokers. https://www.juul.com/
Book	Gordon, S. M. (2019). *Everything you need to know about smoking, vaping, and your health*. Rosen.
Journal article	Walley, S. C., Wilson, K. M., Winickoff, J. P., & Groner J. (2019). A public health crisis: Electronic cigarettes, vape, and JUUL. *Pediatrics, 143*(6), Article e20182741. https://doi.org/10.1542/peds.2018-2741
Newspaper article	Kaplan, S. (2019, September 18). Teenage vaping rises sharply again this year. *The New York Times*. https://nyti.ms/2LBhSjD
Online news story	Nedelman, M. (2019, October 2). Vaping-related deaths in United States rise to 17. *CNN Health*. https://www.cnn.com/2019/10/01/health/virginia-vaping-lung-death-bn/index.html
Magazine article	Satel, S. (2019, October 23). The vaping overreaction. *The Atlantic*. https://www.theatlantic.com/ideas/archive/2019/10/danger-vaping-bans/600451/
Blog post	Tan, R. T. (2019, October 29). State vape ban laws. *Vapor4Life*. https://www.vapor4life.com/blog/vape-ban-laws-by-state/
Conference paper	Obbert, J. O. (2019, May 20-21). *E-cigarettes and smoking cessation* [Paper presentation]. 26th Annual Nicotine Dependence Conference, Rochester, MN, United States.

• **conference paper** A report of research that has been accepted for presentation at an academic meeting.

A **conference paper** is a report of research that has been accepted for presentation at an academic meeting. Many scholars share their work at conferences in order to receive feedback from other researchers and to keep their peers informed of what they are working on. Conference papers often constitute the first public presentation of a study, before the study is published. You can find conference papers about a particular topic by searching the online programs of professional conferences in your field.

When researching a topic for your speech, you can often find information from many or all of the different sources we have addressed thus far, as well as others. Let's suppose you have decided to write your speech about the topic of vaping. Figure 3 gives examples of multiple sources where you might find information.

DATABASES

• **database** An electronic storehouse of specific information that people can search.

A **database** is an electronic storehouse of specific information that people can search. Using a research database is much like using a research search engine. The major difference is that databases tend to be narrower and more specialized in the sources they include. Most research databases, that is, are focused on specific academic disciplines. Such databases include Comindex for communication studies, PsycINFO for psychology, Sociological Abstracts for sociology, ERIC for education, and Criminal Justice Abstracts for criminal justice.

Many college and university libraries offer access to databases on their websites, but you can also visit your library in person and ask for help. One of a library's most valuable assets is its staff of trained professionals who can help you navigate the library's resources, including its databases. If you are uncertain where to begin searching for supporting material, don't be afraid to ask a library staff member for help.

PERSONAL OBSERVATIONS

When you think of doing research, you may—if you are like many students—think only about locating information that already exists in books or on websites. However, an additional option is to do original research by gathering information yourself. One way is by observing a phenomenon and taking notes about what you see and hear.

Let's say you were preparing a speech about nonverbal greeting behaviors, and you wondered how they differed in same-sex and other-sex pairs. To learn about the topic, you might spend a few hours watching people at the airport. You could sit close to the area where arriving passengers meet their friends and relatives, and you could observe and take note of their greeting behaviors. Specifically, you could note similarities and differences in how people greet women and men, and see whether any patterns emerge.

As part of your speech, you might describe how you conducted your observations and what you found:

> To observe greeting behaviors in same-sex and other-sex pairs, I spent two hours on the visitors' side of the main security screening gate at the airport and watched how people greeted arriving passengers. Within two hours, I observed almost 100 greetings. In that time, I noted some stark differences in greeting behavior. Specifically, arriving male passengers were much more likely to kiss and hug women than they were to display that behavior with other men. When greeting another man, male passengers were more likely only to shake hands. Arriving female passengers, however, were equally likely to kiss and hug men and other women.

When using personal observations as supporting material, remember that your observations may not accurately reflect the behaviors of the population at large. After observing people for two hours at one security gate at one airport, you could not say with certainty that *all* women and men differ in their greeting behaviors. You could, however, use this personal observation in conjunction with other forms of data, such as findings from published research, to illustrate how patterns of behavior are enacted in a local environment.

In addition to collecting your own personal observations, you can also use observations made by others as supporting material. Perhaps you're crafting a speech about Venice, Italy, and you want to describe how people travel the city's many canals on boats called gondolas. Even though you haven't visited Venice yourself, you might base your description on the personal observations of your roommate, who spent a semester studying there. For additional material, you could also consult the personal observations of other visitors by reading their travel blogs or Facebook pages.

SURVEYS

Personal observation is a good way to collect original data, but it is effective only if the topic is directly observable, such as public behavior at an airport or tourist travel on a gondola. What if you want to learn about something you cannot directly observe, such as people's attitudes, beliefs, or histories? To learn about those topics, you can conduct a **survey**, which means collecting data by asking people directly about their experiences.

One of the most valuable library resources is the trained professional who can help you to navigate the library's research assets.

Hill Street Studios/ Getty Images

Pictac/Getty Images

• **survey** A method of collecting data by asking people directly about their experiences.

• interview A structured conversation in which one person poses questions to which another person responds.

• questionnaire A written instrument containing questions for people to answer.

One method of surveying people is to interview them. An **interview** is a structured conversation in which one person poses questions to which another person responds. Some interviews are brief, making use of a few questions that probe the person's experiences. Others are in-depth conversations in which the respondent speaks in great detail about his or her experiences. Many interviews take place in a face-to-face setting, but you can also conduct them over the telephone, via text messaging or e-mail, or over Zoom, FaceTime, or Skype.

A second method of surveying people is to distribute a **questionnaire**, a written instrument containing questions for people to answer. Like interviews, questionnaires help you to learn about people's attitudes, preferences, values, and experiences. Using a questionnaire, you might survey students at your school about their use of the campus health service or their preferences for community arts and entertainment. Compiling people's responses allows you to find out which preferences or experiences are the most common. Let's say you discovered that 87 percent of students have visited your campus health service within the previous six months. You could use that information to argue for expanding health services for students.

Compared to interviews, questionnaires have the advantage of allowing you to collect data from a large number of people efficiently. Using a questionnaire, for instance, you could collect data from every student in your communication course in the same amount of time it might take you to interview one person. The disadvantage of questionnaires is that you usually cannot get the detailed answers that are possible in an interview. For those reasons, surveys that include data from both in-depth interviews and questionnaires are often more informative than those that rely on only one method.

Internet research, library research, personal observations, and surveys can all yield quality supporting material for your presentation. Because these sources differ in the information they provide, however, it's often to your advantage to use more than one when you're preparing a speech.

SHARPEN Your Skills: *Informal interviewing*

Select a current issue on which people's opinions vary, such as how the government should address unemployment. Conduct informal interviews with eight or so family members, coworkers, and classmates in which you ask what people's opinions are on the issue and why they hold those opinions. As you conduct each interview, try to keep your own opinions private so you don't influence what others say. Write a paragraph describing the results of your interviews, which could be one form of evidence you use in a speech.

▶ For REVIEW

• **For what reasons might you plan a speech?**

People plan speeches to inform their listeners of information, persuade their listeners to think or act in a particular way, entertain their listeners, introduce someone to their audience, and give honor to a person, place, or event.

• **How can you select a topic that is right for you and your audience?**

You can brainstorm to identify a list of potential topics. Choose one by considering what you know and care about, what your listeners will know and care about, and what would work well for the occasion.

• **Where can you find supporting information?**

The Internet, the library, personal observations, interviews, and questionnaires can all give you access to supporting material that will assist you with planning your speech.

KEY TERMS

audience analysis 321

general search engine 329

research search engine 329

conference paper 332

database 332

survey 334

interview 334

questionnaire 334

NOTES

1. www.kiva.org/about/impact
2. Lockhart, P. R. (2019, October 25). "A man of noble and good heart": Read Barack Obama's eulogy for Elijah Cummings. *Vox.com.* https://www.vox.com/policy-and-politics/2019/10/25/20932171/elijah-cummings-funeral-barack-obama-eulogy-transcript
3. See Lippa, R. A. (2010). Gender differences in personality and interests: When, where, and why? *Social and Personality Psychology Compass, 4*(11), 1098–1100. https://doi.org/10.1111/j.1751-9004.2010.00320.x
4. factfinder.census.gov
5. Sinclair, H. (2018, July 15). Papa John's founder says he used N-word but "it wasn't a slur." *Newsweek.* https://www.newsweek.com/papa-johns-founder-says-he-used-n-word-it-wasnt-slur-1024688
6. Semega, J., Kollar, M., Creamer, J., & Mohanty, A. (2019, September). *U.S. Census Bureau current population reports, P60–266: Income and poverty in the United States: 2018.* U.S. Government Printing Office.
7. See, e.g., Westerwick, A., Johnson, B. K., & Knobloch-Westerwick, S. (2017). Confirmation biases in selective exposure to political online information: Source bias vs. content bias. *Communication Monographs, 84*(3), 343–364. https://doi.org/10.1080/03637751.2016.1272761

12

Denisenko/Shutterstock

ORGANIZING AND FINDING SUPPORT FOR YOUR SPEECH

When Evaluating Evidence, Consider Credibility

Many speeches require evidence—and with the Internet, evidence has never been easier to locate. How do you know whether something you find online is true, though? It turns out that separating truthful stories from fake news is more difficult than you might guess. In a 2019 study, undergraduates read news headlines and were asked to judge whether or not the stories were credible.[1] Simply flipping a coin would have given them a 50 percent chance of being right—yet the students gave a correct answer only 44 percent of the time. What's more, participants were overwhelmingly likely to rate stories that matched their own political beliefs as true instead of false. This study illustrates what researchers have long known: We tend to believe what we *want* to believe, rather than considering where the information came from and seriously questioning its accuracy. Good speakers remember, however, that their claims are only as good as the evidence they present and that scrutinizing the credibility of information is critical.

▶ As You READ

- What are the important elements of any speech?
- Why are formal outlines and speaking notes useful?
- What evidence should you use to support your claims?

As you learned in the chapter on choosing, developing, and researching a topic, preparing a good speech requires choosing an appropriate topic and having a clear understanding of the audience. It also requires developing a detailed speaking plan, creating an effective outline, and—as the chapter opening story implies—finding support for your claims from credible sources.

State Your Purpose and Thesis

There is a famous old proverb that says, "By failing to prepare, you are preparing to fail." Indeed, success in many endeavors relies on solid planning, and public speaking is no exception. One of the first steps in planning a successful speech is to choose the message of your speech. That is, once you've selected your topic, you must consider what you want to say about it.

Suppose you've identified Australia as your topic. You could use your presentation to teach your audience about the nation's cultural history or political climate. You could try to persuade your listeners to visit the country's famous Great Barrier Reef. You could amuse your audience with bits of Australian humor. The point is that Australia is a broad topic that you could address in many possible ways. To be effective, you'll need to narrow the scope of your speech by choosing what, in particular, you want to address. That process involves two related but different concepts. The first is clarifying the **specific purpose** of your speech, which is the primary goal that you want to accomplish in your presentation. Your specific purpose is the answer to the question, *What am I trying to achieve in my speech?* The second is crystalizing your **thesis**, which is the main message of your speech. Your thesis is the answer to the question, *What am I trying to say?* In this section, you'll learn how to address each of these key aspects of speechwriting.

DRAFT A PURPOSE STATEMENT

We saw in the chapter on choosing, developing, and researching a topic that a speech can have several *general* goals, such as to inform, to persuade, to entertain, to introduce, and to give honor. The first step in preparing your speech is to narrow down the goals of your speech, and identify your specific purpose.

Let's say the topic of your speech is Italian food. With that topic in mind, consider the range of specific goals you might have. You could choose to describe the varieties of Italian wines. You could demonstrate pasta making. You could explain the similarities and differences between Italian and French cuisine and argue for the superiority of one. Most likely, you would not attempt to meet all those goals in the same speech. Rather, you would select one purpose on which to focus. You can articulate that specific goal in the form of a purpose statement. A **purpose statement** is a declaration of your *specific* goal for your speech. It expresses precisely what you want to accomplish during your presentation.

To draft a purpose statement, first identify your topic and your general goal. Sticking with your topic of Italian food, let's say your general goal is to inform. Next, consider exactly what you want to inform your listeners *about.* In other words, make your general goal—to inform—specific. Perhaps you decide to teach your audience how to make ravioli. In that scenario, you might articulate your purpose statement in this way:

Purpose statement: *Demonstrate the process of making ravioli.*

Suppose instead that you want to inform your audience about Italian wines. You might express your purpose statement in this way:

Purpose statement: *Teach listeners the differences among five Italian red wines.*

Notice that each of these purpose statements reflects the general goal of your speech, which is to inform. At the same time, however, each makes your general goal more focused and specific.

What if your goal is to persuade rather than to inform? In that case, you will need to consider exactly what you want to persuade your listeners to think or do. Once

---

• **specific purpose** The main goal for a speech or oral presentation.

• **thesis** The main message of a speech or oral presentation.

• **purpose statement** A declaration of the specific goal for a speech.

Spike Mafford/Getty Images

again, you can use your purpose statement to make your general goal more specific. For example, you may want to persuade your listeners that Italian cuisine is better than French cuisine. In that case, you might articulate your purpose statement in this way:

Purpose statement: *Persuade listeners that Italian cuisine is superior to French cuisine.*

Suppose instead that you want to encourage consumption of Italian olive oil because of its benefits for heart health. You might articulate your purpose statement in this way:

Purpose statement: *Persuade listeners to consume more Italian olive oil.*

Notice again that each purpose statement reflects the general goal—to persuade—but it makes the goal specific.

In addition to informing and persuading, the last chapter identified three additional goals for a speech—to entertain, to introduce, and to give honor. Suppose you're preparing an entertaining speech on the state of U.S. politics. You might structure your purpose statement in this way:

Purpose statement: *Make my listeners laugh by making fun of U.S. politics.*

Let's say you are asked to introduce a visiting pastor to your church congregation. You could express your purpose statement in this way:

Purpose statement: *Introduce Rev. Adams by telling the story of how he and I first met.*

Finally, imagine you're giving a toast at your mother's retirement party. You might articulate your purpose statement in this way:

Purpose statement: *Bring recognition to my mother's career by describing her proudest accomplishments.*

A focused purpose statement can launch the creation of a great speech. Constructing a workable outline for your presentation becomes much easier after you have articulated a specific goal. Indeed, your purpose statement will help you to determine the content of your speech, in ways we will explore below.

To develop a strong purpose statement, follow these guidelines:

- *Be specific.* A purpose statement such as "Teach my audience about the weather" is vague because the weather has so many facets. Thus, that statement won't help you to determine the content of your speech as effectively as a sharper, more specific purpose statement, such as "Teach my audience how tornadoes form."

- *Be declarative.* Write your purpose statement as a directive, such as "Explain the process of creating a Twitter account." Simply posing a question, such as "How does someone create a Twitter account?" doesn't indicate as clearly what you plan to accomplish in your speech.

- *Be concise.* Focus your purpose statement on one specific goal for your speech. A statement such as "Persuade my listeners that government should provide universal health care and that the free market economy hurts working families" is too broad because it expresses more than one distinct purpose. Limiting your purpose statement to one goal will help you to organize your speech effectively.

Once you have selected your topic and drafted your purpose statement, you're almost ready to begin constructing your speech. One task remains, however—to articulate the message you want to get across. You can express that message in the form of a thesis statement, as we'll see next.

DRAFT A THESIS STATEMENT

During the 2009 Super Bowl, a 30-second television commercial cost a staggering $3 million—and by 10 years later, that cost had jumped to more than $5 million.[2] That high price prompted the Miller Brewing Company to run an advertisement lasting only one second, just long enough for the announcer to mention the name of the product. Suppose *you* had only one sentence in which to deliver an entire speech. What would your sentence be? What single specific message would you want your listeners

Paul Spinelli/AP Photo

• **thesis statement** A one-sentence version of the message in a speech.

to remember? You can formulate an answer to that question by drafting a **thesis statement**, a one-sentence version of the message in your speech.

Let's say your speech topic is alternative medicine and your purpose statement is "Teach about the effectiveness of herbal supplements." Before you develop your speech, consider what you want your take-home message to be. You might articulate your message in this way:

Thesis statement: *Although sales of herbal supplements are growing, medical research shows they are no more effective than placebos.*

As another example, suppose your topic is personal finance, and your purpose statement is "Persuade my listeners to invest in gold." You could convey your message in this way:

Thesis statement: *Because gold prices rise even in a weak economy, investing in gold is a sound financial decision.*

Notice how each of those thesis statements expresses the *message* of the speech. That is, it identifies what you would want your listeners to take away from your presentation. With a strong thesis statement, you'll find it much easier to construct the rest of your speech because you'll know exactly what you want to say to your audience.

To develop a strong thesis statement, follow these guidelines:

• *Be concrete.* Good thesis statements should be concrete, not vague or abstract. For an informative speech about the massive earthquake that hit Indonesia in 2018,

THE DARK SIDE OF COMMUNICATION

Stretching the Truth: Exaggeration or Deception?

Most people would consider it lying if you were to use a thesis statement in your speech that is blatantly false. What if you were just exaggerating beyond what the evidence shows, however? While preparing a persuasive speech about antibacterial soap, for example, suppose

Mike Watson Images/moodboard/Getty Images

you were to discover research indicating that the product provides minimal health benefits. Would you therefore be lying if you claimed in your thesis statement, "Washing with antibacterial soap is a good way to stay healthy"? Or would you simply be exaggerating—that is, stretching the truth?

According to communication researchers, exaggeration is a form of deception. If your thesis statement makes claims that you know your evidence doesn't fully support, then you are lying to your audience just as surely as if your thesis statement were a complete fabrication. The reason is that by stretching the truth, you are knowingly giving your audience a false impression. If your listeners discover that you have been less than forthright with them, that knowledge is likely to damage your credibility as a speaker. Once your credibility has been damaged, it can be difficult—if not impossible—to regain. Even if your audience never discovers your exaggeration, however, stretching the truth beyond what your evidence supports is always an unethical communication act.

a concrete thesis statement is "A magnitude-7.5 earthquake struck the island nation of Indonesia in September 2018, killing more than 4,000 people." In contrast, the thesis statement "A massive earthquake hit" is vague, because it doesn't specify where the earthquake was, how many deaths it caused, or when.

- *Make a statement.* Frame your thesis statement as a sentence rather than a question. In a persuasive speech calling on listeners to focus more attention on religious persecution in Nigeria, the thesis statement "Twelve thousand Nigerians have been killed in a decade of violence between Christians and Muslims" works well because it declares the point of your speech. In comparison, a question—such as "What religious persecution is occurring in Nigeria?"—doesn't indicate the point you plan to make, only the topic you intend to discuss.

- *Treat your thesis statement as a work in progress.* During the process of preparing a speech, it's best to remain flexible with your thesis statement. As we'll see, creating a draft of your thesis statement will help you organize your outline and your research. Remain open, however, to revising your thesis statement as you work. During your research, for instance, you may uncover details that warrant tweaking or even rewriting your thesis statement, so good public speakers stay open to that possibility.

- *Tell the truth.* Good speakers communicate ethically with their listeners. To speak ethically, you must be sure you believe in the truth of your thesis statement, so that you don't knowingly mislead your audience. Drafting an ethical thesis statement doesn't just mean avoiding claims you know to be false. It also means ensuring that you don't exaggerate your claims beyond what your supporting evidence warrants. To do so risks deceiving your listeners, a topic explored in "The Dark Side of Communication."

Table 1 presents examples of good thesis statements for three different speech topics. Armed with a topic, a purpose statement, and a thesis statement, you are ready to build your presentation. In the next sections, we'll explore the organization of a speech and see how to create a useful outline.

SHARPEN Your Skills:
Purpose and thesis statements

Select a topic you find interesting. Write a purpose statement and thesis statement for an informative speech about that topic. Then write a purpose statement and thesis statement for a persuasive speech about the same topic. In a brief journal entry, describe how your purpose and thesis statements differ for the two speeches.

TABLE 1
WRITING AN EFFECTIVE THESIS STATEMENT

Topic	Goal	Purpose Statement	Thesis Statement
Human rights for sexual minorities	To persuade	Persuade listeners that the United States should take a more proactive role in ensuring human rights for sexual minorities.	The United States should issue severe economic sanctions against countries that impose capital punishment or life imprisonment for homosexual or bisexual behavior.
New York Marathon	To inform	Teach listeners about the qualifications for entering the New York Marathon.	Prospective competitors in the New York Marathon must have achieved a minimum time in an approved marathon within the year prior to the event.
New high school library	To dedicate	Mark the opening of the new high school library and acknowledge those who made it possible.	Thanks to the selfless contributions of multiple individuals, a new high school library is now available to meet the needs of students and community members.

Organize Your Speech

On occasion, you've probably had the frustrating experience of listening to a disorganized speech. Maybe the speaker jumped from point to point with little apparent direction. You might have wondered whether anyone—including the speaker—was following along. Chances are, you didn't learn much about the topic of the speech, and you left with a poor impression of the speaker's competence. If you've had such an experience, then you already understand the benefits of a clearly organized speech.

As an expert public speaker in the making, you can use that negative experience to your advantage by learning how to organize your speech for maximum effectiveness. Even if you have a fascinating topic and a compelling thesis statement, your audience will quickly lose interest if your presentation lacks coherence and order. Several studies conducted in educational settings have formally demonstrated that effect. Research shows that when teachers present material in an organized, coherent manner, their students are more motivated to learn,[3] take more detailed course notes,[4] and recall more of the material than when teachers' presentations are disorganized.[5]

As you'll see in this section, an organized presentation has several features:

- An *introduction* that previews the information to be presented.
- A *body* composed of specific main points.
- *Transitions* that connect the main points to one another.
- A *conclusion* that summarizes the main points.

Figure 1 summarizes how these elements come together to form an effective speech.

THE INTRODUCTION TELLS THE STORY OF YOUR SPEECH

You get only one chance to make a good first impression. The same is true when you're giving a speech. A good presentation starts with an introduction that accomplishes two goals: It captures your listeners' interest in your topic, and it previews the points you plan to make.

The Introduction Generates Interest in Your Topic First, your introduction should grab your listeners' attention and arouse their interest in your topic. One

When teachers present material in an organized, coherent fashion, their students are better motivated to learn.

David Planchet/McGraw-Hill Education

way to accomplish that goal is to open with a story that will spark your audience's curiosity. Imagine a speech that begins with the following:

> *I was running late that morning, so I threw my belongings in my backpack and rushed out of my house. I set my coffee on the roof of my car while I opened the driver's side door and tossed my bag in the back seat. No sooner had I done so than I heard car alarms all around the neighborhood going off. I saw my coffee cup fall to the ground and shatter. It felt like someone was jumping up and down on the back bumper. Then, as quickly as it started, it was over. It took me a few moments to realize I had just experienced my first earthquake.*

That story would be an effective start to a speech about earthquakes because it begins with an easily relatable experience ("I was running late that morning"), describes unusual events (coffee cup shattering, car shaking), and reveals the explanation for those events (an earthquake) only at the end.

Another way to spark your listeners' interest in your topic is to use statistics that illustrate its magnitude. For example:

> *Children in the United States are dealing with a growing problem, literally speaking. Over 9 million of them are overweight or obese. That's more people than the populations of Los Angeles, Chicago, San Antonio, and Detroit put together. Unfortunately, the problem is getting worse. In the past three decades, the childhood obesity rate has more than tripled for children aged 6 to 11. Obesity raises the risks of a range of health problems, including diabetes, hypertension, and heart disease. The annual cost of treating obesity-related disorders for children is nearly $150 million.*

This introduction uses a few well-chosen statistics to illustrate the gravity of the problem of childhood obesity. It also provides an example to help the audience to interpret the number of obese children. Simply saying obesity affects 9 million children may be ineffective if listeners aren't sure whether that's a large or small group. Explaining that the number exceeds the combined population of four major U.S. cities gives them a context for understanding its importance.

In addition to using a story or a statistic to generate interest in your topic, you can use any of the following techniques:

- *Present a quotation.* Many speakers capture attention with a well-phrased quotation relevant to their topic—for instance: "As former U.S. senator Elizabeth Dole once said, 'Power is a positive force if it is used for positive purposes.'[6] Today, I'd like to discuss some of the many ways we can use power to improve the lives of others."

- *Tell a joke.* Opening your speech with a joke can be a particularly effective way to capture your listeners' attention, put them at ease, and generate positive feelings about you. Always make certain that your humor is appropriate for your audience and for the occasion and that it won't be interpreted as offensive.

- *Pose a question.* Beginning your speech with a question is a great way to get your audience thinking about your topic. You could ask something you want listeners to answer, such as "By show of hands, how many of you have ever been called for jury duty?" You can also pose a *rhetorical question*, one you want your listeners to think about but not respond to—for instance: "Why do you suppose you can't tickle yourself?"

FIGURE 1

PUTTING IT ALL TOGETHER: THE PARTS OF AN ORGANIZED PRESENTATION

Introduction
1. Generate interest in topic
2. Preview main points
Transition

Body
1. First main point

Transition
2. Second main point

Transition
3. Third main point

Conclusion
1. Reinforce central point
2. Create memorable moment

An organized presentation features an introduction, a body, a conclusion, and transitions to link the main points.

SHARPEN Your Skills:
Finding and using statistics

Identify a topic for an informative speech, such as immigration, canine anatomy, or the worldwide digital divide. Using the Internet, locate three different statistics you could use in an introduction to generate interest in that topic.

Dmitriy Shironosov/123RF

- *Cite an opinion.* Provocative opinions from well-known people can also get your listeners' attention—for example: "World-renowned physicist Stephen Hawking once warned scientists that making contact with aliens would be disastrous for the human race. In this speech, I'll be exploring some of the reasons he may have been exactly right."

- *Startle your listeners.* Saying or doing something unexpected can be an effective way to capture the attention of your audience. Begin your speech by singing, for example, or by speaking in a foreign language. People tend to pay attention to what is unusual, so if you start your presentation in an unexpected way, your listeners are likely to take note.

- *Note the occasion.* Particularly if you are speaking to give honor to a person, place, or event, you can generate attention by noting the importance of the occasion—or instance: "We have come together in this beautiful place to honor the 50th wedding anniversary of two very special people."

- *Relate your topic to the audience.* An excellent way to establish rapport with your listeners is to relate your topic to them by referring to something with which they are familiar. If you're speaking in a very small community, for example, you might start by saying "As I was driving in this morning, I was a little unsure of my directions, which simply said to 'turn left after the big red house.' Once I got to town, though, it made perfect sense!" By noting something with which your audience is familiar—in this case, the smallness of the town—you make a personal connection with your listeners.

- *Incorporate technology.* Regardless of what you say in your introduction, you can use various forms of technology to generate listener interest. As you present a quotation or cite an opinion, for instance, show a photo of the person you're referencing. If you're telling a suspenseful story, play suspenseful music in the background.

The Introduction Previews Your Main Points Once you have aroused your listeners' interest in your topic, your second goal is to preview the points you plan to make in your speech. A preview will help your listeners pay attention to the body of your speech by identifying ahead of time what they should listen for. Previews can be simple and straightforward, like the following example from a speech about music education:

> Today I'd like to talk about the importance of funding music education in our public schools. First, I'll explain how learning about music helps children both intellectually and socially. Then I'll discuss the challenges to music education funding that our public schools have faced in recent years. Finally, I'll offer some ideas for ensuring that music education is supported for generations to come.

Notice that this preview clearly identifies the major ideas the speaker plans to address. It isn't necessary to explain or justify the ideas during the preview; that's the purpose of the body of the speech. Rather, it's only necessary to identify the points you intend to make. If you put your preview at the end of your introduction, it will also help you transition to the body of your speech by serving as a lead-in to your first main point.

Some speeches focus on topics to which listeners will be sensitive, perhaps because they are uncomfortable or embarrassing to talk about. When you select such a topic as the focus of your speech, it's important to frame your introduction accordingly, as the "Difficult Conversations" box explains.

THE BODY EXPRESSES YOUR MAIN POINTS

If the introduction is the warm-up for your presentation, the body is the main act. The body will be the longest part of your speech, because it's where you will deliver the message you previewed in the introduction.

Difficult Conversations

Introducing a Sensitive Topic

Imagine this: Many potential speech topics can be somewhat sensitive for your audience. We tend to find some issues uncomfortable to think about, such as end-of-life planning or dealing with significant debt. Other topics can be embarrassing to talk about, such as having hemorrhoids or sexual dysfunction. On occasion, a topic can be sensitive because of what is happening in the environment, such as speaking about suicide shortly after a fellow student has taken his own life.

Now, consider this: Just because a topic is sensitive, that doesn't necessarily mean you shouldn't choose it as the focus of your speech. When you do anticipate that your audience may be sensitive about your topic, however, it is helpful to introduce that topic in a caring, tactful way. Consider these strategies:

- Acknowledge that your topic is sensitive, and recognize why. One of the worst ways to introduce a sensitive topic is to ignore the fact that it's sensitive and hope your audience doesn't notice. Instead, be upfront with listeners: "I know it isn't easy to talk about end-of-life planning. Pondering our own mortality can be scary. Nonetheless, I plan to show how having an advance health care directive can ease the emotional and financial stress on our loved ones should we become incapacitated or terminally ill."

- Preview what you plan to say about your sensitive topic. In any introduction, offering a preview of your main points helps you explain to listeners what they can expect to hear during your speech. This is especially useful when introducing a sensitive topic, because it lets listeners know that everything you plan to say about your topic will be relevant and worthy of their attention; in other words, you won't be asking your audience to think about your topic for unimportant reasons.

- Try to avoid euphemisms for your sensitive topic. To lessen listeners' discomfort, some speakers refer to their topics using euphemisms, which are mild or indirect terms that are substituted for terms we find too harsh or blunt. For instance, a student speaking about male sexual problems might use the euphemism "floppy jalopy" in place of "erectile dysfunction." Although euphemisms can be successful in reducing audience discomfort, they can also trivialize the topic, making it seem less important than it is.

Many issues are worthy of attention in public speeches, even if they are uncomfortable to think or talk about. We do listeners a disservice by sticking only to topics that are comfortable and "safe." Nonetheless, when you have chosen a topic that you expect to be sensitive for your audience, it helps to introduce that topic in a caring and competent manner.

To organize the body of your speech, identify the main points you want to address. A **main point** is a statement expressing a specific idea or theme related to the speech topic. Most speeches have between two and five main points; if you have more than five, your audience may have difficulty remembering them. As you'll see in this section, you want to ensure that your main points are related, distinct, and equally important. You'll also want to consider your best option for arranging them.

• **main point** A statement expressing a specific idea or theme related to the speech topic.

Main Points Should Be Related Suppose you wanted to draft an informative speech about hormones, using the following purpose and thesis statements:

Purpose statement: *Explain the structure and function of the human hormone system.*

Thesis statement: *The human hormone system releases chemical messengers to direct the activity of organs and tissues in the body.*

You might then propose the following main points:

Main point 1: *Hormones are chemicals that affect the cell metabolism of organs and tissues.*

Main point 2: *Hormones are produced and released into the bloodstream by a system of glands.*

Main point 3: *Hormones produce different effects on the body, depending on their chemical compositions.*

Notice that the main points relate to one another because they all address the speech topic, the hormone system. The first main point defines what hormones are, the second indicates where they come from, and the third identifies the different effects they can have. You don't want any of your points to seem out of place or unrelated to the topic of the presentation. For example, suppose you had proposed the following main points:

Main point 1: *Hormones are chemicals that affect the cell metabolism of organs and tissues.*

Main point 2: *Hormones are produced and released into the bloodstream by a system of glands.*

Main point 3: *The immune system also releases chemicals into the bloodstream that affect the body.*

The third main point may interest you, but it does not relate to the purpose statement and thesis statement of your speech. If you wanted to keep the third main point in your outline, you would need to expand your purpose and thesis statements to include information about the immune system. Otherwise, you are better off replacing the third main point with one that better relates to your topic.

Main Points Should Be Distinct Main points must also be distinct from one another. Although they all address the same topic, each main point in the preceding example expresses a different idea: what hormones are, where they come from, and what they do. If two points express the same idea, they do not constitute distinct points. Let's say, for instance, that you proposed the following main points:

Main point 1: *Hormones are chemicals that affect the cell metabolism of organs.*

Main point 2: *Hormones are chemicals that affect the cell metabolism of tissues.*

These two statements are probably not different enough to justify being separated into two main points. Rather, you should combine those messages into one main point:

Hormones are chemicals that affect the cell metabolism of organs and tissues.

Main Points Should Be Equally Important A third consideration about your main points is their relative importance, which will dictate how much time you spend discussing each one in your speech. Ideally, you want to give each approximately the same amount of time.

Let's say you have three main points but plan to spend 95 percent of your time discussing the first two. That leaves only 5 percent of your time for your third point. In this situation, you would need to reconsider the relative importance of your three points. Perhaps you actually have only two main points, in which case you might delete the third. Or perhaps you aren't devoting sufficient time to the third point, in which case you should spend less time discussing the first two. If all the main points in the body of your speech are relatively equal in importance, you should give them roughly equal time.

Main Points Can Be Organized in Various Patterns In addition to being related, distinct, and equally important, your main points should be organized in a manner that makes sense for your topic. You can organize them in several different patterns, depending on what they are and how they are related to one another. Consider which of the following five options might work best for your speech:

1. *Arranging points by topic.* When you adopt a **topic pattern**, you organize your main points to represent different categories. Let's say you are preparing an informative speech about aquatic life. You might include separate main points about different categories of aquatic life, with an outline that looks like this:

   A. Fish

   B. Amphibians

   C. Reptiles

   D. Mammals

   If your points don't lend themselves to already-established categories, you can create categories of your own. In a speech about friendships, for instance, you might distinguish various types of friends along the lines of this outline:

   A. Good-time friends: those you always have fun with

   B. Counselor friends: those with whom you share your problems

   C. Downer friends: those who frequently put you in a bad mood

   D. Connected friends: those who seem to know everything about everyone

2. *Arranging points by time.* A second option for organizing your main points is to use a **time pattern**, which means arranging them in chronological order. This option is particularly useful when you are describing the steps of a process, such as designing a scientific study:

   A. Pose a testable question

   B. Construct a hypothesis

   C. Collect data

   D. Analyze data and draw a conclusion

   A time pattern is also useful when your main points describe a historical sequence of events, such as in this outline of a speech about the events leading to the decline of the Roman Empire:

   A. Reign of Theodosius I

   B. Crossing of the Rhine

   C. Rise of the Hunnic Empire

   D. Deposition of Julius Nepos and Romulus Augustus

3. *Arranging points by space.* A **space pattern** organizes your main points according to areas. In a speech about the earth's atmosphere, you might arrange the various atmospheric layers as they exist from the ground up:

   A. Troposphere

   B. Stratosphere

   C. Mesosphere

   D. Thermosphere

   E. Magnetosphere

4. *Arranging points by cause and effect.* In a **cause-and-effect pattern**, you organize your points so they describe the causes of an event or a phenomenon and then

• **topic pattern** A pattern of organizing the main points of a speech to represent different categories.

• **time pattern** A pattern of organizing the main points of a speech in chronological order.

Hulton Archive/Getty Images

• **space pattern** A pattern of organizing the main points of a speech according to areas.

• **cause-and-effect pattern** A pattern of organizing the main points of a speech so that they describe the causes of an event and then identify its consequences.

identify its consequences. If you wanted to discuss the effects of acid rain, you could arrange your main points in this way:

A. Causes of acid rain

   1. Natural causes, such as volcanic eruptions

   2. Human-made causes, such as industrial pollution

B. Effects of acid rain

   1. Effects on plants and wildlife

   2. Effects on surface waters and aquatic animals

   3. Effects on human health

5. *Arranging points by problem and solution.* A **problem-solution pattern** is similar to a cause-and-effect pattern, except that you are organizing your points so they describe a problem and then offer one or more solutions for it. Notice that pattern in this example of a speech about victims of identity theft:

A. The problem of identity theft

   1. Use of your name, Social Security number, or bank accounts without permission

   2. Increases in incidence of identity theft

B. What you should do if you're a victim

   1. Inform credit bureaus

   2. Notify the police

   3. Check your bank statements for any discrepancies

Some ways of organizing your main points are likely to work better than others, depending on what those main points are. If they describe a series of events, then a time pattern will work better than a space pattern. If they identify types or categories of something, then a topic pattern is probably best. Consider what your main points are and how they are related to one another to select the organizational method that will work best for your speech.

TRANSITIONS HELP YOUR SPEECH FLOW SMOOTHLY

A **transition** is a statement that logically connects one point in a speech to the next. Good public speakers use transitions to link the introduction to the body of the speech, and the body to the conclusion. They also use transitions to connect the main points in the body of the speech to one another. Effective transitions give a speech "flow" by bridging each part of the presentation to the next. Some transitions are full statements that provide previews and internal summaries of the material. Other transitions are single words or phrases, called "signposts," that help to distinguish one point from another. Finally, many nonverbal behaviors can signal transitions.

Some Transitions Preview and Internally Summarize One type of transition is a **preview transition**, a statement alerting listeners that you are about to shift to a new topic. Notice how each of the following examples previews a change of topic:

- *Next, I'd like to discuss recent innovations in standardized testing.*
- *Let's now turn our attention to the health implications of managed care.*

As you can see, previews need only be short statements and do not present any new information. By signaling a change of topic, they help your listeners to track where you are in your speech.

ronnarid somphong/123RF

• problem-solution pattern A pattern of organizing the main points of a speech so that they describe a problem and then offer solutions for it.

• transition A statement that connects one point in a speech to the next.

• preview transition A statement alerting listeners that a speaker is about to shift to a new topic.

A second type of transition is the **summary transition**, a statement that briefly reminds listeners of points you have already made. For example:

- *As we've seen, some military personnel lack adequate training and resources to accomplish their missions.*
- *So far, we have discussed two of the three forms that water can take: gas and liquid.*

Notice that each statement simply identifies the points already covered. Each reminds listeners about what they have learned so far and signals that those points are complete.

It is possible to combine summaries and previews. Many speakers will use a summary when they are finishing a point and then use a preview to start the next point. For instance:

- *At this point, we have covered the early life and reign of Mary, Queen of Scots. Next, let's examine her imprisonment and trial.*

Some Transitions Are Signposts Previews and summaries are typically full sentences, but you can also use single words or phrases to distinguish one point in your presentation from another. Such words and phrases (such as "for example" and "on the other hand") are known as **signposts** because they serve as signs to help listeners to follow the path or outline of your speech.

As you'll see in Table 2, signposts can serve several specific functions, including comparing or contrasting points, indicating a sequence of events, providing an explanation, and emphasizing the importance of a point. The signposts that will work best for your presentation will depend on the particular points you intend to make.

Some Transitions Are Nonverbal In addition to using verbal transitions, you can also help listeners to follow your speech by incorporating specific nonverbal behaviors, including

- *Body movement.* Unless you are standing behind a podium during your speech, use the available space to move around during your presentation. You can highlight transitions from one point to the next nonverbally by changing where you are standing as you discuss each point.
- *Vocal inflection.* Inflection refers to variation in the pitch and volume of your voice. You can increase your volume and pitch to emphasize that a specific point is very important. As you prepare to transition between points, let your volume and pitch drop as you conclude one point and then rise again as you begin the next point.
- *Pauses.* The brief silence of a pause is an effective way to signal that you have finished your current point and are about to start the next one. You can also pause for effect, such as after you've made a very important statement that you want your listeners to think about before you move on.
- *Gestures.* You can use hand movements to punctuate your speech. If you intend to present three main points in the body of your presentation, you might signal the start of your first, second, and third points by holding up

TABLE 2
FOLLOW ALONG: SOME EFFECTIVE SIGNPOSTS

SPECIFIC FUNCTION	EXAMPLES
Compare or contrast points	*On the other hand* *In contrast* *Similarly*
Indicate a sequence of events	*First, Second, Third* *Primarily* *Now, Then* *Finally*
Provide explanation	*For instance* *To illustrate* *In other words*
Emphasize importance	*Most important* *Remember that* *Above all*
Show cause and effect	*If, Then* *Consequently* *Therefore*
Give additional examples	*Likewise* *In a similar way* *As a second example*
Summarize	*Finally* *As I've explained* *In summary*

one, two, or three fingers, respectively. If you're comparing two arguments, you might hold out your right hand and say "on the one hand . . ." and then hold out your left as you say "on the other hand . . ."

Nonverbal transition behaviors are generally effective only to the extent that they seem natural rather than staged. As you rehearse your speech, practice using movement, inflection, pauses, and gestures until they feel natural. When you can incorporate these behaviors without consciously thinking about them, they are likely to look and seem natural to your audience.

Using effective transitions ensures that the shifts from one part of your speech to the next don't seem abrupt. You want all parts of your speech to fit together seamlessly so that your listeners can easily follow your presentation from start to finish.

THE CONCLUSION SUMMARIZES YOUR MESSAGE

If your introduction is the warm-up for your speech and the body is the main act, then your conclusion is the grand finale. Your conclusion should accomplish two main tasks: reinforce your central message and create a memorable moment for your listeners.

Good speakers use gestures and movement to signal transitions between topics.

PictureNet/Corbis

The Conclusion Reinforces Your Central Message First, you want your conclusion to reinforce your thesis statement, which is your speech's central message. Good speakers often accomplish this goal by repeating the thesis statement and then summarizing the main points they have made in support of it.

Suppose you're concluding an informative speech about the recent increase in U.S. families' adoptions of children from foreign countries. Here's an example of how you might reinforce your message:

> *As I've explained, foreign adoptions are on the rise in the United States for three primary reasons. First, the number of children in foreign orphanages is growing. Second, increasing numbers of American adults are choosing to adopt instead of having biological children of their own. Finally, changes in foreign adoption laws have streamlined the process of adopting children from overseas. Although foreign adoptions still have their challenges, more and more American families are deciding to pursue them.*

Notice that the conclusion begins with the central idea of the speech (foreign adoptions are increasing in the United States), repeats the three main points of the speech (number of children in foreign orphanages, numbers of Americans choosing to adopt, changes in adoption laws), and then restates the central idea even more strongly (more and more American families are pursuing foreign adoptions). By accomplishing these three tasks, the conclusion clearly reinforces the speech's thesis statement.

The Conclusion Creates a Memorable Moment The second goal for your conclusion is to create a *memorable moment* for your audience. A memorable moment is something your listeners will remember about the speech even if they no longer recall all your specific points. You can probably think of movies that had memorable endings, for instance—although you may not remember every detail of the plot, you remember how they ended. Creating a memorable moment in your conclusion will similarly help your listeners to recall your presentation.

One strategy for making your speech memorable is to end it with humor. If the concluding lines of your presentation make the audience laugh, your listeners are likely to remember your speech—and remember it positively. Another option for creating a memorable conclusion is to surprise your audience. You might begin your speech by telling part of a story, for instance, and then give the story an unexpected ending in your conclusion.

Finally, many great speeches end on an emotionally stirring note. In 2009, on the steps of the U.S. Capitol Building in Washington, D.C., Barack Obama concluded his inaugural address with this dramatic appeal:

> *America, in the face of our common dangers, in this winter of our hardship, let us remember these timeless words. With hope and virtue, let us brave once more the icy currents, and endure what storms may come. Let it be said by our children's children that when we were tested, we refused to let this journey end, that we did not turn back nor did we falter. And with eyes fixed on the horizon and God's grace upon us, we carried forth that great gift of freedom and delivered it safely to future generations. Thank you, God bless you, and God bless the United States of America.*

Many great speeches end on an emotionally dramatic note that captivates the audience.
Brooks Kraft LLC/Corbis/Getty Images

Whether you use humor, surprise, or drama, creating a memorable moment in your conclusion will help to ensure that your audience remembers your presentation.

Now that you know how to construct an introduction, a body, transitions, and a conclusion, it's time to create an outline for your speech. Preparing a good outline requires some effort, but it is a useful step in the development of an effective speech.

Create an Effective Outline

In architecture, a blueprint is a technical drawing that reflects the design of a structure, such as a house, ship, or bridge. Engineers use the blueprint as a guide for determining the types of materials required to build the structure effectively. When you're building a speech, a good outline serves the same purpose: it reflects your speech's design and helps you decide what materials you'll need.

We begin this section by examining three rules of outlining. Next, we'll walk through the process of creating a working speech outline. Finally, we'll see how to convert your working outline into useful speaking notes. As we do so, bear in mind that the outlining process is done in conjunction with finding supporting materials—which we discuss toward the end of this chapter—and that you may need to modify your outline as you consider what your supporting evidence has to say.

• **rule of subordination** A rule of speech organization specifying that some concepts in the speech are more important than others.

Andrew Jones/Image Source/SuperStock

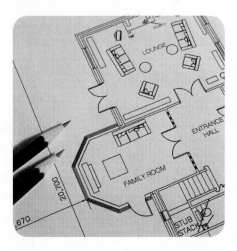

KNOW THE THREE RULES OF OUTLINING

Following three basic rules will help you to create an efficient outline for your speech. These rules govern subordination, division, and parallel structure.

Rule of Subordination First, the **rule of subordination** specifies that some concepts in your speech are more important than others. As a result, you want to make the most important concepts your main points and the less important concepts your subordinate points, or *subpoints*.

Let's say you're preparing an informative speech about how to become an FBI agent. When considering what you want to say, you compile the following list of points:

1. Prospective agents must meet specific criteria.
2. Prospective agents must be U.S. citizens.
3. Prospective agents must be between 21 and 37 years of age.
4. Prospective agents must have 20/20 eyesight.
5. Prospective agents must pass an extensive training program.

If the purpose of your speech is to explain how to become an FBI agent, then all these points are important, but they are not *equally* important. Specifically, the first and fifth points are broad statements about the requirements for agents. The second, third, and fourth points, however, are specific examples of the criteria referred to in the first point. Thus, it would make more sense to organize your points in this way:

1. Prospective agents must meet specific criteria.
    a. Prospective agents must be U.S. citizens.
    b. Prospective agents must be between 21 and 37 years of age.
    c. Prospective agents must have 20/20 eyesight.
2. Prospective agents must pass an extensive training program.

Notice that this outline still includes all five of your original concepts, but they are now organized according to the rule of subordination. The most important concepts are the main points, and the less important concepts are subpoints.

The Rule of Division The second rule of outlining is the **rule of division**, which specifies that if you divide a point into subpoints, you must create at least two subpoints. Suppose the only criterion for becoming an FBI agent were U.S. citizenship. In that case, your outline would look like this:

1. Prospective agents must meet specific criteria.
    a. Prospective agents must be U.S. citizens.
2. Prospective agents must pass an extensive training program.

According to the rule of division, however, if a point has one subpoint, then it must have at least one more. The reason is that if there is only one subpoint, it communicates the same amount of information as the main point. In that instance, it would be better to replace the main point with the subpoint so that your outline looked like this:

1. Prospective agents must be U.S. citizens.
2. Prospective agents must pass an extensive training program.

Notice that this outline gives the same amount of information as the one before it.

The Rule of Parallel Structure The third requirement of outlining is to follow the **rule of parallel structure**, which states that all points and subpoints in your outline should have the same grammatical structure. If you write some points as complete sentences, you should write them all that way. Avoid writing some points as complete sentences, others as incomplete sentences, and others as single words. Giving all your points a uniform structure helps them to fit together to form your speech.

Notice that our three subpoints from the previous example are all worded in the form of complete sentences and are therefore parallel:

1. Prospective agents must be U.S. citizens.
2. Prospective agents must be between 21 and 37 years of age.
3. Prospective agents must have 20/20 eyesight.

• **rule of division** A rule of speech organization specifying that if a point is divided into subpoints, it must have at least two subpoints.

• **rule of parallel structure** A rule of speech organization specifying that all points and subpoints in an outline should have the same grammatical structure.

Suppose instead that we had worded our three subpoints as follows:

1. Prospective agents must be U.S. citizens.
2. How old do prospective agents have to be?
3. 20/20 eyesight

These subpoints violate the rule of parallel structure because the first is a statement, the second is a question, and the third is a sentence fragment.

Once you've mastered the rules of subordination, division, and parallel structure, you're ready to develop a working outline for your presentation.

CREATE A WORKING OUTLINE

A **working outline** is a structured set of all the points and subpoints in your speech. Creating a working outline helps to ensure that you're covering all the points you wish to make. It also assists you with identifying the places in your speech where you will need to include supporting material. Compiling a working outline takes some time and effort, but it will pay off by helping you to develop a high-quality speech.

Most working outlines for a speech include the following elements:

- Title
- Purpose statement
- Thesis statement
- Introduction
- Main points and subpoints comprising the body of the speech
- Conclusion
- Bibliography of sources

We have already covered the process of creating a purpose statement, a thesis statement, main points, and subpoints. When compiling a working outline, you'll want to start with those elements and add the title, introduction, conclusion, and bibliography, all in outline form.

Let's say you're preparing a persuasive speech about the dangers of buying prescription medications online. Figure 2 provides an example of what your working outline might look like.

Several characteristics of this working outline warrant attention. The title expresses what you intend to say in your speech. The purpose and thesis statements are clear and easy to understand. The introduction leads listeners into your speech. The body is composed of three main points, each supported by two subpoints. The conclusion indicates the exact message you want your listeners to remember.

Your working outline will often conclude with a **bibliography**, a list of the sources you used in preparing your speech. To develop a speech about buying prescription drugs online, you will likely consult books, journal articles, websites, and/or other sources to learn more about Internet drug sales, laws that govern them, and people who have been hurt by such transactions. You will probably cite some of those sources directly when delivering your speech and use others only as a source of background information. Usually you will include all of them in your bibliography.

To list your sources in a bibliography, you'll need to follow a particular format. Of the several available citation formats, most people in the

• **working outline** A structured set of all the points and subpoints in a speech.

• **bibliography** A list of the sources used in preparing a speech.

> ### SHARPEN Your Skills: *Outlining*
>
> Construct a working outline for a speech on a topic of your choosing. Make sure it contains all the required elements. Also take care to follow the rules of subordination, division, and parallel wording. Trade your outline with a classmate's and offer suggestions on each other's efforts.

TITLE: Buying Prescription Drugs Online Is Risky

Purpose statement: Persuade my audience that buying prescription medications online involves some risks.

Thesis statement: Buying prescription medications online is too risky to do.

INTRODUCTION

I. Buying prescription medications online entails many risks.
   A. According to the National Institute of Drug Abuse, online sales of prescription medications have nearly quadrupled in the past five years.
   B. My friend Terrie bought an antidepressant from an online pharmacy and ended up seriously ill and in legal trouble.
   C. **Thesis:** Buying prescription medications online is too risky to do.

Transition: We will now look at three of the biggest risks of buying prescription medications online: financial risks, medical risks, and legal risks.

BODY

I. **Main Point 1:** Buying prescription medications online poses financial risks.
   A. Purchases made from online pharmacies may not be covered by insurance, leaving consumers to bear the cost.
      1. Many insurance plans identify specific pharmacies from which patients can order medications.
      2. Out-of-pocket payments for medications can pose a large financial burden for a middle-class family.
   B. Some pharmacies may not ship products that online customers order, causing consumers to lose money for purchases they never receive.
      1. Consumer research indicates that unfilled online orders are increasing in frequency.
      2. Patients who do not receive their products have few options for legal recourse against an online pharmacy.

Transition: Many people have lost significant amounts of money buying prescriptions online. Others have encountered medical risks.

II. **Main Point 2:** Buying prescription medications online poses medical risks.
   A. Online pharmacies may not be subject to government safety standards.
      1. Pharmacies registered outside of the United States are not subject to oversight by the U.S. Food and Drug Administration the way that U.S. pharmacies are.

2. Some online pharmacies are registered in countries with few, if any, government standards for pharmaceutical safety.
   B. Consumers may receive medications containing unsafe ingredients.
      1. Medications sold online may contain inconsistent quantities of active ingredients.
      2. A study by the World Health Organization found that more than half of the medications sold online contained dangerous levels of potentially toxic substances.

Transition: Using medications bought online can put people's health at risk. It can also pose legal risks.

III. **Main Point 3:** Buying prescription medications online poses legal risks.
   A. Some online pharmacies may not be properly licensed to dispense medications.
      1. In the United States, a pharmacy must be staffed by a registered pharmacist who has a license to dispense medication.
      2. Online pharmacies registered outside the United States may employ few people, if any, with the credentials to practice pharmacy.
   B. Consumers may be violating the law by purchasing prescription medications from unlicensed vendors.
      1. Purchasing controlled pharmaceutical products without a prescription is illegal in the United States, even if the products were purchased outside the country.
      2. U.S. customs officials have recently announced that locating and confiscating illegally purchased medications is an agency priority.

Transition: Many people find themselves in trouble with the law after buying prescription medications from online pharmacies.

CONCLUSION

I. Review of main points
   A. Ordering medications over the Internet may be convenient.
   B. The financial, medical, and legal risks it entails make it irresponsible and unwise.
II. Final remarks
   A. It is crucial to exercise extreme caution when buying medications online.
   B. People are much safer purchasing their prescription medications from reputable, licensed pharmacies in their own communities.

communication field use either the American Psychological Association (APA) format or the Modern Language Association (MLA) format. Both formats specify how to cite a source properly. Table 3 provides examples of APA and MLA formats for citing books, journal articles, and other sources. You can learn more about both formats by visiting the websites listed in Table 3.

When you prepare speeches for class, your instructor may assign you a minimum number of citations to include in your bibliography and may indicate which citation format to use. You will learn more about finding appropriate sources for your speech—and evaluating whether they are credible—in the final section of this chapter.

TABLE 3

APA AND MLA CITATION
FORMATS

Book	APA:	Geddes, B., Wright, J., & Frantz, E. (2018). *How dictatorships work: Power, personalization, and collapse.* Cambridge University Press. https://doi.org/10.1017/9781316336182
	MLA :	Geddes, Barbara, et al. *How Dictatorships Work: Power, Personalization, and Collapse.* Cambridge University Press, 2018.
Magazine article	APA:	Oreskes, N. (2019, November 18). Put your faith in science. *Time,* 23–24.
	MLA:	Oreskes, Naomi. "Put Your Faith in Science." *Time,* November 2019, pp. 23–24.
Journal article	APA:	Longman, K., Daniels, J., Bray, D. L., & Liddell, W. (2018). How organizational culture shapes women's leadership experiences. *Administrative Sciences, 8*(2), 8–23. https://doi.org/10.3390/admsci8020008
	MLA:	Longman, Karen, et al. "How Organizational Culture Shapes Women's Leadership Experiences." *Management Communication Quarterly,* vol. 8, no. 2, 2015, pp. 8–23.
Newspaper article	APA:	Kristof, N. (2016, May 7). A confession of liberal intolerance. *The New York Times,* SR1.
	MLA:	Kristof, Nicholas. "A Confession of Liberal Intolerance." *The New York Times,* 7 May 2016, p. SR1.
YouTube video	APA:	Aranda, M. [scishow]. (2017, July 16). *Viroids: Possibly the smallest pathogen on Earth* [Video]. YouTube. https://www.youtube.com/watch?v=fhYbQHP44-c
	MLA:	Aranda, Michael. "Viroids: Possibly the Smallest Pathogen on Earth." *YouTube,* 16 Jul. 2017, youtube.com/watch?v=fhYbQHP44-c
Online publication	APA:	Belluz, J., & Zarracina, J. (2016, April 28). Why you shouldn't exercise to lose weight, explained with 60+ studies. *Vox.* http://www.vox.com/2016/4/28/11518804/weight-loss-exercise-myth-burn-calories
	MLA:	Belluz, Julia, and Javier Zarracina. "Why You Shouldn't Exercise to Lose Weight, Explained with 60+ Studies." *Vox,* 28 Apr. 2016, www.vox.com/2016/4/28/11518804/weight-loss-exercise-myth-burn-calories.
Blog posts	APA:	Gates, B. (2016, April 21). Opening minds on ed tech. [Web log Comment]. https://www.gatesnotes.com/Education/Tech-for-Teaching
	MLA:	Gates, Bill. "Opening Minds on Ed Tech." *gatesnotes,* 21 Apr. 2016, www.gatesnotes.com/Education/Tech-for-Teaching.
Website	APA:	Centers for Disease Control and Prevention. (2018, January 23). *People at high risk of developing flu-related complications.* https://www.cdc.gov/flu/about/disease/high_risk.htm
	MLA:	*People at High Risk of Developing Flu-Related Complications.* 23 Jan. 2018, www.cdc.gov/flu/about/disease/high_risk.htm
Published interview	APA:	Franco, J. (2016, April 7). Understanding James Franco, Interview by J. Weiner. *Rolling Stone,* 36–41.
	MLA:	"Understanding James Franco." Interview by Jonah Weiner. *Rolling Stone,* 7 Apr. 2016, pp. 36–41.
Radio or television interview	APA:	Whitford, B. (2019, January 9). Interview. *The Late Show with Stephen Colbert.* CBS, New York, NY. https://www.cbs.com/shows/the-late-show-with-stephen-colbert/video/g550ZB1_669UGpUx76xLyWgx3qDVhRje/why-bradley-whitford-misses-the-west-wing-/
	MLA:	Whitford, Bradley. Interview. *The Late Show with Stephen Colbert,* 9 Jan. 2019, https://www.cbs.com/shows/the-late-show-with-stephen-colbert/video/g550ZB1_669UGpUx76xLyWgx3qDVhRje/why-bradley-whitford-misses-the-west-wing-/.

The table compares the APA and MLA formats, both of which are popular in the communication field. APA examples are from the 7th edition of the publication manual, released October 2019. (For more about APA format, go to owl.english.purdue.edu/owl/resource/560/01/. For more about MLA format, visit owl.english.purdue.edu/owl/resource/557/01/.)

CONVERT YOUR WORKING OUTLINE INTO SPEAKING NOTES

• **speaking notes** An abbreviated version of a formal speech outline; also known as *speaking outline*.

• **speaking outline** An abbreviated version of a formal speech outline; see also *speaking notes*.

As we've seen, a working outline helps you to organize the structure and content of your speech. When you're delivering your speech, however, you may find your working outline too long and detailed to help you. For that reason, many speakers convert their working outlines into a set of speaking notes. **Speaking notes**, also called a **speaking outline**, are an abbreviated version of your working outline. Their purpose is to aid your delivery by reminding you of each of your points and subpoints. Remember that you will construct your outlines in conjunction with researching support for your points. We will cover the process of research later in this chapter.

Suppose you're preparing to deliver the speech about buying prescription drugs online that we outlined previously, and you want to convert your working outline into speaking notes. First, delete the title, purpose statement, and thesis statement. Replace those elements with a brief reminder about your speech's introduction. Let's say you want to begin with an anecdote about a friend whose health was compromised by medications purchased online. To remind yourself, you might use the phrase "Story about Terrie" in your speaking notes.

Next, abbreviate each of your main points and subpoints into a *keyword*—a word or short phrase that will help you to remember it. For instance, you could abbreviate the first main point, "Buying prescription medications online poses financial risks," with the phrase "Financial risks." Your purpose is to use as few words as possible to remind yourself about each point and subpoint. Finally, abbreviate your conclusion in the same way. When you've finished your speaking notes, you should have a brief outline that will be quick to read and easy to follow as you present.

Figure 3 provides an example of how you could convert your working outline about buying medications online into useful speaking notes. Notice that each note contains only a few words—just enough detail to jog your memory about the purpose of each point. A brief outline such as this will help you stay on track as you deliver your speech, without forcing you to ignore your listeners by reading long strings of text.

FIGURE 3

SPEAKING NOTES: BUYING PRESCRIPTION DRUGS ONLINE IS RISKY

INTRODUCTION
I. National Institute of Drug Abuse: Near-quadrupling of online sales of prescription medications in past five years
Ii. Friend Terrie's problems with antidepressants bought online
III. **Thesis:** Buying prescription medications online = too risky
Transition: Review financial, medical, legal risks

BODY
I. **Main Point 1:** Financial risks
  A. Insurance coverage
    1. Insurance plan restrictions
    2. Out-of-pocket costs
  B. Orders not shipped
    1. Increasingly frequent problem
    2. Few options for recourse
Transition: Significant money lost buying prescriptions online; medical risks

II. **Main Point 2:** Medical risks
  A. Safety standards lacking
    1. No FDA oversight for foreign pharmacies
    2. Some countries with few pharmaceutical safety standards
  B. Unreliable, unsafe ingredients

    1. Inconsistent quantities of active ingredients
    2. WHO study: potentially toxic ingredients
Transition: Health risks of medications; legal risks, too

III. **Main Point 3:** Legal risks
  A. Unlicensed pharmacies
    1. U.S. requires licensed pharmacies
    2. Online pharmacies—possibly lacking credentials
  B. Violating prescription laws
    1. Purchasing controlled medications without prescription illegal
    2. U.S. customs increasing surveillance

Transition: Legal problems after buying prescription medications from online pharmacies

CONCLUSION
I. Review of main points
  A. Convenience of online ordering
  B. Magnitude of financial, medical, legal risks
II. Final remarks
  A. Extreme caution needed when buying medications online
  B. Safer to purchase from reputable, licensed pharmacies in community

COMPETENT COMMUNICATOR

Speech Preparation Checklist—Dot Your i's and Cross Your t's

You have learned about several tasks essential to preparing a good speech. You will soon put your new knowledge and skills into practice by preparing a speech of your own. How will you know you have prepared adequately? Use the checklist below to ensure that you have completed each required step.

*Hill Street Studios/
Blend Images/Getty Images*

Speech Preparation Tasks

_____ I have drafted a purpose statement reflecting the specific goal of my speech.

_____ I have written a thesis statement summarizing the principal message of my speech.

_____ I have created an introduction that generates interest and previews my main points.

_____ I have organized my speech around related, distinct, and equally important main points.

_____ I have drafted a conclusion that summarizes my message and creates a memorable moment.

_____ I have used transitions throughout my speech to preview and review.

_____ I have created an outline that follows the rules of subordination, division, and parallel wording.

_____ I have converted my outline to a set of speaking notes.

_____ I have included a bibliography of all the sources I used when preparing my speech.

"The Competent Communicator" provides a handy checklist for preparing a speech. Consulting it will help ensure that you have completed all the steps necessary to develop a successful speech.

Now that you have created a working outline and speaking notes, you need to identify appropriate supporting material to help you to make your points convincingly. Let's turn to that essential task.

Find Support For Your Speech

Especially when your goal is to inform or to persuade, you will require supporting material to back up the claims you make in your speech. Finding supporting material is not difficult. However, as you will see in this section, to use it effectively you will need to

- Identify places in your speech outline where you need support.
- Determine the type of support you require.

- Evaluate the quality of supporting material.
- Avoid plagiarism.
- Deliver effective verbal footnotes during your speech.

IDENTIFY PLACES WHERE YOU NEED RESEARCH SUPPORT

Before locating supporting material for your speech, you must determine where you need it. Consult your outline to identify where you are making points that would benefit from supporting data. For instance, you need to provide research support whenever you make a factual claim. Recall from the chapter on how we use language that a factual claim is a statement asserting that something is objectively true. Each of the following statements is a factual claim because it argues that something is true in an objective sense:

- The Ebola virus causes high fever, abdominal pain, dizziness, and exhaustion.
- Chinese is the most commonly spoken language in the world.
- Syrah is a dark-skinned type of grape used for making red wine.
- Islam is the world's most widespread religion.

We can distinguish factual claims, which are statements about what *is* true, from opinions, which are statements of belief about what *ought to be* true. The statement "Every person should learn to speak Chinese" is an opinion, because it conveys what the speaker believes *should be*. The speaker might argue persuasively for that opinion and even cite opinions of political scientists or expert linguists as support. He or she cannot cite evidence showing that the statement is true and factual, however, because opinions are never true or false in an objective sense.

In contrast, the statement "Chinese is the most commonly spoken language in the world" is a factual claim because it is either true or false no matter how the speaker thinks or feels about it. When you make such a factual claim in a speech, you need to provide evidence that it is true. To locate effective supporting material, therefore, start by identifying the factual claims you intend to make, and then search for appropriate material to support each one.

DETERMINE THE TYPE OF SUPPORT YOU REQUIRE

Your options for supporting your speech claims include definitions, examples, statistics, quotations, and narratives. As we'll see, different types of claims require different types of support.

- *Definitions.* When your speech focuses on a concept that may be unfamiliar to your audience—or one that can have multiple meanings—you can support your use of that concept by defining it explicitly. In a presentation about conjunctivitis, you might say "According to *Stedman's Medical Dictionary*, conjunctivitis is an inflammation of the mucous membrane that lines the inner surface of the eye." By identifying the source of your definition, you give that definition credibility.
- *Examples.* Another way to help your audience understand a concept is to give examples of it. Suppose you're giving an informative speech about conspiracy theories. Even if your listeners understand in principle what a conspiracy theory is, they may benefit from hearing specific examples, which might include the conspiracy theories surrounding the assassination of President John F. Kennedy in 1963 and the attacks on the World Trade Center and Pentagon in 2001.
- *Statistics.* Statistics are numbers—usually identified through research—that you can use to support your claims. If your focus is on teen pregnancy, for instance,

you might support the importance of that topic in this way: "According to the Centers for Disease Control, the United States has the highest rate of teen pregnancy among all industrialized nations. Nearly 500,000 babies are born each year to mothers aged 15 to 19, and almost two-thirds of those pregnancies are unintended." By providing such statistics, you support your claim that teen pregnancy is a significant issue. Because some statistics are more reliable than others, however, it is always important to identify their source. The next section will give you some hints for determining the merit of your statistics.

- *Quotations.* Quotations from people who are recognized experts on your topic can serve as valuable supporting material. Suppose your presentation is about the 2020 outbreak of the coronavirus in the United States. To address the question of whether businesses closed during quarantine were reopening prematurely, you might say "As Anthony Fauci, director of the National Institute of Allergy and Infectious Disease, noted before testifying in front of Congress, 'The major message that I wish to convey to the Senate HLP committee tomorrow is the danger of trying to open the country prematurely.'"[7] As with definitions and statistics, it is critical to identify the source of the quotation and his or her qualifications for speaking on that topic.

- *Narratives.* Many speakers use narratives—such as personal stories or testimonies—to support their claims. If you're speaking about the benefits of laser eye surgery, you might relate stories of individuals who have had the procedure and experienced improvements in their life. When speaking about something that is personally relevant to you, you may also elect to share a story or testimony of your own. Narratives can be especially compelling for listeners because they often make a topic feel personal in a way that examples or statistics do not.

KNOW HOW TO EVALUATE SUPPORTING MATERIAL

Not all supporting material is equally valuable. You'll want to find the best possible supporting material, and that means checking carefully for three particular characteristics: credibility, objectivity, and currency.

Credibility As you learned in the language chapter, information has credibility if it is believable and trustworthy. Using credible supporting material helps you to make the points in your speech convincingly. To be credible, supporting material must come from a trustworthy source. A source is convincing if its experience, training, and expertise give its claims more authority than the claims of others.

Suppose your speech focuses on adolescent health. Which of the following statements do you think has more credibility?

- *According to Wikipedia.org, most adolescents have dietary habits that elevate their risk of cardiovascular disease.*

- *According to a report from the U.S. Surgeon General, most adolescents have dietary habits that elevate their risk of cardiovascular disease.*

These statements make exactly the same claim. The first statement attributes the claim to Wikipedia.org, a website that anyone—regardless of his or her credentials—can edit. The second statement attributes the claim to the U.S. Surgeon General, a recognized national authority on public health. As such an authority, the Surgeon General is a more credible source to cite on matters of public health than Wikipedia. The health information on Wikipedia isn't necessarily inaccurate. Rather, the Surgeon General—because of his or her professional training and medical expertise—is a more trustworthy source of medical information.

Corey Jenkins/Image Source/ Getty Images

By far the most terrifying film you will ever see.

aninconvenienttruth

A GLOBAL WARNING

www.climatecrisis.net

Hollywood movies, even documentaries, may be entertaining or provocative, but they are not necessarily good sources of credible, objective information.

AF archive/Alamy Stock Photo

Besides coming from an appropriate source, credible supporting material often also includes statistics that enumerate an effect. Statistics are simply numbers that you can use to help make a point more informatively. Imagine that you're speaking about safe driving, and you want to argue that talking on a cell phone while driving is dangerous. Which of the following statements makes that point more credibly?

- *According to the National Safety Council, talking on a cell phone while driving increases the chances of a collision.*

- *According to the National Safety Council, talking on a cell phone while driving increases the chances of a collision by 400 percent.*

The second statement specifies *how much* the risk of collision increases when the driver uses a cell phone. Saying that cell phone use increases the chance of a collision may be interesting, but it doesn't help your audience to understand the magnitude of the risk. That is, your listeners won't know whether cell phone use poses a relatively minor risk—which may cause them to ignore your point—or a significant risk—which may cause them to pay close attention.

Objectivity Some people think that any material they agree with is authentic and accurate, whereas anything they disagree with is "fake news." Human have a natural tendency to favor information that confirms their beliefs while ignoring material that does not. Whether we believe or agree with supporting material tells us absolutely nothing about that material's accuracy, however.

When you are evaluating the potential usefulness of supporting material, consider how objective the source is. A source is *objective* to the extent that it presents information in an unbiased fashion. In contrast, sources are *subjective* when they offer information in a manner that supports only their favored position on an issue. That distinction matters because many people will consider data from subjective sources to be untrustworthy.

Let's say you're preparing a speech about the effects of global warming on arctic animal life. Which is a more objective source to cite—a university study of climate change funded by the National Science Foundation or the movie *An Inconvenient Truth,* based on a book of the same title written by former U.S. vice president Al Gore? To what extent is each source objective? Most people would consider the scientific study to be more objective because the scientific method requires conclusions to be dictated by data. That is, regardless of what scientists *want* to be true, they can claim only what their data tell them. Moreover, a scientist's work is heavily reviewed and scrutinized by other scientists before it can be published. The scientific process therefore demands objectivity. Hollywood movies, in contrast, do not require objectivity. The purpose of most movies is to entertain, not to inform the audience of objective facts. That doesn't necessarily mean that statements made in a movie are untrue, but it does mean that movies are more subjective than scientific studies. Even though many people consider Gore to be an expert on the topic of climate change, his documentary would still have less objectivity than a scientific study that presents original, heavily scrutinized data.

When you are evaluating a source's objectivity, consider the extent to which that source has a political or financial interest in the content of the message. Some media sources routinely present information in a manner that is biased toward one political viewpoint or another, for instance, and that bias should be considered when evaluating the objectivity of news reports. In November 2019, for example, U.S. Congressional committees interviewed diplomats regarding president Donald Trump's interactions with Ukrainian leaders earlier in the year. The televised hearings were watched by millions, but viewers experienced quite different coverage depending on the news source they followed. Politically conservative Fox News framed the diplomats' testimony as lacking credibility and timed commercial breaks to coincide with questions from democratic congressional leaders. Some Fox News affiliates chose not to air the hearings at all.[8] On the contrary, politically liberal MSNBC framed the testimony in more dramatic terms, scrolling the heading "IMPEACHMENT: WHITE HOUSE IN CRISIS" as one of the diplomats spoke.[9] Although both news sources were reporting on the same event, their coverage reflected drastic differences in their political biases. As these news organizations know, viewers will tend to believe the coverage that reflects their own biases. Good speakers realize, however, that neither source provided objective coverage, because each source had a stake in framing its coverage to reflect its viewers' viewpoints.

Currency A final consideration when selecting supporting material is the currency of the information. Information that was produced or published recently is likely to be more up-to-date than older information. Using recent supporting material is particularly important when you're speaking about issues that change continually, such as technology and world politics.

Suppose you're developing a speech about how people communicate online. Which of the following sources would provide better supporting material?

> Lea, M., & Spears, R. (1992). Paralanguage and social perception in computer-mediated communication. *Journal of Organizational Computing, 2,* 321–341.

> Treem, J. W., Leonardi, P. M., & van den Hooff, B. (2020). Computer-mediated communication in the age of communication visibility. *Journal of Computer-Mediated Communication, 25,* 44–59.

Because of its more recent publication date, the second article would clearly provide more up-to-date information than the first. Given how rapidly computer-mediated communication technology develops, having the most recent information to support the points in your speech will be very advantageous.

As you search for appropriate supporting material, remember that credibility, objectivity, and currency are all important, but they are not necessarily equally important. When preparing a speech on Roman history, for instance, you may find the credibility of your sources to be more important than their currency, because the facts about Roman history don't change as rapidly as the facts about computer-mediated communication. If you're speaking about the safety of a new treatment for muscle pain, then the objectivity of your supporting material may be paramount, to ensure that the facts you present are as unbiased as possible. You should always consider the credibility, objectivity, and currency of potential supporting material, but you'll want to think about which of those properties are most important for your particular topic.

Several careers require the ability to find high-quality evidence and make sure that claims are aligned with the data. For one example, see the "Putting Communication to Work" box.

SHARPEN Your Skills: *Finding credible websites*

Consider the claim "Vaccines cause autism." Find three websites that offer data either supporting or refuting that claim. For each site, address the following questions: (1) Who created the site, and does that person or group have a reason to want this claim to be true or false? (2) What kind of data are presented? Are they the results of academic research or the observations of parents with autistic children? Based on your responses to those questions, write a short paragraph explaining which of the three websites is the most credible and why.

Job Title >

Work Responsibilities >

Fact Checker, News Media or Publishing Industry

As the unsung heroes of newsrooms around the country, fact checkers review reporters' and authors' materials to verify that the facts presented are accurate and supported by appropriate sources, and that material has not been plagiarized. Fact checkers must understand the nature of different sorts of claims to determine which ones need to be verified and which do not. They are also diligent reporters themselves, as they are frequently tasked with tracking down written sources and interviewing individuals to confirm everything from facts to quotes to spellings of names. Solid research, organizational, and communication skills are crucial.

Finding appropriate supporting material is essential. So, too, is our next topic: using that material appropriately and responsibly, to ensure that you aren't passing off someone else's work as your own.

DON'T COMMIT INTELLECTUAL THEFT

To support our claims or arguments in a speech or paper, many of us routinely use someone else's words, ideas, or data. Although incorporating material from other sources is perfectly acceptable, you must take care to avoid committing intellectual theft when you do so. A common form of intellectual theft is **plagiarism**, which means using information from another source without giving proper credit to that source. You plagiarize, that is, when you misrepresent someone else's words or ideas as your own.

Intellectual theft also comes in the form of **copyright infringement**, which means using materials that are owned by others—such as photos, videos, or songs—without gaining permission or giving proper recognition to their source. Many of these materials are protected by copyright, a legal recognition that the owner or creator of the material has the right to control its use. Copyright law generally allows people to use or make reference to copyrighted materials for academic purposes, including a class speech, so long as proper credit is made to the source. This chapter describes how to refer to sources during your speech, and the chapter on presenting a speech confidently and competently illustrates how to report copyright information when you include photos or video in your presentation slides.

Intellectual Theft Can Take Several Forms When people prepare speeches, they may commit intellectual theft in at least three different ways. Understanding each will help you avoid plagiarism or copyright infringement when you put together a public presentation.

- *Global theft* means stealing your entire speech from another source and presenting it as if it were your own. You would commit global theft if you

• **plagiarism** Knowingly using information from another source without giving proper credit to that source.

• **copyright infringement** The use of materials that are protected by copyright—such as photos or works of art—without gaining permission or giving proper recognition to their source.

downloaded a persuasive speech from the Internet and passed it off as your own, for instance. Similarly, if a friend allowed you to use an informative speech he wrote for another class as your own, that would also constitute global theft because you are representing the words as yours rather than his.

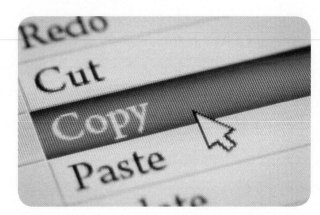

- *Patchwork theft* occurs when you copy words from multiple sources and put them together to compose your speech. Suppose you took large sections of your introduction from a magazine article, portions of your main points from a website, and the bulk of your conclusion from a television show. Even though you compiled those sources and wrote portions of your speech to tie them together, you would still be committing plagiarism because you are passing off someone else's words as your own. Similarly, if you download images from the Internet and include them in your presentation slides without making reference to their source, you are also committing patchwork intellectual theft.

Pavel Ignatov/Shutterstock

- *Incremental theft* means failing to give credit for small portions of your speech—such as a phrase or paragraph—that you did not write. It is entirely acceptable to quote other people's words in your speech, particularly if those words generate audience interest or support a claim. Whenever you do so, however, it is essential that you use a verbal footnote, a statement giving credit for the words to their original source. For example, you might say "According to the April 2020 edition of *Psychology Today*, . . . " or "As renowned opera singer José Carreras once noted, ..." If you are using the person's words exactly as he or she wrote them, say "quote" when you begin reciting the quoted passage and "end quote" when you have finished.

Intellectual Theft Is a Serious Offense Students who commit intellectual theft are stealing someone else's work and committing academic dishonesty by passing that work off as theirs. Colleges and universities enforce codes of student conduct that prohibit plagiarism and copyright infringement and identify punishments for offenders. At many schools, students convicted of intellectual theft can be given failing grades for a course, suspended from school, or even permanently expelled. Being found guilty of intellectual theft can also cast doubt over your credibility in the future. Professional associations in the communication discipline, including the National Communication Association and the International Communication Association, condemn plagiarism and copyright infringement as serious professional offenses.

Given the amount of information readily available online, some students are tempted to commit plagiarism in their speeches and papers because they believe the likelihood of getting caught is small. To combat plagiarism, however, instructors at many colleges and universities now employ plagiarism-detection software, such as SafeAssignment, iThenticate, or Turnitin. These programs check the text of speeches and papers against a wide variety of sources online, and they clearly identify passages of text that have been copied verbatim from another source, making it increasingly easy to spot plagiarism. For that reason alone, it is worth ensuring that you properly cite your sources and clearly identify any verbatim quotes in the speeches you prepare. You can learn more about plagiarism and the Internet by reading the "Fact or Fiction?" box.

The Internet also provides resources to help students to avoid intellectual theft. Table 4 describes three such websites you might find useful when you prepare a speech.

DELIVER EFFECTIVE VERBAL FOOTNOTES

Suppose you have collected all the information you need for giving proper credit to each of your sources. Now you must make it known to your audience as you cite each source during your speech. The way to do so is to use a **verbal footnote**, an oral

- **verbal footnote** A statement giving credit for quoted words in a speech to their original source.

TABLE 4	Website		Materials
AVOIDING INTELLECTUAL THEFT: SOME HELPFUL WEBSITES	plagiarism.org		Types of plagiarism; instructions for citing sources; frequently asked questions about plagiarism
	owl.english.purdue.edu/owl/resource/589/1		Specific tips for avoiding plagiarism; an exercise to identify properly cited sources
	paragondigital.com/blog/how-to-avoid -copyright-infringement/		Instructions for avoiding copyright infringement when using photos and images found online

Fact or *fiction*?

Using Information from the Internet Constitutes Plagiarism

Plagiarism is presenting someone else's words as your own. If you use a passage from a magazine article or dialogue from a television show in your speech without properly acknowledging the source, you are committing plagiarism because the words belong to someone else.

Some people believe that words posted online are an exception to that rule because the Internet doesn't technically **belong** to anyone in the way a magazine or television show does. According to that perspective, using words from the Internet in your speech would not constitute plagiarism, even if you represented those words as your own. That way of thinking is incorrect, however. If you did not write the words in your speech but you represent them as though you did, you are committing plagiarism, regardless of where those words came from. The rules are no different for the Internet than for any other source. You can use words in your speech from any source—including books, movies, and even websites—but you must indicate clearly that you are quoting someone else's words, and you must identify who wrote them.

ASK YOURSELF

- How is plagiarism a form of intellectual dishonesty?
- What can you do to ensure you aren't plagiarizing in your speech?

statement that gives credit to the original source of information. Verbal footnotes are also called *oral citations*, and when used correctly they can powerfully communicate the relevance, credibility, objectivity, accuracy, currency, and completeness of your evidence—all the features of good supporting material. Using verbal footnotes also demonstrates to your audience that you have done your research and prepared your presentation carefully and thoroughly.

Verbal footnotes are necessary whenever you refer to outside sources. That doesn't mean they have to sound boring, though. You can incorporate verbal footnotes into your speech in a variety of ways, as Table 5 illustrates.

In addition, you can create and deliver verbal footnotes that are as engaging as the rest of your speech by using these strategies:

TABLE 5

GO FOR DIVERSITY: VARY YOUR VERBAL FOOTNOTES

This table illustrates several ways to introduce the same verbal footnote.

In his 2016 book *Half-Earth*, Edward O. Wilson explains why preserving the planet's biodiversity is critical.

Preserving the Earth's biodiversity is critical, Edward O. Wilson observes in his 2016 book *Half-Earth*.

According to Edward O. Wilson's 2016 book *Half-Earth*, preserving the planet's biodiversity is critical.

Edward O. Wilson claims that preserving the Earth's biodiversity is critical in his 2016 book *Half-Earth*.

As Edward O. Wilson points out in his 2016 book *Half-Earth*, preserving the planet's biodiversity is critical.

- *Provide detailed information the first time.* You will refer to some pieces of evidence in your speech more than once. The first time you use a piece of evidence, give enough detail that your listeners could locate the source themselves, such as by saying "In his 2012 book, *The Science of Love*, Robin Dunbar explains . . . ." Here, you're omitting some of the information that would be included in a formal citation, such as the name of the book's publisher, but you're providing sufficient detail—the author's name, the book's title, the year of publication—that most listeners could locate the source if they wanted to.

- *Make shorter references to a source later.* Suppose you want to make another point in your speech using the same source. It's not necessary to repeat the statement "In his 2012 book, *The Science of Love*, Robin Dunbar explains . . ." to introduce your new point. Rather, you can abbreviate your verbal footnotes after the first time you refer to a source. Your second reference to the source might include only the author's last name and the book title, and for subsequent references to the same book, just using the author's last name suffices.

- *Cite sources where you use them.* To show that they've done their research, some speakers cite all of their sources at the same time near the beginning of their speech (or as they start a new point). Here's an example of what you want to *avoid* doing:

  The sources I used for my speech are the 2016 New York Times *article "Pope Francis' Race Against Time to Reshape the Church"; the 2016 book* Pilgrimage: My Search for the Real Pope Francis, *by Mark K. Shriver; and the official website of the Vatican.*

The problem with grouping the verbal footnotes in this way is that listeners won't know which source of evidence supports which claims in your speech. The best method is to cite the source of evidence only when you are referring to that evidence.

For REVIEW

- **What are the important elements of any speech?**

  When preparing a speech, you will draft purpose and thesis statements to guide you, as well as the introduction, body, conclusion, and transitions that will make up your speech.

- **Why are formal outlines and speaking notes useful?**

  Creating a formal outline helps to ensure that you have made all the points you wish to make in a logical manner. Speaking notes help you to remember each of your points while you are delivering your speech.

- **What evidence should you use to support your claims?**

  To support claims you have made in your speech, you need evidence that is credible, objective, and current. When using evidence in your speech, you must take care not to plagiarize someone else's work.

KEY TERMS

NOTES

1. Moravec, P. L., Minas, R. K., & Dennis, A. R. (2019). Fake news on social media: People believe what they want to believe when it makes no sense at all. *MIS Quarterly, 43*(4), 1343–1360. https://doi.org/10.25300/MISQ/2019/15505

2. Calafas, J. (2019, February 3). Here's how much it costs to buy a commercial during Super Bowl 2019. *Money.* http://money .com/money/5633822/super-bowl-2019-commercial-ad-costs/

3. Kiemer, K., Gröschner, A., Pehmer, A. K., & Seidel, T. (2015). Effects of a classroom discourse intervention on teachers' practice and students' motivation to learn mathematics and science. *Learning and Instruction, 35,* 94–103. https://doi .org/10.1016/j.learninstruc.2014.10.003

4. Titsworth, B. S. (2004). Students' notetaking: The effects of teacher immediacy and clarity. *Communication Education, 53*(4), 305–320. https://doi.org/10.1080/0363452032000305922

5. Titsworth, S., Mazer, J. P., Goodboy, A. K., Bolkan, S., & Myers, S. A. (2015). Two meta-analyses exploring the relationship between teacher clarity and student learning. *Communication Education, 64*(4), 385–418. https://doi.org/10.1080/03634523 .2015.1041998

6. Elizabeth Dole, speech to the 300 Group, London, November 15, 1989.

7. Anthony Fauci, NIAID Director, quoted in Berkeley Lovelace, Kevin Breuninger, & William Feuer, "Dr. Anthony Fauci warns Congress reopening risks more outbreaks and backfires on local economies." CNBC Health and Science, May 12, 2020.

8. Saacks, B. (2019, November 16). Fox News and CNN covered the impeachment hearings very differently. Here are some of the biggest divergencies. *Business Insider.* https://www.businessinsider.com/fox-news-and-cnn-covered-trump -impeachment-hearings-differently-2019-11

9. Garber, M. (2019, November 14). Fox News covered the impeachment hearings in the Fox Newsiest way possible. *The Atlantic.* https://www.theatlantic.com/entertainment/archive/2019/11/how-fox-news-covered-day-1-impeachment-hearings/602020/

13

Borja B. Hojas/Getty images

PRESENTING A SPEECH CONFIDENTLY AND COMPETENTLY

Speaking Words of Wisdom

College commencement speakers often use the occasion to impart words of wisdom on new graduates, and Chimamanda Ngozi Adichie is no exception. Speaking to the graduates of American University in 2019, the best-selling author of *Americanah* noted how the cliché "life is short" is full of meaning and relevance. "*Life is short* means 'be open,'" she explained. "It means decide what you will do with the regrets in your life. There will always be something to regret. You can waste more time regretting your regrets, or you can put it aside and learn from it. *Life is short* really means 'have a purpose.' And purpose does not need to be grand. I think that the smaller the purpose, the more meaningful. To be kind. To have empathy. To avoid sanctimony. To think of the humanity of other people—to try."[1]

··· ▶ As You READ

- What are the most common forms of speech delivery?
- How can you manage public speaking anxiety?
- How can you deliver a speech effectively?

kasto/123RF

Few of us may ever have occasion to speak before a large audience, such as at a college commencement ceremony. For many people, however, giving a speech—even in front of a small group of peers—can be a challenge. In the previous two chapters, you saw how to plan and prepare a successful speech. In this chapter, you'll learn what it takes to deliver your speech confidently and competently. You'll discover the various delivery options, examine ways to deal effectively with anxiety, see how to practice delivering a speech, and learn to use presentation aids to maximize the impact of your presentation.

Styles of Delivering a Speech

As you learned in the chapter on choosing, developing, and researching a topic, people prepare speeches for many different reasons, such as to inform, to persuade, to entertain, to introduce, and to give honor. No matter *why* you're speaking, however, you have various options for *how* to deliver your speech. In this section, we examine four basic styles of delivery: impromptu, extemporaneous, scripted, and memorized. Because each style has specific benefits and drawbacks, you'll want to consider which works best in the context in which you are speaking.

SOME SPEECHES ARE IMPROMPTU

• **impromptu speech**
A speech delivered with little or no preparation.

An **impromptu speech** is a speech you deliver on the spot, with little or no preparation. Suppose you're meeting with your project team at work and your manager asks you to share your marketing ideas with the group. If she had mentioned a week ago that she wanted you to speak at the meeting, you might have used that time to consider your message and prepare your remarks. Instead, she expects you to speak without the benefit of planning. Making an impromptu speech requires you not only to think spontaneously about what you want to say but also to organize your thoughts quickly into a set of speaking points. Being asked to speak impromptu can be nerve-wracking, particularly for individuals who are already anxious about public speaking.

If you're called on to deliver an impromptu speech, these hints can help you to succeed:

- *Don't panic.* Many people feel pangs of fear when asked to speak impromptu. That's a normal response, and it needn't prevent you from speaking well. If you react that way, take a deep breath and tell yourself "I can do this." Remember that you wouldn't be asked to speak if you didn't have something worthwhile to say.

- *Think in threes.* Whatever the topic of your impromptu speech, identify three points you want to make about it. Ask yourself "What three things do I want my audience to know?" Make these messages the three main points of your speech. If you include more than three points, it will be harder for your listeners—and you—to remember them all.

- *Draw from what's happened.* Consider what else has been said or done in the context you're in and make reference to it. For example, you might begin your speech by responding to someone else's earlier observations. Likewise, you might end your remarks by commenting on the occasion or on the audience.

- *Be brief.* Because impromptu speeches are spontaneous, people usually expect them to be short. Giving a long, detailed description of each point in your speech is usually unnecessary and will reduce your listeners' ability to remember what you've said. Instead, make your points concisely, provide a brief conclusion, and then thank your audience for listening.

Although impromptu speaking can be stressful, it is certainly possible to do it well. As with many communication skills, you'll get more comfortable with it the more you practice.

SOME SPEECHES ARE EXTEMPORANEOUS

One benefit of giving an impromptu speech is that listeners may believe your words are genuine or from the heart because you didn't have time to prepare them in advance. Another style of delivery that gives you that advantage—but also allows you some planning time—is the extemporaneous style. An **extemporaneous speech** is one that is carefully prepared to *sound* as though it is being delivered spontaneously.

Preparing to speak extemporaneously relies on steps we examined in the chapter on organizing and finding support for your speech: constructing purpose and thesis statements; organizing your speech with an introduction, main points and subpoints, transitions, and a conclusion; creating a working outline; and crafting a set of speaking notes. Using your speaking notes, you can practice making your speech sound off the cuff or not heavily prepared. As an extemporaneous speaker, you want to communicate in a natural, conversational manner—to give the impression that you are simply *talking with* your listeners instead of *formally addressing* them. Analyzing and understanding your audience (see the chapter on choosing, developing, and researching a topic) will help you to relate to your speakers as effectively as possible.

Extemporaneous speaking offers some advantages over other styles of delivery. Because extemporaneous speakers use minimal notes, they can maintain audience eye contact, which helps their listeners to be attentive and engaged. They can also speak in a more relaxed tone of voice than if they were reading a script. Yet using speaking notes helps ensure that extemporaneous speakers won't forget their main points or lose their place.

Despite those important advantages, the extemporaneous style of delivery is not the best option in every situation. For instance, many speakers would find it difficult to deliver an extemporaneous speech within a narrow time frame, such as might be required if they were speaking on television or on the radio. If a speech *must* last a specified period of time, then it is safer to read from a script that has been timed to fit that period. The extemporaneous style can also be challenging if the speech must have perfect grammar or large sections must be exactly worded. Such instances call for the use of a script.

- **extemporaneous speech** A speech that is carefully prepared to sound as though it is being delivered spontaneously.

SHARPEN Your Skills:
Drafting three speaking points

Suppose you were asked to deliver an impromptu speech addressing the question "Why should people in the United States learn about cultural diversity?" Identify three points you would make in such a speech.

SOME SPEECHES ARE SCRIPTED

Unlike an extemporaneous speech, a **scripted speech** is composed word for word on a manuscript and then read aloud exactly as it is written. Scripted speeches are particularly common in situations when the exact wording of the speech is crucial or when the speech must fit within a predetermined time frame. For instance, politicians often use teleprompters when delivering important speeches before large audiences, such as the president does when delivering the State of the Union speech every year. In such cases, the manuscript is projected onto the teleprompter in such a way that only the speaker can see it. Similarly, television news anchors read the day's stories word for word from a manuscript that is projected next to the cameras they are facing. A scripted speech allows the speakers to deliver grammatically accurate, well-planned messages within a specified time frame. A reporter or elected official must also ensure that facts are presented accurately, and going "off script" risks mistakes that can damage the speaker's credibility.

- **scripted speech** A speech composed word for word on a manuscript and then read aloud exactly as it is written.

News anchors frequently read the day's stories word for word from a teleprompter.

withGod/Shutterstock

Many people opt for scripted speeches when they are nervous about speaking. Perhaps you've noticed that it is easy to become distracted when you're nervous. Distraction can cause you to stumble over your words or forget parts of what you want to say. You might have experienced nervousness while giving a speech in class or before a student organization. On such occasions, having a manuscript with all your words can be comforting because it ensures that you will always know exactly what you want to say.

Scripted delivery is probably the easiest form of speaking because it requires speakers simply to recite the words of the speech from a manuscript. It has some clear disadvantages, however. First, compared to impromptu and extemporaneous speeches, scripted speeches often take much more time and energy to prepare. Not only must you create a detailed outline for a scripted speech—as you would for an extemporaneous speech—but you also must then compose every part of the speech word for word. That process can be time-consuming, particularly when you generate several drafts.

Second, unless you are using a teleprompter, delivering a scripted speech requires you to manipulate a manuscript—a potentially tricky chore, especially when you're nervous. If you were to drop your manuscript or shuffle the pages in the wrong order, you could lose your place. Even if you're reading your speech from an iPad or tablet, scrolling from page to page can distract your listeners from your words. Finally, because you use your voice differently when you read something aloud than when you engage in conversation, reading a speech can make you sound stiff or uninteresting[2] rather than energetic and sincere. The best way to deal with that challenge is to practice reading your speech while varying your tone, volume, and speaking rate, as you would during a conversation. In that way you can help to ensure that your speech doesn't *sound* read, even if you are reading it.[3]

SOME SPEECHES ARE MEMORIZED

Perhaps you like the control over your words that a scripted speech gives you, but you can't use or don't want to use a manuscript. In that case, you probably want to give a **memorized speech**, a speech you compose word for word and then deliver from memory. Memorizing their words allows people to speak without having to handle a script or set of notes. They can then gesture naturally and maintain an effective level of eye contact with their listeners. As we'll see later in this chapter, both those behaviors can enhance the credibility of a speech. Going "noteless" also frees a speaker to move around during a speech.

Like scripted speeches, memorized speeches are useful when individuals must speak within a specified time frame. In political debates, for instance, candidates are often allowed only a certain number of minutes for their opening and closing statements. They can, therefore, prepare and rehearse memorized speeches that conform to those time limits.

- **memorized speech**
A speech composed word for word and then delivered from memory.

Novelists and poets—including Toni Morrison, shown here—often present their own work, which they know very intimately, making memorization an appropriate strategy.

Daniel Boczarski/ FilmMagic/Getty Images

Like all forms of delivery, memorized speeches have some drawbacks. One is that, like scripted speeches, they take a good deal of time and energy to prepare. Not only must you write the speech itself, you must also commit it to memory—a possibly burdensome task, especially if it is relatively long. Another drawback of memorized speeches is that they can come across as excessively prepared and overly formal. As a result, they may not sound as sincere as impromptu or extemporaneous speeches often do. You can overcome that disadvantage by rehearsing to make your speech *seem* as though you are presenting it for the first time.

A third disadvantage of giving a memorized speech is that a speaker's memory can fail. Many people have had

TABLE 1

BENEFITS AND
DRAWBACKS OF FOUR
STYLES OF DELIVERY

Style	Benefits	Drawbacks
Impromptu	Requires little preparation. Often makes the speaker sound genuine.	Lack of opportunity to prepare can be stressful. Thinking on the spot can be difficult.
Extemporaneous	Provides the speaker with notes while making the speech sound spontaneous.	Takes time to prepare. Difficult to do well under strict time constraints or if perfect grammar is required.
Scripted	Provides maximum control over the verbal content. Ensures the speaker always knows what to say.	Takes much time to prepare. Use of a manuscript can be distracting for speaker and audience.
Memorized	Allows high control over verbal content. Requires no notes, so speaker can use natural gestures and maintain eye contact.	Requires considerable effort to write and memorize. Can sound insincere. Speaker's memory can fail during delivery.

the experience of practicing a speech so many times that they can practically recite it in their sleep, only to forget the words in the middle of their delivery. If you ever encounter that problem, the best way to recover is to improvise. Consider what you were saying right before your memory failed and then speak extemporaneously about it. Improvising for even a few moments may jog your memory, allowing you to resume your memorized speech without anyone's noticing that you temporarily forgot your words.

Impromptu, extemporaneous, scripted, and memorized speeches offer a range of options for delivery. As summarized in Table 1, each style of delivery provides specific benefits but entails certain drawbacks. To succeed at any of these forms of delivery, however, you must first learn how to manage public speaking anxiety, our next topic.

Managing Public Speaking Anxiety

Every few years, various organizations poll American adults about what they most fear. In a 2014 survey of over a thousand people conducted by Chapman University in Orange, California, the most commonly mentioned fear, at 25.3 percent, was public speaking.[4] Incidentally, the fear of death didn't make the top 10 list, a finding suggesting that some respondents were more afraid of giving a speech than they were of dying. That reality once prompted comedian Jerry Seinfeld to joke that at a funeral, most people would rather be in the casket than giving the eulogy.

All joking aside, public speaking can be a terrifying prospect for people who suffer from **public speaking anxiety**, sometimes also called *stage fright*: nervousness or fear brought on by performing in front of an audience. As you'll learn in this section, public speaking anxiety is a type of stress that affects individuals psychologically, physically, and behaviorally.[5] It can sometimes be debilitating, causing people to deliver poor performances. Fortunately, you can learn to use stage fright to your advantage by overcoming some of its problematic effects.

• **public speaking anxiety (stage fright)** Nervousness or fear brought on by performing in front of an audience.

PUBLIC SPEAKING ANXIETY IS A COMMON FORM OF STRESS

Adele is more than a singer and songwriter. She's become a musical phenomenon, winning six Grammy Awards in 2012 alone. The previous year, she became the first artist in history to have a number-one album and three chart-topping singles at the same time. By the time she was 27 years old, she had performed in more than 200 venues in Europe and North America and had sold more than 100 million combined albums and singles, making her one of the best-selling artists in the world. What you might not know is that Adele suffers from debilitating stage fright. "I'm scared of

John Shearer/WireImage/
Getty Images

• **stress** The body's
reaction to any type of
perceived threat.

• **anxiety** A psychological
state of worry and unease.

• **anticipatory anxiety**
The worry people feel
when looking ahead to a
speech.

audiences," she said in an interview with *Rolling Stone*.[6] At a 2011 concert in Amsterdam, she was so nervous that she even tried to escape the concert hall through a fire exit just before going onstage.

As Adele's example illustrates, even seasoned performers can suffer a fear of being in front of a crowd. The anxiety or fear that many people feel before giving a speech or performing in front of a crowd is a form of stress. **Stress** is the body's reaction to any type of perceived threat. You may feel stress, for instance, when you see a growling dog running toward you, when you sit down to take a final exam, or when you are laid off from a job. Although those are different situations, each poses some type of threat, whether it's to your physical health, academic record, or financial well-being. Scientists use the term *stressor* to refer to events that cause the body to experience stress.

As communication scholar James McCroskey documented, public speaking is a common stressor.[7] Research indicates that the anxiety associated with public speaking affects more than one in five adults,[8] a figure that has remained stable for the last four decades.[9] Public speaking stress is so common, in fact, that many scientific experiments about stress purposely use a public speaking activity to elevate participants' stress levels.[10]

Although public speaking may not threaten a person's physical, academic, or financial well-being as do other stressors, many people feel that it threatens their emotional well-being. For instance, they might worry about experiencing embarrassment, disapproval, or ridicule if their speech doesn't go well. Those may seem like mild threats, particularly when compared to being physically harmed, failing a class, or losing a job. As anyone who has experienced public speaking anxiety can attest, however, giving a speech can be just as stressful as—if not more stressful than—many more serious threats.

One speaking situation that can be particularly stress-inducing is having to take a position that you know some members of your audience will disagree with or even be offended by. For some suggestions on how to handle that stressful task, check out the "Difficult Conversations" box.

When we feel stress, our body reacts in ways that affect us psychologically, physically, and behaviorally. Let's examine how those components of the stress response are related to public speaking anxiety.

Psychological Effects of Public Speaking Anxiety

Public speaking anxiety represents a specific form of **anxiety**, a feeling of worry and unease. Communication scholars Ralph Behnke and Chris Sawyer devoted much of their careers to studying the anxiety associated with public speaking. One of their most important findings is that anxiety often begins long before speakers stand in front of an audience. According to Behnke and Sawyer, many people experience **anticipatory anxiety**, which is the worry they feel when looking ahead to a speech.[11] Research shows that anticipatory anxiety often starts when the speech is assigned. Perhaps you can recall feeling worried or stressed when you learned you would have to make a speech in class or at work. Anticipatory anxiety usually decreases as individuals begin preparing their speeches, probably because preparation gives them a sense that they can control their performance.[12] Then, just before delivering the speech, people's anxiety peaks as they feel the pressure to perform.

Not every speech will evoke the same level of anxiety. For instance, you've probably found that you're less anxious when speaking about a topic you understand well than one that is less familiar. The reason is that having a command of your topic gives you confidence in what you're saying. Delivery style also appears to affect how much anxiety people experience about public speaking. One study found that speakers had the most anxiety when anticipating an impromptu speech, less anxiety when anticipating an extemporaneous speech, and the least anxiety when anticipating a scripted speech.[13]

Difficult Conversations

Addressing the "Elephant in the Room"

Imagine this: You are preparing a persuasive speech for your communication class in which you argue that the United States should stop invading foreign countries. Your thesis is that the United States should respect cultural diversity instead of trying to force its own way of living on other countries through the use of military power. In particular, you plan to claim that the 2003 invasion of Iraq, and the war that followed, were completely unjustified. You know, however, that two other students in your class are military veterans who have done tours of duty in the Middle East. You know that your remarks might be considered offensive to the two veterans, as well as to students who support the military or have veterans in their families, but you aren't sure whether or how to address this.

McGraw Hill

Now, consider this: This situation can create an "elephant in the room," which refers to a context in which there is an obvious truth that is being ignored because it would be awkward to acknowledge. In this case, as you lay out your arguments against military intervention, everyone in your class may realize that there are veterans present who could be offended by your words. This creates an uncomfortable situation for your listeners as well as for you. To avoid having an "elephant in the room," consider these strategies:

- First and foremost, acknowledge the issue instead of ignoring it. In this case, you might say "I know we have some veterans in the audience today, and many of us may have military members or veterans in our families. I recognize that some of them may disagree with the position I'm taking." Acknowledging the issue is useful because audiences often grow increasingly uncomfortable the longer it is ignored.

- Make clear that your opposition is not to military members themselves. To defuse tension, in fact, you might offer praise for active duty or veteran military members, by saying "these women and men put their lives on the line for us every day, and they deserve our utmost respect and gratitude." You can then be clear that your opposition is to the government policies that direct military action, not to the troops who carry out those orders.

- Whenever you disagree with a large proportion of your audience, especially on a sensitive topic, point out that people on both sides of the issue feel strongly about their positions. Then, focus on what you believe you have in common with your listeners: "We may not agree on government policies for military action, but I think we can all agree that it's important to respect the sacrifices of our men and women in uniform and to avoid putting them in harm's way whenever we can."

An "elephant in the room" can emerge whenever an uncomfortable truth is avoided instead of addressed. By acknowledging such conflicts, treating the opposing side with respect, and focusing on your similarities instead of just your differences, you can reduce the tension that such situations create.

Public speaking anxiety often starts long before we face an audience.

Jozef Polc/123RF

• **fight-or-flight response** A reaction that helps prepare the body either to confront or to avoid a stressor.

People vary with respect to how many of the psychological effects of speaking anxiety they experience. Those who are outgoing,[14] uninhibited,[15] intellectually sophisticated,[16] and not prone to worry[17] typically experience the lowest levels. Women in one study had higher levels of anticipatory anxiety than did men[18]—perhaps a reflection of differences in how women and men react physically to stressful situations.[19]

Physical Effects of Public Speaking Anxiety Beyond their psychological impact, stressful situations such as public speaking affect the body. Try to recall a time when you experienced stress. Perhaps your heart beat faster, you breathed more heavily, and you perspired more than normal. Other physical changes were occurring outside your conscious awareness. Your body was producing more stress hormones, for instance, and the pupils of your eyes were dilating. Those physical effects of stress are part of the body's **fight-or-flight response**, a reaction that helps prepare the body either to confront the stressor (by fighting) or to avoid it (by fleeing).[20] Your heart and breathing rates increase to get more oxygen to your muscles so that you have more energy for fighting or fleeing from the stressor. You perspire more to keep from overheating. Your stress hormones temporarily increase your strength, and your pupils dilate so that you can take in as much visual information about the situation as possible.[21] In these ways, the physical effects of stress enable you to deal as effectively as possible with the stressor.

Public speaking anxiety produces many of the same physical stress reactions, including increased heart rate and blood pressure and elevated stress hormones.[22] These are also similar to the effects of other forms of stage fright, such as people might experience before acting in a play or dancing in a recital. One study found that people training to be professional musicians experienced increases in heart rate and stress hormones when they performed in front of an audience as opposed to practicing on their own.[23] Even college instructors are sometime prone to experience anxiety before they teach.[24] Fears of making a mistake and being embarrassed can invoke physical stress for anyone performing in front of a crowd, including public speakers. You will find more detail about one study of speaking anxiety in "The Dark Side of Communication" box.

Like psychological anxiety, stress varies from person to person in the level experienced when speaking in public. Some studies have demonstrated, for example, that individuals with a strong tendency to worry experience more physical stress when anticipating, preparing, and delivering a speech than do non-worriers.[25] Moreover, those who react strongly to other stressful situations tend to experience highly elevated stress during a speech.[26] There are also some sex differences in public speaking stress. Although women report more psychological anxiety than men do about public speaking, research shows that men experience more physical stress overall while delivering a speech. In particular, men demonstrate greater elevations in stress hormones[27] and blood pressure,[28] although women appear to experience greater elevations than men do in heart rate.[29]

SHARPEN Your Skills: *Breathing to reduce stress*

When you feel your body getting worked up over the stress of public speaking, close your eyes and pay attention to your breathing. Focus on the sensation of each breath entering and leaving your body. Research shows that focusing on breathing for 15 minutes helps people to deal more effectively with stressful situations.[30]

THE DARK SIDE OF COMMUNICATION

Stressing Out: Public Speaking Elevates Stress Hormone Levels

The ability to speak in public is critical for success in a range of careers. For many individuals, however, public speaking has a dark side: it causes them to experience physical stress. Some of the effects of stress are relatively noticeable, such as increases in heart rate and perspiration. The experience of stress also causes rises in stress hormones, which, although they may not be immediately obvious, have multiple effects on the body.

Research by communication scientists James Roberts, Chris Sawyer, and Ralph Behnke indicates that when college students deliver a speech in front of a group of their peers, their level of the stress hormone cortisol rises. Specifically, students showed a dramatic increase in cortisol from before the speech to eight minutes after they began speaking. Cortisol level

continually decreased from that point on, as students recovered from their stress.

Stress hormones such as cortisol prepare the body in multiple ways to deal effectively with a stressor. For instance, they reduce blood flow to the extremities—the reason why our hands and feet may feel cold when we're nervous—so that more blood is available to our internal organs. They also increase the level of sugar in our blood so that our muscles have more fuel than normal, and they activate the immune system in case it needs to respond to an injury. Such reactions can be helpful in the short term by giving us more physical resources to manage a stressor. However, repeated exposure to stress has many negative effects on the body, including reduced muscle mass and decreased immune system strength.

ASK YOURSELF

- What physical reactions do you notice in your body when you're under stress?
- Instead of studying students, what if the researchers had studied teachers, television reporters, or others who speak in public for a living? How do you think their results would have been different, if at all?

SOURCES: Roberts, J. B., Sawyer, C. R., & Behnke, R. R. (2004). A neurological representation of speech state anxiety: Mapping salivary cortisol levels of public speakers. *Western Journal of Communication, 68*(2), 219–231. https://doi.org/10.1080/10570310409374797; Bodie, G. D. (2010). A racing heart, rattling knees, and ruminative thoughts: Defining, explaining, and treating public speaking anxiety. *Communication Education, 59*(1), 70–105. https://doi.org/10.1080/03634520903443849

Behavioral Effects of Public Speaking Anxiety In addition to its psychological and physical effects, public speaking anxiety also influences the way people behave.[31] You can probably recall from your own experience how you act when you're nervous. Perhaps you fidget or pace. Maybe you find it difficult to speak. Researchers have been examining those and other behavioral effects of anxiety for several decades.[32] Their work indicates that public speaking anxiety—as well as other forms of stage fright—affects behavior in at least five separate domains:

- *Voice.* Public speaking anxiety often causes the voice to quiver or sound tense—or to sound higher than normal.[33]
- *Mouth and throat.* People experiencing public speaking anxiety often swallow and clear their throat more frequently than normal.
- *Facial expression.* Muscle tension in the face causes a general lack of expression and eye contact. It can also make the face twitch slightly.
- *General movement.* Public speaking anxiety frequently causes people to fidget or engage in random movement. It can also cause them to pace, sway, or shuffle their feet.
- *Verbal behavior.* People experiencing public speaking anxiety often stutter more than usual. They also increase their use of filler words, such as "um" or "uh," and they are more likely to forget what they want to say.[34]

As we'll discover in the next sections, the psychological, physical, and behavioral effects of speaking anxiety can inhibit your ability to speak effectively, but speaking anxiety can also *improve* your performance if you know how to manage it successfully.

PUBLIC SPEAKING ANXIETY CAN BE DEBILITATING

When public speaking anxiety is particularly intense, it can become debilitating—that is, it can overwhelm people and prevent them from speaking or performing effectively. Adele's stage fright nearly prevented her from giving her concert in Amsterdam. Like a deer caught in the headlights, people with debilitating speaking anxiety can become immobilized and unable to deliver their speech, even if they have rehearsed extensively. More intense forms of social anxiety can even affect people economically, in the form of lost productivity and increased health care costs.[35]

Debilitating public speaking anxiety often causes two distinct sensations. The first is that your mind seems to go blank, and the second is that you are motivated to try to escape the situation. In the grip of intense stage fright, you become distracted by your body's efforts to manage the emotion you are feeling, and you can easily forget words or information you would readily remember under normal circumstances.[36]

We've seen that stressful events often trigger a fight-or-flight response, so you may not be surprised to learn that the second sensation sometimes triggered by debilitating anxiety about public speaking is an urge to escape.[37] Because stress and fear make you perceive that your well-being is threatened, you want to get away to protect yourself from harm.[38] If you feel intensely nervous about giving a speech, for example, you may find yourself wishing you could postpone the speech or trying to get it over with as quickly as possible. You may also avoid eye contact with your listeners as a subconscious way to escape their attention.

It's difficult to speak effectively when your mind goes blank and you feel the urge to escape. Just because speaking anxiety *can* have those debilitating effects, however, doesn't mean that it *must*.

MAKING PUBLIC SPEAKING ANXIETY AN ADVANTAGE

Although speaking anxiety is common, you can learn to turn it to your advantage. This section offers six pieces of advice for making it your friend, a particular benefit for those with jobs like the one profiled in "Putting Communication to Work."

The stress of public speaking anxiety can cause the face to appear expressionless, much like the look of a deer caught in a car's headlights.

Erin Patrice O'Brien/Digital Vision/Getty Images; Bryan Allen/Getty Images

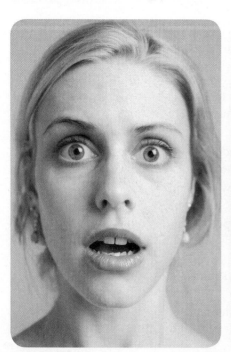

putting**communication**to**work**

Job Title >

Work Responsibilities >

Undergraduate Recruiting Specialist

Undergraduate recruiting specialists work for the admissions and outreach departments of a college or university. Their job is to "sell" the school and its programs to potential undergraduates and their parents. To accomplish that task, they frequently speak to audiences about degree programs, financial aid options, and other topics relevant to their listeners' school choice. Although a friendly, outgoing personality is useful in such a position, the ability to speak effectively to a variety of audiences is even more essential. For that reason, effective recruiting specialists often practice extensively the skills taught in this chapter.

MachineHeadz/Getty Images

Accept Public Speaking Anxiety as a Normal Response When you are working to become a better speaker or performer, you might be inclined to focus on trying to eliminate your public speaking anxiety. You may reason that if it inhibits your ability to perform well, it makes sense to get rid of it. Such efforts would be largely wasted, however. All forms of fear, including speaking anxiety, are deeply rooted in humans' ancestral experiences. The fear response is largely innate, and although people who perform frequently in front of audiences usually become less nervous over time, this visceral response rarely goes away entirely. Thus, rather than trying to eliminate it, accept it as a normal part of the performance experience. In fact, speaking anxiety can even help you to perform better than you would if you didn't feel nervous.

Focus Your Nervous Energy Recall that the stress of public speaking causes bodily changes—including elevated heart rate, breathing rate, and stress hormone levels—that increase your energy stores. That energy boost is meant to help you to deal effectively with a threatening situation. You can train yourself to focus your nervous energy on the goal of giving the best speech possible rather than letting it distract you. Just as many athletes try to get psyched up before a game so they have more energy to channel toward their performance, so, too, can you use your nervousness to energize your speech.

Visualize a Successful Performance A technique that often helps individuals perform well, even if they are experiencing anxiety, is **visualization**: developing a particular mental image of winning or giving a successful performance.[39] Practice visualization by closing your eyes and imagining yourself delivering an expert speech.

• **visualization**
Developing a mental image, such as an image of oneself giving a successful performance.

As you visualize, see yourself giving your entire speech in a confident and relaxed manner. Research shows that people who visualize a successful speech performance experience less speaking anxiety and fewer negative thoughts when they actually deliver their speeches, compared to people who don't use visualization.[40]

Desensitize As we've seen, people generally avoid what they fear. For instance, if you're afraid of flying, you will tend not to fly. The more you avoid flying (or something else you're afraid of), however, the scarier it often seems. In contrast, when people face their fears and encounter the situations that frighten them, they often realize these aren't as scary as they once seemed. Your fear of flying may lessen after you have taken a flight and experienced a safe take-off and landing, and you will gradually feel less and less afraid each time you fly.

• **desensitization** The process of confronting frightening situations directly, to reduce the stress they cause.

The process of confronting frightening situations head-on is called **desensitization**, and it can significantly reduce the anxiety individuals experience about all sorts of fears, including public speaking.[41] The more you practice speaking in front of people, the less frightening public speaking will become, because over time you will become desensitized to it.

Practice in Virtual Reality One way to desensitize yourself to public speaking anxiety is to take every opportunity you have to speak in public, even if the prospect scares you. Remind yourself that you're facing your fears so you can overcome them, and you will be stronger and more confident after each speech.

• **avatars** Graphic representations of people.

Another way to desensitize yourself to the anxiety of public speaking is to practice speaking in front of a computer-generated audience. Using a virtual world such as Second Life, find an area with several **avatars**, which are graphic representations of other people. Then deliver speeches to that virtual audience before you deliver them to real-life listeners. In the safety of a computer-mediated environment, you will gain practice in the public speaking context. Research has shown that practicing with an online audience can help to desensitize you to public speaking anxiety.[42]

Another way to generate a virtual audience is to use an app called VirtualSpeech, which is available for both Android and iOS platforms. When paired with a virtual reality headset, such as Google Cardboard or Gear VR, this app simulates the experience of standing in front of a group of people.

MachineHeadz/Getty Images

Stay Positive Finally, approach the delivery of your speech with a positive, optimistic attitude. Tell yourself that you can—and will—succeed. This positive self-talk can be difficult, particularly if you're very nervous or if you have had negative experiences with previous performances. Staying as positive as you can is important for two reasons, however. First, positive thoughts and emotions help to relieve the negative physical effects of stress.[43] Therefore, you'll approach your speech in a more relaxed manner than you otherwise would. Second, recall from the chapter on perceiving that negative thoughts can turn into a self-fulfilling prophecy, causing you to have a poor performance simply because you expect that you will. Approaching your speech with an optimistic attitude, in contrast, can encourage the behaviors that will help you to succeed.

In summary, public speaking anxiety is a common experience that can either inhibit or enhance your ability to give an effective speech. The key is knowing how to manage it and make it work to your advantage. Yet even if you feel nervous about delivering a speech, you don't have to look or sound nervous. In the next section, you'll discover how to deliver a speech so you come across as calm and confident in the eyes of your audience.

Practicing Effective Delivery

Think about the most memorable speech you can recall hearing. What makes it stick in your mind? Perhaps it's partly what the speaker said, but what you probably remember most is the speaker's delivery. After all, we don't usually read others' speeches—instead, we watch and listen to them. As we considered in the chapter on communicating nonverbally, most of us pay more attention to the way people look and sound than to what they say. An effective speech therefore requires an effective delivery. We can categorize the behaviors of effective delivery as either visual elements or vocal elements. We can also note some of the ways in which speakers' cultural norms affect the styles of delivery they prefer.

VISUAL ELEMENTS AFFECT DELIVERY

Humans have a strong tendency to evaluate a situation—including a speech—according to what they see. Visual cues are thus important elements of effective speech delivery. This section describes how you can use facial expression, eye contact, posture and body position, gestures, and personal appearance to your advantage.

Facial Expression Recall from the nonverbal communication chapter that the face communicates more information than any other nonverbal channel. For that reason, you can use your facial expressions during a speech to add impact to your words and credibility to your message.

Research indicates that two aspects of your facial expression are particularly important for an effective speech. The first is that your facial expressions should match the tone of your words. When your words are serious, your facial expression should be serious as well. You should smile when telling positive stories and express concern when telling troubling stories. Doing so creates congruence between your facial expressions and your verbal message that makes your audience more inclined to believe what you're saying.[44]

The second aspect of using facial expressions effectively is that your expressions should vary over the course of your speech. Presenting the same expression throughout your speech may cause listeners to tune you out. Speakers who vary their facial expressions—as long as they do so in ways that are appropriate to their words—are seen as competent and credible.[45]

Eye Contact A second element of effective delivery is eye contact. Inexperienced presenters often stare at the floor or the ceiling while speaking. If they look at their audience at all, it is only with short glances, often over the top of their listeners' heads.

Avoiding eye contact with your audience is a response to fear that makes you feel hidden and protected. When you avert your eyes, your subconscious is saying "If I can't see my listeners, they can't see me." In contrast, looking your audience in the eye can make you feel vulnerable, because it acknowledges that your listeners are evaluating you.

Effective speakers know that maintaining eye contact with their listeners is extremely important.[46] Imagine carrying on a face-to-face conversation with someone who never looks you in the eye. You would likely get the impression that the person isn't interested in you or perhaps that he or she isn't being honest with you. Your listeners will probably form the same impressions of you if you don't look them in the eye while speaking.[47]

Of course, it's not necessary to stare at your listeners. Rather, you should make eye contact with one person in your audience, hold it for a moment, and then make eye contact with another audience member. Focus on one section of the audience at a time. Look at people in the front row for a minute or two and then direct your eye contact to

Good eye contact helps keep speakers and listeners engaged.

Inti St Clair/Blend Images

those in the back corner or in the middle of the group. Try to make eye contact with each person at least once during your speech. When you look your listeners in the eye, you come across as confident and believable even if you feel nervous.[48]

Posture and Body Position Whether you're sitting or standing during your speech, it's important to adopt a posture that is relaxed but confident. Slouching or hanging your head will make you appear uninterested in what you're saying. Instead, keep your back straight, your shoulders square, and your head up. That posture makes you appear strong, composed, and in control.[49]

You should also be aware of your body movement and position, particularly if you're standing. First, make sure that you stand facing your listeners. That advice may seem obvious, but it is particularly easy to forget if your speech incorporates visual aids, such as a **slideshow**, which is a selection of images and text created in a presentation software and projected on a screen for the audience to see. When presenting a slideshow, for instance, some speakers turn away from the audience and speak in the direction of the screen on which the slides appear. Doing so makes it seem as though they are ignoring their audience and can also make it difficult for listeners to hear them. A better approach is to stand alongside the screen so you are still facing your audience, and to turn your head—instead of your whole body—when you need to see the next slide.

Depending on the size and layout of the room in which you're speaking, you may also have the option of walking around during your speech. Even if you're presenting a slideshow, you can use a remote-control clicker to advance your slides while you walk around. Moving around can make your presentation more visually interesting to your audience than standing in one spot, and natural gestures can also help the audience understand what you are saying, as the chapter on organizing and finding support for your speech's discussion of nonverbal signposts suggested.[50]

If you are able to move around during your speech, it's important that your movements appear casual but deliberate. Move slowly to one position, stay there for a few minutes, and then move slowly to another spot. A particularly good time to move from one place to another is during a transition in your speech, because your change in position will correspond to a change in your remarks. You want to avoid random movement, which will suggest you are moving simply to expend nervous energy. Similarly, avoid movement that looks overly contrived and thus unnatural, such as circulating continuously around three specific spots. If you can move in a natural and relaxed manner, you will hold your listeners' attention and enhance your credibility.

Gestures As we saw in the chapter on communicating nonverbally, gestures are movements of the hands, arms, or head that express meaning. Most of us gesture naturally as we converse with other people, and the use of gestures also enhances the effectiveness of a speech.[51]

Three factors are particularly important when gesturing during a speech. First, gestures should look spontaneous rather than planned. Spontaneous gestures naturally follow what you are saying and thus appear well connected to your verbal message. Planned gestures, in contrast, can appear contrived and insincere. Perhaps the best way to keep your gestures from looking planned is not to plan them but to let them arise naturally from the words you're speaking. Even if you do rehearse your gestures, follow the advice in the chapter on organizing and finding support for your speech by rehearsing them until they look and feel natural.

A second key factor is that gestures should be appropriate in number. Some speakers, especially when they're anxious, gesture almost constantly because the motion helps them to get rid of excess

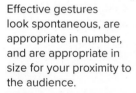

• **slideshow** A selection of images and text created in a presentation software and projected on a screen for the audience to see.

Effective gestures look spontaneous, are appropriate in number, and are appropriate in size for your proximity to the audience.

Photodisc/Getty Images

nervous energy. If you've ever listened to such a speaker, however, you know that using too many gestures can distract an audience and make it difficult for listeners to concentrate on the speaker's words. While some speakers show nervousness by overdoing gestures, others become physically tense and barely gesture at all. As a result, they appear stiff and rigid. Effective speakers, then, use a *moderate* number of gestures—not too many, not too few.

Finally, gestures should be appropriate in size for your proximity to the audience. If your listeners are relatively close to you, as in a conference room or a small classroom, you should use gestures similar to those you would use in face-to-face conversations. The same is true if you are speaking to your audience via a webcam; you'll want to keep your gestures somewhat small so they are easily captured by the camera. If you are farther away from your listeners, as in an auditorium, using larger, more dramatic gestures is appropriate so that your audience can see them.

Personal Appearance A final visual element of an effective delivery is personal appearance—clothing, accessories, and grooming. As a general rule, your appearance should be appropriate for your audience and for the occasion on which you're speaking. Select clothing that will match the formality of—or will be slightly more formal than—the clothes your listeners will be wearing. The more your personal appearance reflects theirs, the more your listeners will perceive you as similar to them, and that perception enhances your credibility.[52] In contrast, dressing far more formally or far less formally than your listeners will lead your audience to see you as more of an outsider.

When presenting a speech, it's best to wear clothing that matches the formality of your listeners' attire.

Steve Debenport/Getty Images; Fuse/Getty Images

Jewelry and accessories should complement your clothing but not attract attention. Long, flashy earrings or multiple bracelets that clang together whenever you move your arm will distract your audience. Effective speakers also know it's important to be well groomed when giving a speech. You can use the checklist in "The Competent Communicator" to ensure you've attended adequately to your personal appearance before presenting a speech.

An exception to this advice arises when you are using your personal appearance as a presentation aid. If you are speaking about stereotypes, for example, you might deliberately dress or project yourself to evoke certain judgments from your listeners, which you can then discuss in your speech. Likewise, if your speech is about military uniforms, you might choose to wear one. Unless your appearance is a presentation aid, however, it's best to dress similarly to your audience, to wear conservative jewelry and accessories, and to be well groomed.

Your facial expressions, eye contact, posture and body position, gestures, and personal appearance all influence the effectiveness of your speech by affecting what your audience *sees*. However, effective delivery also relies on what your audience *hears*.

VOCAL ELEMENTS AFFECT DELIVERY

Several elements of the voice influence how people understand and evaluate what the speaker says. Here we'll examine the importance of rate, volume, pitch, articulation, and fluency as vocal elements of effective speech delivery.

COMPETENT COMMUNICATOR

Personal Appearance Checklist

When you're getting ready to present a speech, use this checklist to make sure you have given adequate attention to your personal appearance. Check either "True" or "False" following each item.

Hill Street Studios/
Blend Images/Getty Images

	True	False
1. My clothing is far more formal than that of my audience.	____	____
2. I am wearing jewelry that makes noise when I move.	____	____
3. I am dressed far more casually than my listeners are.	____	____
4. My appearance is unkempt.	____	____
5. I am wearing accessories that will attract attention.	____	____
6. My clothing is similar to what my listeners will be wearing.	____	____
7. I look well groomed.	____	____
8. Everything I am wearing is clean.	____	____
9. I'm not wearing any flashy jewelry.	____	____
10. I believe my appearance will make the impression I want to make.	____	____

As you might guess, you should answer "False" to the first five items and "True" to the second five. If any of your answers are otherwise, recheck your personal appearance before your speech to ensure you are making the visual impression on your listeners that you intend to make.

Rate One vocal factor in effective delivery is your speech rate, or the speed at which you speak. In normal conversation, most U.S. adults speak approximately 150 words per minute.[53] Studies find, though, that speaking at a faster rate makes a speaker seem more persuasive[54] and more credible.[55] The explanation may be that speakers who talk at a fast rate appear to be in command of what they're saying, whereas slower speakers sound less sure of themselves.

There are two important caveats about speaking rate, however. The first is that it is possible to speak *too* fast. If you speak unusually fast, your listeners may not understand your message but may instead simply focus on how fast you're talking. The second caution is that you should adapt your speaking rate to your audience. Speaking at a brisk rate may work well with most audiences, but you'll likely need to speak more slowly if your audience is composed of young children, the elderly, people with developmental disabilities, or people who don't speak your language fluently, so they can understand you.

Volume Vocal volume is the loudness or softness of the voice. The appropriate volume for your speech depends on several factors, such as the size of your audience, the size of the room in which you're speaking, and whether you're using a microphone.

Just as you would in a face-to-face conversation, you want to ensure that you are speaking loudly enough for your listeners to hear you but not so loudly as to make them uncomfortable. In general, you will speak more loudly if you have a large audience than a small one, but only if you aren't using a microphone. Because a microphone amplifies the volume of your voice, you need only speak at a normal conversational volume to be heard. If you know you'll be using a microphone for an upcoming speech, it is useful to practice your speech with a microphone if you're able to do so.

Effective speakers also vary their volume during their speech to create certain effects. They may speak more loudly when making particular points to express enthusiasm or conviction about those points. At other times, they may speak softly to create a serious tone or to encourage the audience to pay close attention. Varying your vocal volume will add variety to your speech and help to keep your listeners engaged in it.

Frequent speakers know that varying their vocal pitch helps to capture and keep their listeners' attention.

Diego Cervo/123RF

Pitch Vocal pitch is a measure of how high or how low the voice is. Every voice has a range of pitches that it typically produces. Some voices have a naturally high pitch, others have a medium pitch, and still others have a deep, low pitch. When speakers are nervous, however, their vocal pitch becomes higher than normal. As a result, high-pitched speech often makes the speaker sound nervous and unsure, whereas a deeper pitch may convey greater confidence. If you focus on relaxing while you speak, your voice may also relax, allowing you to speak at a deeper pitch.

Perhaps more important than pitch itself is the variation in pitch you use while speaking. Speakers who vary their pitch sound energetic and dynamic and are judged by others as friendly[56] and caring.[57] In contrast, those who speak in a monotone voice, with little or no variety in pitch, often come across as tired or annoying.[58] Just as effective speakers vary their volume to create certain effects, so too do they vary their pitch to hold their listeners' attention.

Articulation Articulation is the extent to which the speaker pronounces words clearly. A speaker who mumbles has poor articulation, which makes it difficult for listeners to understand what he or she is saying. In contrast, a speaker with good articulation enunciates each word clearly and correctly.

• **articulation** The extent to which a speaker pronounces words clearly.

You can improve your articulation by avoiding five common articulation problems:

- *Addition* is caused by adding unnecessary sounds to words. For example, a person might say "real-ah-tor" instead of "realtor" or "bolth" instead of "both."
- *Deletion* occurs when a speaker omits part of a word sound, usually at the beginning or end of the word. Someone may say "frigerator" instead of "refrigerator," or "goin" instead of "going."
- *Transposition* means reversing two sounds within a word. Examples include saying "hunderd" instead of "hundred" and "nucular" instead of "nuclear."
- *Substitution* is caused by replacing one part of a word with an incorrect sound. A person might say "Sundee" instead of "Sunday" or "wit" instead of "with."
- *Slurring* occurs when a speaker combines two or more words into one. "Going to" becomes "gonna" and "sort of" becomes "sorta."

Articulation errors such as these aren't necessarily problematic when they occur in face-to-face conversations. Many of us are so used to committing such errors in our everyday communication that we don't even notice them. In a speech, however, poor articulation can damage the speaker's credibility.

Fluency Whereas articulation refers to the speaker's clarity, **fluency** refers to the smoothness of the speaker's delivery. Speeches that are fluent have an uninterrupted flow of words and phrases. There is a smooth rhythm to the delivery, without awkward pauses or false starts. In contrast, disfluent speeches are characterized by the use of filler

• **fluency** The smoothness of a speaker's delivery.

SHARPEN Your Skills: *Improving articulation*

Record yourself practicing the delivery of a speech. Afterward, ask someone who has not heard your speech to listen carefully to the recording and to point out any words and phrases that you did not articulate clearly. Re-record your speech, taking care to correct any articulation errors.

• **stuttering** A speech disorder that disrupts the flow of words with repeated or prolonged sounds and involuntary pauses.

words, such as "um" and "uh," and by the unnecessary repetition of words. Researchers have known for several decades that people who speak with fluency are perceived as more effective communicators than people who do not.[59]

Speaking with fluency is a particular challenge for individuals who stutter. **Stuttering** is a speech disorder that disrupts the flow of words with repeated or prolonged sounds and involuntary pauses.[60] Stuttering usually strikes individuals early in life and can significantly impair their ability to communicate.[61] With treatment, many can overcome their stuttering before reaching adulthood. For those who do not, ongoing speech therapy can often help to improve the fluency of speech, even if it doesn't eliminate the person's stuttering entirely.[62] Former U.S. Vice President Joseph Biden, actors Julia Roberts and James Earl Jones, journalist John Stossel, and sports star Bo Jackson are among many famous people who have dealt with stuttering and gone on to lead successful lives in the public sphere.

Rate, volume, pitch, articulation, and fluency aren't the only vocal elements of an effective speech delivery, but they are among those most noticeable to listeners. Paying attention to them as you speak will help you to sound confident and credible.

CULTURAL NORMS AFFECT PREFERRED DELIVERY STYLES

Although the visual and vocal elements just described often accompany speech performances that are considered effective in U.S. culture, speakers with other cultural backgrounds may prefer different delivery styles.[63] For example, many Asian cultures teach students to behave modestly and quietly, especially around adults such as their teachers, which can make delivering a speech in a classroom setting especially uncomfortable for Asian American students. Similarly, whereas U.S. audiences generally appreciate speeches that are organized linearly—so that each topic flows logically into the next—norms in some Asian cultures value more circular presentations in which the speaker comes back to the same point multiple times.

Cultural norms can affect the content of a speech as well as its delivery. Many in the United States enjoy speeches that identify a problem and then persuade listeners to adopt a particular solution to it. Political speeches often take that form, for instance. Some Arab cultures, however, regard problems as "severe twists of fate that cannot be solved," making speakers from those cultures less likely to adopt the problem-solving model common among many U.S. speakers.[64]

When listening to speakers whose cultural backgrounds differ from your own, remember that their cultural norms and values may lead them to prefer styles of speaking that seem foreign to you. Although competent speakers work to adapt their behaviors to their listeners' expectations, competent listeners also respect the diversity of ways in which people around the world are taught to express themselves.

Using Presentation Aids

• **presentation aids** Anything used in conjunction with a speech or presentation to stimulate listeners' senses.

The Home Shopping Network (HSN) airs infomercials for everything from jewelry and handbags to steam cleaners and computers. The speakers in infomercials don't simply *tell* you about their products—they also *show* you what the products are and how they work. They may demonstrate the products in use, show photographs of the sizes and colors in which they are available, or present video-recorded testimonials from satisfied customers. They may also display the item name, dimensions, and price on the television screen. Their sales strategies center on **presentation aids**, which consist of anything used in conjunction with a speech or presentation to stimulate listeners' senses. Presentation aids help the viewing audience to understand the products those HSN presenters are pitching.

You can similarly incorporate presentation aids into your speech to make it memorable and engaging for your listeners. In this section, we look first at the benefits of using presentation aids and then at the electronic and non-electronic forms available. Finally, we focus on some tips for choosing and using presentation aids effectively.

PRESENTATION AIDS CAN ENHANCE YOUR SPEECH

Although presentation aids take time and energy to prepare, research shows that using them properly can dramatically enhance a presentation. They work by improving at least three audience responses—attention, learning, and recall.

Presentation Aids Improve Attention One benefit of using presentation aids is that the audience will pay more attention.[65] Most listeners can think much faster than you can talk, so if all they have to attend to are your words, their minds will likely wander. Incorporating one or more presentation aids will better hold your listeners' attention.

Presentation Aids Improve Learning A second benefit of using presentation aids is that the audience will learn more from the speech. One reason is that they are paying closer attention, as we just considered. Another is that most people learn better when more than one of their senses is engaged. If the speaker incorporates materials that activate the listeners' sense of sight, hearing, touch, or smell, then listeners will learn more from the presentation than if they are only listening to the speaker's words.[66]

Presentation Aids Improve Recall Listeners will also remember more of what is said if the speaker incorporates presentation aids. One study compared listeners' recall of material from a speech that included visual aids to recall from one that did not. Three hours after the speech, audience members recalled 85 percent of the content if visual aids were used but only 70 percent if no visual aids were used. The difference was even more striking three days later, when listeners exposed to visual aids still remembered 65 percent of the content, compared to only 10 percent for listeners who did not have the benefit of visual aids.[67]

Improving attention, learning, and recall are three ways that presentation aids can benefit your listeners, thereby enhancing the effectiveness of your speech. You have several options to choose from when selecting presentation aids, from simple demonstrations with samples and props, to hand drawn charts and graphics, to multimedia presentation software.

Speakers in infomercials don't simply *tell* you about their products— they also *show* you what the products are and how they work.

Digital Stock/Corbis

LOW-TECH PRESENTATION AIDS

Some of the most engaging presentation aids are decidedly low tech. As we explore in this section, you can make presentation aids from objects, flavors, textures, odors, handouts, and even people.

Objects Almost any physical object can be an effective presentation aid if it is relevant to your topic and if it can be incorporated easily and safely. If your speech is about Mexican cooking techniques, you might bring in a molcajete—the traditional stone mortar and pestle that is used to grind spices—to use as a visual aid. If you're speaking about French fashion, you could bring several different pairs of high-heeled shoes to demonstrate the French influence on women's footwear.

If it isn't feasible to bring the actual object you want to show your listeners, you may be able to bring a *model*, which is a representation of the object. Suppose you're explaining how the human brain is divided into four different lobes. You probably won't have an actual brain to use as a visual aid, but you can bring a plastic model. In this instance, a model could be particularly effective because you might be able to pull apart its various components to show your listeners where the different lobes of the brain are located.

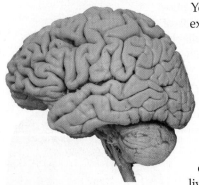

You can also use objects to demonstrate processes. Let's say your goal is to explain how to decorate a wedding cake. Rather than simply telling your listeners about the process, you could bring a cake and decorate it as you describe what you're doing. That way, your listeners hear your description and see the process at the same time.

Before incorporating any object into your speech, consider whether it will be feasible for the space in which you're speaking. Make sure it is large enough to be seen by everyone in your audience but not so large that it dominates your presentation. Check with your instructor or the person in charge of the venue before bringing any type of object that might be considered dangerous or unsanitary, such as a weapon, a power tool, a hot plate, or a live animal. Some school policies prohibit having such objects on campus.

Flavors, Textures, and Odors You can also use presentation aids to appeal to your listeners' senses of taste, touch, and smell. For example, a speech about citrus fruit might incorporate slices of orange, lemon, tangerine, and grapefruit that your audience can sample. A presentation about interior design might use swatches of different types of carpeting that your listeners can feel. If you're speaking about men's cologne, you might bring fragrance samples for your audience to smell. When your topic relates to something that is tasted, touched, or smelled, using those types of presentation aids can be a particularly effective way of demonstrating your speech points.

·text slide An electronic display of text used to accompany a speech.

Handouts Another type of nonelectronic presentation aid is a handout. Most handouts are copies of written material that listeners keep after the speech is over. They can be especially effective when you want your listeners to have more information than you can reasonably address during your presentation. When incorporating a handout, make certain to bring enough copies for everyone in the audience. If you need your listeners to see your handout while you're speaking, distribute it at the beginning of your speech. If not, distribute it at the end so it doesn't distract your listeners' attention while you're speaking.

Sometimes the most effective presentation aid is a person.

Tom Kola/Stock Image/ Getty Images

People Finally, you can use people—including yourself—as presentation aids. Suppose your speech is about the Chinese martial art of tai chi. You might choose to show your audience some of the fundamental movements of tai chi by either performing them yourself or having someone else perform them. Similarly, if you are speaking about the procedure for measuring blood pressure, you might perform a blood pressure test on someone to demonstrate the technique. In both cases, using a person as a presentation aid is more engaging than showing your audience photographs or video recordings because your demonstration is live.

MULTIMEDIA PRESENTATION AIDS

Technology provides a wealth of opportunities for creating interesting and memorable computer-mediated presentation aids. Presentation software programs allow speakers to integrate many different kinds of presentation aids into a unified display. In this section, we'll look at the use of text slides, graphic slides, video, and audio.

Text Slides One form of electronic presentation aid is a **text slide**, an electronic display of text used to accompany a speech. Perhaps some of your instructors use text slides created in presentation software such as Microsoft PowerPoint, Apple Keynote, Google Slides, or Prezi to convey course material in the classroom. Text slides often take the form of lists of words or phrases that are relevant to the presenter's topic.

Effective text slides are clear and brief. Notice, for instance, that the slide in Figure 1 doesn't go into detail about how much sleep a person should get or what a healthy diet should include. That detail is for the speaker to present. The slide itself should give only enough information to introduce each new point. We'll continue the discussion about maximizing the effectiveness of presentation aids later in this chapter.

Graphic Slides Text slides work particularly well for presenting a list of items, such as tips for staying healthy. Another practical electronic presentation aid is a **graphic slide**, the electronic display of information in a visually compelling format that can enhance listeners' attention. Graphic slides include

- *Tables.* A **table** is the display of words or numbers in a format of columns and rows. It is a particularly effective option when you want to compare the same information for two or more groups. For instance, Figure 2 compares starting salaries for high school and college graduates in various fields. This simple illustration makes it easy to spot large and small differences.

- *Charts.* A **chart** is a graphic display of numeric information. Like a table, it is also useful for comparing data between two or more groups. Whereas a table presents the actual text or numbers being compared, a chart converts numbers into a *visual* display. Three types of charts are common. A **pie chart**, as seen in Figure 3, is a graphic display of numbers in the form of a circle divided into segments, each of which represents a percentage of the whole; for example, a pie chart could illustrate the percentages of people around the world who practice various religions. A **line chart**, as shown in Figure 4, is a graphic display of numbers in the form of a line or lines that connect various data points; for example, a line chart could illustrate the percentage of U.S. children living in poverty in various years. Finally, a **bar chart**, in Figure 5, depicts numbers as bars on a graph, such as the percentages of people in various parts of the world who regularly use the Internet.

- *Pictures.* Visual images can be very provocative, so many speakers use pictures as presentation aids. You can embed drawings or photographs directly into a slideshow. For instance, Figure 6 illustrates the use of a photograph in a presentation about Central America. If the picture you want to use is already in electronic form, you can easily add it to a slide. If you have only a hard copy of the picture, you will need to scan it first and save it in a digital format.

Video and Audio Text and graphic slides are excellent options for displaying information, but there may be occasions when you want your audience to listen to or see an audio or a video recording. Perhaps you've been in classes, for example, in which the instructor had you watch part of a movie or listen to a musical recording.

- **graphic slide** An electronic display of information in a visually compelling format.

- **table** The display of words or numbers in a format of columns and rows.

- **chart** A graphic display of numeric information.

- **pie chart** A graphic display of numbers in the form of a circle that is divided into segments, each of which represents a percentage of the whole.

FIGURE 1 EXAMPLE OF A TEXT SLIDE

Tips for Staying Healthy

- Get enough sleep
- Eat a healthy diet
- Take a multivitamin
- Avoid smoking
- Exercise daily

FIGURE 2 EXAMPLE OF A TABLE SLIDE

Average Starting Salaries
Source: *Wall Street Journal, February 12, 2019*

Field	High School Graduate	College Graduate
Sales	$21,000	$38,500
Health care	$28,500	$52,000
Law enforcement	$46,500	$47,000
Event planning	$19,000	$24,750

• **line chart** A graphic display of numbers in the form of a line or lines that connect various data points.

• **bar chart** A graphic display of numbers as bars on a graph.

You may choose to use audio or video recordings in a speech as well, when they will aid your presentation. If your speech were about the career of singer Kenny Rogers (who died in March 2020), you might have your audience listen to one of his many musical hits. You can play audio directly from a media player, such as on a smartphone, or you can embed it in a multimedia presentation.

CHOOSING AND USING PRESENTATION AIDS

If they are used well, presentation aids can greatly enhance a speech. However, if they are not incorporated correctly, they can be distracting or even dangerous, greatly diminishing the effectiveness of a speech. This section gives tips for choosing and using presentation aids for maximum effectiveness.

Remember the Goal No matter what type of presentation aids you choose, remember they are meant to *aid* your speech. They should never themselves become your focus. Instead, they should be like accessories, embellishing your delivery but not overpowering it. Your listeners' primary focus should be on you and what you have to say.

Consider the Context Think about which presentation aids will work best for your audience, the layout of the room, and the resources available to you. Pay particular attention to these factors:

- *The size and arrangement of the room.* Make sure everyone will be able to see, hear, touch, taste, or smell the presentation aids you plan to use. If you're creating a slideshow presentation, use a font large enough for everyone to read comfortably. Before your speech, try your presentation aids in the space where you'll be speaking and confirm that every listener will be able to take advantage of them.

- *The time available for the speech.* Be certain you'll have adequate time to set up and use your presentation aids effectively. If you will be running a slideshow from the computer in the presentation room, try to load your slideshow onto that computer before your speech so you need only to open the document when you are ready to speak. Also be sure you don't have too many slides to get through in the time allotted for your speech. You don't want to have to rush through or skip slides to stay within your time limit. This is an excellent reason to rehearse your speech with your visual aids, as discussed below.

- *The resources available.* Determine beforehand that you will have everything you need to make your presentation aids work. If you're bringing an object that requires electric power, make certain there

FIGURE 3 EXAMPLE OF A PIE CHART SLIDE

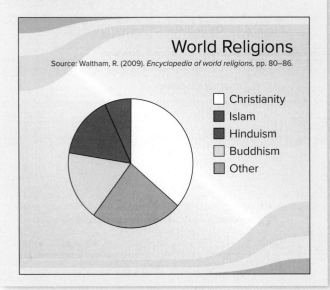

FIGURE 4 EXAMPLE OF A LINE CHART SLIDE

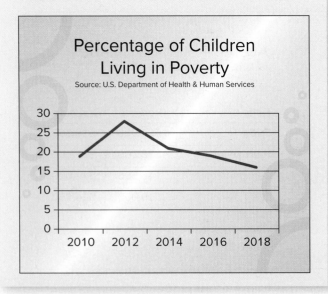

is an accessible outlet and that you have a long enough power cord to reach it. If you plan to use a multimedia presentation, ensure ahead of time that the necessary equipment—such as a projector and screen—is all available. Particularly when you're speaking in an unfamiliar room, don't take anything for granted. Rather, double-check to be sure you will have everything you need.

Strive for Simplicity Choose or create presentation aids that are as simple and straightforward as possible so your listeners will pay attention to their content instead of their form. For example, develop slides that are clean and uncluttered. Stay away from sound effects, fancy slide transitions, and pictures or photographs that are irrelevant to the content of the slide. As you'll discover in "Fact or Fiction?" distracting features can reduce your listeners' ability to learn.

Strive for simplicity in the timing of your presentation aids as well. Make a presentation aid visible to your audience only when you are ready to use it. Then turn it off or put it away when you no longer need it. In this way, you will encourage your audience to pay attention to your aids only when you are using them.

Be Ethical Stay away from any presentation aid that might harm your audience physically or emotionally. In that category are horrifying or disgusting photographs, audio or video recordings with profane or offensive language, and objects that produce dangerously loud sounds or noxious fumes. Using those sorts of presentation aids is unethical, because it places your listeners in danger of being hurt, either physically or emotionally. If you must use a potentially harmful aid in your speech, explicitly warn your audience about it at the beginning of your presentation and again right before you introduce it. For instance, if you're speaking about open-heart surgery and feel you should include a photograph of the surgical procedure, tell your listeners beforehand that your presentation includes graphic depictions of surgery, so they have the option to look away.

In addition, give credit to the source of any information you present. When you prepare a slide with data that you did not generate yourself, include the source of the data on the slide. Notice, for instance, that the slides in Figures 2 to 5 specifically identify where the data in those slides came from. Making reference to these sources is an important way to avoid plagiarism (see the chapter on organizing and finding support for your speech).

Moreover, when you use photographs, videos, or other visual elements in your slide that came from another source, make reference to that source. Notice that the slide in Figure 6 includes, in small type, the source of the photograph featured on that slide. If you did not generate the photo or video you are using, then you run the risk of committing copyright infringement if you do not identify their source (see the chapter on organizing and finding support for your speech).

Practice with Your Presentation Aids If you will be incorporating presentation aids when you deliver your speech, be sure to use them when you rehearse. Practice advancing from slide to slide in your multimedia presentation—manually or

FIGURE 5 EXAMPLE OF A BAR CHART SLIDE

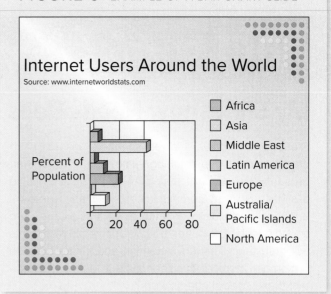

FIGURE 6 EXAMPLE OF A PHOTOGRAPHIC SLIDE

Fact or *fiction?*

My Slideshow Needs Bells and Whistles—Right?

Presentation software gives speakers the ability to create colorful, eye-catching audiovisual aids for their presentations. Even if their primary purpose in using a slideshow is to communicate text, many speakers enhance their slides with features such as pictures and sound effects. They often believe such embellishments will grab their listeners' attention and cause them to remember more of the speech. Is it fact—or fiction— that these special effects work?

Research has found that they usually do *not* serve that intended purpose. Although pictures and sound effects might successfully capture your listeners' attention, they will draw that attention away from the content of your speech. As a result, your audience will learn and remember less from your presentation than if you use simple, straightforward slides with text only. A study by behavioral scientists Robert Bartsch and Kristi Cobern found that pictures in slides were particularly distracting if they were not directly relevant to the content of the text. To use a slideshow effectively, therefore, it's best to forgo unnecessary sights and sounds, making sure that the effects you do include are directly related to your points.

SOURCE: Bartsch, R. A., & Cobern, K. M. (2003). Effectiveness of PowerPoint presentations in lectures. *Computers & Education, 41*(1), 77–86. https://doi.org/10.1016/S0360-1315(03)00027-7

If you plan to incorporate presentation aids into your speech, be sure to use them when you rehearse.

Elena Elisseeva/123RF

with a remote control—so you can do so effortlessly during your speech. Perhaps you must set up or uncover your presentation aid *during* your speech instead of beforehand. If so, rehearse those moves so you can continue speaking while doing the necessary tasks. That way, you will avoid disrupting the flow of your speech with long, awkward pauses. As mentioned above, it is also helpful to practice speaking in the direction of your listeners, instead of facing your slideshow while you talk. Rehearsing with your slideshow is also a good way to ensure you don't have too many slides for your allotted time.

Have a Backup Plan Regardless of the type of presentation aid you plan to use, something can always go wrong that will prevent you from using it. You might forget the USB drive containing your slides, or the computer you planned to use might fail. The light bulb in your projector could burn out, or the room's wifi, which you intended to use, could be out. The photocopier on which you planned to duplicate your handouts might be jammed, or the person who was to demonstrate tai chi moves might get sick and cancel.

Before using any presentation aid, it's thus crucial to think through everything that might go wrong and to have a backup plan. Bring a laptop computer or tablet containing your slideshow in case you forget your USB drive or the room's wifi fails. Copy your handouts a day or two before your speech. Learn the tai chi moves well enough to demonstrate them yourself if you have to. Being prepared to respond to such contingencies will help your speech to succeed under any circumstances.

- What are the most common forms of speech delivery?

  Most speakers deliver their speeches in one of four formats: impromptu, extemporaneous, scripted, or memorized.

- How can you manage public speaking anxiety?

  Remember that speaking anxiety is normal, and try to channel your excess energy toward a good performance. Practice visualizing a successful speech, and maintain a positive attitude.

- How can you deliver a speech effectively?

  Pay attention to what you look like (including your facial expressions, eye contact, posture, gestures, and personal appearance) and what you sound like (including your vocal rate, volume, pitch, articulation, and fluency). Select presentation aids that will enhance your speech, and incorporate them appropriately.

KEY TERMS

impromptu speech 370

extemporaneous speech 371

scripted speech 371

memorized speech 372

public speaking anxiety
(stage fright) 373

stress 374

anxiety 374

anticipatory anxiety 374

fight-or-flight response 376

visualization 379

desensitization 380

avatars 380

slideshow 382

articulation 385

fluency 385

stuttering 386

presentation aids 386

text slide 388

graphic slide 389

table 389

chart 389

pie chart 389

line chart 390

bar chart 390

NOTES

1. Snow, R. (2019, May 28). The 10 most inspiring graduation speeches of 2019. https://www.shondaland.com/inspire/a27558629/inspiring-graduation-speeches-of-2019/
2. Wolvin, A. D. (2010). Listening engagement: Intersecting theoretical perspectives. In A. D. Wolvin (Ed.), *Listening and human communication in the 21st century* (pp. 7–30). John Wiley & Sons.
3. See Tanveer, M. I., Hassan, M. K., Gildea, D., & Hoque, M. E. (2019). Predicting TED Talk ratings from language and prosody. *arXiv,* preprint arXiv:1906.03940.
4. Ingraham, C. (2014, October 30). America's top fears: Public speaking, heights and bugs. *The Washington Post.* https://www.washingtonpost.com/news/wonk/wp/2014/10/30/clowns-are-twice-as-scary-to-democrats-as-they-are-to-republicans/
5. Niles, A. N., & Craske, M. G. (2019). Incidental emotion regulation deficits in public speaking anxiety. *Cognitive Therapy and Research, 43*(2), 419–426. https://doi.org/10.1007/s10608-018-9954-1

6. Toure. (2011, April 28). Adele opens up about her inspirations, looks and stage fright. *Rolling Stone.* http://www.rollingstone.com/music/news/adele-opens-up-about-her-inspirations-looks-and-stage-fright-20120210?page=3

7. Teven, J. J., Richmond, V. P., McCroskey, J. C., & McCroskey, L. L. (2010). Updating relationships between communication traits and communication competence. *Communication Research Reports, 27*(3), 263–270. https://doi.org/10.1080/08824096.2010.496331

8. Ogden, J. S. (2010). *Public speaking anxiety, test anxiety, and academic achievement in undergraduate students* [unpublished master's thesis, Bucknell University]. Digital Commons. http://digitalcommons.bucknell.edu/masters_theses/51.

9. See, e.g., Somers, J. M., Goldner, E. M., Waraich, P., & Hsu, L. (2006). Prevalence and incidence studies of anxiety disorders: A systematic review of the literature. *Canadian Journal of Psychiatry, 51*(2), 100–113. https://doi.org/10.1177/070674370605100206

10. Allen, A. P., Kennedy, P. J., Dockray, S., Cryan, J. F., Dinan, T. G., & Clarke, G. (2017). The Trier Social Stress Test: Principles and practice. *Neurobiology of Stress, 6,* 113–126. https://doi.org/10.1016/j.ynstr.2016.11.001

11. Behnke, R. R., & Sawyer, C. R. (1998). Conceptualizing speech anxiety as a dynamic trait. *Southern Communication Journal, 63*(2), 160–168. https://doi.org/10.1080/10417949809373086

12. Behnke, R. R., & Sawyer, C. R. (1999). Milestones of anticipatory public speaking anxiety. *Communication Education, 48*(2), 165–172. https://doi.org/10.1080/03634529909379164

13. Witt, P. L., & Behnke, R. R. (2006). Anticipatory speech anxiety as a function of public speaking assignment type. *Communication Education, 55*(2), 167–177. https://10.1080/03634520600566074

14. MacIntyre, P. D., & Thivierge, K. A. (1995). The effects of speaker personality on anticipated reactions to public speaking. *Communication Research Reports, 12*(2), 125–133. https://doi.org/10.1080/08824099509362048

15. Freeman, T., Sawyer, C. R., & Behnke, R. R. (1997). Behavioral inhibition and the attribution of public speaking state anxiety. *Communication Education, 46*(3), 175–187. https://doi.org/10.1080/03634529709379089

16. MacIntyre & Thivierge, 1995.

17. Mladenka, J. D., Sawyer, C. R., & Behnke, R. R. (1998). Anxiety sensitivity and speech trait anxiety as predictors of state anxiety during public speaking. *Communication Quarterly, 46*(4), 417–429. https://doi.org/10.1080/01463379809370112

18. Behnke, R. R., & Sawyer, C. R. (2000). Anticipatory anxiety patterns for male and female public speakers. *Communication Education, 49*(2), 187–195. https://doi.org/10.1080/03634520009379205

19. Ordaz, S., & Luna, B. (2012). Sex differences in physiological reactivity to acute psychosocial stress in adolescence. *Psychoneuroendocrinology, 37*(8), 1135–1157. https://doi.org/10.1016/j.psyneuen.2012.01.002

20. Derakhshan, A., Mikaeili, M., Nasrabadi, A. M., & Gedeon, T. (2019). Network physiology of "fight or flight" response in facial superficial blood vessels. *Physiological Measurement, 40*(1), Article 014002. https://doi.org/10.1088/1361-6579/aaf089

21. White, S. F., Lee, Y., Phan, J. M., Moody, S. N., & Shirtcliff, E. A. (2019). Putting the flight in "fight-or-flight": Testosterone reactivity to skydiving is modulated by autonomic activation. *Biological Psychology, 143,* 93–102. https://doi.org/10.1016/j.biopsycho.2019.02.012

22. Casteleyn, J. (2019). Playing with improv(isational) theatre to battle public speaking stress. *Research in Drama Education: The Journal of Applied Theatre and Performance, 24*(2), 147–154. https://doi.org/10.1080/13569783.2018.1552129

23. Arch, J. J., & Craske, M. G. (2006). Mechanisms of mindfulness: Emotion regulation following a focused breathing induction. *Behaviour Research and Therapy, 44*(12), 1849–1858. https://doi.org/10.1016/j.brat.2005.12.007

24. Fredrikson, M., & Gunnarsson, R. (1992). Psychobiology of stage fright: The effect of public performance on neuroendocrine, cardiovascular, and subjective reactions. *Biological Psychology, 33*(1), 51–61. https://doi.org/10.1016/0301-0511(92)90005-F

25. Perciavalle, V., Blandini, M., Fecarotta, P., Buscemi, A., Di Corrado, D., Bertolo, L., Fichera, F., & Coco, M. (2017). The role of deep breathing on stress. *Neurological Sciences, 38*(3), 451–458. https://doi.org/10.1007/s10072-016-2790-8

26. Witt, P. L., Brown, K. C., Roberts, J. B., Weisel, J., Sawyer, C. R., & Behnke, R. R. (2006). Somatic anxiety patterns before, during, and after giving a public speech. *Southern Communication Journal, 71*(1), 87–100. https://doi.org/10.1080/10417940500503555

27. Finn, A. N., Sawyer, C. R., & Behnke, R. R. (2009). A model of anxious arousal for public speaking. *Communication Education, 58*(3), 417–432. https://doi.org/10.1080/03634520802268891

28. Bouma, E. M. C., Riese, H., Ormel, J., Verhulst, F. C., & Oldehinkel, A. J. (2009). Adolescents' cortisol responses to awakening and social stress: Effects of gender, menstrual phase and oral contraceptives. The TRIALS study. *Psychoneuroendocrinology, 34*(6), 884–893. https://doi.org/10.1016/j.psyneuen.2009.01.003

29. Traustadóttir, T., Bosch, P. R., & Matt, K. S. (2003). Gender differences in cardiovascular and hypothalamic-pituitary-adrenal axis responses to psychological stress in healthy older adult men and women. *Stress, 6*(2), 133–140. https://doi.org/10.1080/1025389031000111302

30. Heponiemi, T., Keltikangas-Järvinen, K., Kettunen, J., Puttonen, S., & Ravaja, N. (2004). BIS-BAS sensitivity and cardiac autonomic stress profiles. *Psychophysiology, 41*(1), 37–45. https://doi.org/10.1111/1469-8986.00118_41_1

31. See Sadikaj, G., Moskowitz, D. S., Russell, J. J., & Zuroff, D. C. (2015). Submissiveness in social anxiety disorder: The role of interpersonal perception and embarrassment. *Journal of Social and Clinical Psychology, 34*(1), 1–27. https://doi.org/10.1521/jscp.2015.34.1.1

32. Clevinger, T., & King, T. R. (1961). A factor analysis of the visible symptoms of stage fright. *Speech Monographs, 28*(4), 296–298. https://doi.org/10.1080/03637756109375328

33. Pisanski, K., Nowak, J., & Sorokowski, P. (2016). Individual differences in cortisol stress response predict increases in voice pitch during exam stress. *Physiology & Behavior, 163,* 234–238. https://doi.org/10.1016/j.physbeh.2016.05.018

34. Bulleted list was adapted from Table 1 of Mulac, A., & Sherman, A. R. (1974). Behavioral assessment of speech anxiety. *Quarterly Journal of Speech, 60*(2), 134–143. https://doi.org/10.1080/00335637409383219

35. Konnopka, A., & König, H. (2020). Economic burden of anxiety disorders: A systematic review and meta-analysis. *PharmacoEconomics, 38,* 25–37. https://doi.org/10.1007/s40273-019-00849-7

36. See de Quervain, D., Schwabe, L., & Roozendaal, B. (2017). Stress, glucocorticoids and memory: Implications for treating fear-related disorders. *Nature Reviews Neuroscience, 18*(1), 7–19. https://doi.org/10.1038/nrn.2016.155

37. Moons, W. G., Eisenberger, N. I., & Taylor, S. E. (2010). Anger and fear responses to stress have different biological profiles. *Brain, Behavior, and Immunity, 24*(2), 215–219. https://doi.org/10.1016/j.bbi.2009.08.009

38. See Woestmann, L., Kvist, J., & Saastamoinen, M. (2017). Fight or flight? Flight increases immune gene expression but does not help to fight an infection. *Journal of Evolutionary Biology, 30*(3), 501–511. https://doi.org/10.1111/jeb.13007

39. Ayres, J. (2005). Performance visualization and behavioral disruption: A clarification. *Communication Reports, 18*(1-2), 55–63. https://doi.org/10.1080/08934210500084271

40. See, e.g., Ayres, J., & Ayres Sonandre', D. M. (2003). Performance visualization: Does the nature of the speech model matter? *Communication Research Reports, 20*(3), 260–268. https://doi.org/10.1080/08824090309388824

41. Docan-Morgan, T., & Schmidt, T. (2012). Reducing public speaking anxiety for native and non-native English speakers: The value of systematic desensitization, cognitive restructuring, and skills training. *Cross-Cultural Communication, 8*(5), 16–19.

42. Heuett, B. L., & Heuett, K. B. (2011). Virtual reality therapy: A means of reducing public speaking anxiety. *International Journal of Humanities and Social Science, 1*(16), 1–6.

43. Moneta, G. B., Vulpe, A., & Rogaten, J. (2012).Can positive affect "undo" negative affect? A longitudinal study of affect in studying. *Personality and Individual Differences, 53*(4), 448–452. https://doi.org/10.1016/j.paid.2012.04.011

44. Knapp, M. L.(2009). *Lying and deception in human interaction.* Pearson.

45. Mehu, M., Mortillaro, M., Bänziger, T., & Scherer, K. R. (2012). Reliable facial muscle activation enhances recognizability and credibility of emotional expression. *Emotion, 12*(4), 701–715. https://10.1037/a0026717

46. Yokoyama, H., & Daibo, I. (2012). Effects of gaze and speech rate on receivers' evaluations of persuasive speech. *Psychological Reports, 110*(2), 663–676. https://doi.org/10.2466/07.11.21.28.PRO.110.2.663-676

47. Vrij, A., Hartwig, M., & Granhag, P. A. (2019). Reading lies: Nonverbal communication and deception. *Annual Review of Psychology, 70*, 295–317. https://doi.org/10.1146/annurev-psych-010418-103135

48. Nunamaker, J. F., Burgoon, J. K., Twyman, N. W., Proudfoot, J. G., Schuetzler, R., & Giboney, J. S. (2012, June). Establishing a foundation for automated human credibility screening. *2012 IEEE International Conference on Intelligence and Security Informatics* (pp. 202–211). IEEE.

49. See de Gelder, B., de Borst, A. W., & Watson, R. (2015). The perception of emotion in body expressions. *Wiley Interdisciplinary Reviews: Cognitive Science, 6*(2), 149–158. https://doi.org/10.1002/wcs.1335

50. Munhall, K. G., Jones, J. A., Callan, D. E., Kuratate, T., & Vatikiotis-Bateson, E. (2004). Visual prosody and speech intelligibility: Head movement improves auditory speech perception. *Psychological Science, 15*(2), 133–137. https://doi.org/10.1111/j.0963-7214.2004.01502010.x

51. See, e.g., Congdon, E. L., Novack, M. A., Brooks, N., Hemani-Lopez, N., O'Keefe, L., & Goldin-Meadow, S. (2017). Better together: Simultaneous presentation of speech and gesture in math instruction supports generalization and retention. *Learning and Instruction, 50*, 65–74. https://doi.org/10.1016/j.learninstruc.2017.03.005

52. Elsbach, K. D. (2004). Managing images of trustworthiness in organizations. In K. M. Roderick, & K. S. Cook (Eds.), *Trust and distrust in organizations* (pp. 275–292). Russell Sage Foundation.

53. Wolvin, A. D. (Ed.). (2010). *Listening and human communication in the 21st century.* John Wiley & Sons. https://doi.org/10.1002/9781444314908

54. Guyer, J. J., Fabrigar, L. R., & Vaughan-Johnston, T. I. (2019). Speech rate, intonation, and pitch: Investigating the bias and cue effects of vocal confidence on persuasion. *Personality and Social Psychology Bulletin, 45*(3), 389–405. https://doi.org/10.1177/0146167218787805

55. De Waele, A., Claeys, A. S., & Cauberghe, V. (2019). The organizational voice: The importance of voice pitch and speech rate in organizational crisis communication. *Communication Research, 46*(7), 1026–1049. https://doi.org/10.1177/0093650217692911

56. Floyd, K., & Ray, G. B. (2003). Human affection exchange: IV. Vocalic predictors of perceived affection in initial interactions. *Western Journal of Communication, 67*(1), 56–73. https://doi.org/10.1080/10570310309374758

57. Ray, G. B. (1986). Vocally cued personality prototypes: An implicit personality theory approach. *Communication Monographs, 53*(3), 266–276. https://doi.org/10.1080/03637758609376141

58. Miley, W. M., & Gonsalves, S. (2003). What you don't know can hurt you: Students' perceptions of professors' annoying teaching habits. *College Student Journal, 37*(3), 447–455.

59. Miller, G. R., & Hewgill, M. A. (1964). The effect of variations in nonfluency on audience ratings of source credibility. *Quarterly Journal of Speech, 50*(1), 36–44. https://doi.org/10.1080/00335636409382644

60. Smith, A., & Weber, C. (2017). How stuttering develops: The multifactorial dynamic pathways theory. *Journal of Speech, Language, and Hearing Research, 60*(9), 2483–2505. https://doi.org/10.1044/2017_JSLHR-S-16-0343

61. Watts, A., Eadie, P., Block, S., Mensah, F., & Reilly, S. (2017). Language skills of children during the first 12 months after stuttering onset. *Journal of Fluency Disorders, 51*, 39–49. https://doi.org/10.1016/j.fludis.2016.12.001

62. Anderson, M. R., & Stuart, A. (2017). Speech-language pathologists' perceptions of persons who stutter before and after speech therapy. *International Journal of Speech & Language Pathology and Audiology, 5*, 5–14.

63. Kragh, S. U., & Bislev, S. (2005). Universities and student values across nations. *Journal of Intercultural Communication, 9*, 48–63.

64. Stewart, E. C., & Bennett, M. J. (1991). *American cultural patterns: A cross-cultural perspective.* Intercultural Press. Quote is from p. 155.

65. Alley, M. (2003). *The craft of scientific presentations: Critical steps to succeed and critical errors to avoid.* Springer.

66. Kim, D., & Gilman, D. A. (2008). Effects of text, audio, and graphic aids in multimedia instruction for vocabulary learning. *Educational Technology & Society, 11*(3), 114–126.

67. Zayas-Baya, E. P. (1997). Instructional media in the total language picture. *International Journal of Instructional Media, 5*, 145–150.

14

Production Perig/Shutterstock

SPEAKING INFORMATIVELY

Fake News Can Cause Real Problems

Fewer than half of U.S. American adults get a flu shot each year—and for many, misinformation is the reason. According to the Centers for Disease Control and Prevention (CDC), a common misconception is that getting the flu vaccine will actually cause people to contract the flu.[1] When speakers or websites present this false information as though it were fact, they run the risk of persuading people not to protect themselves against a virus that the CDC estimates killed more than 80,000 people in 2018 alone.[2] These observations illustrate the point that information is powerful, and when it is false or misleading, it can have real effects on people's lives.

As You READ

- What methods can we use to inform?
- In what ways should we frame an informative speech?
- Through what strategies can we hone our informative-speaking skills?

We rely on accurate information from websites, newspapers, interpersonal encounters, and many other sources to make decisions in our personal and professional lives. Having good information can empower us to make wise choices. Often, however, the manner in which information is presented matters as much as the information itself. If the information we receive from others isn't accurate, complete, or understandable, or if it doesn't grab our attention, it may lead us to make poor decisions. The same is true when we have occasion to speak informatively to others. Unless we convey our message clearly and completely and in a way that engages our listeners' attention, their decision making might be compromised.

In this chapter, we explore the various methods for informing an audience and ways to frame the speech topic for maximum effectiveness. We'll also examine several techniques for presenting successfully and we'll peruse an award-winning informative speech.

Choosing a Method of Informing

In the past two decades, more than 50,000 college graduates have participated in Teach for America, a nonprofit organization that recruits individuals to teach for two years in low-income communities throughout the United States.[3] Unlike traditional teachers who have earned undergraduate degrees in education, most Teach for America instructors have no training in teaching practices when they apply for the program. However, many recruits quickly learn that there are several ways to impart knowledge to their students and that although one method may be ineffective, another often works well. The same can be said for any type of informative speaking.

- **informative speaking**
Publicly addressing others to increase their knowledge, understanding, or skills.

We can approach **informative speaking**—publicly addressing others to increase their knowledge, understanding, or skills—in several different ways. The techniques available to us include defining, describing, explaining, and demonstrating. The method or methods we choose depend on our speech topic and audience.

INFORMATIVE SPEECHES CAN DEFINE

- **defining** Providing the meaning of a word or concept.

One method of informing an audience is **defining**: providing the meaning of a word or concept. Let's say you want to educate your listeners about the credit industry. You might focus part of your speech on defining the term *FICO score*, a widely used personal credit score calculated by the Fair Isaac Corporation. An individual's FICO score strongly influences his or her ability to obtain credit, so knowing what a FICO score is can help your audience to understand how the credit industry works.

Teach for America instructors learn to try various strategies for imparting knowledge to their students.

Thomas Barwick/Getty Images

Defining a term may sound like a straightforward task because it requires only that you connect the term to its meaning. Meanings can be highly contested, however. The way a society defines the word *marriage*, for instance, differentiates those who can enjoy the benefits of such a relationship from those who cannot. Likewise, the way a government defines the word *torture* dictates what methods its military personnel can use in combat and interrogations. Individuals often have dramatically different perspectives on how words such as *marriage* and *torture* ought to be defined, largely because the definitions have consequences for so many people.

If defining a word or concept will help you to inform your listeners, you can choose from several methods:

- *Identify the denotative meaning.* You may recall from the chapter on how we use language that a term's denotative meaning is its dictionary definition. In a speech about global warming, for instance, you could define *greenhouse gases* as "atmospheric gases that absorb and emit radiation." If you choose this method, bear in mind that many words have more than one definition in the dictionary, so you would want to select the most appropriate definition to focus on.

- *Explain the connotative meaning.* A term's connotative meaning is its socially or culturally implied meaning. One connotative meaning of the word *home*, for example, is "a place where you feel safe and secure."

- *Provide the etymology.* The **etymology** of a term is its origin or history. In a speech about affectionate communication, you could explain that the word *affection* derives from the Latin word *affectio*, meaning "an emotion of the mind."

  - **etymology** The origin or history of a word.

- *Give synonyms or antonyms.* You can define a word by identifying **synonyms**, words that have the same meaning as your word, or **antonyms**, words that have the opposite meaning. Synonyms for the term *normal* include *usual*, *ordinary*, and *typical*, whereas antonyms include *abnormal*, *irregular*, and *odd*.

  - **synonyms** Words that have the same meaning.

  - **antonyms** Words that have opposite meanings.

- *Define by example.* You may help your audience to understand a concept by providing examples that illustrate its meaning. In a speech about the immune system, you might define the term *pathogen* by giving examples of types of pathogens, such as viruses, bacteria, fungi, and parasites.

- *Use compare-and-contrast definitions.* You can discuss similarities and differences between two or more definitions of a term. To some people, the definition of *family* is limited to legal and biological relationships; to others, it includes anyone to whom they feel emotionally close. If you were speaking about the concept of family, you could compare and contrast those two definitions of the term.

SHARPEN Your Skills: *Defining a term in multiple ways*

Select one word or concept and define it according to its denotative and connotative meanings, etymology, synonyms, antonyms, and examples. Write a brief paragraph or journal entry commenting on which approaches seemed to work best for your word, and why.

INFORMATIVE SPEECHES CAN DESCRIBE

A second way to inform your audience about something is to describe it. **Describing** means using words to depict or portray a person, a place, an object, or an experience. You might describe the arrangement of rooms in the campus student center or the experience of having your eyes dilated by an optometrist, using language that creates a mental image for your listeners.

- **describing** Using words to depict or portray a person, a place, an object, or an experience.

Two forms of description are common in informative speeches. With the first, **representation**, you describe something in terms of its physical or psychological attributes. You could represent the Great Wall of China by telling your audience what it looks like or what kind of awe it inspires when people see it. When you describe by representation, you are helping your listeners to imagine their physical or emotional experiences if they were to encounter what you are describing.

- **representation** Describing something in terms of its physical or psychological attributes.

An informative speech about the Great Wall of China could describe its physical dimensions or detail the awe it inspires in visitors.

John Wang/Getty Images

• **narration** Describing a series of events in sequence.

• **explaining** Revealing why something occurred or how something works.

The second form of description common in informative speeches is **narration**, with which you describe a series of events in sequence. You can think of narration as storytelling. In an informative speech about the field of veterinary medicine, for instance, you could describe what your aunt went through to become a veterinarian or tell a story about your first visit to an animal hospital.

Many speakers combine representation and narration. Let's say you wanted to teach your audience about the life of model and author Chrissy Teigen. You could use representation to describe some of her television appearances. You could use narration to explain how Teigen began her high-profile modeling career or how she met her husband, singer John Legend. Incorporating both forms of description can produce a richer mental image for your listeners than either form can evoke on its own.

INFORMATIVE SPEECHES CAN EXPLAIN

In many informative presentations, the speaker explains something to the audience. **Explaining** means revealing why something occurred or how something works. For example, you might explain how Larry Page and Sergey Brin, then Ph.D. students at Stanford University, developed the search engine Google. You could also explain how cancer cells spread through the body or why people in Great Britain drive on the left side of the road.

When offering an explanation, speakers must use clear, concrete language and avoid jargon that will be unfamiliar to listeners. Suppose that in an informative speech about statistics, you hear a speaker explain: "Mean scores are considered significantly different only if the p-value is smaller than the critical alpha." Although that explanation would make perfect sense to a statistician, it won't make sense to you unless you already understand what mean scores, p-values, and critical alphas are and why they matter. It is always useful to assess how much your listeners already know about your speech topic and then adapt your words to their current knowledge. That consideration is particularly crucial when you are explaining something, to ensure that your audience will understand all the elements of your explanation.

People can offer different explanations for the same event, such as the 2019 shooting of De'Von Bailey. When you offer an explanation, you may be implicitly persuading your audience to accept it as accurate.

Erik McGregor/LightRocket/ Getty Images

TABLE 1

TO INFORM OR TO PERSUADE?

Avoid turning an informative speech into a persuasive speech by keeping in mind these fundamental differences.

	Persuasive Speech	Informative Speech
Focus	What should be	What is
Evidence	Facts and opinions that support the predetermined conclusion	Facts and information relevant to the topic
Goal	To convince listeners to adopt a particular belief or action	To educate listeners about the speech topic

For a speech intended to inform, it is very important to be aware of how your own beliefs can influence your explanations of events. In the chapter on choosing, developing, and researching a topic, we examined the various goals a speaker might have in planning a public presentation, and we differentiated between speaking to inform and speaking to persuade. Of all the techniques speakers can use to inform an audience, explaining most often risks crossing the line from informing to persuading. The reason is that people's opinions and perspectives frequently influence their explanations of events or processes.

In August 2019, for instance, 19-year-old De'Von Bailey was shot and killed by two police officers after the officers questioned Bailey and another man about an alleged armed robbery. The officers told investigators that Bailey had reached for a gun and that they reacted out of self-defense. After the release of body-cam footage showing that Bailey never drew a weapon on the officers, however, many in the community called the officers' actions an example of overt racism. Either explanation—justified self-defense or unjustified racism—may have merit, but the explanation you believe may be influenced by your own attitudes about race or your own experiences with law enforcement. An informative speaker who explained Bailey's shooting as the product of either self-defense or racism would implicitly be persuading the audience to believe the explanation being offered.

You can avoid crossing the line from informative to persuasive speaking by keeping your remarks **objective**—that is, based on facts rather than opinions. When you speak objectively, you avoid trying to convince listeners of a particular point of view. In comparison, remarks in a persuasive speech are **subjective**—that is, biased toward a specific conclusion. Consult Table 1 for some key differences between informative and persuasive speaking.

• **objective** Based on facts rather than opinions.

• **subjective** Biased toward a specific conclusion.

INFORMATIVE SPEECHES CAN DEMONSTRATE

Many people learn better by *seeing* how to do something rather than by simply hearing how to do it. Therefore, one way to maximize the effectiveness of an explanation is to incorporate a demonstration. **Demonstrating** means showing how to do something by doing it as it is explained. For instance, you could teach listeners how to play Call of Duty, clean a camera lens, or stretch properly before exercise by demonstrating those activities during your speech.

• **demonstrating** Showing how to do something by doing it as it is explained.

When you're demonstrating a process, it's important to describe each step as you do it. Let's say your informative speech is about how to prepare a Caprese salad. You might start by identifying each of the ingredients you'll be using: tomato, mozzarella cheese, basil, black pepper, and balsamic vinegar. Then, as you slice the tomatoes and mozzarella, tell your audience what you're doing ("I am slicing the tomato and cheese into equal-size pieces so they'll be easier to eat"). When you chop the basil, describe how you're doing it ("First I'm going to cut the stem off each basil leaf; then I'll roll the leaves together and give them a rough chop"). Explain how you are arranging the tomatoes, cheese, and basil on a plate ("I'm interspersing slices of tomato and cheese on the plate and then sprinkling the chopped basil over the top"). Describe seasoning the salad with black pepper and

Foodcollection

Fact or *fiction?*

Show and Tell: People Learn Best by Seeing *and* Hearing

Speech instructors often encourage students to use demonstrations on the assumption that listeners learn best by seeing *and* hearing rather than by just seeing *or* just hearing. Is that assumption fact or fiction?

Research suggests that it is a fact. Let's say that in addition to describing how to download applications on an iPad, you also *demonstrate* by downloading applications during your speech. Some of us seem to be primarily *visual learners*, who learn best by seeing. Others seem to be primarily *auditory learners*, who learn best by hearing. Yet studies show that students who encounter both visual and auditory stimuli accurately recall 11 percent more of what they learn than do students exposed only to visual stimuli and 8 percent more than students exposed only to auditory stimuli. The explanation may be that we process

Pixtal/AGE Fotostock

verbal and visual information separately, so when we are presented with both types of information, they reinforce each other and enhance our ability to learn.

ASK YOURSELF

- How do you learn best? In what ways is your own learning influenced by verbal and visual stimuli?

- Based on the research described here, how do you think listeners' learning would be affected if a speaker engaged an additional sense—such as their sense of touch or smell—in addition to using visual and auditory stimuli?

SOURCE: See Berk, R. A. (2009). Multimedia teaching with video clips: TV, movies, YouTube, and mtvU in the college classroom. *International Journal of Technology in Teaching and Learning, 5*(1), 1–21.

balsamic vinegar as you do so. In this way, your audience will both *see* and *hear* every step of the process.

Does demonstrating while giving a speech enhance listeners' ability to learn? Check out the "Fact or Fiction?" box to find out.

If you want to include a demonstration in your informative speech, take note of the advice offered in the chapter on presenting a speech confidently and competently about using presentation aids. In particular, make sure you will have everything you need to run your demonstration, such as adequate space, the right equipment, and access to a power supply if you require one. Ensure that you can conduct the demonstration safely and that it won't pose a threat to anyone in your audience. Be certain you can complete the demonstration within the time allocated for your speech, and have a backup plan in case any elements of your demonstration fail.

Selecting and Framing the Topic

Students who compete in speech and debate know the importance of choosing a compelling topic and framing it appropriately for their listeners. They put their speaking skills on the line in every tournament, so they can't afford to bore their audiences.

Imagine that *you* are taking part in an informative-speaking competition with undergraduates from around the country. How will you choose an intriguing topic? How can you frame your presentation in such a way that your listeners will care about and pay attention to the content? In this section, we explore eight categories of topics for informative speeches, and we'll see that effective informative speakers frame their presentations in two connected ways: first by relating themselves to their topic and then by relating the topic to their audience.

SELECT A CAPTIVATING TOPIC

When planning an informative speech, many people have difficulty selecting a topic that will capture and hold their listeners' attention. That decision needn't be a challenge, however, because the list of potential topics for an informative speech is virtually unlimited. Communication scholars Ron Allen and Ray McKerrow have identified eight categories of topics that work particularly well for informative speeches:[4]

Kevin Mazur/Getty images

- *Issues.* According to Allen and McKerrow, *issues* are problems or points of controversy about which people desire resolution. You could choose to speak on a contemporary issue facing the United States, such as unemployment, immigration, or the war on terror. You might also select an issue that has been controversial for some time, such as affirmative action or sex education in public schools. When you focus your informative speech on an issue, your purpose isn't to persuade your listeners to adopt any particular point of view but rather to give them the facts necessary to form their own opinions.

- *Events. Events* are occurrences that are noteworthy for the meanings they represent. You may choose to speak about an event that was publicly experienced, such as the NCAA basketball Final Four or the death of playwright Larry Kramer. You might also elect to speak about a significant event in your personal life, such as a visit to a foreign country or a religious conversion. In each instance, you can educate your audience about the event and communicate the significant meaning it has, either for your listeners or for you.

- *People.* Many informative speakers focus their presentations on other people. You might choose to discuss an individual who made history, such as Misty Copeland, the first African American principal ballerina with the prestigious American Ballet Theatre. You could talk about someone who is noteworthy for acts of charity, such as Pope Francis or the late Princess Diana of Great Britain. You might talk about the life of a person in the public spotlight, such as golfer Dustin Johnson or pop singer Ariana Grande. You could also focus your remarks on a group, such as the Amish or the Apollo 11 astronauts.

- *Places.* Cable television's Travel Channel is popular because it informs viewers about interesting and exotic places. You can do the same by focusing your speech on a place you find significant or intriguing. It might be a place you have personally visited, or it could be a locale where daily life is substantially different than it is for your listeners, such as Cuba, Iceland, or Yemen. You can even focus on a place in a specific historical period, such as China during the Shang Dynasty or Moscow before the breakup of the former Soviet Union.

- *Objects.* Allen and McKerrow have categorized as *objects* any entities that are nonhuman, including living or animate objects, such as the California giant redwoods and the critically endangered Sumatran Tiger, and inanimate objects, such as the guillotine and the Empire State Building. Effective speeches about an object often educate listeners about the object's evolution and development or its significance in history, culture, politics, or ecology.

• *Concepts.* Whereas objects are tangible items, *concepts* are abstract ideas. Oppression, compassion, integrity, bias, and forgiveness are all examples of concepts because each is a notion or an idea rather than a concrete object. Some powerful speeches have focused on concepts that were significant to their audiences. In June 2018, for instance, actor Andrew Garfield used his Tony Award acceptance speech to advocate for inclusion and acceptance of the LGBTQ community. Inclusion isn't an object that can be seen or felt; it's a complex idea that affects millions of lives as a social concept.

• *Processes.* As we saw earlier in the chapter, many informative speeches describe or demonstrate a *process*, a series of actions that culminates in a specific result. For instance, you might focus on a natural process, such as how coal becomes diamond or how a canyon forms from water erosion. Or you might choose a human-created process, such as the design of currency or the functions of a CT scanner. You can also use your informative speech to teach your listeners a process, such as how to tie a bowline knot or crop a digital photo.

• *Policies.* Finally, informative speeches can focus on *policies*—that is, programs that aim to guide future decision making or to achieve some goal. For instance, you might inform your listeners about policies that existed in the past but were overturned, such as school segregation in the United States and apartheid in South Africa. You might also speak on current policies, such as those that regulate interrogation tactics in the military. Some humorous informative speeches focus on bizarre policies and laws, such as the New Jersey prohibition against frowning at police officers and the Nevada law against riding a camel on public highways.

As we've seen, a wide range of topics is available for an informative speech, so be creative! Consider issues, events, people, places, objects, concepts, processes, or policies you feel are well suited to yourself and your audience. As you do so, however, remember that your listeners' cultural background can influence what topics are appropriate. Although to U.S. audiences few topics are considered *taboo*—or inappropriate for public discussion—listeners from other cultures may be surprised or even offended by certain topics. Table 2 presents some examples of culturally taboo topics.

Once you have selected your topic, you will want to frame it for your listeners in a compelling way, as we'll see in the next two sections.

TABLE 2 CULTURAL DO'S AND DON'TS: MANAGING TABOO TOPICS	Teachers of English as a second language (ESL) are taught to avoid particular topics when speaking to certain groups around the world. If your audience consists largely of listeners from one of these societies, you, too, may find it prudent to avoid certain speech topics—or at least to exercise sensitivity when discussing them. What topics, if any, would you consider taboo in *your own* culture?

Country	Topics to Avoid
China	Tibet and the Dalai Lama; the Falun-Gong movement
France	Jobs, financial success, and wealth; immigration
India	Poverty; religious beliefs; India's relationship with Pakistan
Muslim countries	Sex and sexual practices
Japan	World War II
Korea	Politics; personal family matters; the relationship between North and South Korea
Mexico	Pollution; illegal immigration; sexuality
Taiwan	Politics; Taiwan's relationship with mainland China
Thailand	National security; criticisms of the monarchy

Children of deaf adults, or CODAs, often learn to communicate through sign language even before they can speak.

Huntstock/Getty Images

RELATE YOURSELF TO YOUR TOPIC

Recall the discussion of the advantages of choosing a speech topic you know and care about from the chapter on choosing, developing, and researching a topic. By choosing a topic you care about, you ensure you'll have both the knowledge and the enthusiasm to speak in a way that engages and informs. In some instances, your personal connection to the topic may be evident to your audience when you begin speaking. For example, if everyone in your public speaking class knows that you come from abroad, your listeners will understand why you have chosen to speak informatively about international students' experiences. On some occasions, however, your personal connection to your topic may not be immediately evident. In such cases, it is important to explain why your topic is meaningful to you. For example, one student expressed her personal connection to the topic of the children of deaf adults in this way:

> Unlike most of you, I didn't speak my first word. Rather, I communicated my first word—mother—in American Sign Language. You see, I'm what is commonly referred to as a "CODA," a child of deaf adults. As the only person in my immediate family who can hear, I learned to sign before I learned to speak. I'd like to tell you today about what it's like to grow up as a CODA, straddling the fence between the deaf and hearing worlds.

To make her connection to the topic of CODAs more evident to her audience, this student augmented parts of her speech with sign language. By explaining her background and demonstrating her fluency in signing, she made clear to her listeners why the topic of CODAs and their experiences was relevant to her.

Relating yourself to your topic is advantageous for two reasons. First, it establishes for your audience that you have the credibility to speak with authority about the topic. If you have training, personal experience, or a vested interest in what you're discussing, you are likely to be knowledgeable about it. Explaining your connection to the topic establishes you as a qualified speaker whose words can be trusted. The second advantage is that your listeners will care more about the topic if they believe it matters personally to you than if they do not. You may know from your own experience that it is difficult to get excited about a speech when not even the speaker seems to

SHARPEN Your Skills: *Generating informative speech topics*

Generate a list of eight topics—one representing each of Allen and McKerrow's categories—about which you could speak informatively.

care about the topic. In contrast, when you make clear to your listeners that you are enthusiastic about or deeply invested in the topic of the speech, they are more likely to care about what you have to say.

RELATE YOUR TOPIC TO YOUR AUDIENCE

Seeing that *you* know and care about your topic will matter to your listeners. What will matter to them even more, however, is seeing why *they* should know and care about it. To frame an informative speech effectively, you must therefore make clear how the topic is relevant to your audience.

Establish Listeners' Vested Interest in Your Topic Some topics will be easy to relate to your listeners' current experiences. Suppose you are speaking to a group of college-bound high school students about strategies for getting financial aid. That topic will matter to your listeners because many of them will require financial assistance to get a college education. They therefore have a **vested interest** in your topic—an inherent motivation to pay attention to it—and you need only point that out to relate it to them successfully.

Establish Your Topic's Relevance to Listeners In other instances, it's necessary to tell your listeners why they should care about your topic. Even if your audience doesn't have direct experience with the topic of your speech, you can often make it relevant by asking your listeners to imagine themselves in a hypothetical situation. Notice how the following introduction accomplishes that goal:

> *Imagine this: You're spending the holidays with family and you've just gotten up from a delicious dinner when you see your dad stumble and fall to the floor. At first, you think he just tripped, but his eyes are closed and he isn't moving. Your mom runs to call 911, but it could be several minutes before anyone arrives. Would you know what to do to keep your father alive until help gets there? You would if you'd been trained in cardiopulmonary resuscitation, or CPR. Today, I'm going to tell you what CPR is, how it works, and where you can learn to perform it. If you know how to administer CPR properly, you may be able to save the life of someone near and dear to you.*

In this introduction, the speaker makes clear why the topic of CPR is relevant to the listeners. The speaker relates the topic to listeners, even if they have no direct experience with it. Check out "The Competent Communicator" to practice framing topics for an informative speech.

Honing Your Informative-Speaking Skills

Even if you have chosen a compelling topic and successfully framed it for your audience, you must still deliver your speech in a way that will draw—and hold—your listeners' attention. In this section, we'll explore several strategies for delivering an informative speech effectively, including creating information hunger, being organized, making learning easy, involving your audience, and being ethical.

CREATE INFORMATION HUNGER

Perhaps you've had the experience of taking a high school or college course that you thought would be boring, only to be surprised by how interesting the instructor made the material. The instructor inspired your interest by creating **information hunger**, the desire to learn. As an informative speaker, you can do the same with your listeners by sparking their curiosity and giving them reason to want the information you have. In short, you can show your listeners "what's in it for them" if they pay attention to your speech.

• **vested interest**
An inherent motivation to pay attention.

• **information hunger**
The desire to learn.

It's All Relative: Framing Your Informative Topic

When selecting the topic of your informative speech, consider how you can relate yourself to your topic and how you can relate your topic to your audience. Doing so with a few different topics can help you to decide which topic is best for your presentation. In this exercise, select three potential informative-speaking topics, each of which represents a different category in Allen and McKerrow's list. List two ways you could relate yourself to each topic and two ways you could relate the topic to your audience.

Hill Street Studios/Blend Images/Getty Images

Topic	How the Topic Relates to Me	How the Topic Relates to My Listeners
1. _____	_____	_____
_____	_____	_____
2. _____	_____	_____
_____	_____	_____
3. _____	_____	_____
_____	_____	_____

Based on your responses, which of the three topics you chose do you think you could frame most effectively? Why?

Recall from the introductory chapter the five types of needs—physical, relational, identity, spiritual, and instrumental—that communication helps us meet. An excellent way to generate information hunger is to connect your topic to one or more of those needs. By doing so, you imply the benefits of listening to the information you have to share, creating a desire for that information among your listeners.

Imagine that you're preparing a speech about food. Let's look at some examples of how you might connect that topic to each of the five needs:

- *Physical needs.* Teach listeners to cook a meal that is healthy and flavorful.
- *Relational needs.* Discuss the importance of cooking rituals—such as preparing a holiday dinner—in maintaining family relationships.
- *Identity needs.* Explain how individuals with an eating disorder view their consumption of food as a central component of their identity.
- *Spiritual needs.* Explore various real and symbolic uses and meanings of food and drink in religious ceremonies, such as Christian communion.
- *Instrumental needs.* Teach your listeners how to find the best deals on food staples, such as fresh fruit, vegetables, and milk.

By connecting the information in your speech to one or more of your listeners' needs, you make that information relevant to *them* and thereby motivate the audience to pay attention to your words and message.

An informative speech about food presents many opportunities to connect to your listeners' needs, including their relational needs.

Ryan McVay/Getty Images

BE ORGANIZED

Studies confirm what you probably already know: We learn better from presentations that are well organized.[5] That may be so because most of us process information best in a limited number of segments at a time; thus, a speech that presents "chunks" of information in a coherent order is easiest for listeners to follow.[6] Just *appearing* organized, in fact, is enough to boost your listeners' retention of what you say—that's how powerful organization is.[7]

Creating a well-organized informative speech is easy. Recall the different components of a speech—introduction, body, conclusion, and transitions—and the role each component plays in making your presentation coherent. As you prepare your informative speech, work on each component individually to ensure that it is serving its necessary functions. If each component does its job, your speech will have a logical, organized structure, and you will be poised for success.

Use the checklist in Table 3 to make certain that your informative speech includes all the elements necessary for an organized presentation.

MAKE IT EASY TO LISTEN

We've all encountered speakers who seem oblivious to their listeners' needs and desires—for example, presenters who talk too long or use unfamiliar technical jargon. It is difficult to pay attention to such speakers or to care about what they're saying. To avoid that reaction from your own audience, make it easy for them to listen to you by keeping your message short, using clear language, starting with familiar concepts, repeating your key points, and sprinkling in humor when it's appropriate.

Keep It Short In most instances, you will have a specific time slot for your informative speech. Your time frame will limit the amount of material you can effectively discuss in your presentation, so make sure you include only as much information as you can reasonably cover.

Keep It Simple It might seem obvious that your listeners must understand what you're saying before they can learn from it, but many speakers forget that crucial consideration. A common mistake for informative speakers is to use technical language or jargon that most people in their audience will not understand. A better

As you prepare an informative speech, remember your priorities for each component of your presentation.

TABLE 3

PULL IT TOGETHER: ORGANIZE YOUR INFORMATIVE SPEECH

Section	Priorities
Introduction	**1.** Generate interest in your topic.
	2. Present your thesis statement.
	3. Relate your topic to yourself and to your listeners.
	4. Preview your main points.
Body	**1.** Present each of your main points, with appropriate transitions between them.
	2. Make sure you have at least three main points and that they are sufficiently related to each other.
Transitions	**1.** Use transitions to review the material you've presented already.
	2. Use transitions to preview material yet to be presented.
Conclusion	**1.** Reinforce your central idea by reviewing your main points.
	2. Create a memorable moment for your audience.

approach—particularly if you're unsure whether certain words will be familiar to your listeners—is to use plain, simple language that everyone will understand.

Start with What's Familiar Many of us feel uneasy when we're asked to learn a new skill or understand new information. To reduce that anxiety among your listeners, begin your informative speech by describing something that is familiar to them. Then discuss how that familiar concept is related to the new information or skill you intend to describe. For instance, being "psychologically flooded" means experiencing thoughts and feelings so intense that you become unable to continue interacting with others. To describe that phenomenon, you might begin by reminding your listeners what happens to a car engine when it gets flooded. As most drivers know, a flooded engine won't start. You can then make comparisons between that familiar concept and the new knowledge you wish to impart.

Effective speakers make it easy for the audience to listen to their presentations.

wonderlandstock/Alamy Stock Photo

Repeat Key Points Research shows that repetition of critical points will help your listeners to remember more of what you say.[8] Take advantage of that fact by repeating your most important points during your speech. To use repetition effectively, however, repeat only the important points, not trivial ones, and do not repeat them so many times that your audience tunes out.[9]

Make It Fun Like repetition, humor can also enhance your presentation and increase your listeners' retention if you use it appropriately. Humor in informative presentations promotes relaxation that allows listeners to understand and assimilate the information.[10] Remember to consider who your listeners are and what they are likely to find funny. Humor that is distasteful, obscene, or disrespectful of others is never appropriate in an informative speech *unless* the humor itself is the topic.

INVOLVE THE AUDIENCE

Many of us learn better when we're somehow engaged in the lesson than when we're passively receiving it. Skillful informative speakers use several techniques to involve listeners in their presentations.

Invite Direct Participation In this method, you ask your listeners to perform some action that helps them understand your topic. In an informative speech about relaxation techniques, you might instruct your listeners to close their eyes, let their facial muscles go slack, and breathe slowly and deeply, to help them grasp how the techniques work.

Ask for Volunteers If your lesson is too complex for everyone in the audience to participate in it, ask for one or more volunteers with whom you can demonstrate it for the rest of the listeners. In a speech about self-defense, you could ask for a volunteer on whom to demonstrate ways of fending off an attacker.

Poll the Audience A good way to gauge your listeners' opinions or experiences is to take an informal poll related to your topic. You might ask "How many of you have ever known anyone who has suffered from asthma?" If you're speaking in a room with a classroom response system—commonly known as *clicker technology*—your audience can respond to your questions anonymously.

Pose a Hypothetical Situation A technique similar to polling your audience is to ask your listeners to consider a hypothetical situation. For example: "Imagine you're driving late at night along a back road, hit a patch of ice, and end up in a ditch with no way to get out. You're alone, the temperature is below freezing, and there's no cell phone coverage where you are. What would you do?" Asking listeners to picture themselves in such a situation can spark their interest in your speech. The difference between that technique and polling your audience is that you are not asking your listeners to respond.

Refer to Individual Listeners Particularly if your audience is small, an excellent way to connect to your listeners is to refer to them individually during your speech when appropriate. For instance, "Last week we heard Tariq describe his life-changing experience of visiting Mecca. Today, I'd like to tell you about the two major denominations of Islam: the Sunni and the Shi'a." Even though you're referring only to one specific listener, the technique connects all your listeners to you and to your presentation.

Inviting and responding to questions can be an excellent way to draw listeners into your presentation.

Kristin Murphy/WireImage/Getty Images

Invite Questions At the end of some informative speeches, presenters involve listeners by inviting and responding to their questions. If you have the time and wish to use that technique, it's often helpful to tell your audience early in your speech that you'll be taking questions at the end. That way, you encourage listeners to think of questions as you speak. During a question-and-answer period, be mindful of the time allotted so you don't run over.

The ability to involve and adapt to the audience is useful in a variety of careers that require public speaking. For one example, check out the "Putting Communication to Work" box.

BE ETHICAL

Finally, treat your listeners ethically. In the context of an informative speech, one of the most important requirements of ethical behavior is truthfulness. Because your purpose is to impart information to your audience, you have a responsibility as an ethical speaker to ensure that your information is true and accurate. Specifically, you should:

putting**communication**to**work**

Search

Job Title >

Work Responsibilities >

Community Outreach Educator, Health Care and Insurance Industries

Hospitals, health care insurers, and other providers invest in community outreach programs to improve health outcomes and lower health care costs. Community outreach educators deliver presentations on preventive health and wellness (such as breastfeeding, nutrition, safe sex, and accident prevention) and on managing chronic health conditions (such as diabetes, hypertension, and arthritis). Community outreach educators must have solid public speaking skills, as well as an ability to adapt their communication style and content to suit audience needs.

- *Use information only from reputable sources.* Scientific journals and major newspapers are more reputable sources than tabloids and Wikipedia pages, for instance, because information in journals and large mainstream newspapers is checked for accuracy before being published.

- *Understand the information you're reporting.* If you're unsure how to interpret the meaning of a report or a statistic, ask an instructor for help. If you don't, you risk drawing conclusions from your information that are unwarranted.

- *Incorporate verbal footnotes.* When you use information in your speech from another source, identify that source while you're speaking. For example, you might say: "According to the U.S. Bureau of Labor Statistics, occupational therapy is one of the fastest-growing professions."

- *Be clear about when you're speculating.* Many sources of information allow us to infer ideas or speculate about possibilities, and it is fine to include those inferences or speculations in an informative speech as long as you make it clear that they aren't facts. Ethical speakers also avoid using offensive language, exposing their audience to sensitive sights and sounds, and engaging in behaviors that would make their listeners uncomfortable—*unless* they have specifically warned their listeners in advance.

One situation when it is especially important to treat your listeners ethically is when you are called on to deliver bad news. This can be a very uncomfortable task, but you can perform it ethically and effectively by following the tips in the "Difficult Conversations" box.

SHARPEN Your Skills: *Audience involvement*

Take a specific informative speech topic and generate a list of five or six concrete ways you could involve your audience in a presentation about that topic.

Difficult Conversations

johnkwan/123RF

Delivering Bad News

Imagine this: You are the manager of a restaurant whose owners have informed you will be closing in three months. This means that you and everyone on your staff will soon be out of a job.

Now, consider this: The owners have asked you to tell your employees about the upcoming closure of your restaurant, so you have called a staff meeting to break the bad news. How can you share this disappointing news effectively and compassionately? Here are some strategies to consider:

- Preface your remarks by indicating that the news you have to share is negative. Instead of simply announcing that the restaurant is closing, let your listeners know that bad news is coming. For instance, you could say "I'm afraid I have some very disappointing news to share." This will help to prepare listeners to hear what you have to say.

- After you've let people know that bad news is on the way, explain the situation. Once listeners know you have negative news to share, they may feel increasingly anxious until you actually share it.

- As you describe the bad news, be clear about what you do and don't know. When they learn that your restaurant will be closing, your employees are likely to have many questions. As you respond to them, be willing to share what you know. If people ask questions that you don't have the answer to, however, say that you don't know the answer but will try to find out.

- Let your listeners know that you share their disappointment. The closure of your restaurant will cost your job as well as the jobs of your employees. Telling your employees that you are as frustrated as they are can convey the message that you empathize with their situation.

Breaking bad news is never easy or fun. By being sensitive to your listeners, you can prepare them to receive the news and minimize its negative effects.

One highly unethical use of informative speaking is to coerce your audience into believing or doing something. If your purpose is to persuade individuals to adopt a particular belief, opinion, or behavior—a topic we'll examine in the chapter on speaking persuasively—you owe it to your listeners to be upfront about that objective. Speakers who hide their persuasive intentions in seemingly objective informative speeches often cross an ethical boundary by engaging in propaganda. Read more about propaganda—and learn how to identify it—in "The Dark Side of Communication."

A Sample Informative Speech

When we're learning or polishing a skill such as informative speaking, it's often helpful to study excellent examples provided by others. Below is the text of an informative speech by Eric Dern, an economics major at Arizona State University and a member

THE DARK SIDE OF COMMUNICATION

Listener Beware: When "Information" Becomes Propaganda

It's easy to think of informative speeches as offering only objective details and facts. Some speakers, however, use "informative" speeches to disguise their attempts to persuade or coerce their listeners. When they do, they are no longer simply informing but engaging in propaganda.

Informative speeches whose true purpose is coercive often contain one or more of the following elements. How many political speeches have you recently heard that included these elements?

- *Moral labeling.* Using terms with negative connotations to refer to your opponent. Politicians denounce "special-interest groups," for instance, to put down those whose priorities contradict their own. They may use words such as *radical* and *extremist* to describe people with whom they disagree. In recent years, it has become fashionable to call one's opponents "Nazis," drawing comparisons to the fascist German group responsible for killing millions of Jews, Gypsies, homosexuals, and others in the twentieth century. The problem with such labeling is that calling someone a "radical," an "extremist," or a "Nazi" doesn't mean the person actually has any of the characteristics of such groups. Therefore, the labels are meaningless, although highly provocative.

- *Glowing generalizations.* Using positive terms to refer to yourself or your allies. While applying negative terms to their opponents, lawmakers might refer to people and policies in their own parties as "patriotic," "loyal," "democratic," and "fair to working families." Likewise, food and drug companies might describe their products as "100 percent natural" to highlight their quality, even though many 100 percent natural substances are poisonous! Just as denouncing an opponent with negative terms doesn't mean those terms are accurate, referring to yourself or your products with positive terms doesn't necessarily make them any more positive in reality.

- *False dichotomy.* Conveying the idea that "if you aren't *for* us, you're *against* us" to cast anyone with a different opinion as an opponent. Such a ploy categorizes everyone into one of two groups: us or them. It separates people and discourages attempts at reaching compromise or finding common ground.

- *Ordinary folk.* Describing yourself as "of the people" while depicting your opponent as "out of touch with the average citizen." A particularly common tactic among U.S. politicians is to campaign on the premise that the federal government is "broken" and "out of touch with" the realities of U.S. life and that the candidate is a "Washington outsider" who will "fix" the system once he or she is elected. That approach garners support because it casts the speaker as "one of us."

Keep in mind that propaganda does not mean everything you disagree with when you're listening to a speech. Rather, propaganda is a speaker's deliberate attempts to make coercive messages sound like objective information. Knowing the common techniques of propaganda can help you to resist its influence when you encounter it.

SOURCES: Caplan, A. L. (2005). Misusing the Nazi analogy. *Science, 309*(5734), 535. https://doi.org/10.1126/science.1115437; for further information see Jowett, G. S., & O'Donnell, V. (2006). *Propaganda and persuasion.* Sage.

of the school's speech and debate team. The speech describes the Golden Shield surveillance project in China. In April 2009, Eric tied for first place in informative speaking with this speech at the national tournament of the American Forensics Association, a teachers' association dedicated to cultivating excellence in public speaking and debate. Alongside the text are comments about what makes each section of his speech—the introduction, body, and conclusion—so effective. Figure 1, which precedes the speech, provides the formal outline for Eric's speech and helps you to appreciate its organizational structure.

FIGURE 1 FORMAL SPEECH OUTLINE: CHINA'S GOLDEN SHIELD SURVEILLANCE PROJECT

TITLE: China's Golden Shield Surveillance Project

General purpose: To inform

Purpose statement: Inform audience about the Golden Shield surveillance project in China.

INTRODUCTION

I. The Chinese fishing community of Shenzhen has been transformed into a metropolis and a unique lab for Golden Shield, history's largest surveillance project.

II. Golden Shield's more than 2 million cameras watch the population's every move.

   Thesis: The Golden Shield surveillance project has far-reaching implications regarding U.S. foreign policy, privacy rights, and the role of government in individual lives.

   Transition: To understand Golden Shield's impact, we first examine its technology, then its applications, and finally its implications.

BODY

I. Golden Shield stands out due to its technological sophistication.
   A. *Brunei Times:* Golden Shield has advanced camera technology.
      1. Subjects' facial features and walking mannerisms can be tracked.
      2. *Blink:* Detection of involuntary facial microexpressions allows authorities to read motives and predict behavior.
   B. Golden Shield can listen in on every cell phone signal in the city.
      1. *China's Golden Shield:* Voice recordings are saved in a huge database.
      2. Surveillance is constant and exceeds the level of most countries.

   Transition: Now that we know how Golden Shield works, we can see its applications in the world.

II. Golden Shield has applications related to crime prevention and security in China and the United States.
   A. *Shenzen Daily:* Golden Shield is extremely effective in preventing crime.
      1. Shenzhen's crime rate has fallen by nearly 14 percent.
      2. The city is much safer and more secure.
   B. Several U.S. companies are investors in Golden Shield.
      1. *International Herald Tribune:* American hedge funds paid for 91 percent of Golden Shield's face- and behavior-recognition software in the last year.
      2. Golden Shield has an excellent relationship with major U.S. firms.

C. *New York Times:* Thousands of the same high-tech cameras used by Golden Shield have been installed in New York and Chicago.

   Transition: There are three far-reaching implications for Golden Shield.

III. Golden Shield has three far-reaching implications.
   A. By affecting the foundation on which the United States advances democracy, Golden Shield may alter U.S. foreign policy.
      1. *American Prospect:* American investment is helping China suppress internal political activism.
      2. U.S. policymakers must rethink the long-held notion that capitalism and democracy go hand in hand.
   B. MSNBC: Golden Shield may redefine privacy as Americans understand it.
      1. *United States v. Dionisio:* The Fourth Amendment does not protect Americans against Golden Shield's ability to read emotions and motives.
      2. Golden Shield has prompted a redefinition of "probable cause."
   C. *Discipline and Punish:* Promotion of citizen self-policing could free governments to suppress political opponents.
      1. A precedent for self-enforcement among Chinese citizens implies that Golden Shield could be turned off and citizens would police themselves.
      2. The state would thus be freed to carry out repressive agendas.

   Transition: After examining Golden Shield's technology, applications, and implications, we better understand the system's worldwide effects.

CONCLUSION

I. Review of main points
   A. Golden Shield is unique in its size and technological sophistication.
   B. Golden Shield has applications related to crime prevention and security.
   C. Golden Shield has implications for U.S. foreign policy, the meaning of privacy rights, and the intrusion of government into individual affairs.

II. Final remarks
   A. Golden Shield has profound implications for how U.S. democratic society functions.
   B. It seems inevitable that a population control system such as Golden Shield will become a larger reality in the United States.

COMMENTARY	SPEECH
This introduction opens with a short story introducing listeners to the topic of the speech, the Golden Shield.	Southeastern China's Shenzhen was once a simple fishing community, only truly notable for its proximity to the border of Hong Kong. In 1979, the Chinese Communist Party stepped in and chose Shenzhen as the first of four Special Economic Zones, areas where capitalism would be allowed on a trial basis. Today, this Gotham-like metropolis, widely known as China's organized crime capital, is home to 12.4 million people—twice the size of Los Angeles—and is a city of pure commerce.
Notice here how the speaker relates his topic to his audience.	But this rags-to-riches story has its own interesting twist. *Rolling Stone*, on May 29, 2008, reports that it's only fitting that this concoction of crime and capitalism should once again serve as a laboratory, this time for the largest surveillance project in history. Golden Shield, a system of over 2 million cameras, not only watches every move of the city's population but also detects emotion and predicts thoughts. And surprisingly, the communist country's best imitation of George Orwell is far more American than some would like to admit. *Rolling Stone* reports $30 billion of the $33-billion Golden Shield system consists of American investments, so just like everything else made in China with American parts, "Police State 2.0" is ready for export to a neighborhood near you.
Here, the speaker previews the topics to be covered in the body of the speech.	Golden Shield not only is significant for its giant leaps in human tracking technology, but also has implications for how our democratic society functions as a whole. To understand the impact Golden Shield will have on the world, we will first examine the technology of Shenzhen's Golden Shield, next understand its applications, and finally draw some implications from China's massive social experiment.
In the body of the speech, the speaker uses transitions to indicate when he is beginning a new topic.	What separates Golden Shield from London's famous security set-up or the surveillance of the Patriot Act is the system's sheer size and sophistication. To get a full picture of Golden Shield, let's first examine the technology that makes up the system, which is intended to be able to "see" and "hear."
The speaker is careful throughout the speech to cite his sources properly.	First, if I were to stand at the corner at Shenzhen's Civic Centre, the area of the city where most security and government buildings are located, I would be watched by 38 different cameras. The *Brunei Times* of August 30, 2008, details the cameras' technology that allows subjects' eyes, facial features, and walking mannerisms to be checked against a database containing names, photos, and even reproductive information. Additionally, Malcolm Gladwell's 2002 book *Blink* chronicles the exploration of involuntary facial "microexpressions," explaining "When we experience a basic emotion, a corresponding message is sent to the muscles in our face." Golden Shield's software is so advanced that it is capable of reading these involuntary microexpressions within a millisecond, giving authorities the ability to instantly read motives and predict behavior. "The smallest thing could give you away. A nervous tic, a look of anxiety, a habit of muttering to yourself—anything that carries with it the suggestion of having something to hide is itself a punishable offense." This may sound familiar. George Orwell wrote this prediction of a dystopian future in his novel *1984*. Orwell's fantasy may certainly become a reality.
By saying "second," the speaker signals that he is shifting to a new dimension of his topic.	Second, Golden Shield has been equipped to "hear" the sounds of the city. According to the 2006 essay *China's Golden Shield*, the system is capable of listening in on every cell phone signal in the city and saving these voice recordings in a huge database. So, if I were standing on that same corner in the Civic Centre, my cell phone would be constantly tracked and recorded, and my voice could be immediately recognized if I uttered a single word on the street. By utilizing the system's ability to both see and hear, China has reached a state of constant surveillance that few countries can rival.
	Now that we know how Golden Shield works, we can see its applications in the world. Golden Shield has applications on crime and security not only in China but also right here in the United States. But first, let's admit it, 2 million cameras spying on every move you make sounds pretty wrong. And creepy. But in a post-9/11 era, when terrorism and mass attacks are very real possibilities, China doesn't necessarily seem so out of line in installing Golden Shield. In fact, Golden Shield is devastatingly effective at preventing crime in Shenzhen. According to the January 24, 2007, *Shenzhen Daily*, in the very first week of Golden Shield's installation, robberies in the city dropped by 15 percent. Since then, the city's crime rate, once 9 times higher than Shanghai and 3 times higher than New York City, has fallen by nearly 14 percent. Golden Shield has time and time again proved its ability to make Shenzhen a much safer and more secure city.

COMMENTARY	SPEECH
Here, the speaker uses a quote from an expert as supporting material for the point he is making.	But Golden Shield is not simply a Chinese security system. It is a cooperative effort between Chinese communism and American investment. The *International Herald Tribune* of September 10, 2008, reveals that 91 percent of Golden Shield's face- and behavior-recognition software was paid for by American hedge fund money in the last year. Robin Huang, chief operating officer of China Public Security, stated that Golden Shield has "a very good relationship with U.S. companies like Google, Honeywell, IBM, Cisco, HP, and Dell." *Rolling Stone* speculates that "these global corporations currently earning profits from Golden Shield are unlikely to be content if the lucrative new market remains confined to Shenzhen." And, accordingly, this technology is already being applied by these companies in the United States. The *Huffington Post* of August 7, 2008, reports that the same Golden Shield backers are also the companies invested in a Defense Department project auspiciously named "Operation Noble Shield." This virtual database can create constantly updated dossiers and surveillance footage for every U.S. citizen. The July 9, 2008, *New York Times* reports that the first 3,000 of these high-tech cameras were installed in New York, while another 2,200 were installed in Chicago in the past year.

There is a good chance that half of everything you own was made in Shenzhen: iPods, sneakers, maybe your car, and almost certainly your cell phone. And now population surveillance devices. There are three far-reaching implications for Golden Shield, related to American involvement in foreign policy, the meaning of privacy rights, and the intrusion of government into individual affairs.

First, Western powers claim that by doing business in China, they are spreading democracy. But in an August 7, 2008, blog posting, journalist Naomi Klein points out, "We are now seeing the reverse: investment is helping China … actively repress a new generation of activists." This means America must disenthrall itself from one of its most cherished cornerstones in foreign policy: the idea that capitalism and democracy go hand in hand. As Klein states, "Remember how we've always been told that free markets and free people go hand in hand? That was a lie. It turns out that the most efficient delivery system for capitalism is actually a communist-style police state, fortressed with American 'homeland security' technologies, pumped up with 'war on terror' rhetoric." By changing the foundation on which the United States spreads democracy, the existence of Golden Shield may very well alter the course of American foreign policy.

Next, privacy rights. Mike Sullivan, a police technology consultant, states in a November 24, 2008, MSNBC interview that "the difference between the Noble Shield and Golden Shield is the Supreme Court. We have the ability as U.S. citizens to cry foul. In China, citizens do not." However, in the 1973 decision *United States v. Dionisio,* the Supreme Court found a person's physical characteristics, like the eyes or face, are not protected by constitutional privacy rights. This means that while the Fourth Amendment protects us from searches and seizures without probable cause, it does not protect us against Golden Shield's ability to read one's emotions and motives. Golden Shield is redefining the term "probable cause" and may even redefine what we all consider to be privacy.

Finally, in his book *Discipline and Punish,* philosopher Michel Foucault examines Jeremy Bentham's panopticon, a prison layout where prisoners are allowed to roam freely under the permanent visibility of guards in a central tower. Foucault further explains that these guards do not even have to be in the tower for the panopticon to work; the very potential of visibility traps prisoners into disciplining themselves. Golden Shield works in the same way, using cameras instead of towers to ensure the automatic functioning of power. |
| In his conclusion, the speaker reiterates the main points he has made in the speech. He ends with a quote that will make his conclusion memorable. | When Beijing was awarded the Olympic games, the theory was that international scrutiny would force China's government to grant more rights to its people. Instead, the Olympics opened up a back door for the regime to massively upgrade its systems of population control. After examining how Golden Shield works, its applications, and finally its implications, we better understand how the system affects China and the world. No longer is Golden Shield confined to distant and unfamiliar worlds where most of us have probably never been. With the Olympics potentially coming to Chicago in 2016, it seems like only a matter of time before Operation Noble Shield brings this reality closer to home. Maybe George Orwell was right when he wrote, "Big Brother is watching." |

- **What methods can we use to inform?**

In an informative speech, we can define, describe, explain, and demonstrate.

- **In what ways should we frame an informative speech?**

We should begin by relating ourselves to the topic of the speech. We should then relate the speech topic to our listeners.

- **Through what strategies can we hone our informative-speaking skills?**

We can create information hunger, present a speech that is well organized, make it easy for our audience to listen, involve our listeners in our presentation, and communicate in an ethical manner.

KEY TERMS

informative speaking 398	describing 399	subjective 401
defining 398	representation 399	demonstrating 401
etymology 399	narration 400	vested interest 406
synonyms 399	explaining 400	information hunger 406
antonyms 399	objective 401	

NOTES

1. Centers for Disease Control and Prevention. (2019). Misconceptions about seasonal flu and flu vaccines. https://www.cdc.gov/flu/prevent/misconceptions.htm
2. CNBC. (2018, September 26). 80,000 people died of the flu last winter in US. https://www.cnbc.com/2018/09/26/80000-people-died-of-the-flu-last-winter-in-us.html
3. www.teachforamerica.org
4. Allen, R. R., & McKerrow, R. E. (1985). *The pragmatics of public communication* (3rd ed.). Kendall/Hunt.
5. See Mikeska, J. N., Holtzman, S., McCaffrey, D. F., Liu, S., & Shattuck, T. (2019). Using classroom observations to evaluate science teaching: Implications of lesson sampling for measuring science teaching effectiveness across lesson types. *Science Education, 103*(1), 123–144. https://doi.org/10.1002/sce.21482
6. See, e.g., Branco, F., Sun, M., & Villas-Boas, J. M. (2015). Too much information? Information provision and search costs. *Marketing Science, 35*(4), 605–618. https://doi.org/10.1287/mksc.2015.0959
7. Pascarella, E., Edison, M., Nora, A., Hagedorn, L. S., & Braxton, J. (1996). Effects of teacher organization/preparation and teacher skill/clarity on general cognitive skills in college. *Journal of College Student Development, 37,* 7–19.
8. McCoy, S., Everard, A., Galletta, D. F., & Moody, G. D. (2017). Here we go again! The impact of website ad repetition on recall, intrusiveness, attitudes, and site revisit intentions. *Information & Management, 54*(1), 14–24. https://10.1016/j.im.2016.03.005
9. So, J., Kim, S., & Cohen, H. (2017). Message fatigue: Conceptual definition, operationalization, and correlates. *Communication Monographs, 84*(1), 5–29. https://doi.org/10.1080/03537751.2016.1250429
10. Garner, R. L. (2006). Humor in pedagogy: How ha-ha can lead to aha! *College Teaching, 54*(1), 177–180. https://doi.org/10.3200/CTCH.54.1.177-180

15

Franco Origlia/Getty Images

SPEAKING PERSUASIVELY

A Papal Persuasion

As leader of the Catholic Church, Pope Francis has earned a reputation for speaking his mind on issues that matter to him. In September 2015, the 78-year-old pontiff did so in an historic address to a joint meeting of the U.S. Congress. His remarks, marking his first official visit to the United States, called on lawmakers to embrace millions of immigrants displaced by conflicts around the globe. "I say this to you as the son of immigrants, knowing that so many of you are also descended from immigrants," the Pope said. Urging the United States to help immigrants fleeing war-torn areas such as Syria, Francis remarked, "We must not be taken aback by their numbers, but rather view them as persons, seeing their faces and listening to their stories, trying to respond as best we can to their situation." In what was clearly intended to be a persuasive speech, these pleas joined calls for the United States to take a more active role in curbing climate change and the global arms race. Through these statements, the Pope endeavored to persuade U.S. lawmakers to act in what he considered a more effective and appropriate manner regarding the pressing issues of the day.

As You READ

- What does it mean to persuade?
- In what ways can we craft a persuasive message?
- Through what strategies can we hone our persuasive-speaking skills?

Director Alfonso Cuarón used the occasion of winning the Academy Award for best director in 2019 to make a persuasive statement about the plight of domestic workers.

Kevin Winter/Getty images

• **persuasive speaking** Public speech that aims to influence listeners' beliefs, attitudes, and actions.

• **persuasion** An attempt to motivate others, through communication, to adopt or to maintain a specific manner of thinking or doing.

We have many occasions to persuade others for our own personal gain. Perhaps we're trying to convince someone to buy the car we wish to sell or to support a political cause we care about. In some situations, however, our attempts at persuasion are for the benefit of others. When he addressed U.S. lawmakers, Pope Francis urged them to act not for his own benefit but on behalf of millions of displaced immigrants from around the world. Our ability to persuade can therefore have significant effects on other people's lives. In this chapter, you'll discover what it means to persuade others and how you can craft a successful persuasive message. You'll also learn several techniques for presenting effectively, and you'll see an example of an award-winning persuasive speech.

The Meaning and Art of Persuasion

Performers who win major awards frequently use their acceptance speeches as an opportunity to persuade their audiences to adopt their views on politically controversial issues. Upon winning the 2019 Academy Award for best director for the film *Roma*, Alfonso Cuarón used his acceptance speech to highlight the harsh and sometimes dangerous working conditions faced by domestic workers around the world. In his speech, Cuarón remarked: "Thank you to the Academy for recognizing a film centered around an Indigenous woman. One of the 70 million domestic workers in the world without worker rights, a character that historically has been relegated to the background. As artists, our job is to look where others don't."[1] By expressing these sentiments, Cuarón wasn't merely conveying his own viewpoint—he was trying to persuade others to share that viewpoint and to act accordingly. In this instance, Cuarón was using **persuasive speaking**—public speech that aims to influence listeners' beliefs, attitudes, and actions.

We can think of **persuasion** as an attempt to motivate others, through communication, to adopt or to maintain a specific manner of thinking or doing. Some persuasion—including national advertising campaigns and Alfonso Cuarón's speech in front of a television audience of millions—occurs on a broad scale and seeks to motivate large numbers of people at once. Other persuasion—including the types most of us undertake in our daily interactions—occurs one-on-one or with small groups, such as a family or a work staff. In this section, we'll see that persuasion can influence beliefs, opinions, and actions. We'll also discover that good persuasive speakers support their arguments with appeals to integrity, emotion, and reason.

WHAT IT MEANS TO PERSUADE

When we try to motivate people to adopt a specific manner of thinking or doing, we usually have one of three concrete goals in mind:

- To persuade them to believe that a claim we're making is true.
- To convince them to share our opinion on a particular issue.
- To get them to do something.

We may also be working toward more than one of those goals at a time. Let's take a close look at how we can use persuasion to influence others' beliefs, opinions, and actions.

• **belief** Perception about what is true or false, accurate or inaccurate.

Some Persuasion Affects Beliefs Our **beliefs** are perceptions about what is true or false, accurate or inaccurate. When others attempt to persuade us to believe something, they are trying to convince us that their words are a valid reflection of reality.

Suppose that several weeks after having a traffic accident, you and the other driver appear before a judge. Each of you tells the judge, in your own words, what led to your collision. You indicate that the other driver made an illegal turn, hitting your car. The other driver claims the collision occurred because you failed to stop completely at a stop sign. Each of you is trying to convince the judge that your description of the events is true in an objective sense—that is, an accurate depiction of what *really* happened. To help your case, you might offer evidence that supports your description, such as photos from the collision scene or statements from witnesses.

Some Persuasion Affects Opinions Whereas our beliefs are our perceptions of what's true and false, our **opinions** are our evaluations about what's good and bad. Opinions reflect what we think *should be*, not necessarily what is. When people use persuasion to influence our opinions, they want us to evaluate something in the same way they do.

• **opinion** Evaluation about what is good and bad.

Perhaps you've attended rallies at your school where the speakers are voicing an opinion on a specific issue, such as unemployment or government-funded health care. Although they may present facts in support of their position, their goal is not simply for you to accept the facts as true. Rather, it's to cause you to agree with their position on the issue— that is, to arrive at the same evaluation of the facts that they hold. To help their case, the speakers might appeal to your morals or your sense of fairness.

Some Persuasion Affects Actions Our beliefs and opinions are what we think, but our actions are what we do. **Actions** are the behaviors we undertake, and many persuasive messages attempt to influence them.

• **action** A behavior someone undertakes.

Suppose you see a television commercial advertising an extra-strong kitchen garbage bag. The commercial first shows people who are frustrated when their garbage bags break, spilling garbage everywhere. The same people then appear happy and unencumbered while using the advertised bags. The commercial claims that similar bags are more expensive or poorly manufactured, implying that the featured product is a good value. By suggesting that the bag is both strong and reasonably priced, the commercial's producers are attempting to motivate you to take a specific action—to buy the product.[2]

People attending rallies in support of controversial issues often try to persuade others to accept their position.
Alex Wong/Getty Images

TABLE 1

CYBERPERSUASION: WHAT MAKES US CLICK THROUGH?

Internet advertisements—such as the boxes and banners that pop up on websites—persuade people to spend billions of dollars annually on the products or services they tout. The ads are usually effective, however, only if people click on them to get the details of the advertised product or service. What persuades us to click through? According to research, three features of an Internet advertisement draw us:

- *Size matters.* We are more likely to click on large ads than small ones.
- *Specificity matters.* Online ads that describe their products or services specifically, rather than vaguely, are more effective.
- *Amount of text matters.* We favor online ads with lots of text over ads with little text.

SOURCES: Brettel, M., & Spilker-Attig, A. (2010). Online advertising effectiveness: A cross-cultural comparison. *Journal of Research in Interactive Marketing, 4*(3), 176–196. https://doi.org/10.1108/17505931011070569; Robinson, H., Wysocka, A., & Hand, C. (2007). The effect of design on click-through rates for banner ads. *International Journal of Advertising, 26*(4), 527–541. https://doi.org/10.1080/02650487.2007.11073031

Many companies use the Internet as a major channel for advertising their products or services. What characteristics make Internet advertisements persuasive? Check out Table 1 to find out.

THREE FORMS OF RHETORICAL PROOF

• forms of rhetorical proof Ways to support a persuasive argument, including ethos, pathos, and logos.

In one of his major writings, *Treatise on Rhetoric,* the Greek philosopher Aristotle (384–322 B.C.) described three **forms of rhetorical proof**, which are ways to support a persuasive argument. These proofs are appeals to ethos, pathos, and logos.

Ethos Imagine listening to a speaker you do not know as he makes a persuasive appeal for money to help the victims of the massive earthquake that claimed more than 4,300 lives in Indonesia in September 2018. He says that if you donate your funds to him, he will use them directly for the benefit of the Indonesian people instead of deducting a large proportion of the money to fund his operating costs. Moreover, he claims to know where the needs in Indonesia are most dire, and he assures you that he will fund those needs first. Do you donate?

• ethos A speaker's respectability, trustworthiness, and moral character.

Many people, although inclined to help the victims of natural disasters, would want to know more about the speaker before they decided whether to give him their money. The reason is that a speaker who's respectable and trustworthy is generally more persuasive than one who isn't.[3] Aristotle recognized that, to be persuaded, people needed to have positive regard for the person whose message they were considering. He used the term **ethos** to refer to a speaker's respectability, trustworthiness, and moral character.[4]

Speakers can establish ethos with listeners by displaying these specific qualities:

- *Knowledge, experience, and wisdom with respect to the topic.* Does the speaker have adequate expertise with the issue to be persuasive? The individual appealing for your donations to Indonesia could establish knowledge, experience, and wisdom by describing his extensive experience working in Indonesia and his many professional connections in Jakarta, its capital.

- *Integrity and virtue.* Is the speaker honest and trustworthy, or do you have reason to doubt his or her integrity? The fundraiser for Indonesia could establish integrity and virtue by mentioning his moral standards and his intolerance for individuals who cheat or steal.[5]

- *Goodwill toward the audience.* Does the speaker care about the welfare of listeners, or is he or she only trying to use them? The speaker asking for donations could establish goodwill by acknowledging his audience's concerns about giving money and addressing them to his listeners' satisfaction.

Library of Congress, Prints & Photographs Division, photograph by Carol M. Highsmith [reproduction number, LC-HS503-2800]

Note that judgments about ethos belong to the audience. Listeners decide for themselves how much experience, integrity, and goodwill a speaker has. Good persuasive speakers therefore establish and reinforce their ethos with every audience, knowing it will enhance their persuasive abilities.

Hooked on a Feeling: Emotion Persuades

From advertisers to political candidates to addiction counselors, many people appeal to emotion based on Aristotle's idea that feeling can affect beliefs, opinions, and behaviors. Is it fact or fiction that emotion has this effect?

A wide variety of experiments indicates that it's a fact. When researchers examine the findings of multiple studies, they conclude that appeals to positive emotion are often most effective at persuading people to change their attitudes or opinions, whereas appeals to negative emotion (particularly fear) are frequently most effective at inducing behavioral change. Some social scientists believe we are most likely to change our mind about something when we feel good, because then we don't scrutinize the arguments very closely, but are most likely to change our behavior when we feel bad, because we want to end the bad feelings. You can use the findings from this research to compose your own persuasive messages, depending on whether you are trying to change someone's beliefs, opinions, or actions.

ASK YOURSELF

- Besides happiness or joy, to what other positive emotions could you appeal?
- Which emotions most strongly affect your own behaviors?

SOURCES: Tannenbaum, M. B., Hepler, J., Zimmerman, R. S., Saul, L., Jacobs, S., Wilson, K., & Albarracín, D. (2015). Appealing to fear: A meta-analysis of fear appeal effectiveness and theories. *Psychological Bulletin, 141*(6), 1178–1204. https://doi.org/10.1037/a0039729; Nabi, R. L. (2015). Emotional flow in persuasive health messages. *Health Communication, 30*(2), 114–124. https://doi.org/10.1080/10410236.2104.974129

Pathos Many compelling persuasive appeals are memorable and effective because they stir people's emotions. Although it's helpful for a speaker to convince listeners of his or her integrity, it's often much more powerful if the speaker can generate a strong emotional reaction from the audience. The reason is that when people are emotionally aroused, their receptivity to new ideas is enhanced. Aristotle used the term **pathos** to refer to listeners' emotions, and he understood that emotion can be a significant persuasive tool. Was he right? Check out "Fact or Fiction?" to find out.

Consider Brooks, who began taking powerful pain medication following an injury and has become addicted to the prescription painkillers. Many people have tried to persuade him to seek treatment for his addiction, but he never has. Reasoning with drug addicts that they should end their harmful behaviors is often ineffective because that approach underestimates the powerful force of addictions.[6] Even if addicts rationally understand *why* they need help, they may not be sufficiently persuaded to seek it until they have had a significant emotional experience. Afraid for his safety, his family and close friends stage an intervention in which they read aloud letters and other testimony explaining how Brooks's behaviors have negatively affected them. Unless Brooks accepts help, his

Advertisements try to persuade us to buy a product or a service.
Image Source/Getty Images

- **pathos** Listeners' emotions.

TABLE 2	Suppose you were designing a message to persuade people to stop smoking. Here are examples of appeals to pathos that you might use.	
SOME EXAMPLES OF EMOTIONAL APPEALS	**Type of Appeal**	**Example Statement**
	Appeal to fear	Thousands of people die from lung cancer every year; you could be next.
	Appeal to guilt	Think about how many children you're hurting with second-hand smoke.
	Appeal to joy	Imagine how happy you'd be if you were free of your nicotine addiction.
	Appeal to disgust	See this charred skin tissue? That's what your lungs look like right now.
	Appeal to shame	You're an embarrassment to your family when you smoke.
	Appeal to anger	If you're sick and tired of nicotine controlling your life, then kick the habit.
	Appeal to sadness	Imagine saying goodbye to your kids because smoking is claiming your life.

friends explain that they will end their relationships with him and his parents indicate that he will no longer be welcome in their home.

When friends and family members read their letters aloud during the intervention, their intent is to elicit emotional reactions in Brooks that are strong enough to persuade him to get medical help. To generate sorrow and guilt, they describe the negative effects of his behavior on their own lives. To generate fear, they spell out the consequences of continued prescription drug abuse. And to generate hope, a professional counselor at the intervention describes the treatments available. The emotions of sorrow, guilt, and fear about current behavior—and hope for changing it—can often persuade people like Brooks to modify their behavior significantly, if reasoning alone was ineffective.

Although stirring virtually any emotion can be persuasive, emotional appeals often focus on generating negative emotions such as fear, guilt, disgust, anger, and sadness.[7] The reason is that we generally dislike experiencing such emotions, so we are motivated to respond to the persuasive appeal as a way of reducing them. Table 2 presents examples of emotional appeals that might be used in a campaign to encourage people to quit smoking.

Logos A third way to persuade people is to appeal to their sense of reason. If a particular belief, opinion, or behavior makes good sense, then people will be inclined to adopt it if they have the capacity to do so. As we saw in the preceding example, appealing to reason doesn't always work, particularly if some other force—such as an addiction—influences a person's behavior. When people are free to choose their beliefs, opinions, and behaviors, however, they are frequently persuaded by a solidly logical argument. Aristotle used the term **logos** to refer to listeners' ability to reason.

To **reason** means to make judgments about the world based on evidence rather than emotion or intuition. When we appeal to logos, we provide our listeners with certain evidence, hoping they will arrive at the same conclusion we have reached. People can engage in the reasoning process in two ways: inductively and deductively.

Inductive Reasoning In **inductive reasoning,** we first consider the specific evidence and then draw general conclusions from it. As the evidence changes or as new evidence becomes available, we modify our conclusions accordingly.

For example, when you get sick and visit the doctor, she asks you about your symptoms, runs diagnostic tests, and examines your medical record. Each of those sources provides evidence. Let's say your symptoms are a rash, fever, and persistent headache. After considering those symptoms, looking at results of your blood tests, and noticing from your records that you haven't had chicken pox, the doctor diagnoses your condition as chicken pox.

- **logos** Listeners' ability to reason.

- **reason** To make judgments about the world based on evidence rather than emotion or intuition.

- **inductive reasoning** A form of reasoning in which one considers evidence and then draws general conclusions from it.

gulfimages/Alamy Stock Photo

To apply inductive reasoning, that is, the doctor started with the specific evidence and drew her general conclusion from it. It is possible, of course, that her conclusion is incorrect. Even though your symptoms are consistent with a diagnosis of chicken pox, they may also be consistent with another diagnosis, such as meningitis or Rocky Mountain spotted fever. When making an inductive claim, your doctor considers the evidence available to her and draws the conclusion she believes that evidence best supports. If you later developed symptoms inconsistent with a diagnosis of chicken pox, she would have to reconsider her conclusion based on that new evidence.

Deductive Reasoning In **deductive reasoning**, we start with a general conclusion and then use it to explain specific individual cases. Deductive claims often make use of a **syllogism**, a three-line argument consisting of a major premise, a minor premise, and a conclusion. In a valid syllogism, if both the major and minor premises are true, then the conclusion logically *must* be true.

Consider the following example:

Major premise: All fruits contain seeds.

Minor premise: Tomatoes are fruits.

Conclusion: Therefore, tomatoes contain seeds.

Let's consider the logic of that argument. If it is true that all fruits contain seeds, and if it is true that tomatoes are fruits, then logically it must be the case that tomatoes contain seeds. There is no logical way the major and minor premises could be true and the conclusion false. We therefore say the conclusion *follows from* the premises, producing a valid syllogism.

When using a syllogism to persuade, we must first establish the accuracy of the premises. Listeners may not be convinced by the logic of your argument if they don't believe both premises are true. Suppose everyone in your audience accepts that all fruits contain seeds, but some listeners believe tomatoes are vegetables, not fruits. They may not find your argument persuasive unless you first convince them the tomato is a fruit. To do so, you might quote an authority on botany or plant biology to support that claim.

Establishing the truth of the premises is necessary, but it isn't sufficient for producing a valid argument. Consider the following syllogism:

Major premise: All mothers are women.

Minor premise: Lucy is a woman.

Conclusion: Therefore, Lucy is a mother.

That syllogism is not valid. The reason is that, even if both premises are true, the conclusion could still be false. Just because Lucy is a woman and all mothers are women, it doesn't follow that Lucy is a mother, because even though all mothers are women, not all women are mothers.

A second way we can reason deductively is with an enthymeme. An **enthymeme** is a syllogism in which one of the premises is already so widely known and accepted that it isn't mentioned.[8] Consider the now-famous statement made by seventeenth-century French philosopher René Descartes: *I think, therefore I am.* If we were to state his argument in the form of a syllogism, it would look like this:

Major premise: Anyone who thinks must exist.

Minor premise: I think.

Conclusion: Therefore, I exist.

Descartes may have believed the major premise ("Anyone who thinks must exist") was so obviously true that it didn't require articulating. If so, then he could safely construct his argument based only on the minor premise and the conclusion, which results in an enthymeme. Enthymemes can be just as persuasive as full syllogisms, but only if listeners accept the validity of both the omitted premise and the stated one.

Whether we do it inductively or deductively, appealing to reason provides our audience with the evidence and explains how it led us to our conclusions. Our goal in doing so is to persuade our listeners to adopt the same conclusions we have.

• **deductive reasoning**
A form of reasoning in which one starts with a general conclusion and then uses it to explain specific individual cases.

• **syllogism** A three-line argument consisting of a major premise, a minor premise, and a conclusion.

Foodcollection

• **enthymeme** A syllogism in which one of the premises is already so widely known and accepted that it is omitted.

Creating a Persuasive Message

In 2019, the Oregon Supreme Court ruled that when police officers in that state pull over a driver, they are prohibited from asking questions that are not directly related to the reason for the stop. Supporters of the ruling argue that police can unfairly use a traffic stop to search for evidence of other crimes, such a drug possession, so they should not be allowed to question drivers outside the scope of the traffic violation. Opponents say that small talk is normal during a traffic stop and that if officers have reasonable suspicion that other crimes have occurred, they should have the right to investigate those crimes.

Suppose you had the opportunity to persuade citizens to vote one way or the other on the rules for police officer conduct during a traffic stop. Your success would rely not only on the strength of your convictions but also on your ability to communicate them in a compelling way. In this section, we'll consider the types of persuasive propositions you can employ, the options you have for organizing your persuasive message, and the logical fallacies you should avoid.

TYPES OF PERSUASIVE PROPOSITIONS

• **proposition** That which a persuasive speech attempts to convince an audience to accept.

As we saw in the chapter on organizing and finding support for your speech, preparing a speech includes drafting a thesis statement, a one-sentence version of your message. In persuasive speaking we sometimes call the thesis statement a **proposition** because we are proposing something we want our audience to accept. Recall that some persuasive messages influence beliefs, others influence opinions, and others influence actions. As we'll see next, we use different types of propositions to achieve these different persuasive goals.

We Influence Beliefs with Propositions of Fact

• **proposition of fact** A claim that a particular argument is supported by the best available evidence and should therefore be taken as factual.

When we ask people to believe a statement, we are also asserting that the statement is true. To achieve our persuasive goal, we use a **proposition of fact**, a claim that a particular argument is supported by the best available evidence and should therefore be taken as factual. Some examples of propositions of fact are

- Russia interfered in the 2016 U.S. presidential election.
- Flying is the safest mode of transportation.
- Genetically modified foods are not safe for human consumption.

Notice that the first and second examples make a claim about *what is,* whereas the third example makes a claim about *what is not.* All three are propositions of fact, however, because in each case we are asking our listeners to accept what we say as true. If it's true that Russia interfered in the 2016 election, then that's our proposition, and our speech must provide the evidence to support that claim. Similarly, if it's true that genetically modified foods are not safe to eat, we would give the evidence necessary to support that argument.

Propositions of fact are claims about reality. It isn't a matter of opinion whether flying is the safest mode of transportation—either it is or it is not. When we assert propositions of fact, our persuasive goal is to make our listeners believe in the objective truth of what we're saying. That goal requires us to support propositions of fact with credible—that is, believable—evidence.

We examine what makes evidence credible and strong later in this chapter.

We Influence Opinions with Propositions of Value

• **proposition of value** A claim that evaluates the worth of a person, an object, or an idea.

Whereas propositions of fact are statements about what is objectively true, **propositions of value** are claims that evaluate the worth of a person, an object, or an idea. When we assert propositions of value, our persuasive goal isn't to make someone *believe* us—it's to make someone *agree with* us. Some examples of propositions of value are

- Fathers are just as important as mothers.
- Animal cloning is immoral.
- Our country is right to do anything it can to protect its citizens.

Some persuasive speakers include propositions of fact, value, and policy in their presentations.

Dave and Les Jacobs/Blend Images LLC

Notice that all three statements make claims, but they are not claims about facts. Rather, they are judgments that reflect the speaker's opinions about what is important, moral, and right. Unlike facts, opinions are never true or false in an absolute sense—they are only correct or incorrect in the minds of the people who discuss them. Therefore, we can't *prove* an opinion in the way we prove a factual claim. We might use facts to establish a basis for advocating a specific opinion—for instance, we may quote evidence about threats of terrorism and the safety of U.S. citizens—but the facts themselves will never settle the issue. One person might interpret that evidence as justifying our nation's right to defend itself against its enemies. Another person might interpret the same evidence as proof of our failed foreign policy and the need for greater diplomacy. Who is right? That's a matter of opinion.

We Influence Actions with Propositions of Policy

Closely tied to propositions of value are **propositions of policy**, claims about *what we should do*. Speakers offer propositions of policy to suggest a specific course of action for listeners to follow or to support. Some examples of propositions of policy are

- The federal government should ban the use of human stem cells in medical research.
- Hate crimes against ethnic, religious, and sexual minorities should be capital offenses.
- Everyone should patronize only local, family-owned businesses whenever possible.

• **proposition of policy**
A claim about what should be done.

Notice that each statement contains the word *should*, a characteristic that makes it closer to a proposition of value than a proposition of fact. Whereas propositions of value suggest what we should *think*, however, propositions of policy suggest what we should *do*. Each of the examples, that is, suggests a specific course of action, either for individuals ("patronize only local, family-owned businesses") or for the government ("ban the use of human stem cells"). When advocating for individual action, speakers attempt to persuade listeners to adopt the action themselves. When advocating for government action, speakers are usually trying to persuade listeners to support the action, such as by voting for it or encouraging their elected officials to do the same.

Some Persuasive Speeches Include More Than One Type of Proposition

Although each type of proposition can be persuasive on its own, many persuasive speeches integrate two or even all three types to support their message. Let's say, for instance, that you wanted to advocate expanding affirmative action laws that help members of minority groups to get jobs. You might begin your speech with a proposition of value, such as "Diversity in the workplace is important," and persuade your listeners to adopt that opinion. Next, you might introduce a proposition of fact, such as "Affirmative action laws have increased workplace diversity by 27 percent in the past three decades," and provide the evidence for your listeners to believe that factual claim. Finally, you might assert

SHARPEN Your Skills: *Propositions of value, fact, and policy*

Write a proposition of value, a proposition of fact, and a proposition of policy you would use if you were persuading lawmakers how to vote with respect to doctor-assisted suicide.

a proposition of policy, such as "The U.S. government should expand affirmative action laws to increase workplace diversity even further," and use your earlier claims about values and facts to persuade listeners to support that action. In this speech, each new proposition you introduce is supported by the propositions that preceded it, and the result can be a powerfully persuasive argument.

In a face-to-face speech, you can incorporate propositions of fact, value, and/or policy to achieve your persuasive ends. Research shows that the same strategies work in computer-mediated persuasive messages. Several studies, for instance, have found that value appeals and fact appeals sent by text message can influence recipients' health behaviors, including their attitudes toward smoking[9] and the amount of physical exercise they achieve.[10] Given how commonly people use text messaging and other forms of computer-mediated technologies to communicate with each other, persuasive messages are likely to be increasingly frequent.

FOUR WAYS TO ORGANIZE A PERSUASIVE MESSAGE

The way you organize a persuasive message often matters as much as the message itself. Even good arguments can lose their persuasive appeal if they aren't presented in a meaningful sequence. In this section, we look at four options for organizing a persuasive message.

Problem-Solving Pattern One way to organize a persuasive speech is to use a **problem-solving pattern**, in which you establish the existence of a problem and then propose a solution to it. The problem-solving approach requires you persuade your listeners on two separate points. First, you must show that the problem exists and is serious enough to warrant intervention. Second, you must establish that your proposed solution is possible and practical and will be effective at reducing or eliminating the problem.

• **problem-solving pattern** A way of organizing a pervasive speech in which the speaker establishes the existence of a problem and then proposes a solution to it.

Suppose your persuasive speech is about slowing the loss of family farms. You might begin by pointing out how many family farms in the United States have gone out of business in the last 50 years because of competition from corporate mega-farms. Next you need to explain why that's a problem worth solving. For instance, you could show it has eliminated thousands of jobs and required stores to buy food grown hundreds of miles away, decreasing its nutritional value.

Perhaps your proposed solution is that the government increase its subsidies to family farms to help to keep them in business. You then need to provide evidence that such a solution is *possible* (the government has the money to fund the subsidies), *practical* (an infrastructure exists to dispense the subsidies to family farmers), and *effective* (providing the subsidies will keep more family farms in business).

Refutational Approach A problem-solving pattern can work well when your audience is open-minded about the problem and solution you describe. Sometimes, however, your audience may be predisposed toward a certain position you plan to refute. Let's say, for instance, that you're speaking in favor of capital punishment, and you already know some of your listeners oppose it. In this instance, you might use a **refutational approach**, whereby you begin by presenting the main arguments against your position and then immediately refute them.

• **refutational approach** A way of organizing a persuasive speech in which the speaker begins by presenting the main arguments against his or her position and then immediately refutes those arguments.

One common argument against capital punishment is that it won't bring crime victims back. That statement is often persuasive because it's true, and many people use it to argue that capital punishment is therefore futile. If you plan to advocate the death penalty in your speech, you might begin by acknowledging that statement and admitting that it is true. You could then point out, however, that *no* form of punishment will bring the victims back. The fact that the victims won't come back is therefore not a valid argument against capital punishment.

In the refutational method, after you've acknowledged and responded to the main arguments against your position, you then state your own position and argue for it. The refutational approach is designed to dispense with the arguments against your position first—or at least to weaken them—so your own position looks stronger by comparison.[11]

Comparative Advantage Method On occasion, you may find yourself speaking to people who already agree that a problem exists—they just can't agree on the best way to solve it. In that situation, it's often best to use the **comparative advantage method**, in which you explain why your point of view is superior to others on the same topic.

Imagine you're speaking to a group of schoolteachers on the topic of teacher evaluations. Your listeners all agree that evaluations are important, but they have little consensus about how evaluations should be done. To persuade the audience to adopt *your* suggestion, you begin by reminding everyone of the importance of the problem: "Although teacher evaluations are critical to school success, there's no fair way of conducting them."

Next, you identify the various alternative viewpoints and explain why each one is deficient:

> *Evaluating teachers on the basis of student test scores is unfair because that rewards the teachers who "teach to the test." Having principals evaluate teachers is unfair because principals can play favorites. Evaluating teachers based on student feedback is unfair because only popular teachers receive good evaluations.*

After identifying the shortcomings of the alternatives, you propose your own solution to the problem:

> *The only fair way to evaluate teachers is by using expert evaluators from other school districts. Because they won't know the content of student exams, they cannot reward teachers for "teaching to the test." Because they don't know the teachers they're evaluating personally, they won't be inclined to play favorites. Finally, because they are experts, their evaluations won't be swayed by teacher popularity.*

By using the comparative advantage method, you acknowledge that other viewpoints exist, but you give your listeners reason to discount them in favor of the viewpoint you are advocating.

Monroe's Motivated Sequence A final way of organizing a persuasive speech is with **Monroe's motivated sequence**, a problem-oriented structure for persuasive arguments. The sequence, developed by former Purdue University professor Alan Monroe, has proved to be particularly effective at motivating listeners to adopt a specific *action*, such as buying a product or giving money to a charity.

Let's say you must give a speech persuading people to donate blood. Monroe's motivated sequence has five stages you address in order:

1. *Attention.* The attention stage arouses people's interest and sparks their desire to listen, often by making the topic personally relevant to them. Your message at the attention stage is: *Please listen!*

   Example

   Imagine you're badly injured in a head-on car crash, and you're quickly losing blood. After you arrive by ambulance at the emergency room, the doctor says you need an immediate blood transfusion to save your life. The only problem is, they don't have enough blood to give you.

2. *Need.* Once you've aroused your listeners' attention, your next priority is to identify the need or problem that requires their action. Your message at the need stage is: *Something must be done.*

   Example

   In the past few years, community blood drives have been less and less successful at collecting enough blood to meet our area's medical needs. Our supply of healthy, usable blood is drying up fast.

• **comparative advantage method** A way of organizing a persuasive speech in which the speaker explains why his or her point of view is superior to others on the same topic.

• **Monroe's motivated sequence** A way of organizing a persuasive speech consisting of appeals to attention, need, satisfaction, visualization, and then action.

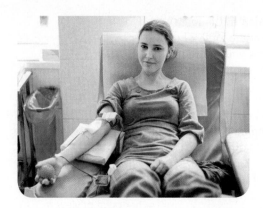

JanekWD/Getty Images

3. *Satisfaction.* After you've established the problem at the need stage, you use the satisfaction stage to propose your solution. Your message at the satisfaction stage is: *This is what should be done.*

Example

We need an association of healthy, committed volunteers who will donate blood on a regular basis and will encourage their friends, relatives, coworkers, and acquaintances to do the same. That will ensure an ongoing supply of blood to meet our needs.

4. *Visualization.* At the visualization stage, you ask your audience to imagine how much better their situation will be if they do what you're proposing. Your message at this stage is: *Consider the benefits.*

Example

With a continuous supply of blood on hand, our area hospitals will be well equipped to respond to a wide range of medical situations, ensuring the health and welfare of the people in our community.

5. *Action.* Finally, at the action stage, you tell your listeners what you want them to do. Your request could be that they change their opinions or their beliefs, but often it's that they change their actions. Your message at the action stage is: *Act now!*

Example

You can make a difference by filling out the blood donor cards I'm passing around and dropping them in the cardboard box at the back of the room as you leave.

Each of the four options for organizing a persuasive speech that we've reviewed in this section has its strengths. Every situation is different, and you will need to choose the best option for the specific circumstances. As you consider ways to organize your presentation, think about what you are trying to accomplish and how sympathetic you expect your audience to be. You can use that information to select the organizational approach that will work best for you.

No matter how you organize your persuasive appeal, it's critical that you use valid arguments. Many arguments that seem valid when you first hear them may actually be problematic on closer inspection, as we consider next.

AVOIDING LOGICAL FALLACIES

• **logical fallacy** A line of reasoning that, even if it makes sense, does not genuinely support a speaker's point.

A **logical fallacy** is a line of reasoning that, even if it makes sense, doesn't genuinely support a speaker's point. Competent speakers avoid logical fallacies because they offer invalid or incomplete evidence for claims. Instead, good speakers focus on providing valid logical arguments and evidence to support their points.

Some logical fallacies are easy to spot; others are subtle and more difficult to identify. The most common fallacies are as follows:

• **ad hominem fallacy** A statement that attempts to counter an argument by criticizing the person who made it.

• Ad hominem *fallacy.* A common but illogical way to counter arguments is to criticize the person who makes them—for instance, "I wouldn't believe anything Senator Rodgers says about fiscal responsibility; the man's an idiot." That line of reasoning, called an **ad hominem fallacy**, implies that if a person has shortcomings, his or her arguments must therefore be deficient. That implication is a fallacy, however. Consider that, in our example, even if the speaker doesn't respect Senator Rodgers, the senator's arguments about fiscal responsibility aren't necessarily wrong. To show they are, the speaker must attack the arguments themselves.

• **slippery slope fallacy** A statement that attacks an argument by taking it to such an extreme that it appears ludicrous.

• *Slippery slope.* A **slippery slope fallacy**—also called a *reduction to the absurd*—unfairly tries to shoot down an argument by taking it to such an extreme that it appears ludicrous. An activist advocating a ban on same-sex marriage might state: "If we continue to allow gay marriage, pretty soon we'll be allowing people to marry animals." Such a method tries to persuade people not to adopt an argument by extending it to a ridiculous and undesirable extreme.

- *Either/or fallacy.* An **either/or fallacy** identifies two alternatives and falsely suggests that if we reject one, we must accept the other. Take the statement, "Either we make condoms available in public schools or we prepare for an epidemic of sexually transmitted infections among our teenagers." That statement argues for providing condoms by identifying an epidemic of infections as the only possible alternative. The reasoning is invalid—a fallacy—because it ignores the possibility that there may be other ways to keep sexually active adolescents healthy.

- *False-cause fallacy.* A **false-cause fallacy**—also known as the *post hoc ergo propter hoc* fallacy—asserts that if an event occurs before some outcome, the event therefore caused that outcome. Consider the claim "I started taking ginseng and fish oil supplements three years ago, and I haven't gotten sick once during that time." That claim implies that because the speaker's streak of wellness *followed* her use of supplements, it was therefore *caused by* her use of supplements. Her reasoning is a fallacy, however, because she has no way of knowing whether she would have been healthy even if she hadn't taken the supplements. The fact that one occurrence preceded the other doesn't mean it caused the other.

Stockbyte/Getty Images

- *Bandwagon appeal.* **Bandwagon appeal** suggests that a listener should accept an argument because many other people have. Think about the assertion "Over 15 million people buy Vetris motor oil each month, and you should too—15 million satisfied customers can't be wrong!" The implication is that if an argument (such as to use a particular brand) is popular, it therefore has merit. That may well be true—good products are often popular *because* they are good—but it isn't necessarily true. Can 15 million people be wrong? Absolutely—so the popularity of an argument is no guarantee of its merit.

- *Hasty generalization.* A **hasty generalization** is a broad claim based on insufficient evidence, usually one or two isolated examples. Suppose you were to claim in your speech that it is unsafe to travel in Turkey. To support your claim, you tell of having had your passport stolen from your hotel room during your study-abroad experience in Turkey last year. Your argument is a hasty generalization because your evidence is limited to one incident in one hotel.

- *Red herring fallacy.* When people are unable to respond legitimately to an argument, they sometimes introduce an irrelevant detail—thus committing what is known as the **red herring fallacy**—to divert attention from the point of the argument. Suppose you hear someone say "We shouldn't prosecute people for prostitution when there are so many more dangerous crimes going on." Prostitution is still illegal even if other crimes are more dangerous, so the danger of other crimes is irrelevant to the claim that prostitutes and their customers shouldn't be prosecuted.

- *Straw man fallacy.* A speaker uses a **straw man fallacy** when he or she refutes a claim that was never made. Let's say the governor of your state proposes to reduce the drinking age in your state to 19 for beer and wine. A legislator responds in a televised interview by saying "Our governor thinks kids should be able to sit in bars drinking martinis! I doubt most parents in this state want to see children getting hammered with hard liquor after school." In that instance, the legislator is trying to refute an argument that the governor hasn't made. After all, the governor's proposal is about 19-year-olds, not children, and about beer and wine, not hard liquor.

- *Begging the question.* **Begging the question** means supporting an argument using the argument itself as evidence. Suppose a speaker says "The use of cell phones while driving should be banned because people shouldn't talk on the phone while driving." That statement presents a claim—cell phone use while driving should be banned—but then supports that claim simply by restating it in another way. No evidence is offered in support of the claim beyond the claim itself.

- **either/or fallacy** A statement that identifies two alternatives and falsely suggests that if one is rejected, the other must be accepted.

- **false-cause fallacy** A statement asserting that if an event occurs before some outcome, the event therefore caused that outcome.

- **bandwagon appeal** A claim that a listener should accept an argument because of how many other people have already accepted it.

- **hasty generalization** A broad claim that is based on insufficient evidence.

- **red herring fallacy** A statement that responds to an argument by introducing an irrelevant detail to divert attention from the point of the argument.

- **straw man fallacy** A statement that refutes a claim that was never made.

- **begging the question** Supporting an argument using the argument itself as evidence.

Although comedian Ellen DeGeneres is a vegan, she is not a physician, nutritionist, or medical scientist. Therefore, despite her high public profile, she is unqualified to comment with authority on the health benefits of veganism.

Richard Rodriguez/ Getty images

• **non sequitur** A conclusion that does not logically follow from a premise.

• **appeal to false authority** A claim that uses as evidence the testimony of someone who is not an expert on the topic.

• *Non sequitur.* The Latin phrase **non sequitur** means "it does not follow." In this fallacy, the speaker makes an invalid deductive argument by offering a premise and then drawing a conclusion that is not logically supported by it. Consider the claim "Fewer people are marrying these days, so therefore, the divorce rate is obviously going down." That conclusion may be true, but it is not implied by the premise. A drop in the number of marriages doesn't necessarily mean anything about the divorce rate. The fact that the conclusion does not logically follow from the premise makes this claim a non sequitur.

• *Appeal to false authority.* An **appeal to false authority** uses as evidence the testimony of someone who is not an expert on a given topic. In a persuasive speech about the benefits of a vegan diet, for instance, a student might say "According to an interview with Ellen DeGeneres, a vegan diet is the healthiest way to eat." The problem is that although DeGeneres is a vegan, she is not a physician, nutritionist, or medical scientist. Therefore, despite her high public profile, she is unqualified to comment with authority on the health benefits of veganism or any other diet.

The lines of reasoning described above are fallacies because they each represent an illogical way of supporting an argument. Two important caveats are worth noting, however. First, *arguments supported by logical fallacies may still be true.* Although Ellen DeGeneres is not a medical authority, that fact does not mean, by itself, that she's inaccurate in saying a vegan diet is healthful. It simply means she does not have the credibility (about which we will read shortly) to make that claim. Knowing whether the claim is true or false would require more believable evidence.

Second, *even though they are illogical, fallacies may still be persuasive.* Consider that politicians frequently use *ad hominem* attacks during campaigns, pointing out, say, that an opponent has failed in her business or his marriage. Although such a statement doesn't logically mean the individual is unfit for public office, people aren't persuaded only by logic, as you'll recall from the earlier discussion of rhetorical proof. They are also persuaded by emotion. If politicians can arouse negative emotion about their opponents, even with illogical arguments, they can be—and often are—persuasive in discrediting their rivals. That practice, known as *negative campaigning* or *mudslinging*, is highly controversial and often considered unethical, particularly when politicians make misleading statements about each other. Although the practice is an example of the dark side of communication, research indicates that negative campaign ads can be just as persuasive as positive ads.[12]

Those caveats aside, however, good persuasive speakers know how to avoid committing logical fallacies. To do so, they first have to be able to spot them accurately. Check out "The Competent Communicator" to see how well *you* can identify some of the most common fallacies.

Honing Your Persuasive-Speaking Skills

Just as an exceptional salesperson can sell almost anything to almost anyone, an outstanding persuasive speaker has the skills to persuade even the most resistant audiences. In this section, we'll explore several strategies for delivering a persuasive speech effectively, including adapting to your audience, building rapport, and establishing your credibility.

ADAPT TO YOUR AUDIENCE

As we've discussed in earlier chapters, it's always important to know who your listeners are and adapt to their needs. Accommodating listeners' needs is useful when you give an informative speech because it helps to ensure that you present information your listeners can understand and don't already know. It is equally important when you are speaking persuasively, because it gives your message the best chance for

COMPETENT COMMUNICATOR

Name That Fallacy!

It's time to put your understanding of logical fallacies to the test. Match each of the fallacies listed below with the statement that exemplifies it.

Hill Street Studios/Blend images/Getty Images

Fallacy

_____ 1. bandwagon appeal

_____ 2. either/or argument

_____ 3. *ad hominem* attack

_____ 4. red herring

_____ 5. slippery slope

_____ 6. hasty generalization

_____ 7. appeal to false authority

_____ 8. false cause

Statement

A. If we restrict oil drilling in Alaska, then eventually we won't be able to drill for oil anywhere and we'll be back in the Stone Age.

B. You should get an LCD television because that's the type 9 of 10 consumers prefer.

C. Joining a fraternity made my son an alcoholic. He never drank before he moved into that frat house.

D. My pediatrician overcharged me for some tests last year. Doctors are crooks!

E. Richard Jones would make a terrible mayor; his daughter's in rehab, for goodness' sake!

F. You should try acupuncture; Michael Phelps swears by it, and he's won 28 Olympic medals.

G. Grading on a curve is unfair because teaching shouldn't be a popularity contest; it's about educating our students.

H. If you're not pro-life, then you're in favor of killing millions of innocent babies.

Spotting logical fallacies can be tricky, but it's a skill you can improve with practice. Answers for this exercise appear below. Not all fallacies addressed in the chapter are included here, because some are impossible to identify without knowing the arguments that preceded them.

ANSWERS: 1-B; 2-H; 3-E; 4-G; 5-A; 6-D; 7-F; 8-C

acceptance. Adapting to your audience requires identifying its general disposition and neutralizing hostility when you encounter it.

Identify Your Audience's Disposition Before presenting a persuasive speech you should know how your audience is likely to react. Some audiences will be receptive to your message, others will be neutral, and still others will be hostile. Connecting with each type of audience requires a different presentational style:

- A **receptive audience** is composed of people who already accept and agree with all or most of what you plan to say. We sometimes use the phrase "preaching to the choir" to describe speaking to a receptive audience. When you have such an audience, your persuasive task is relatively easy because your listeners are likely to respond favorably to whatever you say.

• **receptive audience**
An audience composed of people who already accept and agree with all or most of what a speaker plans to say.

- A **neutral audience** doesn't have strong feelings for or against the topic of your speech. Perhaps such listeners don't know enough about your topic to have formed a strong opinion on it, or maybe they don't care enough about your topic—or see enough of a personal connection to themselves—to bother forming a strong opinion. When speaking to a neutral audience, you should thus inform listeners about what your topic is and why it should matter to them. Once you make it relevant to them, you'll find it easier to persuade them to adopt your viewpoint on the topic.

- The most difficult group to persuade is a **hostile audience**, whose members are predisposed to disagree with you. Their hostile disposition may reflect that they already have a viewpoint on the issue that conflicts with yours, or it may be that they dislike you personally. Whatever the reason, hostile audiences are challenging because they are against you even before you start speaking. Good persuasive speakers can neutralize hostility, however, as we will see later.

Your audience's disposition—and the kinds of persuasive appeals to which it will respond—can also depend on your listeners' cultural background. Research shows that people from different cultures are persuaded by different types of messages. See Table 3 for specific examples.

Neutralize Hostility Many people find it difficult to listen to—let alone to be persuaded by—someone toward whom they feel hostility. If a portion of an audience already is disapproving of a speaker, his or her ideas, or the occasion on which the person is speaking, it is challenging to convey the message effectively. Many speakers are so uncomfortable with such situations that they ignore the hostility, hoping their message will be enough to persuade their listeners. Skilled persuasive speakers, however, acknowledge the listeners' negative feelings and then identify points on which they and their listeners agree.

When President Barack Obama delivered the commencement address at the University of Notre Dame, he faced just such a situation. As a Catholic institution, Notre Dame opposes abortion, as do many of its students, so they protested the selection of pro-choice Obama as speaker. Instead of shying away from their concerns, the president acknowledged them respectfully and focused on points on which he and his audience could agree:

> When we open up our hearts and our minds to those who may not think precisely like we do or believe precisely what we believe, that's when we discover at least the possibility of common ground. That's when we begin to say, "Maybe we won't agree on abortion, but we can still agree that this heart-wrenching decision for any woman is not made casually, it has both moral and spiritual dimensions. So let us work together to reduce the number of women seeking abortions, let's reduce unintended pregnancies. Let's make adoption more available. Let's provide care and support for women who do carry their children to term. Let's honor

TABLE 3

CULTURE MATTERS: CULTURAL DIFFERENCES IN PERSUASION

Cultural background can influence the persuasive strategies to which listeners respond. In one study, researchers from Stanford University observed employees of the same international corporation in four different countries. Each employee was asked to comply with a request from another employee. The researchers found noteworthy cultural differences in what persuaded the employees. How might you use this information to understand your audience better?

Culture	Most Effective Persuasive Strategy
Chinese	Authority: Chinese employees complied with requests made by higher-status individuals.
Spanish	Liking: Spanish employees complied with requests made by people they liked.
German	Consistency: German employees complied with requests if such requests were consistent with the organization's rules.
U.S.	Reciprocity: U.S. employees complied with requests made by people who had recently done something for them.

SOURCE: Morris, M. W., Podolny, J. M., & Ariel, S. (2000). *Innovations in international and cross-cultural management*. Sage. https://doi.org/10.4135/9781452205502

putting**communication**to**work**

Job Title >	Work Responsibilities >
Sales Associate for Financial Services Firm	Financial services firms often offer a broad range of products geared toward diverse audiences, such as first-time investors, parents saving for college costs, and retirees. A sales associate meets with various groups of people and must determine which products would appeal to each crowd. He or she then explains what the financial services firm can do and persuades listeners to buy the firm's products. Besides requiring good public speaking skills, this position also benefits from a keen ability to analyze audiences and ascertain how best to appeal to each group of listeners.

Mike Kemp/Blend Images LLC

the conscience of those who disagree with abortion, and draft a sensible conscience clause, and make sure that all of our health care policies are grounded not only in sound science, but also in clear ethics, as well as respect for the equality of women." Those are things we can do.

By giving voice to his opponents' views on abortion, Obama made his critics feel respected instead of maligned. Further, by identifying points on which he and his critics agreed, he provided a way for people on all sides of this divisive issue to communicate with one another, neutralizing much of the opposition that surrounded his selection as commencement speaker.

To read about one career in which you could use your audience analysis skills, check out the "Putting Communication to Work" box.

During his commencement speech at the University of Notre Dame, President Barack Obama respectfully acknowledged differences of opinion regarding the controversial issue of abortion.

Gerald Herbert/AP Photo

BUILD RAPPORT WITH YOUR LISTENERS

Knowing your audience will also help you to build rapport with your listeners. To **build rapport** is to create the perception that your listeners and you see things similarly. It establishes trust and encourages audience members to listen even if they disagree with you.

Several behaviors can help you to build rapport with your audience:

• **build rapport** Create the perception that listeners and the speaker see things similarly.

- *Interact with listeners before your speech.* Particularly when you're speaking to people you don't know well, spend time talking to them—and listening to them—before your speech. Not only will you get information about who your listeners are and what they're thinking; you will also signal to your audience that you care about them.

- *Maintain eye contact while you speak.* According to research, many people believe a lack of eye contact indicates the speaker is being deceptive.[13] If you don't look at your audience while you speak, you're likely to come across as untrustworthy—an undesirable effect when you're trying to persuade. Practice establishing and maintaining eye contact with each person in your audience for three to four seconds at a time.

- *Open with a story.* Because everyone loves a good story, an excellent way to build rapport with your audience is to open with one. Stories are especially effective when they include information to which your audience can relate. If you live in a cold climate but are speaking in a hot one, for instance, you could describe your experience of dealing with the heat, because your listeners will be able to relate to it themselves.

- *Use humor when appropriate.* It's difficult not to like people who make us laugh. Therefore, a particularly effective way to establish rapport is to use humor in your presentation. Humor can consist of short jokes or one-liners and can also be reflected in the stories you tell. Incorporating humor can help your listeners to relax and enjoy your presentation—and be receptive to your message. When considering the use of humor, however, think carefully about what your audience is likely to find funny and in good taste. It is best to stay away from jokes that risk offending listeners and that your audience may not understand or appreciate.

ESTABLISH YOUR CREDIBILITY

Earlier in this chapter, we considered the value of appealing to ethos, which is the integrity, trustworthiness, and goodness of the speaker. Knowing that ethos is important, good persuasive speakers work to establish credibility with their audiences. **Credibility** means believability—if you're credible, people will believe what you have to say. If you have a good deal of credibility, audiences will take your words seriously and be open to new ideas. If your credibility is low, however, you will find it hard to persuade, even if your evidence is strong. Establishing credibility is thus vital for persuasive speakers. Researchers believe credibility has three different components: competence, character, and charisma.[14]

• **Credibility** The extent to which others perceive us to be competent and trustworthy.

Demonstrate Your Competence People have *competence* when they have the required skills, knowledge, and organization to perform a task well. Think back to the first day of this class. What impressions did you have of your instructor? Did he or she seem knowledgeable, organized, well prepared, and professional? If so, those characteristics probably gave you confidence in what your instructor had to say. In comparison, when you've had instructors who appeared ignorant, disorganized, unprepared, and unprofessional, you probably lacked confidence in their abilities.

Just as you have more confidence in a competent instructor, listeners will have more confidence in you if you come across as a competent speaker. Describing the experience and knowledge you have of your topic, and speaking in a polished, well-organized manner, will demonstrate your competence.

Charismatic speakers are often more persuasive than speakers who lack energy and excitement.

Susan See Photography

Accent Your Character A person's *character* is his or her degree of honesty. People who appear honest are more credible than those who appear dishonest because we can have greater confidence that what honest individuals say is accurate and true. In jury trials, for example, lawyers frequently cast doubt on the testimony of their opponents' witnesses by questioning their character. If an attorney can establish that an opposing witness has been caught lying in the past, that history makes the witness appear to be of questionable character and can cause the jury to doubt his or her testimony.

Good persuasive speakers establish their character by incorporating stories and anecdotes about themselves that demonstrate their honesty. In addition, speakers who enact *high-immediacy behaviors*—such as standing close to others, leaning forward, using eye contact, and maintaining an open posture—are judged to be of more positive character than speakers who do not enact those behaviors.[15]

Communicate with Charisma A final component of credibility is *charisma*, which is a speaker's enthusiasm. As you know, it's much easier to listen to—and be persuaded by—someone who speaks dynamically and energetically than by someone who seems bored by his or her own words. So, when you're giving a persuasive speech, approach your topic and your audience with enthusiasm. Smile! Use gestures and vary your tone of voice to keep your presentation interesting. Look at your audience and use facial expressions that reflect the mood of your message. Bringing energy and excitement to your presentation will encourage your listeners to pay attention and make them receptive to your words.

Table 4 provides a brief summary of the three components of credibility.

When people take actions that damage their credibility, one of the most effective ways to repair that damage is to issue an apology. The "Difficult Conversations" box offers suggestions for making apologies—especially ones that are public—more effective.

Competence—Competent speakers appear knowledgeable, organized, professional, and prepared.

Character—Speakers of good character appear honest and trustworthy.

Charisma—Charismatic speakers are energetic, dynamic, and excited about their message.

TABLE 4

THAT'S CREDIBLE!
THREE COMPONENTS OF
CREDIBILITY

Difficult Conversations

Making a Public Apology

Imagine this: You hold a leadership role in your school's student government association. Last month, you helped to organize a public forum in support of cultural diversity and inclusion. While participating on a discussion panel, you were asked questions from the audience regarding a recent student-led march protesting the practice of abortion, and in a moment of anger, you made flippant and disparaging remarks about religious conservatives being intolerant and bigoted.

Now, consider this: Since the discussion panel, you have received several angry e-mail messages from students, parents, and community members who are upset with your comments about religious conservatives. Some went so far as to call *you* bigoted for claiming to promote diversity while disparaging a large group of people based solely on their beliefs. You recognize that you have lost some credibility with the campus community over your heated remarks, so you decide to issue a public apology. Here are some tips for using your apology to restore your credibility:

- Own up to your behavior and acknowledge why it has upset some people. Even if you disagree with their anger or believe they are overreacting, make it clear that you understand why listeners were upset with your comments.

- Acknowledge the role that your emotions played. Instead of trying to defend your words—which could make your apology seem insincere—admit that you were angry and frustrated in that moment, and that, like many people, you said something in anger that you probably shouldn't have said.

- Say you're sorry. To be effective, an apology needs to include an expression of regret, not simply an explanation for one's behavior. Indicate sincerely that you are sorry for having offended listeners with your comments, especially given that the point of the public forum was to support diversity and inclusion.

- Tell listeners what you have learned from the experience. Instead of simply promising not to make the same mistake again, explain the lesson you have learned, such as "I now realize that supporting diversity means supporting people's rights to believe as they do, and to act in accordance with their beliefs, even if I think differently."

Apologizing isn't always easy, especially when you are called upon to apologize in a public manner. Apologizing with sensitivity and sincerity, however, can do much to restore your credibility in the eyes of others.

The Bottom Line: Credibility Matters In the business world, a company's credibility often directly affects its profits. Corporations therefore go to great lengths to establish and maintain their credibility.

In 2018, for instance, Facebook faced widespread public criticism after a security breach that failed to protect the personal data of millions of users. After taking a significant hit to its stock prices, Facebook placed advertisements on U.S. television and in major publications reinforcing its commitment to customer security.[16] By taking that action, the company has tried to restore consumer confidence and repair damage to its credibility that could have resulted in additional financial losses.

THE DARK SIDE OF COMMUNICATION

Misleading to Persuade: A Threat to Credibility

RidingMetaphor/Alamy Stock Photo

Many companies these days recognize that consumers appreciate socially responsible business practices. Among them is the Tyson Food company, known worldwide for its chicken, pork, and beef products. On its website and social media platforms, Tyson advertises its commitment to sustainable environmental practices and the humane treatment of animals. Such messages are meant to persuade consumers to buy Tyson's products.

Two consumer advocacy groups are unpersuaded, however. In July 2019, Food & Water Watch (FWW) and the Organic Consumers Association (OCA) filed a lawsuit in a Washington, DC, superior court alleging that Tyson engages in deceptive advertising practices meant to trick consumers. Specifically, the suit claims that Tyson regularly violates federal environmental laws, contributing to excessive air and water pollution. FWW and OCA also allege that Tyson raises and butchers its chickens in a distinctly inhumane manner.

The lawsuit does not seek monetary damages against Tyson. Rather, the advocacy groups are asking only that the company change its advertising practices. Although the suit is still pending, media coverage of the controversy may have cast doubt on Tyson's credibility in the minds of its customers and perhaps served as an example for other companies wishing to protect their own credibility.

In contrast, companies found to use false or misleading statements to persuade customers often lose credibility and suffer decreased profits as a result. Consumers find deceptive practices in advertising to be unethical. To read about the problems one company encountered after losing credibility due to misleading statements, see "The Dark Side of Communication."

A Sample Persuasive Speech

A good way to develop persuasive-speaking skills is to study excellent examples. Below is the text of a persuasive speech by Jennifer Wells, a former communication studies major at the University of Alabama and a member of the school's speech and debate team. Jennifer's speech advocates expanding laws that protect people from sexual harassment in the workplace. Jennifer was a quarter-finalist in persuasive speaking with this speech at the American Forensics Association National Tournament in April 2009. Alongside the text are comments about what makes each section of her speech so effective. The formal outline for Jennifer's speech appears in Figure 1.

CLOSING THE LOOPHOLE ON SEXUAL HARASSMENT

COMMENTARY	SPEECH
This introduction opens with a compelling story introducing listeners to the problem described in the speech, same-sex sexual harassment in the workplace.	Joseph Oncale is not a household name . . . at least, not yet. After taking a job as a roughneck on an oil rig with Sundowner Offshore Services, Oncale's outgoing personality was incorrectly perceived as stereotypically homosexual behavior by his coworkers. They verbally and physically abused Oncale, culminating in an episode in which Oncale's arms were pinned behind his back in the shower while cheering coworkers looked on as a Sundowner supervisor simulated raping Oncale with a bar of soap. Certain that he would be protected against such unrestrained subjugation and cruelty, Oncale sued Sundowner for sexual harassment. According to the *Labor Law Journal* of April 1, 2005, the Louisiana Supreme Court found that the atrocities committed against the heterosexual Oncale by Sundowner Services were perfectly excusable under the law. After all, boys will be boys. A loophole in Title 7—the federal safeguard protecting against sexual harassment and discrimination—permits heinous same-sex sexual harassment.

COMMENTARY	SPEECH
Here, the speaker makes her persuasive appeal. Notice that she offers a proposition of value: *people deserve protection from same-sex sexual harassment.* Later, she will advocate changing the law, which is a proposition of policy.	The starkest ramifications of this loophole can be seen in discriminatory practices between men. According to a report from the Equal Employment Opportunity Commission, or EEOC, between 1997 and 2007, 1 out of every 6 reports of sexual harassment was filed by a man. While significant, the scope of the issue is blurred by the fact that, according to the *Mondaq Legal News Network* on July 31, 2008, of those incidents, only a few make it to the verdict stage of a trial, and even fewer survive the appellate proceedings.
Regardless of one's moral, ethical, or religious views on sexuality, everyone deserves the protection of a safe workplace. Therefore, it is our duty as a vigilant society to ensure that we recognize the extent of this social injustice, identify the sources allowing this backwater practice to persist, and unite to protect those whose fundamental human rights have been ignored.
Notice how the speaker effectively previews the topics she plans to address.	To understand this problem better, let's first examine the ramifications of a hostile work environment, and second, the loophole in the law. First, men deciding to report harassment risk escalating a hostile work environment into an openly discriminatory work environment. Servers who filed suit against the Cheesecake Factory stated in the July 11, 2008, *Los Angeles Times*, "It's just different when it happens to a guy; there's always the fear that they're going to question your manhood." The fact that the servers reported anything is unusual, because on top of the vulnerability involved in reporting harassment, coworkers and companies often make it even harder. *PR Week* of May 2, 2008, reports a case in which a finance director assaulted his male assistant during a trip. When the assistant reported it, he was forced to leave his job, but the finance director remains unpunished.
The speaker is careful throughout the speech to cite her sources. These citations help to give her words credibility.	Second, those brave enough to report sexual harassment often do so without the support of the law. The protection of Title 7 of the Civil Rights Act of 1964 extends only to individuals who are discriminated against on the basis of race, color, religion, sex, or national origin. This wording means that the law provides no protection from harassment based on sexual orientation or assumed sexual orientation, or from a member of one's own sex. Therefore, if you are a man and another man sexually harasses you in some way, you have no federally secured recourse. Contending that it is impossible for a man to sexually harass another man, the courts and Congress have repeatedly refused to acknowledge same-sex sexual harassment as an actionable discrimination, especially harassment based on sexual orientation. The December 2006 *Journal of Individual Employment Rights* succinctly explains that, as a federally unprotected class, homosexuals remain extremely exposed to discrimination in the form of sexual harassment.
Here, the speaker offers another brief preview of points she plans to make. By doing so, she helps her listeners to follow the organization of her speech.	The same misconceptions that permitted the Title 7 loophole in 1964 perpetuate today. To better understand why, we must first understand the motivations behind sexual harassment and then examine the short-sighted view many take of it. First, although most people blame sexual desire for demeaning behavior, more often than not desire has nothing to do with motivating perpetrators. The *Journal of Individual Employment Rights* asserts that same-sex sexual harassment usually cannot be attributed to the sexual orientation of the victim or the perpetrator. Instead, it is a "power issue." A 2004 *Journal of Sex Roles* study clarifies that hostile sexism results from the belief that heterosexual men are superior to women and effeminate or homosexual men. That motivation means that the loophole in Title 7 not only permits heinous discrimination but also perpetuates behaviors that invoke heterosexual as the "normal" or "superior" lifestyle. This desire to maintain the status quo propels perpetrators to exploit positions of power, resulting in increasingly hostile work environments.
Here, the speaker uses a quote from an attorney involved in the lawsuit as a way of supporting her point.	The second reason why same-sex sexual harassment is so often overlooked is because of general attitudes toward interpersonal relationships between men. When the law was written over 40 years ago, the sexual harassment tenet was included solely to safeguard women from men. That concentrated focus kept lawmakers from realizing that sexual harassment may occur in ways outside of their hetero-normative viewpoint. As the attorney in the lawsuit against the Cheesecake Factory stated in the *Los Angeles Times,* "There's this expectation that this doesn't happen to men. It's almost this boys-will-be-boys attitude of 'Oh, it's just hazing, it's just teasing, you can't take it seriously.'" The servers of the Cheesecake Factory restaurant in the lawsuit reported harassment that included simulated gang rape. The managers—who were fully aware of the problem—seemed amused and took no action to prohibit the offensive behavior. Their attitude of amusement carried into the court proceedings where, according to the previously cited article from *Mondaq Legal News Network,* in the appeal of *EEOC v. Harbert-Yeargin, Inc.,* the court furthered the "horseplay" excuse and overturned the original guilty verdict by asking, "What's next? Towel slapping in the locker room?"
The speaker introduces her proposition of policy, which is a change in Title 7.	This shamefully outdated view of sexual harassment provides a breeding ground for hostility and degradation. However, solutions exist on the government and personal levels. We as citizens must petition our government officials, letting them know that we do not agree with the loophole in Title 7 but we do agree that action must be taken. I have with me a petition. At the end of this speech round, please add your name to the list alongside those who disagree with allowing a law that permits discrimination to stand. At the end of the year I will send this petition to the EEOC, the organization spearheading the movement to close the loophole in Title 7. This petition will show our support of their activism and our willingness to add our names to the cause. In an open letter released on February 28, 2008, President Obama told the LGBT [lesbian, gay, bisexual, and transgender] community that he would end workplace discrimination based on sexual orientation or gender identity. Hopefully, our outpouring of support will further encourage the president to make good on his promise and move toward equality for all by closing the loophole.

COMMENTARY	SPEECH
	A mandate on the national level would force corporations to update and streamline their policies in accordance with federal law. On a personal level, we can all take a stand against sexual harassment in any form. Most important, we must reshape our paradigms regarding what constitutes harassment. If you see something that would be considered harassment were it to take place between a man and a woman, it is harassment. Teasing is never an excuse. After all, as a community that generally prides itself in promoting acceptance, if change does not begin with us, where will it begin?
In her conclusion, the speaker reminds her listeners of her opening story, a technique that personalizes the issue.	Anytime sexual harassment occurs it is disgraceful, yet when sexual harassment is all but sanctioned under the law it is despicable. Fortunately, Joseph Oncale took his case before the U.S. Supreme Court, who decided that what happened to Oncale was indeed sexual harassment. The decision read by Justice Antonin Scalia laid the foundation to eventually protect the rights of all workers. Hopefully, the name Joseph Oncale will eventually be remembered as a pioneer in defending those whom the government had left to defend themselves.

FIGURE 1

FORMAL SPEECH OUTLINE: CLOSING THE LOOPHOLE ON SEXUAL HARASSMENT

TITLE: Closing the Loophole on Sexual Harassment

General purpose: To persuade

Purpose statement: Persuade my audience that it is the duty of a vigilant society to protect individuals from same-sex sexual harassment in the workplace.

INTRODUCTION
I. Joseph Oncale was subjected to simulated rape by his fellow male oil rig workers.
II. Despite his protests, no punishment ensued because same-sex sexual harassment is not recognized under the law.

    Thesis: Regardless of one's moral, ethical, or religious views on sexuality, everyone deserves the protection of a safe workplace.

    Transition: Describe ramifications of hostile work environment; identify loophole in sexual harassment law; offer solutions.

BODY
I. What is same-sex sexual harassment?
   A. Reporting same-sex harassment risks escalating hostility.
     1. Reporting harassment can turn a hostile work environment into an openly discriminatory one.
     2. *PR Week:* Financial director accused of assault of a male subordinate was allowed to keep his job.
   B. Those brave enough to report sexual harassment often do so without the support of the law.
     1. Title 7 of the Civil Rights Act of 1964 provides no protection from same-sex sexual harassment.
     2. *Journal of Individual Employment Rights:* As a federally unprotected class, homosexuals remain exposed to discrimination.

    Transition: To understand why same-sex harassment is permitted by the loophole, we must understand the nature of sexual harassment.
II. The law overlooks same-sex sexual harassment.
   A. Power is a motivator of demeaning behavior.
     1. *Journal of Sex Roles:* Hostile sexism results from the belief that heterosexual men are superior to women and homosexual men.
     2. The loophole therefore perpetuates the stereotype of heterosexuality as "normal."
   B. Outdated attitudes and beliefs persist about interpersonal relationships between men.
     1. Sexual harassment laws were originally intended to protect women from men.
     2. *Mondaq Legal News Network:* Courts accept the "boys will be boys" explanation for same-sex harassment.

    Transition: Obsolete views of sexual harassment encourage hostility and degradation. Solutions exist, however.
III. Solutions exist at government and personal levels.
   A. The Title 7 loophole needs to be closed.
     1. Sign petition to the Equal Employment Opportunity Commission.
     2. Obama: I will end workplace discrimination based on sexual orientation or gender identity.
   B. People should take individual stands against sexual harassment.
     1. We must reshape our ideas about what constitutes sexual harassment.
     2. Any sexual harassment should be reported to authorities.

    Transition: Any sexual harassment is disgraceful, but when sexual harassment is all but sanctioned under the law, it is despicable and must be legally prohibited.

CONCLUSION
I. Review of main points
   A. People deserve protection from sexual harassment, whether same-sex or other-sex people.
   B. Sexual harassment that is sanctioned by law is despicable.
II. Final remarks
   A. Joseph Oncale's case has been heard by the U.S. Supreme Court.
   B. His case hopefully will prompt changes to federal sexual harassment laws in the United States.

For REVIEW

- **What does it mean to persuade?**

  Persuasion is an attempt to motivate others to adopt a specific belief, opinion, or behavior. We persuade others by appealing to ethos, pathos, and/or logos.

- **In what ways can we craft a persuasive message?**

  Persuasive messages can propose facts, values, or policies. They are organized in a compelling manner and avoid the use of logical fallacies.

- **Through what strategies can we hone our persuasive-speaking skills?**

  We can adapt to our audience, build rapport with our listeners, and establish our credibility.

KEY TERMS

persuasive speaking 420

persuasion 420

belief 420

opinion 421

action 421

forms of rhetorical proof 422

ethos 422

pathos 423

logos 424

reason 424

inductive reasoning 424

deductive reasoning 425

syllogism 425

enthymeme 425

proposition 426

proposition of fact 426

proposition of value 426

proposition of policy 427

problem-solving pattern 428

refutational approach 428

comparative advantage method 429

Monroe's motivated sequence 429

logical fallacy 430

ad hominem fallacy 430

slippery slope fallacy 430

either/or fallacy 431

false-cause fallacy 431

bandwagon appeal 431

hasty generalization 431

red herring fallacy 431

straw man fallacy 431

begging the question 431

non sequitur 432

appeal to false authority 432

receptive audience 433

neutral audience 434

hostile audience 434

build rapport 436

credibility 436

NOTES

1. McCarthy, J. (2019, February 25). The 11 most inspiring speeches at the 2019 Oscars. https://www.globalcitizen.org /en/content/most-inspiring-oscars-speeches-2019/
2. Kim, D. H., Sung, Y. H., & Um, N. H. (2019). Actual Dove versus ideal L'Oréal: Impact of self-related brand image on advertising persuasiveness. *Journal of Marketing Communications, 25*(5), 535–552. https://doi.org/10.1080/13527266.2108.1561496
3. See, e.g., Wallace, L. E., Wegener, D. T., & Petty, R. E. (2019). When sources honestly provide their biased opinion: Bias as a distinct source perception with independent effects on credibility and persuasion. *Personality and Social Psychology Bulletin,* 0146167219858654. https://doi.org/10.1177/0146167219858654

4. Kallio, K. M., Kallio, T. J., Tienari, J., & Hyvönen, T. (2016). Ethos at stake: Performance management and academic work in universities. *Human Relations, 69*(3), 685–709. https://doi.org/10.1177/0018726715596802

5. Stewart, R. A. (1994). Perceptions of a speaker's initial credibility as a function of religious involvement and religious disclosiveness. *Communication Research Reports, 11*(2), 169–176. https://doi.org/10.1080/08824099409359955

6. See Koob, G. F., & Volkow, N. D. (2016). Neurobiology of addiction: A neurocircuitry analysis. *The Lancet Psychiatry, 3*(8), 760–773. https://doi.org/10.1016/S2215-0366(16)00104-8

7. See, e.g., White, B. X., & Albarracín, D. (2018). Investigating belief falsehood. Fear appeals do change behaviour in experimental laboratory studies. A commentary on Kok et al. (2018). *Health Psychology Review, 12*(2), 147–150. https://doi.org/10.1080/17437199.2018.1448292

8. Burnyeat, M. F. (2015). Enthymeme: Aristotle on the logic of persuasion. In A. Nehamas, & D. J. Furley (Eds.), *Aristotle's "Rhetoric": Philosophical essays* (pp. 3–56). Princeton University Press. https://doi.org/10.1515/9781400872879

9. Rydell, R. J., Sherman, S. J., Boucher, K. L., & Macy, J. T. (2012). The role of motivational and persuasive message factors in changing implicit attitudes toward smoking. *Basic and Applied Social Psychology, 34*(1), 1–7. https://doi.org/10.1080/01973533.2011.637847

10. Prestwich, A., Perugini, M., & Hurling, R. (2010). Can implementation intentions and text messages promote brisk walking? A randomized trial. *Health Psychology, 29*(1), 40–49. https://doi.org/10.1037/a0016993

11. DiSanza, J. R., & Legge, N. J. (2011). *Business and professional communication: Plans, processes, and performance* (5th ed.). Pearson.

12. Dowling, C. M., & Wichowsky, A. (2015). Attacks without consequence? Candidates, parties, groups, and the changing face of negative advertising. *American Journal of Political Science, 59*(1), 19–36. https://doi.org/10.1111/ajps.12094

13. See, e.g., Wright, C., & Wheatcroft, J. M. (2017). Police officers' beliefs about, and use of, cues to deception. *Journal of Investigative Psychology and Offender Profiling, 14*(3), 307–319. https://doi.org/10.1002/jip.1478

14. Kouzes, J. M., & Pozner, B. Z. (2011). *Credibility: How leaders gain and lose it, why people demand it.* John Wiley & Sons.

15. See, e.g., Mazur, J. P., & Stowe, S. A. (2016). Can teacher immediacy reduce the impact of verbal aggressiveness? Examining effects on student outcomes and perceptions of teacher credibility. *Western Journal of Communication, 80*(1), 21–37. https://doi.org/10.1080/10570314.2014.943421

16. Levy, A. (2019, June 17). Facebook will try to fix its reputation with advertisements. https://www.fool.com/investing/2019/06/17/facebook-will-try-to-fix-its-reputation-with-adver.aspx

Appendix

WORKPLACE COMMUNICATION AND INTERVIEWING

AJ_Watt/E+/Getty Images

As You READ

- What communication processes are important in the workplace?
- What communication challenges do workplaces face today?
- In what ways can we improve our interviewing skills?

Nearly all of us will be employed at some point in our lives. Whether we work for a large multinational corporation or a small business with only a few employees, our ability to communicate effectively in the workplace can matter greatly to those whose lives are affected by our work. In this appendix, we explore **workplace communication**, the interactions people have as part of their employment. We can think of workplace communication as a form of *organizational communication,* an area of study within the communication discipline devoted to understanding interactions that occur in structured groups, which often include places of employment.

• **workplace communication** The interactions people have as part of their employment.

Communicating in the Workplace

Many popular television shows—from dramas such as *NCIS* and *The Resident* to comedies such as *Brooklyn Nine-Nine* and *Superstore*—focus their storylines on how the characters communicate in the workplace. Most viewers can relate to the communication behaviors and challenges depicted in such shows. Building and maintaining workplace relationships is often difficult, although it can be highly rewarding. In this section, we survey the challenges and benefits of communicating within the workplace, look at employees' communications with people outside the workplace, and examine some key dimensions of creating a positive workplace culture.

COMMUNICATING WITHIN THE WORKPLACE

Much of workplace communication is **internal communication**, that is, the messages people within the workplace convey to one another. A face-to-face or virtual meeting of managers, a companywide e-mail message, and an employee intranet are all examples of internal communication. Internal workplace communication can be either formal or informal.

• **internal communication** The messages people within the workplace convey to one another.

Formal Workplace Communication
Formal communication consists of messages from the work organization that relate to its operations. Whether written or electronic, memos, official announcements, company newsletters, mission statements, and employee evaluations are all types of formal communication that members of many organizations regularly encounter.

• **formal communication** Messages that come from the organization and relate to its operations.

The tone and content of formal workplace communication vary according to the relative status of the sender and the audience. For instance, few of us would speak in the same way to our boss as to our peers. We can understand the effects of relative status on formal workplace communication by differentiating among communication that is upward, downward, and lateral.

- **Upward communication** consists of messages we send to people at higher levels of the organizational hierarchy than ours. These include messages to immediate supervisors as well as to higher-level employees, such as an e-mail we might send to the company president. When communicating upward, we're most likely to be taken seriously if our statements are clear, concise, and respectful.

• **upward communication** Messages we send to people at higher levels of the organizational hierarchy than we occupy.

- **Downward communication** describes messages we send to people at lower levels of the organizational hierarchy, such as subordinates, interns, and staff members who report to us. Although such messages are often instructions regarding work assignments, they may also be general announcements, explanations of policy, or notes of encouragement. When communicating downward, avoid specialized jargon and use language that anyone—regardless of his or her job—can understand. If your message contains criticism, choose your words tactfully and avoid embarrassing people by singling them out.

• **downward communication** Messages we send to people at lower levels of the organizational hierarchy, such as subordinates, interns, and staff members who report to us.

- **Lateral communication** consists of messages we share with peers, coworkers, and anyone who occupies the same position or level of power in the workplace hierarchy that we do. Effective communication with peers contributes to a positive work environment and makes the work experience more satisfying. Good lateral communication treats people as equals and helps them to accomplish the goals they share.

• **lateral communication** Messages we share with peers or anyone who occupies the same position in the organizational hierarchy as we do.

Informal Workplace Communication Formal communication—whether upward, downward, or lateral—is critical to any organization's ability to manage its image and conduct its operations. However, much of the communication in workplaces is informal. Unlike formal communication, **informal communication** is not necessarily sanctioned by the employer but arises from the social interactions of its members.

Many people say that informal communication travels along a **grapevine**, a metaphor indicating that informal messages are often conveyed in upward, downward, and lateral directions simultaneously. Just as a grapevine twists and turns in seemingly unpredictable ways as it grows, in many workplaces informal messages take a similarly unpredictable path.

Regarding communication grapevines, research tells us that:

- *Grapevines use multiple communication channels.* Much communication along the grapevine is accomplished face to face, as people visit informally (and perhaps even secretly) to share information and gossip. Workplace grapevines also make use of telephone, e-mail, text messaging, instant messaging, and other forms of electronically mediated communication, allowing people to participate who aren't physically present.[1]

- *People rely heavily on the grapevine during a crisis.* When employees feel threatened by a situation, such as the announcement of upcoming layoffs, they can spend as much as 70 percent of their workplace communication time on the grapevine, listening to what others know and speculating about what they've heard. Particularly when a situation is ambiguous, we seem to crave the comfort of our informal communication networks.[2]

- *Communication along the grapevine can be remarkably accurate.* The informality of grapevine communication doesn't mean it's inaccurate. Studies show that grapevine messages are substantially accurate 75 to 95 percent of the time. Equally important, employees tend to *believe* grapevine messages are accurate, maybe even more accurate than the employer's formal communication.[3]

COMMUNICATING TO EXTERNAL AUDIENCES

Nearly all organizations also communicate regularly with external audiences. When conducted effectively, **external communication**—that is, messages people within the workplace convey to others outside the organization—can significantly enhance the company's reputation, productivity, community support, and economic success. In contrast, poorly managed external communication can cause a workplace irreparable harm.

Among the many external audiences with whom companies must communicate are these:

- *Consumers,* or anyone who buys or might buy a company's products or services. For many organizations, a primary vehicle for communicating with consumers is advertising. Companies advertise their goods or services in multiple ways, including television and radio commercials; print advertisements and inserts in newspapers and magazines; electronic ads posted on the Internet or sent via e-mail or smartphone; corporate web pages, social media pages, and Twitter feeds; signs and billboards visible to drivers; unsolicited sales calls made in person or by telephone; and booths at fairs, trade shows, and sporting events. To explore one career requiring frequent communication with consumers, check out "Putting Communication to Work."

- *Potential members,* or anyone who might come to work for the organization as either a paid employee or a volunteer. Corporations, nonprofit groups, and the military frequently recruit employees or volunteers through television, radio, and social network and Internet ads.

• informal communication Communication that is not sanctioned by an organization but arises from the social interactions of its members.

• grapevine A metaphor used to indicate that informal messages are often conveyed in upward, downward, and lateral directions simultaneously.

• external communication Communication with people outside the organization.

putting**communication**to**work**

[   ] Search

Job Title >

Work Responsibilities >

Account Manager for Telecommunications Company

The primary responsibility of an account manager is to communicate with customers and ensure their satisfaction with the company's products and services. Account managers intervene to solve problems when consumers are dissatisfied, and they describe new products and services in which consumers may be interested. The position requires excellent listening skills as well as an ability to anticipate what customers want or need.

Jupiterimages/Polka Dot/Getty Images

- *Stockholders*, or people who own shares of a publicly traded company. Companies communicate with their stockholders primarily through their annual reports, which detail the financial gains and losses of a company's endeavors over the course of a year.

- *The media*, which include broadcast, print, and electronic forms of mass communication. Many organizations have spokespersons or media relations managers who accommodate reporters' requests for informational interviews or statements to include in news features.

- *Lawmakers*, including local elected officials, state legislators, and members of Congress. In October 2019, for instance, the chief executive officer of the aerospace manufacturer Boeing testified before a panel of the U.S. Senate to discuss what his company is doing to prevent future problems with the 737 MAX jet, which made headlines earlier that year when two new 737 jets crashed within five months, killing hundreds.

- *The general public*, which includes current or potential customers and employees and anyone else to whom an employer's reputation matters. Many large companies employ public relations experts who use communication to shape their public image.

WORKPLACE CULTURE

Pixar Animation Studios in Emeryville, California, is an unconventional place to work. To stimulate innovative, outside-the-box thinking, company president Ed Catmull instituted Pixar University. This professional-development program encourages risk taking and invites irrational thought as avenues to creativity. To minimize stress, Catmull makes a physician and a massage therapist available to Pixar employees several times a month, and he requires animators to get special permission to work more than 50 hours in a single week. The animation studio boasts a café, break rooms with pool and foosball tables, and an open area for concerts and lectures. At the urging of former Pixar CEO

Steve Jobs, Catmull even created one giant bathroom for the company's 700 employees so people across the organization would regularly interact and talk. Its innovations have put Pixar on the map as a company with a remarkable workplace culture.

Throughout this text, we have talked about culture as the collective values, customs, and communication behaviors shared among people in a particular country or social group. Communication researchers believe that workplaces and other organizations have their own cultures. We can think of **organizational culture** as the values, customs, and communication behaviors that workplace members share and that reflect their organization's distinct identity. We can understand workplace culture by examining its rites, rituals, and roles.

Workplaces Have Rites

Organizational rites are ceremonial acts and practices that convey characteristics of an organization's culture, which can include the culture of a workplace. Organizational behavior scholars Harrison Trice and Janice Beyer identified six types of workplace rites:[4]

- *Rites of passage* signify people's advancement to a higher status or level in a workplace. Ceremonies to celebrate an employee's promotion are examples of rites of passage.
- *Rites of integration* enhance feelings of inclusion and community in the workplace. Participation in a company's annual picnic, for instance, can reinforce employees' sense of belonging to the group.
- *Blaming rites* are concerned with consequences for poor or unethical performance. For example, attorneys who violate client confidentiality might be reprimanded, demoted, or fired and may lose their license to practice law.
- *Enhancement rites* relate to consequences for superior performance. Excellent salespeople might receive plaques, cash bonuses, trips, or recognition as Salesperson of the Year in acknowledgment of outstanding achievement.
- *Renewal rites* update and revitalize a workplace. After a particularly disappointing year of collecting donations, for example, a nonprofit group might organize a retreat to boost morale and refresh its employees' solicitation skills.
- *Conflict resolution rites* aim to manage disagreements and discord. To resolve conflicts between management and employees, a large corporation might use a mediator to help representatives from each group reach consensus on their disagreements.

Workplaces Have Rituals

Whereas rites occur when circumstances call for them, **organizational rituals** are repeated behaviors that provide a familiar routine to an organization's experiences.[5] In workplaces, three types of rituals are especially common:

1. *Personal rituals* are routine behaviors through which individuals convey their workplace identity.[6] On the first day of each fiscal year, a manager might personally greet each arriving employee as a way of communicating her interest in their well-being.
2. *Social rituals* are recurring events that reinforce personal relationships among workplace members.[7] The custodial staff at a government agency might meet every other Thursday for happy hour, for example, in a ritual that allows them to socialize, share information, and affirm their personal bonds.
3. *Task rituals* are repeated activities that enhance people's abilities to do their jobs. For example, when greeting a patient at a clinic, a medical assistant typically performs a series of ritualized tasks, such as asking about symptoms, current medications, and drug allergies and then taking the patient's vital signs.

- **organizational culture** The values, customs, and communication behaviors that organization members share and that reflect the organization's distinct identity.

- **organizational rites** Ceremonial acts and practices that convey characteristics of an organization's culture.

- **organizational rituals** Repeated behaviors that provide a familiar routine to an organization's experiences.

SHARPEN Your Skills: *Workplace rites*

Identify a rite that is common in your workplace. Observe the communication behaviors that rite affects, and in what ways. Notice especially how it influences your own communication. Write up your observations in a short paragraph or journal entry.

Many rites and rituals reinforce a workplace's current cultural practices. As a workplace culture evolves, however, its rites and rituals often follow suit. In recent years, for instance, the U.S. Transportation Security Administration has changed its task rituals for screening airline passengers. Those changes include requiring passengers to remove their shoes for X-ray screening and limiting the types and amounts of liquid that passengers can bring aboard an airplane.

Workplaces Have Roles As we saw in the chapter on communicating in intimate relationships, people in families enact different *roles*, which embody their functions within the family system. The same can be said of people in workplaces. Each employee has certain responsibilities to the group that reflect his or her role.

Some workplace roles are **formal roles**, functions that are prescribed by the employer itself. The formal role of a receptionist, for instance, may be to greet visitors, provide directions to specific company facilities, issue visitor passes, and answer incoming telephone calls. Formal roles are interconnected in a system that fulfills all necessary functions of the workplace. Organizational charts, such as the one in Figure 1, specify the connections among various roles in a fictitious manufacturing company.

Formal roles are tied to *positions* within the workplace rather than to particular individuals. The formal role of a receptionist is the same no matter who has that job. In contrast, **informal roles** are functions adopted by specific people rather than being dictated by the workplace. Whereas formal roles serve the organization's professional needs, informal roles often evolve to serve social and interpersonal needs. At his advertising agency, for instance, Jay is known as someone with an exceptional sense of humor who can always be counted on to bring comic relief to stressful situations. We might say that Jay has assumed the informal role of company comedian.

• **formal roles** Roles that involve functions prescribed by the organization itself.

• **informal roles** Functions that are adopted by specific people rather than dictated by the organization.

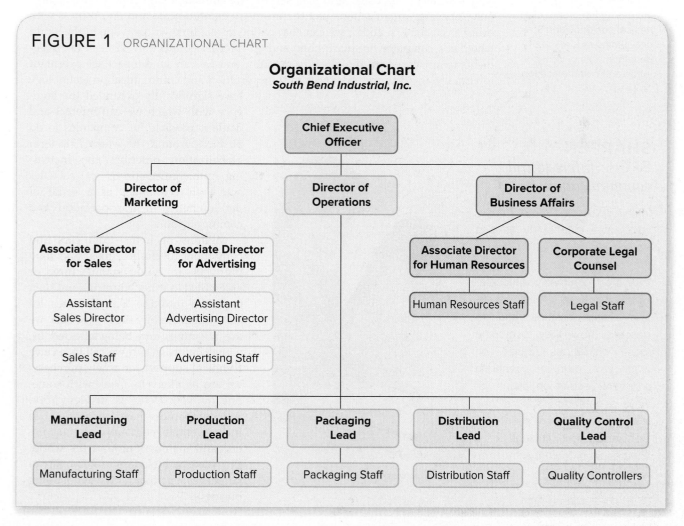

FIGURE 1 ORGANIZATIONAL CHART

Organizational Chart
South Bend Industrial, Inc.

- Chief Executive Officer
  - Director of Marketing
    - Associate Director for Sales
      - Assistant Sales Director
        - Sales Staff
    - Associate Director for Advertising
      - Assistant Advertising Director
        - Advertising Staff
  - Director of Operations
    - Manufacturing Lead
      - Manufacturing Staff
    - Production Lead
      - Production Staff
    - Packaging Lead
      - Packaging Staff
    - Distribution Lead
      - Distribution Staff
    - Quality Control Lead
      - Quality Controllers
  - Director of Business Affairs
    - Associate Director for Human Resources
      - Human Resources Staff
    - Corporate Legal Counsel
      - Legal Staff

No one formally assigned him that responsibility; it wasn't included in his job description or detailed in his contract. Moreover, that role is tied specifically to Jay because of his personality and sense of humor; it would not necessarily be expected of the next person to occupy Jay's position. For those reasons, company comedian is an informal role.

An informal role isn't necessarily any less important than a formal role. Indeed, research shows that sharing humor in the workplace—as Jay does informally—can reinforce company culture,[8] alleviate tension,[9] foster creativity,[10] and enhance interpersonal relationships.[11] Many informal roles employees might play—including conflict mediator, confidante, or social event organizer—are seen by others as indispensable to the group's success.

Managing Workplace Communication Challenges

Everyone in workplace organizations—large and small—encounters communication challenges from time to time. Although no list can enumerate every possible challenge, we can appreciate the communication trials that employees face by examining four issues: globalization, communication technology, work/life conflict, and diversity.

GLOBALIZATION AND CROSS-CULTURAL CHALLENGES

The world has shrunk considerably—figuratively speaking, at least—in the past 100 years. Almost unbelievably, travel time between continents used to be measured in weeks rather than hours. Only a few decades ago, telephone calls to other countries were extremely expensive, and mail service was unreliable and slow. Consequently, only very large organizations had the means to communicate and do business with overseas customers. Today, we can chat online in real time with anyone in the world who has a computer or smartphone and an Internet connection. We can fax documents to any corner of the globe in minutes, and we can send a package overnight to virtually any country. Advances in transportation and communication technology have significantly expanded the audience with which we can interact and made it possible for companies to do business around the world. The term **globalization** describes the increasing interconnectedness of societies and their economies as a result of developments in transportation and communication.

• **globalization** The increasing interconnectedness of societies and their economies as a result of developments in transportation and communication.

Millions of items—from cars and computers to clothes, toys, and food products—are either manufactured or assembled in other countries and then imported into the United States for sale. When we buy those products, we are affecting, and being affected by, globalization. When we call to receive technical support for a new purchase, we are as likely to speak with someone in New Delhi as in New York. As companies have expanded to include employees, suppliers, customers, and members around the world, they have had to adapt to a diversity of languages, customs, and ways of doing business.

ColorBlind Images/Blend Images LLC

COMMUNICATION TECHNOLOGY CHALLENGES

Few organizations today could operate as they do without communication technology. E-mail, videoconferencing, text messaging, telephone and fax machines, and workplace websites allow individuals to work together without *being* together and to communicate with unprecedented efficiency. More than 80 percent of U.S. adults report going online daily, and nearly a third say they are almost constantly connected to some form of online communication, according to a 2019 study by the Pew Research Center.[12] Such technologies have significantly expanded the audience a workplace can reach, while simultaneously making communication faster and more cost-effective. Like many innovations, however, communication technology has also presented new challenges.

Choosing a Communication Channel One challenge of using communication technology in the workplace is deciding which technology to employ in a given situation. Recall from the introductory chapter that some communication contexts are *channel-rich*, meaning they allow people to perceive several communication behaviors at once. The most channel-rich context is the face-to-face conversation because it provides communicators access to each other's words, gestures, facial expressions, vocalic behaviors, touch, and scent. When face-to-face meetings are not feasible, however, a webcam conversation provides the next most channel-rich context. In a webcam conversation, participants can see and hear one another in **real time**, meaning simultaneously, as they are communicating.

> • **real time** A simultaneous form of mediated communication in which messages are exchanged, interpreted, and responded to instantaneously, similar to a face-to-face conversation.

Other communication technologies provide *channel-lean* contexts, which means they restrict the number of communication channels people can perceive. Texting and instant messaging, for instance, allow people to communicate in real time but with only words and emoji that approximate facial expressions. The communicators cannot feel one another's touch, smell their scent, or see their gestures and facial expressions as they can in contexts that offer more communication channels. E-mails and posts to an electronic bulletin board, blog, or Facebook or other social media wall are even more channel-lean than text and instant messages because they normally do not constitute real-time communication and may not be read for hours or even days.

Ensuring Security A second challenge for workplaces—and for many individuals—is ensuring the security of information they communicate, particularly online. Because companies rely so heavily on e-mail to communicate with their internal and external audiences, concerns over the security of e-mail messages have become paramount. In 1986, the U.S. Congress enacted the Electronic Communications Privacy Act (ECPA) to protect the privacy of electronic communication. The ECPA prohibits intercepting a person's private e-mail messages without consent and prevents the government from requiring electronic communication providers (such as Google and Yahoo) to disclose their subscribers' identity except in a narrow range of circumstances. Some workplaces add an addendum to outgoing e-mails notifying the recipient that the messages are protected by the law. Figure 2 provides an example of one such addendum.

Reducing Distraction A third challenge posed by communication technology is the time it takes to keep up with it. According to one survey, the average worker receives over 120 e-mail messages per day.[13] Although some of those messages are related to work, others are personal messages or unsolicited advertisements. Attending to all that e-mail during work hours can be distracting and can reduce productivity.

Distraction is an even bigger danger when employees use the Internet during work hours for personal activities such as shopping, banking, blogging, and social networking. One survey found that 64 percent of workers conduct personal business online during work hours.[14] At least half of all U.S. companies monitor their employees' Internet and e-mail use, and 22 percent of employers have fired someone for inappropriate Internet use during work hours.[15] Know your employer's policy on using the Internet for personal business, and be mindful of the ways it can reduce your own productivity.

FIGURE 2 E-MAIL MESSAGE ADDENDUM REGARDING PRIVACY

| Send | Save draft | Spell check | Attach | Cancel |

To:

Subject:

B *I* <u>U</u> ▀ ▀ ▀ ▀ ▤ ▤ ▤ ▤ ▤ ⬤ ≝ **A**

```
CONFIDENTIAL COMMUNICATION
This Email is covered by the Electronic Communications Privacy Act, 18 U.S.C.
2510-2521 and is legally privileged. The information contained in this Email
is intended only for use of the individual or entity named above. If the
reader of this message is not the intended recipient, or the employee or agent
responsible to deliver it to the intended recipient, you are hereby notified
that any dissemination, distribution or copying of this communication is
strictly prohibited.
```

WORK/LIFE CONFLICT

• **work/life conflict** The pressure of balancing the demands of work with those of nonwork life.

The typical U.S. family of the 1950s was supported financially by only one parent, usually the father, working full-time. In the twenty-first century, however, *dual-career families*—in which both adults work full-time—and *single-parent families*—in which one parent works full-time and takes care of children—are more common.[16] The pressure of balancing the demands of work with the rest of life's activities creates a **work/life conflict** for many people that can be highly problematic for them and their employers if not managed constructively.

Two types of work/life conflict occur. The first is *life interference with work*, which happens when people's life responsibilities impede their job performance. If Ramon's elderly mother falls ill and requires his help, for instance, he may miss work or important deadlines. The second type is *work interference with life*, which happens when people's job responsibilities hinder their ability to fulfill personal obligations. If Simi's position requires her to travel frequently, for example, her repeated absences may make it difficult to maintain close friendships.

Advances in communication technology may actually contribute to increased work/life conflict. Consider that if you carry a smartphone or use an Internet-connected tablet, you may receive work-related e-mail messages even when you aren't working, such as during evenings, weekends, or holidays. Some people are successful at ignoring such messages until they return to work, but others read and even respond to such messages outside of their work hours, which can allow work to interfere with their family time and nonwork life.

• **burnout** Chronic sense of exhaustion or apathy that can come from long-term frustration and stress.

Studies have shown that individuals with significant work/life conflict are at elevated risk of health problems such as depression[17] and sleep disorders.[18] They also experience increased job stress and reduced satisfaction with life,[19] marriage,[20] and family relationships.[21] Finally, individuals with substantial work/life conflict aren't very happy.[22] One of the most harmful effects of work/life conflict is **burnout**, a chronic sense of exhaustion or apathy that can come from long-term frustration and stress. Burnout isn't a component of work/life conflict; it's a result of it. When their employees experience burnout, workplaces suffer in the form of increased absenteeism,[23] lost productivity,[24] and decreased communicative effectiveness.[25]

Individuals can also feel conflicted about their work lives when they experience sexual harassment in the workplace. See "The Dark Side of Communication" to explore this problem.

THE DARK SIDE OF COMMUNICATION

Sexual Harassment in the Workplace

richyrichimages/Getty Images

A serious problem arises in the workplace when employees feel they have been sexually harassed by their superiors. In the United States, the Equal Employment Opportunity Commission (EEOC) defines sexual harassment as unsolicited, unwelcome behavior of a sexual nature in the workplace. You might intend to be friendly or supportive by putting your arm around a subordinate, for instance, but if the subordinate feels uncomfortable by your behavior, it may constitute harassment.

According to the EEOC, sexual harassment can occur in two forms. The first, *quid pro quo* (a Latin phrase meaning "this for that") harassment, happens when a supervisor offers an employee rewards in exchange for sexual favors. A statement such as "I'll give you tomorrow off if you have a drink with me tonight" can qualify as quid pro quo harassment if it is directed at a subordinate. The second form, hostile work environment harassment, occurs when work conditions are sexually offensive or intimidating. Telling sexually suggestive jokes when both men and women are present, or making derogatory comments about a person's sexual orientation, can qualify as hostile work environment harassment.

Sexual harassment is a serious and pervasive problem in some workplaces, and its victims often suffer long-term emotional and psychological harm. If you ever feel you are being sexually harassed, it can be hard to speak up, but ignoring the situation won't make it go away. Remember that sexual harassment is illegal and you have a right not to be victimized.

Sometimes, all it takes to stop harassment is for you to speak up and tell another person that his or her behavior offends you. If you're uncomfortable doing so, or if the offensive behavior continues afterward, report the situation to your organization's human resources department or affirmative action office.

SOURCE: www.eeoc.gov/laws/types/sexual_harassment.cfm

WORKPLACE DIVERSITY

In many workplaces, employees represent a mix of different cultures, religious beliefs, mental and physical abilities, educational achievements, ages, genders, and political orientations.[26] It's therefore likely that workplace experiences will expose us to people with backgrounds, customs, and ways of thinking that are quite different from our own.[27] Many organizations regard such diversity as an essential asset because it may produce more innovative ideas than a homogeneous staff would.

Yet diversity can pose challenges for communication and interpersonal interaction. Working with people whose capabilities, beliefs, and life experiences differ dramatically from our own can be frustrating. Our personal background leads each of us to take certain ideas and experiences for granted that others may not. For instance, when scheduling a meeting of a work team, it may not occur to you that the date you set is an important religious holiday for some in the group. Recognizing and adapting to people's differences can improve our ability to work harmoniously and productively with others.

You can improve your adaptability to workplace diversity if you:

- *Check your assumptions.* When you send an e-mail to coworkers, for instance, do you tend to assume everyone will understand your terminology? Do you assume the recipients will all share the priorities your message conveys? If there's a chance your assumptions may not be valid, adjust your message before sending it.

- *Remember that being different doesn't mean being wrong.* If, say, your religious beliefs are very important to you, you might tend to see alternative ideas as wrong. That tendency can make it difficult to communicate openly and respectfully with people whose beliefs differ from yours. There are many ways to think about religion, and your beliefs are "right" to you only because *you* believe them. Others see their beliefs as right because they believe them. Having a different orientation from you doesn't make someone else wrong, only different. Just as you want others to treat your beliefs respectfully, you should extend that courtesy to them.

- *Help others to adapt.* Being adaptable to diversity doesn't mean only respecting and accommodating others—it also means informing others when they're ignoring your needs or beliefs. Through your honest input, they can learn to be more adaptable as well. When someone doesn't acknowledge your uniqueness, point out—tactfully and respectfully—that your background gives you experiences, beliefs, priorities, and needs he or she may not be recognizing.

Interviewing Successfully

People conduct interviews for various reasons, many of which are related to the workplace. Your ability to participate successfully in interviews can therefore be an asset when communicating in the workplace. We'll begin this section by exploring the diverse purposes of interviewing. We'll then consider how you can land, and subsequently prepare for, a successful job interview and how you should respond to discriminatory questions if you encounter them.

WHAT IS AN INTERVIEW?

- **interview** A structured conversation in which one person poses questions to which another person responds.

A useful and versatile component of workplace communication is the **interview**, a structured conversation that focuses on questions and answers.[28] When we hear the word *interview*, many of us think immediately of a job interview. The job interview—which we will examine below as an example of a *selection interview*—is critical in the workplace; after all, most of us won't be hired in the first place unless we succeed at the job interview. There are, however, *many* forms of interviewing, some of which occur commonly in the workplace.

TYPES OF INTERVIEWS

Interviews are of different types and have varying purposes, including these:

- **appraisal interview** A discussion focused on an employee's performance and goals for the future.

- *The appraisal interview.* Whenever you sit down with someone to discuss your performance and your goals for the future, you're taking part in an **appraisal interview**. In many lines of work, managers and supervisors conduct appraisals of all their employees on a yearly basis. The appraisal interview can encourage you to continue what you're doing well and guide you in ways to improve.[29]

- **problem-solving interview** A discussion conducted to identify solutions to a problem or conflict.

- *The problem-solving interview.* A **problem-solving interview** occurs to understand the nature of a problem and identify potential solutions. You take part in problem-solving interviews, for instance, when you discuss treatment options for an illness with your physician or financial options for a mortgage with your banker.[30]

- **exit interview** A conversation about an employee's experiences with an organization that he or she is leaving.

- *The exit interview.* If you've resigned from an organization to take a job elsewhere, you may be asked to complete an **exit interview**, a conversation about your experiences with the organization you're leaving. During an exit interview, you usually would describe both positive and negative aspects of your job, your supervisors, and the organization.

- **counseling interview** An interaction aimed at supporting an individual through a personal problem.

- *The counseling interview.* When you go through a difficult time, you might reach out to close friends, relatives, or a professional therapist. With those people, you can express your feelings, receive empathy, and gain an outside perspective on your situation. That type of conversation—whether conducted with a therapist or a loved one—constitutes a **counseling interview**, an interaction aimed at supporting an individual through a personal problem.

- *The service-oriented interview.* A **service-oriented interview** is a conversation oriented toward helping you with a product or service you have purchased. When you tell the customer service representative at the clothing store that you've discovered a torn lining in a jacket you just bought, he may examine the jacket and offer either to refund your money or to exchange your damaged jacket.

- *The persuasive interview.* If you've ever received a telephone call asking you to support a political candidate or vote a certain way on a proposition, you've participated in a **persuasive interview**, a conversation intended to affect your belief, opinion, or behavior. During elections, it's common for campaign workers to call or visit registered voters to encourage them to vote in a particular way. You also take part in persuasive interviews when people try to convince you to donate money or volunteer your time.

- *The survey interview.* Each decade, the federal government conducts a *census*, a survey to count and gather information about the U.S. population. To collect census data, government workers may visit or call households and businesses. If you were to be visited by a census surveyor, you would likely be asked a variety of questions, including "How many people live in your household?" and "How many of you are employed full-time?" Your conversation with the census worker constitutes a **survey interview**, an interaction aimed at gathering information.

- *The selection interview.* A **selection interview** is a conversation intended to help the interviewer to choose the most appropriate person for a position, an assignment, a promotion, or an award. When you interview for a job, you are taking part in a selection interview. The ability to succeed in selection interviews is critical to your chances for employment.

LANDING A JOB INTERVIEW

Your first conversation with a potential employer is likely to occur during a selection interview in which you're competing for a specific job. Only rarely do jobs come looking for you. Landing a job interview typically requires identifying employment opportunities in your field of interest and preparing a professional résumé and cover letter to submit for those vacancies. This section contains tips for accomplishing those tasks and also for ensuring that your hard work is not undermined by your online persona.

Conduct a Job Search The first step in landing a job interview is to identify positions for which to apply. An excellent place to start is with your friends, family members, instructors, and anyone you know who works in your field of interest. Tell those people the kind of work you want to do, and ask for ideas about where to look. They may be able to put you in touch with employers in your field who are looking for people to hire and also give you pointers for connecting with other potential employers.

Most colleges and universities also have job placement centers where employers can post announcements of vacancies. Because those centers exist specifically to help students find jobs, they can be a valuable resource for identifying opportunities. Get to know the staff at your placement office and find out about the resources available to you there.

You can also search for job openings on your own. Websites such as Indeed.com, Monster.com, CareerBuilder.com, and CollegeRecruiter.com help you search for jobs by location, field, or company. They describe available openings and allow you to apply for the jobs online. Some websites specialize in advertising positions within a specific field. For instance, TeacherJobs.com posts vacancies for educators, and MedicalJobs.org lists openings for positions in a variety of health care fields. You can also identify vacancies at specific companies by looking at their individual websites, often at the page called "Employment" or "Careers."

Prepare a Cover Letter and Résumé When you find job postings that catch your interest, the next step is to communicate that interest to the employers. In many cases, you will make your first contact with an employer in the form of a cover letter and résumé. Because many employers receive dozens or even hundreds of applications for each available position, you need to ensure that your cover letter and résumé make a positive first impression.

• **service-oriented interview** A conversation oriented toward helping people with a product or service they have purchased.

• **persuasive interview** A conversation intended to affect beliefs, opinions, or behaviors.

• **survey interview** An interaction aimed at gathering information.

• **selection interview** A conversation intended to help the interviewer choose the most appropriate person for a position, an assignment, a promotion, or an award.

The Cover Letter A **cover letter** is a short letter in which you describe the type of position you are interested in. In your cover letter, you have the opportunity to explain why you are seeking the kind of job you want and to indicate how your education, skills, and experience would benefit the employer.

Some applicants write long, detailed cover letters describing their every qualification for the position. That approach is almost never a good strategy. The reason is that your potential employer will likely have stacks of cover letters to read and may not have the time to peruse yours in depth. Remember that the goal of your cover letter isn't to land you the job—it's to land you the job *interview*. Cover letters shouldn't contain your life story; they should hit the highlights and make the employer want to know more about you.

On some occasions, you will print and sign your cover letter and then mail or hand-deliver it to a prospective employer. At other times, you will send your cover letter as an e-mail attachment or upload it onto an organization's human resources website. When sending a cover letter as an e-mail attachment, it is often best to save the letter in a PDF format, which will preserve the exact look you want your letter to have and will also prevent anyone in the organization from intentionally or accidentally making changes to your document. Human resources websites usually have specific formatting guidelines for uploading cover letters, so make sure to read and follow those exactly.

To write a compelling cover letter, pay attention to these tips:

- *Remember that your cover letter makes a first impression.* You want an employer's first impression of you to be entirely positive. A perfect, error-free cover letter can immediately set you apart from other job applicants.

- *Clearly identify the position you are seeking.* Your potential employer may be reviewing applications for several—sometimes hundreds of—positions at the same time. To ensure that your application is routed appropriately, clearly and prominently identify the position you are applying for in your cover letter.

- *Be focused and concise.* Given large applicant pools for every opening, potential employers prefer shorter, more concise cover letters. Aim for three to five targeted paragraphs that focus on your main selling points—your key abilities and attributes—and how they match the employer's needs.

- *Use a tone that is confident but not arrogant.* One of the most challenging aspects of the cover letter is getting the tone right. Employers are looking for employees who can contribute, so you should mention how your unique abilities can help the company. Yet, hiring managers may view excessive self-praise as arrogance.

- *Tailor your cover letter to the job posting and the employer's needs.* By carefully reading the job announcement, you can prioritize your selling points so they are tailored to the position of interest. This approach not only accentuates your ability to do the job; it also shows you have researched the position and are responsive to the needs of the company.

Figure 3 contains a sample cover letter. Notice how the writer expresses his interest in the job, mentions his qualifications, and then says he looks forward to discussing the position further. For most positions, a brief and direct letter such as the sample is best.

The Résumé A **résumé** is a short document listing your employment qualifications. When you're applying for an entry-level position, it is usually best to keep your résumé to one page. As you progress in your career, your résumé may grow in length, but you should always strive to keep it straightforward and clear.

There are several ways to compile a résumé. You'll generally want to include the following details:

- *Name and contact information.* Be certain that your name appears at the top of your résumé and is followed by your mailing address, telephone number, and e-mail address. Ensure that the telephone number you provide has a clear, professional voice mail message.

FIGURE 3 SAMPLE COVER LETTER

1001 Main Street
Seattle, WA 98195
(206) 555–4844
d.shaffer@gmail.com

May 2, 2020

Ms. Ellen Hurston, Sales Manager
Chrysalis Publishing
342 Eighth Avenue, Suite 11
Chicago, IL 60603

Dear Ms. Hurston:

In response to your advertisement in the April 28, 2020 issue of *The Chicago Sun-Times*, enclosed is my résumé for the position of sales associate with Chrysalis Publishing. I am currently a senior majoring in communication at the University of Washington and have a strong interest in using my sales experience and interpersonal skills in the field of academic publishing.

Currently I am the Sales Manager for *The Daily*, the student newspaper at the University of Washington, which has a daily circulation of nearly 30,000. In my position, I coordinate the sale of classified advertising for both campus and corporate clients, and I oversee a staff of 12 part-time student salespeople. This position has given me valuable experience with building and maintaining professional relationships and ensuring high-quality customer service for the newspaper's clients. I would love the opportunity to put those skills to use for Chrysalis Publishing.

My publishing experience also includes work as a copyeditor for Grand Systems Publishing, a producer of technical writing textbooks, and as a sales associate for Barnes & Noble. Both of those positions have helped me to hone my communication, sales, and customer service skills, which I believe would be advantageous in the academic publishing industry.

I am fluent in both English and Spanish and have experience working with people from diverse ethnic and cultural backgrounds. I am also proficient in Microsoft computer programs, including Word, Excel, PowerPoint, and Pages. If you would like a list of personal and professional references, I would be glad to furnish it.

Thank you for the opportunity to apply for the position of sales associate with Chrysalis Publishing. I will look forward to discussing my skills and experience with you in person.

Sincerely yours,

David Shaffer

David Shaffer

- *Employment objective.* Briefly describe the type of position you are seeking and the kind of employer for whom you wish to work. If you will be applying for several different types of jobs, create different versions of your résumé so you can keep your employment objectives as specific as possible.

- *Education.* Identify the schools you have attended and the degrees or certificates you have earned (or are expecting to earn) at each. Note your academic major and areas of concentration, and list your grade point average if you think it will help to make your application competitive.

- *Employment experience.* Starting with your current or most recent job, list the jobs you have had that are relevant to the type of employment you are seeking. For each job, identify your job title, employer, dates of employment, and primary responsibilities. Even if you worked on a volunteer basis in some cases, include the positions most relevant to the work you are seeking now.

- *Skills and interests.* In this section, tell your potential employer about any special skills you have and about your major interests. If you're fluent in sign language, certified in CPR, or proficient at computer programming, say so. Potential employers may find your skills and interests to be particularly attractive.

- *References.* Your employment references should be individuals who can attest to your skills, work ethic, and character. They typically include current or former employers, college instructors, coaches, and others who can verify that you are responsible and proficient. It is usually best not to include relatives, romantic partners, and others whose assessments of you would seem biased by their personal feelings. You can either list your references and their contact information on your résumé or indicate that you will provide those details on request. Be sure to ask permission from your references before including their contact information on your résumé.

As with cover letters, you may submit your résumé in printed form or you may send it by e-mail or upload it onto a human resources website. Once again, a PDF format often works best for e-mail attachments, as that will ensure your résumé looks exactly the way you want it to when a recipient opens it. Be sure to read and follow any formatting directions when uploading a résumé onto a website.

Figure 4 illustrates a sample résumé. You might consult the placement office at your college or university for additional examples.

Check Your Online Persona In your job search, you have carefully crafted your résumé and cover letter to portray yourself as competent, professional, and responsible. Don't make the mistake, however, of believing those documents constitute all the information a potential employer could find about you. What would a human resources director learn about you if he or she Googled your name? Would there be overly personal comments on Twitter? Would he or she read on Facebook that your interests include "getting smashed every weekend"?

There's a simple way to find out. Google your own name, and see what comes up. Whatever information you can find about yourself online will be easily accessible to any potential employer. You may consider it an invasion of your privacy for employers to consult the Internet for information about you. Once you post something online, however, it becomes accessible not only to your friends but also to anyone seeking information about you, including a prospective employer.

If your Google search on your name returns anything that you wouldn't want a potential employer to see, take that information down or make it accessible to authorized viewers only (such as your closest Facebook friends). Alternatively, change your name on social media—temporarily, at least—so that prospective employers would have a difficult time finding you online. The last thing you want is to lose a job opportunity because a human resources manager sees your spring break pictures on Facebook and concludes that you don't have the character or the maturity to perform competently in the job.

FIGURE 4 SAMPLE RÉSUMÉ

David Shaffer

1001 Main Street, Seattle WA 98195
(206) 555–4844 d.shaffer@gmail.com

Employment Objective
To obtain an entry-level sales position for an academic publishing company.

Education
Bachelor of Arts, Communication, University of Washington   May 2020
    Cumulative GPA: 3.69/4.00
    Dean's List five out of six quarters

Associate of Arts, Liberal Studies, Seattle Community College   May 2018
    Cumulative GPA: 3.80/4.00
    Graduated *magna cum laude*

Employment Experience
Sales Manager, *The Daily*, University of Washington, August 2018–present
    Coordinate sales of advertising for major university student newspaper. Maintain business relationships with nearly 100 corporate accounts. Provide customer service and editorial support. Responsible for increasing advertising revenue by 15%.

Copyeditor, Grand Systems Publishing, Seattle WA, February 2017–August 2018
    Edited technical writing book produced for undergraduate and graduate students in engineering, city planning, and design. Developed software to reduce copyediting errors.

Sales Associate, Barnes & Noble, Seattle WA, September 2015–January 2017
    Assisted customers with locating books. Conducted sales transactions. Stocked book shelves. Provided assistance for publication deliveries. Responsible for closing store at night.

Skills and Interests
Computer skills: Word, Excel, PowerPoint, Pages.

Language skills: Fluent in English and Spanish.

Other interests: Writing, software design, cross-country skiing.

References
Furnished upon request.

SUCCEEDING IN A JOB INTERVIEW

Now that you've landed a job interview, how can you ensure that you're ready to negotiate the interview successfully? Job selection interviews can be stressful and even daunting, but you can manage those challenges if you're prepared. In this section, we survey some crucial strategies for winning the job.

Research Your Potential Employer One of the best ways to prepare for a successful job selection interview is to learn as much as you can about your potential employer. Let's say you are interviewing for a marketing position at a major sportswear retailer. Before your interview, you will want to find out about the company's size, the location of its headquarters and major divisions, its top officers, and its past and recent history. Explore the company's website and other sites that discuss the firm for that information, or look for it in the company's annual report, which you may be able to download. You can also get a sense of the company's culture by searching online for recent stories about it.

In addition, learn as much as you can about the specific position for which you're applying, such as the facility where you would be working, the size of the marketing division, and the manager to whom you'd be reporting. Carefully reading the job description and searching the website for information about the marketing division—if there is one—should give you some clues.

Anticipate Likely Questions A major reason job selection interviews are stressful is that you don't usually know beforehand what questions the interviewer will ask. However, you can anticipate many and prepare for them. Let's first briefly examine the most common types of questions and identify successful responses to each.

- *Open-ended questions* invite a broad range of answers. Examples include "Tell me about yourself," and "What are your goals for the future?" An open-ended question gives you the opportunity to reply in a way that reflects positively on you. In response to a question about your goals, for instance, you can focus on two or three that are relevant to the job and explain how you are already working toward attaining them.

- *Closed-ended questions* prompt brief, specific answers. Some call for a simple yes or no, such as "Can you work weekends?" Others elicit particular pieces of information, such as "What was your college major?" When you're asked closed-ended questions, it is best to provide short, direct answers. If the interviewer wants you to elaborate on your answer, he or she will ask you to do so.

- *Hypothetical questions* describe a realistic situation and ask you to speculate about how you would react if you encountered it. An interviewer might ask "Suppose a customer asked you to refund an item without a receipt. How would you handle that?" By posing such a question, the interviewer assesses how you would analyze and approach the situation.

- *Probing questions* request more detail on answers you have already provided. Let's say you are asked why you left your previous job, and you cite the lack of opportunities for advancement as the reason. A probing question will ask "What opportunities for advancement make a job more appealing to you?" Use probing questions as your chance to elaborate on what you've said.

Most job selection interviews include a mix of general and position-specific questions. Interviewers commonly begin with broad, open-ended questions, such as "Tell me a little about yourself." From there, they typically move to more specific, closed-ended, hypothetical, and probing questions about the candidate's education, work history, skills and talents, and qualifications for the job. Many interviewers end by asking whether the applicant has any questions. Although it is impossible to anticipate every question, you can prepare for your interview by formulating answers to commonly asked questions such as those in Table 1.

Generate Questions of Your Own Always prepare at least three or four questions to ask if given the opportunity. Some strategies for formulating good questions are these:

- *Ask questions that allow the interviewer to reflect on his or her own experiences.* An excellent question to ask the interviewer is "What have you most enjoyed about working here?" That type of question allows the interviewer to tell you about himself or herself and also to identify the aspects of the employer he or she most appreciates.

- *Ask questions that indicate your long-term interest in the job.* A question such as "What opportunities would this position offer for someone who is interested in growing with this company?" suggests you are thinking about your career in the long term and will be serious about your commitment to your employer.

- *Don't ask for details about the company that you should already know.* Recall that part of preparing for a job selection interview is researching your potential employer. Therefore, you don't want your questions to reveal ignorance about the company, such as "Where is this company's headquarters located?"

- *Never ask about salary or benefits unless the interviewer has brought up those subjects.* Some interviewers may ask you about your salary requirements. However, unless the interviewer introduces the topic, don't inquire about the salary, vacation time, or medical benefits. Those are questions to be posed after you have a job offer.

Follow Up after the Interview Finally, send your interviewer a thank-you note shortly after your interview. As illustrated in Figure 5, indicate that you appreciate the interviewer's having taken time to speak with you, note how you benefited from the interview experience, and express your excitement about the position. You might want to close by saying you look forward to hearing back. Sending a thank-you note requires only a few moments but may be the one gesture that sets you apart from equally qualified competitors. After you send your note, however, resist the urge to call or e-mail the interviewer with a question such as "When do you expect to make a hiring decision?" Although the temptation to do so can be great, you run the risk of annoying the interviewer and reducing—or eliminating—whatever goodwill you created during your interview.

Some suggestions for what to do and what to avoid in successful interviews appear in Table 2.

IDENTIFYING AND RESPONDING TO ILLEGAL QUESTIONS

In the United States, the Equal Employment Opportunity Commission (EEOC) is the federal agency that monitors unfair discrimination in hiring and firing decisions. For the last four decades, the EEOC has enforced guidelines that specify what an employer may and may not ask prospective job candidates during employment interviews and

---

TABLE 1

QUESTIONS COMMONLY ASKED DURING SELECTION INTERVIEWS

Tell me about yourself.

What are your primary strengths?

What do you consider your most serious weaknesses?

Why are you interested in this particular job/company?

Describe a difficult situation you've been in and how you handled it. Would you handle it differently today?

Who have been the biggest influences in your life? Why?

What can you do for this company? Why should we hire you instead of someone else?

What are your professional goals for the next five years? Ten years?

What do you value in a coworker?

Are you willing to relocate if necessary?

How is your academic background/work experience relevant for this job?

Do you have any questions for me?

SHARPEN Your Skills:
Preparing for a job interview

Think of a job you would like to have when you graduate. Review the questions in Table 1, and write out a short answer for each. Afterward, ask a trusted relative or advisor to go through your answers and offer you feedback about how you might improve them.

FIGURE 5

SAMPLE THANK-YOU NOTE

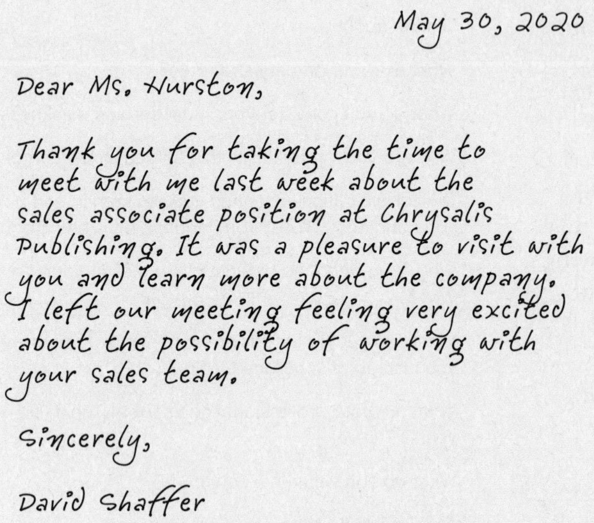

May 30, 2020

Dear Ms. Hurston,

Thank you for taking the time to meet with me last week about the sales associate position at Chrysalis Publishing. It was a pleasure to visit with you and learn more about the company. I left our meeting feeling very excited about the possibility of working with your sales team.

Sincerely,

David Shaffer

on application forms. The guidelines are intended to ensure that employers ask only for information relevant to the position being sought.

During a job selection interview, you might be asked a question that violates federal employment discrimination laws, often as the result of an honest mistake reflecting the interviewer's lack of awareness of the EEOC guidelines. On occasion, however, it represents an intentional attempt to gain information about you that the prospective employer doesn't need. When faced with an illegal question, many job candidates feel caught in an impossible position. They may recognize the question as discriminatory but feel compelled to answer anyway. If you find yourself in such a situation, you can respond effectively by knowing the law and dealing with the question tactfully.

Companies can make employment decisions based only on information that is relevant to job performance. In most cases, the law prohibits employers from considering factors such as a person's sex, age, ethnicity, sexual orientation, religion, marital status, political orientation, or disability status in decisions to hire, promote, or fire. Exceptions are allowed only when there is a *bona fide*, or legally legitimate, reason for them. For instance, if the position legitimately requires someone of a certain sex (such as a men's locker room attendant), a certain ethnicity (such as an actress playing an ethnic-specific movie role), or a certain physical ability (such as a firefighter, who must be able to walk and carry loads of a certain weight), these factors may be considered in employment decisions.

Most jobs, however, require only the skills and training necessary to perform the assigned tasks. If there is no bona fide reason to require applicants to fit a specific demographic profile (such as being of a particular age, marital status, or religion), employers cannot legally ask about those characteristics during a job selection

TABLE 2	Do	Don't
PREPARE TO SUCCEED: INTERVIEW DO'S AND DON'TS	Find out as much about the company as you can.	Ask questions about the company to which you should already know the answer.
	Anticipate likely questions and practice your answers to them.	Go into a job interview intending to "wing it."
	Keep your answers short and to the point.	Monopolize the conversation by giving long, rambling answers.
	Dress professionally.	Look as if you gave no thought to your appearance.
	Arrive on time or a few minutes early.	Arrive late.
	Prepare thoughtful questions to ask of your interviewer.	Indicate a lack of interest in the position by asking no questions about it.
	Follow up with a thank-you note.	Think sending a thank-you note won't make any difference.

Difficult Conversations

Keeping Your Cool When Asked an Illegal Question

Imagine this: You're interviewing for a job you really want. You have prepared three questions to ask at the end—but the interviewer answers all of them during your interview, leaving you with nothing new to ask. Therefore, you're already flustered when the interviewer tries to fill the gap by asking you a question that you recognize as illegal for an employer to ask.

Now, consider this: Even though you realize that the question is inappropriate, you want this job and you don't want to cause a scene by pointing that out. Instead, try these strategies:

- Answer directly but briefly. "Do you go to church?" "Yes, I do."

- Pose a tactful inquiry. "What is your political orientation?" "Why do you ask?"

- Tactfully refuse to answer. "Do you plan to have children?" "My family plans won't interfere with my ability to do this job."

- Neutralize the question. "What happens if your spouse gets called for military duty?" "My spouse and I would discuss the logistical requirements of any change in our circumstances."

- Take advantage of the question. "Do you have any disabilities?" "As someone with mild dyslexia, I've learned to treat people with a wide range of abilities empathically and respectfully."

Although you may feel uncomfortable or even offended when asked an illegal question, it is seldom best to respond defensively ("You can't ask me that; it's none of your business"). Instead, use one of Stewart and Cash's strategies to defuse the tension and show that you can react tactfully and professionally in an uncomfortable situation.

---

interview. Even if one characteristic, such as ethnicity or physical ability, is a bona fide job requirement, the employer can ask only about *that* attribute, not the others.

As a job applicant, you benefit by knowing the laws regarding employment and illegal discrimination. Table 3 offers a list of questions that are generally illegal for employers to ask in an interview, alongside similar, job-related questions that *are* legal to ask.

If you are asked an illegal question during a job interview, there are ways you can provide the necessary information without embarrassing the interviewer or causing everyone discomfort. Communication professors Charles Stewart and William Cash suggest five potential ways of responding effectively to illegal questions, which you can read about in the "Difficult Conversations" box.[31]

TABLE 3

WHAT CAN AND CAN'T BE ASKED DURING A JOB INTERVIEW

Legal to Ask	Illegal to Ask
Are you authorized to work in the United States?	Are you a citizen of the United States?
What languages do you speak, read, or write fluently?	What is your native language?
Are you available to work on the days this job requires?	What religious holidays or days of worship do you observe?
Are you 18 years of age or older?	How old are you?
Have you worked or earned a degree under another name?	Is this your maiden name?
What is your experience with such-and-such an age group?	Do you have children?
Are you able to perform the specific duties of this position?	Do you have any disabilities?
Do you have upcoming events that would require extensive time away from work?	Are you a member of the National Guard or military reserves?
Are you willing to relocate if necessary?	Do you live nearby?
Tell me about your experience managing others.	How do you feel about supervising men or women?

SOURCE: HRWORLD.COM/FEATURES/30-INTERVIEW-QUESTIONS-111507

For REVIEW

- ### What communication processes are important in the workplace?

  In the workplace, people must communicate in upward, downward, and lateral ways to others within the organization, and to multiple constituencies outside of the organization. Organizational culture is reflected in an organization's rites, rituals, and roles.

- ### What common communication challenges do workplaces face today?

  Many workplaces struggle with the communication challenges of globalization, communication technology, sexual harassment, work/life conflict, and diversity.

- ### In what ways can we improve our interviewing skills?

  We can succeed at job selection interviews by researching a potential employer, anticipating likely questions, formulating questions of our own, and writing a thank-you note after an interview.

KEY TERMS

NOTES

1. Robinson, K. L., & Thelen, P. D. (2018). What makes the grapevine so effective? An employee perspective on employee-organization communication and peer-to-peer communication. *Public Relations Journal, 12*(2), 1–20.

2. Gould, E. W. (2009). "I heard it on the grapevine"—Blogging, Facebook, YouTube, and student self-organization during a faculty strike. *Lecture Notes in Computer Science, 5621*, 336–345.

3. Brady, D. L., Brown, D. J., & Liang, L. H. (2017). Moving beyond assumptions of deviance: The reconceptualization and measurement of workplace gossip. *Journal of Applied Psychology, 102*(1), 1–5. https://doi.org/10.1037/apl0000164

4. Trice, H., & Beyer, J. (1984). Studying organizational cultures through rites and ceremonials. *Academy of Management Review, 9*(4), 653–669. https://doi.org/10.5465/amr.1984.4277391

5. Erhardt, N., Martin-Rios, C., & Heckscher, C. (2016). Am I doing the right thing? Unpacking workplace rituals as mechanisms for strong organizational culture. *International Journal of Hospitality Management, 59*, 31–41. https://doi.org/10.1016/j.ijhm.2016.08.006

6. Koschmann, M. A., & McDonald, J. (2015). Organizational rituals, communication, and the question of agency. *Management Communication Quarterly, 29*(2), 229–256. https://doi.org/10.1177/0893318915572386

7. Better Teams. (2018, March 3). 8 workplace rituals that boost employee engagement. https://better-teams.com/2018/03/03/8-workplace-rituals/

8. See Balazs, S., Kuchinka, D. G., Mantz, T., & Bracken, D. (2017). Creating an innovative workplace: Effects of humor style and supervisor support. *European Journal of Management, 17*(2), 37–48. https://doi.org/10.18374/EJM-17-2.4

9. Sliter, M., Jones, M., & Devine, D. (2017). Funny or funnier: A review of the benefits (and detriments) of humor in the workplace. In C. L. Cooper, & J. C. Quick (Eds.), *The handbook of stress and health: A guide to research and practice* (pp. 523–537). John Wiley & Sons. https://doi.org/10.1002/9781118993811

10. Lussier, B., Grégoire, Y., & Vachon, M. A. (2017). The role of humor usage on creativity, trust and performance in business relationships: An analysis of the salesperson-customer dyad. *Industrial Marketing Management, 65*, 168–181. https://doi.org/10.1016/j.indmarman.2017.03.012

11. Mesmer-Magnus, J., Glew, D. J., & Viswesvaran, C. (2012). A meta-analysis of positive humor in the workplace. *Journal of Managerial Psychology, 27*(2), 155–190. https://doi.org/10.1108/02683941211199554

12. Perrin, A., & Kumar, M. (2019, July 25). About three-in-ten U.S. adults say they are "almost constantly" online. *Fact Tank.* https://www.pewresearch.org/fact-tank/2019/07/25/americans-going-online-almost-constantly/

13. Campaign Monitor. (2019, May). The shocking truth about how many emails are sent. https://www.campaignmonitor.com/blog/email-marketing/2019/05/shocking-truth-about-how-many-emails-sent/

14. Grensing-Pophal, L. (2018, October 12). How much time are employees wasting on the internet? *HR Daily Advisor.* https://hrdailyadvisor.blr.com/2018/10/12/how-much-time-are-employees-wasting-on-the-internet-2/

15. Ibid.

16. Bureau of Labor Statistics. (2017, April 27). Employment in families with children in 2016. https://www.bls.gov/opub/ted/2017/employment-in-families-with-children-in-2016.htm

17. Peter, R., March, S., & du Prel, J. B. (2016). Are status inconsistency, work stress and work-family conflict associated with depressive symptoms? Testing prospective evidence in the lidA study. *Social Science & Medicine, 151*, 100–109. https://doi.org/10.1016/j.socscimed.2016.01.009

18. Berkman, L. F., Liu, S. Y., Hammer, L., Moen, P., Klein, L. C., Kelly, E., Fay, M., Davis, K., Durham, M., Karuntzos, G., & Buxton, O. M. (2015). Work–family conflict, cardiometabolic risk, and sleep duration in nursing employees. *Journal of Occupational Health Psychology, 20*(4), 420–433. https://doi.org/10.1037/a0039143

19. Goh, Z., Ilies, R., & Wilson, K. S. (2015). Supportive supervisors improve employees' daily lives: The role supervisors play in the impact of daily workload on life satisfaction via work–family conflict. *Journal of Vocational Behavior, 89,* 65–73. https://doi.org/10.1016/j.jvb.2015.04.009

20. Fellows, K. J., Chiu, H. Y., Hill, E. J., & Hawkins, A. J. (2016). Work–family conflict and couple relationship quality: A meta-analytic study. *Journal of Family and Economic Issues, 37*(4), 509–518. https://doi.org/10.1007/s10834-015-9450-7

21. Michel, J. S., Mitchelson, J. K., Pichler, S., & Cullen, K. L. (2010). Clarifying relationships among work and family social support, stressors, and work-family conflict. *Journal of Vocational Behavior, 76*(1), 91–104. https://doi.org/10.1016/j.jvb.2009.05.007

22. Tangsathapornphanich, P., Senasu, K., & Sakworawich, A. (2017). What makes the Thai workforce happy? The effects of socio-economic status, work-life balance, and mental health on happiness. *NIDA Development Journal, 57*(4), 48–80.

23. Jourdain, G., & Chênevert, D. (2015). The moderating influence of perceived organizational values on the burnout-absenteeism relationship. *Journal of Business and Psychology, 30*(1), 177–191. https://doi.org/10.1007/s10869-014-9346-9

24. Woo, H., Park, S., & Kim, H. (2017). Job satisfaction as a moderator on the relationship between burnout and scholarly productivity among counseling faculty in the US. *Asia Pacific Education Review, 18*(4), 573–583. https://doi.org/10.1007/s12564-017-9506-5

25. Dessy, E. (2009). Effective communication in difficult situations: Preventing stress and burnout in the NICU. *Early Human Development, 85*(10), S39–S41. https://doi.org/10.1016/j.earlhumdev.2009.08.012

26. Guillaume, Y. R., Dawson, J. F., Otaye-Ebede, L., Woods, S. A., & West, M. A. (2017). Harnessing demographic differences in organizations: What moderates the effects of workplace diversity? *Journal of Organizational Behavior, 38*(2), 276–303. https://doi.org/10.1002/job.2040

27. See Anglim, J., Sojo, V., Ashford, L. J., Newman, A., & Marty, A. (2019). Predicting employee attitudes to workplace diversity from personality, values, and cognitive ability. *Journal of Research in Personality, 83,* Article 103865. https://doi.org/10.1016/j.jrp.2019.103865

28. Lumsden, G., Lumsden, D., & Wiethoff, C. (2009). *Communicating in groups and teams: Sharing leadership* (5th ed.). Wadsworth.

29. MBA Skool. (2019). Appraisal interview. https://www.mbaskool.com/business-concepts/human-resources-hr-terms/15103-appraisal-interview.html

30. Coulehan, J. L., & Block, M. L. (2006). *The medical interview: Mastering skills for clinical practice* (5th ed.). Davis.

31. Stewart, C. J., & Cash, W. B. (2017). *Interviewing: Principles and practices* (15th ed.). McGraw-Hill.

A

accommodating style   A style for managing conflict that represents a high concern for the other party but a low concern for the self.

action   A behavior someone undertakes.

action model   A model describing communication as a one-way process.

ad hominem fallacy   A statement that attempts to counter an argument by criticizing the person who made it.

adapt   To modify one's behavior to accommodate what others are doing.

adaptors   Gestures used to satisfy a personal need.

advertising   Communication intended to promote the purchase of a product or service.

advising   Communicating advice to a speaker about what he or she should think, feel, or do.

affect displays   Gestures that communicate emotion.

agenda-setting theory   The theory that media tell people what to think about by determining what they watch, read, and hear.

alternation   A strategy for managing dialectical tensions that entails going back and forth between the two sides of a tension.

alternative media   Media channels that give voice to a wider range of viewpoints than mainstream media.

ambiguous language   Words that can have more than one meaning.

American Medical Association (AMA)   A professional association for physicians and medical students in the United States.

analyzing   Providing your own perspective on what a speaker has said, such as by explaining your opinion or describing your experience.

anchor-and-contrast approach   A persuasion technique by which one precedes a desired request with a request that is much larger.

antecedent phase   Phase of group socialization in which people develop certain beliefs, attitudes, and expectations about a group.

anticipatory anxiety   The worry people feel when looking ahead to a speech.

anticipatory phase   Phase of group socialization in which people decide to join a group and make judgments about what they expect from that group and its members.

antonyms   Words that have opposite meanings.

anxiety   A psychological state of worry and unease.

appeal to false authority   A claim that uses as evidence the testimony of someone who is not an expert on the topic.

appraisal interview   A discussion focused on an employee's performance and goals for the future.

articulation   The extent to which a speaker pronounces words clearly.

artifacts   Objects and visual features that reflect a person's identity and preferences.

assimilation phase   Phase of group socialization in which members decide to accept the group's culture and the group acquires its own identity.

attending   Paying attention to someone's words well enough to understand what that person is trying to communicate.

attraction theory   A theory that explains why individuals are drawn to others.

attribution   An explanation for an observed behavior.

audience analysis   Carefully considering the characteristics of one's listeners when preparing a speech.

authority rule   A decision-making process in which the leader of the group makes the decisions.

autocratic style   A leadership style in which leaders see themselves as having both the authority and the responsibility to take action on a group's behalf.

autonomy face   The need to avoid being imposed on by others.

avatars   Graphic representations of people.

avoiding stage   The stage of relationship dissolution at which partners create physical and emotional distance from each other.

avoiding style   A style for managing conflict that represents a low concern for both the self and the other party.

B

backchanneling   Using facial expressions, nods, vocalizations, and verbal statements to let a speaker know you are paying attention.

balance   A strategy for managing dialectical tensions that entails trying to compromise, or find a middle ground, between the two opposing forces of a tension.

bandwagon appeal   A claim that a listener should accept an argument because of how many other people have already accepted it.

bar chart   A graphic display of numbers as bars on a graph.

begging the question   Supporting an argument using the argument itself as evidence.

belief Perception about what is true or false, accurate or inaccurate.

bibliography A list of the sources used in preparing a speech.

blockbusters Films that are highly successful financially.

blog Short for *web logs*, blogs are websites providing news, commentary, and personal diary entries from the user—the *blogger*—often along with comments from visitors.

bonding stage The stage of relationship development at which partners make a public announcement of their commitment to each other.

brainstorming An idea-generating process in which group members offer whatever ideas they wish before any are debated.

breadth The range of topics we self-disclose to various people.

build rapport Create the perception that listeners and the speaker see things similarly.

burnout Chronic sense of exhaustion or apathy that can come from long-term frustration and stress.

C

caregivers People with the responsibility of tending to the mental and physical health needs of others.

catalytic theory The theory that watching violence in the media can encourage real-life violence, but only if other influences are also present.

catfishing Using false information, including stolen or edited photos, to create a fake online persona.

cause-and-effect pattern A pattern of organizing the main points of a speech so that they describe the causes of an event and then identify its consequences.

centralized power structure An organizational structure in which a small number of people—such as a company president and board of directors—holds the majority of the decision-making ability.

channel A pathway through which messages are conveyed.

channel-lean contexts Communication environments involving few channels at once.

channel-rich contexts Communication environments involving many channels at once.

chart A graphic display of numeric information.

chronemics The use of time.

circumscribing stage The stage of relationship dissolution at which partners begin to decrease the quality and quantity of their communication with each other.

civil dialogue A process of engaging in honest, authentic, and respectful conversation with others, even about points of deep-seated disagreement.

closed-mindedness The tendency not to listen to anything with which one disagrees.

closed systems Organizations that interact little with people or groups outside the organization.

co-cultures Groups of people who share values, customs, and norms related to mutual interests or characteristics other than their national citizenship.

code-switch To shift between jargon and plain language in order to be understood by others.

coercive power A form of power that comes from the ability to punish.

cognitive complexity The ability to understand a given situation in multiple ways.

cohesion The force by which the members of a group work together in the service of a common goal.

collaborating style A style for managing conflict that represents a high concern for the self and for the other.

collaborative communication A model that encourages patients and providers to interact as partners or peers in their communication.

collectivistic culture A culture in which people believe that their primary responsibility is to their families, their communities, and their employers.

collegial stories Stories that people tell about other people in their organization, often to comment on their positive and negative attributes.

commitment The desire to stay in a relationship no matter what happens.

communication The process by which people use signs, symbols, and behaviors to exchange information and create meaning.

communication apprehension Anxiety or fear about communicating with others.

communication codes Verbal and nonverbal behaviors whose meanings are often understood only by people from the same culture.

communication competence Communication that is effective and appropriate for a given situation.

communication privacy management (CPM) theory A theory explaining how people in relationships negotiate the tension between disclosing information and keeping it private.

comparative advantage method   A way of organizing a persuasive speech in which the speaker explains why his or her point of view is superior to others on the same topic.

comparison level   A realistic expectation of what one wants and thinks one deserves from a relationship.

comparison level for alternatives   An assessment of how much better or worse one's current relationship is than one's other options.

competence face   The need to be respected and viewed as competent and intelligent.

competing style   A style for managing conflict that represents a high concern for the self but a low concern for the other party.

competitive interrupting   The practice of using interruptions to take control of the conversation.

complementarity   The beneficial provision by another person of a quality that one lacks.

compromising style   A style for managing conflict that represents a moderate concern for everyone's needs and desires.

conference paper   A report of research that has been accepted for presentation at an academic meeting.

confirmation bias   The tendency to pay attention only to information that supports one's values and beliefs, while discounting or ignoring information that does not.

confirming messages   Behaviors that convey how much another person is valued.

conflict   An expressed struggle between at least two interdependent parties who perceive incompatible goals, scarce resources, and interference from the other party in achieving their goals.

connotative meaning   The ideas or concepts a word suggests in addition to its literal definition.

constraint   The limitations imposed on creativity by the context in which you are working.

contempt   Hostile behavior in which people show a lack of respect for each other.

content dimension   Literal information that is communicated by a message.

context   The physical or psychological environment in which communication occurs.

coping   Efforts to eliminate or reduce the effects of a stressful situation.

copyright infringement   The use of materials that are protected by copyright—such as photos or works of art—without gaining permission or giving proper recognition to their source.

corporate stories   Stories that organizations tell about their histories, goals, and identities.

counseling interview   An interaction aimed at supporting an individual through a personal problem.

coupons   Documents a consumer can exchange for discounts or rebates on a product or service.

cover letter   A one-page letter in which a person formally applies for a specific position.

creativity   The freedom to make independent choices.

credibility   The extent to which others perceive us to be competent and trustworthy.

critical listening   Listening to evaluate or analyze.

criticism   Words that pass judgment on someone or something.

cultivation theory   The theory that television encourages or cultivates a distorted view of the world among heavy viewers.

culture   The totality of learned, shared symbols, language, values, and norms that distinguish one group of people from another.

D

database   An electronic storehouse of specific information that people can search.

deception   The act of leading others to believe something the speaker knows to be untrue.

decode   To interpret or give meaning to a message.

deductive reasoning   A form of reasoning in which one starts with a general conclusion and then uses it to explain specific individual cases.

defamation   Language that harms a person's reputation or image.

defensiveness   Seeing oneself as a victim and denying responsibility for one's behaviors.

defining   Providing the meaning of a word or concept.

democratic style   A leadership style in which every member of a group has the right to participate in decision making.

demonstrating   Showing how to do something by doing it as it is explained.

denial   A strategy for managing dialectical tensions that entails responding to only one side of a tension and ignoring the other side.

denotative meaning   The literal meaning of a word.

depth   The degree of intimacy of our self-disclosures.

describing   Using words to depict or portray a person, a place, an object, or an experience.

desensitization   The process of confronting frightening situations directly, to reduce the stress they cause.

desensitization theory   The theory that people's acceptance of real-life violence grows as they see more violence reflected in the media.

diagnosis   A determination of the medical problems a person has.

dialectical tensions   Conflicts between two important but opposing relational needs or desires.

differentiating stage   The stage of relationship dissolution at which partners begin to view their differences as undesirable or annoying.

diffused power structure   An organizational structure in which decision-making ability is spread evenly among the organization's members, with no one member or group holding excessive power.

disconfirming messages   Behaviors that imply a lack of respect or value for others.

disorientation   A strategy for managing dialectical tensions that entails ending the relationship in which the tension exists.

divorce   The legal discontinuation of a marriage.

doctor–patient privilege   The assurance that health professionals will keep patient information confidential.

downward communication   Messages we send to people at lower levels of the organizational hierarchy, such as subordinates, interns, and staff members who report to us.

E

either/or fallacy   A statement that identifies two alternatives and falsely suggests that if one is rejected, the other must be accepted.

e-mail   Electronic mail messages exchanged through a computer network—one of the earliest mass uses of the Internet.

emblems   Gestures that have a direct verbal translation.

emoji   Cartoon depictions of faces and other objects.

empathic listening   Listening to experience what the speaker thinks or feels.

empathizing   Conveying to a speaker that you understand and share his or her feelings.

empathy   The ability to think and feel as others do.

encode   To put an idea into language or gesture.

encounter phase   Phase of group socialization in which the group meets for the first time.

enculturation   The process of acquiring a culture.

enthymeme   A syllogism in which one of the premises is already so widely known and accepted that it is omitted.

equal time rule   Requires stations to offer competing political parties equal access to the airwaves.

equity theory   Theory that a good relationship is one in which a person's ratio of costs and benefits is equal to his or her partner's.

e-therapy   The use of communication technology for delivering or receiving psychotherapy.

ethics   Principles that guide judgments about whether something is morally right or wrong.

ethnicity   People's perceptions of ancestry or heritage.

ethnocentrism   The tendency to judge other cultures' practices as inferior to one's own.

ethos   A speaker's respectability, trustworthiness, and moral character.

etymology   The origin or history of a word.

euphemism   A vague, mild expression that symbolizes and substitutes for something blunter or harsher.

evaluation   Assessing the value of information we have received.

exit interview   A conversation about an employee's experiences with an organization that he or she is leaving.

exit phase   Phase of group socialization in which people leave a group.

experimenting stage   The stage of relationship development at which people converse to learn more about each other.

expert opinion   Recommendations of individuals who have expertise in a particular area that are sometimes the basis of a group's decision-making process.

expert power   A form of power that stems from having expertise in a particular area.

explaining   Revealing why something occurred or how something works.

explicit rules   Rules that have been clearly articulated.

extemporaneous speech   A speech that is carefully prepared to sound as though it is being delivered spontaneously.

external communication   Communication with people outside the organization.

extroversion   A personality trait shared by people who are friendly, assertive, and outgoing with others.

F

face   A person's desired public image.

face needs   Important components of one's desired public image.

face-threatening act   Any behavior that threatens one or more face needs.

facework   The behaviors people use to establish and maintain their desired public image with others.

facial displays   Facial expressions that are an important source of information in nonverbal communication.

fairness doctrine   A law that required broadcasters to air all sides of a public issue.

false-cause fallacy   A statement asserting that if an event occurs before some outcome, the event therefore caused that outcome.

false consensus   An outcome wherein some members of a group say they support the unanimous decision even though they do not.

family of origin   The family in which one grows up, usually consisting of parents and siblings.

family of procreation   The family one starts as an adult, usually consisting of a spouse or romantic partner and children.

family rituals   Repetitive activities that have special meaning for a family.

feedback   Verbal and nonverbal responses to a message.

fellowship face   The need to be liked and accepted by others.

feminine culture   A culture in which people cherish traditionally feminine qualities and prefer little differentiation in the roles of women and men.

fight-or-flight response   A reaction that helps prepare the body either to confront or to avoid a stressor.

fireside chats   Evening radio speeches President Franklin D. Roosevelt made to the United States between 1933 and 1944.

fluency   The smoothness of a speaker's delivery.

forgiveness   The process by which a wronged person stops feeling angry or resentful about an offense.

formal communication   Messages that come from the organization and relate to its operations.

formal roles   Roles that involve functions prescribed by the organization itself.

forms of rhetorical proof   Ways to support a persuasive argument, including ethos, pathos, and logos.

friends-with-benefits (FWB) relationships   Friendships in which friends engage in sexual interaction with each other, even though they do not consider their relationship to be romantic.

fundamental attribution error   The tendency to attribute others' behaviors to internal rather than external causes.

G

general search engine   A website on which one can search for other websites containing information on a specified topic.

George Gerbner   Communication professor who was a leading researcher on media violence. He estimated that by the age of 18, the average U.S. viewer had witnessed 32,000 murders and 40,000 attempted murders on television.

Gerald Levin   A young executive at *Time* magazine who developed the idea for a cable television network in the 1970s.

gesticulation   The use of arm and hand movements to communicate.

ghosting   Suddenly and unexpectedly stopping all contact with someone on social media.

glazing over   Daydreaming or allowing the mind to wander while another person is speaking.

globalization   The increasing interconnectedness of societies and their economies as a result of developments in transportation and communication.

gossip   Informal, and frequently judgmental, talk about people who are not present.

grapevine   A metaphor used to indicate that informal messages are often conveyed in upward, downward, and lateral directions simultaneously.

graphic slide   An electronic display of information in a visually compelling format.

groupthink   A situation in which group members seek unanimous agreement despite their individual doubts.

H

halo effect   A predisposition to attribute positive qualities to physically attractive people.

haptics   The study of the sense of touch.

hasty generalization   A broad claim that is based on insufficient evidence.

hate speech   Language used to degrade, intimidate, or dehumanize specific groups of people.

Hays Code   Same as the Motion Picture Production Code, which distinguished acceptable from unacceptable content for movies in the United States.

health campaigns   Coordinated media messages that encourage the audience to take specific steps to increase or protect physical and mental health.

health care providers   Professional caregivers.

Health Insurance Portability and Accountability Act (HIPAA) A law giving patients access to, and control over, their personal health information.

hearing The sensory process of receiving and perceiving sounds.

hierarchy The division of people into levels of authority.

high-context culture A culture in which people are taught to speak in an indirect, inexplicit way.

high-power-distance culture A culture in which certain groups, such as the royal family or the members of the ruling political party, have much greater power than the average citizen.

hostile audience An audience in which listeners are predisposed to disagree with the speaker.

HURIER model A model describing the stages of effective listening as hearing, understanding, remembering, interpreting, evaluating, and responding.

I

ideawriting An idea generating process in which members independently list their own ideas and then systematically evaluate one another's ideas before they are considered by the group.

identity The set of stable perceptions a person has about who he or she is; also known as *self-concept*.

illustrators Gestures that go along with a verbal message to clarify it.

image The way one wishes to be seen or perceived by others.

image management The process of projecting one's desired public image.

immediacy behaviors Nonverbal signals of affection and affiliation.

implicit rules Rules that have not been clearly articulated but are nonetheless understood.

impromptu speech A speech delivered with little or no preparation.

individualistic culture A culture in which people believe that their primary responsibility is to themselves.

inductive reasoning A form of reasoning in which one considers evidence and then draws general conclusions from it.

infidelity Romantic or sexual interaction with someone outside one's romantic relationship.

informal communication Communication that is not sanctioned by an organization but arises from the social interactions of its members.

informal roles Functions that are adopted by specific people rather than dictated by the organization.

information hunger The desire to learn.

information overload The state of being overwhelmed by the enormous amount of information encountered each day.

information-seeking behavior A series of actions to find out more about a health issue.

information transfer model Model of organizational communication in which communication is seen as a pipeline through which information flows from one source to another, and which assumes that receivers will assign the same meanings to a sender's words that the sender did.

informational listening Listening to learn.

informational power A form of power that stems from the ability to control access to information.

informative speaking Publicly addressing others to increase their knowledge, understanding, or skills.

in-groups Groups of people with which a person identifies.

initiating stage The stage of relationship development at which people meet and interact for the first time.

instant messaging A form of text communication that occurs simultaneously between two or more connected users on a computer.

instrumental communication Communication about day-to-day topics and tasks.

instrumental needs Practical, everyday needs.

integrating stage The stage of relationship development at which a deep commitment has formed, and the partners share a strong sense that the relationship has its own identity.

integration A strategy for managing dialectical tensions that entails developing behaviors that will satisfy both sides of a tension simultaneously.

intensifying stage The stage of relationship development at which people move from being acquaintances to being close friends.

interaction model A model describing communication as a process shaped by feedback and context.

interdependence The state in which what happens to one person affects everyone else in the relationship.

internal communication The messages people within the workplace convey to one another.

interpersonal attraction The force that draws people together.

interpersonal communication Communication that occurs between two people in the context of their relationship.

interpretation   The process of assigning meaning to information that has been selected for attention and organized.

interview   A structured conversation in which one person poses questions to which another person responds.

intimacy   Significant emotional closeness experienced in a relationship, whether romantic or not.

intimate distance   The zone of space willingly occupied only with intimate friends, family members, and romantic partners.

intrapersonal communication   Communication with oneself.

introversion   A personality trait shared by people who are shy, reserved, and aloof.

investment   The commitment of one's energies and resources to a relationship.

investment model of commitment processes   A theoretic model proposing that relationship commitment is a function of satisfaction, resources (or investments), and the perceived quality of relational alternatives.

I-statement   A statement that claims ownership of the communicator's feelings or thoughts.

J

jargon   Technical vocabulary of a certain occupation or profession.

Johannes Gutenberg   German publisher who invented the printing press in the 1440s.

Johari window   A visual representation of components of the self that are known or unknown to the self and to others.

K

kinesics   The study of movement.

L

laissez-faire style   A leadership style in which leaders offer minimal supervision.

language   A structured system of symbols used for communicating meaning.

lateral communication   Messages we share with peers or anyone who occupies the same position in the organizational hierarchy as we do.

legitimate power   A form of power in which leaders' status or position gives them the right to make requests with which others must comply.

life story   A way of presenting oneself to others that is based on one's self-concept but is also influenced by other people.

line chart   A graphic display of numbers in the form of a line or lines that connect various data points.

listening   The active process of making meaning out of another person's spoken message.

loaded language   Words with strongly positive or negative connotations.

logical fallacy   A line of reasoning that, even if it makes sense, does not genuinely support a speaker's point.

logos   Listeners' ability to reason.

low-context culture   A culture in which people are expected to be direct and to say what they mean.

low-power-distance culture   A culture in which people believe that no one person or group should have excessive power.

M

main point   A statement expressing a specific idea or theme related to the speech topic.

mainstream media   Those media channels that reach the broadest audiences.

majority rule   A decision-making process that follows the will of the majority.

masculine culture   A culture in which people cherish traditionally masculine values and prefer sex-specific roles for women and men.

mass communication   Communication to a large audience that is transmitted by media.

media   A collection of various channels of communication.

media activism   Coordinated efforts to express displeasure with media messages and to force changes in their content.

media convergence   The increasing interconnection of media content and communication technology.

media effects   The influences media have on people's everyday lives.

media literacy   An assessment of your competence in evaluating media messages and their effects.

media sites   Websites on which people can share audio-visual messages.

memorized speech   A speech composed word for word and then delivered from memory.

message   Verbal and nonverbal elements of communication to which people give meaning.

metacommunication   Communication about communication.

microblogging   A combination of blogging and texting supported by the website Twitter.

mindfulness   Awareness—as in being aware of how other cultures' behaviors and ways of thinking are likely to differ from one's own.

minority rule   A decision-making process in which a small number of members makes a decision on behalf of the group.

mnemonics   Devices that can aid short- and long-term memory.

model   A formal description of a process.

monochronic culture   A culture that sees time as a valuable commodity that should be used wisely and not wasted.

monogamy   The state of being in only one romantic relationship at a time and avoiding romantic or sexual involvement with others outside that relationship.

Monroe's motivated sequence   A way of organizing a persuasive speech consisting of appeals to attention, need, satisfaction, visualization, and then action.

Motion Picture Production Code   Distinguished acceptable and unacceptable content for movies in the United States.

motion picture rating system   A means of evaluating a film's suitability for various audiences.

N

narration   Describing a series of events in sequence.

nationality   One's status as a citizen of a particular country.

need to belong theory   A psychological theory proposing a fundamental human inclination to bond with others.

neutral audience   An audience lacking strong feelings for or against the topic of a speech.

noise   Anything that distracts people from listening to what they wish to listen to.

nominal group technique (NGT)   An idea-generating process in which group members generate their initial ideas silently and independently and then combine them and consider them as a group.

non sequitur   A conclusion that does not logically follow from a premise.

nonverbal channels   The various behavioral forms that nonverbal communication takes.

nonverbal communication   Behaviors and characteristics that convey meaning without the use of words.

norm of reciprocity   The social expectation that favors should be reciprocated.

O

objective   Based on facts rather than opinions.

oculesics   The study of eye behavior.

olfactics   The study of the sense of smell.

open systems   Organizations that communicate and share information with other people or groups, including government offices, media outlets, advertisers, and benefactors.

opinion   Evaluation about what is good and bad.

orbiting   Continuing to interact with someone on social media after having ghosted that person.

organization   The process of categorizing information that has been selected for attention.

organizational communication   An area of study devoted to examining the interactions that occur in structured groups.

organizational culture   The values, customs, and communication behaviors that organization members share and that reflect the organization's distinct identity.

organizational rites   Ceremonial acts and practices that convey characteristics of an organization's culture.

organizational rituals   Repeated behaviors that provide a familiar routine to an organization's experiences.

out-groups   Groups of people with which a person does not identify.

over-benefited   A state in which one's relational benefits outweigh one's costs.

P

paralanguage   Vocalic behaviors that communicate meaning along with verbal behavior.

paraphrasing   Restating in your own words what a speaker has said, to show that you understand.

parasocial relationship   A one-sided friendship with someone who isn't aware of your existence.

pathos   Listeners' emotions.

peer   A person similar to us in status or power.

perception   The process of making meaning from environmental experiences.

perceptual schema   A mental framework for organizing information.

perceptual set   A person's predisposition to perceive only what he or she wants or expects to perceive.

personal distance   The zone of space occupied with close friends and relatives.

personal stories   Stories in which people describe how they see themselves and how they want others to see them.

persuasion   An attempt to motivate others, through communication, to adopt or to maintain a specific manner of thinking or doing.

persuasive interview   A conversation intended to affect beliefs, opinions, or behaviors.

persuasive speaking   Public speech that aims to influence listeners' beliefs, attitudes, and actions.

phonological rules   Rules that deal with the correct pronunciation of a word.

physical attraction   Attraction to someone's appearance.

physical traits   The body's physical attributes.

physician-centered communication   A model in which medical professionals dictate the duration and scope of communication with patients.

pie chart   A graphic display of numbers in the form of a circle that is divided into segments, each of which represents a percentage of the whole.

pilot test   A small-scale version of a health campaign meant to spot problems and generate feedback.

plagiarism   Knowingly using information from another source without giving proper credit to that source.

platonic relationship   A relationship that is nonromantic and nonsexual.

political advertising   Media messages designed to influence people's political decisions.

polyamory   Having more than one consensual romantic or sexual relationship at once.

polychronic culture   A culture that views time as holistic, fluid, and infinite.

polygamy   The state of having two or more spouses at once.

power   The ability to influence or control people or events.

pragmatic rules   Rules that specify the implications or interpretations of statements.

presentation aids   Anything used in conjunction with a speech or presentation to stimulate listeners' senses.

preview transition   A statement alerting listeners that a speaker is about to shift to a new topic.

primacy effect   The tendency to emphasize the first impression over later impressions when forming a perception.

problem-solution pattern   A pattern of organizing the main points of a speech so that they describe a problem and then offer solutions for it.

problem-solving interview   A discussion conducted to identify solutions to a problem or conflict.

problem-solving pattern   A way of organizing a pervasive speech in which the speaker establishes the existence of a problem and then proposes a solution to it.

product placement   An advertising strategy involving featuring particular brands in the storyline of a movie, television show, book, or even comic strip.

profanity   Language considered to be vulgar, rude, or obscene.

prognosis   A prediction of the course of a medical condition and the chance of recovery.

proportionality   The relative sizes of facial or body features.

proposition   That which a persuasive speech attempts to convince an audience to accept.

proposition of fact   A claim that a particular argument is supported by the best available evidence and should therefore be taken as factual.

proposition of policy   A claim about what should be done.

proposition of value   A claim that evaluates the worth of a person, an object, or an idea.

proxemics   The study of the use of space.

proximity   Closeness, as in how closely together people live or work.

pseudolistening   Pretending to listen.

psychosocial traits   Characteristics of one's personality and ways of relating to others.

public communication   Communication directed at an audience that is larger than a small group.

public distance   The zone of space maintained during a public presentation.

public speaking anxiety (stage fright)   Nervousness or fear brought on by performing in front of an audience.

purpose statement   A declaration of the specific goal for a speech.

Q

questionnaire   A written instrument containing questions for people to answer.

R

reaffirmation   A strategy for managing dialectical tensions that entails embracing dialectical tensions as a normal part of life.

real time   A simultaneous form of mediated communication in which messages are exchanged, interpreted, and responded to instantaneously, similar to a face-to-face conversation.

reason   To make judgments about the world based on evidence rather than emotion or intuition.

rebuttal tendency   The propensity to debate a speaker's point and formulate a reply while that person is still speaking.

recalibration A strategy for managing dialectical tensions that entails reframing a tension so the contradiction between opposing needs disappears.

receiver The party who interprets a message.

recency effect The tendency to emphasize the most recent impression over earlier impressions when forming a perception.

receptive audience An audience composed of people who already accept and agree with all or most of what a speaker plans to say.

red herring fallacy A statement that responds to an argument by introducing an irrelevant detail to divert attention from the point of the argument.

referent power A form of power that derives from attraction to the leader.

refutational approach A way of organizing a persuasive speech in which the speaker begins by presenting the main arguments against his or her position and then immediately refutes those arguments.

regulators Gestures that control the flow of conversation.

relational dimension Signals about the relationship in which a message is being communicated.

relational maintenance behaviors theory Theory specifying the primary behaviors people use to maintain their relationships.

relational needs The essential elements people seek in their relationships with others.

relational repair Efforts to fix problems in a relationship so that the relationship can continue.

relational transgression A behavior that violates an important expectation in a relationship.

representation Describing something in terms of its physical or psychological attributes.

research search engine A website on which one can search for research published in books, academic journals, and other periodicals.

resources Assets that enable a group to be productive.

résumé A short document listing a person's employment qualifications.

reward power A form of power based on the leader's ability to reward another for doing what the leader says.

role A pattern of behavior that defines a person's function within a group, such as a family.

rule of division A rule of speech organization specifying that if a point is divided into subpoints, it must have at least two subpoints.

rule of parallel structure A rule of speech organization specifying that all points and subpoints in an outline should have the same grammatical structure.

rule of subordination A rule of speech organization specifying that some concepts in the speech are more important than others.

S

Sapir-Whorf hypothesis A theory that language shapes a person's views of reality.

scripted speech A speech composed word for word on a manuscript and then read aloud exactly as it is written.

segmentation A strategy for managing dialectical tensions that entails dealing with one side of a tension in some aspects of a relationship and with the other side of the tension in other aspects of the relationship.

selection The process of paying attention to a certain stimulus.

selection interview A conversation intended to help the interviewer choose the most appropriate person for a position, an assignment, a promotion, or an award.

selective attention Listening only to what one wants to hear and ignoring the rest.

selective exposure A process by which we seek media messages that match our values rather than those that do not.

self-concept The set of stable perceptions a person has about who he or she is; also known as *identity*.

self-disclosure Act of intentionally giving others information about oneself that one believes is true but thinks others don't already have.

self-efficacy A belief that one can perform a desired action.

self-esteem One's subjective evaluation of one's value and worth as a person.

self-fulfilling prophecy An expectation that gives rise to behaviors that cause the expectation to come true.

self-monitoring Awareness of one's behavior and how it affects others.

self-serving bias The tendency to attribute one's successes to stable internal causes and one's failures to unstable external causes.

semantic rules Rules that specify the meanings of individual words.

service-oriented interview A conversation oriented toward helping people with a product or service they have purchased.

sexual harassment Unsolicited, unwelcomed behavior of a sexual nature in the workplace.

signposts Single words and phrases that distinguish one point in a presentation from another and help listeners follow the speaker's path.

skepticism   A method of questioning that involves evaluating evidence for a stated claim.

slang   Informal and unconventional words often understood only within a particular group.

slideshow   A selection of images and text created in a presentation software and projected on a screen for the audience to see.

slippery slope fallacy   A statement that attacks an argument by taking it to such an extreme that it appears ludicrous.

small group   A collection of people working interdependently to accomplish a task; small groups typically include 3 to 20 members.

small group communication   Communication occurring within small groups of approximately 3 to 20 people.

social attraction   Attraction to someone's personality.

social distance   The zone of space occupied with casual acquaintances.

social exchange theory   Theory suggesting that people seek to maintain relationships in which their benefits outweigh their costs.

social loafing   The tendency of some members of a group to contribute less to the group than the average member does, particularly as the group grows in size.

social media   User-generated websites offering content that individual users construct for delivery to mass audiences, allowing people to build and maintain social connections.

social network sites   Websites (such as Facebook) that allow users to meet, communicate, and share information online.

social penetration theory   Theory suggesting that the depth and breadth of self-disclosure help us learn about a person we're getting to know.

social support   The verbal and nonverbal behaviors people enact when they are trying to be helpful to others.

social validation principle   The idea that people will comply with requests if they believe that others are also complying.

societies   Groups of people who share the same culture.

source   The originator of a thought or an idea.

space pattern   A pattern of organizing the main points of a speech according to areas.

spam   E-mail messages sent indiscriminately to thousands of recipients at once, often to advertise a product or service.

speaking notes   An abbreviated version of a formal speech outline; also known as *speaking outline*.

speaking outline   An abbreviated version of a formal speech outline; see also *speaking notes*.

specific purpose   The main goal for a speech or oral presentation.

stagnating stage   The stage of relationship dissolution at which the relationship stops growing and the partners feel as if they are just "going through the motions."

stalemate   An outcome where members' opinions are so sharply divided that consensus is impossible to achieve.

stereotype   A generalization about a group or category of people that is applied to individual members of that group.

stonewalling   Responding to another person's words with silence and lack of expression.

strategic ambiguity   Leaving parts of a message open to different interpretations intentionally to accomplish a specific goal.

strategic control approach   Model of organizational communication that recognizes that people in an organization can use communication to control their environments and act in organized and mutually satisfying ways.

straw man fallacy   A statement that refutes a claim that was never made.

streaming TV   The online distribution of television content.

stress   The body's reaction to any type of perceived threat.

stressor   Any event that causes a perceived threat to well-being.

stuttering   A speech disorder that disrupts the flow of words with repeated or prolonged sounds and involuntary pauses.

subjective   Biased toward a specific conclusion.

summary transition   A statement that briefly reminds listeners of points a speaker has already made.

supporting   Expressing your agreement with a speaker's opinion or point of view.

survey   A method of collecting data by asking people directly about their experiences.

survey interview   An interaction aimed at gathering information.

syllogism   A three-line argument consisting of a major premise, a minor premise, and a conclusion.

symbol   A representation of an idea.

symmetry   The similarity between the left and right sides of a face or body.

symptom   A sign of a potential health problem.

synergy   A collaboration that produces more than the sum of its parts.

synonyms Words that have the same meaning.

syntactic rules Rules that govern the order of words within phrases and clauses.

T

table The display of words or numbers in a format of columns and rows.

task attraction Attraction to someone's abilities or dependability.

Telecommunications Act of 1996 A federal law requiring (among other things) that all television sets 13 inches or larger manufactured after January 1, 2000, include a V-chip.

telemedicine The use of communication technology for health consultation.

terminating stage The stage of relationship dissolution at which the relationship is officially deemed to be over.

text slide An electronic display of text used to accompany a speech.

texting Instant messaging with a cell phone.

theory of structuration Anthony Giddens's theory that all human behavior, including communication behavior, is influenced by an ever-present tension between creativity (or *agency*) and constraint *(structure).*

thesis The main message of a speech or oral presentation.

thesis statement A one-sentence version of the message in a speech.

Thomas Edison U.S. inventor who greatly influenced the lives of people worldwide in the 1800s with his inventions of the incandescent light bulb, the phonograph, and a motion picture camera, among many other patents that he held.

threat A declaration of the intention to harm someone.

time pattern A pattern of organizing the main points of a speech in chronological order.

topic pattern A pattern of organizing the main points of a speech to represent different categories.

traits Defining characteristics of a person that are often relatively enduring and not easily changeable.

transaction model A model describing communication as a process in which everyone is simultaneously a sender and a receiver.

transactional approach A model of organizational communication that makes no distinctions between senders and receivers of messages. According to this approach, everyone in an interaction is simultaneously encoding and decoding.

transition A statement that connects one point in a speech to the next.

treatment plan A course of action to remedy or manage a medical condition.

TV parental guidelines A system for rating the content of television shows.

U

unanimous consensus Uncontested support for a decision—sometimes the only option in a group's decision-making process.

uncertainty avoidance The extent to which people try to avoid situations that are unstructured, unclear, or unpredictable.

uncertainty reduction theory Theory suggesting that people find uncertainty to be unpleasant, so they are motivated to reduce their uncertainty by getting to know others.

under-benefited A state in which one's relational costs outweigh one's benefits.

upward communication Messages we send to people at higher levels of the organizational hierarchy than we occupy.

uses and gratification A theory that leads researchers to explore needs other than validation that media messages fulfill for people.

V

V-chip A device allowing television owners to block access to certain types of programs, such as those featuring excessive violence or adult themes.

verbal footnote A statement giving credit for quoted words in a speech to their original source.

vested interest An inherent motivation to pay attention.

visualization Developing a mental image, such as an image of oneself giving a successful performance.

vividness effect The tendency of dramatic, shocking events to distort one's perceptions of reality.

vocalics Characteristics of the voice that communicate meaning.

W

work/life conflict The pressure of balancing the demands of work with those of nonwork life.

working outline A structured set of all the points and subpoints in a speech.

workplace communication The interactions people have as part of their employment.

Y

you-statement A statement that shifts responsibility for the communicator's feelings or thoughts to the other party in the communication.

A page number with an *f* indicates a figure; a *t* indicates a table.